THE OXFORD HISTORY OF ENGLISH LITERATURE

General Editors
JOHN BUXTON, NORMAN DAVIS,
BONAMY DOBRÉE, *and* F. P. WILSON

IX

THE OXFORD HISTORY OF
ENGLISH LITERATURE

Certain volumes originally appeared under different titles (see title-page versos).
Their original volume-numbers are given below.

THE EARLY
EIGHTEENTH CENTURY
1700–1740
Swift, Defoe, and Pope

BONAMY DOBRÉE

CLARENDON PRESS · OXFORD

Oxford University Press, Walton Street, Oxford OX2 6DP

Oxford New York Toronto
Delhi Bombay Calcutta Madras Karachi
Petaling Jaya Singapore Hong Kong Tokyo
Nairobi Dar es Salaam Cape Town
Melbourne Auckland

and associated companies in
Berlin Ibadan

Oxford is a trade mark of Oxford University Press

Published in the United States by
Oxford University Press, New York

© *Oxford University Press 1959*

First published 1959
Reprinted (with corrections) 1964, 1968, 1990

Originally published as volume VII with the title English Literature
in the Early Eighteenth Century, 1700-1740 (*ISBN 0-19-812205-5*)

British Library Cataloguing in Publication Data
data available

Library of Congress Cataloging in Publication Data
data available
ISBN 0-19-812235-7

Printed in Great Britain by
Courier International
Tiptree, Essex

TO

VALENTINE DOBRÉE

*I dedicate
the most sustained labour
of my life*

PREFACE

THERE is no general agreement as to how, or to what end, a history of literature should be written. My object here has been to give a general view of the literary activity of the period, and to be descriptive in such a way as, I hope, by breaking down barriers, will make the reader free of the realm here treated of, so that he may know what to expect should he adventure into it. It is written, that is, for the inquiring student and the interested general reader, rather than for the expert, or the sleuth-hound of trends and influences. Thus many small fry are referred to, some even discussed at length, as indicating the general approach at the time, out of which the bigger figures emerge for more thorough treatment. These are the writers that matter to us now; but however high the great ones may tower, it is as well to remember that Grub Street is always there. If I have quoted more generously than some may consider necessary, that is for two reasons: the first, that dogmatic statements unsupported by evidence seem to me to imply a certain arrogance; the second, that in inviting a reader to make the acquaintance of an author, I feel he should be given a taste of what he will find.

To give a real sense of the activity of a period it would be necessary to take each five years in such detail as to be wearisome—even if it were not impossible in the space; but so far as these forty years are concerned, it is clarifying to divide them into two periods, separating them roughly half-way. As illustrated in the text, the great writers, Swift, Pope, Defoe, wrote largely in forms different from their earlier choices, and in another manner; moreover the ethos changed. We are not at all in the same world in 1725 as we were in 1705; new sensibilities are making themselves felt. This, however, is true more particularly of creative writing, apart in the main from drama, which I have kept as a whole, together with philosophy, and criticism, which exhibit a more even flow, and history, memoirs and travel which were not so much affected.

It is one of the objects of the Oxford History of English Literature to embody the latest results of scholarship, a counsel of perfection over a field including so many aspects, an ideal rendered all the more difficult by this book having taken more than twenty years to write, partly because of the scandalous dark night of interruption, World War II; to have embodied the latest findings in the earliest written chapters would have been impossible: but I have, I hope, made note of all important discoveries and findings.

To make full acknowledgement of all the help received would be equally impossible. Conversations with my colleagues at Leeds University, and discussions with students, have often given me fruitful ideas, and even supplied me with phrases. But I must not omit to thank experts who have been kind enough to read through certain sections; namely Professor John Butt who scanned and criticized my Pope chapters, Mr. J. M. Cameron who helped me with the philosophers, Mr. Herbert Davis who looked over my Swift, Professor James Sutherland who kept me straight with respect to Defoe, upon whom I received some light from Mrs. Jane Jack who lent me a copy of her thesis. I have especially to express gratitude to my co-editor, Professor F. P. Wilson, who read the whole script, and offered many helpful suggestions as well as being indefatigable in correcting my errors. In compiling the bibliography I have received help and advice as regards Defoe, Pope, and Swift from the scholars mentioned above, and for Berkeley from Professor T. E. Jessop, while in the general portion I have depended greatly upon Mr. Peter Meade of the British Museum, who compiled the greater part of it.

My acknowledgements would be woefully incomplete if I did not include the name of Miss A. C. Stead of Leeds University, whose careful typing saved me immense labour in correcting the text, and for whose disentangling of my first drafts I have nothing but admiration. And, finally, I owe a debt to my wife for reading the book through attentively, and saving me from many obscurities of expression and clumsiness in the phrasing.

B. D.

London
May 1959

CONTENTS

PART ONE

1700-1720

I

THE BACKGROUND

I. SOCIAL

THE picture of society which the historian of literature would wish to realize is different from one constructed for other historical purposes. What invites his study is not the elements which brought about say, the growth of life-insurance, nor those which made the Cabinet an important instrument of rule, but those which called forth certain forms of writing, which modified others, and, in short, set their stamp upon the literature of the time. From this standpoint certain questions seem to thrust themselves forward for answer. Was it, for instance, the popular taste for reading about voyages that made *Travels* a suitable mould for Swift to pour the metal of his satire into? Was it a delight in seeing the issues plain after a confused period of religious polemic that made the *Tale of a Tub* a bookseller's success? If it was a time when social and moral values were changing with marked rapidity, does this account for the unusual proportion of satirical work? And, again, can we find in a variation of social emphasis one of the reasons why the poetry of the eighteenth century differs so greatly from that of the seventeenth?

It is fatally easy for us, looking back in perspective, to simplify too much, to see the year 1700 as ending a phase. Did not Dryden in his at once nostalgic and courageous swan-song of that year declare:

'Tis well an Old Age is out
And time to begin a New;

and Congreve stop writing comedies as though he felt that what he had to say belonged to a previous era? Certainly the scope and intention of literature after 1700 strike us as decidedly different from what had latterly defined it. However arbitrary the date may be, something important in life and significant to literature seems to have happened; so that in passing from one century to the other we have the sense of emerging into a world altogether more comprehensible, one which it takes us less effort to inhabit—or so we perhaps delude ourselves. The old voices go on for a time; Halifax, Temple, Clarendon are published and read side by side with the works of new writers; but these at the turn of the century abandon the old forms, which, unsuited to carry what they have to say, would inevitably clog their utterance. The drama dwindles; at first poetry, a thin trickle of clear water in a marsh of exhausted turgidity, tentatively seeks new forms, or tries variants of older ones; the historians begin to develop method; a new popular philosophy—the Enlightenment we have come to call it—grows into the general consciousness; the busy world looks forward to Baconian and mercantilist conquests, while the scholars gather strength in looking back; a new class becomes dominant, not in taste—that was a sad variant reserved for a hundred years later—but in morality. The picture, naturally, is confused. Some authors, such as Defoe, seem clearly to mark a new age; others, such as Swift, are as evidently linked with the old.

General statements are necessarily in part false; the most we can hope for is to provide a frame which does not distort too much: yet perhaps for our purpose we may say that the age 'began' with the Revolution of 1688 which was felt finally to have swept away most of the remaining vestiges of medievalism. Or put it that a process of profound change which had been going on for over a century now increased its pace, to crystallize out in 1720, or thereabouts, when a new phase becomes apparent. All origins we know can be traced further and further back, all premonitions ante-dated; but to be niggling about refined points of scholarship, to hedge and hover over minute particulars when considering the period before us would be to miss the whole significance of what was happening on a large scale. What we have to take account of, even if we cannot 'explain' it, is the change which indubitably came over literature between the Revolution (some might prefer to put the date back a few years) and about 1740. Writings were no longer addressed in the main either to courtly or highly educated cliques such as could relish Restoration drama, or even to those who responded to the ratiocinative poems of Dryden. And we can note that literature is no longer proffered by men who speak with the voice of authority, but by men whose tone is persuasive; the reader is not being addressed from above, he is being spoken to as an equal.

Since literature itself is part of our sense of what life was like at a given moment, it is hazardous to try to determine their relation; but there are some periods where literature seems very immediately to reflect the political and social scene. This occurs apparently when there emerges a measurably large public which has not been trained to enjoy the books earlier generations delighted in, and which, if not exactly hungry for 'Literature', is ready for some sort of reading, eager indeed to taste anything which seems specially addressed to it. Our period is just such a one, for at that time a new class was coming into being, the class of merchant 'citizens', which, if still the milch-cow of the aristocratic ruling classes, was beginning to feel its power over the latter, and therefore its equality in mental vigour. Its claim was lucidly stated in 1722 by Mr. Sealand in Steele's *The Conscious Lovers*:

I know the Town and the World [he declared]—and give me leave to say, that we Merchants are a Species of Gentry, that have grown into the World this last Century, and are as honourable, and almost as useful, as you landed Folks, that have always thought yourselves so much above us. . . .

This was echoed by Defoe in *Roxana* (1724), and later by Gay, not only in *Polly* but in *The Distress'd Wife* (1734):

Barter. Is the name then [of merchant] a term of Reproach?— Where is the Profession that is so honourable?—What is it that supports every Individual of our Country? 'Tis Commerce—On what depends the Glory, the Credit, the Power of the Nation?—On Commerce.—To what does the Crown itself owe its Splendor and Dignity?—To Commerce.

and Joseph Butler, in a sermon preached in 1740, reminded 'the enlarged middle rank of people' of their responsibilities.

This business class, largely dissenting, which hitherto had had the time to read no more than contentious literature on political or religious topics, was now producing leisured sons, and, still more to the point, leisured daughters, who wanted to read something which bore directly upon the life they knew and lived. The womenfolk who did not merely aspire to ape 'quality' would willingly accept diversions (especially if they had a strong moral tone) other than those of cheapening gloves in the Exchange, paying rounds of gossiping visits, or compromising themselves at basset, in short, plunging into the usual refuges from boredom which are the recourse of the uneducated rich.

Mr. Sealand is symptomatic of one aspect of a general process which was going on, and was completed, say, in the thirties, namely the convergence from above and below of distinct reading classes, which came together to form one large homogeneous group. Naturally there is always reading for the very few—recondite philosophy, for instance—in our period Berkeley and Hutcheson, or, say, Granville fatigued and aloof, and at the other end there will always be the Ned Wards[1] bustling, vociferous, demotic, or the infantile reading represented at this time by almanacs and prognostications, ballads or street songs, and the literature summed up in Swift's gay gibe as the '*Sixpenny Worths of Wit*, Westminster *Drolleries*, *Delightful Tales*, *Complete Jesters* and the like, by which the writers of and for Grub-Street have in these ages so nobly triumphed over time'. These last we shall ignore. But what we have to note as an indication of what broadly was happening is that instead of one group of people reading, perhaps, the Cambridge Platonists, and another the virulent controversies of Penn, Faldo, and Muggleton, 'everybody' will be reading Butler's *Analogy*. Instead of a few relishing Cowley, perhaps, and the others, if they read poetry at all, such things as *Covent Garden Drolleries*, in 1750 'everybody' will enjoy Dodsley's *Miscellanies* and Gray's *Elegy*. No doubt, the main factor in there being a variation in literary matter was political and religious change; but at any rate something was bound to replace the mass of religious polemics, devotional treatises, and political pamphlets, which, now that the moulds disrupted by the metaphysical as well as economic civil strife were settling down into new shapes, could no longer nourish

---

[1] Edward Ward, 1667–1731, of 'low extraction', managed to visit the West Indies, 'ape and monkey climes' as a young man, and on his return became a publican in successive parts of London. He scribbled incessantly, and was not always well advised, being pilloried for certain passages in *Hudibras Redivivus*.

the minds and imaginations of the intelligent middle class. And since it was this class which was to dominate the literary scene for over a century, it is worth our while to glance at it.

This particular middle class now rising (there is always a rising middle class) was that which flourished in unusually large numbers, thanks to mercantile expansion, and of which Mr. Sealand represented the most successful element. Leslie Stephen described it as

a class of comparatively educated and polished persons, large enough to form a public, and not so large as to degenerate into a mob, distinct from the old feudal nobility, and regarding the life of the nobles with a certain contempt as rustic and brutal, more refined again than that class of hangers-on to the Court, of merchants and shop-keepers stamped with the peculiarities of their business, which generated the drama of the Restoration, and, on another side, beginning to despise the pedants of colleges and cathedrals as useless and antiquated encumbrances. . . . After the long struggle at the end of the preceding century, the society called 'the Town' definitely emerges, and is inclined to identify itself with the nation. . . .

In short London itself was emerging, with a close-packed population of about half a million, seventeen times larger than its nearest rival Bristol. It was swelling rapidly as England became ever more urban, for since the Dutch wars and the seizure of the carrying trade by England, the seaports, especially London, had grown in importance. Far more than the place of residence it was later to become, it was a centre of business and politics, its ideas largely set by the City and Whitehall, its intellectual life active only during the legal terms: it is in this buzzing hive that we must seek the new class of readers, and we may for a moment look at its structure.

The great trading companies were being consolidated, new ones were being launched, imports and exports alike were increasing at an inspiring rate, all indicating that directing and business staffs must already have been big, clerical employees numerous, while the considerable number of government clerks of all grades added ever more and more to the reading public. Mingling with these were to be found the smaller citizenry, the tradesmen large and little, the kind of people Moll Flanders moved among, the middlemen, clerks, and those employed in what Defoe described as 'a new trade, which we call by a new name, stock-jobbing', not to mention the footmen (one of whom was called Joseph Andrews) and the servants of the new class; in short, the smaller fry of the spreading mercantile interest and the ever more concentrated capitalism. Whether there was a general rise in literacy it is hard to say: Leslie[1] of *The Rehearsal* complained with acerbity: '. . . the greatest Part of the *People* do not Read Books, Most of them cannot *Read* at all. But they will Gather together about one that can *Read*, and Listen to an *Observator* or *Review* (as I have seen them in the streets)'. But it is probable that the excellent new Dissenting elementary schools, largely attended by children of Churchmen—exempt from the Schism Act and not to be confused with the Academies—did much to raise the standard. So did the Charity Schools against which Mandeville inveighed, since by teaching letters to the lowly, they gave desires for better things to people who should be hewers of wood and drawers of water. There were, of course, the old groups of readers—the Inns of Court young men, the people generically known as the gentry, and the old puritan and dissenting elements that were freeing themselves into wider realms of thought than works of devotion; there were, moreover, large numbers of Huguenots who would help to raise the standard of general literature.

The mass of argumentative people surging through a London which gives so strong an impression of energetic life would probably be devourers of all the flimsier literature hawked about the streets, whitening the stalls of the booksellers, and lying about on the tables of the coffee-houses or taverns they habitually called in at for their pipe, their glass, and their gossip. They were probably agog for anything new or fresh; but what drew them most was discussion or comment, cry and counter-cry, upon the subjects of bitter and vociferous faction, religious, political, commercial, shot with vituperation and libel, which characterized this unquiet time till about 1720. The reign of Queen Anne, far from being the age of exquisite grace and Augustan quiet it was so long presented as being, was actually a virulent one. Harsh and cruel beneath an irregularly polished surface, it was torn by strife over religious issues interwoven with the equally ferocious political squabbles

---

[1] Charles Leslie, 1650–1722, proceeded from Enniskillen to Trinity College, Dublin. He was ordained in 1680; but, a non-juring divine, he left Ireland in 1689. He finally adhered to the Pretender, lived some time in Italy, and returned to Ireland to die.

over the war, the succession, and a dozen other nodes of crisis. And, as at all times of stress, the average man in the street asked for something which dealt directly with the affairs which affected his own way of living as a citizen, the appetite for that sort of reading having been stimulated by the lapse of the censorship in 1695, tempered though it had been by the tax on paper in the next year. Now any scribbler could publish free of 'the fescue of an *Imprimatur*', and newspapers other than the official Gazette could flutter their sheets unabashed. Papers had appeared intermittently before the reign of Queen Anne, notably Sir Roger L'Estrange's *Observator*, but it was not until 1702 that the first daily paper, the *Daily Courant*, came into being, though still the older three-times-a-week papers were more important, such as the very Whig *Flying Post* or the extremely Tory *Post Boy*. Soon there were evening papers. And in these sheets which cost little and were ready to hand, the man who could just read comfortably for pleasure would find his large concerns touched upon, his thoughts expressed, and even his doings described.

But for us, the interest of this literature lies not in what it in itself was, but in what it led to, for sometimes even the most practical of journals would suddenly assume strange garb. For instance, *Great Britain's Postmaster*, which three times a week enlightened the world on matters historical, political, or commercial, including occasional lists of bankrupts, one day in 1707 saw fit to devote a whole issue to an execrably bad poem, *The British Court*, which celebrated the beauties of Queen Anne's entourage. It was possibly in this way that a mass of new readers, intent in the first instance upon the actual, the practical, the useful, came to regard verse as a natural medium, would read at first, perhaps, Defoe's *True Born Englishman*, then go forward to, say Lewis Theobald's *Pindarick Ode on the Union* (1707) with its superb apostrophe,

Hail, Purple Union! lovely, long-expected Child,

and finally to better things such as Tickell's *Ode on the Prospect of Peace* and even Pope's *Windsor Forest*. Such were the steps to Parnassus. In earlier days there had been journals for such as were curious, or even for the literati, for instance, Dunton's *Athenian Mercury*; now we have the newspapers proper, leading through Defoe's *Review* to the various ventures of Steele and

Addison, with their philosophic or at least moralistic comment. These popular successes, reading matter for both the educated and the innocent, would seem to show the coalescence of the upper and lower reading groups in a unification of interests, and agreement as to literary standards.

These, we gather, were continually being discussed in the coffee-houses, which, founded at about the middle of the previous century, were in the first half of the eighteenth an important part of the social scene. Their influence as generators of culture has perhaps been exaggerated, since they were far too much the haunts of cliques to help much in the spread of ideas. Most men are addicts to a set of notions as much as to any other drug, and of every profession it could probably be said, as Swift said of the clergy, 'They have their particular Clubs, and particular Coffee-Houses, where they generally appear in Clusters.' It is true that consciously self-formative young men, such as Dudley Ryder, would go to several, largely to learn to talk, and fit themselves for society; but they were already reading men. However, each coffee-house would seem to have provided the ephemeral literature of the day, whether haunted by parsons, men of letters, City clerks, chairmen, footmen, or wool-traders. And together with the ephemeral reading matter there would be some items which although as topical as could be, and thus popular, would also, by the chance that they were written by men of genius, induct the unsuspecting into the house of Literature. That the dialogue enjoyed so great a vogue may indicate the degree to which discussion made up the mental atmosphere of the time. It had, of course, been used for centuries to give an air of reasonableness to what was stark propaganda, but from the time of Dryden it had been used, rather, for discussion, even for mere talk about matters, as with Defoe. It issued from Shaftesbury's country study, and burst forth from Grub Street. Hervey might object that any argument in dialogue was 'stiff, forced, and unfair', but most seemed to feel with Stubbs that dialogue 'enlivens Philosophy with the Charms of Poetry'. So the townsman who could not live without the sound of voices in his ear could get something of the atmosphere of the coffee-house in the seclusion of his own room.

The flood of new readers in London was augmented by recruits from and in the country districts, for there too the economic processes were being quickened. The wool trade, the new Merchant Adventurers, mercantilism generally, produced people with the leisure and the desire to read. And just because the population of England was becoming more urban, communication, though not easier or swifter than it had been earlier, became far more frequent. Gazettes, lampoons and pamphlets, and occasionally weightier books, especially the classic English works issued in fascicular series, would radiate all over the country, perhaps by the regular post, which went out three times a week on the days the newspapers appeared, perhaps with the news-letters, such as Dawks's and Dyer's, carried by the couriers of Members of Parliament. No doubt, too, they were spread through the hands of the 'merchant manufacturers', industrial magnates whose business it was to travel over the country to collect cloth for home and foreign markets, or to send their agents. They, at least at a certain level, would be reading men, probably wishing to distribute amusing print in the outer districts. Copies of a few of the latest publications could easily be stuffed into wallet or holster to beguile the odd moments of leisure in the jog from croft to cottage in the Yorkshire dales, or along the pleasant windings of the Waveney, and to be left casually in the houses of the country business men, of the factors, or even in the homes of the weavers. Books and pamphlets were sold also at country fairs, as well as by the booksellers in the provinces. At all events there was a big enough reading public in the country in 1713 to justify the printing off of a whole edition of *The Conduct of the Allies* solely for their benefit.

That, at least, would seem to be the way society at this time built itself up; but our sense of what a society was is inevitably composed partly of what its literature suggests about it. At all events with this period we have a curious sense of watching a very self-conscious society, reaching out for what it feels it lacks to become complete. From the turbulent conflict of the first three lustres, when the Whigs, largely Chapel and trading, gradually overcame the Tories, mainly Church and land, there emerges a new concept of culture, that is of values, and the relationship of people towards each other. In the seventeenth century literature in the main sprang from and was addressed to a society living by the idea of semi-divine royalist authority, with its most fruitful contentions and its deepest poetry concerned with religion. By 1750 literature belongs to a trading-manufacturing society governed by an oligarchy, its dominating literature being concerned with morals—not Milton or Crashaw, but Richardson and Dr. Johnson. What the upsurging middle class wanted in the early years of the century was to a large extent materially didactic literature; towards the middle it demanded the morally didactic. It is remarkable how in the first portion of the century—or even earlier—the emphasis is on the severely practical, something to further trade or politics, together with something which was not exactly religion so much as politico-religious controversy which would further peace. Everywhere there seems to be exhibited the desire of people who feel themselves insufficiently educated to be taught about the world.

It is true that throughout the century the most constant subject of the presses, and material for their bulkiest output, was devotion, as it had been in the previous century. *The Practice of Piety* continued to be issued in various forms as did *The Companion to the Altar*, and *The Whole Duty of Man*, and these, while society was changing over from its aristocratic to its middle-class basis, were flanked by pleas for the reformation of manners. Sermons abounded, such as those of Parson Adams, in nine volumes—possibly routine paid-for publications—and were in this phase largely political, while a vast number of works were devoted to the controversies which diversified that age of delightfully exploratory heresy. Fierce wrangles over occasional conformity pursued a noisy course for about fifteen years; terrific polemics upon the dangerous inroads of Socinianism or Arianism assailed the ears of a possibly amused public, varied by warnings against the spirit of free thinking and atheism so alarmingly rife in the works of Asgill, Toland, Woolston, and others, which Parson Adams inveighed against. The literature of the Sacheverell trial, a politico-religious event of the first order, has itself become the subject of a bibliography; but the sweetening element of the religious writing of this time is the still touching devotional verse of Isaac Watts. The new departures were those of men trying to reconcile science with revelation such as Ray and Derham, to be treated of later.

But this undercurrent of religious writing, being, it would seem, a constant factor in the literature of England (it was even quite latterly the largest single section in English publishing) does not affect the picture of what elements may have been changing. It cannot be said that the bulk of political writing altered much, though it is possible to look on the spate of pamphlets which accompanied the crisis at the end of Queen Anne's reign as the last of the torrent which had overwhelmed England since 1642. But it is addressed, not to an equalitarian society, as were the various *Agreements of the People*, nor to a nonconformist group simply because it was nonconformist, as had been Halifax's brilliant *Letter to a Dissenter*, but to an audience that wished for peace that trade might flourish. Again, instead of Filmer's semi-mystical defence of royalty, we get such works as Defoe's popular *Original Power* (1701) or Charles Davenant's far stiffer *Essay on the Balance of Power* of about the same time. No doubt the appearance of Clarendon's *History of the Great Rebellion* published from 1702 onwards did much to educate the new reading public; and what we actually find both in prose treatises and the patriotic verse of the period is that a mystique of commerce was replacing the mystique of royalty. The dominant idea, from being aristocratic was becoming middle class, and this supplied the presses with their political material until the time of Adam Smith's *Wealth of Nations*, which was perhaps the culmination of this sort of political writing, being in its turn opposed by the new mystique introduced by Burke.

It may have been the fierce tensions of the early part of the century that prevented the appearance of much imaginative literature, but it is more likely that it was a public eager for the factual that determined the bulk of reading, for a factual literature that would be educative, enlarging into wider realms. The chief imaginative literature came from abroad or in translation: L'Estrange's *Aesop's Fables* continue to be reprinted; there was *Don Quixote*; but what seemed most to nourish the imagination were the numerous travel books, such as Dampier's often reprinted *Voyages* (1699), George Psalmanazar's[1] seductive, plausible yet wholly fantastic *Description of Formosa* (1704), and

---

[1] George Psalmanazar (his real name is unknown), 1679?–1763, was a native of the south of France, and was educated at a Dominican convent. He served in the army of the Duke of Mecklenburg, from which he was abstracted by an English chaplain, and came to England. Pretending to be a native of Formosa, he concocted his *Description*, and invented a Formosan language which for a short while he taught to aspiring missionaries at Christ Church, Oxford. His later writings, and his character, earned him the veneration of Dr. Johnson.

Woodes Rogers's *Cruising Voyage round the World* (1712). In these the imagination is given actuality to work upon, and perhaps at this stage that was all it asked for. For next divinity in importance figures history, ecclesiastical or lay, followed by a modicum of law, medicine, mathematics, and geography; treatises on mensuration and arithmetic (Cocker's famous work ran into thirty editions in about as many years), books on gardening, on trade, on how to get rich. There were works on children, on education, on marriage ceremonies, on architecture; and in 1708 Dr. William Oliver, who earned immortality by his biscuits, gave to the gouty his *Practical Dissertation on Bath Waters*. What we are aware of is a society intensely eager to cultivate itself, to find out, first about things, then about general ideas, and we see the great journalists of the time, Defoe, Steele, and Addison, jumping to meet the demand. Men and women striving to become 'polite', that is educated and mannered, read the *Spectator* to learn how to live, and what one ought to know.

And it is in the second decade that we cannot avoid noting that literature is being influenced by the great and growing confraternity of successful merchants and their families chiefly living in London but also scattered over the country, together with all the smaller beings who lived on them and by whom they lived: from now we begin to be aware of a great middle-class literature, a literature which was to improve with astonishing rapidity in the next few years, and was soon to constitute the main reading of the country. For it was the establishment in its own proud right of Mr. Sealand's class which proved directive. It came to dominate the field of writing till little by little all good literature, which under the Stuart kings had been in the main written by and for an aristocracy (not by any means altogether of birth) or for religious partisans, came to be written for a great middle group. Now we get, not one section being nourished upon the high religion of Jeremy Taylor, and another wrestling with Satan in *The Pilgrim's Progress*, but the great mass pondering over the moral issues raised in *Clarissa*.

The citizen coming into his own had an enormous effect, especially as he had now grown to be the main patron of literature. The support given by London and the dissenting elements to the Whig cause secured the City and Dissent a strong place in the social scheme. It was no longer practical politics to assume that England was governed by coteries of county magnates who alone were civilized, to whom alone the arts could be addressed; nor, since the foundation of the Bank of England in 1694, could there be any pretence that the great landed gentry were aloof from usury, or above enriching themselves by commerce. The tastes, therefore, of the new trading class were developed, their literary curiosity enlarged, by contact with members of the ruling class engaged in trade. So it came about that the older education of the universities met the new of the dissenting academies on common grounds, those of the daily avocation, and of political manœuvring.

As the century advances we feel the tremendous sense of power and of energy which animated the new class, expressed most fully perhaps in Dyer's *The Fleece* of 1757. Everything is expanding, swelling, bursting into a sort of bloom. And the significance for us lies in the fact that these new people demanded a literature of their own. They were given it in the popular magazines, and most of all in the novel, which now is written, not about great or fantastic folks, nor about rogues—so we get neither the Romance nor the picaresque tale—but about ordinary people, the people the great mass of readers knew, or moved among—Moll Flanders, Clarissa Harlowe, Squire Western, Uncle Toby Shandy. The little country squire, the *hobereau*, secured new consideration—since his lands provided the exports—appearing honourably first as Sir Roger de Coverley, later as the hunting squire who hunted Parson Adams. The novel then, the main vehicle of communication of the middle class, almost exclusively described middle-class life, and, what is more important still, debated what we have come to call bourgeois morality; for two hundred years or so that was the main social function of the novel. It may be that the greater education of the ordinary woman had something to do with it. By 1737 Pope could say 'Our Wives read Milton and our Daughters Plays'—then, as soon as Richardson wrote *Pamela* to read aloud to a sewing bee the novel became the chief pabulum.

On the other hand—and here again perhaps the feminine element operated—the theatre was never able to adapt itself to the new social values. The old tragedy had been of the 'heroic' kind, reflecting the ideas of a quite different society; with Rowe it tried to domesticate the heroic, but the attempt, though immediately popular, was doomed to failure, and the result was sentimentality, and flowers of rhetoric. Worse still, the old sharp critical comedy of the Restoration, in which the citizen had cut such a sorry figure of fun, in trying to present realistically a level of society it was not designed to handle was from the first marked by commonplace emotion and muddled morality; it soon declined to the *comédie larmoyante*, as early indeed as Steele's. It was partly, of course, that the strong puritan element of the new patrons of literature tended to keep serious elements away from the theatre, but it was mainly that the conservatism of the stage condemned it to unreality. It is of interest that the greatest successes were the mock dramas, such as *The Beggar's Opera* and Fielding's *Tom Thumb*; and it constitutes a criticism that George Lillo's *George Barnewell; or, The London Apprentice*, the one original, if clumsy play, which considered that the trading class might contain matter for tragedy, had no successor.

It was about 1720, when the country seemed safely assured of a long peaceful period under the Whig régime, that the new social structure finally became stable. Poetry lost all traces of courtliness, and for a long while was didactic, either physically and scientifically with Thomson and others, or philosophically and morally with such as Pope. We are still conscious of a society moulding itself, anxious to learn. Though until about 1730 the newspapers and magazines are chiefly political, the *Gentleman's Magazine* of 1731, a journal admirably adapted to a middle class, spoke more generally for it, as the far more learned organs that graced the reign of King William, such as the *Athenian Mercury*, had for the upper strata of those days, and as the more brutally popular irregular periodicals such as Tom Brown's[1] *Amusements Serious and Comical* or Ned Ward's *London Spy*, catered for the lower masses. Again we see the coalescence of the upper and lower reading strata.

At the same time, though there had been a social revolution, it had not been a cataclysm. The middle classes were newly strong and numerous, but they were still ruled by the oligarchy they nourished. So though they were strong enough—being the

---

[1] Thomas Brown, 1663–1704, went from Newport School, Salop, to Christ Church, Oxford. After three years as schoolmaster at Kingston-on-Thames, he went to London to live on his wits. Among other things, he translated Scarron's *Roman Comique*.

patrons—to have their morality expressed in their poetry and fiction, and to destroy the drama by sentimentalizing it, they still aspired to the standards of aesthetic taste of the educated and travelled magnates; architecture, pictures, gardening, furniture—all that they copied, admirably, so that museums and academies of the arts sprang into being: the first painters' studio for study from life was established in 1711. At the next social revolution, which brought up a new social stratum—the manufacturing one—the middle class imposed not only its own morals, but its own taste. It no longer aspired to better taste; it declared its own was the best. But in the eighteenth century the new sentimentality, combined with the old taste, produced for a short fifty years a happy state of ever-increasing humanity. There was still much brutality, but society was becoming aware of it. Soon the sentimental man, the man of feeling, was to loom large. For in the period of political stability attained in what we may roughly call the age of Walpole, religious controversy lost most of its old acerbity; an energetic people whose imagination was turned to practical matters had leisure to be busied about itself, its way of living and the bases of it. The physical basis was trade and farming; and we may now turn to see what were the spiritual conceptions that animated this people; what were the currents of vital ideas that formed their culture.

2. THE ETHOS

Just as the picture of society sought by the literary historian differs from that of the social historian, so does his view of the spiritual concepts which inform a society differ from that of the historian of philosophy or of religion. What we are concerned with here then is not to justify or arraign philosophies: our affair is the complex of assumptions, recognized or unconscious, by which, in the main, the people of the age lived; for what is more important than any system of philosophy is the inherited and modified attitude towards existence of the great mass of men. Philosophers may or may not enter into the picture: in our period Locke does enormously, since he appears in everybody's writings; whereas Berkeley had the minimal effect, at least immediately.

When we come to inquire into what was the general ethos of the mass of people at this time, that is, the body of assumptions the common reader of the day would suppose to lie behind any piece of writing, we are faced in an exaggerated form with the eternal contradiction that what people say they think does not always tally with what they do. Often quite contradictory sets of assumptions coexist, not only in the same society but in the same person; these antinomies are not always very apparent at the time—we are blissfully unconscious of our own—but they are more evident to a later generation. Of course in every age a national group lives on a basis of assumptions which seems to itself reasonable and homogeneous, but to us the assumptions of the Augustan age seem amazingly tangled, more so even than was apparent to Leslie Stephen, who did not pursue them back to medieval sources, and touched too lightly upon the scientific invasion. But in a work such as this, it is impossible to do more than suggest certain lines of thought which seem most to have affected literature, leaving aside what turn out to have been minor accidents without issue, however much they may have excited popular opinion at the time. We may, for instance, ignore the Bangorian controversy, which, though its social effect was to block the streets of the City and put the Royal Exchange out of action for a day, seems to us a dreary waste of Hoadlyian and other bad temper and futility.

The 'age of reason', the phrase is familiar—and shallow. It has latterly been modified by calling it 'an age of uneasy romanticism'; or, it has been regarded as one which smoothed out the metaphysics of the previous era. Such 'transition' explanations will not serve, since this age had something of its own to contribute. For though it could not be called an age of reason (as we shall see), and would not have laid claim to be such, it might very well be called an age of attempted clarity, of trying to define the limits of reason, of seeking a balance that must from now on replace the old impossible harmony. There was a new attempt to distinguish, and the clearer-headed men of this time, such as Tillotson, Swift, and Bishop Butler would have regarded as muddle-headedness the old fusion that we think (perhaps fallaciously) to have existed in men such as Donne or Sir Thomas Browne. Again and again, not only in the three mentioned above, but in Locke, John Norris of Bemerton, Synge, Sherlock, and Dean Stanhope,[1] there is stated the

---

[1] John Norris, 1657–1711, was educated at Winchester and Exeter College, Oxford. He was elected a Fellow of All Souls, was given the living of Newton St. Loe

doctrine of 'implicit belief', of accepting things on authority, reason being used only to assess the validity of the source. Not that authority made the things more understandable, since man has only a limited measure of reason: he cannot even understand nature; how should he understand God? And if it may not unjustly be said that the error of this period lay in its *esprit simpliste*, its readiness to believe that plain solutions could be found for its major problems, at least the men of those days tried to separate what could be known from what could not. Defoe, for instance, as perfect a representative as can be found, stated quite clearly in the first chapter of *The Storm* (1703) that certain things were meant to be kept secret by God—such as the cause of winds; for

. . . in Nature, the Philosopher's Business is not to look through Nature, and come to the vast open Field of Infinite Power. . . . Philosophy's [Science] aground if it is forc'd to any further Enquiry. The Christian begins just where the Philosopher ends; and when the Enquirer turns his Eyes up to Heaven, Farewel Philosopher: t'is a Sign he can make nothing of it here.

The spheres of reason and revelation were quite distinct.

In matters of general thought the early eighteenth century was one of great and sometimes brilliant activity, busied as it was in digesting the scientific revolution of the preceding hundred years. If the previous fifty had been an era of ratiocination, the second half of the Augustan period (the whole of which might be said to run from 1660 to 1740) may well be named the age of reason so long as no pejorative sense is implied; for it was an age of passionate reasoning, of reasoning which had at all costs to make the new ideas of the nature of man and the universe somehow come to terms with actual living. It would appear that the age, after the metaphysical, political, and economic war of the previous century was settling down to a vigorously revised, rather than a new basis of assumptions. Partly from the effect of the Revolution of 1688 producing a generation eager to learn, and to adjust itself to the new

in 1689, and of Bemerton in 1691. Edward Synge, 1659–1741, educated at Drogheda and Trinity College, Dublin, finally became Archbishop of Tuam. William Sherlock, *c.* 1641–1707, passed through Eton and Trinity College, Cambridge, eventually becoming Dean of St. Paul's. George Stanhope, 1660–1728, was schooled at Uppingham, Leicester, and Eton, graduated to King's College, Cambridge, and became Dean of Canterbury.

social pattern; and partly through the liberating sense of the Enlightenment (itself a part of the Revolution), the average reader of the early eighteenth century was unusually near to the philosophers of his day, notably Locke and Shaftesbury. Yet matters of high philosophy do not affect the ordinary man till the assumptions involved have become part of the pattern of life, probably without its being noticed, and it is not often that a drastic change occurs. But at this particular moment there came about so great a shift as almost to justify the adjective. For it was not till now that men in general were accepting a vaguely Copernican cosmogony (thus preparing themselves for the Newtonian universe): Milton had, at least for poetical purposes, accepted the old; and in 1693 William Holder, a Canon of St. Paul's and a Fellow of the Royal Society, wrote a textbook containing the remark: 'I shall therefore in this Discourse . . . suppose the Sun to move according to the Ptolemaic system.' Even as late as the second decade of the eighteenth century, Derham, in his *Astro-Theology*, while upholding 'the new system', would not argue 'so rigorously and obstinately as utterly to exclude or oppugn any other system', since some men were 'wedded to the Aristotelian principles or prejudiced to the Ptolemaic'. The old cosmogony, still largely held, taught that

from his supposedly fixed place [to quote Sir Charles Sherrington] man looked at the heavenly spheres enclosing him, and supposed himself the focus of a nine-fold heavenly shell. Around him the seven planets—and sun and moon were of them—journeyed without pause. Their pivot and fixed point was man. To influence him seemed the object of their being. . . . Over him marched each year the procession of the constellations. . . . Over man's head, under his foot, to either side of him, the macrocosm revolved. . . . Each and all of the planets exerted 'powers' on man. Why else should they wheel unceasingly around him?

If we compare this with the picture offered by Addison in *Spectator* 565 (he had adumbrated it in No. 420) as the ordinary educated man's vision of the indifferent universe, we can sense the kind of turmoil that might be produced in minds which possibly held both views at the same time, at different levels:

Were the Sun which enlightens this part of the Creation, with all the Host of Planetary Worlds that move about him, utterly extinguished and annihilated, they would not be miss'd more than a grain of Sand upon the Sea-shore. The Space they possess is so exceedingly little in Comparison of the whole, that it would scarce make a *Blank* in the Creation. The Chasm would be imperceptible to an Eye, that could take in the whole Compass of Nature, and pass from one End of Creation to the other.

The change in knowledge took place amid the upheaval of the seventeenth century, the idea becoming what we might call 'operative' in literature, that is a part of common apprehension, only in the eighteenth. But by 1733 Pope could, in perfect confidence that he would startle nobody, blithely refer to

> Atoms or systems into ruin hurl'd,
> And now a bubble burst, and now a world,

illustrating one of the crucial changes of the Enlightenment, the release, as it was hoped, from the constriction of the medieval vision.

It was, thus, an exciting period; but however enthusiastic for secular ideas it may seem, the stout framework of its assumptions was still the Christian metaphysic, to a large extent the medieval one, while at the same time the Christianity of the Cambridge Platonists merged strangely with the physico-theology of the scientific divines, and the Newtonianism of the new science. It was a motley of ideas in which could happily flourish either the optimism of a Shaftesbury, the pessimism of a Swift, or the cynicism of a Mandeville. The age welcomed from abroad the generous Stoic scepticism of Montaigne, or the sharp acid of La Rochefoucauld. That there were no longer the desperate dogmatic religious cults such as existed in all their violence in the previous century (together with currents of scepticism) is abundantly clear: nor is there the fine Christian humanism of a Milton or a Herbert: there is a whole tangle of threads illustrated by such terms or titles as Locke's *The Reasonableness of Christianity* (1695), Toland's *Christianity not Mysterious* (1696), or Sir George Cheyne's[1] *Philosophical Principles of Religion; Natural and Revealed* (1715). There is a temporary crisis produced by a widespread awareness of the scientific discoveries announced by the Royal Society, which affected the mass of the population.

It might have been differently resolved had the alliance between scientific and clerical thought continued after the

---

[1] George Cheyne, 1671-1743, was educated at the school at Aberdeen, and Edinburgh University. M.D.

twenties. But such an alliance we would commonly judge impossible; yet at the turn of the century scientists and theologians alike believed that to get closer to nature meant to get closer to God without in the least threatening the basis of revealed religion, and Boyle founded his lectures on science for 'The Proof of the Christian Religion against Atheists, and other notorious infidels'. How many of the lectures penetrated the general consciousness it would be hard to guess, but the *Physico-Theology* (1713) of Derham,[1] a Fellow of the Royal Society, and at the time (1711–12) when he gave these Boyle lectures rector of Upminster, must have had many readers after the puff Steele gave it in *Guardian* 175; it reached a twelfth edition before fifty years were out. 'The plain good man', Steele tells his readers,

does, as with a Wand, shew us the Wonders and Spectacles in all Nature, and the particular Capacities with which all living Creatures are endowed for their several Ways of Life; How the Organs of Creatures are made according to their different Paths in which they are to move, and provide for themselves and Families; whether they are to creep, to leap, to swim, to fly, to walk; whether they are to inherit the Bowels of the Earth, the Coverts of the Wood, the muddy or clear Streams, to howl in Forests or converse in Cities. All Life, from that of a Worm to that of a Man, is explained; and as I may so speak, the wondrous Works of the Creation, by the Observation of this Author, lie before us as Objects that create Love and Admiration, which, without such Explications, strike us only with Confusion and Amazement.

Soon he goes on to declare that the intelligent man 'will behold the Light with a new Joy, and a sort of reasonable Rapture', and (he has Burnet's *Theory of the Earth* in mind) will contemplate the distribution of earth and waters and see how perfect is the whole scheme of creation.

Steele, as distributing agent of ideas, is doing two things here: not only is he indicating the exquisite fitness of things, but also man's right to rejoice in it, to which latter we shall return. The first theme, that of perfect adaptation, was common enough in this age of reflection, of consolidation of ideas, and was neatly

---

[1] William Derham, 1657–1735, went to Trinity College, Oxford, after his schooling at Blackley Grammar School. He was vicar first of Wargrave and then of Upminster, and became Canon of Windsor in 1716. He was elected President of St. John's College, Oxford.

expressed by Pope in the famous, if to us somewhat comic couplet:

> Why has not Man a microscopic eye?
> For this plain reason, Man is not a Fly.

In his beautifully ordered encyclopaedia of current philosophies, the *Essay on Man* (1733), Nature, Providence, God, are blandly equated.

Derham's ideas cohered quite naturally with the age-old conception of the 'chain of being', which is largely the basis of the argument in Archbishop King's *De Origine Mali*. Though it does not seem to have been so popular as that other concept of the late Middle Ages, the Wheel of Fortune, it was a constant background. It was bound up with the idea of 'plenitude', in our period still generally accepted. Here, for instance, is Addison in *Spectator* 519:

> Infinite Goodness is of so communicative a Nature, that it seems to delight in the conferring of Existence upon every degree of Perceptive Being. . . . The exuberant and overflowing Goodness of the Supreme Being . . . is plainly seen . . . from his having made so little Matter . . . that does not Swarm with Life: Nor is his Goodness less seen in the Diversity than in the Multitude of living Creatures. Had he made only one Species of Animals, none of the rest would have enjoyed the Happiness of Existence: he has, therefore, *specified* in his Creation every degree of Life, every Capacity of Being. The whole Chasm in Nature, from a Plant to a Man, is filled up with divers Kinds of Creatures, rising one over another, by such a gentle and easie Ascent, that the little Transitions and Deviations from one Species to another, are almost insensible.

This assumption is everywhere to be found, in almost all the poets—Pope, Mallet, Thomson: Young expresses it with his usual turgid fullness in a passage which begins:

> Look Nature thro', 'tis neat *Gradation* all.
> By what minute degrees her scale ascends!
> Each middle Nature join'd at each Extreme,
> To that above it join'd, to that beneath.
> Parts, into Parts reciprocally shot,
> Abhor Divorce . . .

to drone on to consider the place of man through analogy, 'man's surest guide below'—an unconscious medieval touch.

For whatever new ideas of nature as revealed by microscope

and telescope might excite or agitate the age, man still had to ponder his place in the universe. The new cosmogony of infinite space popularized by Addison was accepted even by the orthodox clergy, as witness Derham in his *Astro-Theology* (1715), of which the sub-title was 'or a Demonstration of the Being and Attributes of God from a Survey of the Heavens'. But did man's new position make him more humble, or less? Though the old cosmogony had placed him at the centre of the universe, that centre was the lowest pit of matter, at the farthest remove from heaven and the pure incorruptible bodies. So the new cosmogony, in which the solar system was a barely perceptible speck, did not degrade him further. But if in neither system did man have anything to be proud of, evidently if God had thought it worth while to send His son to die for him, man cannot have been unimportant in God's eyes. So in either case humility must be preached: and the poets of our period seldom fail to remind man that it is through erring pride that he makes his gravest mistakes. But at any time much is bound to depend on the individual attitude: a *contemptus mundi* may engender pride or humility—maybe both at the same time. For some, no doubt, it would appear that in the vast scheme of things security had gone; the silence of the infinite spaces terrified, we may be sure, more people than Pascal, though others, possibly, felt with Fontenelle, when concerned with space alone, that at last they had room to breathe. Yet it would now seem unlikely that man was God's only concern; he might not even be His main concern, an idea that had occurred to the Cambridge Platonists before that of the plurality of worlds had been popularized by Fontenelle.

Yet many still clung to the belief, so hard to avoid, that the universe had been created for man. So Blackmore[1] in *The Creation* (1712):

> What Skill on all its Surface is bestow'd,
> To make the Earth for Man a fit Abode . . .
> Did not the Springs and Rivers drench the Land
> Our Globe would grow a Wilderness of Sand;
> The Plants and Groves, the tame and savage Beast,
> And Man, their Lord, would die with Drought opprest.

---

[1] Sir Richard Blackmore, *c.* 1655–1729, went from Westminster to St. Edmund's Hall, Oxford, but took his degree of M.D. at Padua. He was made physician in ordinary to William III, who knighted him in 1697, and to Queen Anne.

Now, as you see, the floating Element
Part loose in Streams, part in the Ocean pent,
So wisely is dispos'd as may conduce
To Man's Delight, or necessary Use.

The notion was combated, by Pope more pithily than by anyone, in a passage echoing Gay:

Know, Nature's children shall divide her care;
The fur that warms a monarch warm'd a bear.
While Man exclaims, 'See all things for my use!'
'See man for mine!' replies a pamper'd goose.

But here the scale of being came to the rescue; just as there were infinite gradations below man down to the 'most despicable insect', so must there be a similar stretch between him and God. Addison states this, in the *Spectator* just quoted, and then, resting upon the authority of Locke, states that man 'fills up the middle Space between the Animal and Intellectual Nature, the visible and invisible World'.

The word 'intellectual' slips in unobtrusively; but what, it might be asked, was in fact man's intellectual nature? And here again the age had to adjust itself, for by Locke's great authority the belief that man came into the world with 'innate ideas' was no longer generally received; his argument that at birth man's mind was a blank, a *tabula rasa*, gained almost immediate and complete acceptance—though there were stubborn conservatives such as Swift and Prior. What man thought and felt, how he reasoned, and so on, was determined by his experiences; and seeing how this affected his theory of knowledge, it naturally made a difference to his idea of himself; it enabled him to fit more readily into the new conception of the universe, one of a clockwork regularity rather than of moral order.

From one point of view it might be said that the age was adjusting itself to the notion of the machine. The Cartesian presentation of the automatic animal, the compulsion of Newtonian gravitation, and so, in spite of adjustments of the medieval concept of an ordered creation, the replacement of the mystic universe by Locke's apparently mechanistic one, the separation of soul and body, mind and matter, all these things needed digesting, and proved indigestible. If at one moment it seemed possible to adore, not so much the God of the universe, but

God in his universe (the universe as representing God: the Deistic position) as science became ever less biological and more and more mathematical and astronomical, the object of adoration became so very remote, inorganic, and indifferent that the attempt of the Church to absorb the new point of view had to be abandoned. Nevertheless, while the new conceptions which attributed importance only to what could be measured or weighed, so substituting quantity for quality, seemed dominant, the old idea of value latent in the chain of being still had enormous imaginative force; even the medieval idea of 'degree' still persisted—it is endemic in the *Essay on Man* and appears even in the *Whig Examiner* (No. 5). And, it may have been as a compensation, the organic sense prevailed in the new taste in 'natural' gardens, a taste which reacted against the formality of the seventeenth century in which God geometrized; and again we find the imagination, first descanted on by Shaftesbury, and then by Addison (popularizing Locke), becoming a creative principle, and in poetry addressed as such, first by Mallet in *The Excursion* (1727), and then, more notably, by Akenside during the forties.

All this, of course, is a monstrous simplification; but if in many ways the thought of this period seems extremely diversified, its expression in educated circles freer than ever before, there was at least, as already suggested, the unifying influence of Christianity, a Christianity which had for the most part abjured 'enthusiasm' since this seemed to bring only strife and greater divergence. But whose Christianity? Catholics apart, who at the moment were not very numerous, who had no political power and only, one imagines, small cultural influence, it would be difficult to find even within the Churches themselves more than a rather superficial verbal agreement on Christian fundamentals. Defoe's Christianity was clearly something different from Swift's, though both in many respects held, intellectually, much the same view as to where reason ended and revelation should be accepted. But they held it with a different intensity of passion; the view of Addison (who was perilously near Deism) would differ from both of theirs, as becomes clear from the moment we give the smallest attention to these authors. One does not imagine that Berkeley's religion held for him at all the same sense of divine immanence as it may have for Swift, or in a different sense again for Joseph Butler, or Peter Browne,[1] whose *Divine Analogy* (1733) is an answer to Berkeley's *Alciphron*. Outside the Churches there were the professed Deists, while the words Arian and Socinian were bandied about with a pleasant sense of freedom from consequences. Yet if there was no formal Christian faith behind the philosophies of such opposite thinkers as Mandeville and Shaftesbury, there was a great deal of common Christian sentiment.

The Christianity, moreover, as almost throughout its history in England since Tudor times, was strongly if patchily tinctured with Stoicism, which had been popular in England not only as a result of the Renaissance, but of the Reformation also, with its dependence on St. Augustine. But its vogue during the eighteenth century is remarkable for its extent, more especially among those who insisted upon man's insignificance, the oneness of humanity, and its being part of some divine process, some 'stupendous whole'. L'Estrange's presentation of *Seneca* reached its tenth edition in 1711: Jeremy Collier published his *Meditations* of Marcus Aurelius in 1701, the first of the fifty-eight editions which appeared during the century. It is not surprising then that the more educated poets should exhibit the influence; what is more significant is the general level down to which it reached. The most striking example, perhaps, is that of Stephen Duck,[2] the thresher poet, and his labourer friend. Spence tells us in the 'Account of the Author' which prefaces the *Poems* of 1736 that '*Seneca's* Morals had made the name of *L'Estrange* dear to them', and again: 'He had liked the little he had read of *Epictetus*; but it was *Seneca* that had made him happy in his own mind.' That is the strongest evidence possible of how widely Stoicism was diffused: we find it in the most diversely opposed places.

But whatever the divergencies might be, there was, in contradistinction with the older Christianity, a sense that the world itself was enjoyable in a way pleasing to God, and that beauty was not of the Devil. There was nothing new in this—one need think only of the then unknown Traherne—but it was new for the mass of people to have this sense, untinged though it was for them with the deep mystic exaltation that makes every

---

[1] Peter Browne, 1662?–1735, of Trinity College, Dublin. Was made Provost 1699, and Bishop of Cork and Ross, 1710.

[2] Stephen Duck, 1705–56, largely self-educated, was ordained in 1746, and became Rector of Byfleet in 1752. He was librarian to Queen Caroline.

sentence of Traherne glow on the page, and is not lacking in Marvell. 'I persuade myself', Ray[1] tells us in *The Wisdom of God in the Creation* (1691), 'that the bountiful and gracious Author of man's being and faculties and all things else, delights in the beauty of his creation and is well pleased with the industry of man in adorning the earth with beautiful cities. . . .' Such a statement, Canon C. E. Raven comments, 'represents an attitude towards Nature which is new and vastly important'.

This delight in the worth of the world as aesthetically satisfying, intellectually educative, and spiritually significant reflects the best Hebrew, Greek and Christian thought; . . . the direct insistence upon the essential unity of natural and revealed religion as alike proceeding from and integrated by the divine purpose, had not found clear and well-informed expression until Ray's book was published.

For Canon Raven the importance lies in the relation between religion and science; but though for us also this aspect is important, the passage is of the highest interest to the amateur of literature as helping to determine the way poetry was to take from the twenties. There were, inevitably, other influences on poetry leading in the same direction as Ray's; the whole philosophy of Locke, which to the common view seemed mechanistic, and the strong Deistic tendency within Christianity, which could produce the passages that occur in Addison's *Spectators*, in, for example, No. 531, where we read: 'We exist in Place and Time; the Divine Being fills the Immensity of Space with his Presence, and inhabits Eternity.' This, however, is to consider Him only 'by the light of reason and philosophy. If we would see him in all the wonders of his mercy, we must have recourse to revelation. . . .' The Theism, if it be such, and not an expression of the sense of God's immanence (to distinguish if from Deism is no more than a logical quibble), is still clearer in No. 565, where he also quotes Newton's description of infinite space as 'the sensorium of the godhead'. This came alarmingly near the pantheistic, Spinozist, conceptions into which Pope, it seemed to some, was inadvertently trapped. No doubt we today need not fear these slippery paths; they were, it is evident, gaily

[1] John Ray, 1627-1705, passed through Braintree Grammar School. He transferred from St. Catherine's College, Cambridge, to Trinity College, of which he became Fellow. 'The father of English Natural History', he lectured on Greek, mathematics, and the humanities.

enough trodden in the first years of the eighteenth century, until safer, if duller, notions prevailed, perhaps, as some may think, not altogether to the benefit of the Churches. It was all a part of the Enlightenment.

Freed, as they felt, from the shackles of the old dispensation, living in an age when men could for the first time, if discreet enough (and well born enough), fairly openly declare their disbelief not only in Church doctrine but even in God, men were forced to find a new explanation of moral being. So the age seems to have been concerned to an unusual degree with the problem of evil, the solution of which it based largely on scholastic arguments, themselves derived through Neoplatonism and Aristotle, lightly glossed by scientific discovery. Much of the argument is stated in Archbishop King's[1] *De Origine Mali* of 1702, translated in 1730 by Edmund Law.[2] Secondly it was concerned with the absorption into revealed religion of scientific discovery, an attempt which failed; and thirdly it struggled to make scientific discovery itself a basis for religion, which led, on the whole, to Deism. In the process good and evil ceased to have their old connotations; evil was no longer willed by an individual, but was something implicit in the nature of things, and that had to be explained. All partial evil was universal good, a sentiment which may account for there being in this period so little conflict at a deep level. Among the major imaginative writers Swift alone reveals the stress of this great conflict, and among the theologians Joseph Butler and, perhaps, William Law. Faced with this general situation and the consequent problems, and believing that scholastic thinking was merely another name for scholastic cobwebs, humanity, it was obvious, should not presume to scan God, and the proper study of mankind was man. And here we find the real importance of the conception of plenitude and the scale of being, for it provided help towards solving the problem of evil. How it did so seemed clear to the popular philosophers of the time, and was well expressed by King:

God might indeed have refrain'd from creating, and continu'd

---

[1] William King, 1650–1729, was educated at Dungannon and Trinity College, Dublin. He became Bishop of Derry and finally Archbishop of Dublin.

[2] Edmund Law, 1703–87, went from Kendal Grammar School to Christ's College, Cambridge. He became University Librarian, was elected Master of Peterhouse, and in 1768 was made Bishop of Carlisle.

alone, Self-sufficient, and perfect to all Eternity; but his Infinite Goodness would by no means allow it; this oblig'd him to produce external things; which things, since they could not possibly be perfect, the Divine Goodness preferr'd imperfect ones to none at all. Imperfection then arose from the Infinity of Divine Goodness.

So, since they were possible, even the most horrible beasts of prey had to be, the stronger devouring the weaker. King recognized 'a perpetual war between the elements, between animals, and men'. So evil was not due to man's wilful choice, as Milton held, but from something inherent in nature itself: that is why Pope's 'vindication' of God's ways to man differs from Milton's 'justification'. There is no Grace, for there is no possible flouting of God. All things, even evil things—there being some confusion between imperfection and evil—were the result of God's goodness; thus whatever was was right. Even wicked men:

> If plagues or earthquakes break not Heav'n's design,
> Why then a Borgia, or a Catiline?

and since that philosophy had the support of such great thinkers as Spinoza and Leibnitz, Pope and Bolingbroke could quite happily accept it.

But Pope and Bolingbroke did not by any means belong to the group of optimists; they were too Tory for that. For remarkably enough—and it is perhaps a tribute to the sincerity of political feeling in those days—the line of demarcation was Trade–Dissent–Whig–Optimist, following on Locke, and Land–Church–Tory–Pessimist, following on Hobbes (politically), and the fidelity with which the dichotomy works out is almost comic, though there were, naturally, exceptions. Thus on the one side we get Addison, and Shaftesbury with his belief in the essential goodness of man and the kindness of his instincts, and all Button's, with Steele especially in support; their optimism was supported by the idea of progress then beginning to be generally accepted. On the other side there are the Tories in general, Prior and the Brothers' Club merged with the Scriblerians, with Butler to follow, Mandeville playing opposite to Steele; and with them, above all, Swift, who believed man to be a fallen creature, redeemable only by grace, and holding no belief whatever in human progress.

That Pope should, even from his Tory position, at least look towards the optimists is because his main philosophic work was written after 1730, when the sharp definitions of the Enlightenment were beginning to get a little blurred. Things were not quite what they had seemed, and even optimism turned out to be a philosophy of endurance (almost a Stoicism), or at least one of somewhat austere acceptance: in short it was in about the thirties that the picture began to change a little. The poets, excited as they were at one time by the new scientific revelation of the mysterious ways God moved his wonders to perform, were forced as soon as they accepted any subjectivist psychology to refuse the metaphysical implications of the *Principia* and the *Opticks*. It became clear to them, as Whitehead has pointed out, that by this philosophy 'Nature is a dull affair, soundless, scentless, colourless, merely the hurrying of material, endlessly, meaninglessly'.

The reaction against science, its anti-rationalism (in the scholastic sense), its threat to humanism, is apparent in satirists besides the Tories such as Swift and Pope. And, again, towards the forties it was felt that the chain of being did not quite fit in. If it was fixed, all was not for the best in the best of all possible worlds; and though the time had not come for Johnson's criticism of the whole idea in *Rasselas*, nor Voltaire's derision in *Candide*, a certain uneasiness was becoming apparent. In a fixed scale nobody could rise unless someone fell, and this was morally monstrous. Also, if partial evil really was universal good, there could not possibly be any improvement. 'The optimist's proof of the rationality of the general constitution of things', Lovejoy tells us, 'turned out to be a proof of its essential immorality.' And besides, this sort of notion was far too static for an age which had the Baconian vision, an age in which the idea of progress was already fairly potent, though still new. Even Addison—who could be relied upon to touch every kind of feeling that was in the air—had dallied with the notion of the progress of the soul, though indeed before him Henry More had vaguely foreshadowed it. In *Spectator* 111 he develops the idea that:

To look upon the Soul as going from Strength to Strength, to consider that she is to shine for ever with new Accessions of Glory, and brighten to all Eternity; that she will be still adding Virtue to Virtue, and Knowledge to Knowledge; carries in it something wonderfully agreeable to that Ambition which is natural to the Mind of Man.

Leibnitz supported the view in his *The Principles of Nature and Grace.* 'Our happiness', he said, 'never will consist, and ought not to consist, in a full enjoyment in which there is nothing more to desire, and which would make our mind dull, but in a perpetual progress to new pleasures and new perfections.' And Edmund Law, departing a little from King when glossing him, suggested that God cannot have meant to make progress impossible.

In the forties the poets came out full in support of the doctrine of progress, of 'temporalizing the Chain of Being' as Lovejoy puts it: Young in *Night Thoughts*, and Akenside in *Pleasures of the Imagination*. Young was certainly a Christian, and Akenside probably was; but it is interesting to find the Deist Thomson beforehand with them in arguing in *Liberty*, as a Pythagorean, for the progress of the soul. But he expresses it best in the Deistic Hymn at the end of *The Seasons* (1730), in the splendid last paragraph,

> . . . I cannot go
> Where Universal Love not smiles around,
> Sustaining all yon orbs, and all their sons;
> From *seeming Evil* still educing *Good*,
> And *Better* thence again, and *Better* still,
> In infinite progression. But I lose,
> Myself in Him, in Light Ineffable! . . .

The idea of the perfectibility of man was well launched.

All this, evidently, is partly an attempt to rationalize the irrational; and so far the period might be dubbed the age of reason. But it was rather, as suggested, the age of attempted clarity, for though the men of this age appealed to reason, they never believed in its supremacy. Swift was sceptical of it, even grew to hate speculative reason, though he believed that man could be guided by reason if only he would let himself be. 'In *Gulliver's Travels* he found that reason, a human quality, was hardly to be found in humanity.' Pope, in the *Essay on Man*, constantly puts instinct before reason, and Prior in *Solomon* asks:

> Instinct and Reason how can we divide?
> 'Tis the Fool's Ign'rance, and the Pedant's Pride.

Indeed, in a mechanistic universe, or with such a predestinate man as is glanced at in Prior's incompleted poem on *Pre-*

destination, how can reason be effective? Prior's *Alma* is in its whole intention against the brain being the seat of the mind. Of further interest is the adumbration of the idea of the sub-conscious: here, for instance, in *Alma*:

> As well your Motion, as your Thought
> Is all by hidden Impulse wrought:
> Ev'n saying, that You Think or Walk,
> How like a Country 'Squire you talk!

In Fenton's[1] Ode 'What art thou, Life?':

> Instructed then by intuition we,
> Shall the vain effort of our wisdom see—

namely at the Judgement Day; and again in Epistle I of Pope's *Moral Essays*.

It is necessary to try to gather together the threads which compose the background tapestry of the period, in the hope of seeing what general attitude towards life suffused the literature of the time. How does it fit in with the picture of the seething society, the rising middle class? Fairchild, after stressing the importance of Whig ideas up to the end of Queen Anne's reign, goes on:

Their work shows how puritan Protestantism gradually became permeated with latitudinarian views which are sometimes so 'broad' as to be indistinguishable from those of deism. Furthermore, their tendency to reject outward authority, and to regard God, or nature, or reason, or conscience, as a universal faculty of the human heart contains the seed of a new literature and a new religion.

And this represents the new start. The religion did not de-velop, or was absorbed and transformed in Methodism, while the Church, with Butler, returned to orthodoxy and its traditional pessimism. In literature the effect was more lasting.

For the total result of the politico-religious struggle, the scientific approach, the renewed consciousness of the chain of being, the legitimacy of delight in nature, the revived Stoicism

---

[1] Elijah Fenton, 1683-1730, graduated from Jesus College, Cambridge, in 1704. After accompanying the Earl of Orrery to Flanders as his private secretary, he became a schoolmaster, finally obtaining the Mastership of the Free Grammar School at Sevenoaks.

—the last superimposed upon Christianity—was to create, if only temporarily, a strong social sense, with which went a humanitarianism which in about the sixties in some minds degenerated into sentimentality (the word was invented then). The latter chimed in well with the natural trend of the new middle class. It is, however, the former which is the more important in the first half of the century; and we remember that the whole effort of the early essayists was to build up the social conception. There was, however, on the other side, the pull of individualism, a necessary corollary of the extreme Protestantism of trading dissent, producing an attitude of mind well put forward by Professor R. H. Tawney. Speaking of the difference between the England of Shakespeare and the England which emerged in 1700, he says, 'The essence of the change was the disappearance of the idea that social institutions and economic activities were related to common ends, which gave them their significance, and which served as their criterion.' And he goes on to suggest that it was only a mysticism of reason existing together with a mysticism of emotion that enabled this part of the century to find 'in the beneficence of natural instincts a substitute for the God whom it had expelled from contact with society'. The setting of the ethos within a framework of ideas of Nature is a welcome reminder of the theme so admirably developed by Professor Basil Willey; but to suppose that when men agreed with Pope that

> . . . God and Nature link'd the gen'ral frame
> And bade Self-love and Social be the same,

they meant that individual enterprise was given the loose is to miss the social and moral coherence that Pope and his contemporaries were always insisting upon. Butler, for instance, was to go painstakingly into the whole relation between self-love and benevolence. Moreover, the word 'social' was in the early part of the eighteenth century of enormous significance, with a large area of emotional reverberations. Pope was pointing out that man was a dual creature, actuated by 'two consistent motions', 'And one regards itself, and one the whole'. There was, of course, nothing new in this, and it is thoroughly in concordance with the thought of the time that this should once more echo Marcus Aurelius: 'Be you governed by the reason within you; pursue that which is most for your own, and the

Common Interest. For to speak strictly, these Two are but one and the same.' 'If man could govern himself within by reason...', the phrase is Milton's; in this age men so obviously heirs of his thought sighed after reason, but were under no illusions as to the limits of its realm. Perhaps they had lost the concept of 'right reason'.

II

DEFOE TO 1710

THE most sanguine optimist could not hope for a more perfect representative of the changing, seething society of the time than Daniel Defoe, embodying as he does the essence of the new middle class. First and foremost a citizen of action, he relentlessly drove his pen as being the most effective way to become the useful member of the community he earnestly wished to be. Though it is commonly said that had he been successful in 'negoce', as he called it, he would have written little but treatises on trade, monographs on money-making, varied with some political verse; that, in short, the corruption of a tradesman proved the generation of an author; yet it is possible that Dunton was nearer the mark when he wrote apropos of him: 'It is hard to leave off when not only the itch and inclination, but the necessity of writing, lies so heavy upon a man.' His earliest known efforts, not discovered until 1946, take the form of Meditations, pious exercises in Pindarics together with abstracts of sermons, which he compiled at the age of about twenty; but from that time it never occurred to him to write about anything that was not of immediate practical scope, making that claim even for his novels, which he regarded, or at least professed to regard, as contributions towards the reformation of manners; for since his imagination was creative in the world of actuality, he always worked for an immediate purpose in the hope of visible results. Whether he wrote about trade or politics, apparitions or servants, criminals or voyagers, it was always as a reporting journalist, but one whose interest in facts was burningly eager, and whose imagination was like a magnifying glass to make the dim vivid; and as very often the artist in him took charge and made the journalism glorious, the avowed moralistic object is apt to become obscured.

In addition to his being in business, Defoe's position as a Dissenter (the first to write anything impressive other than religious allegory or sectarian controversy), makes him central to that body of readers that was soon to become dominant in the literary field. Already mature when James II attempted his tyranny, he could hardly fail to be Whiggish, a state of mind conducive to his later adoration of William III. His dissent, however, was an eclectic affair. From Samuel Annesley, his first pastor—on whose death he wrote one of his most tedious poems—he derived not only a Calvinistic denial of grace, but a dislike of dogmatic insistence, of fierce politico-religious strife, which the later Defoe would at any rate find contrary to the interests of trade. Annesley, however, dwelt in an atmosphere too rarefied for Defoe, and would never have tolerated the assumption to be found again and again in his sometime charge's work that necessity condones wicked actions. But Charles Morton, later first Vice-President of Harvard, Master of Stoke Newington Academy where Defoe got his schooling, was a disciple of Wilkins, famous in the Royal Society, and he inculcated a firm belief in Baconian progress, making, it would seem, no distinction between the two philosophies, divine and natural. He taught, nevertheless, that there existed an operative providence always at hand to help those strenuous to help themselves. From both, probably, Defoe derived that deep apprehension of the manifestations of supernatural evil seldom absent from the puritanical consciousness. But beyond this, being a Dissenter bred in him two sentiments which we meet again and again as props in the intellectual or emotional structure of his writings. The first is a constant awareness of having something to battle for, an integrity to maintain, supported by a fierce puritan individualism; the second, which was to colour all his imaginative work, the sense of being shut out of communal life. Denied entry into a university, as all Dissenters were, prevented from taking any official part in the government of the country unless he should resort to the dishonourable ruse of Occasional Conformity, cut off to a large degree from the higher social spheres—the sects already marking a class distinction—he felt removed from the main flow of life. No doubt he thought himself lacking in social ease through defects of class habits which his education in a dissenting academy (brilliant though Morton was) had not been able to remedy, and as late as 1712 he was to write with some bitterness:

'Tis evident the great Imperfection of our Accademies is want of Conversation; this the Publick Universities enjoy, ours cannot. . . . Conversation polishes the Gentlemen in Discourse; acquaints 'em with Men, and with Words; lets them into the Polite part of Language; gives them Style, Accent, Delicacy, and Taste in Expression.

And when he said that it was his 'disaster first to be set apart for, and then to be set apart from' the sacred employ of a dissenting minister, he had in mind the presumed uncouthness made fun of by Swift when he discoursed on the Æolists. He exaggerated, as a sensitive man will; for the Dissenters were not such a race apart as he suggests; indeed that Defoe, a wholesale hosier and the son of a butcher and tallow-chandler, should resent not being admitted into the company of the great is merely a sign that he misjudged the level to which his trading class had risen. But there was no real bar, though it was probably harder for a Dissenter to rise if he came of humble parents. After all, Harley himself came of dissenting stock; Annesley was nephew to the Earl of Anglesea; Samuel Wesley, a schoolfellow of his, married Annesley's daughter, who thus became 'the mother of Methodism' though Samuel Wesley himself became an Anglican; and John Wesley could claim cousinship with the Wellesleys, and so with the house of Mornington; Dudley Ryder, afterwards Chief Justice, sprang from exactly the same milieu as Defoe. It would appear, however, that his fellow writers did their best to make him feel an outcast. He seems to have had no friends among them. It may have been that there was something secretive about him; in any case, nearly all of them, giants and pigmies alike, loaded him with contempt and abuse, or twitted him for being an uneducated man devoid of Latin or other university learning. Swift even went so far as to add to the usual shrug of 'illiterate fellow' the crowning insult of pretending to forget his name.

One cannot say how far Defoe's eager interest in politics was born of his sense that his like were oppressed; from the first he was politically minded. He played a minor part in the Monmouth rebellion, and took a hand in the wordy war which raged over the Declaration of Indulgence of 1688, echoing Halifax's warning to the Dissenters that they were to be hugged now that they might be the better squeezed at another time. Urged by the typical panic fear of Popery he declared that 'he had rather the Church of England should pull our clothes off by fines and forfeitures, than the Papists should fall upon the Church and the Dissenters, and pull off our skins by fire and faggot'. He rode in a guard of honour to William III on his accession, and in 1691 was impelled into verse on the occasion of Preston's plot, with *A New Discovery of an Old Intrigue, a*

Satire Levelled at Treachery and Ambition, a work it is wiser not to read.

He announced at the time that this was the first fruit of his pen, and would be the last unless some good came of it. It was evidently not so salutary as he hoped (which is not altogether to be wondered at) for no considerable work of his appeared until 1697, although he had written this book, *An Essay upon Projects,* some four years earlier. Possibly he had been too busy extricating himself from the pit of bankruptcy into which as a trader he had fallen, to the tune of £17,000, in 1692; and only when he was finding his feet again—he never found them completely—was he at leisure to see it through the press. It is a surprising work, both practical and fantastic, going into the minutest details, suggesting moreover schemes, some of which if not altogether visionary, were two hundred years before their time. A few, certainly, were in the air, such as life-insurances (introduced by Barbon), friendly societies, and so on; but it was long before the government founded military academies, took over the roads—and then not on Defoe's grandiose scale—or instituted the income tax; longer still before it sponsored old-age pensions. Here already we see Defoe's imagination working in the realm of fact, an imagination so inclusive and formative that we have barely caught up with it. Most significant, however, in relation to the social change going on was his suggestion for an Academy for Women.

In Defoe's youth the educated middle-class woman was a wonder, if not a bold freak, though there were brilliant exceptions such as the highly cultivated Elizabeth Elstob, who wrote an English-Saxon grammar (but then she was the sister of a don), and Mary Astell, who, following the lead given by the first Duchess of Newcastle, and by Mrs. Maken, in 1694 forestalled Defoe in his ideas as to feminine education. But in the main the average middle-class woman could read, write, and cipher, and little more. She might be given a hint of instruction later on to make her a bearable companion, but it was bestowed upon her condescendingly after the manner of Addison, with a good flavouring of contempt; we are tempted even to wonder exactly what education Swift gave Stella. You could take it for granted, however, that Mr. Sealand's wife and daughters were virtually uneducated; it was the accepted state of things.

Defoe argued a different view, possibly in response to a general sense stirring in the new middle class, which was not that of the universities;

> I have often thought of it [he wrote] as one of the most barbarous Customs in the world, considering us as a Civiliz'd and Christian Countrey, that we deny the advantages of Learning to Women. We reproach the Sex every day with Folly and Impertinence, while I am confident, had they the advantages of Education equal to us, they wou'd be guilty of less than ourselves.

Thus he opens his 'Project', to argue that it is the neglect of the good qualities and senses of women, which he assumes to be greater and quicker than those of men, that ruins them, so that, their virtues running to waste, they degenerate into being 'turbulent, clamorous, noisy, *and the Devil*'. The unbounded faith in education is possibly even more symptomatic of his age than his belief in women; for when a new class comes within reach of what has so far been denied it in favour of an educated coterie, it believes that education will perform every miracle; and in speaking as he did Defoe expressed the determination of the new class to cultivate its brains.

Nor, perhaps, is the style less symptomatic. It has bones and sinews rather than nervous grace: it is simple and appropriate, reflecting the need to express practical things workably. To ascribe the new simplicity in the prose of the latter end of the century entirely to the Royal Society, Glanvill and Sprat, together with L'Estrange and the *Observator*, is to leave out half the tale. These had their effect, certainly, but so had earlier the political pamphleteers of the Civil War and Commonwealth decades, and the unadorned manner in preaching practised as early as 1640 by the 'plaine pack-staffe Methodists'. Here, however, the result arose from the assumption that in speaking of plain things to plain people plain words are best. Defoe's apology at the end of the *Essay* is revealing:

> As for such who read Books only to find out the Author's *faux Pas*, who will quarrel at the Meanness of Stile, errors of Pointing, Dulness of Expression, or the like, I have but little to say to them; ... As to Language, I have been rather careful to make it speak *English* suitable to the Manner of the Story, than to dress it up with Exactness of Stile; choosing rather to have it Free and Familiar, according to the nature of Essays, than to strain at a Perfection of Language, which I rather wish for than pretend to be Master of.

Artist though he was in prose Defoe never pretended to any
artistry in that medium, pluming himself rather upon his
verse: he merely talked, as he supposed, with his pen; and so,
more than any other single person, is responsible for bringing
prose back to the colloquial, to the living norm, a process as
necessary from time to time for prose as it is for poetry. He is
sometimes long-winded, but you never feel ill at ease with him.
There is little aristocracy in his usual style, it is Everyman's style,
and to Everyman it sounds extremely persuasive. Yet it is not
a 'demotic' style; it comprises a wide vocabulary, it is often
suave, even dignified. It can be much in the style of a leading
article in one of our national papers today, and certainly
would not disgrace the best of them. By 1697 he had found its
basis, and in a very few years developed it to a point where it
became the perfect instrument for what he wanted it to do. His
way of writing, however, is enormously varied, since he is
always careful to make it suitable to the manner of any 'story'
he may be engaged with.

Nevertheless the most popular of the many pamphlets which
Defoe showered upon the world at this time was in verse, *The True
Born Englishman* (1701), a reply to Tutchin's peevish poem *The
Foreigners*; and the extraordinary reception it met with—it went
into edition after edition, pirated and otherwise—throws a light
upon, if not the reading public's capacity to appreciate poetry,
for the work was hardly that, at least its ability to enjoy verse,
and its hunger for something that would amuse it with purpose.
Omitting the Introduction, the sort of invocation of Satire to
which Defoe was far too prone, the reader would come directly
upon:

> Where-ever God erects a House of Prayer,
> The Devil always builds a Chapel there:
> And 'twill be found upon Examination,
> The latter has the largest Congregation . . .

What could be more promising than opening with the old
proverb? Anyone might be lured into reading a booklet with
such a beginning, for, as with so many of Defoe's works, the
title might seem to contradic: the contents; and for all anybody knew this might well be a piece in support of Tutchin's
attack on William's Dutch predilections. He would soon be
undeceived, for after describing the ruling aristocracy, Defoe
goes on:

> These are the Heroes who despise the *Dutch*,
> And rail at new-come Foreigners so much;
> Forgetting that themselves are all deriv'd
> From the most Scoundrel Race that ever liv'd;
> A horrid Crowd of Rambling Thieves and Drones
> Who ransack'd Kingdoms, and dispeopled Towns.

Like all Defoe's verse pieces it is rather too dilated, for he was seldom content to make his point once; but it runs along so well, it is so good-humoured, it is such obvious commonsensical truth, and it hits the proud so shrewdly, that nearly everybody could laugh with it. Who could resist the pulse of:

> *Dutch, Walloons, Flemmings, Irishmen*, and *Scots,*
> *Vaudois* and *Valtolins* and *Hugonots,*
> In good Queen *Bess's* Charitable Reign,
> Supply'd us with three hundred thousand Men:
> Religion, *God we thank thee*, sent them hither,
> Priests, Protestants, the Devil and all together;

or deny the logic of

> A *True-born Englishman's* a Contradiction,
> In Speech an Irony, in Fact a Fiction.

The whole thing is a gay performance, even if it does conclude with the prim moral tag, ''Tis personal virtue only makes us great.' Designed for the non-aristocratic reader, making fun of patrician pretensions, it had a sharp political point, yet was so genially written that even the opposite side had to admit the fun for fear of being laughed at. As a successful political pamphlet it ranks with Halifax's *Letter to a Dissenter*, and Swift's *Conduct of the Allies*.

The poetry, like nearly all Defoe's rhyming, is but lively swinging prose, which to judge from the way he constantly breaks into it he wrote as easily as he did the less obvious harmony. 'By his printing a poem every day,' Dunton remarked, 'one would think that he rhimed in his sleep.' The rhymes were no difficulty to him, for he never halted to wait for a good one if an approximation was to hand. Yet his verse is more than doggerel, and sometimes he achieves a good line, as where, in reference to Charles II, he speaks of

> Throughout his Lazy, Long, Lascivious Reign.

His model, which he falls far short of, was clearly Dryden, especially in Part II; and his verse has some qualities in common with that of Swift and Pope, its natural tone, its unstrained word order. Yet it is too careless, too unlopped, ever to achieve the concentration of poetry. His more lofty attempts are unbearably tedious, his vaster pieces drone along fatiguingly; but occasionally, when he gets excited, the verse begins to move, even to dance, and when it is pithy as well, it is in the best tradition of English light verse. Take, for instance, his very long *Jure Divino* of 1706, a satire in no less than twelve books. It is drearily soporific, but now and again you will come upon a passage such as:

> He that invested with the Robes of Power,
> Thinks 'tis his Right the People to devour,
> Will always find some stubborn Fools remain,
> That ha' so little Wit, they won't be slain;
> That always turn again when they're opprest,
> And basely spoil the Gay Tyrannick Jest:
> Madly take Arms, and with their Masters Fight,
> And talk of Nature, Laws of God, and Right.

Put into prose, this is: 'I have heard it publicly preached that if the King commanded my head, and sent his messengers to fetch it, I was bound to submit, and stand still while it was cut off.' Like other doctrines of the extreme high-flying Church party, this theme of non-resistance always gave a livelier flow to Defoe's rarely stagnant ink.

It would be useless to try to give in a short space a regular account of his harried life from 1697 to 1710, or of the more than a hundred works which he thrust through the press in that time. Till 1703 at the height of his good luck, consulted on ways and means by the Chancellor of the Exchequer, to some extent in the counsels of William III, already in confidential service, and employing himself in writing pamphlets in verse or prose, his life was even then as full of affairs as the energy of most men could cope with. But after the disaster of 1703, when he emerged from prison a ruined man, his life became one of fantastic activity. Not only was he ceaselessly engaged on secret service all over the country, including Scotland, where he was sent on intelligence work and to advise upon trade, but he tirelessly produced his paper, the *Review*, always lively, provocative, and entertaining, and added to this continuous writing even more spasmodic books and pamphlets than hitherto. Yet caught up all the while in the furious controversies of his time, hunted by his creditors, and sometimes, if we are to believe him, in danger of his life, his work consistently shows a high quality, often amounting to genius. His glorious talent for magnificent lying, his almost equal talent for supreme honesty, both of these being literary qualities which he put to admirable use, make his life extremely baffling. Nevertheless the outline is plain, since most of his existence was passed in the limelight of notoriety; the chief lines of his thoughts are clear, since these were continuously poured into the press.

His main subjects of discourse were trade, politics, religion, and morals, treated indifferently in prose or rhyme, with such variety, and such organic intermingling of themes that to dissect them out for individual treatment would be to murder the whole and make the parts dull. If throughout he wrote with a tendency to paradox and satire, with a pungency which increased as his style matured, all was invariably based on common sense, common experience, common practice. His originality, and he was the most inventive of geniuses, lay in his treatment. He could be directly forceful, suave, or ironical: prefacing invective with an apology for not being able to descend to the Billingsgate of his opponents, he could be as furious in attack as nimble in defence, and his readers could never guess in what direction he would next leap. His opponents, and most of his work at this time was combative, became uncomfortably aware that he could nearly always turn the laugh on them, and that he would remain imperturbably cool when he should have been goaded into wrath. He was adept at taking the wind out of his enemies' sails. He did not defy even those who threatened him with assassination, but calmly replied:

Gaols, Fetters, and Gibbets are odd Melancholy things; for a Gentleman to *Dangle out of the World in a strang* has something so Ugly, so Awkard, and so Disagreeable in it, that you cannot think of it, without some Regret.

It is the retort whimsical at its most effective, at least as a public gesture; and the order of the adjectives is masterly.

His writings on trade need not concern us; they are lucid expositions of the tradesman's point of view. In economics he was, of course, Whig, a supporter of 'Dutch finance'; but if he was in some ways ahead of his time, it is not certain that he understood the ramifications of the money-market, though he was well aware of its abuses, and loved to trounce the stock-jobbers. In this field his task was easy enough; but in other matters he had the hardest of games to play during a period of extreme faction, that of the pacificator, inevitably misunderstood and fallen upon by both sides. On many matters, however, Defoe could speak clearly as a Whig based on Revolution principles; and up to 1703 often did so in defence of William's measures, his war or peace policies, and again as an enemy of all forms of privilege in support of the liberties of the subject.

This last principle is earliest and very significantly stated in his work in connexion with one of his favourite subjects, the reformation of manners. In *The Poor Man's Plea* of 1698 he asks scathingly what is the good of all this talk of reformation if it merely means that the poor are bullied into virtue by unregenerate masters:

... consider the Coherence of the thing; *the Parson preaches a thundering Sermon against Drunkenness, and the Justice of Peace sets my poor Neighbour in the Stocks, and I am likely to be much the better for either, when I know perhaps that this same Parson and this same Justice were both drunk together but the night before.*

No wonder 'we of the *Plebeii* find our selves justly aggriev'd in all this Work of Reformation': for, quoting the ancient proverb, 'these are all Cobweb Laws, in which the small Flies are catch'd, and the great ones break through'. Not that Defoe was anything of a democrat in the modern sense of the term; he was no Leveller, considering that the land of England belonged to the freeholders of England; and the unemployed got scant sympathy in his *Giving Alms no Charity* (1704). There the tradesman spoke against a dole which served to raise wages, and schemes of public work which would reduce profits. But his middle-class democracy appears very clearly in the part he played in presenting the Kentish petition of 1701, and his large pamphlet of the next year, *The Original Power of the Collective Body of England, Examined and Asserted*, a re-hash of Locke's argument.

Up to 1710, one of Defoe's chief concerns was the position of the Dissenters, and the knotty question of 'this scandalous

Ambo-dexter Conformity'; that, and the monstrous pretensions of the high-flyers. He could hardly keep it out of anything; the most readable part of even his Blenheim poem to Marlborough, *The Double Welcome* (1705), is where he attacks Sacheverell,

> High *Church Buffoon*, the *Oxford's* stated Jest,
> A Noisy, Saucy, Swearing, Drunken Priest . . .

but on this point his true weapon was prose, which he used in an astonishing variety of ways. He needed all his ingenuity, for his declared purpose was to bring peace and union in a field of unrestrained bitterness, taking so high a line with his friends as to make them mistrust him, and adopting so mockingly reasonable an attitude with his enemies as to whip them to still more raging fury. The state of feeling ran as venomously high as is usual when religion is brought into the service of politics and finance, for ostensibly religious as this struggle was, it is impossible to follow it unless it is related to the struggle for power. By so doing we can explain not only Defoe's anxiety for tolerance, but also Swift's almost indecently violent animosity. The Church had within living memory been deprived of all power, mulcted of its revenues, by the dissenting sects, Presbyterian and Independent: it was, a little indecorously perhaps, determined that this should never occur again, and so was inextricably bound up with the Tory party, which was mainly dependent upon the landed interest. On the other side, the Whigs owed their power largely to the trading interest, to a very great extent in the hands of the Dissenters. How far this was so is revealed by the astonishing suggestion made by Defoe in his amusing general satire, *The Consolidator* (1705), in which, taking leaves out of the books of Francis Godwin and John Wilkins, he gave an account of the world in the moon. The lunar Dissenters, the Crolians, defeated the Churchmen by organizing a kind of strike: they lived entirely apart, employed none but themselves, traded with each other only; and finally, by withdrawing their funds to a bank of their own, established a complete domination, a possibility he had treated of more seriously in his second *Enquiry*. This was possibly to exaggerate the power of the Dissenters, but it accounts for the fears of their opponents.

Defoe's first fling into the controversy was on the famous

scandal of the Lord Mayor's appearance in the morning at church, and then in the afternoon, arrayed in all his insignia, at the chapel. The whole argument of Defoe's pamphlet, apparently the earliest on this affair, *An Enquiry into the Occasional Conformity of Dissenters* (1698), is summed up in the epigraph: 'If the Lord be God, follow him: but if Baal, then follow him.' In short, either you were a Dissenter or you were not; if you were, you had no business to bow down in the house of Rimmon for the sake of temporal preferment. 'This is *playing Bopeep* with God Almighty.' His position was clear and perfectly logical, but was so much resented by his co-religionists that he was forced to reaffirm it, as he did in the preface to a new edition of this work in 1700, where he stated that 'Dissenters do allow themselves to practice what they cannot defend', and in another *Enquiry* of 1702, which set out to show 'that the Dissenters are no way concerned in "Occasional Conformity"'. On the other hand, he objected strongly to legislation on the point, as being a further restriction on the liberties of nonconformists. But this position did not satisfy the mass of Dissenters, for they were not able to share his charitable view of the established church, and could not agree that she 'extends her Protection to the tender Consciences of her Weaker Brethren, knowing that all may be Christians tho' not alike inform'd'. Religion to Defoe, unfortunately, was too simple a matter: he did not see the difficulty of what we should now call Church reunion, declaring in his *Reformation of Manners* (1702), virtually paraphrasing Annesley:

> Religion's no divided Mystick Name;
> For true Religion always is the same:
> Naked and plain her Sacred Truths appear,
> From pious Frauds, and dark Enigmas clear.

Moreover, he certainly misjudged the situation in saying that

the Dissenter extends his Charity to the Church of *England*, believing that in his due time, *God shall reveal even this unto them*. If this is not, I wish it were the Temper of both Parties; and I am sure it is already the Temper of some of each side, which few are of the wisest, most Pious, and most Judicious.

'Which few'—that was the difficulty: it was certainly not the temper of the high-flyers from whose rage Defoe was soon to suffer so grievously.

Queen Anne's early declaration that she adhered to the Church had stimulated the High-Church party to an excess of ferocity against the Dissenters, to whose complete abolition they looked forward. In a spate of pamphlets and sermons, notably by Sacheverell, they hung out, to echo the provocative phrase, 'the bloody flag and banner of defiance', in consequence of which Defoe, unaware of the danger of irony, launched his fatal *The Shortest Way with the Dissenters* (1702). It is brilliant, but perhaps not true irony since it does not push the matter discussed over the edge of the plausible; it is, indeed, an admirable but too faithful copy of what the high-flyers were urging. Here Defoe first revealed that element in his genius which is, perhaps, his most distinctive mark, the astonishing capacity so to enter into the being of a person he is portraying as to become the thing he creates, to have that person's emotions, to speak with his or her authentic voice. It is one of the faculties Wordsworth gives the poet, who will wish, he says, 'to bring his feelings near to those of the persons whose feelings he describes, nay, for short spaces of time, perhaps, to let himself slip into an entire delusion, and even confound and identify his own feelings with theirs'. It is, or at least with Defoe it was, that kind of creative imagination which works on actuality raised to the highest pitch. Here he projected himself into the soul of a high-flyer, spoke so perfectly as a High-Church extremist would, that the work was hailed with vociferous delight by the more fanatical members of that sect, who believed *The Shortest Way* to be written by one of themselves. As Defoe confessed ruefully some years later: 'The piece in its outward figure, looked so natural, and was as like a brat of their own begetting, that like two apples, they could not know them asunder.' To us it appears a monstrous fantasy; the irony we would think obvious. Could anyone, we ask, apply to Dissenters, literally, such passages as:

I answer 'tis Cruelty to kill a Snake or a Toad in cold Blood, but the Poyson in their Natures makes it a Charity to our Neighbours to destroy those Creatures, not for any personal Injury receiv'd, but for prevention; not for the Evil they have done, but the Evil they may do.

Or again:

If one severe Law were made and punctually executed, that who ever was found at a Conventicle, shou'd be Banished the Nation, and the Preacher hang'd, we shou'd soon see an end of the Tale. They wou'd all come to Church, and one Age wou'd make us all One again.

Yet this absurd 'spoof', as it seems to us, was taken seriously by both sides, the Dissenters reading it with despondency if not with panic, while one young parson wrote to a friend that he valued it next to the Bible and the Commandments, and hoped that the Queen would act on the suggestions contained in it. In a sense then, it was too good, Defoe writing with a bland plausibility comparable with Swift's: the skill with which he played the shocked pietist was self-defeating.

His *Brief Explanation* only made worse the uproar created by the pamphlet, for both sides looked upon him as their enemy; as the *Observator* remarked on 18 January 1703: 'I don't know what Party stickles for Mr Foe; all good Men condemn'd that Book.' He was proceeded against for uttering a seditious libel, though it is almost certain that the real reason for the government's action was the part he had taken in the Kentish Petition and the writing of the high-languaged *Legion's Memorial*. He gave himself up to save the printer, was flung into Newgate, and condemned to remain in prison at the Queen's pleasure. Further, to his agonized dismay, he was sentenced to stand three times in the pillory. He begged frantically to be let off, but on finding his pleas useless, with magnificent courage he wrote his *Hymn to the Pillory*, the 'hi'roglyphick State Machine', in which he not only defended himself, but in sharply satirical attacks upon political and other figures, declared that it was they who should stand in his ignominious place; and in a defiant taunt at the end he bade the pillory:

> Tell 'em the Men that plac'd him there,
> Are Scandals to the Times;
> Are at a loss to find his Guilt
> And can't commit his crimes;

and whether in appreciation of his bravery, or from political sympathy, the mob turned his humiliation into a triumph. Instead of pelting him with filth, they garlanded the scaffold with flowers, boisterously drank his health, and when he came down, plied him with refreshment.

Nevertheless the episode was disastrous, for not only did it mean the ruin of the flourishing pantile business which was to have been his salvation, and the relegation of his family to poverty, it meant he would for ever be despised and subject to contumely. It exacerbated his sense of isolation; he never again felt, as far as we can judge, that he was a full, and fully free member of the society he so fervently wished to benefit. On reading the autobiographical third part of *Robinson Crusoe*, the 'Serious Reflections', one cannot avoid concluding that he came to be possessed by what we call persecution mania, filled with an abiding sense that he was never given a chance. There he tells, 'too feelingly', of men who have experienced 'the universal contempt of mankind . . . borne down by calumny and reproach'. This bitter sense was to become a main theme through all the work of his great creative period.

And if the affair was spiritually crucial, it was also, where literature is concerned, the turning-point in his career, for after five months in prison (20 May to 4 November 1703) he emerged to undertake the greatest work of his life. Perhaps acceptance of the job was a condition of his release, for the idea was certainly hatched in Newgate during his conversations with Harley's agents. This was the production of a publication which began on 19 February 1704 as *A Weekly Review of the Affairs of France, Purged from the Errors and Partiality of News-Writers and Petty-Statesmen, of all Sides,* and after progressive loppings ended simply as *Review* with the number of 11 June 1713. After six numbers it became a bi-weekly organ, and from 22 March 1705 it appeared three times a week. At a period when the *Little Review* was sandwiched between the numbers, it can be said to have come out five days a week, and the whole was written by himself; an astonishing performance for one man, especially as he had often to conduct it from Edinburgh; and when to this are added a considerable number of tracts and pamphlets, and some large works such as *The Consolidator* and *The History of the Union with Scotland,* and again long poems such as *Jure Divino,* the output is hardly believable. Moreover, the subject-matter of the *Review* was wide; it was practically a comment, and a shrewd well-informed one, on the affairs of Europe, intended to enlighten the public on the issues of the war. To this Defoe again and again returned, but at times he was diverted from his main course by the necessity for enlightening the public as to how to vote in a general election, or for putting them in a right frame of mind with regard to the

Union with Scotland. Nor was he oblivious of the great cause
of the reformation of manners. For instance, when Vanbrugh
was building his theatre, he turned aside from his main objective to belabour it severely in prose and verse.

It is often argued that in consenting to serve Harley, Defoe
lost his freedom as a political writer. But he was not in the main
dishonest, for as Harley's servant he was working with a man
with whom on the whole he agreed. Harley was, to be sure, a
Tory, but like Defoe he was anxious for moderation and unity;
he had no feeling against the Dissenters, would probably not
run counter to Defoe's views on trade, and found in him a man
as eager as himself for the Union with Scotland. To his contemporaries, a man who could write for both Harley and, on
the latter's temporary eclipse, for Godolphin, was a strange
amphibious creature. Defoe had qualms on the question, but
he was quieted by being told that in either case he was working
for his country's good and for the Queen, for whom he had a
great affection. Had she not helped to relieve his necessitous
family when he came out of prison? Defoe had certainly to
perform some strange acrobatic twists and turns; he sometimes
lied outrageously; but it can be affirmed that he consistently
worked for what he thought to be the best for the country, and
always in the same direction, towards peace, unity, and tolerance.
If he was a Whig, as he was on the questions of the succession,
of toleration, and of the rights of the subject, his real belief in
the catchwords 'Peace and Union' enabled him to act honestly
under both Godolphin and Harley, leaders respectively of
Whig and Tory parliaments, though both were middle-way
moderates. But from 1710 it became impossible not to be a
party man, that odious thing repudiated with such horror by
men of letters; and it was the violence of the mob from which
the educated cannot be excluded, fanned into fury by the
newspapers, that made impossible the non-party government
many men still visualized as the normal one.

It is not to be wondered at that Defoe found his popular
manner as a prose stylist during this period. From now onwards
his writing became, normally, sparing of obvious 'literary'
effects. To be sure, he grew more oratorical, as though he were
addressing an audience; after all, he knew that much of his
work would take effect by being read aloud to the illiterate.
Perhaps he always had this in mind, for as early as 1702

something of this quality crept in. For instance, in *A New Test of the Church of England's Loyalty*, where he is arguing that if the Dissenters did kill one king, it was no fault of the churchmen that they in their turn did not kill another, you can almost hear a voice from a platform:

> 'Tis such a Jest, such a Banter, to say, We did take up Arms, but we did not kill him: *Bless us, kill our King, we wou'd not have hurt a Hair of his Head!* Why, every Bullet shot at the Battel of the *Boyne* was a killing the King; for if you did not, 'twas because you cou'd not hit him.

It is delightfully done; again and again Defoe achieves a brilliant stroke of this kind, but he is, we feel, a little chancy. Where, however, he is sure, is in the studied rhetorical effects of his political polemics. It would be enlightening to know whether Morton, who so wisely added training in English to the usual classical-mathematical curriculum of the day, actually taught formal rhetoric. For Defoe often used set rhetorical figures which he infused with all the spontaneous vigour of a man shouting in the street. Here, for instance, is one from *A Challenge of Peace* (1703), when he is ringing the changes on the Queen's phrase about desiring peace and union among Christians:

> First, *Sacheverell's* Bloody Flag of Defiance is not the Way to Peace and Union. . . .
> New Associations and Proposals to divest Men of their Free-hold Right . . . is not the way to Peace and Union.
> Railing Pamphlets, buffooning our Brethren as a Party to be suppress'd, and dressing them up in the Bare's Skin for all the Dogs in the Street to bait them, is not the way to Peace and Union—

the refrain, which he varies, gathering a maddening intensity as he follows up the attack. He is whipping up the mob to a frenzy, and he knows the enormous emotive force of the re-iterated drum beat, as Mark Antony knew it when he spoke over Caesar's corpse.

It is a little crude, but he came to refine upon this by adopting a more confidential air, as though he were speaking to a few men in a room, or a friend at the street corner. He is at his best on the matter nearest his heart, the dissenting question, though on politics and trade he is always clear, informative, and trenchant; but on the first subject his feelings are so warm that the communication has all the effect of art. From this standpoint it is perhaps the second volume of the *Review* which is the best, written in the summer of 1705, before the freshness had worn off, and before feelings became dangerously embittered. The numbers beginning on the 14th of July on 'the *Danger of the Church*' are enormously entertaining even now, and without entering into the refinements of the anti-Marlburian faction. In the opening paper we read:

'Tis necessary therefore for me to Examine this Mighty, this Deplorable Thing, the *Danger of the Church.* . . .
1. *Who they are* that cry out of the *Churches Danger*, and are so Exceeding Solicitous for her Safety? . . .
2. Who is it they pretend the Church is in Danger from? . . .
3. What is the Church in Danger of? . . .

All very cool; but in subsequent numbers the tone is worked up, and soon he can mock, for he assumes he has his audience with him:

Never was there Equal Danger, never a time of such Unaccountable Distress of the Church of *England*; the *Protestant Religion*, of which the Church of *England* is the principal Bullwork, is at the last Gasp, is at the Brink of Destruction.
Well, Gentlemen, and what is the Matter?—Truly Matter enough, and Reason enough: Why the Matter is, the Duke of *Marlborough* has Beat the *French.* . . .

Then, a little later, he hoists himself into a high-Anglican pulpit, to deliver a glorious balloon of a discourse which he suddenly pricks with a superb effect of deflation. Occasionally he let a contemptuous tone creep in: 'Thus Men Banter Vertue, to justifie their own Vices; and think to make their own Practices Tolerable, by throwing Dirt at their Betters.'

It may well be doubted whether the continual goading of his enemies to fury did much to bring about the moderation Defoe so much desired: the fact is that, pen in hand, he was filled with the fighting spirit: if Leslie, or later Swift, smote him, it was not in him to turn the other cheek. But what is interesting from the point of view of literature is the new manner, the new colloquialism of phrase rather than of diction—for Tom Brown and Ned Ward had the latter—a run of everyday phrase which Swift was to catch and to better. In this, as in so many other things, Defoe was a pioneer.

It was in this decade also that Defoe hit upon that other form which he was later to develop into the art which earned him immortality, the form of imaginative yet intensely realistic journalism. His first opportunity came with the historic tempest which ravaged England on 26 November 1703. Defoe's considerable book, *The Storm*, was his first essay in reporting, and though in some ways heavy, prefaced by a weighty mass of popular science, and, as we have seen, of amateur philosophy, it already has those touches which convince the reader that he is being told the truth. For instance, after describing the terrible noise which some thought was thunder, he adds, 'And yet, though I cannot remember to have heard it thunder, or that I saw any lightning . . . yet in the country. . . .' So, with infinite caution, the fact is rammed home that the storm was accompanied 'by unusual flashes of lightning'. The whole account is fully documented, and at the end the reader can hardly doubt that things happened just as described.

That was a beginning, but perhaps the first solid earnest of his gifts as a really creative writer was that enchanting little masterpiece *A True Relation of the Apparition of Mrs. Veal, the next Day after her Death, to one Mrs. Bargrave at Canterbury, the 8th of September, 1705*. It first came out as an appendix to a much read book on death by Drelincourt, and was long considered as a (perhaps ironical) comment on it. We now know that a story of that sort was current, and that Defoe, impelled partly by his journalistic flair, partly by that immense curiosity about the occult which ever and again flares up in his writings, made inquiries at Canterbury. Whether, as now, we recognize the little work as a piece of accurate and inspired journalism, or regard it as once was done as a piece of equally inspired invention—with Defoe it is always impossible to disentangle fact from fiction—the result is an indubitable gem. From the very beginning the verisimility he thrusts upon us compels us to accept it all as a 'true relation'. To give us confidence, he tells us at the outset that Mrs. Bargrave is his intimate friend; he can 'avouch for her reputation for the last fifteen or sixteen years'— the very vagueness of the date is reassuring. So is the statement that his friend is not at all of what we should call the 'psychic' type: she is a perfectly normal and cheerful person; 'notwithstanding the ill-usage of a very wicked husband, there is not the least sign of dejection in her face'. The whole matter is treated as though it were an everyday fact only a fool would dream of questioning; nothing is stressed, so that only at the end do we realize that Mrs. Bargrave never actually touched the apparition, thus had no cause to doubt of its solidity. When, for instance, she expressed a wish to kiss her old friend, Mrs. Veal complied 'till their lips almost touched; and then Mrs. Veal drew her hand across her own eyes and said, "I am not very well", and so waived it'. Thus the story goes on, conversationally, with here and there an 'I should have told you before', or 'it looks to me as if'. It is the first example (if we except the *Shortest Way*) of Defoe's astonishing capacity for living into other people and their experiences, of imagining all the circumstances, so that what he tells has the importunacy of truth.

Here, then, we have a writer who speaks in the new voice of the eighteenth century intent upon actuality, the voice of the middle class which was soon to be almost all-pervasive, on whose ideas nearly all literature was to be based, and which during the century was to determine, if not yet the political structure of the country, at least the economic and largely the social. He was not altogether alone, but among his fellows he was the sole genius. Swift, the only one of his politically active contemporaries to rank above him as a prose writer in that high company, came from a different mould. There was a great tradition behind him, which he had to adapt; he saw deeper, and was the aristocratic heir of ages. Defoe was the child of his time, almost, if one can say such a thing of so very urban a figure, a child of nature, who as often as not spoke as it came to him to speak, with the voice and the accent of the people among whom he had his being, and lived his complicated life.

III

SWIFT TO 1709

SWIFT had arrived at early manhood when in 1689 the state of affairs consequent upon the Revolution made it advisable for him to leave Dublin, where he was preparing for his Mastership of Arts. He landed in England with the sole qualification of Bachelor, and that granted only *speciali gratia*; he had obtained *bene* in his Greek and Latin, but his Latin essay was classed only *negligenter*, yet though his philosophy was noted uncompromisingly *male*, the whole was not the uncompromising *pessime* awarded a large number of his fellow students. The grading in a sense was wilful; for he had as great a contempt for the scholastic philosophy taught at the Trinity College of his day as Milton had had for that offered him at Cambridge half a century before. Swift was to voice his disgust both in his tortured Pindarics and in his prose; but his position might be most succinctly stated by a couplet from his favourite Samuel Butler:

> He knew *what's what*, and that's as high
> As *Metaphysick* Wit can fly;

for his positive mind, always intent upon the practical, upon the relevance of an idea to how life was lived, upon the reality of the emotion felt by an individual, spurned the abstruse from the start. His simplification was perhaps too drastic, but this was a temper of mind admirably suited to his time, and was in due course to have an effect which, if not by itself decisive, contributed powerfully to the moulding of events. It was to make him the outstanding figure of his period, and finally a monument to the courage of man when faced with despair.

He developed slowly to the age of thirty; and then, discovering his method, understanding what he stood for, and based on certain argued positions, he went directly on from strength to strength. He never changed his direction, nor, it would seem, sharpened his sensibility, though experience of power and of disillusion, of triumph and frustration, enriched and deepened his being. His peculiar talent did possibly sprout at an early date, for there is some slight evidence that he sketched out the

fable of *A Tale of a Tub* while yet at Trinity. But like the normal
young man of energy and ambition—in view of the romance
that has condensed round him it is as well to stress his normality
—he first ventured into the literary field with a handful of
Pindarics, just as a generation earlier Dryden had attempted
to win laurels with metaphysical verse, then becoming outmoded in the same way that now, in Swift's youth, the Pindaric was losing its early glamour in face of the forms proper to
the new need for precise utterance.

The leisure to try his hand was granted him, together with
the opportune sense of at least temporary security, when in
Ireland after his first brief visit to Sir William Temple. While
esconced in that cultured household—'he has lived in my house,
read to me, writ for me, and kept all accounts as far as my small
occasions required', Temple wrote to Southwell—he had been
no doubt exposed to the literary currents of the day, or rather
yesterday, for one would expect Temple's household to be a
little old-fashioned in these matters, partly from Temple's
character, and partly from the mere fact of his age. Cowley, we
may be sure, was well thumbed, and Swift would naturally
engage in writing verse in his manner. He took the occasion of
the Battle of the Boyne for his first venture, and early in 1691
painfully engendered his *Ode to the King*. No one could call the
poem successful; but we get the sense of a giant toiling in
chains, especially at the end, where harsh and even gross
images and ideas replace the more obvious 'poetic' strainings,
such as describing bullets as

> Th' impartial Deaths which come
> Like Love, wrapt up in Fire;

in which we should scent an emotional falsity even if we were
unacquainted with the later Swift.

But it would have been strange for Swift to be emotionally
clear at this time; few young men are so, and perhaps no
admirable ones: yet he was already conscious that he was more
profoundly troubled than most. As early as February 1692,
when he was once more with Temple at Moor Park, after a
visit to his mother at Leicester and a fleeting stay at Oxford,
he wrote revealingly to his uncle by marriage, the Rev. John
Kendal, that in seven weeks he had 'writ and burnt and writ
again upon almost all manner of subjects, more perhaps than

any man in England'. That in itself shows an unusual power of concentration, but something more characteristic is to come. 'A person of great honour in Ireland', he goes on to report, 'used to tell me, that my mind was like a conjured spirit, that would do me mischief if I would not give it employment.' His letters at this time tell us further how fiercely he attempted to exorcise this spirit in the Pindaric Ode, how naïvely elated he was when the lucubration to the Athenian Society was printed in the *Mercury*, and commended, and how for five months he laboured at the *Ode to Dr. William Sancroft*. Clumsy, turgid efforts; and Dryden was justified in saying, 'Cousin Swift, turn your thoughts some other way, for nature has never formed you for a Pindaric poet.' He was possibly aware of great power moving beneath the face of the muddy troubled waters, of a mind beginning to mould words to its own uses, unafraid of employing the common word, the colloquial phrase, and here and there, especially in the passages which approach invective, employing them with some success. And already, in 1692, in the *Ode to the Athenian Society*—and what more natural than for this eager youth who hated pedantry to admire and address, as Defoe also did, the group of supposedly learned men who dispensed knowledge so easily?—we come upon Swift's peculiar brand of 'rationalism', which would not allow that man's reason could go beyond common reason, but claimed it to be within its own limits supreme. He speaks, in terms which were to be clearer in the *Argument against Abolishing Christianity*, of

> *The Wits*, I mean the Atheists of the Age,
> Who fain would rule the Pulpit, as they do the Stage,

and he testifies, in a slightly raised voice, against the

> —Madmen and the Wits, Philosophers and Fools,
> With all that Factious or Enthusiastick Dotards dream,
> And all the incohærent Jargon of the Schools.

It cannot be claimed that the poem is successful: the flights are top-heavy and come to grief, the images are the worst sort of poetic jargon, and the lyrical note is singularly absent. Yet all the while we feel that this is no idle exercise, that the poet is trying to express, not himself (that was a much later notion in the history of poetry), but something that he feels to be important and actual, something which has to do with life as it is lived.

To come to Moor Park after Trinity must have seemed to

Swift like being released into fresh air out of a fusty prison. For here were men and women who walked on equal terms with learning since they supplied something learning could not give, who took just so much of it as helped life to be lived intelligently and gracefully, and discarded the rest as ugly foppery. He almost at once expressed his gratitude to Temple in guileless excited terms in the 1692 *Ode to Sir William Temple*. The words do not dance, but the thought, that of a man of action, is incisive. It is a poem throughout which the concepts are clear, and often amusingly stated; and though Swift deluded himself when he ended:

> Whate'er I plant (like Corn on barren Earth)
> By an equivocal Birth
> Seeds and runs up to Poetry,

there is no doubt that the lumbering, galleon-like Pindarics taught him something in expression, and helped him unclog his thoughts.

Some of these are very crude, those of a young country cousin suddenly finding himself in contact with men who live in the great world. It was all very exciting, and had to be got on paper, the form being determined in the first place by what his entourage would consider befitting an educated gentleman. So Swift persisted in it through the twelve laborious stanzas of the even then unfinished *Ode to Sancroft*. But it was clear that the form was stubborn, and the young poet shows himself more at ease in the couplets of the long poem *To Mr. Congreve* (1693), a beautifully generous and unenvious tribute to the friend who had outstripped him. The touch is lighter, the thought moves more freely and is more cleanly stated. For instance, Swift can now dispose of modern scientific pretensions by a mere contemptuous reference to

> A search, no doubt, as curious and as wise
> As virtuosoes' in dissecting flies;

and the greater ease gives an outlet—possibly unlooked for in this poem when he began it—for that vein which, now satirical, was later to express itself in the ironic, and lastly in the sardonic mode. A satirical affectation, honest enough as far as it goes, is not uncommon in young men who have reason to think highly of themselves; and if we knew of no later development we might be inclined to dismiss this note in the early Swift as of no great significance. But two of the three passages italicized (whether by Swift or, in 1789, by the first editor of the poem) are curiously prophetic, especially the couplet

> *My hate, whose lash just heaven has long decreed*
> *Shall on a day make sin and folly bleed;*

which, though something in the tone of a youth setting out to be the Juvenal of his age, seems to come from conviction rather than from the need to strike an attitude. The third italicized passage introduces 'the beast myth' which runs through so much of Swift's work.

There remains of this early phase only the poem *Occasioned by Sir W[illiam] T[emple]'s late Illness and Recovery*, a poem which half-way through abandons its avowed aim and becomes a confession, endowed towards the end with a still dignity coming oddly after the outburst where Swift declares himself governed by

> That scorn of fools, by fools mistook for pride;

for he goes on to admit the gap between his life and his ideals, his poetic desires and their fulfilment. He decides that in him the wish to serve the muse has been a false ambition, a vapour of his brain; and he concludes by telling her that

> from this hour
> I here renounce thy visionary pow'r;
> And since thy essence on my breath depends,
> Thus with a puff the whole delusion ends.

The depression with which the poem is drenched, a state of mind caused partly by his lack of material prospects, partly by his feeling that poetry was not for him, might not need to be taken too seriously if it were not for later events. Yet it is distinctive enough to account to some degree for his peculiar brand of satire, a kind one would imagine to be the growth of a sense of isolation. It was no doubt caused to a certain extent by his feeling himself intellectually superior, more perhaps by being a young man, rather gauche no doubt, and speaking with a brogue, living in the atmosphere that surrounds a famous elder statesman and renowned dilettante. But it seems likely that his depression was mainly the outcome of the error he, a modern young man, had made in trying to express himself in a language and a form appropriate to the outlook of a past age, an age which still included in its poetic material those very metaphysics he so honestly despised. Yet just as he abandoned the muse, he had begun to find the way, the way ultimately trodden by Pope, that of using the easy colloquial phrase, and the 'proper word' that comes, apparently, unbidden to the mind.

So it was not until the whole delusion had ended with a puff, and Swift could move about free of any theoretical shackles as to what poetry might be, that, turning his thoughts some other way, he found, and almost immediately mastered, the easy conversational octosyllable which he might so much sooner have adopted. We meet it first in the *Verses wrote in a Lady's Ivory Table-Book*, written probably as early as 1698, during his last fruitful stay with Temple when he was most likely working at *A Tale of a Tub*, and could regard his verse as a trifling amusement. The piece is imperfect compared with later ones, which at their best, when they dealt with a larger area of human emotions, deserve the name of poetry; but it is lively, and it rings true.

> Peruse my Leaves thro' ev'ry Part,
> And think thou seest my owners Heart,
> Scrawl'd o'er with Trifles thus, and quite
> As hard, as sensless, and as light:
> Expos'd to every Coxcomb's Eyes,
> But hid with Caution from the Wise.
> Here you may read (*Dear Charming Saint*)
> Beneath (*A new Receit for Paint*)
> Here in Beau-spelling (*tru tel deth*)
> There in her own (*far an el breth*)
> Here (*lovely Nymph pronounce my doom*)
> There (*A safe way to use Perfume*)
> Here, a Page fill'd with Billet Doux;
> On t'other side (*laid out for Shoes*)
> (*Madam, I dye without your Grace*)
> (Item, *for half a Yard of Lace.*)
> Who that had Wit would place it here,
> For every peeping Fop to Jear. . . .

The isolated observer has found his weapon; one part of his apprenticeship is over.

Meanwhile another part of the apprenticeship had been going on, an apprenticeship to life, which incidentally, as with Defoe, became the training for prose. It seems to have been in some mood of impatience, or even of despair, that in May 1694 Swift left Temple to go back to Ireland to be ordained. Too much has been made of the sense of humiliation, of servility, that he felt at Moor Park; the impulse to go was more likely born of a sense of frustration. Already not quite so young as he would like to be in making a start in life, uneasy by being 'still to unhappy restless thoughts inclined', he must at this stage have felt immured in this too urbane pleasance, dominated by a man who belonged to an older generation. For though Temple had favoured the Revolution, he had a pre-Revolution mind, whereas Swift was in every mental way post-Revolution. Temple saw life with the eyes of the Clarendons, Danbys, and Cowleys, not with those of the Montagues and Somers, the Garths and Mandevilles; and he regarded science with much the same scepticism, but without the eager interest, of Sir Thomas Browne. Swift caught his attitude to science— though this was not singular among his contemporaries; Pope shared it—but otherwise there was too great a gap. He fretted, feeling in himself a tremendous energy which he knew he combined with an extremely able brain (these made up the conjured soul), neither of which he could use in those surroundings, where he was 'too much treated like a schoolboy'. But the only escape from this prison, gracious as it was, releasing and exciting as it had been at first, seemed to be by way of the Church. To enter it must have needed as severe a self-examination as ever man disciplined himself with; for one thing certainly we know about Swift: he would beware of lying to himself. That he admired the Church there can be no doubt, if only from his *Ode to Sancroft*; that he embraced its tenets with fervour seems unlikely from *A Tale of a Tub*. Its work he could and did approve and labour at, and one must suppose—there is no good reason for not supposing—that his rationalism, which set a limit to what the reason could do, made his acceptance of Holy Orders honest. He longed ardently for an independent situation; so he took the plunge, which carried him to the intellectual desert of Kilroot.

His letters at that period do not let us far into his thoughts, with the possible exception of that strange epistle written on 29 April 1696 to Varina (Miss Waring), proposing marriage in so odd a fashion, a letter which reveals a man who does not know his own mind, and is uncertain of the scale or scope of his emotions. The certitude was to come only after another sojourn with Sir William Temple, this time in a less dependent position, a period to close with one of the chilling disappointments that were to dog him through life; for at Temple's death in 1699 he found himself, at thirty-two, mature but unprovided for. However, in that year he found a place as Chaplain to the Lords Justice at Dublin Castle, and temporary secretary to Lord Berkeley; and in the next year entered into the living of, among other parishes, Laracor, which for the next ten years he was to make his home when not in Dublin or London. There he probably had much time for cogitation, though, besides being a good father to his flocks, he did much to improve his glebe, clearing the stream in which he fished for eel, pike, and trout, planting holly, willow, cherry, and apple trees. He seems to have been a good deal in Dublin, not only at the Castle, but attending to his duties as Prebend of the Cathedral, taking part in diocesan affairs, and, significantly, very early pressing the question of First-Fruits on Archbishop King. In those years he was probably as happy as he was ever to be, more especially as Esther Johnson and Mrs. Dingley had come to live in Ireland, and were usually near him. Yet always, it would seem, he was hankering after a wider sphere in which to exert his intellectual capacities, and his power as a man of action. He felt his place to be at the centre of life, where things were done. He made raids upon London for three long periods until 1704; and then from November 1707 until June 1709, when he came to his proper station as a man of letters, companioning Addison and Steele. It is into this dual background that his writings of the next few years have to be fitted.

It is significant that to the early part of this period belong those clear, foreseeing resolutions *When I come to be Old* of 1699: the emotions were to be, if not banished, severely held in check, especially those instinctive emotions which he may already have felt were to be denied him by his ever-threatening disease, labyrinthine vertigo. Soon there is no doubt of where he stands; there is the all too honest letter to Varina of 4 May 1700. After discussing 'the questions I have always resolved to propose to her with whom I meant to pass my life', in which he asks too much of any woman, expecting her to be at once his creation and his equal, he goes on:

and whenever you can heartily answer them in the affirmative, I shall be blessed to have you in my arms, without regarding whether your person be beautiful, or your fortune large. Cleanliness in the first, and competency in the other, is all I look for.

Already in those displeasing verses *The Problem* he had shown that disgust of the human body which was later to become almost an obsession with him; but here we see the man who carries the positive attitude to the utmost extreme, who will depend entirely upon reason. *Ne pas être dupe*, yes; but whereas Stendhal appears always to suspect that if he looks far enough into himself he will find there a new kind of hero, Swift was buoyed up by no such illusions.

His illusion was of a different nature. In conformity with the trend of thought of his time, with the temper of the Enlightenment, he believed, at any rate for some fifteen years longer, that man was a reasonable animal. 'God has given the bulk of mankind a capacity to understand reason, when it is offered', he was to write courageously in the *Free Thoughts* of 1714, even after the collapse of the Oxford–Bolingbroke partnership; 'and by reason they would easily be governed, if it were left to their choice'. It is this conviction, barren of any of the Christian sense of redemption by love that we might expect from a parson, which informs all his early writing, and much of his later.

His prose work published in the first decade of the century shows a remarkable consistency, varied as its form may be as the artist seeks his vehicle. And now we become aware of three Swifts: the plain straightforward thinker of the Enlightenment who is yet Christian, the hater of all pedantries of thought and useless ornaments of expression, the rationalist anti-intellectual; second the imaginative artist, who can express with full force what the first Swift means only by putting plain thought into a shape which is as fantastic as he can conceive—even if it is the fantasy of extreme logic; and finally the exuberant comic writer, the wit, the mirth provoker, the man whose motto was *vive la bagatelle*. The first we find in *The Dissensions in Athens and Rome* and some of the Church tracts; the second in the *Tale of a Tub* and the *Battle of the Books*, and with splendid certitude in the *Argument against Abolishing Christianity*; the third Swift we find in *Mrs. Harris's Petition*, the *Meditation on a Broomstick*, the *Tritical Essay*, the Bickerstaff pamphlets, and so on. The three manners, naturally, overlap; and when, early in the next decade Swift met such kindred spirits as Pope, Gay, Arbuthnot, and Parnell who formed the Scriblerus Club, all three are to some extent fused. But whatever manner he may be writing in, whatever mood may dictate the manner, the same central

position is held, and the moralistic purpose is dominant from
the beginning.

The Battle of the Books is one of the brighter incidents of that
wearisome contest between the ancients and the moderns; yet
lively as it is, within its covers Swift still largely wears the dress
and draperies of a past age, or those of his own not naturally his,
such as the mock-heroic; and the slight uncertainty one cannot
but feel in it is possibly because the battle was not his own: he was
taking up the cudgels for Temple, skirmishing as an auxiliary.
The central Swift is already here; his scorn of pedantry and
systems generally, of scholasticism, of unjustified pretentiousness, is given full play: the beast myth reappears. Although
basically part of the far greater question of 'the new learning'
as against the old, it was a somewhat confused battle for 'polite'
literature, as the seventeenth century conceived it, rather than
for the rationalism, the 'sweetness and light' for which he himself stood. It was, of course, and still is, good fun; further it
shows Swift beginning to find his skill as a prose-writer. There
is already the ability to handle ideas, to use words richly, and
to think structurally; he can use ornament and dialogue with
immense effect, as in the analogy of the spider and the bee,
referred to above, which is both beautifully placed and beautifully carried out, with just the right amount of weight. There
are hints of that peculiar irony which was to attain perfection
so soon as 1708 in the Argument against Abolishing Christianity,
more than a hint of the supreme contempt which was later to
be one of his deadliest weapons.

If we can with some security place the Battle in 1697, A Tale
of a Tub, with which there are grounds for linking 'The
Mechanical Operation of the Spirit', is harder to place. Though
it may have been begun in 1690, reaching its final form in,
perhaps, 1703, it was probably in 1696 and 1697 that the bulk
of it was written; and indeed while reading it we have an odd
feeling that we are still in the seventeenth century, as perhaps
we should expect, seeing that it is largely a parody of the old
forms. There is the same intricacy of design, the richness of
language, with the sense of the author wishing to put everything into one book, to let no consideration slip by. It is a
decorated work, in the scholastic manner, with its fantastic
piling up of authorities, its purely verbal arguments, of which
the chief ornaments were probably perfected in 1697 or 1698.

If the *Battle* is mock-heroic, it might be said that the *Tale* is mock-scholastic. If Swift, some decades afterwards exclaimed, 'Good God! What a genius I had when I wrote that book', he was, we may think, expressing a feeling that he could not have written it later; it has not the order, the discipline, the clarity of eighteenth-century work, that directness of attack, of which he himself had been so largely the artificer. There is the ruthlessness, the passion to strip appearance, the appeal to reason founded upon knowledge—including knowledge of one's own limitations—that we find throughout Swift; but there is a surface complexity of effect, of style, of allusive wealth, which he came to deny himself for the sake of plainness and speed. Almost incredibly rich and exuberant, it is tremendous, it is Swiftian, full of the terror of thunder and lightning; but it does not show us the new Swift who appeared so suddenly in 1701 with *The Dissensions in Athens and Rome*. Richness of invention he retained to the end, but he learnt to direct it with cleaner, less wasteful skill. There is, in fact, too much in *A Tale of a Tub*; it is impossible to tackle it whole: it must be digested piecemeal.

Indeed it may be that when Swift referred to his genius, he was struck by the immense amount of learning, of reading, packed into the book, the variety of subjects somehow welded into a whole. This is not scholasticism, or manner, or anything but sheer massive brain-power capable of seeing the implication of many things at the same time. As far as the fable goes it is consistently a politico-religious tract, but even that is complex; and when we refer to it as simple and straightforward, it is only by comparison with the whole. Section XI by itself, for example, contains a mass of material and allusion which for any but the most richly read of his contemporaries must have been a feast of unexpected matter, while the transitions from one object of thought to another are sudden and surprising. If *A Tale of a Tub* was really sent out upon the stormy waters of religious faction to give the contending parties something to wrangle over and distract them from becoming politically violent, were such a happy result possible this book certainly gave stuff in plenty. Its very brilliance made it suspect, and to many it seemed in its freedom of expression to topple over into blasphemy. As Mr. Herbert Davis has noted, 'For him no words are sacred; they have good and bad associations, and once they have been perverted for the use of canting hypocrites, he treats them as so much foulness and corruption.' For words too are a clothing, and Swift never made the mistake of confusing the word with the thing.

And besides the richness within the *Tale*, the digressions, covering a number of diverse and fundamentally important matters, deal also with literature. As Mr. Davis remarks, 'the book is more concerned with literature than anything else he wrote' (except, no doubt, *A Tritical Essay* (1707), and the *Proposals for Improving . . . the English Tongue* which he was later to address to Harley); for, as Swift says in the Apology which he prefixed to the 1710 edition, the book was written 'to expose the Abuses and Corruptions in Learning and Religion', and learning he deals with as fully as he does faith. From the point of view of an 'ancient', he ridicules not only scholasticism, but the Baconian pretensions of utilitarian science, the Cartesians and the occultists, for which last he drew largely upon the *Anthroposophia Theomagica* of Thomas Vaughan. As always, Swift is intent to destroy the humbugs, those, for example, who have the affectation to say that their work was the result of a rainy day or a fit of the spleen, or claim merit because they suffer for a cause, and so forth; but he also goes much deeper, as in the splendid Digression concerning Criticks, or in the continual attack upon Bentley and Wotton, where he gives full rein to his anti-pedantic ire, which was later to make him to a large extent the leading spirit of the Scriblerus Club. His treatment of Wotton in the footnotes ascribed to him, the paraphernalia of the dedication to Somers, the statement of the bookseller to the reader, the further dedication to Prince Posterity and the Preface foreshadow the still more elaborate foolery of *The Dunciad* of which he claimed to be part begetter.

Swift, of course, had an overpowering sense of fun, and the book is throughout streaked with delicious humour, some of it sheer sporting with follies, but at any moment it may strike deeper with disturbing certitude. The bland ironic stroke is sometimes so gentle as hardly to be noticed, as when he tells the reader he had intended to write a Panegyric upon the World, with a second part; 'but finding my Common-Place-Book fill much slower than I had reason to expect, I have chosen to defer them to another Occasion'. It is plainly evident in:

But, here the severe Reader may justly tax me as a Writer of short

Memory, a Deficiency to which a true *Modern* cannot but of Necessity be a little subject. Because, *Memory* being an Employment of the Mind upon things past, is a Faculty, for which the Learned, in our Illustrious Age, have no manner of Occasion, who deal entirely with *Invention*, and strike all Things out of themselves, or at least, by Collision, from each other—

precisely Bacon's complaint at the schoolmen for spinning metaphysical subtleties out of their own bowels. Yet if much of the book is high-spirited fooling, in the digressions a continuous attack upon pedants and the moderns, in the fable an unvaried satire upon churches other than the Anglican, we are all through aware of a pressure of driving thought. It seems light, perhaps, in such passages as that which deals with clothes, where the remorseless logic, based on one of the fallacies of living, gently leads the matter home to its absurd conclusion; it is strong in the digression upon the Æolists where the thought becomes urgent. The book is largely the satirist's cry against excess, especially that zealots' enthusiasm which had so lately nearly destroyed both Church and State; yet preach moderation as he may, Swift cannot suffer fools gladly, and already the thought of them is beginning to torture him. Reason based on knowledge, that is the only salvation: for as he had said in the Preface to *The Battle of the Books*:

. . . Wit, without knowledge, being a sort of *Cream*, which gathers in a Night to the Top, and by a skilful Hand, may soon be *whipt* into *Froth*; but once scumm'd away, what appears underneath will be fit for nothing, but to be thrown to the Hogs.

But—and this occurs in the Digression concerning the Original, the Use and Improvement of Madness in a Commonwealth— what the reason reveals is unpalatable to human pride and pretension, hostile to the illusions by which society lives. It is dangerous. Its conclusions have to be accepted, but they must also be forgotten. Reason comes 'officiously, with tools for cutting, and opening, and mangling, and piercing', to show us that surface and substance are not the same. 'Last week I saw a Woman *flay'd*, and you will hardly believe, how much it altered her Person for the worse.' Stick to the superficies, for 'This is the sublime and refined Point of Felicity, called, *the Possession of being well deceived*; The Serene Peaceful State of being a Fool among Knaves.' There a kind of savage despair breaks through; it pierces the surface polished by the resilience of youth; and we catch a glimpse of the master of the grotesque and macabre, who would never accept life on its own terms, and at times could hardly force himself to compromise with living.

The note is not heard again in its fullness till *Gulliver's Travels*: such things come from isolation, from looking too curiously, too honestly within. But after Temple's death, Swift made the effort not to be withdrawn, his continual fear of sudden doom forcing him to assert his being in, to impose himself on, the society in which he was able to move. He was successful in this; he made friends, and we find an atmosphere of gaiety, almost of serenity, in the happy if pungent verses on *Mrs. Harris's Petition* (1701), that admirable, humane character sketch which would be doggerel were it not so controlled; on *Vanbrug's House* (1706–8), full of friendly laughter; in the Prioresque piece *To Mrs. Biddy Floyd* (1708), and above all in the accomplished *Baucis and Philemon* (1706–9), the last better before Addison had passed over it his smoothing chamois leather. He is already well in command of the octosyllable:

> In antient Time, as Story tells
> The Saints would often leave their Cells
> And strole about, but hide their Quality,
> To try the People's Hospitality.
>   It happen'd on a Winter's night,
> As Authors of the Legend write
> Two Brother-Hermits, Saints by Trade
> Making their Tour in Masquerade
> Came to a Villege hard by Rixham
> Ragged, and not a Groat betwixt 'em ... (1706)

he is reaching towards colloquial ease, and the entertaining rhyme. Again there are the admirable if somewhat schoolboy flippancies of the *Meditation upon a Broomstick* (1704?), and of the enormously entertaining Partridge scarifications (1708), serious enough, however, in final intention, since Partridge was chosen out for destruction because he had attacked the Test. These things are very much the product of being, or trying to be, the ordinary mortal among ordinary men; they are addressed to social equals among whom he lives genially. The *Meditation*, a parody of Boyle's pietistic exercises, is really for home consumption only; but the Partridge pamphlets, in

their exuberance, their wit, and especially in their bland statement, their proof that the very much alive and kicking astrologer
is really dead, give a foretaste of what Swift alone had it in him
to do. Yet at that stage of development, Isaac Bickerstaff might
have been personated by others, say by Steele or possibly
Defoe. These things smack a little of a past age.

But already in the apprentice essay, known for short as *The
Dissensions in Athens and Rome* (1701), he had indicated his
possible stature as a figure altogether of his time. In this work
Swift, free and secure, moving among men active in politics, at
once applies himself to an immediate practical question—
whether the newly triumphant Tories should impeach the Whig
leaders. Based perhaps upon Temple, whose 'remains' he was
editing, it is a plea for moderation in an age of rancorous party
feeling; it is in line with Defoe's work, but is backed with
historical examples. The style is pellucid, the colloquial speech
of a man of the Enlightenment, and some of the observation is
so shrewd that many of the generalizations are mortifyingly
applicable at the present day. His party man we recognize:
'He has neither Thoughts, nor Actions, nor Talk, that he can
call his own; but all conveyed to him by his Leader, as Wind
is through an Organ.' The great Swiftian illusion is proclaimed:
'. . . this must be said in Behalf of human Kind, that common
Sense and plain Reason, while Men are disengaged from
acquired Opinions, will ever have some general Influence upon
their Minds', as it had been stated even in the Digression on
Madness: 'the more [a man] shapes his Understanding by the
Pattern of Human Learning, the less he is inclined to form
Parties after his particular Notions.' The general theory of the
State was the commonplace of the day; the cyclic view of history
may have come, indeed almost certainly did come from Temple;
but the pervading idea that the sense common to all humans is
what matters is Swift's, speaking for his age.

He is more clearly himself, because still more free, in the
religious tracts, *The Sentiments of a Church of England Man*, of
1704, the *Project for the Advancement of Religion* and the *Letter
concerning the Sacramental Test* in 1708. In these Swift, in his least
decorated prose, sets out as clearly as he possibly can, perhaps
for his own benefit, exactly where he stands with respect to the
Church, and the three documents can to a certain degree be
regarded as a trilogy. In the *Sentiments* (with respect, we may

note, to religion and government) the problem of the position
of the Church in the State is posed in all its complexity (it was
being lengthily argued at the time by the historians), an attack
on some of its enemies is carried out in the *Letter*, and the
solution is outlined in the *Project*. This is to order too prettily,
especially as the dates are a little dubious, but if read in that
progression they make Swift's position indubitable. As always
it is practical: whatever you think must be fitting with respect
to life as it has to be lived; and here, perhaps, more clearly than
anywhere we feel Swift to be the precursor of Joseph Butler.
As prose, in clarity and balance, it is inimitable, but it ought
to be imitated; for in modelling and speed it is admirable, and
it continually interests not only by abundance of material, but
also by imagery. Seldom has there been a more misleading
phrase than Johnson's 'the rogue never hazards a metaphor';
and if nothing has been sacrificed to grace, that is because
Swift's method of persuasion is always to challenge rather than
to seduce. Much of what he says may be applied to our own
situation; but we are here concerned rather to elucidate Swift
with reference to his time:

. . . A *Church-of*-England *Man* hath a true Veneration for the
Scheme established among us of Ecclesiastical Government; and
although he will not determine whether Episcopacy be of Divine
Right, he is sure it is most agreeable to Primitive Institution; fittest,
of all others for preserving Order and Purity, and under its present
Regulations, best calculated for our Civil State. . . .

We note how careful it is; and though it is not in the least
stilted, and has the colloquial run of phrase, it is not the conversation of even the most educated gentleman: it is far too
incisive. The passage continues:

He would therefore think the Abolishment of that Order among
us, would prove a mighty Scandal, and Corruption to our Faith, and
manifestly dangerous to our Monarchy; nay, he would defend it by
Arms against all the powers on Earth, except our own Legislature;
in which case he would submit as to a general Calamity, a Dearth,
or a Pestilence.

All that is central to Swift's thought.

Many might have written similar statements, though none
could have presented the case so lucidly; but only Swift, the
great imaginative artist, could have created *An Argument to prove*

that the Abolishing of Christianity in England may, as things now stand, be attended with some Inconveniences, &c. (1708). This is a masterpiece of the bland ironic, surpassed some twenty years later by the tremendous *Modest Proposal* only because the latter is, below the cool surface, white-hot with the *saeva indignatio*, which had by that time become one of Swift's main creative impulses. The later work is, in fact, sardonic; in comparison with it this earlier piece is good tempered, partly perhaps because in the first piece he is aiming at the 'polite free-thinker', while in the second he is striking at a less intellectual and more callous dominant group. And whereas the *Modest Proposal* appeals ultimately to the passions—pity and the sense of justice—this piece, in common with the other religious tracts, is built out of plain sense, even though it may be bottomed upon scorn. The arguments are, in inverted form, much the same as those in the directer tracts; they imply tolerance as well as toleration (once more we think of Defoe), the idea of a Church governing through the State, of a State supported by the Church. Yet there are certain contradictions, for the satire is an attack upon hypocrisy, whereas in the *Advancement of Religion* there is a very Addisonian defence of it as 'much more eligible than open infidelity and vice'. The latter tract, together with the *Sentiments* and the *Letter*, is orthodox, middle-way (Swift in this was more Addisonian than high-flying); it is not a very original piece of work unless the suggestions for a private inquisition into the morals of public men and for the early closing of public houses are of Swift's coining. All are the writings of a man attached to no party, of a free man of letters moving among his peers. The direct pamphlets express plainly, in language the plain man cannot fail to understand, the plain man's point of view. Ungarnished, free of all fripperies of thought or manner, though not without metaphor and imagery, more especially drawn from architecture, disease, and medicine, they will certainly have reached Mr. Sealand and his acquaintance; there is no baffling speculation, since all is addressed to that common sense by which men can be ruled.

The same, theoretically, is true of the *Argument against Abolishing Christianity*, even perhaps practically; since, as the Preface to *The Battle of the Books* observes: '*Satyr* is a sort of Glass, wherein Beholders do generally discover every body's Face but their Own.' For us the interest is twofold: not only is it today as fresh, as applicable, as in the year it was written, it is also the first place in which Swift really found that manner which distinguishes him from all other English writers. He found it as surely as he had discovered it in verse in the easy measure of *Vanbrug's House*, and was to do in the material used for the *Description of the Morning* (1709) and *The City Shower* (1710), so deflating of poetic vapour, recklessly free of poetic adornment, bare of connotation, and uncompromising in his determination to see things as they actually are. The *Argument* has these qualities, and, superadded, an irresistibly victorious prose style. Already Swift had attained 'that simplicity, without which no human performance can arrive to any great perfection', and which he had in his mind when he wrote his *Tatler* (No. 180). The tone is set from the first sentence, and, under the dominance of the artist, carried through unfalteringly to the end. The pith of the argument is stated quite early, and carries with it enough satiric force to make the reader look into himself as well as at his neighbour:

. . . I hope, no Reader imagines me so weak as to stand up in the Defence of *real* Christianity; such as used, in primitive Times (if we may believe the Authors of those Ages), to have an Influence upon Mens Belief and Actions: To offer at the Restoring of that, would indeed be a wild Project; it would be to dig up the Foundations; to destroy at one Blow *all* the Wit, and *half* the Learning of the Kingdom; to break the entire Frame and Constitution of Things; to ruin Trade, extinguish Arts and Sciences, with the Professors of them; in short, to turn our Courts, Exchanges and Shops into Desarts. . . .
    Therefore, I think this Caution was in it self altogether unnecessary (which I have inserted only to prevent all Possibility of cavilling), since every candid Reader will easily understand my Discourse to be intended only in Defence of *nominal* Christianity; the other, having been for some Time wholly laid aside by general Consent, as utterly inconsistent with our present Schemes of Wealth and Power.

It is, of course, an attack upon society, a serious plea for religion to be taken seriously; but the bland manner, the puur which lulls the reader till he forgets the claw, the assumption that the outrageous premises of the logic can be accepted by every intelligent cultivated man are so pervading that Swift can here and there allow himself a little bubble of laughter; nevertheless the entire display is so calm that the climax is passed without a flutter: 'Nor do I think it wholly groundless, or my Fears altogether imaginary; that the Abolishing Christianity may perhaps bring the Church in Danger . . '; but here the perilous figure, irony, applied to the common parrot-cry, seems almost to defeat its own object: we shall believe, if we are not careful, that Swift regarded Christianity as important only in so far as it buttressed a political institution, served a vested interest. It all ends with just the suggestion of a growl at what was to become one of his favourite poit s of attack, the money-power, and a note of scorn is allowed to creep in; the claw begins to threaten. All the more effectively, perhaps, in that here Swift lit upon the kind of *persona* he could most triumphantly use in his satirical writing. The *Tale* had been 'written by' an immensely learned if abysmally stupid, or, rather, irremediably naïf man, the *Argument* was put forward by an 'I can see through all that' man of the world; and from now on it is always a 'plain man' of one kind or another, confessedly moderate and open to conviction (unlike Defoe's 'masks', who always tend to be extremists) that Swift will use for his vehicle.

The whole tale of Swift's writings, in prose and verse, for the twenty-odd years we have been considering is a remarkable one of adaptation: he experiments, finds the medium he can best handle, then adapts it to the age in which he lives. The ostensibly simple, plain no-nonsense style he makes capable of a more extreme range of subtlety than we might think possible. He can use it for the sly revealing hint, for the bland statement that by seeming to turn the matter in hand upside down really puts it firmly upon its feet; he will soon be able to use it for the rich orchestration of *The Conduct of the Allies*, later in the cunning dialectic of the *Drapier's Letters*. All these writings are concerned with immediate actuality, with the controversies religious and political bandied about by the man in the coffee-house. They are practical, though informed by the terrific imaginative power which makes actuality vivid, apprehensible; a power which Defoe also possessed. Swift is now master of his medium, and ultimately he will achieve in verse the cool steady denunciation of the *Verses on the Death of Dr. Swift*, and in prose, not merely the dissection of society, but the plumbing of the abyss of his own self and of human nature in the terrible release of *Gulliver's Travels*.

IV

ESSAYISTS AND CONTROVERSIALISTS

I. STEELE[1]

IF the century up to 1709 had been to some extent troubled and agitated, yielding in prose that has survived for common reading hardly anything that was not utilitarian and immediate, the next few years were racked by acute political tension, which in one way or another coloured nearly all prose writing. To those of us who experienced the decade of similar tension from 1931 to 1940, that writing is bound to appear other than it did to earlier commentators on the period, from Macaulay onward. Allowing for the virtually unrestrained speech of those less squeamish days, we can more readily understand the outbursts, the attacks, the dissolution of friendships, and above all the preoccupation with politics which stamps them. For, as we can now see, here was the final battle between the new order and the old, with on the one side the Whigs, that is the moneyed interest, dissent, Deism, free-thinking, and philosophic optimism, and on the other the Tories, the landed interest, the Church, and philosophic pessimism. Every man who was a man, who could not dwell in an ivory tower, was bound passionately to hold opinions, to fight for principles. It may have been easy to mock, meritorious to deplore, party feelings; but when a whole outlook on life is in question, the whole way of living seems to be at stake. It is only a full realization of this ethos that makes Swift's despair comprehensible; for him the Whig triumph meant the collapse of every reasonable assumption for living.

Political passions, then, distort the literary scene from, say, 5 November 1709, when Sacheverell preached his notorious sermon. They disrupted friendships, so that even the 'veritable

[1] Richard Steele, 1672–1729, was at school with Addison at the Charterhouse, and proceeded to Christ Church, Oxford, moving from there to Merton as a Postmaster. He enlisted as a trooper, became Secretary to Lord Cutts, was granted a commission, and retired as a captain. Successful as a playwright, he was made Gazetteer in 1707. Embroiled in politics on the Whig side, on the accession of George I he became a Justice of the Peace, Deputy-Lieutenant of Middlesex, Governor of the Royal Stables and the Royal Company of Comedians. He was knighted in 1715.

triumvirate' of Addison, Steele, and Swift was shattered. Steele and Addison themselves drifted apart. For though the two latter were primarily men of letters, they were also Members of Parliament, the one a rumbustious controversialist, the other full of 'that under-strapping virtue of discretion' which sometimes makes brilliantly unsuitable men Secretaries of State. As tempers rose Steele was driven to increasing outspokenness, and even the cautious Addison occasionally slipped. Defoe wrote nothing but politics, lived nothing but politics, all through these years; while Swift, always politically minded, was from one aspect most fully himself until the Tory collapse in 1714. Till then the period was shot with fears as crisis succeeded crisis—the fall of Godolphin, and of Marlborough, the Occasional Conformity Act, the Treaty of Utrecht, the trembling balance, as it seemed, of the succession accompanied by terror of civil war, the crescendo of excitement when Harley was dismissed, St. John seemed to triumph, and the Queen's death so dramatically timed, bringing with it the dread of a Whig tyranny. After such tension the rebellion of '15 seemed anticlimax. Thus we lose half the meaning of the writers of that time unless we continually bear in mind the social tumult in the midst of which they led their lives and wrote their papers; and it is not surprising that—apart from some philosophic writing and a little poetry (mostly the early Pope)—the best writing, the most original and forceful was journalism. This is partly because it was addressed to the new reading public which demanded matter of urgent interest, but also because the greatest men of letters played the predominant part in it.

It may seem at first sight that the most famous writings of the time, the *Tatler* and the *Spectator*, stand out in direct contradiction to what has been said about the political nature of the liveliest writing of the period. Yet Steele himself proclaimed in the opening paragraph of the *Tatler* that the main design of newspapers 'should be principally intended for the Use of Politick Persons who are so publick-spirited as to neglect their own Affairs to look into Transactions of State'. The *Tatler*, so named in dubious compliment to the fair sex, would instruct 'these Gentlemen, for the most Part being Persons of strong Zeal, and weak Intellects . . . *what to think*'. Yet it scarcely dealt with politics, if we except the not long continued 'Continental Intelligence' with its discreetly Whig tinge: nevertheless it was written, in Dr. Johnson's phrase, 'to divert the attention of the people from public discontent'. He goes on to say that it was 'published at a time when two parties, loud, restless and violent, each with plausible declarations . . . were agitating the nation; to minds heated with political contest, they applied cooler and more inoffensive reflections'.

Addison reinforced this view. Again and again he declared that the virtue of the *Spectator* was that it prevented people from thinking about anything that might stir the passions. It 'drew men's Minds off from the bitterness of Party'—as did indeed 'the Air-pump, the Barometer, the Quadrant, and the like Inventions', thrown out to the public and 'basic spirits' by the Royal Society for precisely the same reasons (*Spectator* 262). Sometimes indeed politics insisted not so much on breaking as on gliding in; as with soothing utterances on Marlborough, upon the sweet reasonableness of the Act of Settlement—to gaze upon which in the Royal Exchange gave Mr. Spectator a 'secret satisfaction'—or upon the beauties of the system of financial credit: *Tatler* 193 indeed, ostensibly about the theatre, was actually an attack upon Harley. But apart from the continual gentle pressure of Whig opinion, the papers in the main kept clear of politics, that is from what was most immediately real; thus there often hangs about them a faint air of falsity, even sometimes of unbearable silliness, a kind of under-age namby-pambyism which can be irritating to the modern reader. Luckily they had other qualities to redeem them.

From the point of view of literary form, the profoundly interesting thing about them is that Steele, and yet more completely Addison, gathered together all those elements of the essay as it had so far existed, and welded them into an amalgam which satisfied the needs of a century. They merged Bacon's epigrams and *sententiae*, the character-writing of Overbury, Earle, and presently La Bruyère, epistolary writing, description as practised by Nicolas Breton, the personal intimate note of Cowley, the discursive musings of Temple (the two last knew their Montaigne), so that these elements made up a unified thing. They made of this a vehicle that could carry all that the average intelligent reader would ask of usable philosophy, of sagacity, of contemplation, or of criticism, one which Dr. Johnson could load up and bowl along with. And the flame which had served them to fuse all the diverse elements together was the pervading sense of the time—developed by the popular philosophers and finally summed up by Pope—that the great object of human endeavour was to find out how to live the social life. Their purpose then was not the description of individual sensibility as Cowley had delightfully achieved and Lamb was to carry to a particular perfection; they had a moralistic purpose, not very profound, by no means daring or original, but directed to teaching men how to live together. That at least was one of the reasons why they were read: they could tell you how to behave. That was largely why, in their collected form, they were read by so typical and intelligent a young man as Dudley Ryder: they trained him for conversation, they expertly hit off the characters of the people he met, and so were extremely useful to him. 'Intend to read [the *Tatlers*] often', he enters on 18 June 1715, 'to improve my style and accustom myself to his way of thinking and telling a story and manner of observing upon the world and mankind.' Such periodicals were useful in that they taught people to live with the amenity of civilized human beings. And the new reading public asked for nothing better; for the emerging middle class was more than anxious to learn how to become worthy of its inheritance, to discover its social *modus vivendi*. Springing as it did from a puritanical background, it could not adopt the immoral manners and intolerably swashbuckling customs of the old aristocracy that had collapsed at the Revolution; and meeting and mixing as its members did in coffee- and counting-house, they wanted to know how to behave to each other, and what sort of people they ought to set up to be. Such papers as the *Tatler* with its successors were thus very largely a series of popular textbooks on etiquette: that is why they contain so many to us insufferably tedious essays on fops, on silly women, on grinning-matches, and so forth, all dispensed with an air of odious school-ma'amish benevolence—'delicate raillery'—which is nothing if not provincial in the worst sense. Luckily they developed; the essays became indicators of good taste in literature and the arts, and with Addison they grew to be miniature treatises. How far they formed the age, how far they reflected it, it is impossible to judge, though Gay's witness cannot be ignored. Writing in *The Present State of Wit* (1712), he bore testimony to the transformation Steele had brought about: ''Tis incredible to conceive the effect his [Steele's] Writings have had on the Town; How many Thousand follies they have either quite banish'd or given a very great check to. . . .' In the next year Felton, in the Preface to his *Dissertation upon Reading the Classics*, commended the *Tatler* and the *Spectator*, with undue optimism, for rescuing criticism from 'Pedantry, Dulness and Ill-Nature', and establishing its 'Place among the Politest Parts of Learning'. The chorus of praise swelled unabated; John Porter in 1720, dedicating his *Epistles of Clio and Strephon* to Steele, hailed him dithyrambically as a supreme teacher, refiner, and reformer, going so far as to say that he had revived the moral laws of England. In a sense, then, these periodicals were part and parcel of the movement for the reformation of manners; but it was sheer journalistic flair for what would tell and what would sell that created them, and gave them their familiar form.

However little they may meet the needs of our own day, it is certain that the most fruitful literary event of the years under immediate consideration was the appearance on 12 April 1709 of the first number of Steele's *Tatler*; and to Steele must belong the credit of having raised to high literary level the kind of newspaper writing of which Defoe had already seen the possibilities. Virtue, however, must also be allowed Dunton, and his predecessors again, the various French *Mercures*, and perhaps the salty vivacious sketches of Tom Brown.

But whatever debt he may have owed, it is certain that Richard Steele had all the qualities necessary for such a task. Born in 1672, he was sent for his schooling to the Charterhouse. There he formed his lasting friendship with Addison, whom he followed to Oxford as a Postmaster at Merton, the latter being already a Demy at Magdalen. Oxford did not hold him long: the excitements of the early years of William III's reign were too enticing for his passionate, adventurous, even reckless temper; and, characteristically sacrificing a legacy in Ireland by so doing, he enlisted as a trooper in the Horse Guards. The dedication to Lord Cutts (the Salamander) of a mediocre poem on the Death of Queen Mary procured him a commission in the Coldstreams. But two or more duels, in one of which he nearly killed his man, and intimacy with Jacob Tonson's daughter which saddled him with the inconvenience of a natural child, made him wish to 'disengage his own mind from deceptive appearances': so during his nights on guard duty early in 1701 he composed his now unread tract *The Christian Hero*, which, though popular among his brother officers, 'had no good effect but that from being thought no undelightful companion, he was soon reckoned a disagreeable fellow'. To counteract the unhappy result he wrote his first comedy, *The Funeral*. Though he remained some time longer in the army, he gradually became the writer-about-town, a Kit-Cat, a man of the theatre—his plays will be discussed later—obtaining in succession such government posts as Gentleman Waiter to Prince George, Gazetteer, and Commissioner of the Stamp Office.

This considerable knowledge of the world, added to his inventive literary talent and his gregariousness, made an admirable basis for his kind of journalism; and a rollicking, vigorous, tempestuous sinning and repenting nature, full of warmth and frankness, of recklessness and generosity, prone to sentimentality, gave him just the understanding he needed for his essays. Always in debt, often 'a little in drink' as he would write with disarming simplicity to his Prue—his second wife, Mary Scurlock, whom he adored and neglected—his life was an unending bustle. To his activities in the theatre, his various papers, his political skirmishings, he would from time to time add such trifles as dabbling in astrology, freemasonry, and schemes for bringing Scotch salmon alive to London. Too impulsive, he sought the public's weal and not his own when it excited him to do so, and he was magnificently loyal in friendship. The only grudge we can feel against him is that he was too humble, even self-abasing, in attempting to balance his riotous overfullness of body and spirit.

His launching of the *Tatler* certainly illustrates his inventive genius, and his daring in taking a chance. He probably consulted Swift—then in England—for it is scarcely likely that he would have borrowed the advantageous name of Bickerstaff without permission, and it is significant that Sir Andrew Fountaine, writing to Swift on 27 June 1710, could refer to 'your bastard the "Tatler"'; there is, besides, the handsome acknowledgement made in the octavo edition. As a journalistic adventure it was an enormous advance on Defoe's *Review*, partly because it appealed to so many interests, idle or otherwise, and partly because of its intimate, easy style, one flexible enough, as the first number showed, to cover a moral intention humorously expressed, the beginnings of a character sketch which promised a romantic love-story, dramatic criticism, and finally (omitting the news, which was always presented more laconically), a further instalment of the Partridge joke. Moreover each section was extremely brief: no one was to be alarmed by a forbidding block of print. It promised never to fatigue. And if it may seem to us that very many of the numbers are addressed to people of the mental age of sixteen, this was apparently just what the general public of that day was ready for, eager indeed to absorb. After the first four numbers, which were free, the paper sold at a penny to an ever-increasing body of readers.

It was 'meerly as a well-bred Man' (*Tatler* 3), not as a Member of the Society for the Reformation of Manners, that Isaac Bickerstaff took upon himself to exhort, admonish, scold, and generally tell people how to behave, which was precisely what the majority wanted to know. They asked to learn the art of 'being pleased in an elegant manner', as was worthy of the people they had become:

The present Grandeur of the *British* Nation might make us expect, that we should rise in our Publick Diversions, and Manner of enjoying Life, in proportion to our Advancement in Glory and Power. . . .

So the theme was expressed in No. 12, and supported by a good scolding:

. . . Instead of that, take and survey this Town, and you'll find Rakes and Debauchees are your Men of Pleasure; Thoughtless Atheists and Illiterate Drunkards call themselves free Thinkers; and Gamesters, Banterers, Biters, Swearers, and Twenty new-born Insects more, are, in their several Species, the Modern Men of Wit.

And though it may be a question whether these objurgations had any effect whatever on the delinquents, it no doubt very much affected the way in which they were regarded in Mrs. Sealand's drawing-room, and in the coffee-house. That, for the moment, was what mattered.

The artistry still keeps fresh the character sketches, and the adumbrations of the novel scattered throughout the whole series of *Tatlers*. That is where Steele's strength lay, because that is where his heart was.

I must confess [he wrote in No. 271] it has been a most exquisite

Pleasure to me to frame Characters of Domestick Life. . . ; to enquire, into the Seeds of Vanity and Affectation . . : In a Word, to trace Human Life through all its Mazes and Recesses.

For though no doubt it is salutary to preach the higher while you pursue the lower, it is also fatiguing, and perhaps in the end not very convincing. Moreover 'it does not often happen, that the Reader is delighted where the Author is displeased'.

A character drawn from the life—not the composite 'character' of the old Theophrastian sort—appeared in the very first number with Cinthio, the absurd nympholept. It may seem to us overdone, but it is an interesting development, not lacking in psychological detail. The first step towards the novel as we know it appears strikingly in No. 13, with the delightful accosting of Isaac Bickerstaff by his guardian angel. It is, outside the drama, the nearest approach since Deloney, to what ordinary people say to each other. And so early as No. 23 we come very near the short story in the account of the lady who took upon herself to govern her husband

. . . by falling into Fits whenever she was repuls'd in a Request or contradicted in a Discourse. It was a fish-day, when, in the midst of her Husband's good Humour at Table, she bethought her self to try her Project. She made Signs that she had swallowed a Bone . . .

and as a result of her lamentations procured a chariot of an elegance equal to her neighbour's. The moral of the story may be, indeed is, tediously obvious; but the lively realism, the sense of middle-class actuality, are nearer to life than anything that had so far been offered the public in the guise of fiction. It is still a trifle 'literary', it still gives too much the sense of being fabricated—a kind of highly proper prose fabliau—rather than a direct reaction to life; but it must have struck its readers as something extraordinarily fresh, a man of their own kind talking to them. But it is not yet a short story; it is the plot for one, or for a short novel such as Chaucer might have given several hundred lines to. It may with some justice be said that Steele unwittingly prepared the way for the novel; but to claim that he was feeling towards it, even when he invented the Coverley group, so much more entertaining than the Staff family, is almost certainly untrue. He aimed at some finality in a certain genre, and he achieved it.

It is that kind of thing progressively bettered that still keeps portions of the *Tatler* alive. Steele himself probably took most pride in those parts; and it is for them that he seems to have been most regarded in his day. A certain amount of pleasure can also be derived from the admirable phrasing, and the *Tatler* from the very start abounded in felicitous sentences, of which the most famous example is Steele's immortal *mot* about Aspasia (the Lady Elizabeth Hastings) in No. 49: 'Yet tho' her Mien carries much more Invitation than Command, to behold her is an immediate Check to loose Behaviour, and to love her, is a liberal Education', bettering even Congreve's description in No. 42.

Steele took all matters of behaviour for his province. *Quicquid agunt homines*, he preluded every number until the 79th, *nostri est farrago libelli*, devoting as much attention to the crime of wearing crimson-heeled shoes as to the more inconvenient offence of duelling. Though often fanciful in ramming home his common sense, he did not give much hint of the deeper imaginative faculty we find as soon as Addison discovered his true bent, as he did in No. 81, in which, building on a hint given him by Swift, he produced his 'Vision of the Tables of Fame'. There a different note is struck, not so much in the handling, trite enough, of its subject-matter as in the sense we get of a wider sweep, of a more controlled form, of a broader rhythm of ideas. But where the matter is domestic, familiar, belonging to the world of common passions and emotions, Steele, free of Addison's superior pose, comes to closer grips with life, especially when a good strong flavour of sentimentality is not out of place. He is most like himself in the description of his father's death (No. 181), which occurred when he was five years old; now he can 'the better indulge [himself] in the Softnesses of Humanity, and enjoy that sweet Anxiety which arises from the Memory of past Afflictions'. The 'man of sentiment' has appeared.

It was no doubt partly through these writings that the tumultuous, rather brutal, strident patrons of the coffee-houses became aware of the complexity of the society they were to a great degree unwittingly constructing. The half-apprehended conflicts of duties, desires, prejudices, generosities, the tensions of manners and religious beliefs, the stresses of the political struggle playing upon character and determining attitudes, were all given a kind of visible being in these pages, in scenes involving personages of both sexes and all ages and occupations, readily linked with persons ordinarily met with. The basis of the vogue of these papers is evident; they fulfilled the old precept of combining pleasure with instruction; they were didactic in the most agreeable way, telling you how to behave by showing you others behaving badly or ridiculously. The method was happily varied by introducing you to the immaculate character, or, for example, as in No. 95, exhibiting a picture of perfect conjugal felicity.

But the lucubrations of Isaac Bickerstaff, setting himself up as a censor of morals and taste, could have been successful only under two conditions: that the actual guise of the censor should give no offence; and that the language he spoke in should be acceptable. Both conditions were brilliantly complied with. Steele himself explained the nature of the first in the number closing vol. ii of the *Tatler* (271).

The general Purpose of the whole has been to recommend Truth, Innocence, Honour, and Virtue, as the chief Ornaments of Life: but I considered, that Severity of Manners was absolutely necessary to him who would censure others, and for that reason, and that only, chose to talk in a Mask. I shall not carry my Humility so far as to call myself a vicious Man, but at the same Time must confess, that my Life is at best but pardonable. And with no greater Character than this, a Man would make but an indifferent Progress in attacking prevailing and fashionable Vices, which Mr. *Bickerstaff* has done with a Freedom of Spirit that would have lost both its Beauty and Efficacy had it been pretended to by Mr. *Steele*.

And again in the last number of the *Spectator* with which he had anything to do (No. 555), he gives the literary reason:

It is much more difficult to converse with the World in a real than a personated Character. That might pass for Humour in the *Spectator*, which would look like Arrogance in a Writer who set his Name to his Work. . . . He might assume a mock Authority, without being looked upon as vain and conceited . . .

and so on. And who could have been better to impersonate the tyrant of society than either the whimsical retired astrologer Isaac Bickerstaff with his instruments and his cat, or the short-faced gentleman who called himself Mr. Spectator? They, presented as they were, could speak out with frankness and pungency without raising ire, so long as their voices were reassuring, human, everyday.

Here really lies the great triumph of Steele, and, imitating and in some ways bettering him, of Addison, that they hit upon the prose (Dryden gone a little soft) which was for long to be the main vehicle of communication, and which still influences the way we write. Swift's is better for the trenchant argument, the final statement, the subtle shattering irony; Berkeley's has a firmer line, a more limpid beauty; but it was Steele and Addison who created the instrument that everybody could use, and that everybody for some decades did use. Defoe's normal prose was in its own way admirable, and more capable of variations in tone; but with Defoe you feel, at least in his journalism, that he is talking at you rather than to you. Steele is always polite, yet full of confidence. His prose has the colloquial run of the spoken phrase, the urbanity of the middle-class man of affairs who has been to a university; he is never strident or urgent (we are not here concerned with his political pamphlets). His phrases are not epigrammatically chiselled as are those of Halifax, but they are never slipshod as they often are with Bishop Burnet: in short, never verbose, never slack, they are cleanly shaped without being pedantic, and they end firmly. His prose admirably carries out the 'one great general Rule to be observed in all Conversation', which, according to *Tatler* 264, is 'That Men should not talk to please themselves, but those that hear them'.

The *Tatler* came to an end on 2 January 1711, partly, it may be, because Steele had a few weeks earlier lost the place of Gazetteer in spite of Swift's efforts to save him, but most likely because Steele was tired of the Isaac Bickerstaff figure, which was wearing rather hollow, and could hardly utter the sort of thing Addison was wanting to say. Moreover, the ostensibly innocuous No. 193 had given great political umbrage, so that it might be wise to discontinue.

However, on 1 March, no doubt after consultation with Addison as to the form the thing was to take, he launched the *Spectator*, which, if we consider the *Tatler* to be chiefly Steele's, we must consider to be mainly Addison's. Yet still the inventive genius was Steele's; it was he who supplied all the creative originality, the dramatic sense, the conception of a group of interacting characters. And if the greater moralizing genius was Addison's, the greater depth, and the completer learning, these qualities carried with them a gradual concentration upon the central figure, Mr. Spectator, so that the creative quality got squeezed out to make way for the not quite first-class commentaries of 'the parson in a tye-wig', as Mandeville called him. But here there was gain as well as loss, for Steele could never have carried his sketches the stage further to the creation of a new form; but Addison was able to establish journalistic literary criticism at a high level, together with the popularization of current philosophy both speculative and natural more authoritatively than hitherto. Thus he further deepened the apprehension of the society that was forming, both as regards itself and the universe around it. Before, however, going on to discuss Addison, it would be fruitful to remind ourselves of the murky politico-literary drama in the acrid dust of which the *Spectators* were written, in which Swift's is the dominating figure.

2. SWIFT, DEFOE, ARBUTHNOT

The curtain may be said to rise in the late summer of 1710 (while the *Tatler* was in full swing) at the moment of the final crumbling of the Whig ministry. On 3 August, five days before Godolphin was dismissed, the first number appeared of *The Examiner*, a weekly paper in which the more brilliant Tories delightedly proposed to belabour the Whigs at a far higher level than Leslie or Tutchin had ever been able to reach. The group was to contain Atterbury, Freind, Prior, and others, all directed by St. John, who gave the journal impetus by his signed *A Letter to the Examiner*. Then, on 7 September Swift again arrived in London, this time grudgingly armed by the Irish bishops with new authority to try once more to extract from the government the remission of Irish First Fruits.

He found himself plunged into all the contagious bustle of the political crisis. Though Godolphin had been dismissed before Swift left Ireland, the news had not reached Dublin, and Swift thought it his duty to call first on the fallen Lord Treasurer. He was scurvily received by the humiliated and depressed Godolphin, and was so enraged that, as he wrote to Stella on 9 September, he was 'almost vowing revenge'. Yet the revenge when it came, as it soon did, was in the comparatively genial verse of *Sid Hamet's Rod*—comparatively that is, if we think of the earlier outrageous *Salamander*, or the subsequent flaying to which he submitted Wharton. It contained indeed only the sort of accusation the men of those days were accustomed to sling at each other—and to receive serenely. To us it is a dull squib, even clumsy; but it is of interest as marking Swift's rapid decision to throw over the Whigs for good. Throw over, not desert, as used for so long to be said: for he had never completely been a Whig. He had, to be sure, been trained in the Whig household at Moor Park, and as far as the succession went he never deserted Whig principles, since there at least they expressed the common sentiment of the people as a whole. And though the *Dissensions in Athens and Rome* of 1701 was on the face of it designed to save the Whig leaders from impeachment, it had been written in the interests of moderation, of tolerance, rather than of party. If as a result he had at once been made welcome by the great Whigs, he had never really been at ease about their principles, however much he may have enjoyed their company. They were not sound on the Church, and their hostility to the 1703 Bill to put an end to occasional conformity was, to say the least of it, perplexing. Swift was not the man to understand the compromises, the shifts and evasions of politics; and at all events he could not possibly see a Church matter in the way the Whig leaders of 1703 had invited him to do. On this issue he appears to us to show a blind and shocking intolerance; but it is essential to grasp what his point was if we are to understand his vigorous, one might even say violent, support of the Tories at this later stage.

His philosophic position, fundamental to the whole of his political attitude during these four years, has been brilliantly summarized by Mr. Quintana. It is, not to flee from the paradox, that at this moment Swift embraced party because he deplored party, which he could describe as 'the Madness of many, for the Gain of a few'. The idea of party was not yet, of course, generally accepted; it was comparatively new-fangled, and it was still open to anyone to think that this was the King's government and that everything else was merely tolerated rebellion. Swift's attitude was not so naïf; but believing as he did that the springs of government resided in the general sense of the people—'common sense'—hating 'enthusiasm' as men in his century in the main did, warned as they were by the experience of the previous one, he regarded 'dissent' in Church or State as factious, and certain, when it got its chance, to be tyrannical.

Where Security of Person and Property [he wrote in the *Sentiments*] are preserved by Laws which none but the *Whole* can repeal, there the great Ends of Government are provided for, whether the Administration be in the hands of *One* or of *Many*. Where any one *Person* or *Body* of men, who do not represent the *Whole*, seize into their Hands the Power in the last Resort; there is properly no longer a Government, but what *Aristotle*, and his Followers, call the *Abuse* and *Corruption* of one. This Distinction excludes arbitrary Power, in whatever Numbers; which . . . I look upon as a greater Evil than *Anarchy* it self.

And just in the way that the government embodied the common sense of the people in political matters, so he argued did the Church embody it in religious belief. The two hung together: to weaken the Church was to undermine the State. So, to sum up in Mr. Quintana's words: 'When he said that dissent was in opposition to civil decrees, Swift meant two things: one, that no law of God gives any church the right to persecute; two, that the law of reason establishes in the commonwealth a church that can be unacceptable only to enthusiasm.' Dissenters, therefore, being out of touch with the State Church, were automatically out of tune with the State itself, and should not share in the government of the country. They might worship as they pleased, they were not to be harried, but govern they should not. Their rule would be a tyranny.

Swift's point of view had been made abundantly clear in both *A Letter concerning the Sacramental Test* of December 1708, and *A Letter to a Member of Parliament in Ireland* of about January 1710. Yet Godolphin had virtually told him in 1708 that the First Fruits would be granted only if the Test were repealed in Ireland, so his visit had been a generous visit of courtesy which deserved something other than a brusque reception. When Swift found that on the other hand Harley, to whom as the newly appointed Chancellor of the Exchequer—not yet Treasurer—he would now naturally apply, was all suavity, strong for the Church, saying after a week's solicitation that the matter of the First Fruits was arranged, how could Swift do otherwise than align himself with the Tories? Or rather, not with the Tories, but with Harley, for Harley was a moderate who attempted to form a coalition government, a procedure that would appear eminently right to a man who had acquired much of his political lore from Temple.

Besides, there was, no doubt, the personal seduction. It was not only that Swift found himself more 'caressed' by the Tories than he had ever been by the other party, invited to intimate dinners, talked with and laughed with as an equal, flattered as a writer of power, but that he found the company congenial. After all, Harley, with his great love of books and his collection of ballads, must have been more to his mind than Godolphin, whose spiritual home was Newmarket; St. John's brilliance must have seemed true lightning compared with the rapid sparkling of Halifax, however good a financier the latter may have been—and Swift at any rate had no ardent love of financiers; Peterborough was with him again, having changed sides; the party medical man, Arbuthnot, had a better mind than Garth, who moreover, though 'the best good Christian he, Although he knows it not', was no Churchman. But if Swift was seduced, carried off to Windsor in the coaches of the great, let in to all their secrets (more completely than has usually been thought), he never lost the clear realism which enabled him to look fearlessly into himself, and was quite aware of what was happening to him. As he described the process in 1713, in the clear-eyed imitation of Horace, 'the Gudgeon took the Bait'.

In his view the Whigs had become an unpopular government, and were therefore no longer the true government; that they would be tyrannous was shown by their impeachment of Sacheverell (not that Swift can have approved of Sacheverell's own immoderation), they were prolonging a hated war, and their desire to repeal the Test was ill-concealed. Harley's government would be the opposite of all this. The Tories' triumph in the October elections proved that it was they who embodied the general sense of the people, and therefore reason; they were determined to end the war, were against Occasional Conformity, and would see that Queen Anne's bounty was extended to Ireland. Besides they would back the landed interest against the money interest which Swift loathed, and he believed they were moderate.

None of these things, however, explain Swift's apparent violence, his continual public fury. But there are two or three factors that may help to account for it, the first being the tense feeling of the time, which no croonings in *Tatler* or *Spectator* could do much to assuage, since fear, fear of what was dimly remembered, fear of the worst, was more than vaguely alive in every man's heart. Politics mattered, because a whole way of

life seemed to be at stake. 'The Church in danger' on the one
hand, and on the other 'The Succession in danger', were cries
which for many carried with them the most vivid omens of
disaster. No wonder there were 'tumults and riots', and the
'heaving and thrusting, the cavilling and clamouring of parties'
(*Review* 23 December 1710). Then there is the controversial
fashion of the time; the invective, and the mud-slinging, for
they were less queasy in those days than we are; the grossest
insinuation, the frankest accusation, were common form. The
method of argument was to bully rather than to persuade, to
slang your opponent rather than to controvert him. Swift, we
cannot but feel, fell a little too easily into this way. It is true
that he nearly always reasoned, though he may too readily have
accepted the facts fed him by Harley and St. John, but he
gave too free a rein to his scorn of others.

No doubt the sense of power, the buoyancy resulting from
a man of action, as Swift partly was, at last being able to act,
sometimes a little carried him away; and the constant introspection which characterizes him, almost daily exercised in the
Journal to Stella, together with the self-critical sense of humour
displayed there and in his poems did not serve as strong
enough correctives. And no doubt he was sometimes animated
by a certain rancour, not so much personal and directed
against the men who had failed to do him justice, as against
those who had refused his appeal to safeguard the Church.
Sometimes also a disgust for persons may have entered in,
and it is possible that when he wrote 'The Character of the
Marquess of Wharton . . .', published towards the end of
the year, the fact that 'He hated Wharton like a toad' loaded
the barbs of his shaft with poison that would have been deadly in
a later age. But here at once we are brought up against a crux
encountered whenever we interpret work in which Swift seems
extreme to the point of being unbalanced: it is that Swift was,
it need not be said above all, but certainly all through, an artist.
When engaged upon doing a thing, he set himself to do it as
well as it could possibly be done. On reading this 'Character'
we are taken out of the realm of politics into that of art: every
great satirist—readers of the day had recognized this with
Dryden, and would again with Pope—partly creates the object
he is intent upon destroying. And as Swift dissects what is
before him, he does it with infinite curiosity, at the same time

constructing a character in the old Theophrastan sense. Here the clean phrases curl round the figure like a lash: 'He seemeth to be but an ill Dissembler and an ill Liar, although they are the two Talents he most practiseth, and most valueth himself upon.' How virulently well done it is we can see at once by comparing it with the reasonably effective but too formally patterned account of Wharton as Verres in the seventeenth *Examiner*, where, at the same time, Swift was turning upon Addison the method the latter had used in the third *Whig Examiner* in his admiring defence of Marlborough as Alcibiades.

Nobody has ever claimed that the *Whig Examiner*, designed 'to censure the writings of others, and to give all persons a rehearing, who have suffered any unjust sentence of the *Examiner*' is exhilarating to read. It is not so feeble as even Addison's greatest admirer, Macaulay, suggests; but Addison, though trained up by Halifax and others for just such a work, had not the mental temper for writing of this kind, and had had no experience, except for *The Present State of the War* of 1708, when animosities were more subdued. He was not the man for the task of replying to vigorous political attacks. The numbers are readable enough; but it does not cut much ice in answering political arguments to criticize the prose in which they are written, as he does in two numbers; the others, though sensible, lack the zest of battle. There is too much literary garniture, too little direct attack, and if the two papers on St. John's *Letter to the Examiner* are not without wit and pungency, it can be felt that the writer had not his heart in the matter. Thus after the fifth number (12 October) he desisted, no doubt with relief, especially if he suspected that Swift was to take over the Tory organ. He would be no match for the man who was still his friend.

The change in the ministry, which both papers were designed to deal with, caused almost panic depression among the Whigs, and jubilation among High-Flyers and even Jacobites. Restraint appears to have cowered down abashed, and the only popular moderating voice in the next few years was that of Defoe, who consistently in *A Review of the State of the British Nation* preached reason in a splendidly combative man-in-the-street style. His is always an appeal to actuality as it must appear to his readers once they have puffed away the whirling vapour of words used by either side. His is not here a great

prose, it lacks the decisive finality of Swift's, it has no graceful
modulations, it makes little appeal to the ear, but it is the living
voice of an earnest man speaking eagerly, often so fast that he
gets out of breath and has to begin again, pleading for clear-
headedness, for common sense, for seeing things as they are.
As a lampoon of 1704 has it, when he speaks of politics, he
'shines like a glow-worm in that night of mysteries'. He is
infinitely patient throughout the troubled period, soothing the
fears of the Dissenters, mocking gently at those who are afraid
that the Pretender will be brought in the next day, refusing to
belabour the Tories until he sees what they actually do. All the
time you feel that here is a man really devoted to the well-
being of his country, honestly disliking party as party, labouring all the while to make people good tempered. The odd thing
is that this very practical political journalism is still delightful
to read. He can even be wittily urbane. When *Examiner* No. 10
referred to 'two stupid illiterate Scribblers, both of them
Fanatics by Profession; I mean the *Review* and the *Observator*',
Defoe very properly asked in his *Review* of 14 December: '*With my
humble service to Mr. Examiner*, I recommend it to him to answer
this civil Question—*If, Sir, you have so much learning, how came
you to have so little manners.*'

Swift's journalism was neither so delightful nor so humane;
his genius was for pamphleteering rather than for the day-to-
day presentation of whatever events might crop up, or notions
flutter their wings. He had to build architecturally to obtain
his full effect; but his whole position in this noisy mell needs to
be kept in mind before judging his work.

Yet the *Examiner*, which he wrote from No. 13 on 2 November
till No. 44 on 7 June of the next year, is not outrageously violent.
It is slashing enough, sometimes scathing, but it is pervaded by
an almost cheerful humour, as befits a writer for whose side
everything is going well. He complains of the dullness of writing
for his party:

> Where is the Merit, or what Opportunity to discover our Wit,
> our Courage, or our Learning, in drawing Pens for the Defence of a
> Cause, which the Queen and both Houses of Parliament, and nine
> Parts in ten of the Kingdom, have so unanimously embraced?

A point he makes again and again to prove that the Whigs
were but a faction. The opposition writers have the excitement

of providing a cordial, he has to provide but milk for babes; but even so, his detractors are so much 'whifflers', with their 'little trifling Cavils and Carpings in the wrong Place', that he is seriously considering whether he will not have to answer himself to keep the game going at a sufficiently high level. Yet he takes up Defoe on the question of passive obedience treated also by Addison in his last number, and again on credit, though here Defoe was really on his side. He can be playful, but he is in the main serious, explanatory, defending the change in the ministry, praising Harley, especially after Guiscard's attempt upon his life, arguing for the better position of the Church. Aimed at a reading public rather more 'polite' than that to which Defoe addressed his journal, his papers do not reveal the popular undercurrent of politics as well as Defoe's do; but to anybody interested in the political history of the time, they are as fascinating as the *Review*. But such journalism was not big enough game for Swift; he is not at his best in the *Examiner*; and once its purpose had been completed, he left it to minor hands, such as those of Mrs. Manley, to whom he occasionally gave hints, and turned to the more important work Harley and St. John gave him to do in justifying the new policy of disentangling themselves from the Dutch.

But Swift's zeal—or zest in his new-found opportunity for influential writing—lured him to take a holiday from his main task, and to write two other pamphlets, on a larger scale than mere weekly *Examiners*. His *Remarks on a Letter to the Seven Lords* (August), those lords who examined the traitor Gregg with the determination to implicate Harley, gave him his first chance of magnificent self-justification, of counter-vituperation, and vociferously heated though beautifully controlled argument. It was big enough to allow him to display various moods of contempt, anger, reasonableness, irony, and bland commonsense explanation, which in their ingenious mixture are at least momentarily convincing. His transitions are admirably modulated:

The cunningest Managers I ever knew among them, are of all others, most detested by the Clergy: Neither do I remember they have ever been able to make any of them *Tools*, except by making them *Bishops*; even those few they were able to seduce, would not be their *Tools* at a lower Rate.

But, because this Author, and others of his Standard, affect to make use of that Word *Tool*, when they have a mind to be Shrewd and Satyrical; I desire once for all to set them right. A *Tool*, and an *Instrument*, in the metaphorical Sense, differ thus: the Former is an Engine in the hands of *Knaves*; the latter in those of wise and honest Men. . . .

And if there is already here a sense of greater power than he had yet shown, in the inventive *A New Journey to Paris*, written to cover up the real course of events when Prior went to France to open the way for negotiations (to be unfortunately discovered by an over-clever customs official on the way back), he was able to give rein to his talent for narrative built up with every appearance of verisimilitude, and a sense of humour undiluted, as far as the details went, by any party purpose. It was 'a pure bite'; but whether, as he told Archbishop King, it succeeded in its design 'of furnishing fools with something to talk of' may admit of doubt. It was obviously good 'bantering', but could not have done much to allay the justified suspicion that the Tories were proposing what was anathema to the Whigs, a 'peace without Spain'. Something bigger had to be done to put the Tory case, and Swift was the man to do it.

The practice Swift had had in political controversy, the exercise in suppleness combined with direct attack, in abuse, in fleeting passages of irony and brief statement of fact, ensured the triumph of *The Conduct of the Allies* published on 27 November 1711. Nothing so far in the party war had been so swiftly and so pervasively effective. Lucid in structure as well as in phrasing, it could be grasped by everybody, so that it went into seven editions in two months, eleven thousand copies being sold before the last edition was issued, 'which is a prodigious run', as Swift remarked to Stella, especially as the first four editions were sold 'as a dear twelve-penny book'. It was outspoken enough for Morphew the printer to be threatened by the Lord Chief Justice; but it was instrumental, if not decisive, in saving the government, and it ensured the making of the Peace of Utrecht.

It is, as so much is with Swift, deceptively simple. 'Swift has told what he has to tell distinctly enough, but that is all', Dr. Johnson remarked. 'He had to count ten, and he has counted it right.' But it is far more complex than a simple sum (and at any rate he had to choose what to count), for not only is the argument beautifully ordered, point after point being attacked with logical precision—the moneyed men, strategy, ambition, and so on—but the pace is varied; all the verbal instruments at Swift's command are used, sometimes more than one simultaneously, so that the effect really is, as suggested earlier, symphonic. Alternating with passages of plain argument, there are some rising in a crescendo of 'ifs' or 'becauses', exciting the reader, warming his blood through the rapidity of his mental motions:

> But if all this be true: If, according to what I have affirmed, we began this War contrary to Reason: If, as the other Party themselves, upon all Occasions, acknowledge, the Success we have had was more than we could reasonably expect: If, after all our Success, we have not made that use of it, which in Reason we ought to have done: If we have made weak and foolish Bargains with our Allies, suffered them tamely to break every Article, even in those Bargains to our Disadvantage, and allowed them to treat us with Insolence and Contempt, at the very Instant when We were gaining Towns, Provinces and Kingdoms for them, at the Price of our Ruin, and without any Prospect of Interest to our selves: If we have consumed all our Strength in attacking the Enemy on the strongest side, where (as the old Duke of *Schomberg* expressed it) *to engage with* France, *was to take a Bull by the Horns*; and left wholly unattempted, that part of the War, which could only enable us to continue or to end it: If all this, I say, be our Case, it is a very obvious Question to ask, by what Motives, or what Management, we are thus become the *Dupes* and *Bubbles* of *Europe*?

Sarcasm he uses, and sheer fun, but irony hardly at all, and then so delicately that it may easily be missed. Time has on some points proved him wrong, and the document is naturally coloured by party prejudice; but his arguments are in the main right, founded upon common sense and a sense of reality. Paradoxical as it may seem, it is a detached piece of writing wherever the bigger issues are concerned, certainly far more detached than any other of Swift's writings in the period.

In the meantime, during this year of 1711, Defoe has been indefatigably instructing the public in the *Review*, as always on the side of moderation, thus incurring the hostility of his own side. He is extraordinarily fair, temperate, and explanatory. He refused to join the outcry against a proposed peace; so long as the Protestant succession was assured, and no 'exorbitant power' allowed to set itself up in Europe, he was no stickler for the exact form. In his admirable racy manner he covers the ground again and again, driving home his points so as to make them plain to the laziest coffee-house reader. It is because his paper is such first-rate journalism, pursuing the argument day after day, that he is not much read now; there is too much of it, it is necessarily too repetitive, but it can be pointed to as a model of what journalism should be. And he still remained above party; but indeed he could not be expected to cling to the Whigs after their scandalous sale of dissenting interests for the sake of purchasing Nottingham and the 'whimsical Tories'. Even there he is grieved rather than violent (he is violent, though often very amusing, only when answering the more brutal attacks upon him in the *Observator*), but he never forgave the Whigs that piece of treachery; he harped on it for many numbers, ignoring even the dismissal of Marlborough and the creation of peers which made it plain that 'the end was not answer'd'. He writes on 3 January 1712:

A miserable divided Nation we have been for many Years past, but never in such a manner as we are now; the Animosities are so great, that the Parties stick at nothing to Overthrow one another; nothing is so Vile, they do not Reproach one another with; nothing so Barbarous they will not *say* of one another, and *do*, to oppose one another; nor can I see which Side to blame most.

And towards the end of the number:

Never open your Mouths after this about publick Faith, the Honour of Treaties, Justice to Allies, the standing fast to Confederacies and the *like*; whoever may complain of these Things, it is not for those I am speaking of, to open their Mouths about it now. . . .

But tempers were too aroused to pay heed, or to soften the asperities of the political conflict; and Swift, having forged his weapon, and being in a state of great anxiety about the fate of a ministry containing such an unstable explosive mixture as Oxford and Bolingbroke, was not going to let it rest, but seized every opportunity of using it. He had his fling at Nottingham in verse in the poetically valueless *Hue and Cry after Dismal*, but followed up the *Conduct* almost immediately with the comparatively humdrum *Remarks on the Barrier Treaty*, and by the vain attempt he made to cool the extremists of his party in the *Advice . . . to the . . . October Club*, a 'ginger group' which had attracted the attention of Defoe more than once. In May he got his chance when the *Spectator* in its 384th number—carefully delayed so that it should not be in time for the Queen to read at breakfast—reprinted a preface that Fleetwood, Bishop of St. Asaph, had added to a volume of his sermons. In this the bishop openly championed the Whig cause. Swift dealt with it in a hugely playful but devastating manner in the form of a letter to the bishop from Wharton on behalf of the Kit-Cat Club, in which the whole Whig policy is lacerated, and Wharton is almost, one would say, gambolled with. Fooling it may appear to be, but it is most effective serious fooling.

Swift's other essays, such as his admirably reasonable *Letter to a Whig Lord*, deserve the attention of the student of Swift together with those already mentioned, if only as illustrations of his varied manner and his various 'masks', as do the essays written by Mrs. Manley with hints from him on occasional incidents, such as Bishop Hare's sermon to the troops, or the further remarks on the Bishop of St. Asaph's sermons, in which the devotee may think to puzzle out what is Swift's, and what his collaborator's. Hare in this year produced an elaborate defence of the conduct of the allies, which, though possibly as good as Swift's attack as far as truth goes, has not survived as literature. But what do still survive as literature are Defoe's *Reviews*, which he began with the shortened title 'Of the State of Parties' from 9 September, the day after the Stamp Act became operative, and Arbuthnot's amusing *Art of Political Lying*, and more important, *The History of John Bull*, of which the first part was published in this year, and the second part in the next.

What is so admirable about Defoe is his immediacy, his common sense, his lucid weighing up of things as they are. He accepts what has happened; he accepts the fact that a treaty is in progress, that Marlborough has been dismissed, that the Whigs sold the dissenting pass to Nottingham, that a Tory ministry is in power. He does indeed, 'to gratifie the Humour of the Age', look a little back also, only to discover that each party has behaved scandalously, without regard to morals. Defoe never makes out that the Whigs are Simon Pures, that all they have done is above criticism; unlike Swift or the opposing Whigs such as Fleetwood or Hare, he does not espouse an interest, such as the Church, or any particular brand of foreign policy; he tests everything by his own standard of dissenting morality. He is the only charitable controversialist. The whole conduct of the *Review* should clear him of the charge of being an opportunist, ready to serve under Harley or Godolphin, whoever should happen to be Lord Treasurer at the time. There was no need to reassure him, as Godolphin did, that in his political intelligence work he was serving not party, but the Queen; he always did serve the Queen, and it is small wonder that his own party turned and rent him. He sometimes interrupted his political journal to discourse upon morals, usually in answer to some *Spectator* in which he found the morals somewhat slack, as in Addison's view of the Fall, in answer to which he also quotes Milton; or when he thought Mr. Spectator carried parental forgiveness too far, arguing that filial disobedience was a crime that God only could forgive (2 October 1711). But for now he was purely political, and followed up his papers on the state of parties with others on the Danger of the Pretender, and the State of the Succession. Both parties accused each other of flirting with the Jacobites, of wanting to bring in the Pretender. What a nation! he scolds his readers.

We Talk much of our Affection to the House of *Hanover* [he opens on 14 October], and the Succession of the House of *Hanover*; for my part, I must own, were I the Prince of *Hanover*, and in his present Circumstances, *hang me* if I would quit the Condition he is in, to take the Crowns of this Government, with the Condition these Crowns are in, and are like to be in.

He is, as always, in the street, arguing, exhorting, with whatever words or ideas come to him first. But in this last year of his paper you feel that even his patience is becoming exhausted, he begins to get a little shrill, his scolding becomes fiercer, till in the last number of all, 11 June 1713, he engages in a magnificent diatribe against everybody, including himself, for being addicted to false gods, revenge, office, bibliophily, drunkenness, shopkeeping, vanity of person, for worshipping the *Examiner* or the *Guardian*, for railing at this, that, or the other, his own failing being too great a love of the *Review*, which he is therefore abandoning. Instead he took a leading part in *Mercator*, instituted to support Harley against the Whig *British Merchant*, and wrote independently. Steele, for his part, instituted the *Englishman*, an almost wholly political paper, which ran from 6 October 1713 until 15 February 1714, where he speaks with 'a direct Intention to destroy the Credit, and frustrate the Designs of Wicked Men' in power. He resumed it in 1715, when it appeared from 11 July until 21 November. Here the Whigs are in the saddle, and the papers are in the best tradition of temperate journalism.

Nor is there anything scolding or shrill about Arbuthnot's[1] *John Bull*, which is even now entertaining reading for those whom allegory does not disgust. It is the story of England during the last few years, in which the war is a lawsuit, England John Bull, successive Parliaments his wives, the Church his mother, and so on. It might be extremely boring, but it is told so slyly, with such zest, and with so much of the liveliness of a novel in its descriptions and conversations, that we are actually eager to know what will happen next, even with 250 years dividing us from the actualities it represents. It must have been enchanting and calming to the Tory reader, and even the Whig would like the description of John Bull given in Chapter V of Part I:

> For the better understanding of the following History, the Reader ought to know, That *Bull*, in the main, was an honest plain-dealing Fellow, cholerick, bold, and of a very unconstant Temper; he dreaded not old *Lewis*, either at Back-Sword, single Faulchion, or Cudgel-Play; but then he was very apt to quarrel with his best Friends, especially if they pretended to govern him: if you flatter'd him you might lead him like a Child. *John*'s Temper depended very much upon the Air; his Spirits rose and fell with the Weather-glass. *John* was quick, and understood his Business very well; but no Man alive was more careless in looking into his Accounts, or more cheated by Partners, Apprentices, and Servants. This was occasioned by his being a boon Companion, loving his Bottle and his Diversion; for, to say Truth, no Man kept a better House than *John*, nor spent his Money more generously. By plain and fair dealing, *John* had acquired some Plumbs, and might have kept them, had it not been for his unhappy Law-Suit.

Something has been borrowed in manner from the *Spectator*, but the language and the rhythms are more homely, the language plainer, and the allegory is crystal clear. Something

---

[1] John Arbuthnot, 1667-1735, seems to have been privately educated, not going to University College, Oxford, until 1692. He graduated M.D. at St. Andrews in 1696, was made F.R.S. in 1704, and in 1705 became Physician Extraordinary to Queen Anne.

is borrowed too from the *Tale of a Tub*, whenever the religious sects are touched upon, but the Church of England has become an old lady whom he describes at the beginning of Part II:

John had a Mother, whom he lov'd and honour'd extremely, a discreet, grave, sober, good-condition'd, cleanly old Gentlewoman as ever liv'd; she was none of your cross-grain'd, termagant, scolding Jades, that one had as good be hang'd as live in the House with. ...She was neither one of your precise *Prudes*, nor one of your fantastical old *Belles*, that dress themselves like Girls of Fifteen. . . . She scorn'd to Patch and Paint, yet she lov'd to keep her Hands and her Face clean. Tho' she wore no flaming Lac'd Ruffles, she would not keep herself in a constant Sweat with greasy Flannel: Tho' her Hair was not stuck with Jewels, she was not ashamed of a Diamond Cross; she was not like some Ladies, hung about with Toys and Trinkets, Tweezer-Cases, Pocket Glasses, and Essence-Bottles: she used only a Gold Watch and an Almanack, to mark the Hours and the Holydays.

His highly coloured portraits of his allegorical figures, the three daughters of John Bull and his first wife (the Whig parliament), War, Faction, and Usury, would make first-rate descriptions in a racy picaresque novel, and the whole thing is extremely shrewd and pointed. Arbuthnot has a distinct style of his own, as different from Defoe's journalistic breathlessness as it is from Swift's studied calm. The rapidity of his phrasing with the heavy stress at the end give an extraordinary sense of hale robustness, and though it would not suit all purposes, it is excellent for relieving the allegory of tedium. How depressing political allegory can be may be discovered by perusing Addison's *Trial of Count Tariff*, which appeared in 1713, the year in which the Treaty of Utrecht was signed, in which Swift wrote three of his most pungent pamphlets, and Steele threw all caution out of doors.

Towards the end of the year 1713, Swift delivered two of his heaviest blows, the one directed against Burnet, the other against Steele, who had at this date dropped the *Guardian* to produce the *Englishman*, and had just become member for Stockbridge. The question of the demolition of Dunkirk had already been ventilated in the *Guardian* (No. 128), to be answered in the *Examiner*, and scurrilously played with by other pamphleteers on either side; but Steele, on being elected Member of Parliament, had reprinted the *Guardian* 'Letter to Nestor Ironside', and added a long discourse, in *The Importance of Dunkirk*

*Considered, in a Defence of the Guardian, in a Letter to the Bailiff of
Stock-Bridge.* Swift, on his return from Ireland, where he had
gone to be inducted Dean of St. Patrick's, fell upon Steele in
The Importance of the Guardian Considered. It is true that he does
incidentally answer the arguments of Steele's somewhat formless and in many ways ill-written document, but his main
purpose is to discredit Steele himself. It is a vigorously slashing
piece of writing, in which Swift's basic political philosophy is
discernible, but it is permissible to wish that Swift had not
written it. It is below the level of his greatest pamphlets, and
though it might be true, as he said of Steele in his *History of the
Four Last Years of the Queen,* that 'his repeated indiscretions, and
a zeal mingled with scurrilities, had forfeited all title to lenity',
after all he and Steele had often co-leagued, and had not easily
allowed 'this damn'd business of party' to estrange them; and
even if, as he thought, Steele had slighted him by not accepting
his help, it should, we feel, have been beneath him to be piqued.
It is admittedly entertaining; but perhaps it is all the less
effective for pursuing Steele in his private life, as he does, for
instance, by a reference to his continually being in debt: 'What
Bailiff would venture to Arrest Mr. *Steele,* now he has the
Honour to be your Representative? and what Bailiff ever
scrupled it before?'

Swift is more on his proper level, using his various weapons
more skilfully and to better purpose, in his *Preface to the Bishop
of Sarum's Introduction,* published at the end of the year. Burnet,
as an advertisement of the third volume of his *History of the
Reformation,* had sent out an Introduction in which he attacked
not only the then ministry as favourable to the Pretender, but
also the average run of Tory country parsons as 'blind, ignorant,
dumb, sleeping, greedy, drunken Dogs', to use Swift's pithy
paraphrase of the bishop's wordier paragraph, and as such
likely to let in Popery. In Swift's scathing document, in which
there are a few side-blows at Steele, you once again recognize
the giant; you can feel it in his use of the verb:

. . . But I will confess, my Suspicions did not carry me so far as
to conjecture that this venerable Champion would be in such a
mighty haste to come into the Field, and serve in the Quality of an
Enfant perdu, armed only with a *Pocket-Pistol,* before his great
Blunderbuss could be got ready, his old rusty *Breast-Plate* scoured,
and his *crack'd Headpiece* mended.

The pamphlet is that of a Churchman rather than that of a politician, but he never forgets that Burnet is a Whig, a member of that bench which Swift intensely disliked as being most of them Whig creations, and he takes occasion once again to defend the now tottering ministry. Burnet is certainly well and truly flayed, as stylist, bishop, politician, and thinker; yet if the violence of his own paper deserved such treatment, it is a little to be regretted that it was Swift who administered it.

Immediately after the publication of this work, he had already begun another round with Steele, in the form of *The First Ode of the Second Book of Horace Paraphrased*, in which he made game of Steele's much heralded *The Crisis*, and warned him:

> Believe me, what thou'st undertaken
> May bring in Jeopardy thy Bacon,
> For Madmen, Children, wits, and Fools
> Shou'd never meddle with Edg'd Tools.

A warning, however, which Steele disregarded, as he naturally would, bringing out *The Crisis* on 19 January 1714. The matter had been largely provided by William Moore, a lawyer, and it had been looked over by Addison, Hoadly, and others, and was not at all a bad, if rather alarmist, picture of the possible dangers in the situation, which was immediately aggravated by the illness of the Queen. It was skilfully advertised and published by subscription, and since it sold 40,000 copies was a real danger to a ministry already disintegrating from within. Swift sprang to the rescue with his *Publick Spirit of the Whigs*, 'the most disgustful Task' that ever he undertook. This pamphlet is directed against Steele not so much as a person, as one of a class of scribblers who dared advise their betters:

> I feel a Struggle between Contempt and Indignation at seeing the character of a *Censor*, a *Guardian*, an *Englishman*, a *Commentator* on the Laws, an *Instructor* of the *Clergy*, assumed by a Child of Obscurity, without one single Qualification to support them.

The conclusion also is personally withering, but one feels all the time that Swift is concerned to defend the clergy, the universities, the ministry, from attacks which were to some extent justified, and not a little damaging.

Meanwhile Defoe had been busily engaged in an anti-Jacobite campaign, opening in 1712 with, to give its short title, *A Seasonable Warning*, purporting to come from an Englishman in Hanover. It contains a vigorous direct statement of the reasons for the Revolution. Then in February 1713 the town was startled with *Reasons against the Succession of the House of Hanover*. 'What strife is here among you all?' it begins, preluding two or three brilliantly novelistic pages describing the furious contentions that agitated the nation, disrupting trade, family life, all peace and quiet; it then settles down to recommend the Pretender's accession as a health-giving vomit. It repays skimming through. But *What if the Pretender should come?*, issued in March, is a little masterpiece in the vein of *The Shortest Way*, though more plainly a skit. It retails with almost Swiftian blandness the advantages of a Stuart succession: as that the Pretender's rule 'will for ever after deliver this nation from the burden, the expense, the formality, and the tyranny, of Parliaments'; nor will poor country gentlemen any longer be harassed to attend them. Or again, since there will be a standing army (the perennial bugbear), 'the whole kingdom will be at once eased of that ridiculous feather-cap's expense of militia and trained-bands'. It is beautifully done; but apart from the literary pleasure obtainable from these opuscules, to which should be added the soberer *What if the Queen should die?* which in April drove home the danger of uncertainty, they reveal the existing tension more than any other popular writing. For it was a period of panic and alarms, of Jacobite scares, during which pamphlets and counter-pamphlets whitened the booksellers' stalls in increasing profusion. On the active side, Steele was expelled from the House for the *Crisis* and for certain numbers of the *Guardian* and the *Englishman*; a reward of three hundred pounds was offered for information as to the author of *The Public Spirit of the Whigs* (an open secret), who, some weeks before the final collapse, despairing of being able to heal the rift between Oxford and Bolingbroke had retired to Letcombe; lampoons on Steele, attacks on Swift, such as *The Hue and Cry after Dr. Swift*, or the assault on both in the form of *A Town Eclogue; or a Poetical Contest between Toby* (Swift) *and a Minor Poet of B—tt—n's Coffee-House* (Steele), enlivened the conflict, and Steele himself produced more controversial literature. The tension reached its height with the Schism Act of June 1714, the dismissal of Oxford in July, and the death of the Queen on 1 August. But the peaceful accession of George I put a fairly quick end to this phase of literary history, apart from a certain spate occasioned by the rebellion of '15, or such defences of Harley as Defoe's *Secret History of the White Staff*, the third part of which appeared in January that year. It is, we may think, a distorting phase; but it is with that tumult as the background that Addison's normalizing work must be looked at.

3. ADDISON[1]

Today we are in two minds about Addison. The phase of lachrymose adoration typified by Miss Aikin, Macaulay, and Beljame has passed, and we are in danger of swinging over too much in the direction of depreciation, fanned by a personal dislike of the man, many of whose actions, and whose general attitude, seem to us odious. Nor do we so greatly admire his prose, preferring Steele's as Landor did, and do not much taste either his humour, nor his oleographic Loves of Hilpa and Shalum, and the Vision of the Temple of Fame. Yet there can be no doubt about his importance and his influence; the difference between ourselves and our predecessors is in where we place the importance, and the virtue we assign to his influence. To us, perhaps, it will seem that where he was really great was as a popularizer, making known as he did the most advanced thought of his time, both philosophically and aesthetically. It is not fair to say with Matthew Arnold—who was comparing him with Pascal—that he had a provincial mind, for after all it was just such minds he was addressing so as to make them less so: he had to speak in their idiom. It is true, of course, that his thought in *Of the Christian Religion* does not stand up to Pascal's in the religious sphere; but then what popular writer's does? Addison, after all, was not a religious thinker, nor a creative artist, but a social moralist; it is as such that he must be judged, and it is in that context that his literary skill must be assessed.

[1] Joseph Addison, 1672–1719, ended his varied experience of schools at the Charterhouse, from which he went to Queen's College, Oxford; but after two years was elected to a Demyship at Magdalen College, and later to a Fellowship. He travelled abroad from 1699 to 1703. In 1705 he became a commissioner of Excise; and in 1708, after being elected M.P., he went as Wharton's secretary to Dublin, where he was appointed Keeper of Birmingham's Tower (Records). He returned to England on the fall of the Whig ministry in 1710, and was not employed until 1715, when he was made Secretary to the Lords Justices, becoming one of the lords of trade in 1716. For eleven months in 1717–18 he was Secretary of State.

And there, given the circumstances of his time, our praise must be very high. He was an able absorber of other people's ideas, he brilliantly gauged the temper of his time—in this he was a journalist of genius—and the language he used to instil urbanity into a somewhat brutal society was well adjusted to persuade, even if it sometimes became a little too dulcet. The tone may have been necessary, since his most important work was produced in the years of violent feeling, 1710–14. As a poet he is not more than mediocre, though he has left two or three pieces still sometimes to be met with in anthologies, and his famous play, if over-rated in his own day, has probably been too much decried since: it will be discussed later.

It might be said that if ever a man made his defects blossom into virtues it was Addison, for a timidity he showed in early youth, a dislike of committing himself, a dread of the *qu'en-dira-t-on*, these his adaptable mind converted to moderation and tolerance. It is congruous with this that what saved him from a life of obscurity in a country parsonage was not any intimation that he might become a man of letters, but that he would be useful in politics. It was for that, after some admired Latin verses, and a translation of some Ovid for the Tonson-Dryden collection—which Dryden, with his usual generosity, over-praised—that Montague, soon to be Lord Halifax, wrested him from Hough, who was then President of Magdalen. He had him given an allowance by Somers, and packed him off to France to mature his mind in the autumn of 1699. He stayed in France, chiefly at Blois, for about a year, and his letters, shockingly schoolboyish for a man of twenty-seven, reveal how he acquired his somewhat smug patriotism and that prejudice against feminine arts which was to make some of his later essays so tedious to others besides Swift. His journey to Italy did little more for him, since, as Horace Walpole was to put it, he travelled through the classics rather than through the country-side. Nevertheless the journey produced his first considerable poem, the verse *Letter from Italy*, addressed to Halifax in 1701; and the *Remarks on Several Parts of Italy*, published in 1705.

The two works obviously carry the stamp of the same mind. Addison is not much interested in people—having noted that the Italians are poor and miserable just as the French were poor and inexcusably gay—he expresses a dutiful if languid interest in the sights to be seen, but is really interested in the antiquities, not for themselves, but for what they remind him of in Virgil, Ovid, Silius Italicus, or whoever may be appropriate:

> For wheresoe'er I turn my ravish'd eyes,
> Gay gilded scenes and shining prospects rise,
> Poetic fields encompass me around,
> And still I seem to tread on Classic ground; . . .

and the poem goes on to say how he searches the hills and woods for celebrated floods, surveys Eridanus with a thousand raptures, and so on; and he was to say in the *Remarks*:

> The greatest pleasure I took in my journey from *Rome* to *Naples* was in seeing the Fields, Towns, and Rivers that have been describ'd by so many *Classic* Authors, and been the Scenes of so many great Actions; for this whole Road is extreamly barren of Curiosities.

But where he meets with curiosities—such as the Cathedral at Milan—his descriptions are without individual touches, his terms of praise extremely general. The prose work is a good guide-book, though not quite so anonymously colourless as most guide-books are, and needless to say it is in no way contemptible; to the latinist of his generation the aptness and profusion of the classical references must have been delightful. But today, though it has a certain interest for the Addisonian, and perhaps for the social historian, it has small literary worth. The poem is livelier, and the conclusion, where the beauty and richness of the landscape is contrasted with the misery of the peasants to evoke a panegyric on English liberty, still has a certain freshness and force.

It is indeed a very fair example of Addison's poetry, which never rose to great heights, but always, after some glaring lapses in his earlier verse—in, for instance, his poem to Sacheverell on the glories of English poetry—maintained a certain decorous level. Joseph Warton might write some forty years later:

> What are the lays of artful Addison,
> Coldly correct, to Shakespeare's warblings wild?

but that is a test few poets can pass (Warton is not among them); and at all events Addison did not fail because he strove too innocently for correctness, which he does not markedly exhibit, but simply because he was not primarily a poet. It was only because he lived in an age where poetry was still the natural medium for the literary man that he wrote poetry at all; but being of great ability, his verse compares well with the general ruck of poets of his day, the Trapps, Dukes, and so on. *The Campaign* never falls to the travesty of such lines as

> Think of ten thousand gentlemen at least
> And each man mounted on his capering beast
> Into the Danube being pushed in shoals,

which caused the governing powers to seek a worthier pen to immortalize their hero: the famous passage of the angel has at least vigour, and Addison always exhibited a certain mellifluousness. His one undoubted achievement is his *Ode* inspired by the 19th Psalm, 'The Spacious Firmament on high' (*Spectator* 465), which can rank among the best devotional poems in the language, though it may smack a little of seventeenth-century rationalism and eighteenth-century Deism; nor are his other devotional verses at all despicable. Perhaps the modern reader finds his translations from Ovid and Virgil his most competent work, for there his artfulness—in Warton's sense—could find scope, while greater poets than himself provided the matter. It is not, of course, Addison's skill as a poet which gives him his place in literary history, but once again an odd accident, an opening with which he had nothing to do.

For it is likely that had Steele's brilliant journalistic invention not caught the public taste, Addison would never have had the opportunity of displaying his real talent, that of a very able, very well-read, and intelligent popularizer of astonishing literary skill. As suggested earlier, he added a deeper note in the chimes of the *Tatler* which sometimes tinkled too easily, and it is interesting to see him developing not only his themes but the sweep of his prose as he became more practised. It cannot be said, however, that in the *Tatler* he achieved anything very profound, but he was becoming more supple, more individual as he went on. If in his vision of the Temple of Fame already referred to he clings too closely to classical models, in his early piece of criticism, the paper on Ned Softly's poetry (163) he is largely reacting so directly to feeble versifying that what he had to say is still fresh; his papers on musical instruments as descriptive of men and women (153, 157) are original in handling, even if their humour, as with so much of the humour of the time, does not appeal to us now. Some of his irritating characteristics are already there—his insufferable patronage of women, his silly hatred of the French, his curious, baffling use of the word 'secret'; but on the other hand, while still confining himself to questions of behaviour, he is extending Steele's boundaries, as in, say, No. 220 on the church thermometer, an essay inculcating moderation. If you compare the two main contributors, you can sense the man of action in Steele, the contemplative man in Addison: take, for instance, Steele on scolds (217), and the next paper, by Addison, on the names given to flowers. The whole tone of the prose is different. Though both are interested in behaviour, Addison is not absorbed in people in the way that Steele is; he has not his ready sympathy, his laughing acceptance of their foibles, but he is deeply interested in motive, and is far more fundamentally the moralist. He is such by instinct and upbringing, and because he desires comfortable order; Steele is such because, hot blooded and impetuous, he desperately wants something to steer by, to save him from himself.

We remember Steele's confession that his delight had been to follow the vagaries of men and women, and to enter into their feelings. This was an honest revelation, as was Addison's in what might be considered his own manifesto, *Spectator* 10, where, after declaring that he would enliven morality with wit, and temper wit with morality, he went on (taking a hint from Shaftesbury) to make the famous statement:

It was said of *Socrates*, that he brought Philosophy down from Heaven, to inhabit among Men; and I shall be ambitious to have it said of me, that I have brought Philosophy out of Closets and Libraries, Schools and Colleges, to dwell in Clubs and Assemblies, at Tea-Tables, and in Coffee-Houses.

That he succeeded in his attempt is to some extent evidenced by the number of times he has been called in as witness in the first chapter of this book; he made the speculations of Locke and Berkeley, of Newton and Ray, matter of common knowledge; thanks to him something of Plato and Lucretius could be bandied about in ordinary conversation. If Steele had raised, and with him continued to raise, the standard of manners, Addison raised the intellectual level of the emergent middleclass society. We are conscious all the while that he lived, as he said, 'in the world rather as a Spectator of mankind, than as one of the species . . . without ever meddling with any practical part in life'. He is, therefore, always a little aloof; his universal benevolence may seem to us priggish, but for his time this was a merit. He is the perfect representative of what the age was trying to be, the man who more than anybody else helped society to go the way that it wanted to go, his own particular sense of morality and behaviour culminating in the Victorian period. He was, it may be said, symptom as much as guide. As H. V. Routh put it, he 'never attempted to enlarge the bounds of thought. His aim was to gather up the best ideas of his time and put them within reach of the ordinary reader.' It is interesting to see which of the ideas of his time he considered to be 'the best'.

Those that he dealt with can conveniently be divided into two well-differentiated categories, the social and the philo-sophical, though these categories were not dissevered, since after all philosophy was to be brought to the tea-table where manners and morals were treated of, and the arts gossiped about. It must be admitted from the outset that the ideas em-bodied and debated in the social essays have little interest for us now, a tribute perhaps to the effect they had. When they do not seem to illustrate—for the social historian amusingly enough —the revolting crudities of a raw middle class, they are of a banality rendered only worse by the tone of voice in which they are discussed, sometimes school-ma'amish, sometimes arch, some-times imbued with a sturdy manly common sense. It is difficult for us to see in perspective the social essays of this 'first Vic-torian'; but there is no doubt whatever that they stated just what the age wanted to hear as it entered with firm tread the path which civilization was to lead it along. They are indeed civilizing essays. The actual statements they utter so com-placently may seem to us vapid or annoying, yet there is about them a sense of broadening, of freeing, as well as of an inculca-tion of manners and discipline, the whole advocating tolerance within the framework of the best Whig conception of the cul-tural value of commerce. Steele in *Spectator* 2 shows at what class—a good paying readers' class—the paper was aimed, the rising man of commerce, for, 'A general trader of good sense is pleasanter company than a general scholar.' Think of Sir Andrew Freeport, wise, debonair, free as a bending angel: Sir Roger is a delightful old gentleman, not very intelligent of course; but then he is just a harmless senile Tory—a point Professor C. S. Lewis has brilliantly stressed. In a sense the essays are a justification of Whiggery, which is throughout discreetly commended, as in No. 3, the Vision of Credit, with the spectre of the Young Pretender wanting to wipe out the national debt—and then, typically, 'Moderation leading in Religion', as a reminder to High-Flyers and extreme Dissenters alike, of sound Erastian doctrine.

Discreetly commended; for discretion, after all, was a prime virtue, one of the main supports, indeed, of the system of social morality which Addison set himself to preach. The theme comes out early enough, as when writing against lampooners in No. 23 he remarks:

... I always lay it down as a Rule, that an indiscreet Man is more hurtful than an ill-natured one; for as the one will only attack his Enemies, and those he wishes ill to, the other injures indifferently both Friends and Foes.

Later we may read (No. 225):

There are many more shining Qualities in the Mind of Man, but there is none so useful as Discretion.

The theme crops up intermittently, and was, indeed, the chief governor deciding the tempo of Addison's life. To us his system may seem a somewhat distasteful mixture of self-regarding qualities which might also be called timidity, far too great a regard of other people's opinion of one's self ('To be negligent of what any one thinks of you, does not show you only arrogant, but abandoned'), and the quiet pride of the superior person. Whether or not he can be ranked among the agelasts—the non-laughers—with his insistence on cheerfulness being preferable to mirth is not certain; but his plea for the introduction of cheerfulness in religion renders him suspect in a way that the Marquis of Halifax's does not. Above all there is the irritating atmosphere of complacency, of 'secret satisfaction' at every phenomenon from the cupolas of the Royal Exchange to the warblings of birds in the meadows of Bilton. To us it seems an odd medley of the sophisticated urbane and the naïf. What Addison was doing, we come to realize, was writing a practical handbook upon how to build up the façade behind which the average man could shelter himself: social man must create the appearance which alone can make society stable, and that is why hypocrisy, though detestable, was 'to be preferred to open Impiety'. It was not a deep morality that he preached, but at

the time it was extremely serviceable in the society then forming
itself; indeed the morals it dealt with were of the kind that can
be considered under the heading of manners, for Mr. Spectator
confined himself to 'those Vices which are too trivial for the
Chastisement of the Law, and too fantastic for the Cognizance
of the Pulpit' (No. 34). Thus to a generation which boasts a
different set of trivial vices, the literary interest of the essays
where he enlivens morality with wit must appear small; they
are in themselves as boring to the adult mind as Sir Roger is to
the millions of schoolchildren who are hopefully expected to be
delighted by him. You may enjoy them as curious revelations
of society, or fascinating glimpses of Addison's oddly arrested
character; otherwise you will most likely come to regard them
with the same distaste as Swift did, and allow him to 'fair-sex
it' to his heart's content, so long as you are not compelled to
read him.

Although the *Spectator* proved immensely popular, being
almost universally read by the literate public of London,
especially the women, and largely listened to by the illiterate,
the short-faced gentleman's air of omniscience, his patronage,
his assumption of the position of *censor morum*, the sense that he
was supported by a clique of admirers, and the frequent solemnity of his prose when inculcating trite sentiment (we might
indicate as an example the conclusion of No. 26) did not fail to
arouse a certain hostility, which had nothing to do with party
politics. Thus whoever it may have been who wrote *The British
Censor* broke out towards the end of 1712 in a protest which was
not unique. After carping at Addison's criticism he goes on:

> All things by Thee are clearly Understood
> From *Homer* to the *Children in the Wood.*
> Maxims of Schools, and the grave Ayrs of France,
> Ethics and Modes, Divinity and Dance;
> Pain, Bliss, Hate, Friendship, Lamentation, Song,
> To thy extended Province, all belong;
> But Poetry is thy peculiar Care,
> And here thy Judgment is . . . beyond Compare.
> Thro' thy Just Praise each arch Pretender shines . . .

to follow up with a satirical reference to Blackmore, and
jeering ones to Tickell, whose verses in commendation of the
supposed author of the *Spectator* (in No. 534)—a little fulsomely
adulatory—might well have called forth the squib.

It is possible that Addison really did very little to reform manners; he was probably merely saying what everybody else was feeling, expressing the desires of society rather than directing it; but where he was clearly of vital importance, and of interest to us now, at any rate as historians of the ideas that have influenced creative writing, was in his popularizing of the philosophic and scientific notions of his day. This need not be stressed here again, but what has already been said may be amplified a little, in pointing out that he made available to the very common reader certain groups of ideas, contradictory among themselves perhaps, yet making up the general vision of the educated man of the time. Addison was well acquainted with what we might call the 'advanced thought' of his day, from Thomas Burnet's *Theory of the Earth*, through Locke's empirical philosophy, to Newton's latest discoveries: he had early been attracted by the philosophy of the Enlightenment, and in his Latin oration of 1693, *Nova Philosophia Veteri praeferenda est*, had shaken off the neo-Aristotelean chains, to be free in the realms revealed by telescope and microscope alike, and declare some sympathy with Descartes.

As valuable an approach as any, since his criticism is shortly to be discussed, may be to see how he integrated the new learning into the experience of living when discussing aesthetics, for there was no division in Addison's mind as there was in Swift's, no inner battling; in this respect at least he was a child of his age, and since he was so universally read, it is possible that the excitement the poets were soon to feel about the new vision of the universe vouchsafed them by Newton was to some extent due to him. The first striking relationship between philosophy—both speculative and natural—and poetry is to be found in the third paper on the Pleasures of the Imagination, where he refers to Locke, and 'that great Modern Discovery . . . Namely, that Light and Colours, as apprehended by the Imagination, are only Ideas in the Mind, and not Qualities that have any Existence in Matter'. This particular 'discovery' was to have somewhat dismal consequences in the poetic apprehension of some fifty years later, but for the moment it was inspiring. In the next paper he refers to the *camera obscura*, while the seventh begins:

We may observe, that any single Circumstance of what we have formerly seen often raises up a whole Scene of Imagery, and awakens numberless Ideas that before slept in the Imagination; such a particular Smell or Colour is able to fill the Mind, on a sudden, with the Picture of the Fields or Gardens where first we met with it, and to bring up into View all the Variety of Images that once attended it . . . ;

and he then proceeds to show how a Cartesian would account for it all. Three papers later he dilates upon the fields opened up by the discovery of the microscope on the one hand, and the telescope on the other:

We are not a little pleased to find every green Leaf swarm with Millions of Animals, that at their largest Growth are not Visible to the naked Eye. . . . But when we survey the whole Earth at once, and the several Planets that lie within its Neighbourhood, we are filled with a pleasing Astonishment, to see so many Worlds hanging one above another, and sliding round their Axles in such an amazing Pomp and Solemnity. If, after this, we contemplate the wide Fields of *Æther*, that reach in height as far from *Saturn* to the fixt Stars, and run abroad almost to an Infinitude, our Imagination finds its Capacity filled with so immense a Prospect, and puts it self upon the Stretch to comprehend it. But if we yet rise higher, and consider the fixt Stars as so many vast Oceans of Flame, that are each of them attended with a different Sett of Planets, and still discover new Firmaments and new Lights, that are sunk farther in those un-fathomable Depths of *Æther*, so as not to be seen by the strongest of our Telescopes, we are lost in such a Labyrinth of Suns and Worlds, and confounded with the Immensity and Magnificence of Nature.

Such a vivid piece of popularization, such an imaginative grasp of the science of the time is in itself a considerable achieve-ment: nor are such passages rare in Addison's work; but the achievement seems still greater when the scientific apprehen-sion is made part of a larger one, part of a mode of being which Addison was attempting to clarify in his various essays in criticism, which deserve more attention than is usually given them.

Indeed it is a long time since Addison's services to criticism have been fairly judged, or, rather, services not so much to criticism itself as to the cultivation of some sort of critical standards in the mind of the average reader: here again he is the enormously valuable popularizer. His observations, as Dr. Johnson said, were framed for those that read only to talk, in contradistinction with Dryden's, who wrote for those who were learning to write. Already, by the time Dr. Johnson wrote his Life, Addison's 'criticism was condemned as tentative or experimental, rather than scientifick, and he was considered as deciding by taste rather than by principles'; that was precisely where he was showing himself sensitive to movements in contemporary opinion, and it was not without some struggle that he had cast away 'principles', that is the pedantry of measuring everything by the neo-classical rod of, mainly, Bouhours, and dared to base his criticism upon feeling, which is, after all, where the common reader wants to be guided, trained, and disciplined. And all the while he was developing his taste so that it should become a sound, workable basis for aesthetic principles. He did not always succeed in escaping from the classical foot-rule, though it is open to us to think that when he suggested that 'Chevy Chase' exhibited the same virtues as the *Aeneid*, he was, as he might have said, 'biting' the pedants. For to some extent at least, here too he was on the side of the moderns, and was content that Steele should mock at Bentley in the *Tatler*, though he suppressed his own *Discourse on Ancient and Modern Learning* (pub. 1739). At all events, once more in the sound Johnsonian generalization, 'his instructions were such as the characters of his readers made proper'.

In the two papers on Chevy Chase (70 and 74) he was in the main weaning the would-be cultured man and woman, 'the buffoon reader', away from the affectation of the Cowleyan Pindaric—which he described as Gothic—to the simplicity his age had by this time reached. He is already, we feel, out of date. Nor did the ballad need either popularizing or making respectable: it was still a part of the literary life of the age; the Pepys and Roxburghe collections had been made, the Harleian collection was coming into being, and there were others from the days of Selden, some of which Addison himself mentions; while the modern ballads met with immediate popularity. What we should say if we met criticism of that sort today is that it was directed at children of twelve or thirteen whose taste had been vitiated:

Earl Piercy's Lamentation over his Enemy is generous, beautiful and passionate: I must only caution the Reader not to let the Simplicity of the Stile, which one may well pardon in so old a Poet, prejudice him against the Greatness of the Thought.

Throughout the terms of commendation are exceedingly vague and general; there is no precision in such words and phrases as 'sounding and poetical', 'majestic simplicity', 'a fine romantic situation', 'natural and moving': all that any reader might gather would be that Mr. Spectator expected him to like the poem, because that was the sort of thing grown-ups would wish children to like. In No. 85, with reference to 'The Two Children in the Wood', he works himself up into a fine scorn of those who cannot 'admire nature in her simplicity and nakedness'.

As for the little conceited Wits of the Age, who can only shew their Judgment by finding Fault, they cannot be supposed to admire these Productions, which have nothing to recommend them but the Beauties of Nature, when they do not know how to relish even those Compositions that, with all the Beauties of Nature, have also the additional Advantages of Art.

Had he written in that way twenty years earlier, the diatribe might have been understandable; we can only wonder at what imaginary enemy he was tilting in the second decade of the century.

The odd truth is that Addison ceased to develop, to change in any way, after, shall we say, 1698. Everything he has to say is implicit in the notes to Ovid's *Metamorphoses* of 1697, and his essay on Virgil's *Georgics*. By that time he had discovered Locke, and on him based the dubious distinction between true, false, and mixed wit which earned him some fame, a distinction perhaps useful at that date, but of little service now with our different philosophy of language; it was more important that he had committed himself to basing any theory of aesthetics on what was then known of the mental processes, and this was a real and lasting contribution. It is true that there is a certain confusion in all this, since, perhaps unavoidably, he tried to combine the new discoveries with the old doctrine, to graft what he found in the empiricist philosophy of Descartes and Newton, together with notions of taste derived from La Bruyère, on to the authoritarian stock of Bouhours and Boileau. The conjunction was original, but the standpoint he then occupied he never deserted, just as he seems never to have noticed that modern poets were writing something different from the older ones, and just as he never changed his views as to French levity or the inferior nature of women. Nevertheless his early critical

essays consolidated a step in English criticism, even if they were
no more than a timely restatement of his seventeenth-century
conclusions, which the public was by that time familiar with,
rather than the discovery of a fresh idea. Basically his standpoint
was the moral one; and in the last resort, in common with others
(as will be shown later), he relied on a taste disciplined by
reading and refined by experience, as Jonson before him had
done and Wordsworth after him was to do. 'A Poet should take
as much pains in forming his imagination, as a Philosopher in
cultivating his understanding.' This comes out most clearly in
his ballad essays, though to make his taste respectable and his
choice approved, he supported himself by neo-classical arguments. He need not have bothered: the public already shared
his taste; but his fellow critics such as Dennis and the author
of *The British Censor*, and at long distance Pope, had no difficulty
in dispatching his argument with ridicule. Nevertheless in his
early papers he is sensible enough, condemning all silly ex-
travagances, punning, rebuses, the Italian Opera (largely
insular prejudice here), and the now meaningless Gothicisms, as
he would call them, of those suffering from the Pindaric disease
or affecting the metaphysics.

But when we come to the Saturday papers on *Paradise Lost*
(the first 267, the last 369) we enter a different realm. There is
considerable thought behind these particular criticisms, Addison having concocted for himself his own boiling of Bouhours,
Bossu, Boileau, and Rapin, with some borrowing from Dennis,
though he bases himself fundamentally on Aristotle and Horace,
with a strong admixture of Longinus who had by this time
become fashionable. But besides this there is the interest they
hold for us in so far as we may be social historians, since they
show how far Addison thought he could carry his public. His
papers really amount to a kind of commented 'Beauties of
Milton', still fitted, we would think, for schoolchildren.
He was probably once more preaching to the converted.
Milton had been well to the fore since Tonson had acquired
the copyright in 1686 and in 1690, *Paradise Lost* having
reached its sixth edition before 1700, and continuing to be
republished. A sign of Milton's being well known as well as
standing high in the estimation of severer critics is to be seen
by the readiness with which he could be imitated either in
burlesque or in all seriousness: Addison, then, was no inno-

vator here, and it is as well to dispel the myth that he rescued
Milton from oblivion. He did nothing of the sort, but he no
doubt made more easy the approach to him by the class eager
to be educated who did not much read closely argued treatises.
It was an education in primitive criticism as well as in Milton.
He began by four papers in which, according to precept, he
treated of the fable, the characters, the sentiment, and the
language, here following Rapin rather than any other predecessor, though he never mentions him. These papers were
succeeded by two containing 'censures', and then he bestowed
a paper on each book. For us, these latter essays have little
interest as criticism; they are admirable popularization of the
Virgilian ideas current about the epic, and of Milton himself.
The chapters are in the main descriptive or explicatory, reserved to blame but eager to commend, and as before the terms
used are extremely general:

> *Milton*'s poem ends very nobly. The last Speeches of *Adam* and
> the Arch-angel are full of Moral and Instructive Sentiments. The
> Sleep that fell upon *Eve*, and the Effects it had in quieting the
> Disorders of her Mind, produces the same kind of Consolation in
> the Reader, who cannot peruse the last beautiful Speech, which is
> ascrib'd to the Mother of Mankind, without a secret Pleasure and
> Satisfaction (No. 369).

No doubt the docile coffee-house reader experienced the sentiments expected of him, but however insipid this sort of criticism
may seem to us to be, Addison from the point of view of taste
is, we would say, right. Moreover, he uses what is after all a
legitimate critical weapon, comparison—comparison of course
with classical models—and is ready to justify Milton in certain
places where he breaks away from the established rules, to
justify him, not so much by the poets who preceded him, as by
the critics that came before Addison. There was also a typical
nice point with relation to the end, one which Dennis had already noted. It might seem that Milton had transgressed an
epic rule by allowing himself an unhappy ending, but it was
just here 'that the Poet has shown a most exquisite Judgment',
for the conclusion is shown after all to be a happy one, since
'Satan is represented miserable in the height of his Triumphs,
and Adam triumphant in the height of Misery' (369).
If it may be doubtful how much Addison affected the popular

view of Milton—he did at least, it is supposed, cause Mulgrave, in the 1717 and 1723 editions of his *Essay on Poetry*, to rate Milton ever higher in the scale of writers of epic—it is certain that his papers on the imagination constituted a step forward in critical presentation. Written originally as a single essay (not printed until 1864), revised and expanded they appeared continuously in the *Spectator* as Nos. 411 to 421 with the heading 'On the Pleasures of the Imagination'. Partly involved as he was in the neo-classical 'imitation' theory, being here much indebted to Dryden as well as to such of the French critics as he did not reject (he thought the worship of some of them exaggerated), he entangled himself worse by his gallant attempt to apply the findings of the new empirical philosophy to his conception of poetry, being among those who were coming to realize that any understanding of poetry must be based on a comprehension of how the mind and the emotion work. What this implied did not emerge clearly. He was no profound philosopher, no very clear logician, but nevertheless, with a fair degree of assurance, he groped towards a doctrine based on his own experience and supported by Hobbes and Locke. Not that he ever mentioned Hobbes—that would have been contrary to discretion—but Locke he continually referred to. And if here and there he picked up contradictory ideas from Shaftesbury, and caught a whiff of what Dennis was saying, it is really only when he deserted his philosophic scaffolding that he adumbrated, almost accidentally it might seem, notions which are really progressive and illuminating, and served to strengthen the basis upon which Akenside could afterwards build his major poem.

As already suggested, it was in his 1693 Latin oration that he rejected the older classical and scholastic philosophies in favour of the new learning, and in the notes to Ovid's *Metamorphoses* that he began to break away from application of 'the rules' and base himself upon taste. His first public confession, however, was in *Tatler* 165, 'On the Impertinence of Critics', where he attacked the pedantry of learning, which 'is like Hypocrisy in Religion, a Form of Knowledge without the Power of it', and mocked the Dick Minims of his day who applied the words of criticism in every part of their discourse, without any thought or meaning, and backed their opinions with the authority of Rapin and Bossu. It is true that here we

might think him merely to be calling the imperfectly educated
to heel (as he did once more in *Spectator* 592) were it not for
successive developments, notably in the fifth of the Milton
essays (*Spectator* 291), where he discusses the business and
qualifications of the critic; but it is perhaps in No. 409, before
embarking upon his Pleasures of the Imagination series, that he
really breaks away and bases himself squarely upon taste,
knowledge, personality.

I must confess that I could wish there were Authors of this kind,
who, beside the Mechanical Rules, which a Man of very little Taste
may discourse upon, would enter into the very Spirit and Soul of
fine writing, and shew us the several Sources of that Pleasure which
rises in the Mind upon the perusal of a noble Work. . . .

In short, the psychological approach. It is, however, in *Spectators* 418, 419, and 421 of the Imagination series that he most
clearly states the new position. In the first he concludes that
the artist 'has the modelling of nature in his own hands'; in
the second he states at the end:

Thus we see how many ways Poetry addresses itself to the Imagination, as it has not only the whole Circle of Nature for its Province,
but makes new Worlds of its own, shews us Persons who are not to
be found in Being, and represents even the Faculties of the Soul,
with their several Virtues and Vices, in a sensible Shape and
Character.

While finally, in No. 421, he declares that the 'Talent of
affecting the Imagination'

has something in it like Creation; It bestows a kind of Existence,
and draws up to the Reader's View several Objects which are not
to be found in Being. . . .

In all this Addison was performing the very useful service in
making known the critical and aesthetic ideas which thinkers
less busied in affairs were discussing, as will be seen in later
sections. His statements confirmed the break with the neo-
classical rules and the doctrine of 'imitation', which even the
new philosophy in some ways supported. He shared, naturally,
many of the ideas of his time—he was eclectically middle-way—
such as the insistence upon 'imaging', to use Dryden's term, or
the supposition that nature was more perfect the more it
resembled art, even in its wildness, but he was, it would seem,

the first generally read critic to claim that beauty was in the mind of the beholder; and—resting a little strangely on the authority of Locke rather than of Shaftesbury—could dwell upon the creative capacity of the artist. If in everything else Addison was nobly orthodox and splendidly timid, here, if none too bold, he at least broke away from orthodoxy, popularized the more 'rebel' doctrines, and prepared the public for Warton, Hurd, and especially Burke.

The *Spectator's* 555 numbers ran from Thursday, 1 March 1711, to Saturday, 6 December 1712. The Club, never very coherent, or much utilized, was played out, and Addison may have been becoming fatigued. The danger of being entrapped in politics was increasing: the Preface of the Bishop of St. Asaph to his sermons, printed as the *Spectator* for 21 May 1712, had been taken action against by the House of Commons on 10 June. Addison, moreover, was now eager to bring his dramatic venture to the test, feeling possibly that he could be more useful politically in the theatre than in the pages of the *Spectator*, which was succeeded by the *Guardian*, running for 175 numbers from Thursday, 12 March 1713, to Thursday, 1 October of the same year. The first part was almost wholly Steele's— apart from the help he got from younger writers, Tickell, Pope, Berkeley, and others; but later on, when Addison was free of the business and the excitements of *Cato*, he contributed his fair share. However, neither Steele nor Addison was at his best in the *Guardian*: the monitory tone is too heavy, and wit does little to enliven morality. The main purpose of the work, the seventy-year-old Nestor Ironside tells his readers,

shall be to protect the Modest, the Industrious, to celebrate the Wise, the Valiant, to encourage the Good, the Pious, to confront the Impudent, the Idle, to contemn the Vain, the Cowardly, and to disappoint the Wicked and Prophane . . . I shall publish in respective Papers whatever I think may conduce to the Advancement of the Conversation of Gentlemen, the Improvement of Ladies, the Wealth of Traders, and the Encouragement of Artificers.

The catalogue is astonishing, but the prospect is not exhilarating. Some fun, however, was to be got from Tickell's essays on the pastoral and Pope's superb retort; much interest is to be derived from Berkeley's pleasant divagations on, for instance, moral gravitation (No. 126); Steele is interesting in reviewing

Derham (No. 175), as we saw in an earlier chapter. Addison evidently took little interest. His essays are laboured, his humour heavy and repetitive; we weary of his jokes about the lion, the fable of the Barmecide feast seems to us to drag. But in the final volume of the revived *Spectator* (556 to 635) which began on Friday, 18 June 1714, and ran till Monday, 20 December, Addison gathered his energies; and himself, with a number of others—though Steele had no hand in it—produced a periodical of considerable character, and rather different from the earlier ones. His own contributions, if not altogether his best, convey his philosophy tinged with more emotion than is usual with him; his fable now is that of Hilpa and Shalum, which though it may seem faded to us, pleased successive generations. The other essays—the authorship of many is still unknown—reach a high standard; Grove is the new name which carries most weight, and it is here that that charming personality John Byrom first makes his appearance, not only in the immediately popular poem 'Phoebe', but in two essays on dreams.

But though these papers form a pleasant enough collection, the volume as such lacks the old driving force. Addison was prematurely played out, as can be seen from his later paper, the *Freeholder*, which does no more than repeat in much the same form as earlier his rather shallower prejudices (the levity of the fair sex and of the French), though his prose is often more trenchant than it had ever been. His political disappointment, which called forth those distressing letters to Halifax which Mr. Spectator would have been the first to censure, his political success as marked by his elevation to the Secretaryship of State, in which he proved so dismal a failure, and the dubious happiness of his marriage, all constitute a melancholy comment on the divergence between theory and practice. His last entry into the arena of literary politics in 1719 embroiled him brutally with Steele, who attacked the Peerage Bill in the four numbers of the *Plebeian*, while Addison in two numbers of the *Old Whig* stood up for the ill-advised project. Addison did not at first know who his adversary was; but the references on either side soon became personal; Addison jibed at Steele, and Steele grew scurrilous about Addison. This *bellum plusquam civile*, as Johnson called it from Lucan, made unmendable the breach which had widened between the two friends; and

Addison died at the age of forty-seven, two months after the controversy had fizzled out.

Tickell's 1721 posthumous edition of his friend's work added two fairly large items to the already considerable bulk of Addison's work, namely the *Dialogues upon the Usefulness of Ancient Medals*, and the possibly incompleted *Of the Christian Religion*. The latter is an unconvincing, laboured document of the 'Evidences' kind, unread tolay, and perhaps never much thumbed; but the former, though it has little of the grace of the dialogue form, and is now, no doubt, superseded, is a good piece of didactics, keen, intelligent, outstandingly accurate for its time, and even today not uninteresting, since the title continues 'especially in relation to the Latin and Greek Poets'. Here and there it is even amusing, as when in the first dialogue Cynthio attacks what seems to be frivolous pedantry, and Eugenius defends it. But neither of these works at all affects Addison's status as a man of letters, though the *Medals* give him an added claim to classical scholarship.

If on his deathbed Addison can have looked back on his achievement, he must have done so with a good deal 'of secret complacency and satisfaction' to use his favourite and to us slightly repellent phrase. As a politician he had been somewhat ineffective, but in letters he had several accomplishments to his credit. The greatest of all his achievements was undoubtedly the fact that he had put 'culture', in Arnold's sense of the word, within reach of vast masses of people who but for him would have found it an inaccessible realm. If he was not the pioneer, he was at least the perfecter; he had both widened and deepened Steele's original conception, and done far more than his friend had done to fix the standard of morals society was searching for. Today his influence is non-existent; we do not go to him for illumination as we do to Swift or Pope or Berkeley; the delight to be got from him is small; but that he is an enormously important figure in the history of English literature there can be no doubt, if importance in literature is at all to be measured by influence on society. If the light of that particular meteor has faded almost to extinction, it blazed brilliantly in the sky for several generations.

V

POETRY

NATURALLY behind all the civil and religious clamour in which the age, after a long struggle of ideas, was settling down to a revised set of assumptions, the ordinary quiet life went on, of social exchange, of personal experience, and of meditation. The picture is necessarily vague; but it would seem safe to say that the writers of that time were not possessed by any sense of cataclysmic change, or stimulated by a heightened awareness of being. The poets might all have said as Mr. Heath-Stubbs makes the ageing Congreve say to Mrs. Bracegirdle:

> And now we live in a rounded time, rounded
> With a low horizon of feeling, until men break it.
> We have forgotten the old high modes of loving
> And the song's poise is gone;

a sentiment echoed in Lady Winchilsea's 'The Prodigy'. We need not be surprised that the poetic tension of the age was low, for now that the bounds of reason were being tested, it is congruous, we may think, that poetry should work towards feeling by way of the intellect rather than attempt to organize the feelings. The contemporary 'employment' of imagery to illustrate a statement rather than itself be the statement serves to reinforce the notion. Thus most of the verse invites a happy collaboration rather than stirs any deep emotion; or if it vivifies our emotions they are such as take up only a part of ourselves, and do not involve the whole man. Yet if this poetry normally lacks a fine excess, the poets were not wanting in excitement. As Mr. Robert Conquest has put it:

> . . . Though they ordered all doubt to disperse
> They were poets. . . .
> . . . And, for the whole of their lives
> Like the mermaid on land in the Hans Andersen story,
> Pretending to notice nothing, they walked upon knives.

Among the best poets there is constantly a sense of sustained balance.

Such large generalizations are made to be riddled with holes, and Pope is always to be left out of account when making sweeping statements of this kind. Nevertheless it is fair to say that the age can offer only minor love poetry, and no great religious poetry, though there is much sensitive verse expressive of the affections, and some very fine, and moving, devotional verse. But with one or two exceptions, these betray nothing of what might be called 'metaphysical tension'; there is no deep conflict, no Coleridgean reconciliation. There could hardly be such in an age set for clarification, trying to distinguish between what was proper for the passions, what, to misuse Swift's phrase, were the mechanical operations of the spirit, and what, by its nature, lay beyond the bounds of reason. Thus they could not make capital, as Donne did, out of what Mr. Eliot has called his confusion of thought, nor out of paradox, though they used ironic contrast. They were suspicious of analogy, which, to quote Mr. Eliot again, is a 'lazy evasion of thought'. This naturally lowered the potential of their poetry, since the lines between metaphor, analogy, and symbol are hard to draw. In a phrase it might be said that in poetry also the age manifested an *esprit simpliste*.

To be set against this is the attempt, already noted as a characteristic of the time, to grapple with the problem of evil. But the means of approach to the problem were so hoary with age, so overloaded with the doctrines at once cloudy and cumbrous of plenitude and the chain of being, that even Pope in the splendid first Epistle of the *Essay on Man* could not quite wrest it back from intellectual to intuitional realms. Here again 'metaphysical' tension could occur but seldom; for if a hundred years back the new philosophy had put all in doubt, the newer philosophy now, it seemed, made everything beautifully clear. There was no room for scholastic dialectic, quite apart from its having been cast aside as an outworn mode of thinking. Thus the age was in the main concerned—and this is where it made its most valuable contribution—on the one hand with the relation of man to man, on the other with its adjustment to, one might even say the delighted degustation of, the scientific ideas which the seventeenth century had made an imperative, and in its way exciting, poetic adventure. In the latter part of our period, with preludings in the earlier, 'cosmic' poems abound; and there are numberless passages where, as

Professor Marjorie Nicolson has shown, Newton demanded the muse. There is, however, such a marked change in the poetry of the second half of our period, as there is in most other fields, that it is convenient for the moment to confine ourselves to the first half.

Speaking broadly, then, aware of exceptions, we may say that the first twenty years of the century exhibit poetry at a level which is not, to be sure, dull, but which today fails to provoke any great depth of emotion or height of excitement. Yet if we feel that it is low-powered, that may be because its tensions are different from those we are accustomed to. It may also be that this middle-level verse—it is not what Professor C. S. Lewis would call 'drab'—is the price, heavy enough, that poetry has to pay for being treated as a natural vehicle of expression that anybody is free to use, and which can be used for expressing anything. This state of affairs has its compensations, certainly. It allowed Defoe, for example, to find some of his liveliest as well as his most tedious expression. In the long run such a phase may be good for poetry; it makes it familiar, brings it down from ivory towers into the street—in this period, shall we say, from the Cowleyan Pindaric to Gay's *Trivia*. It ensures its having the virtues of prose at least, since it has to strike the reading masses directly. Moreover, poetry was as much subject as prose to the change of use in language, with the new insistence on compact statement.

Popular in its own day, and, we must suppose, most of it still palatable when the great collections down to the end of the century were made, the great bulk of it now languishes in its formidable rows unread by any save the hopefully long-suffering historian or student. The early years of the century offer in abundance verse which has not now to be read, though it need not be despised; for poetaster after poetaster—and after poet—produced his pindarics, his imitations or paraphrases of Horace, his Virgilian eclogues or Georgics, his entrance-ticket amatory verses, his songs and laments, his ballads, fabliaux, or fables. Many of them have considerable skill, a healthy awareness of what had been written before; but their poems do not often impress us as corresponding with any imaginative apprehension, or to be the result of poetic, as opposed to social, pressure. Even nature poetry, though sometimes breaking free, is more usually compelled within the expected framework.

Soon something was to emerge, not, it may be said at once, merely premonitions of the future glory of the Romantics (foreshadowings were there, of course; the seeds of one age are always to be found in the last), but, shedding, after completion, the last vestiges of the metaphysical tradition, something distinctive, with a flavour that belongs to no other age. One need not make too high claims in redeeming this poetry from the blight cast on it by Wordsworth's remarks or the strictures of Matthew Arnold. Its virtues reside in its honesty, its determination to say 'something in verse as true as prose', its refusal to be led away by words, as the imitators of Cowley had been. Its great merit lies perhaps in its economy, its attempt to achieve an exact correspondence between word and thing or emotion—that is where the tension arises, not in the clash of ideas—and in its faith that the ordinary, universally shared sentiments were proper material for poetry, without flourishes or extraneous imagery. True sons of Dryden, the poets of that age tended to denote rather than to connote. Thus such pieces as Pope's lines sent to Lord Oxford with Parnell's poems, Aaron Hill's[1] verses in an inn at Southampton, or Congreve's epistle to Cobham, have no implications beyond what they state. There is rarely any plunging beneath the surface, for that is not *common* sense: the poets were to voice what every human being felt, 'what oft was thought', and, if possible, 'ne'er so well expressed'. Yet if they made no display of psychology, that is not to say they were bad psychologists. When they are evocative, as they sometimes are—though they are seldom incantatory—it is not from vagueness, but from precision; not from inviting adventure in realms unknown, but from making the reader realize the similarity of their feelings to his. It was not often great art, because all great art is an exploration of reality; the poets lured the reader to look more perceptively at what he had seen before, as Ambrose Philips did in his 'Winter Piece', or, for that matter, Swift did in his 'Description of the Morning'. They did not exalt you to Himalayan heights, but they enabled you to tread firmly, with a grip on your emotions, the Cotswolds. Later, from Mallet's *Excursion* in 1727 onwards, they deliberately

---

[1] Aaron Hill, 1685–1750, completed his early education at Barnstaple Grammar School and Westminster by going to Constantinople in 1700, and pursuing further Eastern travels. Indefatigable in 'projects' which always failed, including one for a settlement in Georgia, which Oglethorpe later carried out, in 1709 he became 'master of the stage' at Drury Lane, and in 1710 of the Opera at the Haymarket.

invoked the imagination, as Thomson did when he took his readers all over the world to compare climates; but for the first twenty years or so they were content with matter of observable fact. Deists they might be, but they were not Pantheists. They did not think that God was in the mountain mist; they might get a sharpened sense of God by looking at the mountain mist, but they liked to avoid confusing things. And if they did little to enlarge the bounds of experience, they did at least make certain areas of receptivity more sensitive. If such works as Swift's *Cadenus and Vanessa* and Prior's *Alma* did not reveal another level of being, they helped men to live alertly on the one they normally inhabited.

Poets, however, are not mere constructs of times and tendencies; they are primarily men and women; but it is commoner in some periods than it is in others to meet poetry that moves and excites, that opens vistas, and seems to touch the fringes of the inapprehensible. Why was it so rare, we may ask, at the beginning of the eighteenth century? Are any reasons discoverable besides the contributory ones already suggested? It is not, certainly, that many of the poets were not skilled writers, or were uneducated hacks; the best poets among them were nearly all university men; they knew the difference, in at least most respects, between good and bad poetry. Perhaps they were too much university men, too sensible of the pattern of classical poetry, too cognizant of the neo-classical criticism which, particularly in its French form, to some extent coloured the aesthetic thought of the period. Moreover, they were consciously completing a tradition, rounding off a classical phase. It was the 'Augustean' Age, as Dryden had told them; and so, feeling that they were dedicated to tradition, they were averse from stepping outside it. Thus the classics tended to creep in everywhere, like a pestilential vapour. And often, the classical allusions, unless they had lapsed to the state of being mere counters or synonyms, contained implications too heavy for the flimsy poetic structure to carry. They were apt to clog everything except what was written by the two or three poets big enough to integrate them in their sensibility.

But there was more than the somewhat fabricated desire to complete an historical cycle. The poets were also groping for a way in which to express the new sensibility, the unmetaphysical awareness so different from the awareness of the early part of the previous century. They inherited, and most of them wrestled with, forms little suited either to the Enlightenment or the domestic feeling which was so soon to demand expression. Nor would even the decasyllabic couplet they would have wished to take over from Dryden suit their purposes, except always for Pope. Unable to adapt classical prosody, though some of them occasionally tried to, they began, at first largely by way of a joke, to imitate Spenser and Chaucer, producing *naïvetés* they thought were like Spenser, and ribaldries they believed Chaucerian; Milton too was first approached by way of burlesque. But by adapting Spenser (who was edited by Hughes in 1715) and Milton—much of Milton's prosody and diction, something of Spenser's lovely sensuousness and simplicity—they in the end found what they wanted in blank verse. There were other experiments; but it is noticeable, and perhaps significant of their moving freely in a native tradition, that many found the happiest measure for most purposes to be the typically English and infinitely flexible octosyllabic couplet, or its close relation in trimeter or tetrameter rhythm. They got the measure sometimes through *Hudibras* (Butler was everybody's favourite, from Dennis to Ned Ward), but more often probably through *L'Allegro* and *Il Penseroso*, thus harking back through Marvell and King to the Elizabethans and right back to *The Romaunt of the Rose*. In using that metre they imitated Chaucer far more successfully than when they thought they were copying him.

In the early years the poetry was mostly very conscious, as it was bound to be in men intent to follow and fix a tradition, and most of it, therefore, to us very tame. The poets might have done better, we may think, to pay more heed to what Dennis[1] wrote in 1701 in *The Advancement and Reformation of Modern Poetry*:

As Passion in a Poem must be every where, so Harmony is usually diffus'd throughout it. But Passion answers the two ends of Poetry better than Harmony can do, and upon that account is preferable to it . . . Passion can please without Harmony, but Harmony tires without Passion.

[1] John Dennis, 1657–1734, son of a saddler, was educated at Harrow and Caius College, Cambridge, from which he migrated to Trinity Hall. After travelling in France and Portugal, he returned to London to live as a man of letters. In 1705 he was given a place as a royal waiter in the Port of London, which he sold in 1715. During his last years he was poverty stricken, subsisting on the charity of patrons.

It was passion that was sometimes wanting, not often harmony, which was sedulously pursued by poets who, whatever else they might be doing, were in this following Waller. But after all, it would appear to be difficult to exhibit or to feel passion, when there was no prospect of saying anything new. As Addison remarked in *Spectator* 253, where he was reviewing Pope's *Essay on Criticism*:

... give me leave to mention what Monsieur *Boileau* has so very well enlarged upon in the preface to his works, that wit and fine writing do not consist so much in advancing things that are new, as in giving things that are known an agreeable turn. It is impossible for us, who live in the latter Ages of the world, to make observations in criticism, morality, or in any art or science, which have not been touched upon by others. We have little else left us, but to represent the common sense of mankind in more strong, more beautiful, or more uncommon lights.

Pope had put it more pithily in the *Essay* itself.

And, voicing most clearly the opinion of his day, he declared in the Preface to the 1717 edition of his poems:

All that is left to us is to recommend our productions by the imitation of the Ancients: and it will be found true, that in every age, the highest character for sense and learning has been obtain'd by those who have been most indebted to them. For to say truth, whatever is very good sense must have been common sense in all times.

It is not surprising then that this age should in its early stages have been one of imitation, mainly from the classics. Most poets offered a few examples of direct translations, but countless poems were professed 'imitations' of Horace's epistles, satires, or odes, or of the *Ars Poetica*; of Virgil in pastoral or Georgic; of Ovid in fable, or especially metamorphosis, or the Heroical Epistle, and in the *Ars Amatoria*; of Lucretius in the philosophic poem; of the comic epic. Something there was from the Greeks, especially from Theocritus in the pastoral, while many produced scraps of Homer. And arising out of this there was a strong sense of the division of poetry into 'kinds', a point which Professor James Sutherland has skilfully touched upon in his *Preface to Eighteenth Century Poetry*, and need not be elaborated here. All this was very real to the poets of those days. It may be that Professor Havens is right in thinking that the classical predilection was 'a cult, a fad, an artificial taste which grew up

under French influence among the more critical'; but influence
is a seed which will grow only in soil ready to receive it; even
without French influence classicism would have been there,
and there are always deeper reasons for fads and affectations
than appear on the surface. And the main reason here, as has
been suggested, may well have been an illusory sense of history.

At all events, given the mass of poetry with which we are
presented, it would be tedious to deal with the poets seriatim,
and it might be equally tedious to follow through the forms or
'kinds' in any detail. Thus a few poets will be picked out for
more affectionate treatment than anyone would wish to accord
to the bulk of them, more especially where they contributed
something to development, and some of the moods will be
touched on. Interest is to be derived from following a few of the
forms, perhaps to watch one of them dying, as the eclogue died,
or developing from infancy into bulky potentates as the 'nature'
poem did. And in view of the trend of poetic thinking at the
beginning of the century, it will perhaps be most entertaining to
take first a form which exhibits an obvious classical heredity, for
after all, it was an age of university wits, though very different
in character, condition, or purpose from those of the Elizabethan
age. It may therefore be fitting to begin with the mock-heroic.

2. SOME FORMS

Yet how far the mock- or the burlesque-epic is directly traceable
to classical influence, it is hard to say, though it may be
significant that Parnell translated Homer's *Batrachomuomachia*
in 1717. It is more probable that Boileau's *Le Lutrin* was the
spur to imitation, and perhaps Tassoni's *La Secchia Rapita* (both
translated by Ozell), though the burlesque—as opposed to the
mock-heroic—effect seems to have been of native growth,
owing something no doubt to *Hudibras*, even if Butler's work is
not so much a burlesque epic as a heightening into mock-
heroic terms of the picaresque novel and the knightly romance.
And at least there had been *MacFlecknoe*, a lampoon with elements
of the heroic. But the epic in reverse, to call it so, affectionate
parody rather than satire, occurs often enough in this period to
invite special attention. There is Garth, and John Philips,
Swift's *Battle of the Books*, and, above all, of course, Pope; there
are traces in works of other poets, as in King's *Furmetary*, and it
was used for different purposes. Garth employed it for satiric

ends, to scarify the money-making doctors afraid that the
apothecaries would filch from them some of their ill-gotten
gains through the dispensary he had fought to get 'set up for
the relief of the sick poor'; Philips used it for sheer fun, Swift to
make his point amid torrents of laughter; and Pope, in *The
Rape of the Lock*, where it is pure 'mock', to produce exquisite
comedy, while in *The Dunciad* he used it—among other things—
to pulverize his opponents. The major examples appear elsewhere than in this chapter; a few minor ones may be treated
here.

It must be confessed that *The Dispensary* which Garth[1] produced anonymously in 1698 is somewhat indigestible, though
taken in small morsels it has a flavour. It is not only that the
circumstances which produced it have now only the dimmest
historical interest and that the characters of the actors elude
us, but that with its six cantos it is too long, too elaborate:
it seems heavily disproportionate to its purpose. Whatever
Garth may have said, he borrowed more than three or four
lines from *Le Lutrin*; a wider debt is obvious, ultimately based
though he may be on Homer and Virgil. Occasional good lines
have a smack of Dryden:

> Each Faculty in Blandishments they lull,
> Aspiring to be venerably dull;

or, echoing another mood of Dryden's:

> Restless Anxiety, forlorn Despair,
> And all the faded family of Care;

but sometimes he looks forward, one need not say to Pope, but
to Johnson:

> Soon as the Ev'ning veil'd the Mountains' Heads,
> And Winds lay hush'd in subterranean Beds,
> While sick'ning Flow'rs drink up the Silver Dew,
> And *Beaus* for some *Assembly* dress anew;
> The City Saints to Pray'rs and play-house haste,
> The Rich to Dinner, and the Poor to Rest.

---

[1] Samuel Garth, 1661–1719, was educated at Ingleton in Yorkshire and at
Peterhouse, Cambridge. After spending three years at Leyden, in 1691 he was
made M.D., and in 1693 Fellow of the College of Physicians. In 1697 he instituted
dispensaries for poor patients, from which developed out-patients' rooms in
hospitals. A stout Whig, he was a member of the Kit-Cat, and in 1714 was appointed
Physician in Ordinary to the King, and Physician-General to the army, as well as
being knighted.

And if the 'machinery' is a little ponderous, his battle, waged with medicaments and medical contraptions, is lively enough, and his descent into the nether regions, to wit, 'the Cave of Spleen', sufficiently grisly. Its contemporary popularity offers no puzzle, especially as in successive editions (quotations are from the final one) Garth kept his matter up to date, to include such figures as Queen Anne and Addison, such events as the battle of Blenheim. Today it amuses only fitfully.

In his three extremely brief cantos of *The Furmetary* (1699), 'a very innocent and harmless poem', William King[1] does not attempt to imitate the epic, except in the last phase, where he gives us the battle, in a succession of such couplets as:

> Hectorvus first, Tubcarrio does attack,
> And by surprize soon lays him on his back;
> Thirsto and Drowtho then, approaching near,
> Soon overthrow two magazines of Beer . . .
>   In the mean time, Tobacco strives to vex
> A numerous squadron of the tender sex;
> With what strong smoak, and with what stronger breath,
> He funks* Basketia and her son to death . . .
>   * blows smoke upon

going on, of course, to a 'So have I seen . . .' passage. King, we know, liked to toy with classical adaptations, his *Art of Cookery* (there are worse advisers) being his 'imitation' of the *Ars Poetica*, his *Art of Love*, to Dr. Johnson's surprise quite inoffensive, springing from Ovid. John Philips,[2] on the other hand, does not seem to have had the itch to imitate in this way, though he submits to classical discipline. He was concerned rather to amuse himself with Miltonic metric and diction (as Lady Winchilsea played with it, feebly it must be confessed, in 'Fanscomb Barn'), and it is interesting to note that Miltonic bone was reintroduced into English poetry partly through ridiculing it. Philips's very short *The Splendid Shilling* (1701) can hardly be described as a mock epic, though it might claim to be a fragment, and Philips had tact enough not to make his poem

[1] William King, 1663–1712, was educated at Westminster and Christ Church, Oxford: he became a lawyer. In 1702 he was appointed to Ireland, where he held various posts: he returned in 1708, and in 1711 was made Gazetteer.

[2] John Philips, 1676–1709, educated at Winchester and Christ Church, Oxford, was trained to become a doctor: but he abandoned this career in favour of a literary life.

longer than his subject could bear. It is an entertaining parody. There is far more vigour in the versification than in Garth's poem, possibly because Miltonic prosody more readily gives a sense of vigour than the couplet, unless a master uses it, but also because Philips had something of a real singing quality; there is native energy in his verse, as he was to show more clearly later; his images are lively, his vowel-sounds varied. His comparisons of the small and the great are amusingly ridiculous:

> Afflictions great! Yet greater still remain:
> My *Galligaskins* that have long withstood
> The Winter's Fury, and encroaching Frosts,
> By Time subdued (what will not Time subdue!)
> An horrid Chasm disclose, with Orifice
> Wide, discontinuous; at which the Winds
> *Eurus* and *Auster*, and the dreadful Force
> Of *Boreas* that congeals the *Cronian* Waves,
> Tumultuous enter with dire chilling Blasts,
> Portending Agues. Thus a well-fraught Ship . . .

and so on in a concluding passage many serious poets would have been glad to contrive.

Burlesque, or parody, or mock, increased until the fifth decade of the century, though there is little that remains of the later work at all alive; one can think only of Browne's *Tobacco* (1736) and of Shenstone's *Mistress* (1742), where the fun is largely in the Spenserian take-off. And so it went on, but it may not be very profitable in this place to pursue the reason why so much of this sort of work appeared at this time. There are many suggestions to serve as pointers. Perhaps it was that all eyes were on the epic, and that, as MM. Legouis and Cazamian suggest, 'aspiration after a big subject not being sustained by a strong creative mood, stops half-way at the compromise of a mock-heroic intention'; that might be true of Pope, who excused himself for not having written an epic by saying that he had translated two; but it would not apply to most of those poets who enjoyed themselves in this form, for they were not writers of a stature to aspire after a big subject, though Blackmore was deterred by no half-way-house modesty. It is more satisfactory to say with Courthope that the 'tendency to use verse as an instrument of dialectic [was] another symptom of the advance of the philosophic spirit in English society', the burlesque, of course, being an answer to the heroic. Professor Richmond Bond prefers to lean on the supposition, difficult wholly to maintain, that 'Burlesque is a characteristic product of a time which glorified the social arts'; but he is on firmer ground when he refers to critical insight being expressed through comic imitation. Yet even this is a trifle uncertain, since it is parody or travesty which is the critical instrument, though it is true that some of the burlesque, as, for example, *The Splendid Shilling*, which criticizes not only Miltonic prosody and grandiosity, but also the inflated pseudo-classical simile, does exercise this function. The form, of course, was one of the 'kinds' to be imitated; and increasing sophistication, heat being replaced by irony and urbanity, as Professor Bond suggests, made the form agreeable and easy to use; but the question is bound up with the whole large query as to why satire flourished rather more at this period than at any other. Yet after all we may simple-mindedly wonder whether it is not merely that it seems to have flourished more because the two greatest geniuses of the time happened, partly by their nature, partly by their particular circumstances, to have found their most natural vehicle in satire.

A transition from these poems to pastorals will not seem startling if we agree with Professor Empson that the pastoral mode is at once complementary to, and critical of, the heroic. Moreover, the pastoral, by which is here meant the eclogue, or at least the poem in which peasants figure, is the clearest example of the impoverishing, as opposed to the enriching side, of the classical fashion. In its Graeco-Roman form it declined to its end in this period; yet though it seemed to be progressively dying of inanition, it died hard, for if ridicule diversified, it did not seem much to hasten its end. Indeed the endeavours of Gay, egged on by his fellow Scriblerians, to dispatch it with laughter almost reinfused it with new life; and, at any rate, in August 1716 Swift could write to Pope:

I believe further the Pastoral ridicule is not exhausted, and that a porter, foot-man, or chair-man's pastoral might do well. Or what think you of a Newgate pastoral, among the whores and thieves there?

—a suggestion which later bore fruit in *The Beggar's Opera*. It may seem curious that the form should have existed at all in so

strident and realistic an age, in a society which tended to become urban—it was written by the most urban of the poets—
except perhaps as an example of the law of primitive survival.
In our own time, it is true, we have poets such as Mr. Graves,
Mr. Auden, Mr. Plomer, and others toying with the ballad,
deliberately giving an artificial twist to the old spontaneous
simplicity, and something of the sort may have occurred here.
Moreover, since the pastoral at least implies the idea of the
noble savage or peasant, it tallied with the Shaftesburian
'optimism' of the time, as it may have with the 'golden age'
primitivism, the idea of which crops up sporadically in such
later poets as Thomson. Yet it can never have meant much to
the average reader of the day, though the friends of Ambrose
Philips did their utmost to puff it into popularity. The form
did not fit the sensibility of the age.

Even Spenser, in attempting to comply with the fashionable
puritan classicism of the Cambridge of his day rather than
follow his own bent, carried a certain conviction into the rebirth
of the form in English, as did, even more clearly, Drayton in
some of his loveliest work, and other Elizabethan pastoralists,
while Quarles had made no bones about his moral intent. How
far they may have fused their sensibility with that of the classical
authors does not much matter, but they did use the form to
convey some intuition of contemporary life: they were serious,
just as had been Theocritus, Bion, Moschus, Virgil, and others,
for whom the eclogue had been a valid vehicle of poetic apprehension. In the earlier time there had still been enough of what
Professor Empson has analysed as the opposition of the heroic
in life with the pastoral, enough real class distinction to make
the idea of pastoral (the hero finding simplicity) still dimly
intuitive. A Philip Sidney could allowably pen an *Arcadia*;
the great lord might still pretend to be a peasant; when,
however, you get little middle-class men pretending to be
rustics, the artificiality becomes meaningless. And for the
writers of our period, it would seem—Walsh, Broome, Philips,
Elizabeth Rowe or Singer ('the Pindaric Lady' as Dunton
dubbed her), or Aaron Hill—the eclogue was not a means of
coming to grips with any sort of reality; it was an escape into a
tradition the meaning of which had been lost, and it is significant that our poets refer only to Spenser among earlier English
writers, unless a mention of Sidney as the friend of shepherds

may be allowed to count. More than once the four great pastoral performers of the world are stated to be Theocritus, Virgil, Spenser, 'and our own Mr. Philips': the inclusion of the last was, of course, pedantic nonsense.

Much of it was written meekly to theory; and if we look at this, and at the aesthetic philosophy through which the eclogue was supposed to appeal as set out in the papers contributed to the *Guardian* (Nos. 22, 23, 28, 32), almost certainly by Tickell (though the first one has strong whiffs of Addison), it would appear that the form was doomed, being so amusingly incongrous with the time. The very insistence on its unreality in that very realistic age is proof enough. 'It is a dream, it is a vision, which we may wish to be real, and we believe that it is true.' Borrowing generously from Fontenelle, Tickell dilates upon primitive times, their affluence and ease—the golden age myth —laying down that 'it is sometimes convenient not to discuss the whole truth, but that part which only is delightful'. Thus the pastoral was to create a 'pleasing delusion', and the poems were to appeal to the human love of ease. We learn that 'simplicity is necessary to the character of Shepherds', though the Arcadians need not be dolts. They are to be simple-spoken people, innocent in their manners, prone to religion and even superstition, given to proverbial sayings: indeed one of the problems of the form was 'to raise a proverb above the vulgar style', one of Philips's triumphs being 'A rolling stone is ever bare of moss'. The other essays are little critical studies of pastoralists past and present, which Dr. Johnson was not much to better in his *Ramblers* 36 and 37. It is clear that this sort of pastoral has nothing to do with the nature poem, however much Tickell might invite the truculent citizens of Queen Anne's London to be 'entertained with all the sweets and freshness of nature'. It was an artefact which attempted to resolve a certain group of social emotions.

Though what emotions are resolved by Ambrose Philips's[1]

---

[1] Ambrose Philips, 1674–1749, was educated at Shrewsbury and St. John's College, Cambridge. Became a Fellow, and may have been ordained deacon. Tried to obtain employment in Holland, but failing, took a commission in the army, and served in Spain. Was much a friend of Addison's, and a prominent member of 'the little senate'. Early in 1709 was appointed Secretary to the Envoy at Copenhagen (Daniel Pulteney); in Feb. 1711 went to Italy as tutor to Simon Harcourt (*aet*. 24), coming back to England in June. In 1724 went to Ireland as Secretary to the Primate of All-Ireland (Boulter); in 1734 he became Registrar of the

Pastorals it is not easy to say, nor why they got so much more applause than they seem to us to deserve. Philips, at this time a favourite of Addison's in his 'little Senate', was tiresomely overpraised by Tickell, who was displacing Steele in Addison's regard; and we cannot but think that it was clique-loyalty that produced the adulations from all sides, honest, no doubt, but none the less suspect critically. At the same time it must be admitted that at any rate he conformed to theory. The pastoral, he said in his Preface, 'gives a sweet and gentle Composure to the Mind', and he attempted to continue the line in the recognized descent. He did not seem to notice that there was a certain harsh realism about Theocritus, a political and prophetic strain in Virgil, an implied opinion on affairs in Spenser —though there are indeed references to events in Philips. Four of his pastorals appeared at the beginning of 1708 in Fenton's *Oxford and Cambridge Miscellany Poems*, and all six in Tonson's sixth volume of *Poetical Miscellanies* (1709), together with Pope's, the first four being refurbished for the new edition, though they did not assume their final polished, heavily revised form till the edition of his poems in 1748. The second version differs in a few respects from the first, losing a little freshness in the interests of the correct, and we are left in no doubt that all were carefully fabricated from their earliest moment in 1700. By 1705 Addison was able to praise them.

There is undoubtedly a certain charm about these pastorals 'pastoralised to the most artificial-trivial extent possible, of pale translations and second hand things in various *rococo* styles', such was Saintsbury's damning conclusion; there is even a good deal of silliness, some of which was corrected by 1748. He took full advantage of the suggestion made by Walsh[1] in his *Essay on Pastoral Poetry* (1697) that the numbers 'ought to be looser and not so sonorous' as in other forms of poetry, yet his eclogues are not lacking in mellifluousness, of a rather obvious sort that relies a good deal on repetition. Though they are imitations, sometimes of imitations, and though the descriptions are for the most part derived from descriptions, there is a soothing and 'pleasing' melancholy running through them as

Court of Faculties and of the Prerogative Court. Resigned in 1748, and died after living a year in London.

[1] William Walsh, 1663–1708, went to Wadham College, Oxford, but took no degree. He became Member of Parliament for Worcester, and then Richmond, Yorks., and was made Gentleman of the Horse to Queen Anne.

they carefully avoid the higher strains of poetry. As good an example as any is the fourth, praised by his latest editor Miss Segar, which is based on the first of Theocritus, and clothed in diction partly borrowed from Spenser. A portion may be culled to indicate his quality:

> O, *Colinet*, how sweet thy Grief to hear!
> How does thy Verse subdue the list'ning Ear!
> Not half so sweet are Midnight Winds, that move
> In drowsie Murmurs o'er the waving Grove;
> Nor dropping Waters, that in Grots distil,
> And with a tinkling Sound their Caverns fill:
> So sing the Swans, that in soft Numbers waste
> Their dying Breath, and warble to the last.
> And next to thee shall *Mico* bear the Bell,
> That can repeat thy peerless Verse so well.

In the 1748 version the uncomfortable distilling grot has gone, together with the caverns, while the swans have mercifully flown; now Philips seems really to have been there, but, alas, though he has no more to say, he says more.

We need not imagine that Pope nursed any Tickellian notions when at the age of sixteen he first set his hand to the pastorals which he was to polish until he was twenty-one. Not for him the idea of restoring ancient simplicity: he was going to write pastorals as an art form, since that was how the dedicated poet began. In following Walsh's exhortation to be the first 'correct' poet in the language, he would certainly ignore the latitude in versification which that very minor pastoralist recommended. So Pope ran true to form; the shepherds indulged in musical contests, panted after the loves they celebrated, bewailed the death of a fellow shepherd; but he made little attempt to bring to Londoners the sweets and freshness of the countryside. Yet here and there we meet touches of personal observation, never far away with Pope, such as '. . . fleecy clouds were streak'd with purple light'; but it was not his intention to represent nature or 'natural' human beings: he meant to make objects of a recognized kind. One might liken a Philips eclogue to one of those charming but rather dimly formal landscapes painted on glass so popular in the nineteenth century, and say that Pope's have all the deliberate artificiality, hardness of outline, and brilliance of Staffordshire figures. He never supposed they were aspects of any reality, even of a

dream; but they themselves were a reality of a kind one could,
so to speak, handle. Since they were to be delicious artefacts he
took good ingredients from wherever he could find them, not
from the ancients alone, but from Cowley and Congreve, and,
as is normal with Pope, from Dryden. We may take as typical
the passage from the second Pastoral, Summer (they follow the
four seasons as an extra grace of form), which was in 1744 to
become a famous Handelian song when inserted into a revival
of Congreve's *Semele*:

> Where-e'er you walk, cool gales shall fan the glade,
> Trees, where you sit, shall crowd into a shade,
> Where-e'er you tread, the blushing flow'rs shall rise,
> And all things flourish where you turn your eyes . . .
> But would you sing, and rival *Orpheus'* strain,
> The wond'ring forests soon should dance again,
> The moving mountains hear the pow'rful call,
> And headlong streams hang list'ning in their fall!

Ruskin's perfervid abuse of this passage—'simple falsehood . . .
hypocrisy . . .' and so on—would have seemed to Pope ludi-
crously beside the mark, as indeed it is. Of course he was not
telling the truth! Why should he be? There is no evidence that
he considered the eclogue a vehicle for expressing anything
very important, but at least he was making a poem, a patterned
object full of melody, of enlivening imagery, with 'correctly'
appropriate diction, and with delightful and varied metrical
effects, here 'imitating' Virgil as later he would, with a freer
mastery, 'imitate' Ovid and Horace. That he did not regard
these toys with high seriousness, except for the seriousness of a
craftsman intent upon making as perfect an object of its kind
as he could, is plain from the dedication of this same pastoral:

> Accept, O *Garth*, the Muse's early lays,
> That adds a wreath of Ivy to thy Bays;
> Hear what from Love unpractis'd hearts endure,
> From Love, the sole disease thou canst not cure!

The least whiff of that sort of humour would have immeasurably improved Philips's work in this genre.

We should probably not pay much attention to these pastorals
'written in the year MDCCIV' if Pope had written nothing further;
yet they are indubitably poetry, as he demurely indicated in his
delightfully malicious *Guardian* No. 40, in which, not unnaturally

smarting at the hoisting above him of the complacent Philips,
he displayed his own theory. Using the ironic mode, he brilliantly overstates the orthodox position, and out-Fontenelles
Fontenelle in his purist objection to the ancients. He has no
difficulty in bedevilling the unlucky Ambrose, in his most
shattering passage quoting lines over which Tickell had crooned
approval:

> O wo'ful Day! O Day of Woe! quoth he;
> And wo'ful I, who live the Day to see!

That Simplicity of Diction, the Melancholy Flowing of the Numbers,
the Solemnity of the Sound, and the easie Turn of the Words, in
this Dirge (to make use of our Author's Expression) are extreamly
Elegant.

Philips might rage, and hang up a cane at Button's to greet
Pope with, but—the lines were duly altered! It is, however, in
the condemnation of himself in this essay that Pope's real
theory of the eclogue is expressed.

> Mr. *Pope* hath fallen into the same Error with *Virgil*. His Clowns
> do not converse in all the Simplicity proper to the Country: His
> names are borrow'd from *Theocritus* and *Virgil*, which are improper
> to the Scene of his Pastorals . . . whereas *Philips*, who hath the
> strictest Regard to Propriety, makes choice of Names peculiar to
> the Country, and more agreeable to a Reader of Delicacy; such
> as *Hobbinol, Lobbin, Cuddy,* and *Colin Clout*.

The whole culminating in the impish but crushing 'Our other
Pastoral Writer [Pope], in expressing the same Thought,
deviates into downright Poetry'. There was, of course, to be
propriety; wolves should not occur in England, nor should 'roses,
lilies and daffodils blow in the same season'; but why absurdly
pretend that the country of eclogues was the countryside
everybody was living in? Besides, to shun all ornament, all
vividness of expression, or that Latin sonority always present
in Pope, would be to deprive the form of anything that made it
worthy to be called poetry.

The most curious figure to appear in this connexion, and
one completely ignored until his recent resuscitation by Mr.
Geoffrey Grigson, is William Diaper.[1] Though according to
Giles Jacob 'he had a fine poetical genius', he appears in no

---

[1] William Diaper, 1685-1717; of Balliol College, Oxford. Held curacies at
East Brent, Somerset, later at Crick, Northamptonshire, and possibly in 1713-14
at Dean near Basingstoke.

contemporary criticism, except for a disdainful couplet in *The Dunciad*, afterwards expunged. Swift, however, whose protégé this obscure country parson for a time was, saw something in him, presented him to Bolingbroke, and collected some guineas for him. Writing to Stella of the *Nereides, or Sea-Eclogues* (1712), he remarked 'they are very pretty, and the thought is new'. Diaper, with a real love of the sea, and a very considerable lore in fishy matters derived largely from Oppian whom he was later to help in translating, found little pleasure in the eternal shepherds and shepherdesses, the constantly recurring formalized descriptions of the country:

> All do not love in clotting Fields to sweat,
> Where clayie Fallows clog the labouring Feet.

He really was original; his were the first sea eclogues, and seem to remain the only ones. There had indeed been Sannazaro, whose Latin piscatory eclogues were duly noted by Tickell and laughed out of court, an example followed with more dignity by Johnson; the sea and sea-shore were dull and horrid; it was not poetical to present a mistress 'with oysters instead of fruits and flowers'. There had also been in England, Phineas Fletcher's *Piscatorie Eclogs* (1633). But as Diaper said in his Preface, those who have attempted to touch the beauties and riches of the sea 'have only given us a few Piscatory Eclogues, like the first Coasters, they always keep within sight of Shore, and never venture into the Ocean'.

The reader of the dedication to Congreve, in many respects the usual formal thing, should have noticed that a new tune was to be heard; for after saying, in not very original verse, that

> The flowry Meadows, and the whispering Trees
> Have oft been sung, and will hereafter please,

he announces the new field in a voice of his own:

> But the vast unseen mansions of the deep,
> Where secret Groves with liquid Amber weep,
> Where blushing Sprigs of knotty Coral spread
> And gild the Azure with a brighter red
> Were still untouch'd. . . .

Yet Diaper, as much as anyone, is avowedly based on the ancients, often directly imitating Theocritus or Virgil. He filches from Ovid as he does from Du Bartas (or at least Sylvester), but he makes a thing of his own by a vivid imagination backed by a naturalist's knowledge of sea life; his epithets are few, accurate, and well chosen. Though as an eclogue-writer he sings of sea-loves, and indulges in the obligatory plaints, his eclogues are not all silly-sooth: there is some philosophy in them. In No. 4 Diaper attempts to account for the then unsolved problem of the tides, and resolves the query scholastically; in No. 8 Proteus describes the creation and would seem to be a Berkeleyan, and No. 13 amusingly argues from the Scale of Being:

> Loose not too much the Reins of wild Desire:
> Shrimps may not grow to Crabs, nor Orks to Whales aspire.

He has plenty of good lines, his imagery never disappoints and is sometimes vivid: thus it would seem to have been the subject-matter that repelled his contemporaries. The sea was acknow-ledged to be a horrid and depressing element, and they were not prepared to believe that

> The Ocean has its Groves, and gloomy Shades,
> And chrystal Springs below, and cooling Glades

nor be won by his surprisingly actual descriptions of the tides. His companion in the translation of the *Haleuticks* did indeed in 1722 defend the scene, and threw not undeserved scorn on Tickell's narrowness in decrying Sannazaro; and in 1726 John Rooke, making *Select Translations from the Works of Sannazarius* also justified the choice, and declared that Tickell 'used a Freedom with Sannazarius, that, to say no more of it, trespasses both upon Decency and good manners'. But it was too late to save Diaper from more than two centuries of virtual oblivion.

With Gay's[1] *Shepherd's Week* (1714) we return to dry land. Originally designed to make game of Ambrose Philips, Gay did not confine himself to this, making, for instance, glorious fun of Blackmore by parodying *The Creation* and 'The Song of Mopas'

---

[1] John Gay, 1685–1732, was educated at Barnstable School, and became a silk-mercer's apprentice; in 1712 he was made Secretary to the Duchess of Monmouth, and in 1714 Secretary to the Ambassador at Hanover (Lord Clarendon), but this lapsed on the death of Queen Anne. He lived largely by the kindness of patrons, Pulteney, Harcourt, and others. He lost the money from the South Sea Stock that Craggs gave him. In 1727 he refused the offer of Gentleman Usher to the Princess Louisa, and spent the last few years of his life as the guest of the Duke and Duchess of Queensberry.

in 'Saturday' and 'The Song of Bowzybeus'. But apart from that by a happy accident it allowed him to make his first durable contribution to the poetic canon. There is no dream-scene fustian about these pastorals; his shepherds really have a rough existence; his shepherdesses, by no means 'lily-handed', actually milk the cows and clean out the pigsty. We can believe in their affections. And for all their labour and discomfort there is an atmosphere of gaiety about them, a spice of humour and light-heartedness which carries back to Nicolas Breton and earlier Elizabethans. He is firmly contemporary and realistic. As he says in his entertaining *Proeme*:

... my love to my native country *Britain* much pricketh me forward, to describe aright the manners of our own honest and laborious plough-men, in no wise sure more unworthy a *British* Poet's imitation, than those of *Sicily* or *Arcadia*; albeit, not ignorant I am, what a rout and rabblement of critical gallimawfry hath been made of late days by certain young men of insipid delicacy, concerning, I wist not what, *Golden Age*, and other outragious conceits, to which they would confine Pastoral. Whereof, I avow, I account naught at all. . . .

Thus the Squabble, the Ditty, the Dumps, or the Dirge, in which the characters are Grubbinols and Blowzelindas, give a far more accurate rendering than was usual of the real spirit of the ancients (at least in some respects), though Gay too based his pastorals on theirs, as his references to Virgil, and once to Theocritus, show. But perhaps in this age, as Professor Empson suggests, it was through burlesque alone that genuine pastoral could be reached. It is his straight descriptions that really count; they are genuinely pastoral. Consider this from 'Tuesday; or, the Ditty':

> Whilom with thee 'twas *Marian*'s dear delight,
> To moil all day, and merry-make at night.
> If in the soil you guide the crooked share,
> Your early breakfast is my constant care—
> And when with even hand you strow the grain,
> I fright the thievish rooks from off the plain.
> In misling days, when I my thresher heard,
> With nappy beer I to the barn repair'd;
> Lost in the music of the whirling flail,
> To gaze on thee I left the smoking pail:
> In harvest when the sun was mounted high,
> My leathern bottle did thy draught supply;

When-e'er you mow'd I follow'd with the rake,
And have full oft been sun-burnt for thy sake:
When in the welkin gath'ring show'rs were seen,
I lagg'd the last with *Colin* on the green;
And when at eve returning with thy carr,
Awaiting heard the Gingling bells from far;
Strait on the fire the sooty pot I plac't,
To warm thy broth I burnt my hands for haste.
When hungry thou stoods't *staring, like an Oaf,*
I slic'd the luncheon from the barly loaf;
With crumbled bread I thicken'd well thy mess.
Ah, love me more, or love thy pottage less!

You are expected to laugh, but you cannot help enjoying the something else that comes through the mockery; there is direct contact with life, and, what is more, an individual poetic quality to be discussed when Gay's work is considered as a whole.

A further example of mockery, directed not at the form, but which by using the form enhances a very mild social satirico-pornographic effect, is to be found in Lady Mary Wortley Montagu's *Town Eclogues* of 1717, piratically used by Curll in his *Court Poems* of the previous year. These also provide a 'week', with such items as 'Thursday, the Bassette Table', and 'Saturday, the Small-Pox', but their poetic value is no more than that of social *vers d'occasion*, though their place in socio-literary history is secure thanks to the connexion with Pope, and Curll's emetic. One might have thought that this variety of mockery might have added just that weight under which the form would have sunk.

But no mockery of any kind could affect a writer such as Thomas Purney.[1] If Gay's pastorals are grotesque, they are so of set purpose; Purney's are unwittingly so. He fell into all the worst pits indicated by Tickell and others as virtues; and into further chasms, since believing all the *Guardian* essays to have been written by Addison, for whose every word he had the deepest reverence, believing him also the author of Pope's wickedly witty No. 40, which he took *au pied de la lettre*, he sailed away in a happy clumsiness, having swallowed everything said in these essays, entirely regardless of their digestibility. He even

---

[1] Thomas Purney, 1695–1727(?), was educated at the Merchant Taylors' School and Clare Hall, Cambridge. He became Ordinary at Newgate, and disappeared mysteriously.

admired the absurdity Gay invented as part of a 'fine old Pastoral Ballad' and which Pope had quoted:

> Rager go vetch tha kee, or else tha zun
> Will quite be go, before c'have half a don.

Thus it is not surprising that his *Pastorals. After the simple manner of Theocritus*, 1717 (actually 1716), are made as simple as can be imagined, and that Purney feels free to take what liberties he likes with current English, believing that he was imitating Spenser by using affected archaisms. His Kentish labourer is not a Kentish labourer, but 'A Gentle Swain yfed in *Kentish Mead*'. This kind of regurgitation produces such passages as:

> But ill I say how sweet the Lasses sate,
> Oh that you'd seen 'em, I'd give any what!
> This sooth I say (for sooth the Shepherds say)
> Soft simpering thus said the Youngling Mey.
> The meaning of the Mey no whit I ween,
> I', sure, when near I came, just thus she sain.
> *Paplet*. How much I marl: 'Tis pretty, if tell Truth!
> But say; Ha, Ha! Be He so soft in sooth?

We are told in a footnote that 'mey' indicates someone younger than a 'maid'; but that the word is used chiefly 'as it has not the vulgarness of *Maid*, and is of a sound particularly sweet and simple'. Yet this incredible namby-pambyism is not without its interest; for Purney abandoned the fashionable pattern in favour of artless stories, which, 'for the ease of the Soft-Sex', were 'specified in the *Arguments*', not without some cause in the interests of lucidity. It is just this streak of originality which perhaps makes it worth while to retain the memory of Purney, for though it would be absurd to say that his work in any way foreshadowed the pastoral romanticism of the nineteenth century, there is something new stirring in the old form, both here and in his other pastorals, *The Bashful Swain; and Beauty and Simplicity*, 1717. That is more than can be said for the pastoral which Mrs. Centlivre wrote to bewail the death of Rowe in 1718, in which Daphnis and Thyrsis praise the departed Colin in the usual allegorical terms, with some melody but at too great length. Of all the dead forms, which should have been left to the undertaker, the pastoral elegy, especially in eclogue form, is the most obvious. It would, however, be interesting to know what Pope thought of the achievement of his sometime collaborator Broome,[1] whose two pastorals (1727), though livelier in versification and feeling than Mrs. Centlivre's funerary plumes, are unoriginal in form and usually in phrase: they adhere to the Anglo-Classical model:

> . . . the falling Day
> Gilds every Mountain with a ruddy Ray;

the breeze whispers and salutes the flowers; the shepherdesses fly their ardent swains—not too swiftly; the fountains murmur, and the birds warble on the vocal bough. But Broome did at least see that swallows skimmed over lakes, and that

> The timid Deer, swift-starting as they graze,
> Bound off in Crowds, then turn again and gaze;

but these things are no more than the mere amusements of a country parson fond of the classics. Of slightly different taste are the *Piscatory Eclogues* of Moses Browne[2] (1729), which he published together with a thickly learned and unilluminating Preface. Among foreign practitioners in the great line he adds Tasso, and at home 'our Spencer, Milton, Congreve, (and I ask pardon if I am mistaken in adding Mr. Philips too)'. He on the whole eschews singing competitions, love-plaints, and so on, being concerned rather to versify *The Compleat Angler*, which he later edited, with 'improvements': his verses might be called fishing Georgics in eclogue form. Except for the subject, there is nothing original about them; the verse and the diction are fatiguingly familiar. Lyttelton's youthful eclogues, *The Progress of Love* (1726, published 1732), exhale a faint flavour of the Popean form, and are sufficiently soothing.

Thus the eclogue as a form seems to have ended at about this time, unless we include Collins's *Persian Eclogues* (1742) which are a rather more subtle matter; henceforth the peasant appears differently conceived and in a different setting, as in Gray's *Elegy* (1751) or Goldsmith's *Deserted Village* (1770), to come triumphantly into his own poetic place with Wordsworth. The Sicilian shepherd is no longer to be met with in England, at least till we come to *Thyrsis*; but Arnold was hark-

---

[1] William Broome, 1689–1745, educated at Eton and St. John's College, Cambridge, became Vicar of Eye, Suffolk.

[2] Moses Browne, 1704–87, a pen-cutter, who was ordained in 1753, and in the same year became vicar of Olney, where Newton sat under him. He was made chaplain of Morden College, and later Vicar of Sutton in Lincolnshire.

ing back to Milton rather than to Spenser, Philips, and Pope. There is a brief and lovely interlude of real English pastoral with Barnes, but when next we meet the eclogue in any memorable form it is in Fleet Street, with John Davidson.

If the pastoral was dying, the descriptive philosophic nature-poem was to swell in the second part of our period to be almost the dominant 'kind'. It had of course been 'there' in the seventeenth century, notably with Cotton and Marvell, and, with a more self-conscious flavour, with Milton; but in the eighteenth century it finds new expression, not through the pastoral, but first through the 'Horatian' element in occasional verse, and then through the Georgic. The term 'Horatian' is here used in Quiller-Couch's sense, as indicating a mood of retirement, of seeking day-to-day contentment in quiet accompanied by frugal pleasures, the state expressed by Milton in the line 'And when God sends a quiet hour, refrain', and earlier by Elizabethan poets. The more classically imitative poets of Queen Anne's day were alive to the Roman derivation, Parnell in 'Health' declaring that 'Tully's Tusculum' revived in his. In the real 'nature' poet this element fades out: Thomson in his 'Hymn on Solitude' of 1729 found the state only 'mildly pleasing', and preferred to experience it where

> I just may cast my careless eyes
> Where London's spiry turrets rise.

And if at the beginning of our period the theme, as old as literature itself, is associated with a countryside not too far from a town, and always linked with utility, it is all quite sincerely felt. Thus Pomfret[1] in *The Choice* (1700):

> Near some fair Town I'd have a private Seat,
> Built uniform, not Little, nor too Great;
> Better, if on a Rising Ground it stood;
> Fields on this side, on that a Neighb'ring Wood.
> It should within no other Things contain,
> But what are useful, necessary, plain: . . .
> A little Garden, Grateful to the Eye;
> And a Cool Rivulet run murm'ring by:
> On whose delicious Banks a stately Row
> Of Shady Limes or Sycamores shou'd grow . . .

[1] John Pomfret, 1677–1703, was educated at a grammar school in Bedfordshire, and Queens' College, Cambridge. He became Rector of Maulden.

a development foreign from Pope's schoolboyishly imitative but happily done 'Ode on Solitude'. When Swift in 1712 came to 'imitate' *Hoc erat in votis* he was 'imitating' in the proper sense, making the version a vehicle for his own thoughts, as Pope was to do later with other epistles. But Pomfret was really expressing himself directly, as was King in 'Mully of Mountown', 1704:

> Mountown! Thou sweet Retreat from *Dublin* Cares,
> Be famous for thy *Apples* and thy *Pears*;
> For *Turnips*, *Carrots*, *Lettuce*, *Beans*, and *Pease*;
> For *Peggy's* Butter and for *Peggy's* Cheese.
> May clouds of *Pigeons* round about thee fly,
> But condescend sometimes to make a Pye.
> May fat *Geese* gaggle . . .

and so on, in a gastronomic manner not surprising in the author of *The Art of Cookery*. Walsh, in his 'The Retirement', is more perfunctory about nature, giving her only the first two lines:

> All hail, ye Fields, where constant Peace attends;
> All hail, ye sacred solitary Groves!

but then in this early part of the century a clear reference to nature was enough. The setting was given, and the reader was expected to fill in the details with whatever attendant delights he might associate with them. It is, after all, courteous; the reader is supposed to have some experience of his own, and to be at least the ordinary sentient being.

But if the vaguely Horatian was one of the elements that went to the making of the nature poem, other elements soon mingled with it, the moralistic one, and that of sheer delight. The moralistic strain is common drugget stuff—everyone's wear; and we get it often enough in this period; but it improved. After all what matters is not so much the sentiment itself, as the conviction with which it is realized. Sheer delight, as illustrated by Wordsworth's 'And then my heart with pleasure fills, And dances with the daffodils' (to ignore here the deeper implications of the whole poem), is not at first very apparent, though it is to be met with here and there. But concurrent with these early stirrings of a new sensibility was the utilitarian interest, which through mere pleasure in the country thing done, carried with it a love of the country.

The best and most famous utilitarian poem is John Philips's
Cyder, a long labour of love in two books published in 1708.

> What Soil the Apple loves, what Care is due
> To Orchats, timeliest when to press the Fruits,
> Thy Gift, *Pomona*, in *Miltonian* Verse
> Adventrous I presume to Sing; of Verse
> Nor skill'd, nor studious: but my Native Soil
> Invites me, and the Theme as yet unsung,

he preludes the work, 'long to be read, as an imitation of Virgil's
Georgick'; and since, to continue Dr. Johnson's quotation, it
'needed not shun the presence of the original', it can still give
pleasure. It is far more than a poem on cider, but in so far as it is
that, it admirably fulfils its utilitarian purpose. Philips evidently
knew a great deal about soils, grafting, budding, and pruning;
he was wise about composts and pests. Familiar with all the
processes of the cider press, he took great delight in it all,
besides ranking cider above every other beverage. It is, as well
as a country poem, a patriotic one, as is Virgil's, and it does not
lack the moralistic note. It may claim cousinship with *Windsor
Forest*, which did not appear till some five years later, and we
must think that when Pope described how the lapwings 'feel the
leaden death', and that

> Oft', as the mounting Larks their notes prepare
> They fall, and leave their little lives in air

he was at least aware of:

> now the Fowler . . . with swift early Steps
> Treads the crimp Earth, ranging thro' Fields and Glades
> Offensive to the Birds; sulphureous Death
> Checques their mid Flight, and heedless while they strain
> Their tuneful Throats, the tow'ring, heavy Lead
> O'ertakes their Speed; they leave their little Lives
> Above the Clouds, præcipitant to Earth;

though he no doubt knew the Virgilian source. Moreover the
poems are alike in other ways; there are apostrophic passages
to living great men, historic passages, and references in either
poem to early Britain, to Edward II, Henry VI, to the battle of
Crécy, to civil wars, the death of Charles I, and, of course, to
the glory of Queen Anne. The country is loved, not only
because it is the country, but because it is England; here too, in
the intrusion of patriotism, their poems are Georgics. There is
no very glowing description of nature, though certain apples

are warmly praised, but there is knowledge, and the observation, that comes from delighted interest:

> It much conduces, all the Cares to know
> Of Gard'ning, how to scare nocturnal Thieves,
> And how the little Race of Birds that hop
> From Spray to Spray, scooping the costliest Fruit
> Insatiate, undisturb'd. *Priapus'* Form
> Avails but little; rather guard each Row
> With the false Terrors of a breathless Kite.
> This done, the timorous Flock with swiftest Wing
> Scud thro' the Air . . .

or again in the description of the wasp traps, in which the pests

> Flap filmy Pennons oft, to extricate
> Their feet, in liquid Shackles bound . . .

though one may not readily absorb the moral that such doom was the result of 'luxury, and lawless Love of Gain'. His description of the country frolic is a lively genre piece *à la* Teniers.

By the time Philips came to write this, his major poem, he had learnt to be free with his Miltonics. *The Splendid Shilling* (1701), extremely popular as it was—though there were some scandalized dissentient voices such as that of 'Philo-Milton' who in 1709 wrote a short poem upbraiding Philips for sacrilege —somewhat overdoes the prosodic tricks. No doubt it was intended to do so, as a parody of Milton as well as of the epic; but if so, Philips fell in love with the prosody; so when, after considerable pressure, he wrote his *Bleinheim*, the Tory 'occult opposition' to Addison's *Campaign*, he fell naturally into it, and produced a poem which some preferred, and may still without shame prefer, to Addison's. *Cyder* is continually reminiscent of Milton, not in the versification alone, but in phrases and imagery, culled from sources other than *Paradise Lost*. Yet with Philips it becomes an original metre; he is singing, or if not singing, at least intoning, with his own voice, so much so as to earn the praises of Edmund Smith, Prior and others, and finally of Thomson, who in *Autumn* pays him the tribute of:

> *Phillips*, Pomona's bard! The second thou
> Who nobly durst, in rhyme-unfetter'd verse,
> With *British* freedom sing the *British* song . . .

and it did indeed take some daring to write blank verse in that decade, or even later. Philips, moreover, was the only poet up to the twenties who had any success in that form, a by no means negligible success, for the poem drives along well; it gathers momentum as it goes; the patriotic passages especially are a step towards Thomson, and one rises invigorated from a reading of it. His earlier *Cerealia* (1706), a burlesque poem in praise of beer and brewing, falls rather flat; it may be regarded as a preliminary exercise.

So far any individual discovery is wanting; the poets enjoy in the country what anyone would naturally expect to enjoy; the conveying of a direct impact of a sensation, it might be called the sense of intimacy, is rare; it comes out startlingly in Lady Winchilsea's 'Nocturnal Reverie' of 1713. Its opening 'In such a night' is suspiciously derivative, and uneasiness grows at being immediately introduced to Zephyr and Philomel; but then, with little transition from poetry-making to poetry, we are taken right into the country at night,

> When the loos'd *Horse* now, as his Pasture leads,
> Comes slowly grazing thro' th' adjoining Meads,
> Whose stealing Pace, and lengthen'd Shade we fear,
> Till torn up Forage in his Teeth we hear.

There is intense realization there, as Wordsworth recognized. Her work, however, exceeds the triumph with this particular theme, and is treated separately.

If disgust at nature, equally with delight in nature, may claim a place in poetry of this kind, then William Diaper may claim a humble one. He is not the only poet to indulge in the anti-nature poem: there was Richards's *Hoglandiae Descriptio* in 1710, and in 1720 the anonymous *Lincolnshire*, both written possibly in reaction to the formal praise of the countryside at this time almost obligatory, perhaps with something of the mock-epic spirit. 'Debunking' is always a useful form of minor criticism. Diaper's complaint of the climate of Brent, which gives the name to his epistolary poem to a friend, is an amusing condemnation of the country he was in. It is not a good poem, but it is wet, soggy, marshy, full of the vapours of the fens. Moreover,

> No joyous birds here stretch their tunefull throats
> And pierce the yielding air with thrilling notes,
> But the hoarse seapies with an odious cry
> Skim o're the Marsh, and tell what storms are nigh.

'Serpents innumerous o're the mountain roam', while the peasants, an 'ungainly brood', are gifted with speech hardly superior to that of the animals. The verses are the opposite of 'romantic', but they express a direct contact with nature; there is nothing conventional about them.

In *Dryades*, however (1712), Diaper produced a more than tolerable poem, not attempting the pastoral, which he now abjures even in its oceanic form, since 'Eclogues but ill become a warlike Age'; now he gives something which owes a debt to, if it does not derive from, *Cooper's Hill*, a few lines from which a lorn the title-page. The poem itself contains a tribute to John Philips as Thyrsis, from whose *Cyder* a hint is here and there taken. If the rhymes are sometimes uncertain, the versification is more than adequate if never very exciting, and there are some passages which can be described as pretty without any pejorative implication. Throughout the poem there is real detailed observation, of glow-worms, of ants, and Diaper evidently loved the country for its own sake; but he has to moralize his song, and often suggests that politicians have much to learn from animals or insects. For the poem is partly political, in praise of Bolingbroke and the Treaty of Utrecht; it is also a patriotic poem, according to the fashion of the time: perhaps this was the Georgic once more. And Diaper here, as in the *Sea Eclogues*, is tinged with the philosophic, or philosophical-moral of the time, besides the delight in microscopy, and expresses it very pleasantly, as with the

> . . . Animals, that careless live at ease,
> To whom the Leaves are Worlds, the Drops are Seas . . .
> The azure Dye, which Plums in Autumn boast,
> That handled fades, and at a Touch is lost,
> (Of fairest Show) is all a living Heap;
> And round their little World the lovely Monsters creep.
> Who would on Colour dote, or pleasing Forms,
> If Beauty, when discover'd, is but Worms?

There is always a sense of originality about Diaper; he is rarely dull, but always keeps one alert for the unexpected adjective or word; snakes, for instance, 'brandish' their tongues. His poetry has precision; worms, for example, trail 'their folding bodies'. In sensibility, in observation, in pleasure, he anticipates much that the poets of the next decade were to give; but the most remarkable foretaste, perhaps, is the one he gives us of land-

scape painting, which was to be developed by Dyer and
Thomson:

> So first the Mountain Tops are touch'd with Light.
> And from the gloomy Vales the Swains invite;
> While Mists below, and intervening Clouds
> Cast a deep Dusk on all the frowning Woods.
> The shaded Meadows view, with Envy, round
> The distant Splendour of the rising Ground;
> But soon the spreading Rays expanded move,
> And streaming like a Deluge from above,
> Sweep o'er the gladsome Field, and dart through ev'ry Grove.

There is in scarcely any of this poetry the ecstasy, the rapturous
sensuous response that you get in, say, Marvell. In its mixed
elements *Dryades* is not unlike *Windsor Forest*, and if as versification it is far from being as enlivening, as a nature poem it is
better, more intimate. Pope was not interested in the change of
seasons, as Diaper was, nor in the cycle of life of birds and beasts
and insects. Pope's is the better poem, but it is not better as a
'nature' poem. This is not to argue that there is any special
merit in a poem being such; nature is perhaps too easy a
counter to play. The early eighteenth-century poets were wary
of it; nearly all played it, but timidly; many used it to express a
vague emotion of décor; it set the scene for the human figures
brought into play. But progressively as the century went on it
became the subject of description, to be used in the next phase as
the major poetic symbol.

It is, perhaps, another sign of the verbally and emotionally
controlled nature of the poetry of the first twenty years of this
century that there was no verse which could be called 'religious
poetry', with that fierce pressure to be found earlier in the
metaphysicals, even as far towards this period as John Norris of
Bemerton, and later in Smart and Blake. But there is much
devotional verse in this great hymn-making century which
includes Bishop Ken, Tate, the Wesleys, Byrom, Toplady, and
Cowper, and the early years are by no means lacking in it.
This verse is seldom great poetry, if ever; it is never so intensely
devotional as George Herbert's; but it has a quality of its own,
a quality of sincerity combined with a sense of song, something
more simple and direct than Addison's 'The spacious firmament
on high'. Much of it is mere droning fustian, as meditative
verse is apt to be in the hands of mediocre performers, and it is

possibly Parnell[1] who first engages our attention, his devotional
poems being far better than others of his more usually cited,
even the 'Elegy, to an Old Beauty' which contains the almost
proverbial couplet

> And all that's madly wild, or oddly gay,
> We call it only pretty *Fanny's* way.

His social verse, in spite of a measure of skill, is very small beer;
but he can rank as one of the moderately skilled practitioners
dans le mouvement. His *Bookworm* is a humorous enough piece
which flirts with satire. But turning to his 'Hymn to Contentment' or the Hymns for Morning, Noon, and Evening, we are
met with a welcome devotional gaiety. In common with so
many poets of this period, he found his happiest expression
in the loose octosyllabic couplet, an excellent vehicle for the
fresh delight in the countryside becoming typical of this part of
the Augustan age. A fragment from the 'Hymn to Contentment'
will give a fair sample of his agreeable fluency:

> Oh! by yonder Mossy Seat,
> In my Hours of sweet Retreat,
> Might I thus my Soul employ,
> With sense of Gratitude and Joy!
> Rais'd as antient Prophets were,
> In heavenly Vision, Praise, and Pray'r;
> Pleasing all Men, hurting none,
> Pleas'd and bless'd with God alone:
> Then while the Gardens take my Sight,
> With all the Colours of Delight;
> While silver Waters glide along,
> To please my Ear and court my Song;
> I'll lift my Voice, and tune my String,
> And thee, great *Source* of *Nature*, sing.

He was always in control of what he wrote; he had thought
about verse, if his verse 'Essay on the Different Styles of Poetry'
may be taken as evidence; for though the poem dedicated to
Bolingbroke is, one might almost say, strikingly derivative—
from Horace, Boileau, Roscommon, Granville, Pope—Parnell
uses his own phrases and illustrations. His most famous poem,

---

[1] Thomas Parnell, 1679–1718, graduated from Trinity College, Dublin. In
1702 he became a Canon of St. Patrick's, and in 1706 Archdeacon of Clogher. He
spent some time in London, but left it when he resigned the archdeaconry in 1716
to become Vicar of Finglass.

'A Night Piece on Death', with its obvious moralizing, does not attain the tension of anything that could be called religious poetry; an adaptation of the baroque tomb, it may have initiated the phase of graveyard verse which was carried on in Young's *Night Thoughts* and Blair's *Grave*, to find its most dignified expression with Gray, and its rapid deliquescence with Monk Lewis. However, it has some freshness. And certainly his religious fable, 'The Hermit', which can be classed with devotional poetry, exhibits considerable mastery in the use of the decasyllabic couplet. Though the tale is somewhat naïf, and as an explanation of evil not very convincing, the change in dramatic tension is well handled, the prosodic pace well adapted to the general movement. The transformation of the apparent felon into the archangel is told in verse that is vivid enough, though the passage does not approach great poetry:

> Wild, sparkling Rage inflames the Father's Eyes,
> He bursts the Bands of Fear, and madly cries,
> Detested wretch—but scarce his Speech began,
> When the strange Partner seem'd no longer Man:
> His youthful Face grew more serenely sweet;
> His Robe turn'd white, and flow'd upon his Feet;
> Fair rounds of radiant Points invest his Hair;
> Celestial Odours breathe thro' purpled Air;
> And Wings, whose Colours glitter'd on the Day, '
> Wide at his Back their gradual Plumes display.
> The Form Etherial bursts upon his Sight,
> And moves in all the Majesty of Light.

Parnell is at least good enough to keep the eye and mind alert, and that, after all, is no small merit.

But a potentially greater poet than Parnell, and a much greater devotional poet, is Isaac Watts,[1] for so long the derision of readers brought up on the Alice books; yet the very fact that Lewis Carroll could parody for the immediate comprehension of the young more than one of the *Divine Songs for Children* (1715), such as 'Let dogs delight to bark and bite' and ''Tis the voice of the sluggard, I heard him complain', is a tribute to their power and popularity, at least at a certain level. But others of

---

[1] Isaac Watts, 1674–1744, was educated at Edward VI Grammar School, Southampton, and Stoke Newington Dissenting Academy. In 1700 he became Pastor of the Independent Congregation in Mark Lane, which rmeoved to Pinners Hall. From 1712 he lived with Sir Thomas Abney at Abney Hall.

his verses lasted longer than that, indeed are still alive and moving, such as 'There is a land of pure delight', and 'Jesus shall reign where'er the sun', and, notably, 'Our God, our help in ages past', which bids fair to last as long as Christianity endures in English-speaking countries. These things are so well known as not to need quotation, as is the lovely 'Cradle Song', which is tender without being sentimental. But beyond these poems, admittedly devotional verse at a high level, Watts is an extremely interesting poet. It is not so much that the bald content of his work holds the attention—it is the expression of nonconformity at its best and sweetest—as his variety, his metrical experiment, and his imagery.

He was among the earliest of the good Miltonists, but no slavish imitator, taking warning perhaps from the burlesque of *The Splendid Shilling*. In the later version of the Preface to *Horae Lyricae* he tells us:

> In the *Essays without Rhime*, I have not set up Milton for a perfect Pattern, tho' he shall be for ever honour'd as our Deliverer from the Bondage. His Works contain admirable and unequall'd Instances of bright and beautiful Diction, as well as Majesty and Sereneness of Thought. There are several Episodes in his longer Works, that stand in supreme Dignity without a Rival; yet all that vast Reverence with which I read his *Paradise Lost* cannot persuade me to be charm'd with every Page of it. The Length of his Periods, and sometimes of his Parentheses, runs me out of Breath: Some of his Numbers seem too harsh and uneasy. I could never believe that Roughness and Obscurity added any thing to the true Grandeur of a Poem: Nor will I ever affect Archaisms, Exoticisms and a quaint uncouthness of Speech, in order to become perfectly *Miltonian*.

That is as level-headed a piece of Miltonian criticism as one could hope to meet with. Smoothness, as we might expect at that date, is perhaps a little too much insisted upon; but it is an admirable example of a warning not to imitate the wrong thing in a poet whom you admire. It could be wished that the Spenserians had taken to heart what follows:

> It is my Opinion that Blank Verse may be written with all due Elevation of Thought in a modern stile, without borrowing any thing from Chaucer's Tales, or running back as far as the Days of Colin *the Shepherd*, and the Reign of the *Fairy Queen*.

Had that advice been adhered to, many painful excesses would have been avoided. But for Watts, anything fanciful, anything obscure or difficult, would have been to defeat the end of his writing, which was 'to promote the pious entertainment of souls truly serious, even of the meanest capacity', as he explained in the Preface to the *Hymns and Spiritual Songs*. These, unlike the Lyric Pieces, were not addressed to 'the politer part of mankind', though he would not wish his *Hymns* to disgust the educated. Nevertheless his pious intention prevented him from being so good a poet as he might have been—he was himself modest enough about his talents—not only because he refused to give so much time as was necessary to the labour (as it was he felt ashamed of having 'written so much and read so little') but because he had to be understood without difficulty.

> . . . if the Verse appears so gentle and flowing as to incur the Censure of Feebleness, I may honestly affirm that sometimes it cost me labour to make it so: Some of the Beauties of Poesy are neglected and some wilfully defaced. I have thrown out the Lines that were too sonorous and have giv'n an allay to the Verse, lest a more exalted Turn of Thought or Language should darken or disturb the Devotion of the plainest Souls.

So the Preface to the *Hymns and Spiritual Songs*. But if the poems addressed to simpler souls occasionally drop into something perilously near doggerel, they also sometimes attain an intensity rare in the poetry of the period. Look, for instance, at 'When I survey the wondrous Cross', with its magnificent third stanza:

> See from his Head, his Hands, his Feet,
> Sorrow and Love flow mingled down;
> Did e're such Love and Sorrow meet?
> Or Thorns compose so rich a Crown?
>
> His dying Crimson like a Robe
> Spreads o'er his Body on the Tree . . .

And what is interesting there is the fusion of image with thought and emotion, in a manner extremely rare with the Augustans, whose images, as Mr. Day Lewis has pointed out, 'aim to make a point or outline a picture, rather than to rocket the poem into a stratosphere of infinite meaning', one of the reasons why they so rarely attained intensity. There are, of course, other ways of attaining this, but they were normally beyond the reach of Watts. He does, however, achieve intensity in the last version of the first part of Psalm xc, when he uses his favourite prosodic form, common metre. What might be called the raw material we meet in the *Hymns and Spiritual Songs* of 1707:

> Our Moments fly apace
> Nor will our Minutes stay,
> Just like a Flood our hasty Days
> Are sweeping us away.

In The Psalms of David, Imitated in the Language of the New Testament of 1719, we get in the first version:

> A thousand of our Years amount
> Scarce to a Day in thine Account;
> Like Yesterday's departed Light,
> Or the last Watch of ending Night.

This being 'A mournful Song at a Funeral', a pause is here enjoined. Then:

> Death like an overflowing Stream
> Sweeps us away; our Life's a Dream;
> An empty Tale, a Morning-flow'r,
> Cut down and wither'd in an Hour.

Then, in the triumphant version known to everybody who has ever sung or heard 'Our God, our Help in Ages Past', we find:

> A thousand Ages in thy Sight
> Are like an Evening gone;
> Short as the Watch that ends the Night
> Before the rising Sun. . . .
>
> Time like an ever-rolling Stream
> Bears all its Sons away;
> They fly forgotten as a Dream
> Dies at the op'ning Day.

The Psalms usually exist in more than one metrical version, sometimes even in three, the short-metre form being employed in addition to the other two, for convenient adaptation to well-known tunes after the manner that persisted well into the nineteenth century, as witness Mr. Percy Lubbock's *Earlham*. But Watts was always experimenting in metre—his was 'the adventurous Muse', as Professor Pinto has remarked, borrowing a title from Watts—in a short-lined Pindaric, in blank verse, in 'trissyllabic Feet' and in his well-known essay in Sapphics, 'The Day of Judgement':

> When the Fierce North-wind with his Airy Forces
> Rears up the *Baltick* to a Foaming Fury,
> And the red Lightning with a Storm of Hail comes
> Rushing amain down . . .

As with so many other poets, a number of his happier effects are obtained in the tetrameter as, for example, his lightly phrased moralistic verses on 'True Riches':

> I am not concern'd to know
> What to Morrow Fate will do:
> 'Tis enough that I can say
> I've possest my self to Day:
> Then if haply Midnight-Death
> Seize my Flesh and stop my Breath,
> Yet to Morrow I shall be
> Heir to the best Part of Me

a lilting little sermon in verse which he can keep up with admirable liveliness for seventy-four lines. Similarly light are his epigrams, or his paraphrases from Horace, such as the one of *nos numerus sumus*, which begins

> There are a Number of us creep
> Into this World to eat and sleep,

and concludes with epigrammatic neatness. But we may end a brief account of Watts with a sample of his blank verse, for he is one of the very few writers, perhaps the only one, apart from John Philips, who in the century, before the emergence of Thomson, could handle this form. Take from 'True Courage', one of the poems in *Horae Lyricae*:

> He, tho' th' *Atlantic* and the *Midland* seas
> With adverse Surges meet, and rise on high
> Suspended 'twixt the Winds, then rush amain,
> Mingled with flames, upon his single Head,
> And Clouds, and Stars, and Thunder, firm he stands,
> Secure of his best Life; unhurt, unmov'd;
> And drops his lower Nature born for Death.
> Then from the lofty Castle of his Mind,
> Sublime looks down, exulting, and surveys
> The Ruins of Creation (*Souls alone*
> *Are Heirs of dying Worlds*;) a piercing Glance

Shoots upwards from between his closing Lids,
To reach his Birth-place, and without a Sigh,
He bids his batter'd Flesh lie gently down
Amongst its native Rubbish, while the Spirit
Breathes and flies upward, an undoubted Guest
Of the third Heaven, th' unruinable Sky.

That is more than a tactful adaptation of Miltonics: the man who could write the last few lines is potentially more than a very minor poet.

Far from these poets being artificial, it was their very naturalness which makes it seem to us that they were so, since it makes them lack the tension arising from conflict. They were, in a sense, too direct, and of this directness a good example may be found in Croxall's[1] *The Vision* (1715): we have come to the purely descriptive phase: ·

Pensive beneath a spreading oak I stood,
That veil'd the hollow channel of the flood;
Along whose shelving banks the violet blue
And primrose pale in lovely mixture grew.
High over-arch'd the bloomy woodbine hung,
The gaudy Goldfinch from the Maple sung . . .
Here every flower that Nature's pencil draws
In various kinds a bright enamel rose:
The silver dazy streak'd with ruddy light,
The yellow cowslip, and the snow-drop white;
The fragrant hyacinth. . . .

and so on in cumulative catalogue. There is no sort of patterning.

The description in Parnell's 'Night-Piece on Death' moves a little further towards poetry.

How deep yon Azure dies the Sky!
Where Orbs of Gold unnumber'd lye,
While thro' their Ranks in silver pride
The nether Crescent seems to glide.
The slumb'ring Breeze forgets to breathe,
The Lake is smooth and clear beneath,
Where once again the spangled Show
Descends to meet our Eyes below.

[1] Samuel Croxall, d. 1752, was educated at Eton and St. John's College, Cambridge, taking his B.A. degree in 1711. He was appointed Chaplain in Ordinary at Hampton Court, and, an enviable pluralist, held various livings, becoming Archdeacon of Salop, and later Canon of Hereford.

The Grounds which on the right aspire,
In dimness from the View retire:
The Left presents a Place of Graves,
Whose Wall the silent Water laves.
The Steeple guides thy doubtful sight
Among the livid gleams of Night . . .

It is still only too plain, simple a statement; or so it seems, clothed as it is in the smooth, apparently easy felicity of sound and measure. Yet the scene is well observed, really felt, and sensitively as well as accurately described. The demand made upon the reader is only that of relating his experience to what the poem suggests vividly enough, and with enough particularity. And what a blessing, the reader might have felt, not to have to think in terms of somebody else's mind, merely, perhaps, to feel with somebody else's feeling. In perusing the older poets he might have lamented, as George Eliot was later to do, 'that intelligence so rarely shows itself in speech without metaphor—that we can so seldom declare what a thing is, except by saying it is something else'.

At this date it should be possible to discount the pejorative notion of the 'artificial' as applied to this poetry: as Lytton Strachey remarked, the only kind of poetry that is not artificial is bad poetry. Our poets could not, evidently, create the sort of tension we are accustomed to in the metaphysical poets, because the latter, based on scholasticism, exploited the scholastic dialectic. Their images, metaphors, and general violence in yoking together heterogeneous things were largely mechanical, really artificial, and did not at all imply an integration of sensibility any more achieved than that of the Augustan poets.

It is true that it would never have occurred to the latter that poetry was the *spontaneous* overflow of powerful feelings. Heaven forbid! Certainly poets and theorists alike insisted again and again that passion or instinct was the basis of all poetry, yes; but then judgement was there to guide, to form, to lick into shape. Whatever might impel the soul, 'Reason's comparing balance' merely gave purpose and direction; it did not provide the motive. It might be argued that they paid too much attention to form, relied too much upon it; but they knew that without form there can be no full communication, and would have agreed, apparently, that *de la forme naît l'idée*, a point forgotten by critics on the trail of expressed morals, or who believe that imagery, or even irony or ambiguity, is all. That sense of form, the appropriateness of 'kinds', of 'decorum' in general, was one of the great benefits conferred by classical studies; but it is, of course, true that here again too steady an eye on the classics provided an over-rigid form, too accustomed a scale of reference which the poets expected the reader to be able to share. This last, however, is a charge that can be levelled at poets of almost any age, not least our own. Their love of artifice was perhaps exaggerated, a fault incident to a generation consciously civilizing itself. How far this pleasure was general it might be hard to say, but to judge from Addison, who usually expressed what a good many people were at least tending to think, it was fairly widespread. In *Spectator* 414 he tells us that though

There is something more bold and masterly in the rough careless Strokes of Nature, than in the nice Touches and Embellishments of Art . . . yet we find the works of Nature still more pleasant, the more they resemble those of Art. For in this case our pleasure arises from a double Principle; from the Agreeableness of the Objects to the Eye, and from their Similitude to other Objects. We . . . can represent them to our Minds, either as Copies or Originals.

A kind of metaphor in nature, perhaps; but still, the artificial was in itself delightful, as was the grotto described in *Spectator* 632, or exemplified in Pope's amazing toy. Such an attitude can, naturally, produce the piffling conceited *vers d'occasion*, but it can often enter as an ingredient into more serious work.

A far more formidable barrier than this kind of enjoyed artifice is the poetic diction, which can, if you like, be called artificial, since it as consciously includes certain forms of speech just as Wordsworth's consciously excludes them. But once it is seen what the poets were after, what this seemingly very mannered idiom implied, the barrier disappears; the 'artificiality' is recognized, and ultimately felt as a habit of thought so ingrained as to become quite 'natural'. Here again we have to thank the classical tradition; but once more it must be stressed that the classics injured only the weaker brethren who could not happily assimilate them. (This is not a question of 'latinisms': that is another issue which arises acutely with Thomson.) For this kind of poetic diction reached English poetry almost entirely through Virgil and translations of the classics generally. It was not a tiresome invention of the Augustan age, but began, as Professor G. Tillotson has shown in his admirable *On the Poetry of Pope*, with Spenser and with Sylvester's translation of Du Bartas, to be reinforced by Sandys's *Ovid* and May's *Lucan*. And there were two elements at work here. First the theory of the sublime, of the heightening of poetry, namely the making low objects worthy of the muse, as Virgil had so excellently exemplified in the *Georgics*, sometimes also making the muse worthy of lowly objects—a matter which our poets did not forget. Virgil, it was noted, was quite aware of what he was doing. As Dryden translated the theory:

> Nor can I doubt what Oyl I must bestow,
> To raise my Subject from a Ground so low:
> And the mean Matter which my Theme affords,
> T'embellish with Magnificence of Words. :

Naturally, to follow such precepts too far lent itself to ridicule, and that was one of the fields in which burlesque poetry could disport itself. That was certainly part of the fun of *The Splendid Shilling*, the butt of which was not only Miltonic prosody, but heightening generally. As Edmund Neale, known as 'Rag' Smith,[1] remarked in his *Poem to the Memory of Mr. John Philips*:

> What sounding line his abject themes express!
> What shining words the pompous shilling dress!

implying that Philips had well performed at least one part of the poet's job.

The other point is the inclusive phrase, the epithet–noun combination: 'feathered tribe', 'fleecy care', 'finny breed', and so on, used, not, it must be insisted, in the interests of generalization and a soothing vagueness, but on the contrary, of precision, or of more attentive observation. 'Fleecy care' was not just a poetic way of saying 'sheep', since when they wished our poets could say 'sheep' as clearly and as often as anybody else. In the first place, 'fleecy' drew attention to wool, and demanded the appropriate visual image of sheep; for aural imagery the poets would refer to 'the bleating kind'; it all depended upon what was happening in the poem. 'Care' was a tremendously inclusive word, we might almost say connotative, expressive of everything in the shepherd–sheep relation, of all the operations of sheep-breeding and their attendant anxieties. Neither 'fish'

[1] Edmund Neale, 1672–1710, who took the name of Smith, was educated at Westminster and Trinity College, Cambridge. He became a captain in the army, but was chiefly notorious for the slovenliness of his dress.

nor 'bird' are rare words in the poetry of the period, and many poets exhibit a considerable knowledge of many varieties of either, and named them when it was appropriate to do so. But they might want to generalize and at the same time draw attention to some special attribute—fins or scales, feathers or songs or wings. If read with an alert mind and an imagining eye, such phrases as 'the finny tribe' or 'the feathered kind' cease to wear the air of a tiresome affectation, and enrich the poem to the limit of the reader's recognition of what the poet is talking about. But the poet of those days could assume in his reader at least a fairly expert acquaintance with country life.

Rhyme demands a different adjustment from the unaccustomed reader, since pronunciation has changed so much that the poets of those days may seem to us to have been abominably inept. Yet it may with confidence be assumed that in ninety-nine cases out of a hundred the rhymes are good, though some indeed resist the heartiest attempts of the most candid reader to make them plausible. In the main we have to think much in terms of the traditional brogue-speaking Irishman, for whom 'creature' and 'nature' rhyme perfectly, and lie down in amity with 'satire'; we have to keep in mind as we read that words recently borrowed from the French are to be pronounced in a vaguely French manner—'obleege' is a well-known instance— so that 'sphere' rhymes with 'air', while 'supreme', 'scheme', and 'theme' rhyme with 'fame'; 'join', it is clear, echoes 'line', and '-ert' is indistinguishable from '-art'. Not that all poets, apparently, pronounced in the same way, any more than they do now; from the rhyming dictionary which Bysshe added to his *Art of Poetry* it is clear that he did not utter every word in the same way as Pope or Blackmore. The intelligent reader, however, will find the rhymes no stumbling-block so long as he endows the poets of that day with as good ears as his own.

Several threads might be followed up, such as the influence of the street ballad; or the treatment of various kinds might be pursued; but to do so would have only a limited interest, and would require too great space. Many and various 'special studies' exist to allure the interested student, and it might be more valuable to indicate some of the surmountable barriers that exist between readers of our own generation and the poets of the period. Some of the barriers are of those inevitably made by time—shifts in sensibility, changes in common knowledge and fields of reference, variations in language, and the differing experiences that fall to the lot of successive generations; these can be minimized, though the present fashion is to make them bulk as large as possible, from what motives it might be ungenerous to inquire. The artificial barriers erected by romantic prejudice, ignorance of the material, and wrong-headed education for the last hundred years or so, are tougher; but there are signs that they are crumbling.

To conclude, there is one virtue these poets had which was lacking in their forerunners and their successors alike, storytellers apart, namely, the sense of a large, alert, critical audience. The earlier poets spoke to individuals or select groups; the later either spoke to themselves or uttered with the voices of prophets. In the main a poem expressed the relation between poet and object; but now a third term was introduced—audience—with an effect of subtlety, of play of position, of varying simultaneous angles of approach (not of different levels as with the metaphysicals) which has since been lost. It is most evident perhaps in Prior and Gay, though it is happily there with Thomson. The song was in process of achieving a different poise.

With such points in mind, it may be profitable to approach some poets as a whole; it will not be ill to begin with Prior, as both varied and representative.

3. SOME POETS

Prior[1] is a singularly attractive person, a slightly whimsical figure, lanky, even a little ungainly, approaching life with a gaiety tempered by an uneasy feeling of something being missed. A man of ardent patriotism yet of continental sympathies, devoid of rancour, full of human weaknesses and generosities, he made poetry so much a part of his life that his poems are full of life as it is daily lived, laughed over, cried over, and

---

[1] Matthew Prior, 1664-1721, was educated at Westminster, The Rhenish Tavern, and St. John's College, Cambridge. He early abandoned poetry for work in the Diplomatic service, was Secretary to the Ambassador at The Hague, and was much concerned with the Treaty of Ryswick. He soon afterwards became Under-Secretary of State, and succeeded Locke as Commissioner of Trade. He gradually veered round from the Whigs to the Tories, and in 1711 went secretly to Paris to initiate the peace talks which led to the Treaty of Utrecht—Matt's Peace. He was imprisoned for some two years after the accession of George I, but was released without being impeached, and was given to live in, by Lord Harley (Oxford's son), Down Hall in Essex.

mused upon. You do not feel with him, as you do with so many lesser poets, that his poetry was a specialized activity he withdrew himself to indulge in, afterwards producing the result for popular applause. It came naturally to him as a ready means of expression. He tells us in his *Essay upon Learning*, where he is speaking of the desire to write, 'As to my own part I found this impulse very soon, and shall continue to feel it as long as I can think. . .', and then, with engaging modesty, he describes how he came to abandon a literary career. This he speaks of even more deprecatingly in his *Letter to Monsieur Boileau Despreaux* (1704):

> But We must change the Style.—Just now I said,
> I ne'er was Master of the tuneful Trade.
> Or the small Genius which my Youth could boast,
> In Prose and Business lies extinct and lost:
> Bless'd, if I may some younger Muse excite;
> Point out the Game, and animate the Flight.

It is doubtful, however, if he would ever have been a major poet, but we may well be inclined to think that his talent was admirably suited to his age, and developed to the utmost extent it was capable of.

He had been publishing some twenty years before, in 1709, he collected his poems—they had been pirated in 1708—his first appearance having been with Halifax—then Charles Montague—in *The Hind and Panther Transvers'd* (1687), from which anyone secure in his devotion to Dryden can derive a great deal of amusement. It uses the form and the personages of the *Rehearsal*, but its motive is political and religious, or at least sectarian, hostility rather than critical exuberance, which however, it does not lack. That Prior, then an undergraduate at Cambridge, had the chief hand in the work, though 'Mouse' Montague was himself at that time an aspirant after literary honours, we have on the authority of Spence, whom Peterborough informed that Montague wrote it only 'just as if I was in a chaise with Mr. Cheselden here, drawn by his fine horse, and should say, "Lord how finely we draw this chaise"'. Prior always evinced a dislike of 'drudge Dryden', a little unfairly, we may think seeing how much *Solomon* and *Predestination* owe to the very *Hind and Panther* so boisterously ridiculed in *The Country and City Mouse*.

That he should have succumbed to the Pindaric disease

endemic in England in his early writing days was only natural; and on reading the more solemn efforts in his early volume— if we do read them, for Dr. Johnson is not the only critic to fail to plough through *Carmen Seculare* of 1700—we may not, in spite of some moving passages, think it a very unhappy chance that caused Prior to abandon letters as a livelihood, to become an active civil servant and distinguished statesman. By so doing he always retained something of the amateur spirit which is so healthy an ingredient in all the arts, enabling them to admit an irresponsible fancy which ensures their vitality. As a reward Prior has from the first been praised—and loved—for his light verse, though it is not so easy to lay one's finger on the precise quality that keeps fresh, and permanently refreshing, what on the surface are mere *vers de société*. We may get a little tired of poems where Cloe is mistaken by gods themselves for the mother of love, and which Swift was later to gibe at (a Jonsonian influence may help to account for that conceit), for with him the classical connexions, far from making the wine sparkle, are like water added to it. Nevertheless, his light verse really is light, in a way that none had been before, and very little has been since.

In all previous 'immoral' verse, from Wyatt through the Elizabethans, through Suckling and Rochester, to Congreve, there is always a touch of weariness, or of defiance, or snickering or sneering, in some form or another a feeling of guilt. What is so admirable about Prior's verses to or about his mistresses, or in his 'cynical' treatment of love, is their complete integrity: the sentiments, the words, the metre, the imagery, are all in perfect congruity. Take one of the 'Songs set to Music':

> Phillis, since we have both been kind,
>   And of each other had our fill;
> Tell me what pleasure you can find,
>   In forcing nature 'gainst her will . . .
>
> We both have spent our stock of love,
>   So consequently should be free;
> Thyrsis expects you in yon' grove,
>   And pretty Chloris stays for me.

The sentiment may not be very deep; but you know that what Prior did feel he felt and expressed with absolute sincerity. He never leers, or giggles, or becomes aggressive; he never regrets and certainly never repents. How should he? He had no sense of sin. And through all his lighter poems, his amorous verses, his tales, his epigrams—and even sometimes in his serious ones—there flows a delicious current of humour, 'which involves sentiment and romance', as Saintsbury said, 'which laughs gently at its own tears, and has more than half a tear for its own laughter'. He is never sentimental, and behind many of his poems there is a vague, half-caught sense of something else stirring; something faintly but persistently suggests awareness of a world beyond; a very delicate quickening flavour is left on the palate after the main taste has gone. For all his innocence and gaiety, his often earthy humour, in much of his verse we catch, very distantly, the small haunting music of disillusioned humanity.

No one would claim for Prior a high place among poets; but because he has this quality of his own he is not of the flat-footed ruck, and has always been looked upon as the master artificer of the occasional poem; Praed, it is said (as though this were the highest possible praise), did not improve upon him. Undoubtedly the stanzaic poems addressed to Cloe, Nanette, Lisette, or whoever it might be, delightfully do what they set out to do; they may not be better or more valuable than what Congreve, say, was doing at the same time, or even Dorset before him; but they have the quality of extreme lightness combined with strength (like a deceptively flimsy-looking steel bridge), which is more in the French tradition than the English. Such a thing as 'The Merchant, to secure his Treasure', is, of its kind, perfect. Yet it may well be held that where he is at his best, at once at his freest and most concise, is where he ap-proaches nearest to Swift in the handling of the octosyllabic verse which Prior at any rate took over from Butler and made more easily readable. Even Addison, when attacking Prior in his first *Whig Examiner*, in answer to Prior's tearing to shreds a very mediocre piece of Garth's belauding Godolphin (*Examiner* 6), praised him unwittingly. Prior, he conceded, had 'a happy talent of doggerel, where he writes on a known subject: where he tells us in plain intelligible language. . .' and then instanced in blunt description *The Ladle* and *Hans Carvel*. Plain intelligible language, yes, free of the imitative solemnities Addison wel-comed in the work of his contemporaries; but Prior's tales, with (as Tickell noted) their Chaucerian smack, are written in a metre which is by no means doggerel. And if in our politer age it may be embarrassing to confess to whole-hearted enjoyment of them, at least *The English Padlock* has left the well-known couplet:

> Be to her Virtues very kind:
> Be to her Faults a little blind:

while *To a Young Gentleman in Love* is as entertaining a moralistic poem, in the realist sense, as could be asked for.

Mention has been made of Swift, and indeed the poetical development of the two men runs remarkably parallel. There was much in Prior's approach to poetry to commend him to Swift, and it was more than political affinities and their both dining at Harley's table that made them exercise together in the park, the one to get fat, the other to get thin. In some ways comparison would be absurd. Prior could sing, whereas Swift could not; the latter could never have written 'If Wine and Musick have the Pow'r', nor achieve the spontaneity of 'My noble, lovely, little Peggy', his Biddy Floyd verses being laboured in comparison; nor would he have approached, even had he wished to, what we might call Prior's 'amoretti', any more than Prior could have achieved the deeply moving quality of the Stella birthday poems. And if we compare their Pindarics (or Pindaresques) we see at once of what much heavier poetic metal Swift was composed. Prior is more slapdash, more Hudibrastic; and we have only to put *Baucis and Philemon* side by side with *The Ladle*, which, till the finale, tells much the same story, to see how refreshingly more exact, more nourished, more disciplined Swift was. Yet both were in some respects trying to do the same thing with words, with the swing of the spoken phrase. Take, for instance, Prior's half-critical, half self-mocking, *The Conversation*; it is half-way between Swift's autobiographical *Imitation of the Sixth Satire of the Second Book of Horace (Hoc erat in votis)*, with its cheerful opening

> I often wish'd, that I had clear
> For life, six hundred pounds a year

and the laughing part of *Verses on the Death of Dr. Swift*. Both poets are in the tradition of Jonson in his 'Inviting a friend to supper', or of Suckling's 'Ballad upon a Wedding', Swift by richness of content being nearer Jonson, Prior in lightness and in music being nearer Suckling. But we could tell that this, from *The Conversation*, belongs to the age of Swift from its directness, its particular humour, and its careful use of the word to say exactly what it means, and not a hair more:

> Matthew, who knew the whole Intrigue,
> Ne'er much approv'd That Mystic League.
> In the vile Utrecht Treaty too,
> Poor Man, He found enough to do:
> Sometimes to Me He did apply;
> But down-right Dunstable was I,
> And told Him, where They were mistaken;
> And counsell'd him to save his Bacon:
> But (pass His Politics and Prose)‎
> I never herded with his Foes;
> Nay, in his Verses, as a Friend,
> I still found Something to commend:
> Sir, I excus'd his Nut-Brown-Maid;
> ‎Whate'er severer Critics said:‎
> Too far, I own, the Girl was try'd:
> The Women all were on my Side.
> For Alma I return'd Him Thanks
> I lik'd Her with Her little Pranks:
> Indeed poor Solomon in Rhime
> Was much too grave to be Sublime.

The joke of the thing is that the man speaking thus did not know Matthew Prior well enough to recognize that it was to him he was talking; it shows that Prior was, like Swift, sufficiently clear-eyed to see what sort of figure he cut in the eyes of others.

And indeed readers have never taken very heartily to *Solomon*, preferring the 'little pranks' of Alma, the mind, which, according to the 'Pritty spanish Conceit' (really from Montaigne) Prior tells us of in his *Essay upon Opinion*, 'as we are born . . . comes in at our Toes, so goes upward to our Leggs, to our Middle, thence to our heart and breast, lodges at last in our head and from thence flies away'. The consequence of it, Prior sums up, 'is Obvious, our Passions change with our Ages, and our Opinion with our Passions'. Though 'a loose and hasty scribble to relieve the tedious hours of imprisonment' (so Prior wrote to Pope), on the surface an almost frivolously light essay in psychology, *Alma* is extremely interesting as a gloss upon the popular philosophies of the day, since, as Professor Monroe K. Spears has shown, it seriously handles Cartesian

and Lockean notions. For Prior there was no 'ruling passion'.
Adhering to no doctrine of the primacy of the reason, he rejected
the medieval-Aristotelean notion that the mind

> Throughout the Body squat or tall
> Is *bona fide*, All in All.

He rejected Locke also, preferring the introspective whimsicality
of Montaigne—as he brings out more fully in the delightful
prose dialogue between the two philosophers—he arrives almost
at an anti-intellectual position; for does not the mind, after all,
come to be amused at anything? So he addresses Alma:

> . . . I view with Anger and Disdain,
> How little gives Thee Joy, or Pain:
> A Print, a *Bronze*, a Flow'r, a Root,
> A Shell, a Butter-fly can do't.
> Ev'n a Romance, a Tune, a Rhime
> Help Thee to pass the tedious Time,
> Which else would on thy Hand remain:
> Tho' flown, it ne'er looks back again.
> And Cards are dealt, and Chess-boards brought,
> To ease the Pain of Coward-Thought.
> Happy Result of Human Wit!
> That ALMA may Her self forget.

The three Cantos are fairly intricate: a freeing philosophy of
morals, including Temple's theory of climate, gives it the
semblance of backbone, and an element of social satire animates
the whole lively epistle; there are little thumbnail sketches of
Rarus, Vento, Curio, and so on, such as Pope was to develop
into his shattering portraits, and there is a friendly tribute to
Pope himself.

It may be that *Solomon* is too grave to be sublime, but it is not
negligible. If Dr. Johnson was bored by *Solomon*, that is to be
expected in a man who had, in *The Vanity of Human Wishes*,
done the same thing, and, of course, in his own mind, better.
If Pope thought less of this poem than he did of *Alma*, that might
well be because it in some ways forestalled what he probably
already had in mind to do in the *Essay on Man*, and because in
Solomon Prior, in giving the couplet the same freedom as blank
verse, was trying to do with it exactly the opposite of what Pope
was striving for, namely progressively crystallizing it. In the
result the poem is pervaded by a haunting nostalgic sense and

by a feeling which is not at all shallow; it really does adumbrate
the *Essay on Man*—less highly geared, less highly powered, but
individual. It has very little connexion with *Ecclesiastes*, on
which it is professedly based; it contains, rather, the cogitations
of a man of Queen Anne's day, reacting stubbornly against
current philosophy, and, as a Tory, experiencing its disillusion.

Here again Prior denies the primacy of the reason, yet it is
reason which provides him with the vision of the universe
which occupies some of the first book, 'Knowledge'. What
carries the poem through, in spite of such obtrusions as Solomon's prophecy of Britannia, and a certain unwitting comic
element in that monarch's misfortunes in love, is a definite
poetic pressure. It is rarely dull, and the movement is sustained;
but though the paragraphing is more happy than Pope's often
is, the structure is not very convincing. The verse, however
much Prior would have denied it, is based on Dryden's, but has
a march of its own, a march tuned by melancholy:

> Thus, thro' what Path soe'er of Life We rove,
> Rage companies our Hate, and Grief our Love: . . .
> Till by one countless Sum of Woes opprest,
> Hoary with Cares, and Ignorant of Rest,
> We find the vital Springs relax'd and worn:
> Compell'd our common Impotence to mourn,
> Thus, thro' the Round of Age, to Childhood We return;
> Reflecting find, that naked from the Womb
> We yesterday came forth; that in the Tomb
> Naked again We must To-morrow lye,
> Born to lament, to labor, and to dye.

It surely derives largely, even to its occasional triplets and
alexandrines, from the end of Dryden's translation of Lucretius
on the fear of death; but this verse has a stoicism of its own, and
a more colloquial directness, a terseness even, foreign both to
Dryden's and to Pope's, between which it stands.

Colloquialism, tactfully handled, is perhaps Prior's great
achievement; there are the delightful second 'Epistle to Fleetwood Shephard', 'When Crowding Folks, with strange Ill Faces',
'As Doctors give physic by way of prevention', or the humanely
witty 'Jinny the Just' in the Longleat Manuscripts, who

> . . . read and Accounted and payd & abated
> Eat and drank, Play'd & Work't, laught & Cryd, lov'd & hated,
> As answer'd the end of her being Created.

which reminds one—it is a reminiscence only—of Swift's 'Betty the Cookmaid's Letter'. Prior was a happy experimenter in verse: he was always ready to slough off old skins in trying to make verse do what he wanted it to do, and even Dr. Johnson, no ardent admirer, owned that his phrases were original. In common with most of his age, he could write with the freedom of blank verse only when using the couplet. When he tried his hand at blank verse, as in the translated 'Hymns of Callimachus', it hobbled along as though he were trying to naturalize the hendecasyllable, most strangely in the fragmentary 'Prelude to a Tale from Bocace':

> . . . uncontroll'd,
> The Verse, compress'd the Period, or dilated,
> As close discourse requires, or fine description.

But that he could use the controlled couplet is shown in the uncompleted 'Predestination', which, finding himself, like nobler beings before him, 'in wand'ring mazes lost', he wisely abandoned. The 'brouillon', however, has merits, and we of the post-Fitzgerald age may be pleased to find so surprising an anticipation as:

> Yet is the great Apostle heard to say,
> Does not the Potter's hand dispose the Clay?
> And shal the Vase his makers Art upbraid
> If or to honour or Destruction made?

Prior's experiments in various quatrain forms are always neat, though variously successful. And if he was one of the first to indulge in the detestable habit of 'imitating' Spenser, in his earliest attempt he did at least try to catch the sensibility of his original rather than hatch out a lugubrious pastiche or 'disfigure his lines with a few obsolete syllables': it might be argued that he helped to point out the way to the more inventive 'Spenserians', for here too he showed the amateur's courage, the virtuoso amateur's taste for adventure, which gives so much of his lighter verse a gay quality lacking in a good deal of his contemporaries' work.

Most nearly contemporary with him in our poetic scene is Lady Winchilsea.[1] If for the quiet reader she has more than a

---

[1] Anne Finch, Countess of Winchilsea, 1661–1720, daughter of Sir William Kingsmill. In 1683 she was one of the Maids of Honour to the Duchess of York. In 1684 she married Heneage Finch, later Earl of Winchilsea, who refused to swear allegiance to William and Mary.

little individual charm as 'an inferior muse' (her own modest phrase), for the literary historian she has the added interest of being an evident link between the modes of feeling of the two centuries. In prosody and emotion alike she seems to move forward from one to the other. Something of the complex melody of the older poets with more than a hint of their metaphysical fusion of moods greets you in her pages, but so do more than a few later Augustan characteristics, to wit the thinning of the contents in her 'songs', and a more staccato use of the octosyllable. She modifies the rigorous idea of solitude, she shows a tendency towards purely social satire, and it might be said that she takes the lead in admitting a happy domesticity as a fit subject for poetry.

In the *Miscellany Poems, Written by a Lady*, which appeared in 1713, she exhibits a wide variety of metre, even within one form, more especially in the tetrameter. She makes it serve her purpose in her 'Invocation to Sleep' in the same manner as Henry King had in 'The Exequy'—for example:

> Whilst still as Death, I will be found,
> My Arms by one another bound,
> And my dull Lids so clos'd shall be
> As if already seal'd by thee:

but she seems in her 'Petition for an Absolute Retreat' to borrow the movement, if not quite the metre, of Marvell's 'Garden':

> Figs (yet growing) candy'd o'er,
> By the Sun's attracting Pow'r,
> Cherries, with the downy Peach
> All within my easie Reach;
> While creeping near the humble Ground,
> Shou'd the Strawberry be found
> Springing wheresoe'er I stray'd,
> Thro' those Windings and that Shade.

This buoyant poem, which errs perhaps in going on too long, including over-abundance of illustrative material, to a large degree expresses what Lady Winchilsea had to say. Developing a hideous boredom with fashionable London life, which she sometimes expressed in amusingly light but nevertheless well-felt satire, as in 'Ardelia's Answer to Ephelia' couched in swift enough heroic couplets, on withdrawal from Court she readily embraced a quiet country existence. 'Imitating' Marvell as she may be in her 'Petition', her retreat was not to be so absolute as her title suggests. It was far from her to think that

> Two Paradises 'twere in one
> To live in Paradise alone

since to share her solitude she prays—not indeed as Thomson was to do, for the peopled loneliness of Norwood—but for a companion:

> Give me there (since Heaven has shown
> It was not Good to be alone)
> *A Partner* suited to my Mind,
> Solitary, pleas'd, and kind;

to share the pleasures of the country. Her feeling for this—the 'Nocturnal Reverie' has already been mentioned—was real and unaffected, not a Horatian attitude adopted for 'poetic' purposes by a number of her contemporaries, who at any rate naturally loved the country without fuss because they lived in it. There is then enough emotional pressure in the 'Petition' to carry it through without faltering, and to impose organization upon the material. It is thoroughly competent work.

Yet she always referred to herself as an amateur, protesting also a woman's right to belong to the mob of gentlemen who wrote with ease. Nevertheless she experimented as an addict, and wrote with the concentration of an artist. She was, moreover, usually able to find the right measure to match what she had to say, as, for instance in 'To Mr. F. . . . now going abroad . . .', a smiling poem of domestic felicity expressed in Suckling's 'Ballad' metre, while quatrains carry 'To my Sister Ogle' at an appropriate amble, and anapaests briskly serve 'The Circuit of Apollo', a modest piece of the 'sessions of the poets' kind on the merits of women writers, altogether free from malice. She has her 'place' or 'estate' poem on Longleat, her pastoral (rather indecisive in form), her fables, and her songs, the better of these last being in common measure: she even dares attempt the single-rhymed octosyllabic tercet.

Her triumph in construction is, however, 'The Spleen' published in Gildon's *Miscellany* of 1701; the other of her Pindarics, such as the one on the great storm of November 1703, are of the usual turgidity; but in 'The Spleen' the form provides just that atmosphere of grotesque comedy the poem is meant to

have. Its elaborate stanzaic structure—derived perhaps from
Dryden rather than Cowley—the invocation, the puffing up
(*ampoulement* we might call it); the classical references, the
satire on the fool, who 'to imitate the wits' pretends to the
splenetic state, indicate a wry-mouthed humour. But the poem
is partly serious. Lady Winchilsea describes the state of nervous
irritability; for

> Now the *Jonquille* o'ercomes the feeble Brain;
> We faint beneath the Aromatick pain, . . .

she herself evidently having been prey to the 'black jaundice'
which prevents her writing poetry, and forces her to the tedious
routine of embroidery:

> Whilst in the *Muses* Paths I stray,
> Whilst in their Groves, and by their secret Springs
> My Hand delights to trace unusual Things,
> And deviates from the known, and common way;
> Nor will in fading silks compose
> Faintly th' inimitable *Rose*,
> Fill up an ill-drawn *Bird*, or paint on Glass
> The *Sov'reign's* blurr'd and undistinguish'd Face,
> The threatning Angel, and the speaking Ass:

and she manages to maintain the odd balance of sensibility,
formalism, satire—the whole shot with streaks of sheer poetic
beauty—which makes it possible to rank this poem with those
of the metaphysicals.

Sensibility—perhaps even of the self-conscious sort which was
later to become a main theme; indeed Lady Winchilsea's
'Moral Song' might almost be a rough note for Mrs. Greville's
'Prayer for Indifference' of some fifty years ahead. She had,
certainly, perceptions so acute as to create in her enough poetic
pressure to break the bounds of direct description and achieve
the poetic image. These are fairly thick-strewn in such pieces as
'The Echo', 'The Tree', 'To the Nightingale', the fragmentary
'Inquiry after Peace', all in octosyllables veering now towards
the Miltonic. Here, for example, from 'The Bird':

> Soft in thy notes and in thy dress,
> Softer than numbers can express,
> Softer than love, softer than light
> When just escaping from the night,

but she tends to over-elaborate, spoiling what has just been
quoted by adding:

> When first she rises, unarray'd,
> And steals a passage through the shade;

the intellectual fabrication blundering upon the intuition. But
she has enough poetic individuality, something especially
feminine, to add to the canon. Certainly her country poems are
happier than her social ones; and though these indeed often
shine with a disciplining wit, we might even say an epigrammatic quality, they are of the surface: the song with her had
already lost its poise, as with Congreve it had not.

For Congreve,[1] who had abandoned playwriting after the
disappointing reception of *The Way of the World* in 1700, constitutes another link with the earlier century. It is possible that
did he not stand out against the looming background of his
plays he would show as a very small figure in the poetic landscape of this period, though one quite distinct, pale almost to
transparency, but tremendously distinguished, fastidious, integral. He had said his main say in the drama, as our earliest
poet, perhaps, to insist on the delicacy of the personal relation,
and had no more to say in that form, though he still retained
his interest in the theatre. But now, partly it seems from a decline
in energy, but also because of his increasing love of music, it
took the form of masque and opera, and of the ode to be set to
music. There is nothing haphazard about this later writing; as
always, he thought about the exigencies of the form he was
writing in, and his *Hymn to Harmony*, the St. Cecilia ode for 1701
set to music by John Eccles, *Semele* and *The Judgment of Paris*
(1701) are admirably adapted for singing, or for recitative,
which, as Congreve said in the 'Argument Introductory to the
Opera of Semele' when it was printed in 1710, 'is only a more
tuneable Speaking; it is a kind of Prose in Musick; its beauty
consists in coming near Nature, and in improving the natural
Accents of Words by more Pathetick or Emphatical Tones'.
It is only in the short lyrics or in the choruses that the verse as
such is tolerable reading.

But it is in his detached songs that he is most his exquisite

---

[1] William Congreve, 1670–1729, was with Swift at Kilkenny school and Trinity
College, Dublin, from which he went to the Middle Temple. He was Inspector of
Hackney Coaches, and Secretary to the Island of Jamaica.

self, the sensitive man dreading lest his emotions should be asked to carry too much; and it is in these that he most belongs to the previous century, being brother here to Suckling. In the determination to express and experience things as they are they have something of the honesty and the attack of Rochester, as we can feel, for example, in 'False though she be to me and love'. And if there is something of the eighteenth-century 'sentiment' in the song he wrote for Rowe's *The Fair Penitent*, 'Ah stay! ah turn! ah whither would you fly...', he is free both of the domesticity which assorts so ill with the form, or of the self-consciousness that sometimes spoils even Prior. There is a curious haunting melody about his verse, evocative of the old fear of disillusion which gives his comedies their fragrance; and with him more perhaps than anybody we feel that the motto *ne pas être dupe* props up the shield over the door of his poetic mansion. His songs always mean something; he did not aim at vacuity as Ambrose Philips and Carey professedly did.

It cannot be said that his translations offer anything outside the ordinary run of such things on the higher level, and the same can be said of his prologues and epilogues. He had sent in to the public his obligatory exercises—his pastoral elegy on the death of Queen Mary, his Pindaric congratulations to William III on the taking of Namur. But he came to see that the Pindaric as then written would not do, and his 'Irregular Ode on Mrs. Arabella Hunt Singing' gains the undoubted if slight charm that it has because of its restraint. But his later odes are worth the historian's glance, if not that of the amateur of poetry, if only for the contribution that he made in illustration of his 'A Discourse on the Pindarique Ode' which, returning to the regularity of the Jonsonian manner, as advocated by Edward Phillips in his *Theatrum Poetarum* (1675), might have infused some order into a form which, however, remained obstinately 'free'. Nevertheless his strictures on the average contemporary performance, which was not the less dull because it was anarchic, may have had a good disciplining effect:

The Character of these late Pindariques, is, a Bundle of rambling incoherent Thoughts, express'd in a like Parcel of irregular Stanzas, which also consist of such another Complication of disproportion'd, uncertain and perplex'd Verses and Rhimes. And I appeal to any Reader, if this is not the Condition in which these Titular Odes appear;

and it must be conceded that his own odes to the Queen and to Godolphin, 'regularly' written in strophe, antistrophe, and epode, exhibit if only by virtue of their form a litheness as refreshing as it is unusual, which in itself imparts a moderate pleasure. Something remains of the old metaphysical ethos, in such things as 'pious Selinda', something of the 'conventional ironic' but immensely sophisticated, as though it were well to be ironic about irony itself.

Yet the most individual things, and the ones which for us at least would seem to have more universal scope, are his two Epistles. The earlier one, 'Of Pleasing', addressed to Sir Richard Temple, is a gay, charming tribute to a friend whom he admires; it has a little good-natured satire and a pleasant movement which gives it the feel of spontaneity. But the later Epistle, addressed to the same friend when Lord Cobham, in the poet's declining years (it was indeed his swan song), has a colloquial freedom which brings Congreve right into the middle of one of the streams of eighteenth-century poetry, a stream which runs at least from Ben Jonson's verse letters to Tennyson's epistle to FitzGerald preluding *Tiresias*. The conclusion is directly simple:

> . . . When Leisure from affairs will give thee Leave,
> Come, see thy Friend, retir'd without Regret,
> Forgetting Care, or striving to forget;
> In easy Contemplation soothing Time,
> With Morals much, and now and then with Rhime,
> Not so robust in Body, as in Mind,
> And always undejected, tho' declin'd;
> Not wondering at the World's new wicked Ways,
> Compar'd with those of our Fore-fathers Days,
> For Virtue now is neither more or less,
> And Vice is only varied in the Dress;
> Believe it, Men have ever been the same,
> And all the Golden Age is but a Dream.

And if the final sentiment both conflicted with Whig optimism and outraged Swift, the whole passage echoes very tunefully the sentiments revealed in Congreve's all too few letters to his friend Joseph Keally.

Had Gay had more capacity for thought, he might have rivalled Prior as the great writer of light verse in this period; he is too artless in his attitude to pierce to any depth, and though his fingering is often deft, there are no great prosodic delights to be extracted from him because not having any thought to struggle with, there is no deep vitality in the expression. One would hardly expect it from the friendly, helpless, childlike man whom it is over harsh to call a parasite; what one does get is a boyish vitality, high spirits, as often as not in doing what he was bid, a certain inventive ease, an immense sense of fun, the morals of a good boy who is healthy enough to be naughty sometimes, and the satisfaction of feeling native skill happily employed. He did something to free poetry from the 'polite' classical trammels, though by no means ignorant of the classics. For however much he may be writing according to an approved mode, as he was in his first publication, *Rural Sports*, which was his Georgic, there is always just a little singing note, something which is his own and not according to pattern. *Rural Sports* (1713) has little value as a country poem; nothing seems to have been freshly felt or seen by Gay, nothing is there to indicate that he has himself fished or been out after partridge or pursued the fox, though he appears to have been present at coursing; yet there is a lilt in the verse which redeems the poem from dullness, especially in the earlier version; if the eye closes on being not very vividly presented with the familiar, the ear is kept amused and alert by some little variation in prosody, more perhaps in the later version:

> Or when the ploughman leaves the task of day,
> And trudging homeward whistles on the way . . .

and in like manner *The Fan*, though justly classed by Johnson as being dull from the staleness of its theme, 'one of those mythological fictions which antiquity delivers ready to the hand', now and again comes alive from some personal touch, and it has at least provided one familiar quotation:

> *Strephon* had long confess'd his am'rous pain,
> Which gay *Corinna* railly'd with disdain:
> Sometimes in broken words he sigh'd his care,
> Look'd pale, and trembled when he view'd the fair;
> With bolder freedoms now the youth advanc'd,
> He dress'd, he laugh'd, he sung, he rhim'd, he danc'd:
> Now call'd more powerful presents to his aid,
> And, to seduce the mistress, brib'd the maid.

It is all, admittedly, very small beer, and it was not until he was to write his pastorals (see p. 140) that he allowed his own real self, compact of childlike humour combined with a good deal of realistic observation, to come to the fore, and it is in this last that certain tendencies of the age gave him scope.

For one of the threads running through the period, to help in the general release of verse, was what might be called the 'down to earth' thread, a deliberate turning away from the 'poetic', what Swift called the 'effusion of the brain'. It was clear that the Cowley way was not that suited to most writers of the period, though poet after poet hoped that it might be. Cowley's constructions need the whole background of metaphysical apparatus, and his success, in spite of the fine odes to Hervey and Hobbes, is dubious. Dryden, by giving the form another turn, by simplifying the metaphysical mode and ridding it of a good deal of lumber, had to a large extent triumphed in his St. Cecilia odes and in 'Anne Killigrew', but for most writers all that was produced was a desert of thorn bushes. Butler had shown a way of escape in the realism he mingled with his burlesque, which was part of the burlesque. But, even so, this was not quite down to earth; it did not yet reach the stage of being able to produce, again in Swift's words, 'Something in verse as true as prose'. Not being realistic enough, it did not deal with what everybody knew and could see or handle or be personally aware of. The impulse which led to the change was therefore only partly that of burlesque, and it appears first, perhaps, in William King's *The Furmetary*, which speaks in a new way. Its opening is significant:

> No sooner did the grey-ey'd Morning peep,
> And yawning mortals stretch themselves from sleep;
> Finders of gold were now but newly past,
> And Basket-women did to Market haste;
> The Watchmen were but just returning home,
> To give the Thieves more liberty to roam,

which, one imagines, Swift must have known when composing his *Description of the Morning*:

> Now hardly here and there an Hackney-Coach
> Appearing, show'd the Ruddy Morns Approach . . .

and so on, in a style developed in *A City Shower*. Not merely is the language familiar, easy, or even sprightly, but the verse is made to handle observation of things hitherto not considered 'poetic', with the result that though nothing of any high poetic value was produced, this coming down to earth made possible the ballad poem such as Carey's 'Sally in our Alley', and perhaps also the homely idiom, though not the form and matter of Matthew Green's *The Spleen*. It has nothing to do with the country realism of such Georgics as Philips's *Cyder*, nor with the Horatian imitations glorifying the blessings of a simple life, nor with the deliberate grossness of the mock epic. Here we meet a natural and refreshing reaction, but it does not appear very often.

Its most important appearance, except for its constant presence in Swift and often in Prior, is in Gay's *Trivia, or the Art of Walking the Streets of London*. There it appears as mockery of the country poem, perhaps of the Georgic, but acute observation, down to earth experience, is the whole time there, far more so than in his *Rural Sports*:

> If you the precepts of the Muse despise,
> And slight the faithful warning of the skies,
> Others you'll see, when all the town's afloat,
> Wrapt in th' embraces of a kersey coat,
> Or double-button'd frieze; their guarded feet
> Defie the muddy dangers of the street,
> While you, with hat unloop'd, the fury dread
> Of spouts high-streaming, and with cautious tread
> Shun ev'ry dashing pool; or idly stop,
> To seek the kind protection of a shop.
> But bus'ness summons; now with hasty scud
> You jostle for the wall; . . .

yet *Trivia*, admirable as it is as a description of London, the most vivid picture that we have, is yet partly mock-classical, the passage going on:

> So fierce *Alecto's* snaky tresses fell. . . .

The two worlds are somewhat roughly linked together, but realism intrudes even into the classical realm with such phrases as 'clotted and straight'. His 'Town Eclogues' adopt the same method, and are indirectly satirical.

For us today, possibly, Gay's most delightful verse is to be found in the songs of *The Beggars' Opera* (1727) and *Polly* (1729). They are the lightest of airy nothings, and though perhaps the well-known tunes have served to make them popular, they are, even without the music, inescapably musical. They are sheer irresponsible fun, imparting all the refreshment of a boyish romp, performed with such economy, such grace, such sure fingering, that they free the spirit. Trifles indeed, but such trifles as 'Youth's the season made for joy', 'O ponder well, be not severe', the dactylic 'How happy could I be with either', or the laughingly sensible 'Can love be controll'd by advice', are delicious iridescent bubbles, which charm and amuse for a moment, and are blown with infinite skill.

But for Gay's generation—and for Gay himself it appears— the *Fables* were his most important poetic work: the success of the 1722 collection encouraging Gay to fuller examples published after his death in 1736. They chimed in admirably with the moralistic part of both the world that knew itself for 'polite', and of the world that wished to be so. The morals are, to be sure, trite and obvious, the satire, we would think, hardly worth attempting to drive home; the whole seems congruous with the still largely adolescent view of the great reading public, and after all, they were written to instruct a boy, the Duke of Cumberland. But their lightness, their geniality, their gaiety, make them still readable in idle moments; some, such as 'The Elephant and the Bookseller', still have their point, and it may be argued that others, such as 'The Lion and the Cub', will always have it. Gay did not confine himself to one form, or, as Dr. Johnson would have it, was not too certain of his form, confusing fable, tale, and allegory; but the lines of demarcation in such an easy, varied author as Gay are not very clear, and the indistinction need not bother the modern reader. His epistolary verses, which contain some of his best work, are equally diverse; 'Mr. Pope's Welcome from Greece', a real epistle embodying warm tributes to his friends, such as the well-known lines in the twelfth stanza:

> Dan Prior next, beloved by every muse,
> And friendly Congreve, unreproachful man!

is a little spoiled for us by containing so many forgotten names; but in the often reprinted epistolary verses 'To a Lady on her Passion for Old China', which should really be called 'On a Lady . . . ', Gay seems for once to join his own person with the general ideas of his time:

> Philosophers more grave than wise
> Hunt science down in Butterflies;
> Or fondly poring on a Spider
> Stretch human contemplation wider;
> *Fossiles* give joy to *Galen's* soul,
> He digs for knowledge, like a Mole;
> In shells so learn'd, that all agree
> No fish that swims knows more than he!
> In such pursuits if wisdom lies,
> Who, *Laura*, shall thy taste despise?

It ends with a pleasant variant of the 'Gather ye rosebuds' theme, which, like most of Gay's work, gives a lively turn to what has often been done before. It is possible that we shall turn more and more to Gay for the sheer pleasure of seeing life presented with such sureness and skill, life not at all evaded, but formalized, civilized, so that even his *Trivia* has a Watteau quality. And whatever he writes, all the while, though he rarely criticizes society or ideas, he is detached, slightly mocking, using words individually enough to keep the reader alert. The kind of delight that he gives is itself a positive value.

It cannot be suggested that the prospect of reading Thomas Tickell[1] offers any likelihood of acute pleasure, but he is interesting because he seems to be the central example of a certain kind of Augustan poetry which received the approval of a good many readers. If he rarely delights, he never offends; and though his verse is not much more than numerous prose, it has all the contraptions of poetry demanded of the general 'polite reader' of that age, the smoothness—the Waller–Granville kind of smoothness—the adulation of noble figures, the discreetly obvious satire, the classical allusions, the formal references to the beauties of nature. His first production, *Oxford* (1706), is at a fair undergraduate prize poem level; the decasyllabic couplets conduct one gravely round a tour of the sights of Oxford, with the expected references to the great men, especially the poets, who had lived there, more especially the recent, living ones; it is all very right and proper (Tickell is always very right and proper); but though it has a certain melody, the regularity of the prosody with a heavy stress nearly always on the second

---

[1] Thomas Tickell, 1686–1740, educated at St. Bees and Queen's College, Oxford, deputized for Trapp as Professor of Poetry, 1710–11. Addison made him his Under-Secretary of State in Ireland in 1717, and he became Secretary to the Lords Justices in 1724.

syllable of each line, renders the whole thing soporific. But he improved his versification, he became a little less derivative, and *Kensington Garden* (1722) is a pleasant enough fable, lightly done, though it 'disgusted' Dr. Johnson, who was unable to endure the bringing together of Oberon and Neptune in one poem. In all his poems his sentiments are impeccable; he is everywhere the perfect gentleman, and even his long and very popular poem on *The Prospect of Peace*, written in the year of stress 1712, failed to ruffle his Whig friends. This poem, however, rises above his usual level, and earned the praises of Pope, then struggling with *Windsor Forest*, who found certain lines too like his own:

> Fearless our merchant now pursues his gain,
> And roams securely o'er the boundless main;
> Now o'er his head the Polar Beam he spies,
> And freezing spangles of the Lapland skies:
> Now swells his canvas to the sultry line,
> With glitt'ring spoils where Indian grottoes shine,
> Where fumes of incense glad the Southern seas,
> And wafted citron scents the balmy breeze.

The protégé and adorer of Addison, whom he was the first to bracket with Virgil, his praises of *Rosamond*, or *Cato* and *The Supposed Author of the Spectator* only just avoid the fulsome; *The Royal Progress* welcoming George I to the shores of England does not do so, while the ballad *Colin and Lucy* (1725) though lilting enough is hardly less ludicrous in its sentimentality than Gay's mockery of the spurious form in *The What D'Ye Call It* ballad ''Twas when the seas were roaring'. Gay, indeed, called it 'the prettier ballad', but only that he might forgive Tickell his peace poem. On the other hand, the poem *On the Death of the Earl of Cadogan* has the merit of a certain bitterness added to the, for him, unusual merit of conciseness (we remember the line where Envy 'To blast the living gave the dead their due'); and the poem addressed to the Earl of Warwick on the death of Addison is, if not the finest poem of its kind in the language, as Johnson declared, yet a poem expressive of real feeling which pierces through the formality of the verse, the pompous exaltation of the departed hero, and the triteness of the adjectives. The *Letter from a Lady in England to a Gentleman at Avignon* is a good example of the light political poem, and has both common sense and humour.

If Tickell carries with him a certain individual dignity, Ambrose Philips is one of the smaller fry distinguished from the others only by a slightly higher degree of 'correctness', Addison's liking for him offset by Swift's contempt, and the notoriety that has attended him on account of the 'namby-pamby' aspect of his poetry. His pastorals are discussed elsewhere in this volume (p. 135), but the rest of his work deserves a moment's fleeting attention. There is not much thought in it, but it has a gentle tunefulness, and a precision which makes him a little different from other poets of occasional verses. His early *Lament for Queen Mary* is ridiculous enough; it compares badly, for instance, with Congreve's; but his later works, especially his Epistles, have an ingredient of observation and self-observation which makes them readable. His downright refusal, in verse, to be effusive on the death of William III has the merit of self-depreciation, and one may think that had he retained his capacity for self-criticism, or perhaps become a humorous poet, he would have deserved better of posterity:

> Why then, in making verses should I strain
> For wit, and of *Apollo* beg a vein?
> Why study *Horace* and the *Stagyrite?*
> Why cramp my dulness, and in torment write?
> Let me transgress by nature, not by rule,
> An artless Idiot, not a study'd fool . . .

and indeed, when in later years he abandoned the fashionable attempt to write by classical rule, and reverted happily to being an artless idiot, his poems have a naïf charm. They are, it must be confessed, silly; and if, as he said in the poem just quoted from, he

> . . . tinkled in the close,
> And sweetened into verse insipid prose,

at least he was enjoying himself and amusing a small coterie. If we take them in the same spirit, and forget that they were portentously included in 'Works', as they should never have been, they can entertain us also.

For his verses, 'little flams', to the Pulteney and Carteret children—in tone and matter more suitable for adolescents than the babes they actually were—together with those to Madame Cuzzoni, those in short of the 'dimply damsel, sweetly smiling' variety of toy, though justly ridiculed in *The Bathos* as examples of the 'Infantine', as well as being mocked, a little cruelly in Carey's wickedly delightful 'Naughty, paughty, Jack-a-Dandy' verses, are not displeasing silly sooth if you are in the mood for silliness; nor indeed are they all silly if thought of as directed to young girls. Yet the moment you compare them with the verses addressed with much the same intonation by Skelton in his *Garden of Laurel* they appear extremely immature, as regards both sensibility and versification. His more solemn attempts, and his translations, are no better and no worse than the average stuff of this low-powered poetic period. His songs are as empty, as neat, and as near-epigrammatic as can be required by his own theory as set out in *Guardian* 16; the only thing he forgot is that they were to be set to music. One poem, however, has other qualities, by no means so rare at that time as usually supposed, namely those of a precise observation of nature, and a concise record of objects. It is true that it might be said of each poet of the period, at least till the middle twenties, that

A primrose by a river's brim
A yellow primrose was to him,
And it was nothing more,

but a simple primrose is a very delightful and interesting object, and there is no reason why it should always be forced into being something more. There is a great deal to be said for liking a thing for its own sake, for seeing the object vividly as it is: one cannot all the time be discovering a world in a grain of sand. Philips, at least in the 'Epistle to the Earl of Dorset' (the 'Winter Piece') addressed from Copenhagen on 9 March 1709 and printed in *Tatler* 12, exhibits a happy delight in the mere spectacle of nature. His description of the country around Copenhagen after a fall of frozen rain evidences a keen and appreciative eye, and a poetic precision he was later to lose:

... ev'ry Shrub, and ev'ry Blade of Grass,
And ev'ry pointed Thorn, seem'd wrought in Glass;
In Pearls and Rubies rich the Hawthorns show,
While through the Ice the Crimson Berries glow ...
When if a sudden Gust of Wind arise
The brittle Forrest into Atoms flies:
The crackling World beneath the Tempest bends,
And in a spangled Show'r the Prospect ends.

It does not, of course, compare with Cotton's boisterous *Winter*;

there is not a striking word, no really imaginative simile; nothing but what seems to be plain statement. Yet it does not give a flat picture; it is a stereoscopic vision contrived by the exquisite adaptation of the words to the thing seen. We react, moreover, to the repetitions of 'ev'ry', the careful choice of adjectives in 'brittle', 'crackling', and 'spangled'. Tactfully, mercifully, there is no comment, except a fanciful little piece at the end about Merlin, since Philips respects his reader, and the result is a holding static picture, seen through a glacial transparency, and the poem looks forward, if not to *Windsor Forest*, which is in a different tradition, at least to *Grongar Hill*.

To pick out a few poets for individual treatment may perhaps give a false impression as to the enormous poetic activity of the age, the constant outpouring of verse in pamphlet, miscellany, or volume. At the beginning some of the old guard were still writing, Sedley, for instance, in the amusing battle of the wits attacking Blackmore, who responded with one of his liveliest pieces, his *Satyr against Wit* (1700). Even such unlikely personages as Godolphin entered the lists, while Garth abandoned the mock-heroic to write a place poem.

VI

POPE TO 1725

I

Pope does not belong to the class of poets that think they are the voice of God, or at least the vessels appointed to transmit the divine utterance; but, rather, to the other class that regard themselves as the mouthpiece of humanity. But the voice is not that of the ordinary man so often as is supposed, for considerable thought went to the making of his suavest couplet. It is deceptive in that the thought is so compressed, stated so smoothly and with such final brevity, that often what is said appears to be superficial when it is really far from that, as Byron was one of the earliest of Pope's defenders to appreciate. It is Pope's misfortune that quotations from his work have become commonplaces—he is still one of the most quoted poets in the language—since as a result we forget how much he sums up. We are apt to ignore, for instance, the large amount of Stoical and neo-classical Renaissance philosophy contained in the already quoted couplet:

> Thus God and Nature fix'd the general Frame,
> And bade Self-love and Social be the same.

The difficulty, however, need not exist for anyone familiar with the intellectual climate of the age. A harder barrier to surmount in arriving at a proper appraisal of Pope is the personal antagonism or the passionate defensive love which his work seems always to arouse. As De Quincey suggested, to one group of persons he is merely dust that is a little gilt, to the other sheer gold no more than a trifle o'erdusted. It is, after all, a tribute to his odd power that with no poet does it seem so hard to be detached, to see his work apart from himself, and himself apart from us.

A man of varying moods, now irritated, now feeling himself above the strife, he could at one moment rejoice in combat, at another genuinely hanker after a haven of retirement and aloofness. If there were times when he wished to show the best side of himself, and seems too much given to self-justification, there is often a streak of impish humour inspiring the defence. It may be said, perhaps, that he was to the end a little raw, that he never attained the amplitude, the urbaneness of his master Dryden; he is at times angular, and may tend to shrillness. But here it is that we are aware of the chronic invalid always nursing his little crazy carcass, by his very nature agonizingly supersensitive, conscious also that he is a member of a religious sect living under disabilities and the threat of penalties. In such circumstances every hurt becomes an agony, every fear a terror. And if he does not spare his enemies, we may well ask, in view of their spite, why he should? What is remarkable about him is the way in which he could turn his physical and moral disabilities to poetic uses. For all his inconsistencies there is a guiding integrity in Pope, the integrity of the artist given to something bigger than himself, a fine aesthetic morality establishing a standard from which he never swerved. We shall not enjoy Pope, not understand him or assess him rightly unless in reading him we rid ourselves of the coxcombry of our perpetual moral pretensions. He exists, he is a quality; he continually gives us an addition to life, a delight which releases in us springs of understanding.

The unusual thing in Pope is not that he lisped in numbers, but that he so early knew the kind of poet he wished to be. Walsh's famous advice, to become the first correct poet in our language, would have had no effect if Pope had not been ready to receive it. He would have agreed with Flaubert that:

La correction (je l'entends dans le plus haut sens du mot) fait à la pensée ce que l'eau du Styx faisait au corps d'Achille: elle la rend invulnérable et indestructible.

Not that he ever supposed that correctness was all. As he was to say in the Preface to *The Iliad*:

Exact disposition, just thought, correct elocution, polished numbers may have been found in a thousand; but this poetic fire, this *vivida vis animi* in a very few.

Correctness had with Pope far wider and richer connotations than those usually given the word, or than Walsh, perhaps, was aware of. With Pope, from the first, it meant an exquisite weighing of sound, of textures, of rhythm, as well as an adaptation of metre to the idea, the congruence of feeling with form, and, one need hardly add, appropriate diction. Moreover, it involved constant labour, a devotion to craftsmanship such as only great artists achieve. 'To write well, lastingly well, Immortally well, must one not leave Father and Mother and cleave unto the Muse?' he wrote to Bolingbroke.

Born in London in 1688—not a happy year for Catholics— of somewhat elderly parents ready to retire to the country (Pope's father having been a luckier wholesale linen-trader than Defoe), his youth from 1700 was passed at Binfield in Windsor Forest. He escaped any damping educational discipline; an aunt taught him to read while the family was still living at Hammersmith, and he at once became a lover of books. As a Catholic he shared neither the advantages nor the constraints of the Protestant system. He had some private tutoring from a priest, some scrappy school education, but from the age of twelve he was almost entirely self-taught. His main instruction came through his father's criticisms of his youthful poems, and the literary conversations he held while out riding with old Sir William Trumbull, who had the taste of a cultured gentle-man, and more erudition than such usually display. Opinions may differ as to the value of such an irregular education; but at least for the next few years the boy was allowed to browse as he would in the English and Latin poets, perhaps also in the Greek, and to dip into the brave show of theological controversy his father had garnered. He was not pestered with other people's opinions about literature, and did not have to justify his own. Thus he was soon intimately acquainted with the main English poets from Chaucer onwards; and if there appear to have been some gaps at this time—Chapman, Daniel, Drayton, and the dramatists as a whole—he was familiar with both threads that run through seventeenth-century poetry, the Jonson–Donne tradition, and that of the lighter lyric poets not to be herded into a school.

He reaped the benefits, and suffered from the defects of the self-taught. He made boyish experiments in varied forms, epic, comedy, and so on, which were duly scrapped, though the epic was kept until, years later, Atterbury advised him to destroy it. The earliest poem of his that we have is an unlicked version of the 'Ode on Solitude' which he sent to Henry Cromwell in a letter of 17 July 1709, saying with an air of deprecation, 'which I found yesterday by great accident, & which I find by the Date was written when I was not Twelve years old'. There is no inherent unlikeliness in this; it was most probably tinkered at for Cromwell, as it suffered further alteration before it was published in 1735. Horatian in metre and in sentiment, vocal of feelings proper to a middle-aged and somewhat disillusioned man of the world, it is ludicrous for a boy of twelve; but if it was really written in 1700, Pope may well have been intuitively reflecting his father's emotions. At all events it is an admirable instance of how he could enter imaginatively into a theme, the 'retirement' one already noted in this volume, its hopes as absurdly at variance with the mature poet's sentiments as they were with those of the boy. This is not insincerity; it is one way in which a poet can work; and as often as not the springs of Pope's imagination were loosed by writing what might seem to be exercises in 'kinds'—the pastoral, the place-poem, the heroical epistle, the mock-epic, the 'imitation'. He served his apprenticeship in this way, and by pastiches of English poets, these last being exercises in metre and verse forms. Skilful as in some ways they are—especially the difficult exercise 'On Silence' written in imitation of Rochester's then still extremely popular triplets 'On Nothing'—these pastiches would not be read now if Pope had not written them; yet even there, in the Cowley, we can find such a happy couplet as

> Where *Lillies* smile in virgin robes of white,
> The thin Undress of superficial Light,

with its interplay of short and long 'i' sounds to enhance the dainty image of whiteness.

But the most important exercise of these early years was the pastorals, which Walsh and others saw, at least in part, in 1705, and which may have been sketched out before. Pope naturally jumped at Tonson's invitation to publish them, and they appeared in the *Miscellany* (No. 6) of 1709. They have been discussed earlier in this volume, and need not be dwelt upon, but we may note how in these Pope had already achieved what he called 'softness', that is an amazing capacity for liquidness in his vowel combinations. In sheer sound, in pure music, they are delicate and sure, and it was in the mastery of sound itself that Pope was to make his next efforts, and undertake in couplet form the sustained *Essay on Criticism.*

It was a bold adventure for a beginner. Though not published until 1711, and then anonymously, it appears to have been written in 1709; and the organizing power required to marshal, and to concentrate into less than 750 lines, the accumulated thought upon criticism of all the centuries since Aristotle, might easily fail a young poet. There is, to be sure, nothing very original in any of the thought; it is in itself an example of the famous couplet:

> True wit is Nature to advantage dress'd,
> What oft' was thought, but ne'er so well express'd.

'Wit' was a trifle ambiguous, and in Pope's view, perhaps, in need of rehabilitation: 'Nature' implied the 'common sense' of mankind throughout the centuries, which it was the function of an Augustan age to sum up. Pope had been clear upon this last matter certainly as early as July 1706, to judge from his letter to Walsh on the 2nd; and Walsh had thoroughly endorsed the argument for plagiarism, when he answered on the 20th. The problem, then, was how to present with gaiety and point what had been attempted in English verse only by Mulgrave and Roscommon in lines that were decently smooth and mildly soporific. Pope, with Dryden's wisdom as a guide, was to do for England what Boileau had recently done for France in displaying the main doctrines of Renaissance criticism, especially perhaps those of 'immortal' Vida (who had said a poet should begin with pastorals), together with those of Longinus, Horace, Petronius, and all the rest, and what of Aristotle's was still current. Pope had been pondering the subject-matter for some years, as can be seen from his correspondence with Walsh and Cromwell; the whole piece was first laid out in prose; so he undertook the work, we see, to clear his own mind as to the principles of his art as much as for any other reason, and to practise such precepts as it might contain; and so it is that his intense interest in his craft gives a surprising warmth to what might otherwise be a coldly brilliant performance, transmuting many passages into sheer lyric.

Even today it carries you dancing along over the common-places, happily hailing the popular quotations as you (unexpectedly sometimes) leap over them. The commonplaces were familiar enough, no doubt, to the educated reader of the day, who would admire the felicity of phrase and illustration, the arrangement of matter, the occasional topical reference while saluting old friends of thought. Yet Dennis's strictures in *Reflections, Critical and Satirical, upon a late Rhapsody called an Essay upon Criticism* (he did not pretend to be unprejudiced) are valid in their sphere. Besides lack of originality in idea, there is considerable confusion, and some inconsistency, but Dennis's main objection was that it failed to be the passionate, simple, and sensuous poetry which, as a good Miltonian, Dennis hoped to see the younger poets trying their hand at. In the main, *sub specie aeternitatis*, he was perhaps right; but he failed to do justice to the merits of the piece, for it is hard to see how the kind of thing it is could have been more persuasively presented. The general public, the new readers perhaps too confidently postulated earlier in this volume, would find it not only easy and conversible, so to speak, but dazzlingly new; and if some of them, like Lady Mary Wortley Montagu, liked it less when they discovered how little it was original in thought, they could not claim that they had been deliberately taken in. Pope could regard it as a contribution to building up the Augustan civilization: he had effected its pastorals; here was its *Ars Poetica*.

Addison could find no plan in it, though Johnson found 'novelty of arrangement'; it does, of course, suffer from being a collection of wise sayings, yet an order is discernible in the three parts, though the architecture is not very secure: the first part states the general philosophic position, the second deals with aesthetic and technical matters, the third indicates the moral standpoint. But if Addison's *Spectator* is any indication, what most entranced the contemporary reader was the 'imitative harmony' (Dryden's term) so brilliantly exemplified in, say, the lines, which close with Virgil's Camilla:

> Soft is the strain when *Zephyr* gently blows,
> And the smooth stream in smoother numbers flows;
> But when loud billows lash the sounding shore,
> The hoarse, rough verse should like the torrent roar.
> When *Ajax* strives, some rock's vast weight to throw,
> The line too labours, and the words move slow;
> Not so, when swift *Camilla* scours the plain,
> Flies o'er th' unbending corn, and skims along the main.

What was not so immediately observable, and what pleases us more, is the magnificent conciseness, the neatness. In one of the couplets just quoted he is translating Vida; Christopher Pitt,[1]

[1] Christopher Pitt, 1699–1748, was educated at Winchester and New College, Oxford, of which he was made Fellow in 1721 on the strength of his first poem; he graduated B.A. in 1722, and was at once made Rector of Pimperne in Dorset, where he remained for the rest of his life.

in his version of 1726, took about fifty lines to say what Pope had managed to convey in eight; and in the above passage Pope abolishes the necessity for four of Pitt's lines by introducing the name of Ajax to stand for 'some giant horrible and grim', with some five descriptive lines added.

Above all, it adumbrates so much of what is to come, partly in its subject-matter, and partly in its form. As we should expect, there are to be found here some of the basic ideas which support the *Essay on Man* and the poems that followed in the final fruition of Pope's genius in the fourth decade of the century; the general concept of 'unerring' Nature; the sense, very faint, of self-love and the ruling passion; and pride as the chief snare of mankind. Here also, before Scriblerus, we meet the sparring at pedantry, and a good deal of the attitude which produced *The Dunciad*. It is interesting to compare the superb passage in the third book of the later poem where the collapse of learning and the arts into medieval blackness is described (whether or not in conformity with modern historical fashion is scarcely to the point) with the passage in the third book of the *Essay on Criticism* where the same event is related.

It is fascinating also to see how in this work Pope was feeling his way towards the form which on the whole characterizes the bulk of his work. It is not to be too much insisted upon, for it never presents itself too insistently in his poems; but if the books or sections of any of his longer works are analysed, or the works which, though not short, are not long enough to be subdivided, a certain structural likeness appears in them all. Each poem (or section) begins with a firm attack; there is an unhesitating, even tread about the first few lines: it settles down to a fairly steady pace, varying indeed a little in urgency, and in pitch of voice, but in the main fairly even. Then, not far from the end, there is a heightening, a greater poetic pressure, which throughout this discussion of Pope's work will be referred to as the 'rise', and either within the rise, or near it, there is a singing passage, a far more lyrical movement, which will be referred to as the 'lilt': the close is normally quiet, and usually rich and varied in sound and in texture. Pope from the beginning modulated his rhythms, his textures, the placing and the depth of his caesuras, his speed and colour, with a skill which is, literally, inimitable; these qualities play over the surface of the not very striking structure and keep it constantly alive. This form, these qualities, will be found at different stages of development in *An Essay on Criticism*, together with insecure dovetailing of paragraphs (never Pope's strongest point), and too great syntactical contraction, but already with some of that colloquial quality which was finally to earn for him a high place among the least artificial of our poets. But before that stage could be reached there was a long apprenticeship to be gone through, a setting up in English of the 'correct' form of most of the 'kinds'; and the one we may first consider is his 'place' poem, or Georgic, *Windsor Forest* which he published in 1713, after the first (1712) version of *The Rape of the Lock*.

At this time Pope was much the amateur painter, in 1713 going to study under Jervas, making the painter's home his London address, developing a lively eye for colour and scenery. As Norman Ault showed, colour words are more thickly abundant in *Windsor Forest* than in any other poem in the language. An almost random quotation will yield:

> Here in full light the russet plains extend:
> There, wrapt in clouds, the bluish hills ascend.
> Even the wild heath displays her purple dyes,

while the glittering scales of fishes, the shining feathers of birds echoing the colours of the countryside, form an integral part of the whole conception. Yet given all this, the question with Pope, as always, was in what form could he make this expressive, what previous model congruous with the classical idea he was to 'imitate', that is, adapt and develop. For Pope was already of the opinion that a poem composed wholly of description would be 'as absurd as a feast made up of sauces', as Warton reports him to have thought; a poem must be given solidity by something beyond the sensuous, by some feeling of wholeness, of integration with man's passions and his deeds, since man too is part of nature. It was thus fairly evident that his work might well be of the 'place' variety; it could spring from what was still the most famous poem of its 'kind', namely *Cooper's Hill*, devoted to a region very near his own, and containing just the elements he would wish to include. Moreover, following a more than broad hint from Denham, he could easily, as Granville suggested, turn his first drafts of 1704–10 into a patriotic poem celebrating the coming peace of Utrecht, and incidentally condemning the Revolution. This would at

once satisfy his already conscious sense that a poem must be of
and for its time, and confirm his alliance with the Tories. But
the poem of 1713 is far more complex than its forerunners; if
Denham was his main model, Pope also drew upon classical
authors, Virgil, Ovid, and Ausonius, and among English predecessors in description, in addition to John Philips as suggested
earlier, Spenser, Drayton, Milton, and Waller. Possibly he
read Cotton and Vaughan. It may be a mere coincidence, or a
common reference back to the Georgics, that his poem and
Diaper's *Dryades* have the strong resemblances in certain
particulars already noted: both of them are peace poems.

Thus enriching and adding to the themes found in *Cooper's
Hill*, his problem was to thread the diverse elements together,
which he did on the whole with uncanny skill; there is some
hint of uneasiness in the transitions of subject and of the
emotions to be aroused. The address to Granville, interwoven
with a reference to 'Sylvan Maids', is in part poetic homage
(he illustrated the 'smoothness' of Waller), in part a tribute to
the Treasurer of the Queen's household and one of the Utrecht
peers. After this opening, Pope weaves in a reminder of Milton,
pagan cities, an Ovidian metamorphosis, a ruin scene, a description of fishes, rural sports, medieval history, and some
Horatian retirement. It leads up to a vision of a golden age in
the future, which includes the emotional appeal of the 'noble
savage' popularized by Mrs. Behn and Southerne in their
respective *Oroonoko*'s. It ends with the full quiet close which was
to become one of the characteristics of Pope's poetry, as the
deflationary close was to be a mark of Swift's. But all the while
he kept close enough to familiar models to make his readers
feel they were on secure ground. So familiar, indeed, that he
found himself in some difficulty, having been forestalled by
Tickell in his poem *On the Prospects of Peace*, notably in the
passage quoted when speaking of Tickell in a previous chapter.
He wrote about it to Caryll in some anxiety (29 November
1712); but he did not need to alter very much.

To read Denham side by side with Pope offers an amusing
exercise in comparative criticism, though little is to be gained
from a comparison of the versification, since the differences are
obvious. Denham had made great steps in the use of the closed
couplet, but Pope's is already brilliant, masterly, and modulated; what is more interesting is to notice the way in which

Pope develops and clarifies certain themes. The 'order in variety' passage, for example, which has been ascribed to his imitating Claudian, he more likely derived from Denham, who speaking of Nature wrote:

> Wisely she knew, the harmony of things,
> As well as that of sounds, from discords springs.
> Such was the discord, which did first disperse
> Form, order, beauty, through the universe . . .

Pope turned this into:

> Here hills and vales, the woodland and the plain,
> Here earth and water seem to strive again:
> Not *Chaos*-like together crush'd and bruis'd,
> But as the world, harmoniously confus'd:
> Where order in variety we see,
> And where, tho' all things differ, all agree.

Again and again there are verbal reminiscences, quite apart from the likenesses in theme and structure noted in a previous chapter.

But it is more important to find what is distinctively Pope's, and the easiest pleasure of the poem for the modern reader is the delight to be obtained from the vivid descriptions of nature—the chequered shadows, the brilliance of fish, the gorgeous colours of the pheasant with his 'purple crest' and 'painted wings'. It may be worth noticing that at Penshurst too the pheasant is purple and speckled, and is a 'painted patriarch'; but Pope's picture is particularized, as a careful painter's might be, for as he wrote in the rough draft of the 'Epistle to Mr. Jervas':

> Like friendly colors our kind arts unite,
> Each from the mixture gathering sweets and light.

It is, inevitably, a period piece. But the movement is compelling, the various rises admirable, as, say, in the Lodona fable, a piece of invented Ovid, preceded by the lilt describing Diana, to subside in a hushed quiet, almost a lullaby, after the swift excitement of Pan's chase of the nymph:

> She said, and melting as in tears she lay,
> In a soft, silver stream dissolv'd away.
> The silver stream her virgin coldness keeps,
> For ever murmurs, and for ever weeps;

the words to be said very quietly, so that the sibilants of the second line come like the soft whisper of autumn leaves on the ground. The great rise occurs in the magnificent vision at the end, when Thames speaks of his glories, and the pageant of the ages passes before him, with Britain bringing peace to all the world, a *pax Britannica* attended by prosperity. It is fervent, it expresses a real patriotic belief in the mission of England, and though to some this faith may seem ridiculous, it is to be noted that the prophecy in it very nearly came true in the fullness of a century and a half. Pope loaded with ore every line of this passage, which though it has its parallels in *Cooper's Hill* and the concluding stanzas of *Annus Mirabilis*, is far from being merely traditional. While asking the mind to hold the whole terrene globe in its vision, a Kipling-like vision of ships like shuttles weaving civilization together, he gives the eye every detail it can hold; he fills it with colour of coral and amber and ruby; he shows cities and peoples. A generous creative process is going on; there is balm and spice in the air; peace and freedom are to ensue, the vices that make for cruelty and conquest are to be expunged, the gasping furies will thirst for blood in vain. The passage is orchestral in its effects, strings and woodwind and brass all contributing to the result; so far, for sheer richness of music, as well as for sheer sensuousness, Pope had achieved nothing so powerful.

Yet it is not until we get to the 1714 *Rape of the Lock* that we hear Pope really singing consistently with his own voice, on his own theme. So far he had been imitative, or he had sung other people's songs: his muse, we can say, had been in leading strings. But now this 'occasional' theme, suggested to him by Caryll on an absurd event that had taken place in Catholic high society (the cutting off of a lock of Miss Fermor's hair by Lord Petre), released what was formatively original in him—precisely because the theme was so trivial, far more so than that of *La Secchia Rapita* by which Pope is influenced in his title alone. True, in one sense he was still imitating, using a form recently recognized, a form by now well understood and relished. There was indeed room for greater correctness; but beyond that there was something else wanting, and this also Pope supplied—another dimension.

This is not so much apparent in *The Rape of the Locke* of 1711 (which came out in Lintot's 1712 *Miscellany*), the extremely elegant trifle of not much more than three hundred lines, which in its own way was as complete and perfect as Addison said it was. The poem is not indeed quite complete until the 1717 version of some eight hundred lines, which included Clarissa's lovely speech, though in everything but that the 1714 edition is virtually the final state: it contains all the 'machinery' of the Rosicrucian system—according that is, to the Abbé Montfaucon de Villars's *Le Comte de Gabalis*, a system Erasmus Darwin was to use in his Botanic Garden, and Anatole France in *La Rôtisserie de la Reine Pédauque*. Pope continued to polish it till his final illness, thus making the Warburton 1751 text in some ways the most authoritative. Whether Pope from the first intended to add some sort of machinery, as he states in the 'Dedication to Mrs. Arabella Fermor', may be open to doubt; but it transforms this astonishing occasional poem from being a witty agreeable toy into a masterpiece. 'I am charmed with the magic of your invention,' Berkeley wrote to Pope on 1 May 1714, 'with all those images, allusions, and inexplicable beauties, which you raise so surprisingly, and at the same time so naturally, out of a trifle.' It is not only because the affectionate parody of the epic was made more perfect, allowing, for instance, of a descent into the lower regions (for that age, the Cave of Spleen, as Garth had indicated) as well as of the enchanting upper realm of divinities ('Milton's thrones, dominations, and archangels reduced to the scale of the fairies in *A Midsummer Night's Dream*') but chiefly because it liberated him into realms till then unexploited by him.

It is possible that we today can understand better than his contemporaries what Pope was really saying. We can sense what is eternal in the poem—and there is something eternal—without the barrier of contemporary allusion, both social and literary. So many lines or passages are echoes, adaptations, or parodies of pieces that the 'polite' reader of the day might be expected to know. He would, for example, recognize Statius in

Where wigs with wigs, with sword-knots sword-knots strive;

and Dryden in

The conq'ring force of unresisted steel.

He would be conscious that he was expected to understand the mockery of the epic form and its various points, the invocation, the sacrifice, the games, and so on, and to compare what he read with at least *The Dispensary* if not *Le Lutrin* and *La Secchia Rapita*. All would seem to him of merely local reference. When, it may be, he read:

> Whether the Nymph shall break *Diana's* Law,
> Or some frail *China* Jar receive a Flaw,
> Or stain her Honour, or her new Brocade,
> Forget her Pray'rs, or miss a Masquerade ...

he would, probably, particularize the image, or, if he were solemn, regard it as a criticism of maids of honour at Court. We can now generalize, and for us the lines describe the attitude of the average human being as he finds a *modus vivendi* in a life of bewildering conflicting duties, impulses, and velleities.

The feeling for texture, for rhythms, for vowel-play, are here very nearly as perfect as Pope was ever to make them; colloquial ease was yet to come, and at any rate was hardly appropriate here. All his concentrated craftsmanship was needed to fuse together the diverse elements—the human story, the exquisite sylphs, the light social satire of the gossiping Court ladies as

> In various Talk th' instructive hours they past,
> Who gave the *Ball*, or paid the *Visit* last;

the rather too easily assumed bitterness of:

> The hungry Judges soon the Sentence sign,
> And Wretches hang that Jury-men may dine;

the gay bantering of Sir Plume, the action of the contest at ombre, of the great battle, the Platonic, Homeric, and Ovidian references. The brilliance of the end of the first canto is enchanting, the sensuous description of the dressing-table which is also an altar, an altar at which the nymph is her own votaress. It is consummate achievement that the symbolism which is so obviously 'artificial', of the 'let's pretend' type, should yet be a deeper symbol of plenitude. A creative sense is wrapped up in a shimmering haze, where such words as 'silver', 'glitter', give the whole tone, as iridescent, as the wings of the sylphs, of whose miraculous beauty *Gabalis* gives no hint.

Notable about the poem is its success on a variety of levels. It was here that for the first time Pope really displayed his affinity with the metaphysicals, to which Mr. Middleton Murry first drew attention, the ability to evoke responses simultaneously from different realms of experience, feeling, and apprehension. *The Rape of the Lock* is not only an exquisite piece of music, a criticism of the heroic form, and a light-hearted piece of fun; it is also a by no means shallow piece of satire, not all on the drawing-room level, as well as a poignant lament for the ephemeral nature of things. Moreover the complex of responses is called upon nearly all the time, together, naturally, with the continual contrast in our minds of the whole grandeur of life conceived as an epic, and the littleness of life as lived from day to day, with the accompanying suggestion that to puff our littleness into epic size is the delusion that makes mankind so lovable and so absurd. Some of this was already there by 1712, in the very last paragraph, for instance, where Belinda's lock becomes Berenice's hair, 'The skies bespangling with dishevel'd light'. This is pure poetry, lyric song; the foolery has gone, Arabella Fermor has vanished: we experience a curious release, a liberation of the spirit into the realm where the dominant emotion is the feeling of pathos for the amusing but touching helplessness of human beings.

Complete as the poem was in 1714, Clarissa's speech added in 1717 forms a brilliant coping-stone, and the passage of Homer parodied, the speech of Sarpedon to Glaucus, was cleverly chosen. Most non-Grecian readers would know the passage, if not from Pope's own version in the 1709 *Miscellany*, almost certainly from the version printed in Denham's *Works*, still current popular reading. The lines add a further level of awareness, now of moral awareness, to deepen the one already suggested by the couplet:

> Safe from the treach'rous Friend, the daring Spark,
> The Glance by Day, the Whisper in the Dark . . .

for profound nostalgia inspires the passage:

> Oh! if to dance all Night, and dress all Day,
> Charm'd the Small-pox, or chas'd old Age away;
> Who would not scorn what Huswife's Cares produce,
> Or who would learn one earthly Thing of Use? . . .
> But since, alas! frail Beauty must decay,
> Curl'd or uncurl'd, since Locks will turn to grey . . .

which thus becomes a comment on the whole of life. Indeed the amazing feat which this poem constitutes is that, besides being a joke it is a profound work of art. Fundamentally the subject-matter of the poem is the quality of life, far more so really than in the Ethic Epistles of some twenty years later, since it is less reasoned, more profoundly intuitive. It is to be sure youthful, tender, a touch sentimental in its laughter; but in the last paragraph the whole story is forgotten; pure poetry has supervened: it is a lament for the passage of time.

Through all these years Pope had been practising, as he had done ever since he began to lisp in numbers. There had inter-mediately been a medley of smaller things, besides the major works, either translations or examples of particular forms, such as his 'Ode to Music', published in 1713, but written, Pope is eager to inform us, for St. Cecilia's Day in 1708. Here, once more consciously following Dryden—as is clinchingly evidenced by the last couplet—Pope gave himself over to often successful, 'imitative harmony', and to experiments in changes of move-ment which are always interesting and sometimes exciting. His most haunting passage is the four lines since used as a theme for variations by Mr. Sacheverell Sitwell, which may derive from the opening of Jonson's 'Elegy on the Lady Jane Pawlett',

> By the hero's armed shades,
> Glittering through the gloomy glades
> By the youths that died for love,
> Wandering in the myrtle grove:

but the poem as a whole, though a much better piece of work than is usually conceded, does not hang together with the inevitability that we associate with the fully developed Pope.

There were, too, the Chaucer translations. There had to be Chaucer translations, since Dryden had set the pace. Moreover, there was undoubtedly an interest in Chaucer, even though he was regarded mainly as the purveyor of indecorous fabliaux (see, for instance, Fenton's 'imitation') as Pope himself appears at one time to have thought him from his amusingly indecent little 'after the manner of', which one imagines to be as early as it is clumsy. 'The Wife of Bath's Prologue' (1713), for which 'The Merchant's Tale', the 'January and May' of the 1709 *Miscellany* was preliminary practice, need not long detain us: 'This Translation was done at sixteen or seventeen Years of Age' Pope tells us. Most readers today will prefer to enjoy them in the more prolix originals, if only because the language is more consonant with the ideas and the atmosphere than Augustan English could possibly be. Nevertheless they are in themselves extremely readable, pungently phrased, and not too long. Something of Chaucer has gone, of course, something of the earthy richness; but certain awkwardnesses have gone too. The result is far more decorous and drawing-room; it smacks a little of the vulgarity of 'refinement'; but it is what the Augustan age would stand. Pope, as Dryden before him, had done a service to the fame of Chaucer, and kept him alive in the national memory in a way the misleading edition of 1687 failed to do. For at that date nobody knew how to scan him, and most were too easily baffled by the presence of obsolete words.

But *The Temple of Fame* of 1715, stated by him to have been written in 1711, is altogether different. Pope is no longer translating; he is imitating, that is, producing an original poem as a variation upon an older theme. The theme indeed is far more than merely Chaucerian; it runs through the seventeenth century in various forms—including the mock form of Sessions of the Poets—the most immediate precursors being Yalden's *Temple of Fame* in 1700, and an anonymous poem of the same title addressed to Congreve in 1709. In this same year the *Tatler* devoted parts of three numbers (67, 74, 81) to a competition for immortal places, and in *Spectator* 439 of July 1712, Addison introduced a warning against government spies with a reference to Ovid's Palace of Fame. So in giving one more instance of a special form, Pope was building upon a fashionable curiosity about Chaucer, the familiarity of a well-known theme, the hankering after the classics, and a taste for imitations. This really gave him complete freedom in his adaptation of the third part only of the *House of Fame*, in a poem which though it scarcely justifies the tedium of the allegorical form, contains some miraculously evocative little insets, such as the description:

> So *Zembla's* Rocks (the beauteous Work of Frost)
> Rise white in Air, and glitter o'er the Coast;
> Pale Suns, unfelt, at distance roll away,
> And on th' impassive Ice the Lightnings play:
> Eternal Snows the growing Mass supply,
> Till the bright Mountains prop th' incumbent Sky:
> An *Atlas* fix'd, each hoary Pile appears,
> The gather'd Winter of a thousand Years,

transforming into poetry accounts travellers had brought back from Greenland, which in search of 'winter pieces' Pope had studied in December 1712. But the importance of the poem is not so much what it is in itself, upon which Professor Wilson Knight has illuminatingly enlarged, as what it looks forward to in Pope, both as a romantic poet and as a moralist. The two sides are carefully differentiated; as Professor Tillotson points out in a passage of brilliant analysis (Section xii of his Introduction), the poem combines two kinds of poetry, each with a different sort of couplet, and different verbal colourings. The descriptive, epic, historical part has splendid official words: 'superior', 'eternal', 'pompous', and with them go adjectival past participles; the romantic passages are adorned with 'poetical' words: 'wild', 'confus'd', 'promiscuous', and with them 'go the scores of adjectival present participles, the present participle usually representing transience, growth, movement'. All these are words commonly used in verse, and among them shine out the 'newly chosen' words which give force to the moral passages, which come thicker towards the end, and it is really as foreshadowing the satirical moralist that the poem has its chief importance.

There is no space here to go further into detail, to compare with Chaucer's tetrameters, or to consider the occasional lapses, with here an uncomfortable inversion, there too sudden a drop from the deliberately statuesque to the ephemeral. Yet the poem is worth lingering over generally because it would seem to some degree to indicate for Pope a possible parting of the ways. This vastly learned poem, drawing as it does from a huge variety of sources, made him a citizen of a good many worlds. Could he inhabit the 'romantick' one which he was soon to essay with yet another 'correct' form—the heroical epistle—or would he so early decide to stoop to truth and moralize his song? He knew, of course, as well as anybody before or since, that didacticism is eventually no more 'moral' than seemingly disinterested works; that there are gains and losses in effectiveness either way. There was, however, as he must have felt, something in the atmosphere of the time that told in favour of direct speech and satire. He had already tried his hand at satirical characters—'Successio', Artemisia, Phryne, and Macer and Atticus, to appear later. But up to this point Pope showed the world mainly the 'pure' poet, intent only to manufacture the most perfect thing of its kind that he can, setting immense if inchoate learning to the tune perpetually running in his head. But, if he was naturally a singer, he was also a moralist, this not naturally, since only born prigs are that, but battered into being one by his experience, by the shocks that had countered his youthful hubristic sallies in the persons of Dennis and Gildon, by his bitter taste of the insecurity of friendships, and, let us add, by an honest looking at his own defects. Pope, one may hazard, was beginning to see where his love of fame might lead him; this was perhaps his first exercise in self-castigation, which with him when brought to the precision of poetry tended to take the form of self-justification.

But before—and then only after some years—Pope was to go on to the work in which his genius finally matured, he had still other forms of which to give a 'correct' exemplar, notably the heroical epistle. Here he could, while pursuing his dedicated task of integrating English poetry into one splendid whole, develop the native tradition, of Drayton and others, and equal (if not surpass) the ancients on their own Ovidian ground. He was, it seems, stimulated to this task by the appearance in 1713 of an English version by John Hughes of Bussy de Rabutin's free translation, with courtly decorations, of the Latin letters of Héloise and Abelard. One may guess—it is just a little more than a guess—that in about 1715 a state of emotional tension caused by his relations with Martha Blount and Lady Mary Wortley Montagu made it inevitable for him to write, if not a love poem in the ordinary sense, at all events a poem about love. It is a poem you can reject as cold and meaningless, or in which, with Byron, you can find deep passion, we might think almost too searingly expressed. And as always with Pope, whatever other feeling may be running through the work—and it is difficult not to agree with Byron that Pope was profoundly moved when he wrote this poem—the whole is informed with his driving need to make as perfect a work of its kind as is humanly possible. Given the theme, given the emotional mood at the time, the heroical epistle would, no doubt, seem to Pope the very form that he wanted. It enabled him, moreover, to round off a fairly handsome collection of pieces of a shape invented by the great poets: Ovid whom he loved, he had not yet modelled himself upon or imitated, though he had, following Dryden, translated some of him, notably *Sappho to Phaon*;

the *Heroides*, then, offered a familiar model which would fall in
very well to versify the prose offered by Hughes; it was, we may
say, the final step in his apprenticeship. Moreover it enabled
him to fill in another, rather different, sort of gap, which Walsh
had found in the earlier English poets: 'Among all these, that
Softness, Tenderness, and Violence of Passion, which the
Ancients thought proper for Love-Verses, is wanting.' There
was, of course, an enormous amount to think about and to do;
the range of diction to be used had to be thought out, the kind
of imagery to be employed; and then the modelling of the
crude material into a shapely, because expressive, form.

For, after all, Pope was the superb craftsman that he was
because of his being a creative artist. Technique is merely the
name given to the way any particular problem of presentation
is solved; but sometimes, when reading Pope, or criticisms and
appreciations of his poetry, we are apt to think that the artifice
is all; there is pleasure to be got from recognizing it, as there
must have been immense satisfaction in achieving it; but it is
nevertheless a side issue. Pope, in taking this ever-moving
story, which in our own day has once again been explored,
notably by George Moore, was evidently animated by the
desire to 'present' it to the utmost possible limit of understanding and sensibility; he worked, we imagine, on the theme, just
as Henry James worked on a theme; but Pope had the good
luck to live in an age when originality of form was deplored
rather than considered essential. His problem was to see how
much he could do within that form, and by modulation, by
imagery, by association, and by change of tempo, impart to
the reader his own vividly imaginative apprehension of a story
that had become almost legendary.

We can see in full detail in the Twickenham edition, what
elements went to making up the mosaic; Milton, of whom he
was the first genuine imitator, especially in the passages of
gloomy romanticism; the romanticism itself residing not only
in the essentials of the story, but in the decorations—the horrid
chasms, the ruins, the ivy, and so on, which we associate with
Gray rather than with Pope; the borrowings from Crashaw,
whom he had studied for years, and who in the fusion of human
and divine eroticism had much to give him for this subject;
there is Dryden again and again. But the poem is far richer
than a mosaic, or an exquisite pattern; the effect is much nearer

something three-dimensional. It is all the time informed with life. Pope's paragraphing in this poem is for once nearly flawless, with all the control of emotional movement which that implies. Here, more than anywhere else perhaps, is Pope master of the rise and fall, in tension and in speed, master too of varying colour.

It is these last qualities which bring home to us so poignantly the tumult of conflicting emotions in Eloisa which is the dramatic—though not the philosophic—theme of the poem, as it is the conflict which makes the poem so much more actively human than any in Drayton's *England's Heroical Epistles.* Splendid as these are, and bold as Drayton was in using modern subjects for the Ovidian form—bolder in this respect than Pope —they are undramatic; the couplets move to their appointed end of establishing a single mood, what element of drama there is being introduced by the pairing of the letters. But Pope is altogether dramatic, even as he follows each subtle change in Eloisa's emotion. The 'romantic' setting, which might have been static, is itself endued with the movement of drama, even for us now in those very passages which might for the modern reader, unused to the diction of the time, seem stillborn and tinselled:

> ... The dying gales that pant upon the trees,
> The lakes that quiver to the curling breeze;
> No more these scenes my meditation aid,
> Or lull to rest the visionary maid:
> But o'er the twilight groves, and dusky caves,
> Long-sounding isles, and intermingled graves,
> Black Melancholy sits, and round her throws
> A death-like silence, and a dread repose:
> Her gloomy presence saddens all the scene,
> Shades ev'ry flow'r, and darkens ev'ry green,
> Deepens the murmur of the falling floods,
> And breathes a browner horror on the woods.
> Yet here for ever, ever must I stay: ...

the quickening movement of the 'Shades ev'ry flow'r' line being premonitory of the resigned outburst that follows.

The 1717 volume which offered these poems contained, except for a few smaller pieces varying in quality, all of major original worth that Pope was to produce for a decade; for since 1713 he had been progressively immersed in his translation of the *Iliad*. This is in a sense a contribution to English poetry, yet, seeing what Pope had so far done, it may be regretted that he had not held himself free from so exacting a task; it did, however, in the end make him free, for it established both his reputation and his income on a secure basis. Thus before considering his Homer, it may be of value to assess his distinct contribution to the corpus of English poetry so far. It was quite clear by now that there was no rival in the field; others were writing, or had within his life written, poetry akin to his own—Lady Winchilsea, Prior, Parnell, Gay, Congreve, each adding a little individual note to the chorus; but Pope clearly was the only poet of real power, of whom it might with certainty be said that he was in process of making, if he had not already made, a difference to the shape of the poetic tradition of the country. He was to add more, perhaps his most important work; but the addition was a development of what he had so far done; the moralist who was to emerge on his final return from Greece was the same poet, though he might have a more determined bias: the romantic singer of Eloisa is essential to the satirist of *Sober Advice*.

It can be said that his triumph was a technical one, provided sight is not lost of the elementary fact that the way a thing is uttered is part of what is said: a man labours at words to make them expressive only if he has something to express. Moreover, within the technical framework was summed up in a special form many of the gains of poetry in the previous century, notably the multiple-layer effect of metaphysical poetry together with the Denham–Waller 'smoothness', which at first sight seems incompatible with the tough thinking and uncompromising feeling as expressed by Donne or even Jonson.

Though this element is discoverable in most of his earlier work—discoverable but not easily to be seen—it is apparent throughout in the poem which in a way is pendent to *Eloisa*, namely the *Elegy to the Memory of an Unfortunate Lady*, 'the rare fineness of which', as Dr. Leavis remarks, 'has not had the recognition it deserves'. Its fineness is threefold—in that it is deeply evocative; that its music and its movement are extremely rich and perfectly controlled, and that it is throughout tautened by 'metaphysical wit'. The actual story upon which the poem is founded remains doubtful, but there is no doubt that when Pope wrote the poem he was deeply agitated by a circumstance with which he became acquainted: it is the sense of this which makes the poem moving; and all the while we feel that Pope is determined to impart his emotion to the reader, and will lose no means at his disposal. He again uses Jonson's 'Elegy to Lady Jane Pawlett,' this time for his opening, but the appeal is soon direct:

> Is there no bright reversion in the sky,
> For those who greatly think, or bravely die?

Then after a little while, a passage that might have come from a later metaphysical:

> Most souls, 'tis true, but peep out once an age,
> Dull sullen pris'ners in the body's cage:
> Dim lights of life that burn a length of years,
> Useless, unseen, as lamps in sepulchres;
> Like Eastern Kings a lazy state they keep,
> And close confin'd in their own palace sleep.

Then, a little more than half-way through the poem comes the poignant passage with three successive lines beginning 'By foreign hands . . .', making a smooth transition to 'By strangers honour'd . . .' which by a subtle but compelling transition inaugurates a new phase with 'What tho' thy friends . . .', so that the metaphysical wit of the 'souls' passage becomes absorbed in the general emotion.

That he should have been able to integrate a metaphysical wit—which implies seriousness and grace—was an immense gain; but we need not value a poem in proportion to its closeness to this form. It was not this quality alone that enabled him to use words with the precision which is the merit of his age, making them say all he needed them to say, but not an atom more. From this point of view it is profitable to examine, so as to get the maximum delight from them—and considerable it is —three lesser poems, something between a real letter in verse and the full-blown epistle 'kind', namely the two poems 'To a Young Lady' and the 'Epistle to Robert Earl of Oxford, and Earl Mortimer' prefacing his edition of Parnell's *Poems*. There is no 'wit' here in the metaphysical sense, no Ovidian ornament, no metaphor: they have the deceptive appearance so common with Pope, and not infrequent with others of the time, of being mere plain statement. But, for example, the poem which went with the letters of Voiture, whether or not addressed to Martha

Blount, provides its own background if Pope's physique is remembered; it is the touching expression of an *amitié amoureuse*, trembling with an intensely civilized, restrained, responsible emotion. In these pieces Pope had achieved something altogether original yet within the traditional framework.

2

Throughout his first period, we can watch Pope discarding a good deal of fustian, and ridding himself of the shackles of a previous age. He is adapting the old tradition to serve a new sensibility, another apprehension of life, progressively achieving his own idiom and diction, much of which derived from Milton as well as from Dryden. Though he is not yet skilful enough to handle the colloquial manner for serious purposes, he is already, when occasion demands it, master of the astringent monosyllable, able normally to use the run of spoken expression, if not yet achieving the rhythm of natural speech. Though the *Homer* will be written to a different formula, his progress was not checked. The influences at work from, say, 1713 to 1725, which seem to have matured, fructified, and become seminal underground, brought about his full flourishing once Homer was done with. These influences, which had their roots in this middle period, combined with the security both poetic and financial he gained from his translations, are so important in shaping his future performance that this would seem the place to touch on them briefly before considering the *Homer* itself.

Pope's beginnings had been under the aegis of older men whom he had impressed—Trumbull, Walsh, Cromwell, Wycherley: after his first publications he came to stand on his own feet, and to begin with, hoping to evade politics (vain hope!), he naturally drifted to the rising group centred about Addison at Button's. He seems first to have made the acquaintance of Steele, who asked him to write for him, and for whom he produced the Hadrian lines, the St. Cecilia 'Ode to Music', the version of the Pollio eclogue known as the 'Messiah', and later, through that connexion, the prose pieces in the *Spectator* and *Guardian*. About this period also he came to full acquaintance with Addison, who invited him to write the Prologue to *Cato*. But contemporaneously with all this there arose the clash with Dennis over the Appius passage in the *Essay on Criticism*, and the other series of prose pieces, beginning with *The Critical Specimen* of 1711, if it is his. From 1711 Pope began to find the life of a wit a continual warfare upon earth, as it was also, we must suppose, at this period that he formed his resolve to be independent, not to have to submit to the humiliations of patronage; and it is possible that his sense that Addison was too patronizing formed the basis of the deep antagonism towards him that soon developed, which was to reach its climax over the Homer affair. There was, for him at least, a pretentiousness about the Buttonians that he found insufferable.

And it was no doubt partly this which sent him over to his natural affinities on the other side of the political fence, to Swift, Prior, Gay, Parnell, and Arbuthnot, and the antagonism to pretentiousness which caused these men—Prior apart, who was largely abroad—to form the Scriblerus Club which vowed perpetual war against pedantry. With Swift it was an old war, which he had waged ever since the days of *The Battle of the Books*, but it was probably Pope who began to give it shape in his essay in *Spectator* 457, 14 August 1712, where he tells Mr. Spectator:

... Now, Sir, it is my Design to Publish every Month, *An Account of the Works of the Unlearned*. Several late Productions of my own Country-men, who many of them make a very Eminent Figure in the Illiterate World, Encourage me in this Undertaking.

The first direct shot the Club fired in the war was Pope's *Guardian* essay (No. 78, 10 June 1713), 'A Receipt to Make an Epick Poem'. But thanks to political developments the Club was short-lived, and collapsed in 1714 with the Tory administration; so that its great work, the *Memoirs of Martinus Scriblerus*, remained in more or less fragmentary form until Pope gathered the pieces together, and considerably rehandled the whole, for publication in 1741. But it had numerous offshoots, Gay's *Shepherd's Week*, *The What D'ye Call It*, and *Three Hours after Marriage*, and there was a great flowering of Scriblerian productions in 1727 and 1728 with *Gulliver's Travels*, *The Dunciad*, and *The Beggar's Opera*.

It was with this group, far more than with the Buttonians, that Pope was spiritually allied, for he found congenial Swift's intense dislike of any philosophic 'system'—a dislike shared by Bolingbroke; and if there was about Pope a good deal of the

Shaftesburian optimist, he shared Swift's Christian pessimism. His political position as a Catholic put him closer to the Tory Church of England than it did to Whig dissent, and this he would most feel during the period of political tension. He also liked the kind of laughter laughed by Swift and Gay and Arbuthnot; he could not bear the 'complacent satisfaction' which shone on the faces of successful Whigs.

Nevertheless it was as soon as the beginning of George I's reign that he began to make the acquaintance of the great Whig magnates, who, besides genuinely admiring his work, gave him the opportunity of indulging his passion for gardening and building, a passion he could himself gratify only on a minute scale. Pope's family sold their property in Windsor Forest in 1716, since as Catholics they were threatened with land-tax, and moved to Chiswick, near Lord Burlington. Pope, however, lost his father at the end of that year, and during the next he rented the house at Twickenham which was to become famous for the garden over the road, and for the connecting grotto which ran under it, that splendid toy which was to be his great solace. It was here that he settled for the rest of his life; it was here that his character, especially his poetic character, grew to full maturity. His life at Twickenham, with his mother and his friends, with his garden and his grotto, is a far more important element in his life than the perpetual war he waged against Grub Street.

It was then as a man experienced in life and in the ways of men that he settled here; he had passed through a phase of youthful exuberance, of tavern friendships, of writing for private circulation such poems as the parody of Sternhold and Hopkins's metrical version of the First Psalm, the amusing 'Worms' poem, and the indecorous revelation of the expression of the emotions of a lady witnessing *Cato*. No one would argue that his indelicacy was such that it would be indelicate to notice it; but he can handle it so as to make the 'Court Ballad' one of his most charming and characteristic things. We get a glimpse of this mood and this life in the 'Farewell to London' he wrote on going to the country in 1715, employing a metre unusual with him, which he yet could handle quite freely: as when

> The gayest valetudinaire,
> Most thinking rake alive

bids

> Luxurious lobster nights, farewell,
> For sober, studious days;
> And Burlington's delicious meal,
> For salads, tarts, and pease!

He gave as excuse for his retreat to the country that 'Homer, damn him! calls'. But even a man with better physique could not have gone on at the pace he was going, living too strenuously the life of the young author, involved in all the fatiguing, if at the moment stimulating, squabbles of literary cliques and partisanships.

For his uneasy alliance with the Buttonians led him into such scrapes as youthful exuberance creates. The hubris of an early felt sense of mastery had caused him to write the lines in the *Essay on Criticism* that had excusably angered Dennis, and brought about an inexcusable revenge. When Steele and then Addison offered him the shelter of their group, he could not but respond. He knew no other, and was glad to be free of any suspicion of party allegiance within the realm of letters. Having written the Prologue to *Cato*, in itself an admirable little critique explaining Addison's departure from the formulas of heroic tragedy, he felt he was entitled to get his revenge upon Dennis, not by replying to Dennis's attack upon himself, but to the virulent, and quite acute, *Remarks upon Cato*. The inspired buffoonery of his *Narrative of Dr. Robert Norris Concerning the Strange and Deplorable Frenzy of Mr. John Denn—*, not, it may be observed, the well-known critic, but an *Officer of the Custom House*, is a quite unmalicious essay in the form of a semi-dramatized and obviously burlesqued short story supposed to be told by Dr. Robert Norris. Steele may have had some hand in it, but the prose is unlike Steele's either in essay or play, and though it is unlike Pope's *Spectator* or *Guardian* style, it is unlike anyone else's, and must be ascribed to him. Take a speech of Dennis's:

Caitiffs stand off; unhand me, Miscreants! Is the Man whose whole Endeavours are to bring the Town to Reason mad? Is the Man who settles Poetry on the Basis of Antiquity mad? Dares anyone assert there is a *Peripataetia* in that vile piece that's foisted upon the Town for a Dramatick Poem? That Man is mad, the Town is mad, the World is mad. See *Longinus* in my right Hand, and *Aristotle* in my left; I am the only Man among the Moderns that support them. Am I to be assassinated?

Pope, we would think, was feeling his way towards dramatic writing, and the glorious high spirits exhibited in the *Frenzy* may have had more than a vague repercussion in *The What D'Ye Call It*, which, though properly ascribed to Gay, was to some extent at least contributed to by Rowe and Pope. That Pope had a hand in it was more than suspected by the Buttonians, who, together with Addison, had no relish for the burlesquing of Cato's reading of Plato which occurs near the end, and which anyone who had seen Addison's play would chuckle over. His only other dramatic excursion was whatever part he may have taken in *Three Hours after Marriage* where Gay, Pope, and Arbuthnot

> . . . boldly did adventure
> To Club a Farce by Tripartite Indenture,

a play which first embroiled him with Cibber. Pope's ventures as a playwright have little importance in themselves, but writing that sort of prose, or helping to write it, may have brought him greater ease in the dialogue form he was to some extent to adopt in his Imitations of Horace.

More important from the point of view of his immediate development as a man, and so his ultimate character as a poet, are the incessant attacks to which he was subject from the time that Dennis made his brutal retort. For most of them there was no justification whatever. They were attacks on his character, his honesty, his ingratitude, his greed, his physique, and his capacity to translate Homer. None of the brawling would matter very much, apart from the conception it gave him of the world of letters (so furnishing matter for *The Dunciad*); and much of it he took light-heartedly enough, in such things as the *Key to the Lock*, where, under the name of Esdras Barnivelt, he brilliantly and good-humouredly satirized political mania. Some of the clapper-clawing however, especially when the attacks seemed to threaten his poetical reputation and his livelihood as the translator of Homer, he felt more bitterly, and took such steps as the administering of an emetic to the grotesque Curll, and pursuing him with lampoons—which, however, probably did no more than tickle the pachydermatous hide. Though the period is important since in those years Pope was driven away from the Whigs at Buttons, into the arms of the more Tory Scriblerians, this event seeming to relate poetry with politics, and destroying for him any hope of tolerance, it might not have been of first importance but for the behaviour of Addison. The smaller fry might stink and sting, and it would not matter much; but it is easy to imagine that to find the great, and for many reasons justly revered, man capable of so much littleness was a decisive experience. It gave an extra dimension to Pope's moral emotions, imped his natural human dislikes with righteous indignation, and was perhaps the efficient cause that directed his genius into the channels of satire. We can therefore confine ourselves in the main to the Homer story, which, however, can be only briefly touched upon.

It is likely that Pope had for some time had in his mind the translation of Homer: it had been among his youthful exercises, and he had published some fragments. When he came, as he did in shall we say about 1712, to regard himself as lineal to the throne of Dryden, he no doubt felt that he might companion Dryden's Virgil with his own Homer. The Preface to his *Iliad* does rather more than suggest this. At the time there existed, after Chapman, whose diction and versification were by no means in the taste of the day, Hobbes and Ogilby who were inadequate and dull, and prose and blank verse translations from the French and Greek respectively by Broome, Oldisworth, and Ozell. The age was ready for a new version done in its own idiom. It was possibly Sir William Trumbull who first put the notion into Pope's head, but it was Addison, probably in the summer of 1713, who, applauding the notion when Pope brought it to him, had set him seriously to the task, as his letter of 6 October (if genuine) would indicate. For in October the proposals were out, and on 23 March Pope signed his contract with Lintot. We now know—though Pope never knew it—that on 31 May Tickell, Addison's young friend and protégé, a good poet and a very good classical scholar, signed a similar contract with Tonson. It seems quite clear that Addison, and perhaps others of his little Senate, were sponsoring a rival translation by which they hoped to humiliate Pope.

The first hint to reach Pope that anything was brewing against him was when in the late summer of 1714 he asked Addison—no doubt largely by way of compliment—if he would 'look over' his first Book of Homer; to which Addison replied that he regretted he could not, since he had just performed that office for a friend of his who was engaged on the same task, and to advise about both would smack of double dealing. The blow to Pope was more than a mere literary disappointment. It was like a betrayal. And it was perhaps from that time that began the war which was to occupy so much of Pope's time and genius, the war against the Dunces which was to have all the bitterness of a struggle for survival—the survival of certain personal values—rather than the detached calm of the Scriblerus Club. This is not the place in which to follow the details of the early parts of this campaign, the extraordinary waiting game which ensued between Pope and Lintot on the one hand, and Tickell and Tonson on the other; nor the violent, unjust, and scabrous defamatory attacks upon Pope by Thomas Burnet, George Duckett, and others, many of them of the Addison clan. The two editions or numbers of *Homerides*, *Æsop at the Bear-Garden*, issues of the *Grumbler* (Duckett's paper), the *Key to the What D'ye Call It*, and other events, including Pope's *Horrid and barbarous revenge by Poison on the body of Mr. Edmund Curll*, belong to biography rather than criticism. The complicated tale of the general defamation of Pope on almost every conceivable moral and physical ground, the Lady Mary Wortley Montagu imbroglio, the Cibber episode of *Three Hours after Marriage*, and so on, have been admirably dealt with by Professor George Sherburn, and may be glossed by reference to Norman Ault's work. What is important for the critic to note is the kind of feeling engendered in Pope by this attack on the work on which he was staking his poetic reputation and his financial security; and the fact that it brought forth the Atticus lines, which made Atterbury suggest to the poet in 1722 that his true bent lay in satire. But with Pope the satire was to come from the deeper levels. 'Who would not weep if Atticus were he!' is no mere literary hope or happy antithesis; it symbolizes the tragic sense implicit in the great third and last phase that was to follow.

The publication of both the translators' work hung fire; but Pope's volume of four Books appeared on 6 June to be followed two days later by Tickell's one. Addison and his faction did all they could to make Tickell's version prevail, some declaring outright that Pope's was comparatively worthless, Addison characteristically remarking that both versions were good, but that Tickell's had more Homer in it—whatever he might have meant by that. But the Pope party was too strong, and even the University of Oxford declared in his favour. Pope's adversary, as he said, sank before him without a blow. Tickell, however, in his Preface stated his intention of relinquishing the *Iliad*, the translation of which had fallen into far abler hands, adding that he published only to gain support for his proposed translation of the *Odyssey*. This surely was in the far future, for in the same year we find him soliciting subscriptions for a Lucan— in which Pope helped him—which in fact never appeared, the field being left clear for Rowe, whose *Pharsalia* is not the least of his achievements. Pope undoubtedly triumphed, and was able to continue the work free of fear of opposition. Nevertheless attacks on his Homer went on for some fifteen years, till after the criticisms aroused by the final Book of the *Odyssey* had died down. Dr. Johnson was not far wrong when he declared that in Spence 'Pope had the first experience of a critick without malevolence, who thought it as much his duty to display beauties as to expose faults; who censured with respect and praised with alacrity'.

We can now turn to the work itself, which occupied so much of Pope's major energies for so long. He brought to bear upon it all his powers of scholarship and poetic transformation. He got all the help he could from better scholars, Congreve, Rowe, and notably Parnell, who in 1717 produced his own version of the *Batrachomuomachia*; and once he had gone into the house at Twickenham largely withdrew from Grub Street and other literary concerns to devote himself to his Greek, his mother, and his friends. How far he had withdrawn is evidenced by Gay's lively, affectionate poem welcoming him on his return from Greece; how far he was absorbed we can judge from his methodical getting through the work—from thirty to fifty lines a day—how far his whole being was committed is evidenced by his telling Spence that it used to haunt him in nightmarish dreams. Though to us the work does not seem of the first importance in the Pope canon, to him it was in a sense the crown of his achievement.

His object in his translation of Homer was to make an English poem which would appeal to the people of his own time; and so much does it embody the ethos of the period, the common assumptions of the day, that Dr. E. M. W. Tillyard ranks it among English epics. Bentley's reported 'It's a very pretty poem, Mr. Pope, but you mustn't call it Homer', was quite beside the point in so far as it may have been meant as a criticism. If it was a very pretty poem, that was all that Pope cared about; he knew that it could not be Homer, certainly not for any classical scholar. What he had to do was to tell the story as Homer had it, in the sort of verse Homer used.

It suffices at present to observe of his Numbers [so Pope wrote in his Preface] that they flow with so much ease, as to make one imagine *Homer* had no other care than to transcribe as fast as the *Muses* dictated; and at the same time with so much Force and inspiriting Vigour, that they awaken and raise us like the Sound of a Trumpet. They roll along as a plentiful River, always in motion and always full; while we are born[e] away by a Tide of Verse, the most rapid, yet the most smooth imaginable.

'The most rapid, yet the most smooth imaginable.' Precisely! It would be no use presenting his readers with the flatness of Ogilby, or the splendid ruggedness of Chapman, which Keats preferred (as many do today). Even Dryden, who had performed patches of Homer, could be improved upon. Thus here criticism by comparison is inapplicable; at any rate we must allow Pope what Matthew Arnold allowed him—the essential speed. For us, perhaps, 'inspiriting vigour' is lacking, but yet:

> Thro' Blood, thro' Death, *Achilles* still proceeds
> O'er slaughter'd Heroes, and o'er rolling Steeds.
> As when avenging Flames with Fury driv'n
> On guilty Towns exert the Wrath of Heav'n;
> The Pale Inhabitants, some fall, some fly;
> And the red Vapours purple all the Sky.
> So rag'd *Achilles*: Death and Dire Dismay,
> And Toils, and Terrors, fill'd the dreadful Day.
> High on a Turret hoary *Priam* stands,
> And marks the Waste of his destructive Hands;
> Views, from his Arm, the *Trojan's* scatter'd Flight,
> And the near Hero rising on his Sight!
> No Stop, no Check, no Aid! With feeble Pace,
> And settled Sorrow on his aged Face,
> Fast as he could, he sighing quits the Walls;
> And thus, descending, on the Guards he calls;
> You to whose care our City Gates belong . . .

And whatever the reaction to such verse may be at any given literary phase, it has to be conceded that Pope knew perfectly well what he was doing, knew also where he was strong and where he was weak, why he used the couplet, the Homeric repetition of phrase, the Virgilian tone, and so on. He also knew exactly why he used the diction that he did, the famous 'diction' which copied by poorer poets in the wrong sort of poem became the type of language against which the Romantics quite rightly rebelled. But it was not the diction of Pope they were determined to expel from poetry, so much as the diction that Pope thought it 'decorous', that is fitting, to use when translating Homer, deliberately to give it an artificiality which would impart a certain ritual ceremony and a certain temporal distance to events and manners and modes of belief which could not be contemporary. He never dreamt of treating Horace in that way; had he done so, decorum itself would have been outraged.

It has too often been said that the couplet is no medium in which to translate Homer; but the fact remains that the two verse translations still most read are those of Chapman, whose *Iliad* is in rhymed sixteeners whose *Odyssey* is in heroic couplets, —and Pope's. Pope had no theoretical objection to blank verse, as is shown by his remark to Atterbury, who was always urging him to write in that form. But he knew he could not manage it. With the couplet he got at least speed, vividness, clarity, the form perhaps being all the more suitable since he deliberately heightened the pathos, here and there introducing Ovidian phrasing and even imagery. As we have seen, nobody at that time, at any rate till Thomson came, could freely handle blank verse. Even Fenton, who might have preferred it, and independently produced Book XI of the *Odyssey* 'in imitation of Milton', did better when translating for Pope in couplets, though how much the effect may owe to Pope's polishing it is impossible to say. Not that the couplet prevented Fenton from being Miltonic. We recognize his master when in Book I of 'Pope's' *Odyssey* we come across a line beginning 'Bitter constraint . . .'; and we wonder whether it is to Homer or to Milton that he is being faithful when we read the line

> With sweet, reluctant, amorous Delay,

and thus are divided in our vision between the Dardan plains and Paradise.

We might take an example or two to illustrate the diction

Pope elaborated for Homer; a very brief comparison with his other work will reveal the difference in idiom. Here, almost at random, from the *Iliad*:

> From Ship to Ship thus *Ajax* swiftly flew,
> No less the Wonder of the warring Crew,
> As furious, *Hector* thunder'd Threats aloud,
> And rush'd enrag'd before the *Trojan* Croud;
> Then swift invades the Ships, whose beaky Prores
> Lay rank'd contiguous on the bending Shores.
> So the strong Eagle from his airy Height,
> Who marks the Swans' or Cranes' embod'd Flight,
> Stoops down impetuous . . .

or take such a phrase as:

> but safe from Harms
> He stands impassive in the ethereal Arms.

And even in the short passages quoted we can see how Pope's treatment of the couplet itself is as different from what his use of it had been in *Eloisa to Abelard*, as it was to be in the *Epistle to Dr. Arbuthnot*, or even the far more formal *Essay on Man*. The effect is more plangent, the vowels more orotund, there is altogether a sense of the grandiose, which Pope was careful to preserve when deliberately mistranslating, or glozing over, words which carried in the England of his day less noble connotations than they had in Homer's Greece, such as the name 'ass'.

There is no need to labour these points. Pope has made most of them himself in his admirable Preface, at once so proudly confident and so humble, in which he dedicated the work, not to some would-be Maecenas, but to Congreve. His theory of translation was, as we would expect, that of his age, of Dryden and of Roscommon, whose verse *Essay on Translated Verse* was still the textbook, so to speak, of the would-be translator. A certain degree of adaptation was necessary, but this was what the age would expect. How much or how little the worth of a rendering would depend on the skill and personal poetic force of the translator can be judged by comparing Pope with Tickell, or realizing that when it came to the turn of the *Odyssey* three translators were involved, writing so much to pattern (though Pope certainly revised to some extent) that the average reader would be unable to assign the books to the right poet. The near

identity of many of Tickell's lines to Pope's may have been due
to Tickell's having seen some Pope manuscripts, but it is considered more likely that mere coincidence is explanation
enough. Certainly it was quite easy for Pope to incorporate
some of Tickell's ideas in his revised edition without any incongruity being apparent. Perhaps the fairest comparison between
the two rivals was made by Tickell himself, in a critique printed
for the first time in Mr. R. E. Tickell's *Life*. He is scrupulously
fair, sometimes awarding the palm to Pope, sometimes not
stinting the praise for himself. For instance:

> When I began to read these translations of the *Iliad*, I was im-
> patient to see how νεφεληγερέτης or *the Raiser of Clouds* was trans-
> lated. I could never be satisfied with *Cloud-compeller* which really
> conveys no Idea to an English Reader. This I was the more curious
> to learn, because the whole Philosophy of Thunder is couched in
> this Epithet. According to every opinion Mr. T. has given us a most
> sublime Interpretation:
>
> > To whom the God Whose Hand the Tempest forms,
> > Drives Clouds on Clouds and blackens Heav'n with Storms,
> > Thus wrathful answer'd:
>
> Mr. P. translated it thus:
>
> > She said, & sighing thus the God replies,
> > Who rolls the Thunder o'er the vaulted Skies
>
> which, in my humble opinion, is a mean, unphilosophical Transla-
> tion, and seems borrowed from the Play-house, where the Tragical
> Engineer makes Thunder by rolling a large Mustard-ball over the
> Ceiling.

an objection contemporaries might have considered more valid
than we are likely to do. For us it might well seem that Tickell
had paid too high a price for his 'sublimity', and consider that
the reply of Zeus was indeed rather in the nature of a sigh
than 'wrathful'; the comparison may serve to show how tactful
Pope was in his 'heightening'.

The venture was so successful, in spite of the bitter and malicious criticisms hurled at Pope from Grub Street, that he decided
to follow it up with a translation of the *Odyssey*. The event had
proved him secure enough in his scholarship, and a reply to
critics was available in the Life of Zoilus prefixed to Parnell's
Battle of the Frogs and Mice, where Pope's methods of translation
were defended. Nevertheless, Parnell being dead, he could rely

a little on the help of his collaborators Broome and Fenton, who took half the work off his hands. To have done the whole would have been too wearisome. Matters were somewhat delayed, however, thanks to the political cloud which for a moment threatened him, partly on account of his friendship with Atterbury, who was exiled in 1721, and partly because of his edition of the Duke of Buckingham's (Mulgrave's) *Works*, for which he had made himself responsible without troubling to look for Jacobite implications. Thus the further Homer 'undertaken' by him (the expression being used to gloze over the fact that he was not the sole translator) was not begun until 1723; the first three volumes were published in April 1725, the remainder in June of the next year.

But while waiting for the political cloud to blow over—for while it threatened he could not solicit subscriptions—he had embarked on a piece of work for which he was to be paid outright, namely his edition of Shakespeare. It was not a work any Scriblerian should have undertaken, since it necessarily involved some of that pedantry to which the Club was sworn enemy. In many ways it is matter for wonder that it was so well done. Pope had at least an inkling of what the job was —which was more than Rowe had had—and collected a good number of Quartos as well as the Folios. 'He was the first that knew, at least,' Dr. Johnson cautiously adds, 'the first that told, by what helps the text might be improved.' If, as Professor D. Nichol Smith says, he approached the work as an executor rather than an editor, the attitude was not without its value. His Preface is impeccable, and had he carried out the doctrines there laid down he would have performed a far more useful work than he did. As matters turned out, the self-styled 'conservative' editor made many outrageous emendations—often from ignorance of the period—though it is true to say that some of his emendations, made from the ear and intuition of a poet rather than from the knowledge and genius of a scholar, have held the field. But when in the next year Theobald, who may claim to be the first of our great Shakespearian scholars, brought out his *Shakespeare Restored*, it was clear to everyone that Pope had attempted something outside his province. Grub Street howled with glee, and for once Pope was really hurt, not by the accustomed abuse, but by the justice of Theobald's criticism; and although he struck back, not so much by making Theobald King of the Dunces as by the Notes ascribed to him in *The Dunciad*, he came to realize that he had made a mistake. The attempt, no doubt, had been worth while; but perhaps its somewhat humiliating conclusion was just as well. For Pope would never be tempted to edit anyone else's work; he would not wish to spare the time and energy for any further large translation: he was free to return to the writing of his own poetry, from his experience in verse-writing and his attention to Shakespeare still more perfectly equipped as a craftsman to make effective what he wanted to say as a poet.

The whole phase, however, from at least 1717 if not from 1714, had 'placed' Pope in his own mind in relation to his fellows, whether writers or not. He now had very precise opinions as to the characters of the people among whom he moved, as to the nature of the society in which he and they together had their being, and as to the kind of position he himself might wish to occupy.

PART TWO

1700–1740

VII

THE DRAMA

THE story of the drama in this period is one of decline, a
story not without its interest for those whom the problem
of literary form excites, especially in its relation to subject-
matter. Briefly speaking, a form attempted to survive into an
age with which it had nothing to do. It was no use to try to
carry Heroic Tragedy into the age of mercantilism and enlightenment, nor to present the conventions of the seventeenth-
century comedy of manners to an audience which resented the
manners and did not understand the conventions. But the
theatre, being, as Shaw told us, the most conservative of all
institutions, went straight on, with the result that it became
merely imitative in form, and so, naturally, was destroyed by the
new elements which the temper and thought of the time, not to
mention the social life, forced it to introduce. The 'legitimate'
theatre to all intents and purposes died, the only contribution
which the age made being the ballad-opera, and that strange
production, Lillo's *London Merchant* (1731), born 150 years
before its time. There is, in short, nothing in the drama of this
period which is at once first class and characteristic of the day.
The prose of the age has long been conceded a peculiar virtue;
its poetry adds something definite to the canon. But the theatre,
with the exception of the items noted above, has nothing to
offer except the spectacle of an old form being corrupted by
vital elements it is unable to absorb—though the question ob-
trudes itself as to whether these elements were really such as the
drama could at that time incorporate in itself, and whether
they were not more properly taken into the novel, which they
transformed, and, in fact, exploded into a new form. The

elements were, we might prelude here, domesticity, and the mental and moral states proper to the vigorous eighteenth-century middle class.

At the opening of the period, comedy, to be sure, gave signs of vitality; but even a flicker of new life was absent from tragedy, and Steele expressed the state of affairs beautifully, if with a touch of exaggeration. Isaac Bickerstaff, discussing tragedies in *Tatler* 22, tells us that he has by him

. . . in my Book of Common Places, enough to enable me to finish a very Sad one by the Fifth of the next Month [which gave him six days at most]. I have the Farewell of a General, with a Truncheon in his Hand, dying for Love, in Six Lines. I have the Principles of a Politician (who does all the Mischief in the Play), together with his Declaration on the Vanity of Ambition in his last Moments, express'd in a Page and a half. I have all my Oaths ready, and my Similies want nothing but Application. I won't pretend to give you an Account of the Plot, it being the same Design upon which all Tragedies have been writ for several Years last past; and from the beginning of the First Scene, the Frequenters of the House may know, as well as the Author, when the Battle is to be fought, the Lady to yield, and the Hero proceed to his Wedding and Coronation.

The criticism in the main was just; tragedies continued to be written in the same design, not only of plot, but of character and diction; there is no marked difference between what Rowe produced at the beginning of the century, what Young gave the public in the middle of our period, and what Thomson wrote at the end. The thing was dead. However, it made quite an attractive corpse when laid out, with all the floral wreaths given it from Rowe onwards.

But before looking at what was being written for the theatre, it may be useful to glance at the conditions prevailing in the theatrical world. If the split in the acting profession which had occurred in 1695, when Betterton had led most of the older actors away to the playhouse in Lincoln's Inn Fields, leaving Christopher Rich to manage, or mismanage, the official building in Drury Lane, had widened the possible scope for dramatic writers, it had also called forth a spirit of rather unhealthy rivalry. Each theatre was forced to pander to an audience without the cultivation necessary to appreciate drama as something better than vapid entertainment, with the result

that there was a lowering of standards; and it is to be suspected that, as is normal with public entertainers, the managers
underrated the brains and sensibility of the people they wished
to attract. Burnaby[1] was probably right in his diagnosis
when he made Sir Solomon Empty in *The Reform'd Wife* (1700)
say:

If I was to write a Play . . . I'd have something to divert every
Body. I'd have your Atheism to please the Wits—some affectation to
entertain the Beaux, a Rape or two to engage the Ladies; and I'd
bring in the Bears, before every Act, to secure an interest in the
Upper Gallery.

Motteux, indeed, in his Prologue to Mrs. Pix's amiable light
comedy *The Innocent Mistress* (1697), makes the actors complain
of the competition of 'scaling Monkies' and 'dancing Swans'.
But for the warnings of his architect, Rich would have produced
an elephant on his stage. Spectacle became important in the
theatres, which vied with one another in the luridness of hell-
fires accompanying rival productions of *Faustus*; there were
what we should call variety turns, such as 'the girl from Devonshire', and, menacing all serious drama, the pantomime and
harlequinade; while the increasing attraction of the Italian
opera, 'the silly diversion of the nobility' as the staling 'legitimate' theatre scornfully termed it, for some seasons nearly
deprived the actors of a living. All these intrusions were hardly
encouraging to the serious dramatist.

Perhaps as good a view as any to be obtained of the literary
drama is that suggested in *A Comparison of the Two Stages* (1702),
possibly by Gildon, a dialogue of mediocre literary value but of
great interest to the literary historian. Possibly the most important side-light it throws on the scene is to be found in the
fact that Betterton, when at his wit's end for a success, fell back
n Shakespeare. The dialogue tells us:

Sullen. . . . the whim fell in very luckily with the humour of the
People, and every body now run to renew their acquaintance
with *Shakespear*.
Critick. I think the people were never more in the right, for no

[1] William Burnaby, 1672/3–1706, of Irish extraction, became a Commoner of
Merton in 1691. Two years later he entered the Middle Temple, where he stayed
some two or three years. After some time at Malmesbury, he lived in London, as
'a fashionable wit', and dabbled in alchemy.

Author ever writ with that Felicity, or had such a prodigious compass of Thought . . ;

and it may as well be said here, once for all in this work, that it was during our period that Shakespeare came to be generally recognized as the supreme figure in our drama. 'No man of taste', Joseph Welwood declared in his Preface to Rowe's *Lucan* (1718), 'but pays to Shakespeare's Memory the homage that's due to one of the greatest Genius's that ever appear'd in Dramatick Poetry'; and Welwood, a physician, represented the ordinary educated man's taste. Later, Gibbon could refer to the 'idolatry for the gigantic genius of Shakespeare, which is inculcated from our infancy as the first duty of an Englishman'. Shakespeare then was, as he is today, the somewhat grudgingly admitted standard of excellence for all drama with any pretence to literature, a drama which had only an accidental connexion with the popular, clever, meaningless theatre of the time, best represented by Mrs. Centlivre. It is not without interest to note that Rich countered Betterton's move with another season of Ben Jonson, not the humour comedies, but the big three, the *Fox*, the *Alchemist*, and the *Silent Woman*. It is, moreover, noteworthy that in *A Comparison*, the comedy picked out as having something new in it is Steele's *The Funeral*—his first venture— and the opinion given that among the new writers of tragedy the only author worth considering is Rowe, though only for his diction.

The continuity in the drama is best shown in comedy, which we may take first; for whereas all the tragedians representing the old tradition were dead or silent—Dryden's last contribution had been the Secular Masque in Vanbrugh's *Pilgrim*—in comedy the comedy of manners overlapped the turn of the century in Cibber and Vanbrugh, and carried on to some extent in Farquhar and others. And if the form—and the content even more than the form—did gradually change, the change was hardly noticeable, and there was no acute controversy; whereas in tragedy there was internecine strife between those who approved and those who opposed the doctrine of poetical justice. The only three comedians who really count, Congreve having ceased to write for the stage, are Vanbrugh, very much the man of his day, saying and feeling what the average man thought and said; Steele saying what he hoped everybody ought to feel; and Farquhar bringing a satirical edge to bear upon aspects of society never at all considered by the writers of the comedy of manners. To distinguish between a school of manners and a school of humours is of small use. Rich's revival of Ben Jonson, and the lesser homage usually paid to Shadwell, perhaps indicate some break away from the manners tradition; but the boundaries between the forms were always vague, and either ingredient is essential in any form of comedy. And at all events, as Professor Allardyce Nicoll remarks: 'More than half of the plays of the time cannot in any wise be esteemed purely of one kind or another. Manners, humours, burlesque, sentimentalism—all often enter into the make-up of one single comedy.'

Thus it may be more profitable to take account of the general ethos—Collier's[1] attack in 1698, which later skirmishers prolonged; the appearance of various Societies for the Reformation of Manners; the foundation by William III of 'The Society for the Propagation of the Gospell in Forreigne Parts' on 6 June 1701, together with the likely responses of an audience far more 'popular' than previously. The question was: what kind of 'instruction' was to be imparted by this particular form of literature? Morals, of course, had always been preached: Wycherley, for example, had demanded a brutal honesty, a clearance of moral cant from the mind, and Congreve had called for sensibility with respect to other people. But now the moral would scarcely seem to be individual at all. There was nothing fierce about it, nothing exquisite—merely a conforming, for whatever reason, even funk, to the accepted moral usages of the day.

Vanbrugh, perhaps, never took the obligation very seriously. 'The business of comedy,' he threw off in the *Short Vindication* which was his answer to Collier, 'is to show people what they should do, by representing them on the stage doing what they should not.' But Cibber,[2] whose influence as dramatist, actor, and manager runs through the whole period, was more representative, and he gradually conformed quite honestly to the

---

[1] Jeremy Collier, 1650–1726, was educated at the Ipswich Free School, and Caius College, Cambridge. Violently opposed to the Revolution, he was imprisoned for a short while in 1688. He was outlawed in 1696, fled, but came back unmolested in 1697. In 1713 he was consecrated by a non-juring bishop.

[2] Colley Cibber, 1671–1757, had his schooling at Grantham, and in 1690 became an actor. Successful as such and as a playwright, in 1709 he became one of the three managers of Drury Lane. In 1730 he was made Poet Laureate; and in 1732 sold his interest in the theatre.

new vogue. He jibes a little in the epilogue to *Love's Last Shift* in saying:

> He's lewd for above four acts, Gentlemen.
> For faith, he knew, when once he'd changed his Fortune,
> And reform'd his Vice, 'twas time—to drop the Curtain:

having in the first four acts given a loose rein to the most lubric fancy. In his *Love makes a Man*, of December 1700, he attempts to redeem the freedom of his first acts by a good deal of high-falutin cant at the end, but by the time of *The Careless Husband*, acted at the end of 1704, he had learnt a more subtle tactic, and came at least half-way to the belief that a comedy was almost avowedly a lay sermon, though he can combine his profession of faith with a sly dig at Collier's *Short View*:

> *Lady Betty.* Lampoons and Plays, Madam, are only things to be laughed at.
> *Lord Morelove.* Plays now indeed one need not be so much afraid of, for since the late short-sighted View of 'em, Vice may go on and prosper, the Stage hardly dare show a Vicious Person speaking like himself, for fear of being call'd Prophane for exposing him.
> *Lady Easy.* 'Tis hard indeed, when People won't distinguish between what's meant for Contempt, and what for Example.

By the time, however, he came to write his Apology (1740), his conversion was whole-hearted:

> I say then, that as I allow nothing is more liable to debase and corrupt the Minds of a People, than a licentious Theatre: so under a just, and proper Establishment, it were possible to make it, as apparently the School of Manners and of Virtue.

'It *were* possible to make it'; there perhaps was the rub; for however much practising playwrights might reform—though to be sure the warning to comedy writers, 'But now no luscious scenes must lard their Plays' (to quote again the Prologue Motteux wrote for Mrs. Pix), was scarcely regarded—the old comedies, such as *The Country Wife*, remained a certain draw. The old convention, perhaps, made it seem to the audiences sufficiently removed from the life they knew to allow them to enjoy it without a twinge either of moral fear or domestic alarm. Steele, of course, was always the moralist, 'all the time on his good behaviour', as Hazlitt remarked, 'as though writing a

comedy was no very creditable employment and the ultimate
object of his ambition was a dedication to the Queen'; and his
last play, *The Conscious Lovers*, was in fact dedicated to the King.
The Preface informed the reader that: '. . . the greatest Effect
of a Play in reading is to excite the Reader to go see it; and
when he does so, it is then a Play has the Effect of Example and
Precept.' The Prologue, by Welsted, made the case plainer still:

> Your Aid most humbly sought, then *Britons* lend,
> And Lib'ral Mirth like Lib'ral Men, defend.
> No more let Ribaldry, with Licence writ,
> Usurp the Name of Eloquence or Wit;
> No more let lawless Farce uncensur'd go,
> The lewd dull Gleanings of a *Smithfield* Show.
> 'Tis yours, with Breeding to refine the Age,
> To Chasten Wit, and Moralize the Stage.

Such an exhortation was hardly calculated to quicken an
audience and render it all agog for comic pleasure; yet in spite
of this damper the play was a great success, running for eighteen
nights—a long run for those days.

Such a close relation between art and life could not but be
ruinous; to load aesthetics with directly stated morals is to
deprive it of its wings. For the method of art is indirect. It
produces its ultimate effect by first inducing a mood of detachment. Thus the comic spirit fled to farce, though the only
notable ones till we come to Fielding are those in which Gay
was the ruling spirit, to wit *The What D'Ye Call It* (1715)—a
tragi-comi-pastoral-farce—and *Three Hours after Marriage*
(1717), in which Pope and Arbuthnot each took a hand. Gay,
however, was to show his real genius in the different form of the
mock-heroic ballad opera. With this preliminary we can look
at some of the more prominent authors.

Cibber, who comes first on the scene, need not detain us long.
His comedies have, it is true, vestiges of ideas. His main theme
throughout was the marriage, basically sound enough, broken
by the 'affected' humour of the typical Restoration hero or
heroine healed by experience on the one hand, and devotion on
the other. All the time, in effect, he is vulgarizing Dryden's
Marriage-à-la-Mode, adding for irrelevant relief, the egregious
fop, here vulgarizing Etherege's Sir Fopling Flutter, his first
re-creation, Sir Novelty Fashion, being his best. But he had a
sense of the stage, and had he been less pleased with himself

might have penetrated deeper. The attraction of most of his comedies must have been the blatantly fleshly treatment of sex combined with a briskness of movement that masks the improbability of the action. His first play, *Love's Last Shift* (1696), was an attempt to inculate a goody-goody moral, and his reformed rake proved an easy butt for Vanbrugh. Lewdness for four acts was an unconvincing preparation for a virtuous fifth, but the attempt chimed with the mood to which Collier so vociferously gave expression; and since, in Congreve's well-known phrase, the play contained a great many things which were like wit but were not really wit at all—so making no demands on the brains of the audience—the play took. Perhaps —to make a selection of two or three of the most successful of the plays of this voluminous writer—*Love makes a Man* (1700) is a trifle less luscious; but it is in the main no more than a cheap 'thriller', quite impossible both physically and psychologically, with a good deal of moral cant at the end. *The Non-Juror* (1717), derived largely from *Tartuffe*, is confessedly a political play written to kill the dead dog of Jacobitism, so dubious in its working out that Pope was able to make fun of it as insidious Jacobite propaganda; yet oddly enough the young heroine in this play, Maria, is a charmingly amusing coquette, who might be described as a kind of sub-Millamant. For all its intrinsic weakness, Cibber's work cannot be denied a brittle vivacity, such as will in some part account for its contemporary success.

Following close upon his heels came a far more important figure, that of John Vanbrugh,[1] who goaded into mirthful protest at the rank improbability of *Love's Last Shift*, in the same year produced his counterblast, *The Relapse; or Virtue in Danger*, a sub-title of some use in answering Collier. But Vanbrugh's notion in writing comedies was frankly to amuse the honest gentlemen of the town, and 'to divert (if possible) some part of their spleen, in spite of their wives and their taxes'. Nothing astonished him more than to find himself accused of 'blasphemy and bawdy' by Collier, and to be told by the Society for the Reformation of Manners that he had 'debauched the stage

[1] Sir John Vanbrugh, 1664–1726, was sent to complete his education in France after leaving the King's School, Chester. In 1686 he obtained a commission in the army. In 1696 Captain Vanbrugh, as he then was, turned playwright; in 1701 he began to build Castle Howard, and the next year became Controller of the Royal Works, viz. chief architect to the Crown. In 1703 he became Clarenceux King at Arms, and in 1705 began to build Blenheim. He was knighted in 1714.

beyond the looseness of all former times'. If so, he had done it in all innocence by the fact of confusing two kinds of realism, the intellectual and emotional realism of Congreve, with the factual realism of, shall we say, Mrs. Behn. This deprived his comedies of the detachment, the aesthetic distance, necessary to the form he thought he was continuing, an effect enhanced by the happy naturalness of his dialogue, which sometimes descended into being no phrasing at all: though that his phrasing has some of the old tang is evident when we compare passages of *The Relapse* with their parallels in Sheridan's *Trip to Scarborough*. What he brought, however, was a robust vigour lacking in most of his contemporaries, sound common sense based on experience, a real inventiveness unusual in the theatre of his day, and a considerable amount of the spirit of comedy. If in Sir Tunbelly Clumsy and Hoyden, and in much of the movement of his plays, he went back to an Elizabethan mode, Sir Tunbelly and his daughter are real creations in that mode, and prove his originality. Lord Foppington is Cibber's Sir Novelty Fashion raised to the peerage, and also raised to a higher degree of the comic. If fops abound in the plays of the time—as no doubt they did in life as travesties of Beau Nash who lorded it at Bath—Vanbrugh's creation has become in fact, and not only in Foppington's own view, the head of that prevailing party. He is more than 'the quintessence of nullity'; more than 'the personification of the foppery and folly of dress and appearance in full feather' as Leigh Hunt and Hazlitt described him, since he has a resilient inner core based on a sense of himself as a man of integrity, and the dignity which should go with aristocratic pretensions.

Vanbrugh had at least one of the qualities of a great comic writer, an ingrained contempt for all cant and humbug; but this a little tied him down to everyday realism, which, however, he turned to admirable effect in his husband and wife quarrel scenes, as in *The Provok'd Wife* (1697), and especially in his unfinished posthumous play, completed by the amiable Cibber, *A Journey to London*, produced in 1728 under the title of *The Provok'd Husband*. These scenes, carried out with a deal of humour, suggest that Vanbrugh might have been a master of domestic comedy; but his interest in the drama was comparatively short-lived, for from the beginning of the century his thoughts were 'hugely turned to architecture'.

His other plays are all adaptations, almost we might say, free translations. *Æsop* from Boursault (1697) is a dreary performance, perhaps written in the interests of a morality which 'honest Van' accepted readily enough but was not greatly interested in; *The Pilgrim* is from Fletcher (1700) and so on, the best possibly being *The Confederacy* from Dancourt in 1705, which gives us the wholly delightful, garrulous Mrs. Amlet, the dressmaker, literally breathing the ethics of a whole class. And it might be taken as a decline in general vigour of comedy at the time that so many plays were adaptations of older English plays or more usually of recent foreign ones. Not that, of course, this kind of borrowing was new; what is significant is the extent of it in this age. There was a good deal too much of 'the frippery of crucified Molière' to argue a healthy state of affairs. Vanbrugh largely breathed his own gustful self into his adaptations, but though he produced something with considerable 'go' about it, he destroyed his originals by missing the point, without substituting any idea of equal worth. He grew content to be derivative; his characters are often remembered characters, his verisimilitude often relying on similitude.

But at least he helped to break fresh ground, and with him a breeze of life swept through the theatre. In this his works are in marked contrast to those of that strange figure William Burnaby who attempted, it would seem, to write comedy in the old witty mode, but failed to see that its movement had to bear some relation to that of real life, and that its emotions have to be sharp. His plays were not successful, but they have an interest for the student of literature in illustrating the bankruptcy of a convention which is no longer fit to reflect the changing temper of an age—or at least of an audience. In his plays, *The Reform'd Wife* (1700), *The Ladies' Visiting Day* (1701), *The Modish Husband* (1702)—we may ignore *Love Betray'd* (1703), a miserable travesty of *Twelfth Night*—his people come on the stage to fire off at each other a series of epigrams and apophthegms, which coming as they do from a translator of the *Satyricon*, often have a certain pithy cogency; but so divorced are they from the realities of the social life either as known to people in actuality or on the stage, that the plays are wanting in one of the essentials Farquhar was to stress in his *Discourse upon Comedy*, namely that of enabling actors to show their art.

Farquhar[1] was the only dramatic writer of any comic power at the beginning of the century who managed to infuse a new spirit into the old form, partly by setting side by side with it a spirit critical of matters which had hitherto lain outside its view. Had he not died at the age of twenty-nine it is possible that he might have discovered some way of expressing the ethos of the century—its domestic sense, its sentimentality, its notion of social morality—in comic form. By his last two plays, he stands out from among his contemporaries for sheer originality, for zest, for acute criticism of social assumptions, and a sense of the stage that transcends tricks. He was brilliantly alert to the ridiculous, while at the same time wielding the Meredithian sword of common sense, and was aware that the method of art is indirect—that comedy must primarily amuse, though it may incidentally teach: it is no mere 'agreeable vehicle for counsel and reproof'. Incidental, certainly, must have been any teaching on the plane of sexual morality of his first play, *Love and a Bottle* (1699), where the love exhibited is redolent rather of a late lascivious reign than of the decorum of William III's; there is, however, a touch of romantic comedy of the girl masquerading as a page (though Wycherley also made use of that Elizabethan trick), common enough in the plays of the next twenty years. In so far as Farquhar shows any originality here it is in his satire of the young fop up from Oxford, learning to dance and push (fence) and sing, an originality not so much in the theme as in Farquhar's zestful enjoyment of it all. He rejoices in the fool as much as he enjoys mocking at the folly. But his next few plays, *The Constant Couple* (1699), *Sir Harry Wildair* (1701) and its sequel, *The Inconstant* (1702), together with *The Twin Rivals* acted at the end of the same year, are dreary rehashes of the theme of *Love's Last Shift*. In them the hero, pursuing his unselective amours through four acts, suddenly vows fidelity to some heroine whom he has approached in the belief that she is a prostitute, or who has—with an interlude as a page—returned from a supposed grave, all being of an unreality both of fact and of sentiment redeemed only by a certain inventiveness of plot and liveliness of conventional

[1] George Farquhar, 1677-1707, was at the age of seventeen entered as a Sizar at Trinity College Dublin, but was (probably) expelled. He commenced actor in Dublin, but in 1698 transferred to London as a playwright. In the same year he obtained a commission in the Earl of Orrery's regiment, but sold out without having seen active service.

dialogue. 'What low pert comedy e'en Farquhar writ' is an understandable comment in the context of these plays. Here and there, it is true, there is a telling phrase, something revealing a mind at work; and in the last we are conscious of a growling discomfort somewhere in the background; but on the whole this Farquhar is merely the able hack playwright earning his sparse living by turning out the expected machine-made goods.

Then after some four years' interval (apart from an adaptation from the French) there appeared *The Recruiting Officer*, the scene laid well outside the tedious precincts of fashionable London, the characters on the whole free of the deadening eroticism of those in Farquhar's previous plays, the themes the live ones of the day—chiefly the recruitment of men for the War of Spanish Succession—the subsidiary figures freshly observed, and a great sense of fun pervading the whole wholesome atmosphere; then in 1707 *The Beaux's Stratagem*, the best of all his work. It is, of course, absurd to say that he in any way approaches Congreve in excellence—except possibly in contrivance of plot, where Congreve was clumsy; there is no modulation of phrasing, no pondered sentiment, no values above the commonplace. But Farquhar brought to English society that cool, appraising glance, that sense of the falsity of assumptions, that mocking critical spirit which is so often the gift of the Irishman. He is, in a sense, the Shaw of his time. He had no very subtle sense of comedy, as is shown by his *Discourse upon Comedy*, which is chiefly devoted to scourging academic critics; but he had an eye for the comic and the incongruous, and a feel for what would go on the stage, including the unexpected. His people in his last two plays are no longer puppets; they are flesh and blood filled with vitality, sometimes a stage vitality (and that is a good deal) but more often that of real life. For the highwayman, when told on his capture 'if you have a short prayer, say it' to retort, 'Sir, I have no Prayer at all; the Government has provided a Chaplain to say Prayers for us on these Occasions', is as far-reaching as it is delightfully surprising, and needs no gloss. The people in both these plays are likeable where they are meant to be, and we feel that Farquhar was possessed of a real humanity lacking in most of his contemporaries.

Steele, from the point of view of high comedy, is on a lower level; yet it is a relief to turn to his plays after a session with Cibber or Burnaby, for at least his people speak with the voices of human beings, and their emotions are such as we should share, in the main, if ever we were to find ourselves in the wildly improbable situations in which Steele places them without, apparently, a tremor. His first play, *The Funeral, or Grief-à-la-Mode* (1701), though based on a situation difficult to swallow, has originality of material, and is full of a sense, if not of the high comic, at least of enormous fun. 'Gildon' was right in classing it as farce rather than comedy, for it is based, to use Dryden's phrase, on what is monstrous and chimerical; but there are in it admirable scenes of comic realism, as in the parade of the undertaker's mourners, while the whole thing served as a happy antidote to *The Christian Hero*, the seriousness of which had considerably perturbed Steele's brother-officers. This was really Steele's sole original contribution to the theatre, for his next play, *The Lying Lover* (1703), derives largely from Corneille's *Le Menteur*, just as *The Tender Husband* (1705) borrows considerably from Molière's *Le Sicilien: ou l'Amour Peintre*, while *The Conscious Lovers* (1722) owes at least two acts to Terence's *Andria*. He distorts his originals even more than Vanbrugh did the plays he borrowed from Dancourt, and though this is in a sense a virtue, in that his plays are further removed from translation, in the result the content seems all the more inappropriate to the form. Yet Steele cannot be denied vigour, movement, and a competence in dramatic handling. He is even now readable, and might be actable because his creatures speak an understandable language conformable with understandable emotions. And he must be allowed the originality which introduces into a form even the element which will destroy it. He is the first example of the sentimentalists who wrote, to quote Hazlitt again, those 'do-me-good, lack-a-daisical, whining make-believe comedies . . . where the author tries in vain to be merry and wise in the same breath'. It was one importantly characteristic side of the early eighteenth-century make-up, and Steele was the first to state it roundly, and bring it into prominence. His plays are, of course, permeated with the domestic sense and domestic virtues—not too evident in the conduct of his own life—and a constant theme with him is the crassness of marriages arranged by parents with a view to good settlements, as opposed to marriages of love. This must have been a reaction fairly commonly felt in the new middle class, for it is largely the theme of

Mrs. Haywood's sole comedy *A Wife to be Let* (1723), a not unamusing piece with a gay handling of a fantastic plot, where at least the couple chosen by the parents are shown to be deeply unsuitable marriage partners. But if Steele's plays have only a minor value in themselves, they are significant as a symbol, and were important as an influence. They are part of the movement which culminated in the *comédie larmoyante* which they did so much better in France than in England that there it exists in its own right as a distinctive form. Symbolic also, and of dread significance, are the plays of Mrs. Carroll, better known as 'the celebrated Mrs. Centlivre',[1] who began her career as a playwright in 1703. It is difficult to imagine anything sillier or emptier, and their popularity does more than anything to attest the extremely low level of taste in the new middle-class audiences. Mrs. Centlivre was one of those writers who have what is known as 'a sense of the theatre' and little other sense at all. Her plays are sheer comedies of intrigue and situation, of silly intrigue and obvious situation. They belong to the history of the theatre rather than to literary history. Again to make a selection, it may be said that *The Gamester* (1705), from Regnard's *Le Joueur*, is a brisk enough play, made up of counters, devoid of any of the grace, the light touch with reality, the intellectual amusement which distinguishes Regnard's work. Mrs. Centlivre spoils it by romanticizing it crudely, disguising her heroine as a man, and giving the play a happy ending. *The Busy-Body* (1709) is an empty comedy of intrigue, without any reality of emotion whatsoever, but *A Bold Stroke for a Wife* (1719), though equally a comedy of intrigue, is more amusing, and is at least free of the sham sex-antagonism which the writers of the Restoration decadence dragged on into an unsuitable ethos. Her butts are the fine gentleman, the virtuoso, the trader, and the Quaker. Nothing very original there, it is true; but still, the change is refreshing. Mrs. Centlivre would hardly be worthy of notice in the company of the others here mentioned, but that she seems in a curious way to have anticipated the light, frivolous, drawing-room comedy of such as the Colemans and Mrs. Inchbald, which captured the stage in about the 1760's, and marked the death of any comedy

---

[1] Susanna Centlivre, *c.* 1667–1723, *née* Freeman, married at the age of sixteen, but twice widowed before the end of the century, took to playwriting under her then name of Carroll. In 1706 she married Joseph Centlivre, chief cook to Queen Anne.

worthy of the name until the late middle of the nineteenth century. There were, certainly, to be found here and there plays which might be called 'something different', such as Charles Shadwell's[1] popular *Fair Quaker of Deal, or, The Humours of the Navy* (1710), which though vapid in sentiment and absurd as regards plot and denouement introduced naval types treated on hereditary Shadwell lines; a second play dealing with the army was a failure, as were the rest of Shadwell's numerous attempts, though he had a period of popularity in Dublin. It was, of course, Gay, who sowed the seeds of something new in *The What D'Ye Call It* (1715). It is largely part of the Scriblerian anti-pastoral spoofing; but mixed with a certain actuality of theme—recruiting for the army, the place of the country squire, and a measure of literary criticism (of Rymer on *Othello*, of Addison's *Cato*)—it provided a mixture which was new, and appealed to many levels in the audience. It is varied and light; it acts well; and it contains that mock-ballad ''Twas when the Seas were roaring' which is so charming as to be as often as not, indeed more often than not, impercipiently quoted as an admirable example of the ballad proper. The play is a delightful trifle, but like all Gay's trifles it has a point, as indeed has the heavier-handed *Three Hours after Marriage*. This play probably remains unread, though it has some passages which are lively enough, in spite of the too forced satire of the fossilist Woodward—Arbuthnot's butt—and of Dennis, the subject of Pope's attention. It was, however, *The Beggar's Opera* (1727) which gave Gay his rank as a playwright. Refused by Cibber, it was taken over by John Rich, who had succeeded his father Christopher in 1714, and it made, as Dr. Johnson records the saying, Rich gay and Gay rich, running for over sixty nights during each of two successive seasons, thus easily beating the hitherto most popular play, Addison's *Cato*.

If it showed vice in its most odious aspect, as Swift said, very justly if we keep in mind the utter irresponsibility of the criminals involved, it delighted the onlookers by its sheer exuberance, the frolicsome reversal of all values, its fun, its consistency within itself, and the charming songs set to tunes everybody knew. It gaily mocked what the audiences were prepared to

---

[1] Charles Shadwell, d. 1720, probably served in the army in Portugal, and was later supervisor of Excise in Kent.

mock—the heroic, the Italian Opera, driving the latter out of Town for one season at least, the under-age adulation of the dare-devil—and it touched on topical points especially in its side hits at politicians, an element probably exaggerated in retrospect, since the *Craftsman*, No. 85 of 17 February 1728, had to rub the point home, if it did not actually suggest it. It was, as already noted, a Scriblerian product, being to some extent the 'Newgate pastoral' Swift had urged Gay to write some years earlier, but it was its originality of form that captivated the public; it was the first of the ballad-operas which held the stage till after the end of the century, and eventually developed into the musical comedy of the late nineteenth. Gay may possibly have got a hint from Addison's strange production *Rosamond* (1707), which in parts so oddly adumbrates musical comedy; but even so, 'Whether this new drama was the product of judgement or of luck' as Dr. Johnson was to comment, 'the praise of it must be given to the inventor'. And it had in it, as recent revivals attest, the elements of permanence, because although human values are reversed, they exist by implication, and serve as a basis for the apparently careless grace and wit of the whole enchanting and virile performance. How far playgoers can be aware of what Gay is actually doing with them is doubtful: the 'double-irony method, out of which the jokes are constructed, is inherent in the whole movement of the story', as Professor Empson analyses it in his brilliant study, and the method takes a little time to penetrate; the actors seem to say one thing while actually implying its contrary; delightful shocks are administered to moral sensibility; Macheath can come out with such a Senecan 'sentence' as

A moment of time may make us unhappy for ever;

and the underlying grimness itself stimulates the gaiety, which is sometimes of a Swiftian order. It is a serious criticism of society delivered as a light-hearted jest.

Its successor, *Polly* (1729), which was banned on political grounds, but from which Gay drew what was most likely a greater reward from a subscribed edition, 'zested' according to Lord Hervey, 'with some supplemental invectives' would probably not have been a success. It is not only that the songs lack the lyrical quality of the earlier piece, but that the atmosphere is not consistent within itself; sometimes the values are 'straight', sometimes turned upside down, and the violent general satire against politicians, the result perhaps of Swift's disillusioned influence, might have wearied an audience intent on amusement. Laid in the Plantations, it would have had its interest, and possibly the noble savage theme, the chief one of the play, might have made its appeal as it had more than thirty years earlier in Southerne's play *Oroonoko* and Mrs. Behn's novel of that name. But it is too easy to feel that Gay's primitivism is not very deep-rooted, and that he is untouched by any Shaftesburian belief in the goodness of the natural man; it is, we suspect, rather that Gay found the theme too useful a stick to beat politicians with. It is easy to understand why it was banned, though Gay protested his innocence not only in his Preface, but in his posthumous, not by any means dull farce, *The Rehearsal at Goatham*. His other posthumous play, *The Distress'd Wife*, which draws something from Vanbrugh's *Provok'd Husband* and *Provok'd Wife*, deserves a better fate than it has met with; for if the plot is somewhat the stock one of the foolishness of fashionable women, the emotions expressed in it are at least real, and the figures believable. It is on an intellectual level far superior to the artificial vapourings of Mrs. Centlivre, or the would-be moralizings of Colley Cibber. His pastoral opera, *Acis and Galatea* (1731), set to music by Handel, contains some charming lyrics.

No more need be said of the comedy of our period. It had not found a form congruous with the matter the audiences wished to be nourished on. Failing new material, Rich, for one, went back to Congreve, who now for some twenty years was given a considerable revival. It may be that his renewed popularity was the result of the new middle-class audience becoming more cultured, more able to grasp what Congreve was 'at': it may be merely that there was a lack of comedy writers. Had Fielding had a free hand it is possible that his farces, which are vigorous enough, might have developed into a medium for the sense of high comedy he was to reveal in his novels. If in themselves his comedies have little new merit, they are of importance in the development of the creator of *Tom Jones*, and will be discussed in the next volume. It must suffice here to note that he produced the most brilliant of the pure mock-heroic series in *The Tragedy of Tragedies; or, the Life and Death of Tom Thumb the Great* (1730 one act, 1731 three acts), since it has more meat in it than either Henry Carey's *Chrononhotonthologos* or the *Hurlothrumbo* (1729) of 'the other' Samuel Johnson. In this 'dance on the grave of heroic tragedy' Fielding far surpassed his other burlesques, extending the satire to the heroic tragedy of the previous century, and to critics and commentators, while the 'Annotations of H. Scriblerus Secundus' make as good reading, and provide as good criticism, as the best work of his predecessor. But comedy as such was temporarily dead, and it is to the post 1700 comedies, rather than to those of Wycherley and Congreve, that the epithet 'artificial' can be applied. For while in the previous century the emotions had been real enough, and often indeed the events, with Mrs. Centlivre and Cibber and their imitators, the emotions themselves were artificial. Nothing can be made out of this material.

If the tragedy also was artificial, it was so in another sense, and while the bulk of comedies of the period are now unreadable, there is a certain pleasure obtainable from these dulcet versions of late seventeenth-century models of tragedy. If in a sense the heroic emotions had been unreal, they had at least corresponded to some ideal; and if the attempt to present the romantic emotions in a classical framework had produced a form not unaptly named baroque, the form had a certain validity and consistency within itself. But once the humdrum feelings as might be understood by, say, Cibber, became the material of tragedy, the form had nothing to combat or discipline, so that the tension which made the heroic play creative almost wholly disappeared. Yet even so dull a dog as Cibber produced work of some dignity, as in his late *Caesar in Ægypt* (1724), even though the surface of our emotions remains unruffled. His *Xerxes* (1699), though it met with 'entire damnation', is a little fiercer, while his *Richard III* (1700), a loose adaptation of Shakespeare's play, which it replaced for some decades, runs to pure melodrama with uneasy transitions: in truth Cibber had nothing of the tragedian in him, and he soon found that his more natural vein lay in his brash comedies. As far as tragedy goes he is of interest mainly as a connecting-link between the two centuries.

With Rowe,[1] however, whose first tragedy appeared appro-

---

[1] Nicholas Rowe, 1674–1718, was educated at Westminster, from which, in 1691, he proceeded to the Middle Temple. He held a number of small government posts, his last being that of Clerk to the Council of the Prince of Wales, and in 1715 succeeded Tate as Poet Laureate.

priately enough in 1700, we are provided with a good start for our study of decay; but before entering upon a brief discussion of his work it would be as well to see what the elements were that suffered a gradual corruption. Rowe, naturally, raised his well-constructed if temporary edifices on the basis of the old heroic tragedy, in which, at its purest, the emotion aimed at was admiration, 'principally for three virtues, valour, beauty, and love', as Hobbes put it. Where these virtues for any reason failed, pity was called for; but tragic terror, the stark perception of what happens to man, the indifference of fate to the individual, the injustice of the gods, was an ingredient almost wholly absent. One essential part of tragedy, the metaphysical sense, was thus missing; but another, not quite so indispensable though normally present, was at least implied, namely, the vision of something noble or fine being destroyed by something meaner than itself, perhaps through the fatal flaw in character. Thomson was fully to exhibit this aspect in the person of Masinissa in his *Sophonisba* written in the fourth decade of the century. In the main, however, the emotions which Restoration tragedy sought to build up in the spectator were terror-admiration balanced with love-pity, a process we see developing from the admirably consistent constructs of Dryden, through the Gothic tensions of Lee and the 'tenderness' of Otway. But while these three dramatists held a certain balance of somewhat abstract sentiments, by the time we come to Rowe the issues were already so confused by the ethos of domesticity as to produce an aura of sentimentality as destructive of tragedy as of comedy, though sentimentality is a word to beware of, since as often as not we apply it to emotions other people feel but which we do not happen to share. The age, with such tendencies, found very happily to hand the notion of poetical justice, promulgated by Rymer, who had declared that 'the end of all is to show virtue in triumph'. In our period, however, it was not always easy to determine what virtue was. Patriotism, heroism, Roman constancy, a passion for liberty, these to be sure were virtues; but whether love could be included in the list admitted of some doubt. Rowe, possibly, began the reaction against regarding love as 'the noblest frailty of the mind', while to go forward once more to *Sophonisba*, near the end of our period, Thomson, sentimentalist though he was, regarded it with the gravest suspicion as a softening emotion fatal to a character aiming at heroic virtue. Nevertheless, such was the force of tradition, that it was love which was almost exclusively made to bear the burden of pity and send the audience away filled with the 'pleasing anguish' readers of the *Spectator* were in due course instructed to expect. Rowe struck the note in his Epistle Dedicatory of *The Ambitious Step-Mother*. The audience

> should be struck with Terror in several parts of the Play, but always conclude and go away with Pity; a sort of Regret proceeding from Good-nature, which, tho' an uneasiness, is not altogether disagreeable to the Person who feels it.

This 'passion' he achieved in this play by the death of Amestris, the injured heroine.

This, however, created a new dilemma; for if the virtuous lover dies, if innocent persons are shown unfortunate, where is poetical justice? Rowe argued that he had satisfied its claims by killing off the villains, and so got the best of both worlds. That formula satisfied most of the writers of the time and, presumably, the audiences, though there were protests and reactions against it in sterner quarters. Dennis in the prologue to *Appius and Virginia* (1709), a 'tremendously' Roman play contrived entirely by a series of unnecessary delays, asked:

> What welcome here can our rude *Romans* find?
> Who love without one word of whining Cant,
> And rage without the buskin'd Bully's Rant.

Nor had the play any truck with 'distress' as usually offered the audiences for their delectation, as for instance by Gay in his Dedication to the Princess of Wales of *The Captives* (1724)— a play much after the usual pattern, but like everything of Gay's with a flavour of its own—when he says: 'I have often been reflecting to what to impute [your approbation], and I think, it must have been the Catastrophe of the fable, the rewarding virtue, and the relieving the distressed.' Or, again, by Young in his *Busiris* (1719), the Prologue to which, written by a friend, stated that:

> Here Pomp and Splendor serve but to prepare;
> To touch the Soul is our Peculiar Care;
> By just Distress soft Pity to impart,
> And mend your Nature while we move your Heart.

Such motives can, and indeed perhaps should, form part of a tragedy, and do so usefully, no doubt, in the greatest; but as

sole springs of creation they cannot produce anything urgent,
anything to provoke thought or brooding, and in none of the
plays of the period is there any metaphysical idea, no great
theme which makes the observer say, 'This is what happens to
man!' That is why all the tragedy of this period is moribund.
It unconsciously pleaded the middle-class virtues in an incongruous heroic framework, with dubious results, of which Rowe,
it is true, became a little uneasy. After dedicating *The Fair
Penitent* to the Duchess of Ormond, with the usual cliché about
the moving 'Misfortunes and Distress' of the play, 'generous
Pity' being one of the main designs of tragedy, he explained in
his Prologue, that though

> Long has the Fate of Kings and Empires been
> The common Bus'ness of the Tragick Scene

all this was too remote:

> Therefore an humbler Theme our Author chose,
> A melancholy Tale of private Woes:
> No Princes here lost Royalty bemoan,
> But you shall meet with Sorrows like your own;

a statement which in itself might pave the way to that domestic
drama for which the age would seem to have been ripe, but
which made only one noteworthy appearance.

Such indecision, such lack of vision, was reflected in the
medium the authors chose to present their scenes in. The new
ideas that seem below the surface to have been seeking for
expression never found a suitable vehicle. The drama, being
constructed on the heroic model, though without the heroic
emotional content which was extravagantly romantic, would
naturally call for the heroic couplet. But the reaction against
using this verse-form in the drama had long ago triumphed, and
the authors were condemned to labour in blank verse they did
not know how to handle. It is interesting to watch the development of stage blank verse exactly paralleling its development in
other poetry, the old writers struggling to express themselves
in heroic couplets from which rhyme had been banished, with,
sometimes, the oddest effects. The better they were as poets, the
worse they wrote dramatic blank verse. Cibber, with his experience as an actor, managed to produce a sort of stage speech
which can by courtesy be called verse, and Dennis achieved
something which, though dull, gives less the effect of floundering

in strange seas. But Rowe, who was after all a poet of some distinction, an able prosodist and versifier, buffeted haltingly along. Opening a volume at random, this confronts the reader —an average example:

> Search not too deep the Sorrows of my Breast;
> Thou say'st, I am indifferent, and cold.
> Oh! is it possible, my Eyes should tell
> So little of the fighting Storm within?
> Oh! turn thee from me, save me from thy Beauties,
> Falshood and Ruin all look lovely there.
> Oh! let my lab'ring Soul yet struggle thro'—
> I will—I would resolve to die, and leave thee.

Turning the pages idly, to discover a few lines in rhyme, a little earlier in the act we find this from Tamerlane himself, in a neat illustration, incidentally, of the current stage attitude towards love:

> Wisely from dangerous Passions I retreat,
> To keep a Conquest which was hard to get:
> And oh! 'tis time I shou'd for Flight prepare,
> A War more fatal seems to threaten there,
> And all my Rebel-blood assists the Fair:
> One Moment more, and I too late shall find,
> That Love's the strongest Pow'r that lords it o'er the Mind.

The reader is at once sensible of greater ease for himself. It is Addison, however, who in *Cato* provides the most startling examples of the sense of release from the Sargasso Sea of the rhymeless couplet masquerading as blank verse, to where the breeze of the rhyme bowls the vessel gaily along. At the end of Act IV, Cato speaks:

> Farewel, my Friends! if there be any of you
> Who dare not trust the Victor's Clemency,
> Know there are Ships prepared by my Command,
> (Their Sails already op'ning to the winds)
> That shall convey you to the wisht-for Port.
> Is there aught else, my Friends, I can do for you?
> The Conqueror draws near. Once more Farewel!
> If e'er we meet hereafter, we shall meet
> In happier Climes, and on a safer Shore,
> Where *Caesar* never shall approach us more.
>   [*Pointing to the Body of his dead Son.*

> There the brave Youth, with Love of Virtue fired,
> Who greatly in his Country's Cause expired,
> Shall know he Conquer'd. The firm Patriot there
> (Who made the Welfare of Mankind his Care)
> Tho' still, by Faction, Vice, and Fortune, crost,
> Shall find the gen'rous Labour was not lost.

The couplets are far freer, infinitely more flexible and suitable for stage speech than the blanks. Young, coming at the end of the second decade of the century, achieved a fair level of stage suitability in either form, being perhaps slightly easier in his blanks, an unexpected conclusion, since the rhyming metres of his earlier discourses in verse are so much livelier than the solemn dronings of *Night Thoughts*. It is not, however, till we get to Thomson that the rhymeless verse seems natural speech, for by that time he had become a master of the form he had so consistently practised. Take from *Edward and Eleonora*:

> Here flow'd her Tears afresh; with burning Lip
> She press'd the humid Couch, and wept again.
> At last, while weary Sorrow paus'd, she rose,
> And, fearing lest immediate Death might seize Her,
> Demanded to be led to see the Prince;
> But Fear of chasing from his Eyes, too soon,
> The salutary Sleep that heal'd his Pangs,
> Restrain'd her trembling Footsteps. On her Couch,
> Abandon'd to Despair, she sunk anew,
> And for her Children call'd.

A little humdrum, perhaps; but however stilted the actual diction may be, a diction Thomson shared with his contemporaries, the verse has something of the flow of colloquial speech, and is suitable as a stage instrument.

Rowe occupies the foremost place as a writer of tragedy in the first part of our period; as closest inheritor of the form he worked in, he is the best of the tragic playwrights of the whole century, which is to make no extravagant claim. To write plays was, it may be imagined, not more than the favourite serious pastime of this apparently not very profound man, whose frivolity scandalized Addison. Nevertheless, his plays are not slapdash; they are well constructed, owing a good deal of their power and readability, and no doubt their stage success, to the arrangement of the acts, and the movement of the emotions within the acts. It is tempting to think that born into an age offering better material to handle, he would have been more important in the history of the drama than he actually is; yet the sentimentality of his diction, his frequent 'Oh!'s, the constantly recurring 'never more' refrain, seem to fit in so pat with the sentiments he dealt with, that it is impossible not to concede that the man superbly fitted the occasion.

Superbly is the right word, for it is difficult to imagine a diction—one which seemed natural to him—which would better bring home the sentiments which were his material; apart from, and perhaps above, construction, his words, as *A Comparison* rightly stated, were his chief merit. It was all very well for Gray to ask '*Approchez-vous, Néron*—who would not rather have thought of that half-line than all Mr. Rowe's flowers of eloquence?', for it was precisely what Rowe called 'poetic coloring' that gave his tragedies their particular flavour. It was not within him to produce a stark final vision; his intention was to offer something which would be charming and soothing to an audience which had its notions as to what constituted the beautiful. His work had to be smooth and gentlemanlike, clothed in neo-classic draperies, with corresponding gestures. As Smollett remarked, it is solid, florid, declamatory. His figures are simplified; strong in their virtue or their vice, with little inner struggle, except against the debilitating effects of love. Only in *The Fair Penitent* (1703) is the serenity, or at least the decorous melancholy of his dramas, ruffled by any turbulence or trouble, and in that play we are less aware of poetic beauties.

In *Tamerlane* (1701), his favourite play, the hero is drawn, it would appear, from that perfect, great, and benevolent monarch William III, and the villain, Bajazet, from that compendium of all horrific wickedness Louis XIV: it is replete (no other word will quite fit) with such beauties. The main appeal, of course, apart from the 'liberty' theme which runs through so much of the Whig writing of the period, is to pity for lovers in distress, but great warriors express themselves in the tones of pastoral poetry. Thus Axalla, towards whom Selima has relented and expressed fears for his safety in battle, answers:

> The murm'ring Gale revives the drooping Flame,
> That at thy Coldness languish'd in my Breast;
> So breathe the gentle Zephyrs on the Spring,
> And waken every Plant, and od'rous Flower,
> Which Winter Frost had blasted, to new Life.

And so it goes on, the good in the play uttering the noblest sentiments in such terms; but the sentiments are not the heroic ones of the older drama so much as those of the Sunday school, while the wicked are purely vicious, without any of the subtlety of the old Machiavells. The odd thing is that it is not boring. Rowe does not in any way explore life or add anything to our knowledge of the emotions, yet he succeeds in taking us into a sort of coherent, self-consistent fairyland, where the fancy can amuse itself, lulled by sounds that are undeniably sweet. Here, if anywhere, a certain peace of the Augustans may be found.

Rowe's attitude to the old heroic values is amusingly dubious. There are echoes of a 'Roman strictness', but ambition has become a passion that pushes man 'beyond the bounds of nature', and love is a softening emotion. Thus Antinous in *Ulysses* (1705) remarks:

> Youth by Nature
> Is active, fiery, bold, and great of Soul;
> Love is the Bane of all these noble Qualities,
> The sickly Fit that palls Ambition's Appetite;

while Seofrid in *The Royal Convert* (1707) frankly states that love 'or call it by the coarser name, lust', is 'what most we ought to fear'. Rowe was shrewdly aware that what passed for love in the plays of his time did usually deserve the coarser name, and this hardly fitted in with the family virtues he was intent to preach. Thus we feel he is more at home, more actual, when he passes from classical scenes to those of English history; and his later plays, if they lack the tension of *The Fair Penitent*, bear a certain relation to life, and are more fitting vehicles for the sense of domesticity which was to pervade the age. His *Jane Shore* (1714), 'written in imitation of Shakespeare' (Professor Nicoll suggests he meant Banks), and his *Lady Jane Gray* (1715), give an effect of greater freedom, while the verse is easier and more flexible, released to greater degree from the shackles of the couplet. The dialogue in the last play between Guilford and Pembroke (IV. i), though still a little flowery, is no longer floral; it gives some sense of power, as it does the 'distressed lady' scene in *Jane Shore* (Act V). Rowe for all his faults, his weaknesses, his sentimentality, and his occasional absurdities, achieved something which is still worth reading for relaxation.

If it is Rowe in the main who fills the tragic scene in the first fifteen years of the century, there were one or two other plays which, for varying reasons, were popular, such as Ambrose Philips's *The Distrest Mother* (1712)—which even though she 'did not love Traidys', Lady Strafford found 'a good won'. This was more than a passably mellifluous adaptation of *Andromaque*, having considerable tension, and being almost wholly free of 'poetic colouring'; it outdoes Crowne's earlier attempt; and, for the comfort of contemporary audiences, bettered Racine by preserving Astyanax with Andromache to ensure the evaporation of all disagreeables, though hardly in Keats's sense. Ushered in by Steele, ushered out by Budgell (or Addison), this Buttonian effort was a considerable success since Andromache was sympathetically treated, and it was acted till near the end of the century. But though it held the stage almost as long as that other Buttonian success, *Cato* (1713), it could not compare with it for popularity, nor did it deserve to. For Addison's play is still worth reading, and should occasionally be revived. It is curious that in spite of its immense popularity, only in the first instance due to political fervour, a great deal of it runs counter to the ethos of the age. It aimed at, and to some extent achieved, that tragic starkness so notably lacking in the period; and it attempted to convey the Christian-Stoic attitude, which if fairly common at the time among 'the polite', can hardly have appealed to the mass of the audience. Pope expressed this quite clearly in the Prologue:

> Our author shuns by vulgar Springs to move
> The Hero's Glory or the Virgin's Love;
> In pitying Love we but our Weakness show,
> And wild Ambition well deserves its Woe.

Moreover, there was to be no pity-mongering on behalf of poetical justice: the play was concerned with

> A brave Man struggling in the Storms of Fate,
> And greatly falling with a falling State!

so that no happy ending would salve the emotional wounds of the spectators.

Romanism and liberty—those are the themes that support the action, the old Romanism of heroic suicide, of baring the naked breast to the knife, of prowess in the pursuit of savage

beasts, of self-immolation in the country's cause; liberty was the
new liberty of the glorious Revolution:

> A day, an Hour, of virtuous Liberty
> Is worth a whole Eternity in Bondage.

It is difficult for us today to respond very immediately or at all
profoundly to these emotional stimuli—even liberty we take
with a greater sense of responsibility; there is, moreover, what
might be called the dramatic idiom of the time, such as brothers
being in love with the same woman, and a certain strident
Machiavellism which rouses little response in us. But even if
beyond this there are certain aspects that repel, such as Cato's
gloating, the word is hardly too strong, over the corpse of his
son 'nobly' killed in battle, there is still much left in the general
vision to make it a play with some emotive quality. The
philosophizings, unlike those of Rowe, are not personal but
general:

> O think what anxious Moments pass between
> The Birth of Plots, and their last fatal Periods.
> Oh! 'tis a dreadful Interval of Time,
> Fill'd up with Horror all, and big with Death!

a poor version perhaps of

> Between the acting of a dreadful thing,
> And the first motion . . .

but nevertheless carrying with it something of foreboding.
Moreover, the language, in spite of the constriction of Addison's
blank verse, has vigour; the people, you feel, mean what they
say; the dramatic tension is well maintained. Though not a
great tragedy, it stands out remarkably from contemporary
works in that genre. Dennis's brutal mauling in his *Remarks on
Cato* has some validity, though his personal rancour carried him
too far; but for all that, it is the only play in the period that is
at all memorable, or has left any traces in the popular record
in the form of common quotation.

If some sense of the worth of Addison's *Cato* is to be obtained
by reading it directly after Rowe's most tense contribution to
the form, *The Fair Penitent*, which has at least due motive for
'distress', a still higher sense is to be obtained by turning to the
tragedies of Young,[1] which would scarcely deserve notice if it

[1] Edward Young, 1683–1765, went from Winchester to New College, Oxford,

were not for their author's other work, and if they did not beautifully exhibit one further characteristic of the drama at the time. His first play, *Busiris* (1719), is chaotic; the heroine, Mandane, wanders indifferently about bedrooms or battle-fields, and the inaction at moments of urgent need for action is more than disconcerting. Though to some extent adorned with poetic passages, the language is mediocre. This is to a large extent explicable if we continue that part of the prologue from which a quotation has already been drawn; it goes on:

> Nor wou'd these Scenes in empty Words abound,
> Or overlay the Sentiment with Sound.
> When Passion rages, Eloquence is mean;
> Gestures and Looks best speak the moving Scene.

In short, put the burden on the actors! This, of course, is fatal. Really good drama occurs only when the playwright, actor, and the man we have come to call 'the producer' are justly related. *The Revenge* (1721), to quote Dr. Johnson, 'approaches much nearer to human practices and manners', but like the previous play, and indeed his third, 'concluded with lavish suicide'. We need not go so far with Dr. Johnson as to say that 'the reflections, the incidents, and the diction are original', but the moral observations are introduced and expressed so as to have all the novelty that audiences require. Thus the play, vaguely derived from *Othello*, is at least readable, in the sense that it provides the gently soothing balm characteristic of tragedies of the period, once the premisses, and the idiom, can be accepted. *The Brothers*, however, written in about 1723, but not acted until 1753, is a return to the old heroic tragedy, with more than a faint whiff of Lee about it. For example:

> *Demetrius.* Curse whom? Curse thee!
> *Erixene.*   Yes, from thy inmost Soul.
> Why dost thou lift thine Eyes and Hands to Heav'n?
> The Pow'rs most conscious of this Deed, reside
> In Darkness, howl below in raging Fires,
> Where Pangs like mine corrode them.—Thence arise
> Black gods of Execration and Despair!
> Thro' dreadful Earthquakes cleave your upward Way,

but transferred to Corpus Christi, in 1708 becoming a law Fellow of All Souls. After an unlucky political life, he took Holy Orders when nearing fifty, was made Royal Chaplain in 1728, and in 1730 became Rector of Welwyn, where he died.

While Nature shakes, and Vapours blot the Sun;
Then thro' those Horrors in loud Groans proclaim,
That I am ——
Demetrius.   What?—I'll have it, tho' it blast me.
Erixene. Thus then in Thunder,—I am *Perseus'* wife.

It is understandable that, in view of the changed audiences,
the play had to wait some thirty years for production, and then
only for an unremunerative performance in aid of the Society
for the Propagation of the Gospel.

More in tune with the time was Thomson, especially as the
later of his five plays have a strong political flavour, good clap-
trap at the time of the strongest anti-Walpole reaction; but
even so they were never very popular. His first play, *Sophonisba*
(1730), has already been touched upon, and although it remains
in the general memory by the unlucky line 'Oh Sophonisba,
Sophonisba oh!' so devastatingly transmuted by Fielding into
'Oh Huncamunca, Huncamunca oh!' (the line disappeared
from later editions of the play), it deserves better. Masinissa's
almost Eloisa-like fluctuations between his passion and his duty
to Rome, though too oscillating to deserve much sympathy,
form a not uninteresting basis. The old 'Roman' appeals are
there, of course; but Thomson gives them a certain freshness by
the handling of the verse. Though it had a fair reception,
Thomson, busied with *Liberty* and revisions of *The Seasons*, and
a little retarded by his natural indolence, did not venture
again in the theatre until 1738, when his *Agamemnon* appeared,
aiming to please, as declared in the prologue provided by 'the
author of Eurydice' (Mallet, not Fielding), 'by noble means,
alone'. The play, a fairly close adaptation of Aeschylus, proceeds well, in spite of a vacillating Clytemnestra, too easily
moved from her remorsefulness by a remorseless Egisthus, and
a too wordy Cassandra; the catastrophe comes rapidly and
excitingly, after a lull in the action provided by a chorus of
Trojan captives. Thomson's sententiae, providing incidentally
some good phrases for the enemies of Walpole, are the most
pithy part of the play; the briskest are even a little savage, such
as Agamemnon's comment on

> . . . those dust-licking, reptile, close
> Insinuating, speckled, smooth Court-serpents,
> That make it so unsafe, chiefly for Kings,
> To walk this weedy World.

But apart from these, and a few moralizings on love, the play lacks any particular hall-mark of either Thomson or the age (though indeed the 'virtues' are glaring), and perhaps for that more easily than other plays of the period obtains a response from the modern reader, to whom it does not convey any political implications, and who can be carried along by the momentum of the story.

Detachment from immediacies, however, was not to be expected for long from such a devoted adherent of the Patriots, to whom the word liberty acted as an emotive gong; and politics were too obvious in Thomson's next venture, *Edward and Eleonora*. This would have been acted in 1740 but for the intervention of the Lord Chamberlain, who, eager to retrieve his error in allowing Mallet's *Mustapha* in the previous year, banned the play for the passages which no amount of disingenuous denial from Thomson could free from 'subversive' intention. Gloster's plea to Edward to return from Palestine:

> To save your Father's old and broken Years,
> His mild and easy Temper, from the Snares
> Of low corrupt insinuating Traitors:

and to help build England's rising grandeur on the firm base of well-proportioned liberty, was too obvious a comment on the position of Walpole and Frederick Prince of Wales to pass unnoticed amid would-be historical slashings against

> *Italian* Leeches, and insatiate *Rome*.

Just as Gay had done when *Polly* was banned, Thomson published by subscription, and gained more than the theatre could have got him. For it is doubtful if the play would have been a success. The story, indeed, was unusual; there was no love-affair except that of Edward for his wife, who sucks the poison from his wound, but is saved by Selim, the villain turned virtuous hero; the criticism of the Crusades was possibly a new note; but though the domestic virtues are exhibited, all is so solemn and grandiose, so lacking in any tension after Leonora's willing self-sacrifice, that tedium would certainly have supervened, as it did not in *Tancred and Sigismunda* of 1745. For this play, as Professor Grant says, was 'inspired by the poet's own disastrous passion' for Miss Young, so that actual emotional experience here finds utterance: Thomson could enter into the

feelings of Tancred baffled of his bride by a father who had
other views for his daughter. The moral is plain, and domestic:

> Taught hence, ye parents, who from nature stray,
> And the great ties of social life betray;
> Ne'er with your children act a tyrant's part:
> 'Tis yours to guide, not violate the heart.

And though Sigismunda tells Tancred that

> The man, whom Heaven appoints
> To govern others, should himself first learn
> To bend his passions to the sway of reason

we feel that neither her heart nor Thomson's really supported
this Rowe-like sentiment. The play is on the favourite 'distress'
theme and, though it was much acted till the end of the century,
is, in common with most of the tragedies of the period, alms for
oblivion, in spite of the slightly more convincing appeal to the
feelings. It is marred in the reading by Thomson's wordiness,
which, in the acting, was considerably curtailed, Lyttelton and
the young Pitt helping in the production. A posthumous play,
Coriolanus, a classical draping of Shakespeare, and a dull play,
was a failure at the time of its acting.

The truth is that the audiences were getting wearied with
these attempts to convey their sense of life in an outworn mode;
there was no vitality in the persons presented to them, who
bore little relation to living as they knew it. Moreover, between
Young and Thomson had appeared a tragedy of which the
source might have taken place on their doorsteps, Lillo's[1]
remarkable *The London Merchant, or The History of George Barnwell*. This, on 22 June 1731, startled a delighted audience by
inviting them to witness, not

> Princes distrest and scenes of royal Woe,

but the good merchant next door and his erring apprentice, the
mercenary pretty lady they might meet in the street, all the
persons moved by emotions they could really share, and speaking, not blank verse, but, with occasional 'heightening', the
language they themselves spoke. The appeal was partly in the
grim and pitiable story of the old ballad, which had come down
from Elizabethan days, which could enable Lillo to make

---

[1] George Lillo, 1693–1739, was brought up in his father's trade as jeweller, and
was his father's partner for some years before abandoning the trade for playwriting.

capital out of the anti-Spanish feeling of the time, partly in the
erecting of the merchant into a high position as the best part of the
social fabric; partly in the moral sentiments well rubbed home.
The play was enormously successful, more so than Lillo's other
attempt to write domestic drama, namely, *The Fatal Curiosity*
(1736), written in blank verse which is workmanlike but un-
stirring, free of poetic beauties, and with no fustian hero raging,
as Fielding said in the Prologue. The audience whose normal
fare was such as what follows from Henry Brooke's *Gustavus
Vasa* (1739) (a play concerning 'a state distress'd', banned
because, Brooke said, it belauded patriotism and 'personal
freedom'), must have found the change in idiom immensely
refreshing. To expect such speech as

> Six Moons have chang'd upon the Face of Night,
> Since here he first arriv'd in servile Weeds,
> But yet of Mein majestic . . .

and to hear

> *Randal.* . . . Shall I forsake you in your worst necessity?—
> Believe me, sir! my honest soul abhors
> The barb'rous thought.
> *O. Wilmot.* What! canst thou feed on air?
> I have not left wherewith to purchase food
> For one meal more!

would at least give the auditors a sense of reality lacking in such
distant scenes as Brooke's. Thus *George Barnwell* is the most
important of Lillo's plays, even though to us it seems sheer
melodrama, with its too contrasted good and evil, its bloodshed,
its repentance, its scenes on the scaffold, redeemed by the
touching figure of Maria, offering an appeal to sympathy if
not to Augustan Pity. If Millwood may have seemed to a contemporary audience a female version of the stage Machiavel, to
us she will appear only as a risible amoral vamp of the flimsiest
shocker. When Mr. Samuel Weller referred to George Barnwell,
he gave it as his opinion that 'the young 'ooman deserved
scragging a precious sight more than he did'. The importance
of the play lies in its being the first indubitably middle-class
tragedy expressing middle-class ideals; not that it was without
forebears, which the age was aware of, since Hill had based a
play (*The Fatal Extravagance*, 1721), on *The Yorkshire Tragedy*,
and Mrs. Haywood was to precede Lillo himself in an adapta-

tion of *Arden of Feversham*. Other attempts at middle-class tragedy had been, and were to be made, notably *The Perfidious Brothers* (1716) by Lewis Theobald, whose other writings in this kind had been on classical themes; but these never came down to the life of next door, as may be seen by the failure of John Hewitt's *The Fatal Falsehood; or Distress'd Innocence* (1733), and Thomas Cooke's *The Mournful Nuptials; or Love the Cure of All Woes* (1739). Yet though Lillo's play was popular, being acted to the end of the century, it had no successor; for if the old form of tragedy was played out, the English theatre was not ready for the new for another hundred and fifty years. But on the Continent it became the inspiration of the tragic domestic drama which is the common run from its greatest master, Ibsen, until almost the present day. Its influence became effective first in Germany, Lessing's *Miss Sara Samson* (1755), the fecund parent of German domestic drama, being based on it; but already, in 1748, it had been translated into French, when it received Diderot's always lively and intelligent notice.

If tragedy at this time became a subsection of contemplative rhetorical poetry, it may be because, as Professor Basil Willey has suggested, the age lacked the tragic sense. This, however, is open to question, since the sense of tragedy is personal, and it may be that, denied its expression on the stage, it found its satisfaction in satire. And though it is true to say that the dramas of the age fail to impart real tragic emotions or attitudes, it was not through lack of public appreciation of serious theatre, as is evidenced by the audiences' turning against the destructively flippant epilogues introduced during the Restoration. It was matter for serious discussion in such papers as the *Universal Spectator* and *Grub-Street Journal*, as well as more expectedly in the *Templer*, the *Comedian*, and especially the *Prompter*, which last Aaron Hill edited from 1734 to 1736. Nor was it through lack of writers trying. Hardly an author known for any other writings but made the attempt, from Mrs. Manley to Aaron Hill himself, whose vapidly sentimental *Merope* (1749), derived from Voltaire, vies in the solemnity of its stilted diction with any play of the time. Many of them it is true were rehandlings of other plays, from the classics, from the French, and our own older drama. It seems all the more likely, therefore, that it was partly the diction which stifled tragedy. The attempt to forge the utterly undialectical verse form of contemplative and philosophic nature-poetry into a stage instrument was doomed to failure, a failure for some time disguised by the skill of the actors. What most hastened its decay was the other attempt to make tragic material out of the softer domestic emotions the new audiences were interested in. Tragedy is a savage animal, with a rough pelt; bring it in with coat brushed, combed, and perfumed, it becomes merely a domestic creature, pleasant to stroke but unlikely to arouse terror. And such the tragedy of our period mostly remains.

VIII

THE PHILOSOPHERS

THE business of the literary historian when discussing the philosophers is not to consider the validity of their systems. It is, rather, to note them as men of letters, and to describe their ideas in so far as they nourished works of imagination. To take an overall view, it might be said that in the early part of our period philosophy reflected the conflict in the popular mind between the 'optimism' of Shaftesbury and the 'pessimism' of Mandeville; and that towards the end of the third decade of the century, Berkeley, together with Butler and Law, helped to resolve the battle between them. Their ideas, merged with those of Locke—treated in the preceding volume—permeate the first half of the century, largely affecting the writing of poetry, and remaining normally implicit in criticism.

At this time, the man of 'large, sound, round-about sense', as Locke put it, or the 'polite reader', was the son of a tradition that ran from Descartes through Hobbes to Locke, the last of whom derived his cosmological ideas from Newton. Often allying these, however uneasily, with Christianity, he on the whole accepted the mechanical account of nature (about which Locke seems to have had some private reservations), though shying at its corollary of necessity; in short, he was prepared to live with the empirical philosophy and the associationist psychology of Locke. Faced with 'a kind of dead and wooden world', in which various congeries of atoms whirled round according to mathematical formulas, resulting in a universe of matter to be described only by extension, weight, shape, and hardness, without colour, smell, or sound (for these were merely secondary qualities added by man); with a mind subject to the same laws, existing only as a photographic plate, a *tabula rasa* that grouped sensations according to laws of association (notwithstanding Descartes's holding by 'innate ideas'), the average man might well become confused, or submit with a dulled stoicism to this necessitarian existence. But man is not so built that he can for long dwell in such circumstances: in actual living he believes ineradicably in the freedom of the will, and in his capacity to act well or badly.

And if the reason, based on empiricism, could find no argument for immortality or for God, some still held by revelation; and those whose faith had been shattered by the scientific approach found refuge in a deep scepticism which questioned the wholesale competence of the reason. Here again it can be observed that this age, far from being given over to reason, was one which sought rather to define its limits. The period, understandably, was rife with theological speculation and heresy, promoted by frank unbelievers, by more dubious free-thinkers, by Spinozists, Arians, and a host of sects including Quakers (Penn did not die until 1718); but theological controversy is a theme too specialized to invite treatment here. All that need be noted is the strong pull towards Deism, the impulse to unravel the problem of good and evil and the nature of conscience. Those who tried to reconcile natural philosophy with religion arrived, as Thomson did, at a kind of 'natural' Deism, which involved the finding of a moral pattern in Nature, and attempting to mould oneself by it. With men and women of vision, or deep moral temper, this attitude could mean something, involve a discipline, be in some sort a way of life; but it readily became an empty cliché, as when Mrs. Eliza Haywood could say in *The Female Spectator*, published in the early forties, that 'the study of *nature* is the study of *divinity*', and that 'Nature is in itself abhorrent of vice'.

At the beginning of the century, however, nature did not appear in so soothing a form, and the moral sense of men who could not accept dogmatic religion rebelled against both the mathematical universe of Hobbes and the psychology of Locke. They found a possible solution in the series of works by Shaftesbury,[1] which appeared between 1708 and 1710, being gathered together and expanded in 1711 as *Characteristics of Men, Manners, Opinions, Times*, which contained *Miscellaneous Reflections on the preceding Treatises and other Critical Subjects*. These had an immediate and considerable success. Appealing to men, especially men of goodwill, who felt naked, helpless, and insignificant in the new world offered them by the dominant philosophers, Shaftesbury could unite the latitudinarian Christian,

[1] Anthony Ashley Cooper, 3rd Earl of Shaftesbury, 1671–1713, was educated privately, at Winchester, and by travel abroad. He was M.P. from 1695 to 1698, succeeding his father in 1700. He took some part in politics, and was for a short time Vice-Admiral of Dorset; but ill health compelled him to live much abroad, and he died at Naples.

the waverer, and the uneasy infidel. Retired from the world, sensitive, cultivated, inherently disliking systems—'The most ingenious way of becoming foolish is *by a System*', he says in *Advice to an Author*—he brought a contemplative rather than a strictly philosophical mind to the dilemma in which men found themselves. Deriving from the Cambridge Platonists, as Professor R. L. Brett has convincingly shown, he loathed the Hobbesian doctrines of religion and of relative morality. Though tutored by Locke in infancy and childhood, imbibing from him perhaps his admirable tolerance, and always holding him in the deepest affection and respect, he rejected both the mechanistic universe and the *tabula rasa*. ''Twas Mr. Locke', he wrote to Michael Ainsworth, the Young Man at the University to whom he addressed the *Several Letters* (1716),

that struck at all fundamentals, threw all *Order* and *Virtue* out of the World, and made the very *Ideas* of these (which are the same as those of God) *unnatural*, and without foundation in our Minds. *Innate* is a word he poorly plays upon.

'Connatural' was the right word; for it did not matter *when* ideas entered a man's mind; the important thing was that at some time or other there did spring up in him, infallibly, inevitably, necessarily, 'the Idea and Sense of *Order*, Administration, and a GOD'. This is almost pure Cudworth; moreover, through the Cambridge men he found in Plato an alternative to the set, ordered universe of Hobbes, with God no more than a prime mover in a system of cause and effect. The universe, as he saw it, was not only God's machine, but, as Mr. Brett puts it, also his work of art, in a process of continuous organic creation. This doctrine directed Shaftesbury's aesthetics (to be treated later); indeed the two are inseparable, for his philosophy, his ethic, is based on aesthetics. To philosophize is 'To learn what is *just* in Society, and *beautiful* in Nature, and the Order of the World'.

Such benevolent doctrine was very well for the *grand seigneur* quietly tending his country estates, and against him the polite reader, without any urgent tendency to philosophic thought, could place Mandeville,[1] the realistic doctor of 'the hypochondriacal and hysteric passions'. This genial cynic, forced to

[1] Bernard (de) Mandeville, 1670–1733, was educated at the Erasmus School at Rotterdam and at Leyden University, where he took his medical degree in 1691. Coming to England 'to learn the language', he remained, earning a none too sumptuous livelihood as a physician, and a pensioner of Dutch distillers.

dwell amid the rugosities of life, an emigrated Dutchman who had been bandied about a little in the world, could not accept the charming picture presented by the well-provided country gentleman. 'His notions, I confess', he wrote, 'are generous and refined: they are a high compliment to human-kind. . . . What a pity it is that they are not true!' So this 'facetious, entertaining companion', as Benjamin Franklin called him, subjected optimistic notions to what might be described as *badinage*. For him the springs of society were actuated by far other motives than Shaftesbury would admit; he belongs, rather, to the honourable line of sceptics, tracing his descent from Montaigne through Bayle, and he often seems to be translating La Rochefoucault. 'Ce qu'on nomme libéralité n'est le plus souvent que la vanité de donner', becomes with Mandeville: 'Thus thousands give Money to Beggars from the same Motives as they pay their Corn-cutter, to walk easy.' This, to be sure, would seem to imply a conscience; at any rate, no man is 'so savage as not to be charm'd with Praise, or so despicable as patiently to bear contempt'. In short, 'The nearer we search into human Nature, the more we shall be convinced that the Moral Virtues are the Political Offspring which Flattery begot upon Pride.' But Mandeville's is not mere shallow scoffing. His absorbing passion was to examine into people's motives, and 'in private he never ceased examining into himself', a course he recommended in *The Virgin Unmask'd* (1709). Once he had come to terms with life he found he enjoyed it; and this very relish of life, he declared, 'was accompanied with an elevation of mind that seemed to be inseparable from his being'. And if this elevation of mind did not preclude a certain impishness, especially as regards parson-baiting, this does not make his attitude any the less respectable.

It is easy to oppose Mandeville to Shaftesbury, but they have in fact much in common. It is not only that, as Leslie Stephen said, they were, rather, complementary, but that they go a long way together. Both defended the free-thinker, the man, not debauched and atheistical as he was commonly gibed at for being, but independent of authority, who relied upon his own experience; they were empiricist in the sense that they were based upon what they knew, and not upon assumptions. Both were anti-puritanical, Shaftesbury because the puritans denied the validity and virtue of beauty, and the emotions connected with it, Mandeville because they either denied or scorned the basic desires of humanity, through which, after all, life is lived. Both recognized the existence of conscience based upon the opinions of our fellow creatures, though—and this is the fundamental difference between them—for Shaftesbury conscience was inborn, for Mandeville it was brought about by the educated reason. They were at one in belauding the social virtues. Further, and this for the average man was the important thing, both asked men to base their philosophy—at all events their moral philosophy—upon the honest report of what they found when they looked into themselves. They appealed to common sense, in the proper use of the term, not to some trained mental procedure. If the credit of philosophy ran low, that was because, Shaftesbury said:

We have immur'd her (poor Lady!) in Colleges and Cells; and have set her servilely to such Works as those in the Mines. Empiricks and pedantick Sophists are her chief Pupils.

They were understandable; they spoke to the average reader. And after all, in an age so imbued with the social sense, what were the most important things to know? Surely, what was the basis of morality? What was the nature of conscience?

Thus in common with most of the moralizing of the time, their philosophy comes under the heading of the ugly word 'utilitarian'—if the wish that most people should lead the good life should be so dubbed—holding, in the phrase that Hutcheson invented and that Bentham was to make popular, that *'that action* is *best,* which procures the *greatest Happiness* for the *greatest Numbers'.* For the optimists, self-love and social were the same, to use Pope's phrase, not because private vices were public benefits, as Mandeville was paradoxically to argue, or because the individual thrives most in a thriving society, but because man derives his greatest satisfaction from the performance of benevolent actions.

Many of Shaftesbury's qualities and ideas, his temper and his approach, are to be found in the first separate work that he published, *A Letter concerning Enthusiasm* (1708), called forth by the desire for martyrdom of some French Protestant refugees. This, in common with all his essays, should be read together with his *Miscellaneous Reflections,* which constitutes a gloss on the earlier parts of his work; each work is, in a sense, a comment upon the others, containing a number of cross-references, not only backwards, but also forwards. His rambling method, though not altogether without structure, with divagations rather than digressions, lends itself to repetition and to the amplifying of notions previously expressed. His style, a little too urbane saving where he waxes rhapsodical, somewhat muffles his attack; but what he has to say comes out clearly enough in the end, though if the writings are taken piecemeal it may seem elusive.

To the casual reader of today, Shaftesbury's work may seem to be a series of somewhat obvious moralizings by a benevolent, liberal-minded tolerant man of culture and taste, sometimes prosy, though in *The Moralists, A Philosophical Rhapsody*, he writes confessedly as an 'enthusiast', indulging in passages of exclamatory rhetoric which in rhythm often approach blank verse. But all the while his intent is plain: to offer an alternative to the self-interested morality of Hobbes, and that which the Christian churches strove to make effective by the fear of condign punishment and the hope of reward; to propose a different system of the universe from that expounded by empirical-scientific philosophy, together with the concept of the mind made popular by Locke; and to solve the problem of evil. And having learnt from Locke that the understanding of the outer world required looking into how the mind (the reason) worked, he found it needful also to see what the heart said. Otherwise how could man discover what justice and beauty were, or what the order of the world might be, for heart and head complete 'the *real* PHILOSOPHER'. Looking into his own admirable heart, he found there certain basic feelings which he supposed everybody must share, if not to the same degree:

'Tis impossible to suppose [he wrote in *An Inquiry concerning Virtue*] a mere sensible Creature originally so ill-constituted and unnatural, as that from the moment he comes to be try'd by sensible Objects, he shou'd have no one good Passion towards his Kind, no foundation either of Pity, Love, Kindness or social Affection. . . . A Soul, indeed, may as well be without *Sense*, as without Admiration in the Things of which it has any knowledg. Coming therefore to a Capacity of seeing and admiring in this new way, it must needs find a Beauty and a Deformity as well in Actions, Minds, and Tempers, as in Figures, Sounds, or Colours.

Man, in short, has a natural moral sense.

And besides, Shaftesbury argues in more than one place, if

man were not just, benevolent, with a sense of beauty, and so on, how could the conceptions of justice, benevolence, and the beautiful arise in him? How could he give to God attributes of which he was not sensible? This may be to make God in man's image, but the General Mind (or Nature) formed man in such a way that he must inevitably develop such ideas. Furthermore, man has a conscience:

... no Creature can maliciously and intentionally *do ill*, without being sensible, at the same time, that he *deserves ill.* ... But besides this, there must in every rational Creature be yet farther *Conscience*: *viz.* from Sense of *Deformity in what is thus ill-deserving and unnatural*: and from a *consequent Shame or Regret of incurring what is odious, and moves Aversion*.

From which many things flowed.

It is clear that this sort of reasoning would appeal to the generality of thoughtful men who did not care for the findings of professional philosophy. His assumptions and premises would appeal to the experience of the ordinary man of the Enlightenment, who, aware of conscience, would hail the doctrine that it was not a matter of fear as taught by some 'dismal religion'. Again and again Shaftesbury insists that to follow virtue for the sake of a bargain is by no means to be virtuous, and for this reason expressly repudiates the teachings of the dogmatic churches. Indeed, how could society come about at all if man were not essentially overflowing with virtue and moral sense? It was no mere Hobbesian contract or commercial pact, nor a bolt-hole for the weak and cowardly:

'Tis ridiculous to say, there is any Obligation on Man to act sociably, or honestly, in a form'd Government; and not in that which is commonly call'd *the State of Nature* . . . *Faith, Justice, Honesty, and Virtue*, must have been as early as the State of Nature, or they cou'd never have been *at all*.

The Hobbesian view, he says in 'raillery', is 'a notable account of the original of moral justice'! So much for 'the Cavils of a Philosophy, which speaks so much of *nature* with so little meaning'! Was it not clear that these moral instincts were those which preserved the species? 'If *eating* and *drinking* be natural, *Herding* is so too.' But it was more than a utilitarian instinct for the safety of the tribe, more than a sense of fellowship that would easily degenerate into love of party and 'cantonizing', that impelled men to virtue; it was the admiration and love of order raised to the height of being an elegant passion of love of beauty. Morals then, as we gather again and again, are ultimately based on aesthetics; and Shaftesbury finally asserts that 'It has been the main Scope and principal End of these volumes to assert the Reality of a Beauty and Charm in *moral* as well as *natural* Subjects.'

Characteristics reads on the whole like the work of an enraptured Deist; we get an account of the exquisite fittingness of everything in the world, and the starry universe, in the manner familiar with the Deists, and to be found, as so much else in Shaftesbury, in the *Essay on Man*. He professed himself a Theist, though he conformed to the rites of the Church, arguing indeed that the condition of being a good Christian was to be a good Theist. To be perfectly such, according to his definition, was to believe 'that everything is govern'd, order'd, or regulated *for the best*, by a designing Principle, or Mind, necessarily good and permanent'. All is for the best in the best of all possible worlds, which is ruled by a Supreme Manager, or a general Mind, which, 'we may rest satisfy'd, . . . is *the best-natur'd one in the World*'. For since it is general, it can have no particular interest, and therefore no malice.

But then, and here is the difficulty with the optimistic philosophy, how account for evil? Pope again phrases the answer most briefly: all partial ill is universal good. Evil exists in the world as shadows or dark parts in a picture; there could be no light without darkness. Indeed the beauty of the world which we admire is 'founded on contrarieties'. The world contains a vast amount of ill, certainly: there are earthquakes, floods, famine and tempest; animals prey upon one another, and there are wicked men who act as wolves on their own kind. But there cannot be anything ill with respect to the whole, for if there were anything really ill, this must have been produced either by design or by chance, which argues either ill will or impotency in the general Mind. There is, however, imperfection, which is itself part of the design, for without it 'Where had been *Temperance* or *Self-denial*? Where *Patience, Meekness, Magnanimity?*' We are to rest assured that it was not the intention of Universal Nature 'to leave us without some Pattern of Imperfection', which would itself not seem so if we could see all: we have limited minds, and 'a Mind which sees not *infinitely*, can see nothing fully'. To the properly balanced man, then, there is no real difficulty in the problem of evil. The man of perception soon sees, if he does not instinctively feel, that to have the natural affections is to achieve happiness, more especially if his affections are exercised in the constant things, namely the intellectual enjoyments, rather than on the physical ones, however benevolent, since the latter pass. From the love of one person grows the love of humanity, which brings with it 'a pleasing Consciousness of the actual Love, merited Esteem or Approbation of others'. From there man can proceed to a satisfaction in the whole scheme of things. But to have the private or self-affections too strong, to indulge in malice, malignity or hatred, 'is to be miserable in the highest degree'.

Such a philosophy, or ethic, would evidently appeal to the new reading public of the time, eager for self-education, learning how to live. How delightful to be shown the way to cultivation along paths which seemed so smooth! It was not difficult to read, but seemed to tread higher paths; and though repetitive, it mingled the strange with the familiar in ways that were entertaining, as when Shaftesbury sketched out and made mock of the now classic theory of evolution. Talking of style, he could hit out such a phrase as 'the gouty Joints and Darning-work of Whereunto's, Whereby's, Thereof's, and the rest of this kind'. So the reader would proceed, his fancy amused, perhaps, by the conduct of the dialogue by means of which Shaftesbury pursues his argument in *The Moralist*, where the well-intentioned free-thinker is converted to Theism, and one or two others, particularly a crusty old gentleman, are introduced to vary the tempo. No wonder that the work was popular, the fourth and seventh editions being published between 1727 and 1733, though later in the century the taste for it waned, no doubt under the impact of *Rasselas* and *Candide*. Certainly the main notions of the *Characteristics* became widely diffused; they are to be found in Addison, Steele, and in all those who aimed at the reformation of manners. Thomson, naturally, welcomed the whole work, on moralistic as well as on cosmological grounds. He hailed 'the generous Ashley . . . the friend of man',

> Who scann'd his nature with a brother's eye,
> His weakness prompt to shade, to raise his aim,
> To touch the finer movements of his mind,
> And with the *moral beauty* charm the heart.

It is true that some might find the rhapsodical portions 'disgusting', as a little later Horace Walpole was to do. If his enthusiasm might not merit the name 'panic', the word he proposed as a synonym for religious enthusiasm, yet there would be some who could not stomach his ecstatic rapture. Among these, naturally, was Mandeville, whose doggerel essay on the moral basis of society, *The Grumbling Hive, or Knaves turn'd Honest*, vastly amused the coffee-houses in 1705, arguing as it did that though the love of money might be the root of all evil, at any rate it was the spring of all progress. You cannot have a prosperous community unless there are people eager for wealth, for luxury, and ready to spend their money. It's no use grumbling that there are some dishonest folk, rapacious merchants, stock-jobbers. The moral of the squib, written with a good deal of Hudibrastic vigour—as Coleridge conceded—is that 'vice' is essential to civilized living:

> Then leave complaints. Fools only strive
> To make a Great an Honest Hive . . .
> Bare Virtue can't make Nations live
> In splendor; they that would revive
> A Golden Age, must be as free
> For Acorns, as for Honesty—

a doctrine for moralists to pounce upon.

But Mandeville was himself a moralist, also very much a man of letters, as evinced by his translations of the fables of La Fontaine in 1713, and of Aesop in 1714—though these might be considered moralistic—his Scarronesque mock-heroic *Typhon* of 1705, and his occasional poems of 1712, which bore the name of its main piece, *Advice to a Godson*. His later manner he hit upon with his *The Virgin Unmask'd* of 1709, a not unamusing if rather too long dialogue between an elderly lady and her niece, but this also was a moralistic work. His medical training, largely psychological, of which he made literary use in his *Treatise of the Hypochondriac and Hysterical Diseases* (1711), later expanded into three still readable dialogues, gave him a specialist's interest in human motives. It also enabled him to accept the human being for what he was, and to dislike hypocrisy. As he was to say later in the controversy his views aroused:

All Passions and Instincts in general were given to all Animals for some wise End, tending to the Preservation and Happiness

either to themselves or their Species: it is our duty to hinder them
from being detrimental or offensive to any Part of the Society: but
why should we be ashamed of having them?

It might be said that the whole tenour of his writings is 'Clear
your minds of cant'. Perhaps it was political faction that caused
him to flick out, as it were, *The Grumbling Hive*, as it was possibly
the tension prevalent in the last four years of Queen Anne's
reign, combined with the attacks on his popular squib, that
made him seriously consider the basis of morals and society.
Certainly *The Fable of the Bees: or, Private Vices, Public Benefits*,
published in 1714, is the work of a thinking and introspective
man. Taking phrases from his poem, he commented on them
in a series of Remarks, which made his position clear, and constituted a serious challenge to the general run of moralists.

It outraged the repressive side of Puritanism, and those who
held that abstention was the basis of wealth. He put forth what
is now known as the expansionist theory, that the more that
goods of any kind are demanded, the more money will flow,
and the more employment there will be; as more wages are
earned so much better off will be the working classes: thus
prosperity all round will be assured. If nobody demanded good
food and drink, fine clothes, splendid, or at least admirable
houses, furniture and so forth, what shocking unemployment
there would be! No nation could thrive without such demands
being made. Even the import of wines, and other foreign
luxuries, such as works of art, helps the importing country
by employing sailors, shipbuilders, transport agents, and such-
like. Not only the greatness, but the happiness, nay the con-
tinuance of a nation depends upon such demands being made
and gratified. If there are spendthrift heirs, they also contribute
to the general prosperity by circulating money; even gambling
may have beneficent repercussions. Thus good, by the better
distribution of wealth, is educed from the seeming evil. In sum,
without vices there would be no trade, only a miserable
agricultural condition, in which wretched men eke out a bare
living.

It is all sensible enough. But Mandeville roused the ire of
those who did not read him carefully, or who missed his point.
He was not advancing some scheme for immoral living, but
launching an attack upon hypocrisy. His critics neglected to
observe that 'Vice is beneficial found' only 'When it's by Justice

lopt and bound', or to take note of his 'rigoristic' definition of vice. Nothing was virtue that was not 'a task of self-denial to be perform'd with the utmost severity against nature'; thus vice was the gratifying of any impulse or appetite, however natural. And how absurd it was of men to pretend to virtue, when all their actions denied it:

... Ask not only the Divines and Moralists of every Nation, but likewise all that are rich and powerful, about real Pleasure, and they'll tell you, with the *Stoicks* that there can be no Felicity in Things Mundane and Corruptible: but then look upon their Lives, and you will find that they take delight in no other.

How then did the idea of virtue come about? It was thanks to the wily machinations of priests and 'skilful politicians', who endeavoured to seek their own advantage, preaching up public-spiritedness '. . . that they might reap the Fruits of the Labour and Self-denial of others, and at the same time indulge their own appetites with less disturbance', giving the name of virtue only to such actions by which men, contrary to the impulse of nature, should try to benefit others, or to conquer their passions 'out of a Rational Ambition of being Good'.

All this was so pungently expressed, with such good humour, and with such a wealth of amusing illustration, that it was widely read, even by those who would not readily understand the argument which was not so simple as the extracts quoted would indicate. It might easily mislead, as being an incitement to evil living, and it was as such that the voices upraised in protest took it. It was largely referred to as a pernicious document, and more than once 'presented' by the Grand Jury when republished in 1723 with the addition of 'An Essay on Charity Schools' and 'A Search into the Nature of Society', nevertheless reaching a sixth edition in 1732. It was replied to in 1724 by Law,[1] and by Dennis, whom Mandeville later referred to as 'a noted Critick, who seems to hate all books that sell, and no other'. Dennis's attack is swingeing enough, vigorous to violence, as his writings tend to be, but without subtlety or real understanding. Law, in his witty and even caustic *Remarks on a Late Book entituled The Fable of the Bees* (considered by John Sterling to be 'one of the most remarkable philosophical Essays

---

[1] William Law, 1686–1761, was educated in his home at King's Cliffe, Northamptonshire, and Emmanuel College, Cambridge, of which, in 1711, after ordination, he was elected Fellow. For further details see text later.

I have seen in English'), was far more damaging. Written in the form of a letter to Mandeville, it accused him of regarding man as no more than an animal, and got in some home thrusts which strike at the root of the whole method of argument:

> You say, *you believe man to be* etc., now I can't understand to what part of you, this believing Faculty is to be ascrib'd; for your Definition of Man makes him incapable of believing any thing, unless believing can be said to be a *Passion*, or some Faculty of *Skin* or *Bones*. . . .
> If Man had nothing but *Instincts* and *Passions*, he would not *dispute* about them; for to *dispute* is no more an *Instinct*, or a *Passion*, than it is a *Leg* or an *Arm*.

But he weakens his case by shifting his ground to the light cast by revelation and God, and tends to play with words rather than to develop ideas. He is, it comes to be seen, really a Shaftesburian. 'Let me tell you, Sir,' he exclaims, '*moral Virtue* came amongst Men in the same manner as *Seeing* and *Hearing* came amongst them', but he fails in the urbanity of his predecessor, and towards his conclusion descends to brash invective.

Hutcheson[1] attempted to reduce the question to common sense in three papers he contributed to a Dublin journal from 1725. In his 'Observations on the *Fable of the Bees*' he argued that though the actions of the intemperate, luxurious, and proud do indeed tend to the consumption of manufactures, that does not make such people any less odious and inhuman. 'The good arising to the public is in no way owing to them, but to the industrious, who must supply all customers, and cannot examine whether their expenses are proportionate to their fortunes or not.' According to him, a man may spend what he likes how he likes—short of immorality—so long as he lives within his means. To live high is not vice if you can afford it. This is quite beside the point of Mandeville's argument, who had never condoned 'vice' that was harmful to the individual or the community; and his conclusion that though vices may be inseparable from civilization they are not necessary to it, glances smoothly off Mandeville. Where he came closer home was in

[1] Francis Hutcheson, 1694–1746, was educated at James McAlpine's academy at Killeleagh, where he imbibed scholastic philosophy, and at Glasgow University. Returning to Ireland he started a private academy. The writings he published in Dublin led to his being offered the Chair of Philosophy at Glasgow, which he occupied until his death, Adam Smith being one of his pupils.

his criticism of Mandeville's tricks as a controversialist, not only in his ridicule of pedantry and the clergy, but also in his affectation of superior learning and broader knowledge of the world. That this last proved irritating to many is borne witness to by another attack in 1726 by John Thorold in *A Short Examination of . . . The Fable of the Bees*, where Mandeville is accused of sharing the vanity of all free-thinkers. A further refutation was that of Archibald Campbell in *An Enquiry into the Original of Moral Virtue* (1734), which supported the Shaftesburian view that 'Virtue is founded in the Nature of Things', an assertion which might have brought comfort to readers of Defoe's *History of the Devil*.

Surely, Mandeville seems to have thought, the prose exposition of his gnomic verses must have made plain how innocuous his matter was; but the 'manifold clamours' and the solemn attacks showed him his error, and in 1729 he published a Part II, consisting of six dialogues between Cleomenes, himself, and Horatio, who has been misled by the attackers. Here Mandeville abandons the paradoxical, provocative tone, and, though still pungent and lively, states his case more acceptably. He in no way retracts, and though not at all abating his assault upon the churches and their servants, professes himself a supporter of the Christian ethical idea. He is humane, tolerant, genial even, and sensible, as he elucidates ideas implicit in the first part. The dialogues throughout are admirably managed, and their style may, to quote Saintsbury, 'challenge comparison with the most famous literary vernaculars in English for racy individuality', having moreover, grace, balance, and a sense of pithy rhythmic effect. His conversations really read like conversations, and there is a refreshing absence of the infuriating Socratic trick of leading a victim into a trap.

In his *Enquiry into the Origin of Honour*, Mandeville takes up the point of the necessity of rewards and punishments. He denies that the idea of futurity keeps in awe the multitude who would otherwise commit crimes. 'It has been said a Thousand times by Divines of all Sects; but No body has ever shewn the least Probability of its being true.' In a series of dialogues in which Cleomenes convinces Horatio, he puts forward the proposition that pride and shame are really the same passion, namely self-liking, which he equates with honour. Religion, certainly, is necessary to government, which through it appeals

to popular sentiment, but honour is a much more useful idea
to the politician than virtue is: it is a later, and far more
ingenious invention. In the third dialogue he stresses the general
fear of the unknown, and claims that honour is a notion highly
important for the soldier, and is very modern in his view that
self-respect is the basis of discipline. It is, however, in the Preface that he puts his general position most clearly: adventuring
into etymology, he deduces virtue from *virtus*, being that which
appertains to man, *vir*: virtue thus is synonymous with manli-
ness. So far good, and then he sums up his whole moral position, especially as regards virtue being, not a spontaneous
impulse, but a matter of training: '. . . it is manifest that this
Habit [of virtue] is the Work of Art, Education and Custom;
and it never was acquired, where the Conquest over the Passions
had not been already made.' The whole performance is very
temperate, very common-sensical, difficult to refute in terms
of common experience, and all most urbanely set out. There is
none of the paradoxical air of *The Fable of the Bees*, none of the
impish humour, and scarcely a trace of parson-baiting. It is
quiet and assured, written by a man unwilling to wound, yet
not afraid to strike—and strike hard.

The struggle about the basis of morality was widely conducted, many, including Lord Hervey, taking part, and it
turned also upon the question of whether, even supposing
Mandeville to be justified, it was right to let people know it.
Would it not make them immoral? The conclusion of the matter
was paradoxical enough, as Mr. F. B. Kaye pointed out in his
admirably commented edition of *The Fable of the Bees*:

. . . The fact is that the cynical Mandeville, who spent his life in
telling how bad people were, really felt enormously more confidence in them than the uncynical Berkeley; and that is why he was
able to call them so many bad names and still be happy.

It was on the whole Hutcheson who, as Shaftesbury's nearest
heir, most effectively maintained the latter's views, in a style
marked by the sobriety proper to a professor of moral philosophy. How much of a temper he was with his elder may be
judged by his popular defence of the doctrine of ridicule in the
Reflections upon Laughter which appeared between 1725 and 1727
in the same Dublin journal that published his *Remarks on the
Fable of the Bees*. The matter of ridicule was giving rise to some

spirited debate. No doubt it was largely Hobbes's view of laughter as due to 'a sudden glory arising from a sudden conception of some eminency in ourselves'—a view popularized by Addison—that had brought the 'engine of ridicule' into some disrepute; at all events, when Shaftesbury, from the time of his *Letter concerning Enthusiasm*, and throughout his writings, maintained its efficacy in disentangling truth from folly, he set going a controversy that was to last some years, and was echoed by Mr. Brooke when he contested the election at Middlemarch. In his defence of the position which he elaborated in the second essay of *Characteristics*, Shaftesbury argued that a freedom of raillery alone made 'speculative conversations any way agreeable'. He had been at once attacked, as he seems to have expected, by the solemn, the pompous, and the pusillanimous, for already in his first Letter he had noted how alarmed 'men of sense' were at the approach of ridicule, as though they mistrusted their own judgement. Hutcheson, himself a man of great good humour with a love of serene good temper and laughter—he was, after all, Hibernian—begins his papers with an easy refutation of Hobbes, and proceeds to distinguish between laughter and ridicule. In his third paper he makes his position plain:

> When in any object there is a mixture of what is truly great, along with something weak or mean, ridicule may, with a weak mind, which cannot separate the great from the mean, bring the whole into disesteem, or make the whole appear weak or contemptible: but with a person of just discernment and reflection, it will have no other effect, but to separate what is great from what is not so.

But the battle went on, the pious objecting to ridicule of any part of any belief they might hold; but as Anthony Collins,[1] the notorious 'free-thinker', pointed out in his *Discourse concerning Ridicule and Irony* (1729), many serious divines had used banter and ridicule against sects to whom their own religion was just as serious as that of the Church to the orthodox, and he cited Hales, Chillingworth, Stillingfleet, Burnet, Sherlock, and others. He asked whether the accounts of some miracles, smacking rather of the poltergeist than the saint, really deserved serious

---

[1] Anthony Collins, 1676–1729, went from Eton to King's College, Cambridge, and thence to the Middle Temple. Living in Middlesex, he was appointed J.P., and Deputy Lieutenant of the county; and on moving to Essex in 1715 held the same offices there.

regard. But besides those he had already named, was not Erasmus guilty of this offence? And even Lucian had chased out jugglers and impostors. 'Laughing, therefore', he summed up, 'and *Ridicule* in *serious Matters*, go round the World with no inconsiderable Applause, and seem highly proper to this World of Nonsense and Folly.' Decency and propriety, he concluded, will stand the test of ridicule. Many others entered the lists, notably Berkeley in his third Alciphron dialogue, and forgetting that he himself had a pretty turn for bantering opinions he himself did not hold, twitted the minute philosophers for their use of it.

To return, however, to Hutcheson. How far he absorbed Shaftesbury's doctrine of the aesthetic basis of morals is shown by certain paragraphs of *An Inquiry concerning Beauty*, &c. (discussed under aesthetics), which prefaces *An Inquiry concerning Moral Good and Evil* (1725). In common with his predecessor he regards a system of rewards and punishments as ignoble, beneath the dignity of man. By arguing that good actions are disinterested, he disposes of Mandeville, and bases his doctrine on the existence of a moral sense. 'Perception of *moral Good*,' he insists, 'is not deriv'd from *Custom, Education, Example*, or *Study*. These give us no new Ideas.' This need not suppose the existence of innate ideas, merely that man by his make-up is ready to receive amiable or disagreeable ideas of actions just as he can recognize an harmonious form. All approved actions appear as benevolent, 'flowing from the love of others', and so on, the theory being built up on grounds which are ultra-optimistic. The amount of good a man can display in view of his aptitudes is debated by means of mathematical equations, which if meant to serve as aids to conviction fail of their purpose, since they do no more than make the plain platitudinous. He admits with Mandeville that the love of honour may be a potent influence in producing goodness, but honour itself presupposes a sense of moral virtue. Having shown to his satisfaction that a moral sense is essential to the happiness of mankind, and that virtue is superior to all other pleasures, he returns to aesthetics, and finally proceeds to establish political freedoms and rights as fundamentals without which virtue cannot have free play. This was good popular Whig doctrine, which, combined with an earlier appeal to the experience of every thinking man, made his book well enough liked to be republished in the next year, and to reach its fifth edition, though not its last, in 1753. For us he may well seem a little tedious; for though his approach is direct enough, his manner simple and not without vigour, there is none of the challenge we experience from Mandeville, nor the interest of following, as we do with Shaftesbury, the mind of a man urgently in pursuit of an originally felt idea.

This, however, we get abundantly in the writings of George Berkeley, who at this point takes his place in a history of literature, since it was in 1732 that he struck the popular mind with his attacks on Shaftesbury and Mandeville, and engaged its attention as a moralist. Standing for the most part, however, aside from this particular controversy, he shines out among all his contemporaries in the philosophic field, not only as a highly original thinker, but as a man of letters, combining an exalted vision with high practical common sense. If he had little effect on the contemporary philosophic scene, that is largely because he was too far ahead of his time.

Born in Ireland in 1685, he followed Swift and Congreve at the great school at Kilkenny, and in 1700 became a member of Trinity College, Dublin, where he rapidly made his mark, becoming a junior Fellow in 1707. Though appointed as a classic, his first published works were two tracts, in Latin, on mathematics. This interest in them he maintained throughout his life, later not so much for their own sake, but rather as a method of thought, excellent in itself, but also leading in the minds of others to inferences which had to be refuted. Thus in *The Analyst* (1734) he argued that no Christian dogma is more mysterious or incomprehensible than the assumptions made by mathematicians, asking in this discourse 'Addressed to an Infidel Mathematician', 'Whether such mathematicians as cry out against mysteries have ever examined their own principles?' Attacking the Newtonian calculus together with Leibnitz's theory of fluxions, which as 'the velocities of evanescent increments' he describes as 'ghosts of departed quantities', he very plausibly offers the common reader the no doubt welcome notion that 'he who can digest a second or third fluxion, a second or third difference, need not, methinks, be squeamish about any point in Divinity'. *The Analyst*, as an aspersion upon the fidelity of innocent mathematicians, provoked a number of heated rejoinders, Berkeley answering them in 1735 with *A Defence of Free-thinking in Mathematics*, which, with a couple of lesser pamphlets, will delight any reader who enjoys good combative controversy. These adventures into mathematics provide admirable illustrative addenda to Berkeley's main writings; they link up well with them, the same mind and temper may be seen working in both. But they need not concern us here, except to make plain to us that in science Berkeley was at the level of the best thought of his time, and that from the first the logic of mathematics, driving its points home to their utmost conclusion, was not foreign to his own procedure.

So much, at least, can be gathered from that remarkable series of notes and detached thoughts, long known as *The Commonplace Book*, but now as *Philosophical Commentaries*, compiled it would seem between 1707 and 1709 while he was resident at Trinity. Confusedly and in embryo, it contains not only the major part of his philosophy, but also much that enlightens us as to the man. He can fling out in one entry, 'I side in all things with the mob', and in another 'I am young, I am an upstart, I am a pretender, I am vain. . . . But one thing I know I am not guilty of. I do not pin my faith on the sleeve of any great man.' What it brings out clearly, together with his unhampered originality, is his early repugnance (a favourite word of his) to abstractions, or at any rate to any doctrine of abstract ideas: it reveals his empiricism, more ruthless than that of any of the empirical materialists whose conclusions he countered by his famous and fruitful 'immaterialism'. His philosophic road is not easy to tread without stumbling, and often, with his own Hylas, the reader may find 'an unaccountable backwardness' in accepting in his bones the propositions he so easily persuades him to in his mind. Coxcombs may vanquish Berkeley by a grin; Dr. Johnson may refute him by stubbing his toe on a stone; but the fact remains that, neglected for so long, even derided in his own day by such staunch lights as Dr. Samuel Clarke it may often be heard said that 'Berkeley' is where every philosopher today starts from. The general reader he can lure by his appeal, all along the line, to common experience (when deftly analysed); some may even be won over by his somewhat delusive statement that 'Sensual pleasure is the *summum bonum*. This is the great principle of morality', though more perhaps will approve of his determination 'To be eternally banishing Metaphisics, &c., and recalling men to

Common Sense'. But common sense with respect to what, for what purpose? the reader might ask; and certainly Berkeley would have more greatly stirred the thoughts of his contemporaries had he brought himself to compose the second part of his *Principles*, designed to deal with morals. The first draft of this, however, was lost during his travels in Italy; and being at least as much a man of letters as a philosopher, he found that he 'never had the leisure . . . to do so disagreeable a thing as writing twice on the same subject'.

An Essay towards a New Theory of Vision (1709), though not in itself a work of art, cannot but give intermittent pleasure to anyone who delights in beautifully clear argument, can relish lucid prose, and enjoy both direct attack and sly humour. It is, however, a matter of finding delectation in morsels, rather than liking the whole, which is of interest chiefly to those eager to trace Berkeley's development, especially in his breaking away from Locke. It may be said to open the door to philosophic possibilities, yet it stops short of Berkeley's true position. This may have been kept deliberately in reserve, for it was to be beautifully stated in the work published in the next year, and probably begun before the *Essay* was finished, namely *Of the Principles of Human Knowledge*. How Berkeley laboured at this as a devoted craftsman of letters, resolute to overcome the hindrances of language, is evidenced by the first draft of the Introduction, which we luckily possess, and which it is a challenging lesson to compare with the final version, not only for structure in the whole conduct of the argument, but also for the handling of paragraph, sentence, and phrase, together with the choice of words. The first writing is vigorous enough, indeed it batters too hard; in the second Berkeley had found, though not yet quite in perfection, his characteristic prose, musical as well as precise, persuasive as well as firm; warm, congenial, humane. He certainly would need to arrive at a prose abounding in these qualities to make his thesis acceptable. It was startling enough, and many would protest with Hylas 'But the novelty, *Philonous*, the novelty!' What made it all the more baffling was that it claimed to be based on common sense—that is, what every man is conscious of without any of the special faculties granted to philosophers. How would the average man respond to the paragraph immediately succeeding the one where Berkeley states of all things that 'Their *esse* is

percipi, nor is it possible they should have any existence out of the minds or thinking things which perceive them'?

It is indeed an Opinion strangely prevailing amongst Men, that Houses, Mountains, Rivers, and in a word all sensible Objects have an Existence Natural or Real, distinct from their being perceiv'd by the Understanding. But with how great an Assurance and Acquiescence soever, this Principle may be entertained in the World: Yet whoever shall find in his Heart to call it in Question may, if I mistake not, perceive it to involve a manifest Contradiction. For what are the foremention'd Objects but the Things we perceive by Sense, and what I pray you, do we perceive besides our own Ideas or Sensations, and is it not plainly repugnant that any one of these, or any Combination of them shou'd exist unperceiv'd?

In addition the disturbed reader will not only be further harassed by being told that the prevailing opinion, by which he no doubt lives, is a pernicious tenet, but, poor matter-of-fact man, will be informed that it will 'be found at bottom to depend on the doctrine of *abstract ideas*'.

Berkeley, as became him, ardently believed that philosophers were engaged in noble subjects; his complaint was that they handled them ill, in contradistinction with the mathematicians, whose method was excellent, but whose subject-matter was trifling. Thus though in a sense he owed most to the philosophies of Locke and Malebranche, it was rather as edifices he could shatter to bits and remould nearer his mind's desire, with here and there a brick or two from Hobbes and Descartes. Again and again, pursuing Locke's thought to a further, and perhaps merely logical conclusion, he makes it out to be 'absurd'. For Locke, in constructing a system to embody the scientific theories of his time, presented a material mindless world, governed by natural law, a corpuscular world responded to by a corpuscular nervous system, conceptions which seemed to Berkeley monstrously contradictory to actual experience, to 'common sense'. To exist is to be perceived, or to perceive. Things certainly do exist; and this being so, they are 'necessarily perceived by an infinite mind; therefore there is an infinite mind, or God'. When men see, hear, feel, have sensations, they are communicating with the mind of God. This, when simplified down to what is possibly a ridiculous extent, becomes a statement that all existence is a mental act, performed by a perceiving mind, the very process postulating an act of will. 'Take away

perceptions and you take away the mind', and 'the very existence of ideas constitutes the soul'. Again, 'While I exist or have
any idea, I am eternally, constantly willing; my acquiescence
in the present state is willing'; and in another *Commonplace
Book* jotting he approaches, as Huxley noted in the margin of
his copy, the Schopenhauerian position of the world being
will. As for the ascription to matter of primary and secondary
qualities, this too was absurd. 'There is an odour, that is, it was
smelt; there was a sound, that is, it was heard; a colour or figure,
and it was perceived by sight or touch', a declaration that comes
early in the *Principles*.

The polite reader might follow him up to this point, though
he might think that 'common sense' was being strained a little
far; yet, after all, the theory of knowledge is no easy business.
Some comforted themselves with the view that Berkeley was
merely an Irishman scattering amusing paradoxes; but others,
such as Shaftesburians accustomed to the idea of man as a
Prometheus under Jove, might not be so bewildered. Nor
would be those who read *Clavis Universalis—or a Demonstration
of the Non-Existence and Impossibility of the External World* put out
by Arthur Collier[1] in 1713. Collier was an original thinker, who
incurred suspicion; not only was he too tolerant of Arianism, but
he 'fell into the heresy of Apollinaris in regard to the Incarna-
tion'. He became aware of Berkeley, whom he mentions in his
Specimen (1730) and, indeed, comes close to him: 'I declare in
the First Place, that in affirming that there is no External World,
I make no Doubt or Question of the Existence of Bodies, or
whether the Bodies which are seen Exist or not. It is with me a
first Principle, that whatsoever is seen, Is. To Deny, or Doubt
of this, is errant *Scepticism*.' At all events the Berkeleyan position
was one that men could discuss, and easily distort to conclude
that there was no such thing as material substance—as indeed
for Berkeley in the Lockian sense there was none—and that all
was mind, that 'things' were no more than human 'ideas'. No
doubt 'it sounds very harsh to say we eat and drink ideas, and
are clothed with ideas'; but when you come to consider how we
come to be aware of victuals and apparel it will be seen that
this is only a question of the use of language. Thus manœuvred

---

[1] Arthur Collier, 1680–1732, educated at Pembroke College, Oxford, and later
Balliol, was in 1704 granted the living of Langford Magna, which he retained till h
death.

some could make themselves feel at home in this world. In his judgement of scientific results, however, Berkeley was some two hundred years ahead of his time. For him they were on a par with mathematical procedures, arriving at pronouncements which were, to be sure, of service in demonstration, reckoning, and prediction, but in no way a statement as to the nature of things, a point of view the scientist of today is not unready to share. *De Motu* seems to him not at all old-fashioned. To attempt to present more than this vulgarized account of Berkeley's philosophy would be outside the scope of this book. It remains only to say that as time went on it seems to have veered a little towards Platonism; but whether this was so, or if it was so to what extent, is still under debate by professional philosophers.

Here we are concerned with the literary quality of Berkeley's writing, and his impact on his age. Throughout his works we feel we are in contact with not only a brilliantly searching mind, but also with a man filled with a sense of the immediate importance of what he had to say, so that men, through a right understanding of the nature of being, might have a proper conception of God. In an age riddled with thinking such as animated Toland's very able *Christianity not Mysterious* (1696), or Collins's *Discourse of Free-Thinking* (1713), and others of the same kind, he felt urgently impelled to combat scepticism. Finding that his *Principles* met with a cool reception, even in quarters where he might have hoped for support, he set himself to put his views in the more easily assimilable form of *Three Dialogues*, which he published in 1713 when he came over to England. In to some extent using the Socratic form of manœuvring a hapless victim into agreement with him, he achieved what Yeats judged to be 'the only philosophical arguments since Plotinus that are works of art, being so well-bred, so sensible'. The setting in the college garden is as engaging as that on the banks of the Ilissus; the argument, though deeply serious, is witty and amusing, conducted with a good deal of humour and some dramatic movement; the prose, always precise, swift but beautifully balanced, is at once urbane and downright, being varied in pace and colour. Throughout Berkeley deals with actuality; his appeal is consistently to common experience, to universal physical sensation; on the other hand, to continue with Yeats's phrases, 'Though he could not describe mystery— his age had no fitting language—his suave glittering sentences suggest it; we feel perhaps for the first time that eternity is always at our heels or hidden from our eyes by the thickness of a door.'

This sense, naturally, does not pervade the whole of *Three Dialogues*, and part of their enduring fascination is the gradation of tone and tempo which characterizes them. Sometimes we are carried away on the wings of the argument; at others we share the delusive hope of Hylas that he is at last going to make a point against his mentor; Philonous on occasion loses patience and scolds his weakly backsliding friend:

I have said it already, and find I must still repeat and inculcate, that it is an unaccountable Licence you take, in pretending to maintain you know not what, for you know not what Reason, to you know not what Purpose:

the securely spaced emphases, the beautifully modulated vowel-sounds at the end of the clauses, serving to drive home the reproof. But it is where he rises to the imaginative height of his great argument against scepticism that Yeats's words seem justified. Take, as a single example, the passage in the second dialogue where he argues from design:

Look! are not the Fields covered with a delightful Verdure? . . . How aptly are the Elements disposed? What variety and use in the meanest productions of nature? What Delicacy, what Beauty, what Contrivance in animal and vegetable bodies? How exquisitely are all things suited, as well to their particular Ends, as to constitute apposite parts of the whole!

You have only to compare those few enchanting phrases with the formless, repetitive passages, of tedious length, with which Derham in *Astro-Theology* lulled his readers, to feel the vivid impulse that animated Berkeley. And when in the same paragraph he invites Hylas (so lamentably steeped in Locke!) to raise his thoughts to 'all those glorious luminaries that adorn the high arch of heaven', the tempo, the intensity change, so that we too share Berkeley's delight in 'the negligent profusion with which [the fixed stars] appear to be scattered throughout the whole azure vault'. However much Hylas may be called upon to bring imagination to his aid to try to grasp 'the energy of an all-perfect Mind displayed in endless forms', still there will stand out 'ungrasped a surplusage immeasurable'. And then, finally, Philonous asks 'How should those Principles be entertained that lead us to think all the visible beauty of creation a false imaginary glare?' Surely such scepticism will 'be thought extravagantly absurd by all men of sense'. It is, indeed, by perpetually challenging the imagination, not by overfeeding it, that Berkeley sustains his effect. Here again we have but to compare him on the same subject with Addison (*Spectator* 565), who, not content to leave a statement alone, is impelled to make it three times in a slightly different context, thus dulling the effect, to realize how Berkeley imparts his own deep excitement, a participation of the whole being in a glorious vision.

Except for the essays he contributed to the *Guardian*, Berkeley wrote little of more than ephemeral value for some twenty years. He was too busied about his own affairs, and his educational schemes. First, by Swift's contrivance, he accompanied Peterborough abroad as his chaplain, later going for some time to Italy as tutor to the son of Swift's friend, Dr. Ashe, Bishop of Clogher. Thus he had little leisure for writing. He did, indeed, keep a journal of his tour in Italy, in which here and there a vivid word or phrase leaps out, but it consists chiefly of factual notes, and reads in marked contradistinction with a brilliant letter he addressed to Arbuthnot in 1717 startlingly descriptive of an eruption of Vesuvius. While at Lyons on his way home in 1720, he offered a Latin treatise *De Motu* as a bid for a prize in a public competition; and after his return to England, finding the country in the throes of the South Sea Bubble crisis, he wrote *An Essay towards preventing the Ruin of Great Britain*. This, though it exhibits the interest in economics he was later to indulge fully in the *Querist*, is chiefly a gloomy indictment of English morals and manners, concluded by a hope that the time may not be near when men shall say of the English, that though once a brave, religious, and sincere people, 'they degenerated, grew servile flatterers of men in power, adopted Epicurean notions, became venal, corrupt, injurious, which drew upon them the hatred of God and man, and occasioned their final ruin'.

That, 'disgusted at an age and clime', and in the belief that 'Westward the course of empire takes its way', he turned his eyes to America, is at least dubious. But at all events he began from now to cherish in his mind a scheme for, as he phrased it, better supplying the churches in foreign plantations, and converting the savage Americans to Christianity, tasks to be furthered by a college to be erected in Bermuda. Money for this was lacking; but in 1723 Esther Vanhomrigh, revoking in her last illness the will she had made in favour of Swift, left all her considerable worldly goods to Berkeley; and this stroke of fortune was followed, in 1724, by promotion to the lucrative Deanery of Derry. Thus partly provided with funds, he further obtained from Walpole and from Parliament the grant of a sum encouraging enough to induce him to proceed with the plan, about which he issued a pamphlet in 1725. By 1728 the money was not forthcoming (it was, in fact, never made over); nevertheless he set out with his newly married wife to carry out his visionary project. On the voyage, however, he changed his mind about Bermuda, and landing at Newport in Rhode Island in January 1729 decided to found his college there. Nothing came of the scheme, except in the end the endowment of three classical scholarships at Yale; but while in Rhode Island he compiled his largest work, *Alciphron; or the Minute Philosopher*, which, on abandoning his venture in 1731, he brought back with him to England. Directed against free-thinkers, the volume has as its underlying theme an epigraph culled from Jeremiah: 'They have forsaken the Fountain of living waters, and hewed them out cisterns, broken cisterns that can hold no water.'

In these seven dialogues 'containing an apology for the Christian Religion', he conducts the argument in the manner of the conversations Landor was to write rather than in the sterner Socratic tone of *Three Dialogues*. Thus Alciphron and Lysicles, townsmen of fashion, maintain against Euphranor and Crito, decent country folk, the tenets of the 'latitudinarians' in thought, such as Collins, Shaftesbury, and Mandeville; or, rather, to say truth, of the opinions their more frivolous followers might irresponsibly come to hold. Thus, in a sense, in these dialogues, beautiful as they are, written in what is perhaps the most seductive prose in the whole of our literature, by distorting the views of his opponents Berkeley did not quite do justice to his own integrity. It was here that he gave an opening to Mandeville, whom he had attacked in the second dialogue, and who made the most weighty of the scattered replies, among them one by Lord Hervey. Mandeville's answer, *A Letter to Dion*, is a dignified and courteous item in controversy, and a sustained effort of sorrowful rather than angry indignation. Almost at once he brings a grave but justified charge against Berkeley:

Whoever reads your second Dialogue, will not find in it any real Quotations from my Book, either stated or examined into, but that the wicked Tenets and vile Assertions there justly exposed, are either such Notions and Sentiments, as first, my Enemies, to render me odious, and afterwards Common Fame had already father'd upon me, tho' not to be met with in any Part of my Book; or else, that they are spiteful Inferences, and invidious Comments, which others before you, without Justness or Necessity, had drawn from and made upon what I had innocently said . . .

the inference being that Berkeley had judged the *Fable* by hearsay, and had never himself read it. In his retort Mandeville develops his basic argument, remarking by the way on the unfairness of his case being given to such 'lawless libertines' as Alciphron and Lysicles. He reinforced his rigoristic position by laying down the proposition that 'the Kingdom of *Christ* is not of this world'; he is writing for a nation that professes Christianity, though its members show by every action that they are all 'closely attach'd to this wicked World'. The outcry against his book arose from its being an attack upon hypocrisy. It was 'a Book of exalted Morality'; but what vexed people most was that it was 'wrote without Rancour or Peevishness . . . free from Pedantry and Sourness'. He makes his position quite plain. 'Vice is always bad, whatever Benefit we may receive from it.' He upbraids Berkeley for his treatment of Shaftesbury, for whom he professes sincere reverence, and allows himself a little raillery. What he most admires in Crito and Euphranor, he declares, is 'the consummate Patience in keeping Company, and bearing for a whole Week together, with two such insupportable, out of the way Rascals, as you have represented Alciphron and Lysicles to be'. Shaftesbury was no longer there to answer for himself the attack on him in the third dialogue, but in a sense Mandeville had already in part done so for him, since in his *Origin of Honour* he had dealt with one of the subjects Berkeley develops in the third dialogue, namely that the idea of future rewards and punishments is necessary, since, thanks to the weakness of man, without it he will certainly err, and give rein to his desires and passions. Berkeley takes his place among the 'utilitarians'.

Whatever the philosophic merit of these dialogues may be, in all of them Berkeley shows himself a triumphant literary artist, resolving attractive plain speaking, scorn, humour, satire, witty repartee, and generous indignation into the kind of prose that can make the reader receptive of suggestion. Not only in his description of the setting in which the conversations take place, but also in the ways he can keep the reader's mind alert, never allowing him to stay too long in one temper, he reveals his mastery of evocation and of movement. The reader is never bored, not only because the prose itself gives positive delight, but because he cannot guess what may be going to happen next. The fifth dialogue, for example, contains a picture of Rhode Island (though the setting is supposedly England) exactly in tune with the sense of men who have been lulled by drinking tea, and a little fatigued by walking up a hill; it proceeds to serious discussion which can be relieved by such strokes as 'Can no method be found to relieve them from the terror of that fierce and bloody animal an English parson?' At one point, the moving, passionately felt arguments of Crito are varied by an entertaining, if a little unfair, twisting of some of Shaftesbury's prose into free verse. You feel all the time that Berkeley is enjoying himself as an artist, as a thinker, as a converter of the infidel, and the result is that you enjoy yourself too.

In his last three dialogues Berkeley was concerned to show that the arrows of the minute philosophers (Cicero's *minuti philosophi*) glanced harmlessly off the shield of orthodox doctrine held by believers. While he does not decry natural religion, he argues that by itself it is not enough, that the great pagan civilizations of the past fall below those of the Christian era in moral and social behaviour. For the rest his argument is much the appeal to scepticism as he used it with the mathematicians, but phrased in a more urbane way. It was, of course, the discussion of what men should believe, on what they should base their morals, on how, in short, they should live, that made these dialogues the most generally discussed of his writings, since they were directly relevant to daily life. It has been complained that his manner of argument is more likely to confirm the believer in his faith than to convert the sceptic; but that criticism can be applied *mutatis mutandis* to most controversialists, at all events by such readers as ridicule cannot abash. We may glean a lively example from the sixth dialogue, where Lysicles delivers himself, one might say delivers himself up, as follows:

I must own I should rather suppose with *Lucretius*, that the World was made by Chance, and that Men grew out of the Earth, like Pompions, than pin my Faith on those wretched fabulous Fragments of Oriental History. And as for the learned Men who have taken pains to illustrate and piece them together, they appear to me no better than so many musty Pedants. An ingenious Free-thinker may, perhaps, now and then make Use of their Lucubrations, and play one Absurdity against another. But you are not therefore, to think, he pays any real Regard to the Authority of such apocryphal Writers, or believes one Syllable of the *Chinese, Babylonian,* or *Ægyptian* Traditions. If we seem to give them a Preference before the Bible, it is only because they are not established by Law. This is my plain Sense of the Matter, and I dare say it is the general Sense of our Sect; who are too rational to be in earnest on such Trifles, though they sometimes give Hints of deep Erudition, and put on a grave Face to divert themselves with Bigots.

It is not only the Emperor Julian, we are made aware, whom Crito makes out to be a 'prating, light, vain, superstitious sort of man'. Yet the whole of the dialogues are conducted with such courtesy, that though the free-thinkers are, inevitably, routed, Berkeley, by submitting to them the basic ideas of his philosophy, all the while treats them as being on his own intellectual level. *Alciphron,* then, together with the much lighter *Guardian* essays (where Berkeley more than tends to berate the free-thinkers) constitute, in the absence of the second part of the *Principles,* his moral writings. These last, according to a jotting in the *Commonplace Book,* should have handled 'The 2 great principles of morality—the being of a God & the freedom of man', which to a large extent *Alciphron* does. At the end of that work freedom is certainly offered the free-thinkers, freedom to choose the way of 'utilitarian' common sense:

. . . Sceptic as you are, you own it probable there is a God, certain that the Christian Religion is useful, possible it may be true, certain that, if it be, the Minute Philosophers are in a bad way. This being the Case, how can it be questioned what Course a wise Man should take? . . . A Minute Philosopher, therefore, that would act a consistent part, should have the Diffidence, the Modesty, and the Timidity, as well as the Doubts of a Sceptic; not pretend to an Ocean of Light, and then lead us to an Abyss of Darkness.

Fear of punishment rather than hope of reward; at any rate, self-interest. But after all—a jotting again—'I'd never blame a man for acting upon interest. He's a fool that acts on any other principles.' One morsel of cant cleared away!

In 1734 Berkeley was nominated Bishop of Cloyne, and, except for a few months before his death early in 1753, spent the rest of his life in Ireland. His first literary work while there was the composition of the *Querist*, a remarkable pamphlet on economics, in which he sought a practical cure for the miseries of his country. In a succession of questions he attempted to undermine the mercantilist theory then prevalent, to destroy the illusion that the wealth of a nation consists, not in what it produces, but in the amount of precious metal it can amass. His queries are so probing as to be valuable to this day. It is too poor a claim to make that in many respects he anticipated Adam Smith; he went further, and may be said to belong to the age of Keynes. Such a phrase as 'Whether we are not in fact the only people to starve in the midst of plenty' has an ominously modern ring. And it was again a practical matter, an epidemic of ill health in Ireland, which Berkeley set himself to relieve by advocating the use of tar-water, that brought forth his next work, one of major importance. But *Siris; A Chain of Philosophical Reflexions and Inquiries* (1744), though it opens with utterances reminiscent of a quack crying his nostrums, proceeds by a series of imaginatively logical steps to a consideration of the nature of God. If Berkeley began with the practical, as he did also in the smaller works that he issued, such as *A Word to the Wise* (1749) in which he asked the aid of the Roman Catholic clergy to rouse the peasantry from sloth, or the witty *Maxims Concerning Patriotism* (1750), he was easily carried away into other realms by his eager spirit. Thus in *Siris*—the name first occurs in the second edition—he came to produce what in many ways is his profoundest work, as it is certainly the most meta-physical, raising issues which are still matters of debate. Tar-water, as a result of this treatise, became the most popular remedy in Europe, and when Horace Walpole asked a chemist 'Do you sell tar-water?' he was answered 'Sir, I sell nothing else!', a sufficient tribute to the practical side. Indeed who would not wish to imbibe a 'luminous spirit' detained in the native balsam of pines, and of a nature so 'mild and benign . . . as to cheer but not inebriate, and to produce a calm and steady joy like the effect of good news'? But from considering the properties of tar-water, then the characteristics of the plants and trees that produce tar, Berkeley went on to ponder causes and effects, and, rejecting all mechanical explanations (which explain nothing), to ask:

. . . what these forces are, which are supposed to be lodged in bodies, to be impressed on bodies, to be multiplied, divided, and communicated from one body to another, and which seem to animate bodies like abstract spirits, or souls.

Through the agency of his prose, always vitally alive, as though issuing naturally from the urgency of the spirit within, he takes the reader on an exciting chase (the phrase is excusable) after the ultimate truth of things, which, however, man cannot hope to see, 'imprisoned' as he now is in his body, 'like an oyster'. Only in this treatise does he make use of authorities, here, *en revanche*, quoting a bewildering number, including the Chinese and the 'Hermaics', veering broadly towards Platonism. The whole, to the general reader, does not in actual impression differ very much from theistic optimism, with the same handling of the problem of evil. The recurring leitmotive of the work, that 'a Divine Agent doth by his virtue permeate and govern the elementary fire or light, which serves as animal spirits to enliven and actuate the whole mass and all the members of the visible world', has much in common with the view set forth by Lysicles some fifteen years earlier, nor is it in essence at variance with the idea of the Great Directing Mind postulated by Blackmore, Pope, or any of the self-confessed Stoics. On the Stoics indeed Berkeley drew (among almost every conceivable ancient authority) in the latter half of this amazing document, which becomes a splendid, flaming extravaganza on the theme of light, or fire, a magnificent prose poem, now invoking the alchemists, now Newton, or the Pythagoreans, now the Egyptians, contemporary Dutch doctors or the Cambridge Platonists; Berkeley is enraptured by the theme of light; at moments we feel that God for him is light, or fire, 'Bright effluence of bright essence increate'. Almost, like Dryden's Damilcar, he reels, he staggers, he is drunk with light. It is with something of a sense of anticlimax that at the end we find him almost perfunctorily connecting the doctrine of the Trinity with the beliefs of the ancient philosophers.

But the great importance to literature of Berkeley is the extraordinary quality of his prose, which seems to put the reader into direct contact with a man imbued with candour, a being of exquisite perceptions and piercing insights. The run of his sentences, their vigour and variation, the tendency to end clauses with polysyllables, and sentences with a firm single sound, the lovely vowel-play, all makes up a music which in no way interferes with the precision, is finally part of the precision.

It is the music that was in him that he imparts to us, so that we do indeed feel when steeped in his writing that eternity is separated from us only by the thickness of a door. Sometimes the result is achieved by the unusual use of words, as Dr. Donald Davie has shown when, in analysing the style in *Siris*, he traces the effect made on us by

a choice of terms which are nicely ambiguous in reference. We speak of a 'mild' purgative as we speak of a 'mild' disposition; and 'mild' therefore can be used so that the reader feels, in the word, the identity of the spiritual and physical worlds. . . .

Again and again, tar-water is described in terms which strike the modern reader as proper only to descriptions of moral or spiritual condition. It is 'unctuous', 'subtle', 'active'. It is 'gentle, bland and temperate'. And 'it is of so just a temperament as to be an enemy to all extremes'—phrasing which one would think to find in Hume, describing a moral man.

Though Berkeley can be pungent and aphoristic, the main effect of his prose is to release the imagination into unaccustomed realms.

If Berkeley's prose is throughout that of a mind imbued with happiness, transfusing a kind of serious gaiety into all that he writes, the prose of Joseph Butler[1] is that of a man bravely and religiously supporting the ills that are the lot of fallen humanity surrounded by uncertainties, hampered by its ignorance. The music in his soul that made him a writer was sad, resigned, and quiet. Even more than the other philosophers here considered, he was primarily a moralist, and it was as such that he affected his generation, first in the *Sermons* (1726) with the Preface added in 1729, then in the famous *Analogy* (1736), more especially in the second Appendix 'Of the Nature of Virtue', and finally in the *Six Sermons* collected in 1749. He saw that to arrive at the idea of morality was a far more laborious business than, for instance, Shaftesbury or Hutcheson had seemed to imagine. But the very carefulness of his thought makes him none too

[1] Joseph Butler, 1692–1752, was sent from under the care of the Master of the Grammar School at Wantage to Samuel Jones's Dissenting Academy, first at Gloucester, then at Tewkesbury. Adhering to the Church, he went to Oriel College, Oxford, in 1715, took his degree and was ordained in 1718, being almost at once nominated preacher at the Rolls Chapel, which post he retained until 1726. In 1721 he became a prebend of Salisbury, and in 1725, Rector of Stanhope. Appointed Clerk of the Closet to Queen Caroline, after her death he was, in 1738, made Bishop of Bristol, to which, in 1740, he added the Deanery of St. Paul's. In 1750 he was appointed to the see of Durham.

easy to read. You feel all the time that he is labouring patiently, searching in the depths of a profound nature for the exact thing he means to talk about. Aware, as Berkeley also had been, of the imperfection of language, in the Preface he warns the reader against isolating any statement: he who would understand must

consider the whole of what is said upon it: Because this is necessary, not only in order to judge of the Truth of it, but often, such is the Nature of Language, to see the very Meaning of the Assertion;

and in the *Analogy*:

Language is, in its very Nature, inadequate, ambiguous, liable to infinite Abuse, even from Negligence; and so liable to it from Design, that every Man can deceive and betray by it.

No wonder that, meticulously anxious to make his statements correspond with the truth of his thought and his experience, the reader may feel with John Byrom that his manner is 'a little too little vigorous'. But then Butler did not think that reading should be easy. He knew that there was a great deal of literature designed for an 'idle way of reading and considering things', and a great many people who conned books to find arguments for some casual purpose rather than to arrive at the truth of things, or 'merely for the sake of talking, or to qualify themselves for the world'. He knew only too well that it is extremely hard, if not impossible, to put difficult things simply without falsifying them.

It must be acknowledged [he says in the Preface] that some of the following Discourses are very abstruse and difficult; or if you please, obscure: But I must take Leave to add, that those alone are Judges, whether or no and how far this is a Fault, who are Judges, whether or no and how far it might have been avoided—those only, who will be at the Trouble to understand what is here said, and to see how far the Things here insisted upon, and not other Things, might have been put in a plainer Manner; which yet I am very far from asserting that they could not.

Butler, then, will not win the reader as Berkeley or Shaftesbury or even Mandeville might (one may leave out the ponderously mathematical Clarke): he may possibly subdue; but anyone eager to pursue what Butler himself is in search of will be greatly rewarded, finding it most readily, perhaps, in his *Charge*, and the *Sermon on Education*.

Though he is to be ranked among the 'pessimists', he cannot be simply opposed to the 'optimists', for he shares a good deal of ground with them. He was ready enough, with others of his age, to accept the viability of natural religion up to a point; he conceded that there were many good natural instincts; but he insisted upon the necessity for judgement, or as Euphranor, a shade more 'utilitarian' than Butler, phrased it to Lysicles, for 'the art of computing'. On the other hand, he was prepared to admit with Mandeville that conscience is often merely the fear of what others will think of us, that self-esteem which rests on the esteem of the world. But always he bids you ask, what sort of actions will your cogitations produce? How far will they be beneficial to yourself and others? What is 'fit', as he would say, for 'such a creature as man is, placed in the circumstances we are in the world'? All this might be dreary, even trivial, but in actual proof it is not. You feel all the time that you are in contact with a man feeling passionately if patiently towards the truth of things, searching for the final reason why we should act thus and not otherwise. He is not concerned with metaphysics, but with the common realizations of being. 'Things and actions are what they are, and the consequences of them will be what they will be: why then should we desire to be deceived?'

Anybody of any faith at all, or of no faith if he is not impenetrably pachydermatous, can today read the sermons with profit, and that delight which good literature brings. The note struck throughout is that 'we are plainly constituted such sort of creatures as to reflect upon our own nature', and we will find that conscience is the 'universal governor' of our actions. Since his preaching was largely to men whom he assumes to be self-seeking, much of it is directed to proving that self-love and social are the same; that self-love, virtue, and duty turn out to be identical. But we must not confuse: 'Everything is what it is, and not another thing', even though it may turn out that benevolence most satisfies the love of self. For

It is plain that there is a Capacity in the Nature of Man, which neither Riches, nor Honours, nor sensual Gratifications, nor anything in this World can perfectly fill up, or satisfie: There is a deeper and more essential Want, than any of these Things can be the Supply of.

Or again:

Reason alone, whatever any one may wish, is not in reality a sufficient Motive of Virtue in such a Creature as Man: but his Reason joined with those Affections which God has impress'd upon his Heart.

There is no evangelical fervour about him; his method is always to ask men to look into themselves, to watch their motives, to be self-critical. The sermon 'Upon Self-Deceit' is salutary reading for anyone today; let him try to answer the question, 'Suppose then an enemy were set about defaming you, what part of your character would he single out?', and he may find uncomfortable matter to reflect upon. The sermons in short are still alive, still disturbingly actual; they are not exciting, they will not dazzle, the ensnaring literary graces are wanting; they do, no doubt, as Matthew Arnold complained, lack the element of joy in religion; but he will be a poor spiritless rationalist whom they will not stir to think to some purpose about himself.

It is not, however, with his sermons, relevant as they are even today, that his name is usually connected, but with that to us rather curious piece of argumentative architecture, *The Analogy of Religion*, of which the title goes on: 'Natural and Revealed to the Constitution and Course of Nature'. Butler's aim was to refute the Deism which with varied ethos pervaded the religious sense of the time. Butler was perhaps unduly alarmed, as a consequence maybe of outspoken declarations he heard at the conclaves he attended in Queen Caroline's drawing-room; it was no doubt from these that Hervey could conclude:

Besides this, the fable of Christianity, as Leo X called it, was now so exploded in England that any man of fashion or condition would have been almost as much ashamed in company to own himself a Christian as formerly he would have been afraid to profess himself none.

This state of affairs Butler lamented in the Advertisement prefixed to the first edition:

It is come, I know not how, to be taken for granted, by many Persons, that Christianity is not so much as a Subject of Inquiry; but that it is, now at length, discovered to be fictitious. And accordingly they treat it, as if, in the present Age, this were an agreed Point among all People of Discernment; and nothing remained, but to set it up as a principal Subject of Mirth and Ridicule, as it were, by Way of Reprisals, for its having so long interrupted the Pleasures of the World.

The remedy was to controvert this attitude 'upon principles of reason', a reason which should, however, be 'cautious'. Thus ever and again we meet such phrases as 'for aught we know', and 'for aught I see', the basis of the argument being stated in the Introduction. Origen, he says,

has with singular Sagacity observed, that 'he who believes the Scripture to have proceeded from Him who is the Author of Nature, may well expect to find the same sort of Difficulties in it, as are found in the Constitution of Nature'.

He might have taken for epigraph a sentence from Swift's *Letter to a Young Gentleman*: 'Neither is it strange, that there should be Mysteries in Divinity, as well as in the commonest operations of Nature'. It is a question of probability, as he insists at the outset, in a passage that will serve admirably as an example of his careful, even hesitating manner:

That which chiefly constitutes Probability is expressed in the Word Likely, i.e. like some Truth or true Event; like it, in itself, in its Evidence, in some more or fewer of its circumstances. For when we determine a thing to be probably true, suppose that an Event has or will come to pass, 'tis from the Mind's remarking in it a Likeness to some other Event, which we observe has come to pass. And this observation forms, in numberless daily Instances, a Presumption, Opinion, or full Conviction, that such Event has or will come to pass; according as the observation is, that the like Event has sometimes, most commonly, or always so far as our observation reaches, come to pass at like distances of Time, or Place, or upon like Occasions.

All this is combined with an appeal to the virtue of prudence (Berkeley, we have seen, made the same appeal), in a manner that attaches him in some sort to the utilitarian school, though this he repudiated in the second Dissertation; for, in the end, the happiness of the world is not man's concern, but God's. Man's business is veracity and justice.

Possibly, as Leslie Stephen suggested, the *Analogy* made more sceptics than it redeemed, for the same charge might be brought against Butler that the not altogether ineffectual Hervey brought against Berkeley in reply to *Alciphron*, that he was a dangerous friend, since you cannot prove by reason what is by definition a mystery, and that in trying to do so you make for infidelity. Butler's aim, however, was not so much to vindicate Christianity, as to induce Deists not to reject it. The difficulties of natural religion, he insists, are of the same kind as those of revealed religion; therefore it seems 'probable' that the Author of Nature is the Author of Revelation. But to the common reader, as Bagehot pointed out in what remains one of the most brilliant, penetrating and balanced pronouncements on Butler, the complement of Matthew Arnold's 'Bishop Butler and the Zeitgeist', 'so far from its being probable that Revelation would have contained the same difficulties as Nature, we should have expected it to explain those difficulties'. Butler, in reality addressing those who already believe, bases his argument on the limited faculties of man to understand, and the suspicion creeps in that he is at one and the same time explaining to us and telling us that we are incapable of understanding the explanation. It all comes perilously close once more to the argument from scepticism.

Yet though the work may not seem to us to offer very sure grounds for belief—any defence of Christianity must today take account of attacks made from a different quarter—no one can read it without feeling an enormous respect for Butler, a recluse urged by the continual need to grapple with ultimate problems, wrestling with thought, with language, with all the difficulties and uncertainties of knowledge; a man with great psychological insight, yet without much imagination as to the impulses, *divers et ondoyants*, of his fellow creatures. The constant pressure makes it literature. His prose is the reverse of Berkeley's, being innocent of imagery, lacking any change of movement, devoid of wit, and with only the smallest traces of humour. According to Leslie Stephen, 'The *Analogy* impresses us in literature like some mass of rockpiercing strata of a different formation, immovable and undecayed, but yet solitary, exceptional, and barren.' The rock may have nourished no growth, but for some generations it provided a secure seat for certain types of 'such creatures as we are'. And to Bagehot, though he found it full of feeble words and halting sentences, it seemed, however oddly, that 'the power of the *Analogy* is in its rhetoric', in 'the strong disinclination to disagree with' Butler that comes over you as you muse over his writings.

Those who are at home with Butler will feel no such

disinclination when reading the philosophical works of Boling-broke,[1] even though the judgement of posterity has always been at variance with what his contemporaries thought of him. At one time Swift was dazzled, and though he felt some reserves as to his character, remained his correspondent; for Pope he held, so long as he was in England, the declared post of guide, philosopher, and friend. Chesterfield, of a younger generation, but who had known him well in the period of opposition to Walpole, could write to his son of the *Letters on the Study and Use of History* (pub. 1752):

It is hard to determine whether this work will instruct or please most. The most material historical facts, from the great era of the treaty of Munster, are touched upon, accompanied by the most solid reflections, and adorned by all that elegancy of style which was peculiar to himself, and in which, if Cicero equals, he certainly does not exceed him; but every other writer falls short of him. I would advise you almost to get this book by heart.

The fact would seem to be that, apart from his elegancy of style, which will be discussed later, he appeals mostly to those engaged in affairs, such as Disraeli, who welcome not only the application of ideas to life, but their formulation from experience, and moreover the testing of them by living. Burke's 'Who now reads Bolingbroke?' is probably no more than one of those chance phrases the tone of which can easily be misconstrued. That he is not much liked by specialists in any field is not to be wondered at; he always refused to be led to conclusions by logic alone, a position he makes clear enough in the third letter on *The Study of History*:

I think then we must be on our guard against this very affectation of learning, and this very wantonness of curiosity, which the examples and precepts we commonly meet with are calculated to flatter and indulge. We must neither dwell too long in the dark, nor wander about till we lose our way in the light. We are too apt to carry systems of philosophy beyond all our ideas, and systems of history beyond all our memorials. The philosopher begins with

---

[1] Henry St. John, Viscount Bolingbroke, 1678–1751, travelled abroad after leaving Eton. M.P. in 1701, in 1704 he became Secretary at War till the fall of the ministry in 1708. Returning with the Tories in 1710, he was made a Privy Councillor and Secretary of State, being created Viscount Bolingbroke in 1712. Dismissed by George I in 1714, in 1715 he fled to France, where for a few months he was Secretary to the Pretender. Breaking with the Jacobites, he was pardoned in 1723, but never regained political rights, though he was not without influence.

reason, and ends with imagination. The historian inverts this order: he begins without memorials, and he sometimes ends with them.

Small wonder that philosophers grow irascible while reading him, and sympathy goes out to Mr. D. G. James when in the course of his brilliant study he cried in exasperation: 'He will not *think*.' Nevertheless, he is forced to say that though Bolingbroke did violence to the empiricism of Locke, he is part of the movement from Hobbes which was to come full circle in Hume. Philosophers will never rank him high, if only because, suspicious of the naked intellect in common with Swift and Shaftesbury and Pope, he failed to evolve a proper structure of thought. It is not in the realm of pure thought that he is interesting, nor should he be judged on that level, and he would have applied to himself Samuel Butler's couplet

> An English Poet should be tryd b'his Peres
> And not by Pedants, and Philosophers.

Yet it is appropriate that he should be considered in this section, rather than among historians, essayists, or memoir-writers, though it is these, and practical statesmen, who are his peers; for after all he studied philosophy in his early retirement when out of office during Queen Anne's Whig ministry; he discussed it at great length with Pope, writing down the results of their conversations. If systems were not to his taste, general ideas were very much so, and he clearly exemplifies the Deism which was so marked a feature of the age, and which receives such short shrift from believers on the one hand, and confirmed agnostics on the other. What precisely his religion was it would be hard to say; possibly that which the first Earl of Shaftesbury had declared to be the religion of all sensible men; which no sensible man ever reveals.

His career as a writer began with his launching of *The Examiner* in 1710 to support the Tory interest, and though this did not occupy him for long, he once more took up political journalism as Humphry Oldcastle in *The Craftsman* of 1725, after his return from exile two years earlier. But it is not in this sphere that his writing is of interest; no doubt the exercise gave his prose a certain flexibility, taught him something of the art of attack, the earliest of his writings to attract the literary historian being the *Letter to Sir William Wyndham*, written in 1717 though not published until 1753. This brilliant apologia, though it does not

yet exhibit the political philosophy, born of practical knowledge, which he was to develop in his later writings, is a lasting
commentary on the ways of politicians and the springs of
politics at a time of crisis, and the mentality of dispossessed
exiles. His often quoted remark on the House of Commons is
still valid: 'You know the nature of that assembly: they grow,
like hounds, fond of the man who shews them game, and by
whose halloo they are used to be encouraged.' If the character of
the Pretender is a little classic in its kind, that is a special—if not
unusual—case; whereas his description of the self-induced
hysteria which took hold of the Whigs after the accession of
George I can be applied to any election today. Already in that
lively writing we find the ability to handle large masses of
material, the beautiful skill in paragraphing—he is perhaps the
first of our writers to handle that difficult art—and his perhaps
too easy disposition to derive general ideas from the idiosyncrasies of human behaviour.

He was to develop all these in his larger works, such as *The
Patriot King*, the *Dissertation upon Parties*, and the *Letters on the
Study of History* already referred to; but anybody wishing to
make a first acquaintance with his writing and his mind, even
to know the bases of his philosophy, political and otherwise,
can gratify himself well enough by conning not only the *Letter
to Sir William Wyndham* but the two booklets bound up with it in
1753, namely *Of the State of the Nation*, left unfinished in 1749,
and *A Letter to Mr. Pope*, written in about 1730, which served as
a Preface to the philosophic *Letters, or Essays, addressed to Alexander
Pope*, published by Mallet in his edition of 1754. The themes he
later developed at too relentless a length are all there, and if
not always fully stated, at least rather more than adumbrated;
moreover, the three works span his active literary life, and we
recognize the same mind working in them all through, a mind,
however, in some ways at least capable of being affected by
experience, but which always refuses to be overpersuaded.

'There has been much noise made about free thinking', he
remarked to Pope; but his was not irresponsible, based as it was
on an enormous amount of reading among the moderns as well
as the ancients. His theism, his moral sense—the wildness of his
youth is no argument against his having one—is much that of
Shaftesbury tempered by Mandeville, the object of his thought
being what he called 'the first philosophy', namely 'natural

theology or theism, and natural religion or ethics'. For this, we do not need 'any other guides than the works and the word of God. In natural religion the clergy are unnecessary, in revealed they are dangerous guides.' A little too contemptuous of 'metaphysical pneumatic', his favourite philosopher, short of complete acceptance, was Locke, and for the layman at least his arguments about Malebranche, Descartes, Leibnitz, and Berkeley have a happy cogency, while his determination not to let words run away with him is a refreshing discipline.

However, in a work devoted to literature, that side of him must be left to the none too tender mercy of philosophers. His chief interest will for many lie in his discourses upon politics or his cogitations upon history, for there he was in direct contact with the theme. He is grappling with something that he knows about. From having been a notable engineer of party, he came to favour a broader basis of government, which he stated first in his *Dissertation upon Parties*, originally published as essays in *The Craftsman*, and was to put more idealistically in *The Patriot King*. As a man of affairs he is perfectly aware that in the second book he is crying for the moon, men being what they are; but like Swift he deplored the rise of the moneyed interest; like Swift he came to think that a minority opposition smacked too much of faction. His account of the rise of party government is full of fascination if only as representing what a brilliantly clever man thought about the political history of his own country in the previous hundred years. Party for him became the instrument by which a governor might divide and rule, a principle he regarded as abominable. Letter VII opens:

I advanced in the *first* of these Essays, something to this Effect; that every *clumsy, busy, Child of Fortune*, on whom she bestows the Means and Opportunity of *corrupting*, may govern by this infamous Expedient; and having gratified his Ambition and Avarice, may have a Chance to secure himself from Punishment, by destroying the *Liberties of his Country*.

The patriot king, therefore, will act on a different principle, selecting men who vary in their admixture of Baconian wisdom and cunning. It was a counsel of perfection, as he must have known when he withdrew abroad after the failure of the opposition to oust Walpole from his supremacy in 1735. It was at that date that he composed, from France, his *Letters on the Study and Use of History*, to which again laymen will give more assent than the professional historians, most of whom he scourges as pedants with Scriblerian ferocity.

For us today Bolingbroke is not of the first importance, though it would be as well if he were more studied by those who utter glib generalizations about the eighteenth century, or vilify him without having made much attempt to understand him. And if few will share Chesterfield's view of the elegancy of his style, this too is worth consideration. If now and again his grammar is a little entangling, he is in the main beautifully lucid. If sometimes he seems a trifle long-winded, too generously multiplying his examples, too insistently making his point, his prose is never dull. It is graceful, it is modulated, it is largely conversational at the level the Augustans aimed at. Hervey, who detested him, judged that 'his writings are always larded with a great deal of knowledge, as well as seasoned with satire; his words are well chosen, his diction extremely raised, and his style so flowing that it does not seem at all studied or forced; and when he makes use of uncommon words, seems to do it from not being in a common way of thinking, rather than seeking them'; a sound analysis. Some may feel his prose to be a little too consciously Ciceronian, but how gently persuasive it can be may be exemplified by an extract from the fifth letter in *The Study and Use of History*:

By comparing, in this study, the experience of other men and other ages with our own, we improve both: we analyse, as it were, philosophy. We reduce all the abstract speculations of ethics, and all the general rules of human policy, to their first principles. With these advantages every man may, tho few men do, advance daily towards those ideas, those increated essences a Platonist would say, which no human creature can reach in practice, but in the nearest approaches to which the perfection of our nature consists: because every approach of this kind renders a man better, and wiser, for himself, for his family, for the little community of his own country, and for the great community of the world. Be not surprized, my Lord, at the order in which I place these objects. Whatever order divines and moralists, who cotnemplate the duties belonging to these objects, may place them in, this is the order they hold in nature: and I have always thought that we might lead ourselves and others by private virtue, more effectually by a due observation of this order, than by any of those sublime refinements that pervert it.

Self-Love but serves the virtuous mind to wake,
As the small pebble stirs the peaceful lake:

The centre mov'd, a circle strait succeeds,
Another still, and still another spreads;
Friend, parent, neighbour, first it will embrace,
His country next, and next all human race.

So sings our friend Pope, my lord, and so I believe. So I shall prove too, if I mistake not, in an epistle I am about to write to him, in order to complete a set that were writ some years ago.

A man of my age, who returns to the study of history, has no time to lose, because he has little to live: a man of your Lordship's age has no time to lose, because he has much to do . . .

The manner is indeed a little easier than usual here, where he is writing for the young Lord Cornbury, the descendant of his admired Clarendon; but even when writing more sternly, as in the philosophical essays, there is always about his phrases the grace of human speech. No small feat when discussing 'the Nature, Extent and Reality of Human Knowledge', 'the Folly and Presumption of Philosophers', or 'the Propagation of Errour and Superstition'.

The only other writer in this period comparable with these is William Law, whose more important work, however, was written after 1740, when he finally came under the spell of the writings of Jacob Boehme. He had, however, become a public figure much earlier, since, till his middle years by no means averse from stout controversy, he had plunged into the Bangorian dispute (1717–19) with *Three Letters to the Bishop of Bangor*. Appearing again where debate was for the moment at its hottest, in 1723 he issued his *Remarks upon the Fable of the Bees*, referred to earlier, which he followed in 1726 with a violent diatribe on *The Unlawfulness of Stage Entertainment*, a somewhat belated contribution to the Collier controversy of the late nineties. In 1731 he replied vigorously to Tindal's *Christianity as Old as the Creation* (the second volume of which was 'quietly burked' by Bishop Gibson), and in 1736 his *Letters to Fanny Henshaw* involved him in argumentation with the Quakers. As yet unwearied, in the next year he returned to the attack upon Hoadly; and in 1740, the year he retired to King's Cliffe, issued two works against Trapp, who invited Law's scorn for being, as well as a sober churchman, a poet and professor of poetry, and had committed the crime of writing a play. But already, in this busy life, in which he had relinquished a Fellowship at Emmanuel on declaring himself a non-juror, become tutor to

Edward Gibbon the elder at Putney, by virtue of which the future historian met him, been ordained a non-juring priest, founded a girls' school, argued with John Byrom, and broken with John Wesley, he had begun that series of works upon which his fame rests, and which place him among the very highest of English mystical writers.

His earliest works in this kind, however, were not too far from mundane living, and were addressed to mortals to whom perilous heights are denied, his first being *A Treatise upon Christian Perfection* (1726), to be followed in 1728 by the still popular, or at all events occasionally reprinted, *A Serious Call to a Devout and Holy Life*. Though this has neither the spiritual charm nor the literary grace of *Holy Living* and *Holy Dying*, it has about it all the sweetness of the unworldly approach; and as a manual of devotion it soars above the numerous versions of *The Practice of Piety* which the booksellers all through the period had found it so profitable to publish. Written with a good deal of humour, and based on acute enough observation of manners, it is couched in urbane straightforward prose split up into very short paragraphs extremely easy to digest, and which always make their point. Thus he appealed to a far larger public than Berkeley or Butler could hope to reach, in fact to the immense public struggling into a civilization it hoped to see moral, to the whole enormous dissenting class, and to the evangelically minded who would not go so far as Wesley or Whitefield. Take, for instance:

You can make no *stand* against the assaults of pride, the meek affections of humility can have no place in your soul, till you stop the power of the world over you, and resolve against a *blind obedience* to its laws.

The basis, of course, was a deep religious emotion:

Prayer is the nearest approach to God, and the highest enjoyment of him, that we are capable of in this life.

It is the noblest exercise of the soul, the most exalted use of our best faculties, and the highest imitation of the blessed inhabitants of heaven.

Such readily understandable calls, interspersed with what might be called 'character sketches' modelled upon those which enlivened the *Tatler* ('*Flavia* would be a miracle of *Piety*, if...'), could not but provide welcome pabulum for the emergent middle class which preferred to follow its worthier instincts rather than distress its mind about the grounds of virtue or the nature of conscience.

For what really makes Law of interest to us at this point is his reaction against 'reason' in this sphere; he is in line with the general trend back to 'enthusiasm', and he shares with Butler a scepticism as to the accuracy of language. In this matter, in his *Demonstration of the ... Errors of ... a Plain Account*, namely of the Lord's Supper (1737), he boldly tackled Hoadly, declaring roundly:

> When you place the Power of your Salvation in your *intellectual* Light or the Strength of your *own reason* you place it in the *weakest* part, in the *poorest*, most *trifling* and *insignificant* Thing that belongs to you and upon that which has the least Effect in human life.
>
> The only good that Reason can do to you is to remove the Impediments of Virtue and to give room to that inward *Instinct* or *Attraction* to God, and Goodness, to display itself; that the inmost Spirit of your Mind may receive its Strength and Assistance from the Spirit of God, from which, as the *Needle* from the Loadstone, it has all its *Instinct* of goodness and *Tendency* towards God.

This Confucian 'The nature of man is originally good', though it may seem to echo Shaftesbury, is to put aside the inquiry into the origins of virtue, and totally to repudiate all that Butler was trying to inculcate. For Law a direct divine message was essential, and his attitude helps to complete the picture of the active religious sense of the early eighteenth century, an age wrongly regarded as one of spiritual apathy. Just as it is misleading to take the energetic distortions of the satirists as a realistic picture of the time, so it is a mistake to accept the dicta of those who attack the religious sloth of their contemporaries. In either case it implies the vigorous health of an opposite outlook. After all, the Society for the Propagation of the Gospel was founded in 1701, only three years after the birth of the Society for the Promotion of Christian Knowledge, and the whole scene from 1700 to 1740 is noisy with religious controversy (which cannot be more than referred to in this book), to which Samuel Clarke's *Dissertation on the Being and Attributes of God* (1705) may be regarded as central. No attack on orthodox doctrines, such as those of Collins or Woolston, went unregarded. Nor was the Church itself by any means sunk in fat slumbers, as can be judged from Burnet's *Letter on*

Pastoral Care (1692) at one end, and Butler's *Charge to the Clergy of Durham* (1750) at the other. It is true that the Church made for quietude, for order and decorum, as was essential after the turmoil, the virulence even, of the previous century; it was on its guard against 'the pretending to extraordinary revelations and gifts of the Holy Ghost', these not being regarded as anything but 'a horrid thing, a very horrid thing', as Butler protested to Wesley. 'Our province', he says in his *Charge*, 'is virtue and religion, life and manners, the science of improving the temper and making the heart better.' Yet all the time, in religion as well as in poetry, the age was searching for a form in which to release its tensions, for a freedom which it did not find in adaptations of the older forms, the boundaries of which were constantly being burst. The creation by Charles Wesley of the Holy Club in 1729, which through the flame of his brother's personality became the Methodist movement, is as characteristic of the general pulse as are the Odes of Collins. It is to give a wrong picture to suggest that Johnson, Gibbon, Burke are the only proper children of the Augustan age; just as legitimate are Cowper, Lord Kames, Macpherson, and Christopher Smart—or William Law, when he devised the supernal dialogues, *The Way to Divine Knowledge* and *The Spirit of Love*.

IX

CRITICS AND AESTHETICIANS

I. CRITICS

TOWARDS the end of the seventeenth century, 'that criticall warr which', according to Davenant, 'never ceases among the learned', began to be waged among those who were less erudite: here too the new reading public demanded to be catered for. Thus from the opening of the eighteenth century we encounter discussion which, though sometimes based on considerable knowledge, more often exhibited the spirits of the minor dabblers in poetry or the drama, who at least were concerned as craftsmen with the problems of literature. Those who figured primarily as critics were regarded with active suspicion. A typical enough observation is that of Edward Pickering Rich, who in his *Original Poems on Several Occasions* (1720) opened his poem 'To the Critics' with:

> To that long snarling useless Tribe I write,
> Which youthful authors too too often fright:

and the chorus of those who regarded criticism as a troublesome cur biting the calves of young writers and snapping at the heels of the great reached such proportions that James Miller,[1] in the Dedication of his *Harlequin Horace* (1731), parodied the position in an amusing paragraph of abuse in which the term 'malevolent mungrills' is among the mildest. Gildon, in the Preface to his *Complete Art of Poetry* (1718), wrote defensively of '... the unpopular Name of Criticism, which by the Ignorant Writers in Vogue, has been represented as an *ill-natured* Thing: and that too many Learned Men ... had incumber'd its Maxims with Abundance of hard Terms....' The last statement might be difficult to refute, even the amiable Henry Felton,[2]

---

[1] James Miller, 1706–44, went to Wadham College, Oxford, and took Holy Orders. He was immediately made lecturer at Trinity Chapel, Conduit Street, and preacher at the private chapel, Roehampton. In 1743 he became Rector of Upcerne in Dorset, as his father had been before him.

[2] Henry Felton, 1679–1740, from school at Westminster and the Charterhouse, matriculated to St. Edmund Hall, Oxford, of which at one time he was Principal. He became Rector of Whitwell in Derbyshire.

in his *Dissertation on Reading the Classics, and forming a Just Style* (1713), remarking that 'Excepting those of some very learned Men, Comments are generally an Art of making Authors difficult, under a Pretence of explaining them. . .', a complaint not wholly outrageous today. Matthew Green, as might be expected, takes the labours of the critics more lightly:

> These Tayl'ring artists for our lays
> Invent cramp'd rules, and with strait stays
> Striving free nature's shape to hit,
> Emaciate sense before they fit.

Probably Aaron Hill did more than any other publicist to set matters on a common-sense level, declaring in the *Plain Dealer*, liv (25 Sept. 1724): 'I am determined to examine into the foundation of this silly Notion That Criticks are Enemies to Wit and Learning . . . the Critick is the Champion of Wit, and defends it from Prophanation.' Yet even as late as 1748 we find Spence, himself a critic rather than an originator, writing to Richardson about *Clarissa*, 'For Heaven's sake, let not those sworn enemies of all good works [the critics] destroy the beauties you have created.' Much of this, of course, was due to the childish perennial gibe, originated perhaps by Wycherley, that critics are 'failed poets': even Dennis was not spared that imputation. Needless to say, rival judges edified the public with noisy personal wrangles among themselves, this traditionally urbane age offering the melancholy sight of the gods engaged in far from benevolent slanging-matches. As Young observed in his essay *On Lyrick Poetry* (1728; prefacing *Ocean. An Ode*): 'The Poetick Clan are more *obnoxious to Vanity* than Others. . . . As soon as they become Authors, they become like *Ben Johnson's* angry Boy, and learn the Art of Quarrel.'

Yet in spite of what was perhaps an undue predominance of eager discoverers, of sorrowful pedants, or of gleeful neophytes, there were some who would feel with Felton—anticipating a remark Goethe made to Eckermann—that 'We can say nothing New, at least we can say nothing Better, that hath been said before; but we may nevertheless make what we say our *Own*.' If many ignored Dryden's dictum that the principal business of criticism is not to find fault, but to reveal those beauties that will delight the reasonable reader, there were such as Spence,[1]

---

[1] Joseph Spence, 1699–1768, was educated at Eton and Winchester, at Magdalen

who makes one of his speakers in the dialogue *Essay on Pope's Homer* (1726) advise 'always to keep our Hearts open to the beauties of a Poem; and never to shut our Eyes against the defects of it'. There was thus a considerable, if minority, body of writers, less rigid and better mannered than the mass of critics, who opened the door to more flexible, we would think more civilized ideas. Yet Broome, in the Preface to his *Poems* (1739), found it necessary to say: 'Modesty is essential to true *Criticism*; no Man has a title to be a Dictator in Knowledge, and the Sense of our Infirmities ought to teach us to treat others with Humanity'; and in the same Preface he has considerable fun with 'envious and Malicious Critics'. Thus for all the strident and sterile squabbling that strikes the reader as characteristic of the age, definite standards of some value finally emerge, together with a more varied and better founded appreciation of the new.

By the beginning of the century peace had to all intents descended upon the two most heated and vociferous fields of contest, those of the Battle of the Ancients and Moderns (the chapter attached to *A Tale of a Tub* being a belated missile) and of the Immorality of the Stage. The former was carried on in revised form, as that of Pessimists against Optimists, the pessimists, far more weighty intellectually, comprising such mutually antagonistic personalities as Pope and Dennis, who could agree at least on this point, even though Dennis might think that Pope served only to illustrate the dire collapse he so much deplored. The optimists, and with them the whole tide of common readers, could boast only names of minor rank, such as that of Welsted,[1] who, in the Dissertation he prefixed to his *Epistles, Odes etc*: (1724), hazarded the opinion that the nation was on the brink of a 'perfect Classical Age', the language, for one thing, being almost as good as it could be. Eusden, in one of his *Three Poems* (1727), assured Augustus (this was before Pope's Epistle to the ruling monarch) that new Virgils would arise under him and

> To *Albion* Thou (if Poets can presage)
> Shalt give another, sweeter, Classic Age!

College, Oxford, and finally at New College, of which he became Fellow. In 1728 he succeeded Thomas Warton the elder as Professor of Poetry, and in 1742 was given the sinecure office of Regius Professor of Modern History.

[1] Leonard Welsted, 1688-1747, went from Westminster to Trinity College, Cambridge, became a clerk in the Secretary of State's office, and later in the Ordnance Office.

but he in turn was blotted out in the general massacre of *The Dunciad*. As to the immorality of the stage, this matter still continued to occupy the critics, such as Dennis and Gildon, who rose to defend the theatre against the attacks of Bedford, Blair, Witherspoon, and Law; but in the main criticism proper concerned itself with poetical justice, chiefly in tragedy, though Edward Filmer,[1] in his *Defence of Plays* (1707), would have had this extended to comedy also. These issues were dead or dying; what was now to concern men of letters for some time was the validity of the neo-classical rules, a matter which had been enriched by the appearance in the last century of Boileau's 'Longinus' and Locke's faculty-psychology. Boileau's 'Longinus' (Hall's version of 1652 seems to have dropped out of cognizance) was translated by Welsted in 1712 and reissued in 1724, to be superseded in 1739 by a translation from the original by William Smith, who, by his commentary freely illustrated from the Bible, Shakespeare, and Milton, widened the application of 'the sublime' to include subtler points of style. So of chief interest in our period was the adaptation of neo-classical principles, in this country never too clearly defined nor too zealously adhered to, so as to fit in with new notions of the creative faculty in man.

If Shaftesbury is the outstanding aesthetician of the time, John Dennis, while having a niche in that hall, is, or was, by common consent 'the critic', earning, in spite of Pope's jeers, considerable respect among the young. Even Rich, in the poem quoted above, could say that 'if great *Pope*, or *Dennis* will approve', he will continue to benefit the world with his 'humble lays'. Dennis might have had a far greater effect if he had not reddened at every word uttered in opposition to his views, and stared tremendous with a threatening eye. It must be admitted that after his early writings his style, apart from a few pungent phrases, is deadening: he is ruthlessly repetitive, he rams his points home, he never lets you off for a moment; yet what he had to say was so fruitful that in due course Wordsworth and Coleridge were, according to De Quincey, 'to have an absurd "craze" about him', Landor was to belaud him unduly, while Swinburne was to put him as far above Addison as he put Coleridge and Lamb above Dennis. In fact, from Cowper to

---

[1] Edward Filmer, *c*. 1657–*c*. 1708, was in 1672 admitted as Founders' Kin Fellow at All Souls, Oxford. He took his B.A. in that year, and became D.C.L. in 1681.

Gosse he has never lacked those who would put in a good word for him, and finally proper justice was done him by E. N. Hooker in his comprehensive Introduction to his edition of Dennis's *Critical Works*. Though beginning his career as poet and playwright, his interest in criticism as a species of writing in itself is plain from the appearance in 1692 of his Preface to *The Passion of Byblis*.

While it may be said that his *The Impartial Critic* (1693) is a gay enough dialogue, there already he stated that 'the Didactick Stile demands succinctness and gravity . . . Pleasantry, indeed, may make Sophistry pass upon us, because it puts the Mind into agitation'; and though he is usually grave enough, succinctness is often lacking, while his pleasantry is of the scoffing kind, as exhibited in his pulverizing of Blackmore in his *Remarks on Prince Arthur* (1696). Yet in his main period or criticism, up to about 1706, his manner is urbane enough; till then he had mixed in literary society, mainly among the Whigs, in common with most poetasters writing his pieces on the death of William III, his celebrations of Blenheim and Ramillies, and so forth. He then retired from the literary scene, enjoying a small post at the Customs Office, writing, besides a few poems, his masque of *Orpheus and Eurydice* and his abortive tragedy *Appius and Virginia*. Then in 1711 he sallied forth in bristling critical armour to attack Pope in the disgracefully personal *Critical and Satirical Reflections upon a Late Rhapsody call'd, An Essay upon Criticism*, his revenge for the unduly impudent Appius passage. His mood had become permanently savage, his critical views reiterative. One illustration of his change in manner will suffice. In *A Large Account of the Taste in Poetry* (1702) he discussed the lowering of standards, as compared with those obtaining in the reign of Charles II, when 'a considerable part of an Audience had those Parts, that Education and that Application which were requisit for the judging of Poetry'. He accounted for the decline in his day in stating that:

there are three sorts of People now in our Audiences, who have had no education at all. . . . A great many younger Brothers, Gentlemen born, who have been kept at home, by reason of the pressure of the Taxes. Several People who made their Fortunes in the late War . . . a 3rd sort of People . . . that considerable number of Foreigners. . . .

In *The Causes of the Decay and Defects of Dramatick Poetry* (1725), the audience now consists of 'upstarts . . . meanly born and more meanly educated'; the foreigners, whose ignorance of the English tradition was once excusable, have become 'shoals of exoticks'; . . . the theatre 'is now in the Hands of Players, illiterate, unthinking, unjust, ungratefull and sordid'. The Doge of Drury, to wit Steele, and Ægyptian Cibber, come in for withering abuse in a treatise which is little more than a sustained exercise in flamboyant vituperation. Not that it is lacking in some just, if overstated, denunciation of errors, nor contemptible as fiercely scathing prose, nor unamusing should one be in the mood for vigorous scarification; but it adds nothing to Dennis's critical stature. The same may be said of his attacks on 'Sir John Edgar', namely Steele, his bombardment of *The Rape of the Lock* and of *The Dunciad*, not to mention *A True Character of Mr Pope and his Writings* (1716). Perhaps his religious tractates are worthier of his mind, which demands respect, or the political pamphlets he issued intermittently throughout his life, including an attack upon *The Fable of the Bees*; but to get the gist of what he had to say it is sufficient to examine the critical works he published between 1700 and 1704, with occasional references to later work, which are largely superb examples in the art of literary fisticuffs.

Where he fits most securely into any picture of his time is in his battle for 'the rules'. Not that he was a cast-iron advocate for them. He could, to be sure, appeal to Aristotle, Horace, and Vida (whom, after all, Pope, who could when he wished make glorious fun of the rules, called 'immortal'), but he was fundamentally as anti-pedantic as any Scriblerian. His main argument was that men are moved in art by what moves them in nature; and since nature is regular—after all, he lived in the Cartesian–Newtonian era—so art must be. Yet seeming irregularities might add to the beauty of a poem: had not Milton triumphed sublimely by his very transgression of the rules? and had not Addison made nonsense of *Cato* by too strict adherence to them? That his advocacy for them became increasingly stern was due no doubt to their being progressively flouted, in both precept and practice, as the century wore on; and since the drama decayed correspondingly, Dennis had some justification in making a connexion. If, he argued, you try to catch popular applause by giving the rabble that the audiences had become what they wanted, which was simply snatches of

amusement devoid of any coherent emotion, your plays will be merely chaotic performances, and therefore meaningless. You defeat your own ends by flouting the rules, which are no more, basically, than generalizations drawn from centuries of experience of how an audience is to be effectively moved, an audience, that is, capable of appreciating what 'Nature' is really like.

There was, it need hardly be said, a great deal of nonsense talked about the rules, as there always is about any fashionable dogma, the mugwumps finally bringing them into ridicule. There were plenty of solemn criticasters, who, in common with Martinus Scriblerus had a most peculiar talent to convert every trifle into a serious thing, and those who, as Farquhar put it, 'take all innovations for grievances'. But the English, Rymer apart, had always felt uneasy at too strict an application of neo-classical principles, Dryden saying that in *All for Love* the unities were 'more exactly preserved than, perhaps, the English theatre requires'. Yet apart from the argument from experience, there was another, plausible enough, in their favour, and easy for the sheerest simpleton to understand. It was put with sufficient clarity by Abel Boyer[1] in the fifth of his *Letters of Wit, Politicks and Morality* (1701): 'To judge aright of a Performance in any Art, we ought to consider the *End*, or Design of that Art, for that *Performance* must certainly be the *Best*, which *best* answers that End.' This position was continually stated in one form or another, by Dennis among others. Charles Gildon,[2] as might be expected from so faithful a watch-dog of Dennis, came down heavily on the side of the rules, as 'against Sir *William Temple*, the *Tatlers* and other enemies of the rules'. He discussed them at great length, without undue heat, in the second of the insufferably puffed-out dialogues of his *Complete Art of Poetry*, a work, incidentally, which does not, as he said, at all trench upon Bysshe's *Art of Poetry* (1702), that simple manual of prosody which, with its rhyming dictionary, lies

---

[1] Abel Boyer, 1667–1729, finding his education at the Academy of Puylaurens interrupted by religious faction, completed his studies at Franeker in Friesland. He came to England in 1689, was tutor to Allen Bathurst, afterwards first Earl, and French teacher to the Duke of Gloucester. His employment then became literary and historical.

[2] Charles Gildon, 1665–1724, was trained for the priesthood at Douay from the ages of twelve to nineteen. He ran through the patrimony he inherited at twenty-one, and resorted to hack-authorship.

before Hogarth's 'The Distressed Poet'. Gildon is quoting Dennis almost verbatim when he writes:

. . . Poetry is an Art; for since it has a certain *End*, there must be some certain Way of arriving at that *End*. No Body can doubt of so evident a Truth, that in all Things, where there may be a Right and a Wrong, there is an Art, and sure Rules to lead you to the former, and direct you to avoid the latter:

and he, in the person of Laudon, seems to have convinced his opponent Tyro, in spite of the beginner's chariness of accepting the findings of so suspect a person as an avowed critic. Those who argued thus had behind them the authority of Joseph Trapp,[1] who in *Praelectiones Poeticae* (1711–15), translated from the Latin in 1742, had laid down: 'That Poetry is an Art, is sufficiently plain. . . . It observes certain Laws and Rules, is brought to the Test of right Reason, and, lastly, it aims at some particular End.'

If only it could be known what the end was! Trapp gave some indication, saying of poetry: 'Rage is indeed its Property; but a Rage altogether divine; not deviating from Reason, but rendering it more ornamental and sublime.' Its end, and this, of course, is familiar enough and only too vague, is 'the Delight and Improvement of Mankind'. But still, why rules? Here again Trapp, in common with a number of others, gave the answer, one equally familiar and equally vague, simply the old doctrine of art being an imitation of nature. But in what sense an imitation? The answer was to hand. Since the celestial orbs go round the world with heat, swiftness, and regularity, 'We see there is no Absurdity to have Rules prescribed to this Art'. Dennis, in his Epistle Dedicatory, addressed to Granville, of *The Advancement and Reformation of Modern Poetry* (1701), had already stated this far more persuasively:

There is nothing in Nature that is great and beautiful without Rule and Order; and the more Rule and Order, and Harmony, we find in the Objects that strike our Senses, the more Worthy and Noble we esteem them. I humbly conceive that it is the same in

---

[1] Joseph Trapp, 1679–1747, was trained at home, and for a short time at New College, Oxford, but proceeded to Wadham College, of which he became Fellow, entering into Holy Orders. He was Professor of Poetry at Oxford (the first) from 1708 to 1718. He became Chaplain to the Lord Chancellor of Ireland, and to Bolingbroke. He was made vicar of parishes in London and Middlesex, and appointed lecturer in several London churches.

Art, and particularly in Poetry, which ought to be an exact Imitation of Nature. . .

and so on, at some length. In much the same vein, Oldmixon,[1] in his *Essay on Criticism* (1728), a piece of writing abounding in plain sense, stated that: 'The Rules laid down by . . . great Criticks are not to be valu'd because they are given by *Aristotle*, *Horace*, &c., but because they are in Nature and in Truth.' It was, however, Felton, who put the matter most flexibly in his very readable *Dissertation*, in which he abjures 'the Pomp of Quotations':

> Rules speak themselves; they draw the Picture of Nature, and give us sure Criterions of an Original in every Performance. . . . For those who first prescribed the Rules of Writing did not take Nature stripped and naked for their Copy; but they looked upon her, as she was dressed and adorned by her Adorers. . . . they knew that every good *Genius* would write and judge by Nature, whether any Rules had been set or no. . . . But now how many Scriblers are there who observe the Rule and neglect the Meaning, and what Numbers of Pedants do we meet with, that keep to the Letter, and lose the Spirit.

Thus he praised Dryden, 'who at once gave the best Rules, and broke them, in spight of his own Knowledge, and the *Rehearsal*'. Farquhar, in his *Discourse upon Comedy*, had seen a little more clearly and practically, though Dennis had said much the same thing in *The Impartial Critic*. Plays were designed for English audiences, not French, nor Spanish, nor ancient Greek. Therefore, 'The Rules of English Comedy don't lie in the Compass of *Aristotle*, or his Followers, but in the Pit, Box, and Galleries.' Not that he would jettison all method, and so 'make the Conditions of the English Stage a State of Anarchy'; but the rules must be new since, given that the points aimed at and the passions appealed to are not the same, the conduct of the play is bound to be unlike others'. 'If our *Utile*, which is the End, be different from the Ancients, pray let our *Dulce*, which is the Means, be so too.'

The tendency to break away from pedantic application naturally led to excesses. Some smaller writers revelled in what they thought to be a new-found freedom; since 'Shakespeare

---

[1] John Oldmixon, 1673–1742, was educated privately in the family of Admiral Blake. He became Collector of Bridgwater in 1716.

writ without rules' they felt they could disport themselves as
they liked. These did not evade the shafts of the versifiers,
James Miller writing in *Harlequin-Horace*—the title is significant:

> Take then no pains a Method to maintain,
> Or link your Work in a continu'd Chain,
> But cold, dull Order gloriously disdain;

so in the same sense Walter Harte in *An Essay on Satire* (1730):

> We grant that *Butler* ravishes the Heart,
> As *Shakespear* soar'd beyond the reach of Art;
> (For Nature form'd those Poets without Rules,
> To fill the World with *imitating Fools*).

Genius, it was suggested, could achieve results free from directions; but those lacking genius had better make what use they
could of them to give coherence to their ideas.

To such as Dennis the loosening process seemed to be approaching anarchy, the influence of the moderates disastrous.
It is unlikely that Felton was much read, but Welsted, who said
much the same as Felton, was a more popular performer, if
only because his verses, according to *Peri Bathous*, flowed with
a quiet thoughtlessness. To the rigorous he must have appeared
as the chiefest sinner, and certainly in the Dissertation prefixed
to his *Epistles, Odes etc*: (1724) he gravely offended against the
formalists. Not that he thought the rules useless; but in truth,
he explained, echoing Felton, 'they touch only the Externals
or Form of the Thing, without entering into the Spirit of it;
they play about the Surface of Poetry, but never dive into its
Depths'. The real graces were unanalysable. He held, however,
that impracticable as the rules might be, it did not follow that
the writing of verses was a 'lawless mystery', as many seemed to
think. Young cleared up the position considerably in remarking
that though the ancients were to be followed, poets 'should
rather imitate their example in the general *motives*, and fundamental *methods* of their working, than in their works themselves'.
Spence, more detached, more philosophic one might say than
the others, saw more clearly that principles had to be adapted
to the emergence of new forms. Talking to Richardson in the
letter already quoted, he remarked: 'A piece quite of a new
kind must have new rules, if any: but the best of all is, following
nature and common sense.' This, derived from Dryden, was
good Popeian doctrine, as might be expected from Spence:

whether Nature and Homer might turn out to be the same would depend upon the common sense of the writer.

Dennis, it is clear, occupied no extreme position in this matter; he was more definite in his views on poetical justice, in arguing about which he again fits into the generally accepted —if largely false—picture of his time, even though he equated it, seemingly, with retributive justice. It was Rymer who had invented the term, borrowing the idea perhaps from La Mesnardière, and brought the notion to the common eye—it had been touched upon by Sidney and Jonson—and in his earlier days Dennis had now and again mentioned it as though taking it for granted, for this battle also had really been fought out in the Restoration period. Gildon, who for once differed from Dennis, expressed the opinion of our period well enough when he wrote in his Preface to *The Patriot* (1703), "'Tis not the Business of the Stage according to *Aristotle* and *Reason* to punish profligate Offences, for the Punishment of those has nothing productive of Terror and Compassion.' Dennis, however, was led, partly by personal resentment, to make a full statement of it in a letter to the *Spectator*, a letter which he printed in his essay on Shakespeare (1711), and again in his collected *Original Letters* (1721). In *Spectator* 40, which Dennis believed to be written by Steele, Addison had attacked, not the whole conception, but its complete and detailed application. He regarded it as an error in contemporary tragic authors to feel that they must deliver a virtuous hero from his troubles and make him triumph over his enemies.

This Errour they have been led into [he wrote] by a ridiculous Doctrine in modern Criticism, that they are obliged to an equal Distribution of Rewards and Punishments, and an impartial Execution of poetical Justice. Who were the first that established this Rule I know not; but I am sure it has no Foundation in Nature, in Reason, or in the Practice of the Ancients. We find that Good and Evil happen alike to all Men on this Side of the Grave.

Dennis's reply, after he had satisfactorily castigated the *Spectator* for ignorance and his 'dictatorian way', was based on two grounds:

'Tis not always that we know Men's Crimes, but how seldom do we know their Passions, and especially their darling Passions? . . .'

But suppose I should grant that there is not always an equal Distribution of Affliction and Happiness here below. Man is a

Creature who was created immortal, and a Creature consequently that will find a Compensation in Futurity for any seeming Inequality in his Destiny here. But the Creatures of a poetical Creator are imaginary and transitory; they have no longer Duration than the Representation of their respective Fables; and consequently, if they offend, they must be punish'd during that Representation.

The argument was not quite so naïf as an extract suggests; and as the contention developed, in *Spectator* 584 and *Remarks upon Cato*, it resolved itself more and more into how far the doctrine should apply to minor figures or to the heroes, and in the end there was no great difference between the contestants.

Vehemence, a violent assertion of his opinions, is Dennis's chief characteristic, but on many points he can be both suave and extremely interesting, as when, in *A Large Account*, he distinguishes between wit and humour, in our sense of the word, arguing for the superiority of the latter as an element in comedy, wit being the effect of fancy, humour the work of the judgement. It gives occasion for action, which is the life and soul of the theatre, and distinguishes the characters better: 'Wit must often be shocking and nauseous . . . because it destroys and confounds the characters.'

But fifthly and lastly, if Comedy is Poetry, 'tis Humour chiefly which makes it so, for that which Characteristically distinguishes Poetry from Prose is Passion . . . and Humour is subordinate Passion.

And since humour is to be found chiefly in 'the lower sort of people', it follows that low comedy is to be preferred to the high. Humour can indeed be found on a high level, but in his view it took a Wycherley, whom he greatly admired, to manage this feat successfully.

The embroilment of Dennis in the points of criticism popular in his age, matters which we today approach from a rather different angle, may be left in favour of the qualities which single him out from his contemporaries, qualities which reveal him as a thinker able to establish principles which will find few dissentients among us, and may even provide needed correctives to current practice; he also sowed the seeds of certain critical concepts which were later to sprout luxuriantly. The basis of his criticism was ethical, in conformity with the then ideas of the Church of England—he was a vigorous opponent of the Deism, covert or otherwise, of his time—and he believed ardently that

'Poetry is necessary for the inforcing Religion upon the Minds of Men': a theory he developed both in *The Advancement* . . . and in *The Grounds of Criticism in Poetry* (1704). In the former treatise, arguing that 'the Design of the True Religion and of Poetry are the same', namely the happiness of man, he also declares that the best poetry is religious.

We have proved that Passion is the chief Thing in Poetry, and that Spirit or Genius, and in short, every Thing that moves, is Passion. Now if the chief Thing in Poetry be Passion, why then, the chief Thing in great Poetry must be great Passion. We have shewn too, that Passion in Poetry, is of two sorts, ordinary Passion, or Enthusiasm. Let us now proceed to convince the Reader, that a Sacred Poem, is more susceptible of Passion, than a Prophane one can be.

The remainder of the essay treats of this at laborious and repetitive length; what is most of interest will be found in the comparisons of Virgil and Ovid with Milton, who, whenever put to the test by particular passages treating of the same thing, as for instance the Creation, emerges triumphantly, if the reader is prepared to accept Dryden's translations of the ancient poets as a fair gauge. And here it may be opportune to dwell upon the service that Dennis did Milton.

Not that Milton had been unappreciated, at any rate by the poets, as already shown; as to the general public, as early as 1690 the Swiss scholar Minotuli could write to Bayle: 'All the educated Englishmen I have known extol to the skies a poem written in English by Milton called *Adam*; they speak of it as the *non plus ultra* of the human spirit.' In 1694 Gildon published a letter 'In Vindication of Paradise Lost' by an author not surely identified; yet it is to be noted that this vindication, of Milton's style only, did not gain universal consent. Welsted, who greatly admired *Paradise Lost* and felt that it disputed the prize with Homer, was impelled to say in 1724 that 'the Phrase and Stile' of the poem 'is a second *Babel*, or confusion of all languages' (Keats would have agreed); adding, however, that if Milton 'had wanted that Fault, he had perhaps wanted a Superior'. But Dennis was the first to subject him to any detailed criticism, usually laudatory, from which Addison borrowed lavishly.

It may also be remarked that Dennis was among the first, perhaps the first, to suggest the relativity of judgement. While admitting, in *The Advancement*, that Virgil was more euphonious than Milton, since English as a language did not yield music so readily as Latin, he claimed that Milton pleased us more than Virgil because a poem based on Christianity must necessarily satisfy us better than one based on paganism; in the same way Virgil was superior to Homer since in the days of the latter 'the Reason of Mankind was satisfy'd at an easier rate'. Then:

And, therefore, when I say that *Virgil* is to be preferr'd to *Homer*, I mean, that he is so in regard to us, because he is capable of giving us the greater Pleasure than *Homer*; but I do not pretend at the same Time, that Virgil is capable of giving us greater Pleasure than Homer gave his Contemporaries. As likewise when I affirm, that the Moderns, by joining Poetry with the True Religion, will have the advantage of the Ancients, I mean only in regard to us, to whom they will give a greater Pleasure than the Ancients can do, but not a greater than the Ancients gave their Contemporaries.

And he goes on to forestall Dr. Johnson's view that classical mythological imagery and allusion are an absurdity in English verse: 'I think we may very well conclude, that in our Time we ought to fling it out of our Poetry, when it has been for so long time utterly exploded, and contemn'd by the very Boys.' True, a poet may imagine himself transported back in time, and may be moved by the old religions; 'and if a Poet be extremely mov'd himself, why they who read him must be mov'd in some measure too', but he doubts if this will apply to the generality of readers. Indeed, 'The Christian Religion alone, can supply the Poet with all that is sublime and majestick in Reason.' Reason! that was essential in great poetry,

For since the Design of every Art is to make Men happy, and that the best and noblest Art, which makes the best Provision for the Happiness of Mankind, and nothing can make Man so happy as the reconciling him to himself, which can be no way so effectually done, as by making all the Faculties find their satisfaction together; it follows, that that must be the noblest Poetry where the Reason, the Passions and Senses, are all of them pleas'd, and pleas'd in the highest Degree together.

He is, in fact, almost saying that poetry is the utterance of reason in her most exalted mood, and it is clear why Wordsworth, who also held that 'poetry is passion', could hunt out Dennis's by then forgotten pronouncements.

What no doubt fostered his unpopularity was his bitter

concern that 'an Art, so Divine [as poetry—the noblest of all the arts] in its Institution, is sunk and profan'd, and miserably debas'd . . . a thing that is confess'd by all'. This was ominous, for he declared in *The Grounds* 'the great Design of Arts is to restore the Decays that happen'd to human Nature by the Fall, by Restoring Order'. If the rules were invaluable because they induced the poets to imitate the order that runs through the creation, they were all the more so because in the process they enabled poetry to attain its final end by rousing the emotions. His standard of value, then, is what happens to the recipient; his approach, in fact, and here he strikes a modern note, is the psychological one. The pleasure of poetry, and poetry must please, is attained by exciting passion, 'because every one who is pleas'd is mov'd, and either desires, or rejoices, or admires, or hopes, or the like'. Then the next step is taken. 'Poetry by the force of the Passion, instructs and informs the Reason: which is the Design of the true Religion.' He then adventures, and formal as his procedure seems to us to be, that is the right word, into the field of what has come to be known as 'the poetic process', in showing how the admirable result described above is the outcome of an organic unity in the poem: thoughts are produced by the subject, they in turn induce the spirit, which then engenders the expression, a process 'which is known by experience to all who are Poets; for never any one while he was rapt with Enthusiasm, wanted either Words or Harmony'. This is not very different from the modern doctrine of immediacy. It was a little unlucky for the success of his theory that he himself was said by Miller to be 'By Inspiration furiously Dull'. However that may be, his theorizing impelled him to try to arrive at the secret of the sublime. He complained of Longinus that though 'he takes a great deal of Pains to set before us the Effects it produces in the Minds of Men; as for Example that it causes in them Admiration and Surprize; . . . and a Fulness of Joy mingled with Astonishment', he had done nothing to show how these desirable effects were brought about.

Dennis, then, is far from being the cold legalistic critic he has so often been assumed to be; moreover he broke new ground. Among other novelties he introduced the detailed criticism of a poem—Dryden had done it for plays—and his line by line discussion of Waller, whom he greatly admired, introduced into his *Remarks on Prince Arthur*, may have served Landor as a model for his dialogues on Milton. Concerned as he was with the 'greater' poetry, he had nothing but contempt for the simplicities of the ballad, and opposed Addison's contention that 'Chevy Chase' was Virgilian. For there is nothing figurative in the ballad, as there must be in all good poetry, while to claim that a poem must have value because it has for long pleased 'the Rabble' is the height of absurdity. If Sidney liked it, and he had merely said that he liked to hear it sung, that was, he 'shrewdly only suspected', because 'there were some martial Notes in this old *Gothick* Tune'. Virgil knew what simplicity was; '*Chevy Chase* . . . shews not a Simplicity, but an Imbecility of Expression'.

Diction, itself subject to rules, and furnishing part of the argument about them, naturally loomed large in discussions about poetry; but the current theory was indeterminate enough. Indeed it was so self-contradictory, offering so splendid an example of eating your cake and having it, that it could receive almost universal acceptance. Gildon, in Dialogue V of his *Complete Art of Poetry*, lays out the prospectus at length. Language in poetry must have five qualities; it must be 'apt, clear, natural, splendid and numerous'. Apt diction has in it 'nothing impure or barbarous'; it must be clear, since 'one of the greatest Faults in the Diction is Obscurity'. To be natural means to be

without Affectation. . . . Studied Phrases, and a too florid *Stile, fine Words*, and terms strain'd and remote, and all extraordinary Expressions are unsupportable in true Poetry.

All this, however, seems to be swept off the board when we read:

Fourthly, the *Language* must be *Lofty* and *Splendid*; for the common and ordinary terms of the Mob, the *Canaille*, are by no means proper for a Poet; he must make use of words that partake nothing of the *Base*, and the *Vulgar*.

Here, having pleaded for current educated usage, he seems to take us on to Gray's statement that the language of the age is never that of poetry.

Giles Jacob,[1] in the Preface to the second volume of his

---

[1] Giles Jacob, 1686–1744, was bred to the Law; apart from diligent compilation and abortive attempts at playwriting, he was occupied as steward and secretary to the Hon. William Blathwait.

Poetical Register (1719), repeats all this in less vivid phrases, though he brings out rather more clearly than Gildon that the theory is based on 'the Rules of Decorum and good Sense'. He does not, however, expatiate so widely on the sublime, of which Gildon remarks:

> But this sublime Stile, is the Rock on which mean Wits always split, they fly out into too vast and boistrous Terms from what is natural, where they aim at being sublime and lofty. For this high and pompous Kind of Speech becomes vain and cold, if not supported with great Thoughts; and the great Words which are affected to heighten the Diction, most commonly only make a noise.

Jacob's contribution consists in saying that though the boldest strokes of poetry are those which most delight the reader, if managed artfully, yet the poet's fancy and wit should be kept within due bounds; 'like luxuriant plants it requires a great deal of pruning'.

The more considerable poets or prose-writers were sure of their diction; they did not need to justify their practice, though they might occasionally, as did Pope and Swift, utter dicta on the matter. Not that many tried to enlighten the world on this subject, feeling perhaps with Savage that,

> Sure, next to writing, the most idle thing,
> Is gravely to harangue on what we sing.

Yet the minor voices are revealing as to general trends. Purney thought that in the drama 'the Immagination is restrain'd by Rule. In the Epick and Pastoral Poem, the Ode, Satyr, &c., 'tis not', though it may direct the stream of the rich fancies of the poets into a proper channel: Spenser might have profited by them. Yet he had his own doctrines, and, going to extreme lengths in expatiating upon the pastoral, declares that in that form 'No Phraze must be admitted till enervated, and wholly void of *Strength*'. Pope, who in the categories defined in *Peri Bathous* cuts right across the 'kinds', made no play with Purney under the heading of 'the Silly', confining his attention largely to Ambrose Philips. Purney indicates indeed that his doctrine applies to all poetry but the sublime: it would have been interesting to read the Preface he would no doubt have written for his epic if it had ever been published.

Some few touched upon prose style, among them Welsted, who would have it allowed greater freedom, 'to unfetter it, as it were, and give it a more unconfined air'. He proposed John Philips—having highly praised *Cyder*—whereas a few years earlier John Hughes[1] had advanced Temple and Tillotson as exemplars. This in his *Of Style* (1698), a book mainly devoted to poetry, where he insists that each writer has his own manner, constituting his style, in which he was followed by Trapp, these, then, standing between George Puttenham on the one hand, and Buffon on the other. Hughes's *On Allegorical Poetry* (1715), and his *Remarks on the Faerie Queen*, the latter a 'candid' examination pointing out faults as well as beauties, are well-tempered exercises in analysis, which, while marking an advance in approach, yield little but the obvious.

John Bancks (or Banks),[2] again, may be taken as representative of the author-critic. Though he later turned historian, finding as he wrote to Pope in his third Epistle on 'The Progress of Petitioning', that

> To seek a livelihood from Rymes
> Suits ill with these prosaic Times,

his *Miscellaneous Works in Verse and Prose* (1728) offer a bulk of, in the main, lively exercises in odes, songs, fables, epistles, together with good middle-way critical matter. A long Preface 'says something' of all the species he wrote in, as though, seeing chaos in the confusion of 'kinds', he was attempting to restore order. His paragraph on the song runs:

> The constitution of the *Song* is less noble and majestic than that of the Ode, but then it is more delicate and tender: As female beauty, though less commanding, is more soft and attractive than manly. The single Thought which constitutes a Song, must be wrought up with the utmost Nicety and Exactness, till it strikes the Imagination in an agreeable Point, altogether free and natural. No Transposition of Words, no affected Phrases, in short nothing but what has the Air of familiar Prose, should enter into its Composition, at the same time that it consists of the most elegant Versification. . . .

He, too, also touches upon prose in his 'A Discourse concerning Language'.

> The Ranging of Words, as well as the Choice of them, deserves a

---

[1] John Hughes, 1677–1720, was contemporary with Isaac Watts at the Dissenting Academy in Little Britain. He obtained posts in the Ordnance Office, and as secretary to the commissioners for purchasing lands for the Royal Docks.

[2] John Ban(c)ks, 1709–1751, was taught by an anabaptist minister, and apprenticed to a weaver. But he abandoned that trade in favour of bookselling, from which he proceeded author.

little to be considered. Not only Cadence and Harmony, but Perspicuity and Strength, depend much on the Knowledge of this Art. But this Knowledge must be attained by Practice and Example, rather than collected from Precepts, which at best are always deficient in the Niceties of every Science. . . .

It is a sensible essay in which he stresses that even given all the qualities, there must still be 'long Application and close Reflection', which goes to show that prose was beginning to be thought about by the generality of authors—the masters by their very nature do so—who, broken loose from the old rhetorical structure, were seeking another effectiveness.

The question of rhyme as against blank verse was matter for some tepid debate, though there was little attempt to discover what it actually did. In the eyes of some, apparently, it could compensate for weaknesses: Stephen Duck, at all events, having composed his *Shunamite* in blank verse, 'upon reading it over . . . found his Language was not sublime enough for it; and that therefore he was forc'd to write it all over again, and turn it into Rhyme'. Oldmixon, praising *Cyder*, asserts that it is 'full of Instances where mean Thoughts are raised by noble Expressions', Philips having evidently solved the problem; but Oldmixon is anxious to distinguish between the sublime, the grand, and the noble, and even, in another place, 'the puffy'. Edward Young, who in his famous *Conjectures on Original Composition* (1759) was to say that blank verse is 'verse unfallen, uncurst', in 1728 professed himself in favour of rhyme, which, provided the difficulties are overcome, gives grace and pleasure; but it must be consistent with perfect sense and expression, 'as though the writer were free from that shackle'. But in the main the arguments about diction were languid, Abel Boyer, for example, thinking that altogether too much pother was made about it. He declared that to discuss it was a great error, perpetuated by 'little Pretenders to Rhyme', who loved to pounce upon slips. But this was before *Peri Bathous*, that glittering and still entertaining thesis, a brilliant early example of that criticism which judges solely by results.

The critical assumptions of the time were, naturally, brought to bear upon Shakespeare, who now began to undergo editorial as well as critical care. Mention has been made earlier of the veneration in which he was already held by the generality of Englishmen; but the critics, though they worshipped him, did so, very sensibly, this side idolatry. Editions began to crowd one upon the other, beginning with Rowe's six volumes in 1709, to which in 1710 Gildon added a seventh containing the poems. Pope's followed in 1725, increased again by Sewell in 1728 by the addition of Gildon's volume, to which he added a Preface. Pope was brought to book in 1726 in *Shakespeare Restored* by Theobald,[1] who in 1733-4 produced his own edition, he himself being followed by Hanmer in 1743, and Warburton, not by any means the first disintegrator, in 1747, he in turn being beautifully reduced—supposing him to be susceptible of reduction— in the next year by Thomas Edwards in *The Canons of Criticism*, an entertaining work it must be salutary for any present-day editor to run through. In this volume, however, the tale ends with Theobald.

Nobody had the least doubt as to the supreme genius of Shakespeare; the tone had been set by Dryden. But the early eighteenth century, as indeed every age in varying degrees, healthily found unacceptable certain sides of the otherwise unmatchable work; the defects they ascribed to lack of knowledge; or found, to quote Edwards's fifth canon, that if an editor does not like an expression 'he may condemn it as a foolish interpolation'; or judged, as latterly did Dr. Bridges, that passages which did not please them were the result of the baleful influence of a mob audience. We of today will not always agree with the early objections; we do not, for instance, greatly cavil at Hector quoting Aristotle; but then, for that matter, neither did Theobald, who boldly declared that 'such *anachronisms* were the effect of poetic licence, rather than of ignorance in our poet'. They were due to 'the too powerful blaze of his imagination; which, when once raised, made all acquired knowledge disappear before it'. Nor do we resent, as Dennis did, that Menenius should be presented, not in accordance with the views of Roman writers, but as a buffoon. Nevertheless, it is of some interest to note what was said in the early years of Shakespearian criticism, to mark the beginnings and development of textual work, and the gradual laying down of the lines on which Shakespearian studies have subsequently run.

[1] Lewis Theobald, 1688–1744, was educated at a school at Isleworth, became an attorney, but abandoned the law for literature, which brought him but poor financial reward.

The question of Shakespeare's learning, though still argued over, has little interest for us now; we know more about his schooling: but for the eighteenth century it was a matter of everlasting argument. Rowe considered that:

Whether his Ignorance of the Antients were a Disadvantage to him or no may admit of a Dispute, for tho' the knowledge of 'em might have made him more Correct, yet it is not improbable that the Regularity and Deference for them, might have restrain'd some of that Fire, Impetuosity and ever beautiful Extravagance which we admire in Shakespeare.

Gildon, however, saw no reason why knowledge of the rules should have tempered Shakespeare's flame any more than it did that of Homer, Virgil, Sophocles, and Euripides. Certainly he knew French; and 'there are many Arguments to prove, that he knew at least some of the *Latin* Poets, particularly *Ovid.* . . . that he had read *Plautus* himself, is plain from his *Comedy of Errors*'. On this last point Dennis more acutely supposed that a translation of the *Menaechmi* must have existed, and there later scholarship has proved him right. Addison thought that Shakespeare was 'a remarkable instance' of those 'who by mere strength of natural parts, and without any assistance of art or learning, have produced works that were the delight of their time and the wonder of posterity' (*Spectator* 160). The whole question may seem to us a little futile, and the general lover of Shakespeare will be content to leave the word with Pope:

But as to his *want of learning*, it may be necessary to say something more: there is certainly a vast difference between *learning* and *languages*. How far he was ignorant of the latter, I cannot determine; but it is plain he had much reading at least, if they will not call it learning. Nor is it any great matter, if a man has knowledge, whether he has it from one language or another.

A very proper remark to issue from the translator of Homer. Sewell,[1] however, took the matter up again, and found he could not place Shakespeare's learning so low as some had done.

Yet this was not an altogether pointless query, and bore closely on the discussion as to whether Shakespeare 'wanted art'; that is, could he handle his material to the best dramatic

[1] George Sewell, *c.* 1688–1726, was educated at Eton and Peterhouse, Cambridge. He studied at Leyden, but eventually took the degree of M.D. at Edinburgh. Failing as a practitioner, he took to the pen, with miserable financial success.

advantage? Addison might say that this question was a stumbling-block to all rigid critics (*Spectator* 592), but it is the eternal one of the well-made play: does the playwright dissipate the emotional responses, or order them to an effectual crisis? In our period it was almost universally deplored that Shakespeare was weak in 'fable', most agreeing with Rowe that 'it is not in this Province of the *Drama* that the Strength and Mastery of *Shakespeare* lay'. Hughes, while praising *Othello*, found 'the economy of the fable . . . too much neglected' (*Guardian* 37). Thus the chronicle plays were not highly estimated, while Dennis regarded *Pericles* as due for dismissal from the canon, and allowed only certain passages of *A Winter's Tale* to be from the hand of the master: *The Tempest*, naturally, was from Rowe onward accounted perfect.

And then, once more connected with 'learning': Were the personages always presented as they should have been? Dennis, complained, for example, that Caesar in all the greatness you would expect of him was hardly shown in the play of which he is the eponymous hero: 'Had *Shakespear* read either *Sallust* or *Cicero*, how could he have made so little of the first and greatest of Men, as that *Caesar* should be but a Fourth-rate Actor in his own Tragedy?' Steele, however, realized the presentation more imaginatively in *Tatler* 53.

In the Tragedy of *Caesar* [Shakespeare] introduces his Hero in his Night-Gown. He had at that Time all the Power of *Rome*; Depos'd Consuls, subordinate Generals, and Captive Princes might have preceded him; but this Genius was above such Mechanick Methods of showing Greatness. Therefore he rather presents that great Soul debating upon the Subject of Life and Death with his intimate Friends, without endeavouring to prepossess his Audience with empty Show and Pomp. . . . When the Hero has spoken this Sentiment, there is nothing that is great, which cannot be expected from one, whose first Position is the Contempt of Death to so high a Degree, as to make his *Exit* a Thing wholly indifferent, and not a Part of his Care, but that of heav'n and Fate.

Sewell, who was to help Theobald in his edition, sided with Dennis on this point: how differently, the latter sighed, would Corneille have treated the theme! Further, it need hardly be said, poetical justice was a second stumbling-block for many, for Dennis especially, who, as already seen, was outraged by Addison's flouting of it in *Spectator* 40, in which, moreover defying Rymer and Tate, he had declared: '*King Lear* is an admirable tragedy . . . as Shakespeare wrote it; but as it is reformed according to the chimerical notion of poetical justice, in my humble opinion it has lost half its beauty.' 'The rules', we see, raised their still formidable but battered head; yet most were ready to follow Gildon in claiming of Shakespeare that there was such a witchery in him that all the rules of art 'vanish away'. Pope was wary: since Shakespeare 'writ to the *people*', and not for the learned, 'To judge . . . of Shakespeare by Aristotle's rules, is like trying a man by the laws of one country, who acted under those of another.'

Though Dennis has appeared above as a destructive critic, it must not be thought that he (to use his own words) 'who admires [Shakespeare's] Charms and makes them one of his chief Delights, who sees him and reads him over and over and still remains unsatiated', was a whit behind others in his praise. In his view it was Shakespeare's blind admirers who showed most contempt for him, an opinion shared by Sewell, who wished to 'distinguish his *Errors* from his *Perfections*, now too much and too unjustly confounded by the foolish Bigotry of his blind and partial Adorers', an attitude taken up by Landor when he criticized Milton. The second paragraph of Dennis's first Letter of his *Essay on the Genius and Writings of Shakespeare* constitutes a panegyric outrivalling Dryden's; and for all his rigidity he admitted that in the plays the passions often touch us more 'without their due preparations' than do those that other poets portray with all the 'Beauties of Design' at their command. Our poet was one of the greatest geniuses for tragedy that the world ever saw (his comedies, especially the romantic ones, were not so much liked), his particular accomplishment being the raising of terror. Here Dennis was at one with the age generally, Rowe stating that 'no Dramatick Writer ever succeeded better in raising *Terror* in the Minds of an Audience', and Felton that he delighted most in terror. All agreed that it was in the realm of the passions that Shakespeare shone above all other dramatists, Pope, alone perhaps, claiming that he was as adept at producing the passions of 'laughter and the spleen' as the tenderer emotions. Rowe possibly meant to include these when he remarked 'how powerful [Shakespeare] was, in giving the strongest Motions to our Souls that they are capable of'.

But how?—since he fell short in fable. By imagination in general, by the liveliness of his characters, and his 'incomparable Expression', though this was, Rowe added, 'perhaps in some Instances a little Irregular'. For him: 'the Greatness of this Author's Genius do's no where so much appear, as where he gives his Imagination an entire Loose, and raises his Fancy to a flight above Mankind and the Limits of the visible World, as in *The Tempest, A Midsummer Night's Dream, Hamlet,* and *Macbeth*.' For Dennis, 'His Imaginations were often as just as they were bold and strong'; Sewell found that 'His Imagination is a perpetual Fountain of Delight, and all drawn from the same Source: even his Wildnesses are the Wildnesses of Nature.' Theobald judged that 'His fire, spirit, and exuberance of imagination, gave an impetuosity to his pen.' Similarly the greatness of his characters was the result of his intuitive, imaginative penetration of nature. All praised their convincing quality, typefied by Theobald's exclamation, echoing Pope, 'What draughts of Nature! What variety of originals, and how differing each from the other!' They were so alive as to be considered, not as imitations of persons, but as persons themselves; and indeed they were often subjected to shrewd analyses, not by the editors alone, but by Hughes and Steele among others. 'Here,' E. N. Hooker judged, 'rather than in the second half of the eighteenth century, do we see the real beginnings of the romantic criticism of Shakespeare's characters.'

If we turn to diction and expression we find some hesitancy; the puns, the quibbles, the 'low' language were distasteful to some; but for such faults the age of Elizabeth was to blame, and the fact that Shakespeare was a player, denied the benefits of gracious society. No doubt many of the peccant passages were interpolations, by actors probably, in those days ignorant folk. It is Pope who argues this at greatest length; and here, wrong-headed as much of this may seem to us, we catch the first glimpse of the method of interpreting a poet in terms of his own age. But in the main there was nothing but extravagant praise. 'His images are indeed ev'ry where so lively', Rowe maintained, 'that the Thing he would represent stands fully before you, and you possess every Part of it', an ingenious variation of Dryden's 'when he describes any thing, you more than see it, you feel it too'. Gildon, of whom it was unfair of Theobald to say that he was more concerned to display his powers by finding fault than in consulting the improvement of the world, is vigorous in the essay preceding his volume containing the poems, a quite acute if rambling performance.

There is not one of [his poems] that does not carry its Author's Mark and Stamp upon it; not only in the Manner of Thinking, the same Turn of Thought, but even the same Mode of Dress and Expression, the Decompounds, his peculiar sort of Epithets.

We would be more convinced of Gildon's acumen if he had not included, together with 'The Passionate Shepherd' and the answer, some very odd stuff. Nevertheless, he was the first to recognize the importance of the sonnets, to include which he laid down should be part of the duty of an editor of Shakespeare, an injunction not followed till Malone produced his *Works* in 1790. The change in language, Gildon hazarded, loses the Augustan reader something, 'yet there is a wonderful smoothness in many of them, that makes the Blood dance to its Numbers'. Felton made an all-embracing statement:

Nothing can be greater and more lively than his Thoughts; nothing nobler or more forcible than his Expression. The Fire of his Fancy breaketh out into his Words, and sets his Reader on a Flame.

Those utterances may stand as types of what was said during the period.

Editorially the work done in these years solidly laid the foundations of the palace of Shakespearian labours from which we benefit. Rowe based himself on the fourth Folio, but consulted the earlier ones and even one or two Quartos. But he was indolent, as Pope was not, who, taking Rowe as his text, corrected from the earlier Folios and a number of Quartos, placing in the margin passages he regarded as spurious, rearranging and sometimes rewriting prose and verse, with Rowe dividing the acts into scenes, and making intuitive rather than scholarly emendations. Theobald, though classing Pope's edition among those 'of no authority', made more than a little use of him, and delved a good deal deeper. As with Pope, however, his professions are better than his practice. His collation may have been 'deep and laborious', but it was patchy. Yet, as Professor Nichol Smith has said, '... he is the first of our Shakespearian editors, and for these reasons. He respected the readings of the older editions and did not give full rein to his taste. He made many emendations ... but he did not emend at sight'; or, as he put it himself in his *Shakespeare Restored* (only in its full title an aggression upon Pope), he refrained from being 'arbitrary, fantastic, or wanton'. An unfamiliar word found in a play he would seek for in others; he studied Elizabethan diction and usage, and other plays in the period besides Shakespeare's and Jonson's. He supposed that some texts derived from shorthand copies; he was aware of 'sophistication', and used the word in the sense present-day editors use it. His great fault was that in improving he over-rode scansion, and was deaf to the music of the phrase, though he did much to emend pointing. It is to him more than to anybody else that credit is due for this period having inaugurated Shakespeare studies on a sound basis.

The picture of criticism in general drawn in this chapter shows a somewhat confused outline, but indeed the critics themselves were not very clear, and it may throw some light on the scene to glance at the aesthetics of the period. Although it is impossible, and perhaps undesirable, to draw a rigid dividing line between criticism and aesthetics, it may be convenient to devote the next section to a different approach, beginning with the philosophers, and coming back to what was thought by the practitioners.

2. AESTHETICIANS

Shaftesbury carried the aesthetics of the time almost immeasurably further than had so far been done; yet, as with his ethical thought, what he has to say is muffled; he never seems to push his cogitations to that point of clarity where the statement is unmistakably plain, but he planted seeds which were to attain their full tree-growth with Coleridge, just as many of his philosophic intuitions find poetic expression in Wordsworth. His influence was enormous on the Continent, where his notions were finally, and much more clearly, taken over by Kant; and at home, more immediately if less clearly by Hutcheson, Akenside, and others, perhaps even so early as Parnell, as Professor R. L. Brett has illustrated. He is important, not so much for what he has to say about the appreciation of art, his insistence upon individual taste (with reservations) in which Addison was to follow him, as in his tentative reachings out to a coherent theory of the creative, as opposed to the reflective imagination. As to taste, he is cautious. Man has a sense of beauty just as he has a moral sense, but he has to judge by his own experience, his own feelings. But then if each man was to judge merely by what he liked, there would be chaos; there would be no standards.

... as long as we enjoy a Mind, as long as we have *Appetites* and *Sense*, the *Fancys* of all kinds will be hard at work.... They must have their Field. The Question is, Whether they shall have it wholly to themselves; or whether they shall acknowledge some *Controuler* or *Manager*. If none; 'tis this, I fear, which leads to *Madness*.... For if FANCY be left Judg of any thing, she must be Judg of all. Everything is right, if anything be so, because *I fansy it*.

Thus he was not too hasty to jettison the neo-classical rules. They existed because man had a sense of unity, of proportion, of harmony, here just as in morals; and the rules were merely a formulation of these things. They were not, however, immediately recognizable by everybody. To perfect taste needs severe training. To achieve good taste, he emphasizes in *Advice to an Author*, a man

shou'd set afoot the powerfullest Facultys of his Mind ... in order to make a formal Descent on the Territorys of the *Heart* ... by which he wou'd be able to gain at least some tolerable insight into *himself*, and Knowledg of his own *natural Principles*.

In fact the man of taste has to be a virtuoso, in the best sense of the word, the kind that Shaftesbury supported, not the exaggerated, distorted kind that he, in common with Swift, was constant in mocking at.

This doctrine of taste, welcome to an age breaking away from all authority, and cultivating its sensibility, soon developed into an accepted orthodoxy. Acceptable enough too, was his conception of sublimity. In the *Advice to an Author* where he pleads for simplicity, he went no further than to comment a little scathingly upon the Longinian doctrine, noting that

... what commonly passes for *Sublime*, is form'd by the variety of Figures, the multiplicity of Metaphors, and by quitting as much as possible the natural and easy way of Expression, for that which is most unlike to Humanity, or ordinary Use.

But in *The Moralists* he puts himself in line with the later seventeenth century by finding the sublime in nature, though he does not use the word:

... Even the rude *Rocks*, [he writes] the mossy *Caverns*, the irregular unwrought *Grotto's*, and broken *Falls* of Waters, with all the horrid

Graces of the *Wilderness* it-self, as representing NATURE more, will be the more engaging, and appear with a Magnificence beyond the formal Mockery of princely Gardens . . .

to appreciate which is to be 'deep in the *romantick* way'. What was harder to accept, had to be, indeed, fought for against the sense of an age steeped in empiricism, was the theory of the imagination, a subject which at any rate would appeal only to the few who read philosophy, and perhaps to the poets. Shaftesbury, just as he refused to accept the doctrine of the *tabula rasa*, rejected the Hobbesian notion of imagination as being merely decaying sense, or the Lockeian idea of association. He relied on his notion of the plastic General Mind, always creating, of which the mind of man was a reflection, even a part. The world he tells us in *The Moralists* is no mere matter modified, a lump in motion. There is a governing Mind: and the mind of man, being in some sense a part of this is formative, plastic; and, as he explains later, all men are spectators and partakers: 'By turns we catch the vital breath and die', as Pope was to say. He develops the idea as he proceeds to his close, talking about art:

. . . the *Beautiful*, the *Fair*, the *Comely*, were never in the *Matter*, but in the *Art* and *Design*; never in *Body* it-self, but in the *Form* or *forming Power*,

a position Coleridge was to adopt. Further, there are dead forms, and the forms which form, that is, human beings. There is beyond these a third order of beauty which forms even the forms which form, something artist-like, in fact the wisdom and spirit of the universe, the creative principle, or the God whose work of art the universe is.

This from the first had been a pervasive idea with Shaftesbury. In *Advice to an Author*, distinguishing the true poet from the mere chimer of words, he had said of the former that he is

. . . a second *Maker*; a just Prometheus under Jove. Like that Sovereign Artist or universal Plastick Nature, he forms *a Whole*, coherent and proportion'd in it-self . . .,

and this is the point he pursued in the *Second Characters*, an incompleted work which remained in manuscript till Benjamin Rand unearthed it, and published it in 1914. Throughout the whole of this rough draft which he heads *Plastics*, and which was to have been the crown of his performance, he insists on the creative power of the imagination: but all this is part of the larger vision, in which reason exists, but which is not the same thing as thought, which is 'pre-eminent'. The sense remains, reason subsists, but thought 'maintains the eldership of being'. Men derive their thought, even more, their conscious existence, from the original and eternally existent thought. The doctrine only emerges as we read; Shaftesbury's sense of his position never seems very clear to himself; the idea seems to be striving for birth. But to us, looking back, it seems fairly plain that he holds Coleridge's notion of man's perception being 'a repetition in the finite mind of the eternal act of creation in the infinite I AM'—the primary imagination—and like Coleridge is groping towards what can only be called what Kant called it, the aesthetic imagination. It is reason in her most exalted mood. Hutcheson, as we shall see, Thomson, Akenside, and others held much the same view as the Romantics, though the latter were, if not clearer, possessed by a far intenser feeling as poets, and as poets of nobler stature, endowed with greater power of utterance.

Stubbs,[1] in a Platonic *Dialogue on Beauty* (1731), in which Socrates asks Aspasia 'a competent number of questions', makes harmony the essential of beauty. The understanding can appreciate symmetry, and the pleasures of the understanding give the highest kind of delight. Thus design and knowledge are the parents of beauty; in the pleasures arising from knowledge 'we even partake of the Divine Happiness or the Contemplation of Beauty'. The mind, indeed, is the first and highest beauty, the body being the lute upon which the mind plays; but minds produce a beauty of their own, so the idea of moral beauty must be formed by our own powers, and thus it is that we delight in 'the pleasing View of Concord and Innocence which are the Shadows of Moral Beauty': we rejoice, for instance, in a flock of sheep and detest wolves. Throughout we feel that Stubbs is tending towards Shaftesbury, dimly groping in a maze of sentimental if elevated notions.

It was, however, Hutcheson who continued the line in the first instance, in this sphere, as well as in the moral one. If, according to Pope, as recorded by Spence, he was 'a very bad

---

[1] Philip Stubbs, 1665–1738, was educated at the Merchant Taylors School, and Wadham College, Oxford, of which he was made Fellow in 1691. After holding livings at Woolwich, and St. Alphage, London Wall, he became Archdeacon of St. Albans, and in 1719 Rector of Launton, Oxfordshire. He was elected F.R.S. in 1703, and was most active in the S.P.C.K.

writer', 'he has struck out very great lights, and made very considerable discoveries by the way.' In the first part of his *Inquiry* (1725), which is concerned with beauty, order, harmony, and design, he modifies the Shaftesburian approach while adhering to the main doctrines which allow aesthetics to enter largely into morals. Decrying the limitation of the word 'sense' to the sensations derived from the five senses, 'Our Philosophers', he complains, 'consider that "the only Pleasure of Sense . . . is that which accompanys the simple Ideas of Sensation": they ignore the greater pleasures of the ideas raised in us which we call by such names as beauty and harmony'. He goes on later to argue that we can call the perception of beauty a sense, since it does not arise from knowledge but strikes us at once; no amount of knowledge can increase this immediate sense, though it may add a rational pleasure from prospects of advantage or the increase of knowledge: nevertheless, aesthetic delight is disinterested, since

. . . it plainly appears that some Objects are *immediately* the Occasions of this Pleasure of Beauty, and that we have Senses fitted for perceiving it; and that it is distinct from that *Joy* which arises from Self-love upon Prospect of Advantage.

The realization of beauty, however—a realization that comes from a universal perception of 'uniformity amidst variety'—is not confined to objects perceived by the material senses. Pleasure can be obtained from abstract ideas, from Euclid, for example, or from history, which is an art. And

This Delight which accompanys Sciences, or universal *Theorems*, may really be call'd a kind of *Sensation*; since it necessarily accompanys the Discovery of any Proposition, and is distinct from bare Knowledge it self, being most violent at first, whereas the Knowledge is uniformly the same.

Moreover, 'those, who after Mr. Locke have shaken off the groundless Opinions about *innate Ideas*' do not make their case, since the agreeable or the disagreeable are agreed to be natural powers of perception. Nor will custom provide a reason for the sense of beauty. It is true that custom may cause a man to connect the ideas of religious horror to certain buildings, 'but *Custom* could never have made a *Being* naturally incapable of *Fear*, receive such ideas'. Though custom and education may influence the internal senses, such arguments presuppose our sense of beauty to be natural. It is clear that such an approach would be welcome to the ordinary thinking man, careless of whether 'our philosophers' were right about the nature of things, for his own empiricism, the appeal to what he knew he felt, would be convincing. So too would be the distinction between absolute and relative beauty, the former being the internal sense we enjoy immediately, the second that derived from comparison—for our minds are strangely prone ever to compare; thus the second pleasure widens the scope of enjoyment for the man who knows enough to compare objects, or works of art, or works of art with the objects they employ.

Hutcheson does not pursue the question of taste with the defensive ardour which inspired Shaftesbury; he takes it for granted, or rather, renames it 'internal sense'. But to anybody aware what was in Shaftesbury's mind, especially when he drafted the *Second Characters*, which Hutcheson may have seen, it is clear that he was on the one hand a little at variance with his leader in that he did not think taste needed the discipline Shaftesbury thought necessary, but on the other hand supported him in his objection to academic minds which would, like the petty virtuosoes', base all taste upon education and knowledge. Shaftesbury was always inveighing against the pretentiousness of those who with a little knowledge and no sensibility criticize works of art—the genus is numerous and active enough in our own day—and apply ill-digested rules; but at the same time, as we have seen, he insisted that taste must be trained. Between them they propagated the idea of taste, and the word became one of common usage. It lent itself well as a criterion in a society anxious to train itself, to shine as the exemplar of civilization, the first number (21 Feb. 1724) of *The Tea-Table* declaring that its efforts would be directed against bad taste. Taste became in many ways the hall-mark of the century, as expressed in such works as Hume's *Essay on Taste* (1760).

In essence all the discussion about the rules was only a part of this wider question, which was naturally of concern to the enlarged circle of readers who wanted to enjoy perceptively without being hampered by the cogitations of men whom they regarded as pedants padlocked in dead academic assumptions. Not that it was supposed that taste was a happy gift of nature; the emphasis always was upon a due degree of knowledge in such matters; it did not need a Wordsworth, quoting Reynolds, to tell the readers of this earlier period that 'an *accurate* taste in poetry, and in all the other arts . . . is an *acquired* talent, which can only be produced by thought and long-continued intercourse with the best models of composition'. It was Dennis's fear, as it was Pope's, that the rise of a reading public, uneducated, and avid for amusement, would destroy all the bases of taste; this the obedient Gildon echoed in his mortally tedious dialogues. In *A Large Account of the Taste in Poetry* (which has a particular application to comedy) Dennis insisted that 'for the judging of any sort of Writings, those talents are in some measure requisite, which were necessary to produce them', chiefly learning, and a knowledge of mankind and of the world. Also, he adds, leisure and serenity are necessary, since the dignity of poetry requires the whole man. He sums up:

> But now, as Parts, Education and Application are necessary to succeed in the writing Poetry, they are requisite in some degree for the forming a true judgment of it. No man can judge of a Beautiful imagination in another, without some degree of it in himself. And as for the judging rightly of any thing without Judgment, that is a contradiction in terms.

He then goes on to deplore, in his usual fashion, the 'degeneracy' of taste, with all that that implied for him, in his own age.

Welsted, as noted, took a more cheerful view; but (modern readers will have some sympathy with him here) he was opposed to the more vocal and extreme applauders of 'common sense'.

> Many of the Graces of Poetry may, I grant, be talk'd of in very intelligible Language, but intelligible only to those who have a natural *Taste* for it, or are born with a Talent of judging. To have what we call *Taste*, is having, one may say, a new Sense or Faculty superadded to the ordinarily [*sic*] ones of the Soul, the Prerogative of fine Spirits! and to go about to pedagogue a Man into this sort of Knowledge, who has not the Seeds of it in himself, is the same thing as if one should endeavour to teach an Art of seeing without Eyes.

He is, in fact, postulating an aesthetic sense, much in line with Shaftesbury's and Hutcheson's views. '*Taste*, or a faculty of Judging. . .', he remarked later, 'cannot be reduc'd to a formal Science, or taught by any sort of Precepts', and it cannot be 'explained' any more than the existence of gravity can be 'explained' by the astronomers.

Moreover, Welsted went deeper into the matter, suggesting, for the first time it would seem, a subject for discourse which occupies us at the present day with increasing urgency, namely, the different modes possible for apprehending truth. Already in his day the dominance of the scientific approach was making men uneasy.

It is certain, every Thing depends on Reason, and must be guided by it: but it is certain, that Reason operates differently, when it has different things for its Object: poetical Reason is not the same thing as mathematical Reason; there is in good Poetry as rigid Truth, and as essential to the nature of it, as there is in a Question of Algebra, but that Truth is not to be prov'd by the same Process or way of Working; Poetry depends much more on Imagination than other Arts, but is not on that Account less reasonable than they.

He seems to be feeling towards some theory of the intuition, going a good deal further than Howard had done in his Preface to *The Duke of Lerma* (1668) when blaming 'the unnecessary understanding of some that have laboured to give strict rules to things that are not mathematical', his argument being merely that a poet has greater latitude to offend against reason. Howard had gone on to declare that liking or disliking a play was a matter of the fancy which any person best relishes; he does not use the word taste, nor suggest that 'fancy' needs to be trained. Most critics had something to say on the point, but little of any trenchancy; Oldmixon, sensible as always, seems to hold the balance between Dennis and Welsted. He reacted strongly enough, however, against Howard's affirmation that 'there can be no Determination but by *Taste*'. No vehement upholder of the Rules, as we have seen, here he bursts out: 'Thus a wrong Taste is as good as a right one, and the Smell of a *Pole-cat* to be preferr'd to that of a *Civet*, if a Man's Nose is so irregular.' James Bramston, in his poem *The Man of Taste* (1733), addressed to Pope, is amusing and lightly satirical, but beyond evidencing the interest the subject held for the general reader, throws no light on the development of the idea.

The emphasis on taste was an indication of the subjective approach in criticism; a work was to be judged, not as a thing in itself, but by its effect on the reader. Trapp saw that some psychological research was needed, suggesting that to understand 'how Delight should flow from Pity and Terror, and even

Sorrow itself' would require our knowing 'the secret Springs of the Soul'. It is surprising to find that the clearest indication of this approach emanates from Purney, whose contribution to the pastoral, and his critical comments on it, would almost seem to be a spoofing of the whole pastoral idea. In the Preface to his somewhat insipid poems in dialogue, *The Bashful Swain: and Beauty and Simplicity* (1717), he stated that to arrive at the bottom and foundation of criticism it was necessary to write:

> *First*, On the Nature and Constitution of the human Mind, and the Pleasure it is capable of receiving from Poetry.
> *Secondly*, How that Pleasure might be best excited.

He would divide poetry, and this, he says, is his great discovery, into Image and Sentiment, the latter being an expression of feeling or thought: images can be great, beautiful, uncommon, terrible. Then there are

> ... the kind of Sentiments, not quite distinguishable from the Image. 1. The Sublime. 2. The Bright or Brilliant. 3. The Satyrick or Biting. 4. The Mournful, Piteous, or Elegiack. 5. The Comick. 6. The Tender. 7. The Agreeable. ...
> *Thirdly*. To show the Rules how to arrive at Perfection in each of these Ways and Kinds of Writing.

But there is no one rule. There are 'many Kinds of Heroick Poems, and all as perfect as *Homers*, yet constituted entirely otherwise, and [he adds with some sense of relief] but a fourth part so long'.

He added also to the family of emotions. In his comments on his later pastorals, he points out that 'That kind of Writing call'd the *Gloomy* also reigns there; such as is not repugnant to the Happiness of Swains'; and he goes on to develop this in such a way as to constitute an interesting sidelight on the grave-yard poetry that was coming into fashion, and a premonition of the Gothick novel of some fifty years later. Incidentally he trenches upon the virtues of ambiguity with which the present age has been so happily entertained.

> The *English* alone ... have Genius's fitted for the *Gloomy*. But as we have never abounded much with *Criticks*, never has any enter'd into the Nature of it. Tho' sure it deserves an entire Discourse. And so sweetly amusing is it to the Soul, That 'twill strike thro' Language even ridiculous; and alone support a Sentiment. As here
>
> *Put out the Light, and then put out the Light.*

The Language is a kind of *Pun*, and therefore to Minds that care not for the Beauty of the Thought divested of it, the line appears absurd.

He went no further in analysis; but how far the aesthetic sensation might be related to physiology made a shy appearance, by implication in Addison (*Spectator* 412), as in Gildon, when speaking of Shakespeare's sonnets. Trapp drew an analogy:

Are the Passions, then, to be purg'd, even by their being put in Agitation? Yes; and why not? Bile and Phlegm, and other Humours in the Human Body, cannot be carried off, unless they are first fermented, and put in Motion: Nay, Humours are often expell'd by Medicines of the same Nature and Temperament . . .

perhaps as good a reason for enjoying tragedy as any given in that age. Addison's *suave mari magno* explanation, that we relish the painful horrors offered us on the stage because we are ourselves free of them, hardly corresponds with experience.

Here and there we find small advances in the field of aesthetics, or, rather, the dropping of a seed or two which barely sprouted. We can note one such let fall by Jonathan Richardson[1] in *Explanatory Notes and Remarks on Milton's Paradise Lost* (1734). It had long been universally recognized that the object of poetry was to instruct and delight, and though it was undisputed that the instruction was to take place in morals, nobody inquired what part of the human being was to be infused with delight. For Richardson the great end of poetry was 'to Please and Inrich the Imagination, and to Mend the Heart, and make the Man Happy'. Happiness, we have seen, was in the mind of Dennis also, but rather by elevating man in the religious sphere than by nourishing the imagination. This seems to have been obscurely in the mind of Addison when he remarked in No. 2 of his series on the imagination, that 'it serves us for a kind of Refreshment, and takes off from that Satiety we are apt to complain of in our usual and ordinary Entertainments'. So in *Spectator* 412, but Steele, in a letter in the next number, got a little closer: 'The Pleasures of the Imagination are what bewilder Life, when Reason and Judgment do not interpose.' Trapp was of opinion that 'the Mind of Man does not love to have too minute a Detail of Particulars; but takes a Pleasure in having

---

[1] Jonathan Richardson, 1665–1745, was apprenticed as a scrivener, but took to painting, succeeding Kneller and Dahl as the fashionable portraitist of his day.

room for the Imagination, and of forming a Judgement of what is not express'd from what is'; and Giles Jacob wrote that 'in Poetry it is equally happy to forbear speaking all one knows, and to leave something for others to employ their thoughts upon; as in Prospects those are best and most pleasing, which leave us room to guess more than the Eye can discover'. There was abroad a confused sense that one of the functions at least of poetry was to release the imagination. Richardson noted Milton's power of affecting the imagination by silence, a contribution Dryden had already made when he said of Virgil that 'he speaks by silences'.

Spence has been credited with a small step forward in discussing grace as the fourth constituent of beauty (the other three being colour, form, and expression) in his *Crito: or a Dialogue on Beauty* (1752), whereby, it is claimed, that he forestalled Kames and Lessing.

> Though Grace is so difficult to be accounted for in general; yet I have observ'd two particular things which (I think) hold universally in relation to it.
> The First is: That there is no Grace without Motion, either of the whole Body, or of some Limb, or, at least, of some Feature . . .

quoting Bacon, Horace, and Virgil as possible supporters for his theory. His second 'particular thing' is Propriety. 'Grace, like Poetry, must be born with a Person, and is never, wholly, to be acquired by Art. . .', which is no more than insisting upon the *curiosa felicitas* of which John Hughes had reminded a generation not unfamiliar with the idea. Dennis, in some not very illuminating remarks about imagery, had laid down that 'Images are never so admirably drawn as when they are drawn in Motion; especially if the Motion is violent', Hogarth later agreeing if not with Dennis, at least with Richardson. For Stubbs's Socrates, regular exercises of motion were delightful to beholders, which Aspasia confirms—perhaps after a visit to the ballet—by adding 'as is confessed by expiring Crowds'. But these are morsels of chaff in little side eddies agitated by the great wind raised by Shaftesbury, which, *via* the Germans, was to blow Coleridge into fame before a century had passed.

X

LETTERS, MEMOIRS, TRAVEL;
HISTORIANS AND ANTIQUARIES

I. LETTERS, MEMOIRS, TRAVEL

THE period is not rich in outstanding background documents of this type, though it can boast two or three relished
examples; but what there is of it repays in fugitive delight
at least a cursory conning. Before, however, entering on a brief
discussion of them, a few preliminary observations are to be
made, for there is a certain difficulty to be faced as regards
dates, especially with respect to the publication of Memoirs.
The two *Histories* of Clarendon (d. 1674) and Burnet (d. 1715),
which are essentially memoirs, are dealt with in the previous
volume, though they did not appear till 1702-4 and 1723
respectively, since they are concerned, in the first case altogether, in the second mainly, with what the writers lived
through in the seventeenth century. The same is true of Ellwood's more intimate journal, published in 1714. Yet it is
impossible to be completely consistent: thus the biographies
and memoirs of Roger North, though treating mainly of the
earlier period, but written within the dates covered by this
volume, and not published till a little later, are included here.
Journals and diaries, however, fit in happily with the chronological division. As regards letters, those of the writers whose
works are discussed separately are not considered in this section,
though those of Swift and Pope, and to a lesser degree of Steele
and Addison, which are subject to editions separate from their
other writings, are in themselves literature. The letters treated
of in this section are those which constitute the chief literary
product of their writers, such as those of Lady Mary Wortley
Montagu (whose later letters will be treated in the next volume),
or of men such as Aaron Hill, who are not considered separately as authors. Though the three most famous letter-writers of
the century, Chesterfield, Wesley, and Horace Walpole, began their correspondence within this period, the bulk belongs

to the next phase, and will be treated of in the succeeding volume.

Biography in this period is almost non-existent; William Oldys's life of Walter Ralegh (1736), or Sewell's of John Philips call for special mention no more than such works as Gildon's life of Betterton and Carte's life of Ormonde, though Middleton's *Cicero* still has a certain place: but Roger North's delightful *Lives of the Norths* (1742–4)—really Memoirs, containing accounts of three of his brothers, and his own autobiography not published till 1890—are of great and varied interest, and as regards style may be looked upon almost as curiosities of literature, so oddly is the old manner mixed with the new. Son of Lord North, Roger was born in 1653, and lived until 1734; though having achieved the position of Solicitor-General to the Queen in 1684, as a staunch, almost rabid loyalist, after the Revolution he retired to his home at Rougham in Norfolk, and studiously 'lived out of the way'. He did not set to writing until 1706, when goaded by what he considered the outrageous treatment accorded to Charles II in White Kennett's Whiggish *History of England*, he prepared a bulky refutation of Kennett's charges, published in 1740 as *Examen*, which, with all its occasional felicities of style, may be left as a quarry for historians. Out of this, apparently, arose his own memoirs (left unfinished), and from these again the lives of his three elder brothers, Francis, Lord Keeper, who became the first Lord Guilford, Sir Dudley, a rich Turkey merchant, and Dr. John North, Master of Trinity, Cambridge. They are rambling, intimate narratives, what is said or told in the autobiography often being repeated in one or other of the lives, which are crammed with detail, usually of the first general interest, but sometimes attractive only to historians of the law, or of economics, or of politics; but nowhere, for anybody interested in human affairs or complex relationships, is time wasted in long leisurely reading. Least of all is it wasted for the multifariously curious, or for tasters of prose.

The editor of the standard edition of 1890, Augustus Jessopp, remarked regretfully (in the *D.N.B.*) that his style was 'defaced' by the use of some unusual words, but for many it will be just those words that give the discourses their flavour. We meet something of this quality at the beginning of his *Lives*, where he explains, speaking of Francis North, that he needed 'a well qualified compurgator of all his thoughts and actions', so as to 'refel calumny', of which there had been a good deal of the idle kind; yet even if this is of no authority

... I cannot but think it in me a sort of duty to puff away such slight dust, because calumny which riseth after a man's death (the most unworthy and degenerous of all) needs most a friend to retund it; because, as a man's authority and power ceaseth, impudence gets ground and thinks to ramp it without check. ...

In contradistinction to the Latin words we meet such vernacular as 'flam'—much as we would use it now; Dr. John North is 'roiled', that is, vexed, disturbed in spirit; a certain virtuoso's house in Bloomsbury is, in the common phrase, a veritable 'knick-knack-atory'; one Pollexfen, who was supported by the family enemy Judge Jeffreys, is 'a thorough stitch enemy to the crown and monarchy'; he himself, at one stage, is 'young and vegete'. Sometimes the language can be direct enough, as this in the *Life* of Sir Dudley North:

Another thing, new to him in London, was the coffee-houses. There were scarce any when he was last before in England; and, for certain, none at all when he first went out. At Constantinople they had coffee, but no coffee-houses; for those were not suffered; it having been found the people, by a tendency to sedition, made an ill use of them.

Or it may attain a symphonic music which makes one suppose that North had read *Urn Burial*, and he need not have apologized for his 'Tenuity of Style or Language'.

The main emotion binding these lives together is one of deep family piety, and the reader would do well to begin his adventure with the 'Notes of Me', which preface the autobiography, giving a vivid picture of affectionate but disciplined family life under the government of Lady North, who to all the graces of the motherly care of a highly educated woman added reproof that was 'fluent and pungent'. Three of the brothers seem to have been closely and loyally connected, if Dr. John, a disagreeable man, apparently, ever at odds with the Fellows of his college, always remained a brother rather than a friend. Though Roger was sent to the Free Schools at Bury St. Edmunds and Thetford, and spent a year at Jesus College, Cambridge, his chief education—apart from music, to which he ascribes enormous importance—was attending Francis, twenty years his senior, on his circuits as a judge. He learnt more about life when his brother Dudley came back from his sojourns at Archangel and in Smyrna and Constantinople, to become a sheriff of London and one of the commissioners of the Treasury. In daily contact with these extremely able men of affairs, Roger mingles accounts of family matters, his own cogitations, as when he argues that suicide is allowable, personal characteristics and individual portraits (such as the brilliant one of Judge Hale) with crucial national events. Detailed political discussion of these last, however, are mercifully relegated to *Examen*, to which the reader of the *Lives* is ever and anon referred. The result is an extraordinary fusion of private and public doings, at all levels, and in many parts of the country, giving a sense of the actuality of life which it is difficult to parallel in any document of this kind. It may seem that the Norths were un-duly virtuous, irritatingly always in the right—though there can be no doubt that they were humane, upright, and intelligent —nevertheless, through them we can get a sense of what living was like in the Restoration period. North is not scandalously personal and intimate as Pepys is, but we get far more sense of general movement, of political clashes as they affect the person, than we do from him or, say, Burnet. Occasionally we get glimpses of drama full of vitality and often entertaining. Take, for example, the occasion when an attempt was made to prove that Sir Dudley had been appointed Sheriff by some intrigue. He was examined before a committee, and in due course was asked

'. . . if Secretary Jenkins did not come down to the City and per-suade him to take the Office of Sheriff upon him?' 'You hear the question,' said the Chairman. After which there was a profound Silence, expecting the Answer. All which time Sir *Dudley North* was gathering as much Breath as he could muster, and, then, came out a long 'N-o-o-o-o!' so loud as might have been heard up to the House of Lords. This was so violent and unexpected that I could see a Start of every one in the House, all at the same Instant, as if each had had a Dash of cold Water in his Face: and immediately all called out, 'Withdraw'; and my Neighbour *Titus Oates*, being, as I suppose, frustrated of his Expectations, cried out 'Aw Laard, Aw Laard, Aw, Aw!' and went his way. Sir *Dudley North* went out, and never was called upon more about this Affair.

So if it cannot be claimed that this work is of the first literary order it ranks as a work of literature. Admitting also that there are occasional tedious passages, as reminiscences covering the legal life of England, the public scene, trade disputes in Turkey, or the contentions of university politics, the three volumes are amazingly rich mines in which the labour of quarrying is itself not disagreeable.

It has, moreover, formative importance in the development of biography; published as it was between 1740 and 1742, it must have influenced Johnson, and through him Boswell, in the handling of material. For with North, even when treating of his own kin—where he is partial enough—biography is never hagiography, as it had more than tended to be in the previous century. He does not hesitate to note 'scars and blemishes', and felt with Johnson that 'the business of a biographer is often to pass lightly over those performances and incidents which produce vulgar greatness, to lead the thoughts into domestic privacies', and so on. In every case he gives us 'a breather, not a statue', and suggests the motives that direct the undercurrents of social and political activity.

To those avid of such, the title *Memoirs of the Secret Services of John Macky* (1733) is disappointingly misleading. A short preface by his son disposes of political activities in a few paragraphs, the rest of the book being made up of somewhat platitudinous 'characters' of the main figures of the day, many of which, it is claimed, appear in later editions of Burnet's *History of His Own Time*, though a cursory examination does not invite conviction. But there is interest in the British Museum copy, since in it are transcribed by Thomas Birch the comments on the personalities that Swift jotted down in his own. For instance, in describing Lord Raby, Macky remarks that he is 'of fine understanding', against which Swift scribbles, 'very bad & can't spell'. But Raby's family was not greatly addicted to correct spelling, as we discover from *The Wentworth Papers 1705–1739* (published 1883), perhaps the most entertaining— and from more than one point of view extremely interesting— bundle of letters of the period. They are all addressed to William Wentworth, Lord Raby, later, shortly before his going to Holland to negotiate the Treaty of Utrecht, Earl of Strafford. The bulk of them are from his family while he was abroad as Ambassador from 1705 to 1714, and give a fascinating picture of the life led by the richer aristocracy during the period, with all their interests, frivolous and serious. The letters of old Lady Wentworth, eager to tell 'My dearist and best of children' anything that might amuse or interest him, or lead him to a profitable marriage, still have the pulse of life as lived from day to day by a *grande dame* of that time, with all its *naïveté*, its humanity, its shrewdness and its innocence:

March 16th, 1705. . . . Lady Windum, Lady Hyde's sister is dead, and Lorde Dalkith, the Duke of Munmuth's eldest son is dead, was abroad a Munday and Tewsday he was about his own house, and dyed Wensday morning at fower of the clock; and there is twoe strang fishis taken up, and fower sons was seen by severell and a flaiming soard. This I was told for truith, but I know not how to afirm it for truith, but this I will afirm for truth that no son was more beloved by a mother then you ar by yours.

Sometimes she will throw a revealing sidelight on the events of the day, such as the Sacheverell trial. But for intimate life and gossip, where houses are to be got, what 'the Dutchis of Molbery' was about, she is inimitable with her fine disregard of spelling, her keen interest in what was going on. It would have amused Pope to have read what Raby's sister Betty wrote the Ambassador in 1710 when asking for 'ten pd for a tickit' for the lottery, since 'mony now adays is the raening passion'.

For the student of politics, wishing to gloss the statements of the historians, Swift included, the letters of Raby's brother Peter are indispensable. The reader can live in the atmosphere of the rumours, the reports of meetings, the speculations that filled the air at the period of Utrecht, and can almost share the tension, feel the significance of why the Duchess of Marlborough cancelled the dancing at her house, or the importance of the Queen's attack of gout. And while all this is going on, and the 'Whimsical Tories' are making their gestures, and the 'Accational Conformity' Bill is going through, both Lady Strafford and Lady Wentworth tell their correspondent about the Mohocks: 'Here is nothing talked about but men that goes in partys about the street and cuts peaple with swords or knives, and they call themselves by som hard name that I can nethere speak nor spell. . . .' Or we hear that Lady Strafford has 'been at Mr Jervises to see our pickturs'; but the mother writes to her son 'pray let Sir Godferry Nelloe draw your Lady's picture, whoe is the best panter we have, nether of her picturs dus her justiss'. Thus family chatter alternates with such things as

Peter Wentworth's account of the stabbing of Harley by Guiscard, or Lord Berkeley of Stratton's flurried report of what happened at Queen Anne's death, when the names of the governors were announced, and 'My Lord Sunderland look'd very pale when the names were read'. Then three years later we find Lord Bathurst, his first cousin, writing to Strafford about improving a house he had just acquired at Boughton. Soon Strafford's daughters appear, first with childish letters; and then Lady Lucy Wentworth develops a taste for music. In January 1737:

My mama has been so good to give me leave to goe to the Opera to night with Lady Anne. 'Tis to be a new one call'd Meropy, but the foolish Buffo's are to be left out which I am very glad of.

And ten days later:

. . . Last Sunday there was a vast deal of musick at Church, too much I think, for I doubt it spoils every bodys devotion, for there was drums and Trumpits as loud as an Oritoria.

The youthful Lord Wentworth is interested in the theatre as well, and we are told that in January 1739 'Young Cibber was vastly hiss'd a Thursday, but his old friend Impudence kept him from being either out of countenance or in the least disturb'd at the noise'; and for the new oratorio, *Saul*, we learn that 'Mr. Handell has borrow'd of the Duke of Argylle a pair of the largest kettle-drums in the Tower, so to be sure it will be excessive noisy with a bad set of singers; I doubt it will not retrieve his former losses'.

The volume provides only intermittent glimpses of literary figures. In 1705 Lord Raby writes, 'I am impatient for those verses you promise me of Prior's, who has an excellent knack of writing pleasant things and tells a story in verse the most agreeable that I ever knew'; and in 1711 he did not seem averse to having 'my old school-fellow and friend Matt: Prior' as a Plenipotentiary for the peace, though the appointment was not made. It is agreeable to find that in 1725 the Duke of Bedford is a devoted admirer of Pope, and is eager to meet him; and though we can understand why Lord Berkeley felt as he did about the poet, it does not add to our esteem of his Lordship to find him writing on 15 January 1732: 'I have not seen Pope's verses ['The Epistle to Bathurst' published on that day?]. These people are all flattery or abuse. They put me in mind of some who cannot be civil to one body without affronting the rest of the company.' Steele appears mainly for political reasons, though Peter Wentworth arranges to send his brother the complete *Tatlers*. Swift, apart from his party writings, is mentioned in connexion chiefly with the death of his protegée, young Harrison, who was Raby's secretary abroad. Lady Strafford tells her husband: 'His brother Poets bury'd him, as Mr Addison, Mr Philips, and Dr Swift.' We hear of 'a most scandalouse Lampoon com out against the Duchess of Somerset', probably Swift's 'The Windsor Prophecy'; and in August 1714 of 'a very cleaver banter come out upon Doctor Swift', no doubt the 'Hue and Cry upon Dr Swift'. If there is no great literary merit in these letters, they are extraordinarily fresh, written in a good running manner without pomposity or reticence.

At the opposite pole to the foregoing lurks that very queer document *The Life and Errors of John Dunton* (1705), inchoate and rambling, whining and aggressive, crushingly derogatory of some men, fervently praising of others, occasionally acute, but phrased in a bubbling vernacular sometimes so uncontrolled as to indicate the insanity to which Dunton[1] at one time succumbed, and often scrambling into verse. Apart from a certain amount of interest in the personality of the man, and some amusement at and with his writing, the main value of the book is in the light it throws upon Grub Street, its scribblers, booksellers, printers, engravers, waste-paper men, and in the emotionally impelled character sketches which make up a large proportion of the work. He professes, indeed, to give more than a thousand brief biographies and characters, which would seem to be true, though how exactly the statistically minded may determine. His excuse, if one is needed, is:

I take this NEW-WAY of writing my Life (*by way of* Characters), as I believe *A History of Living Men* (besides the Novelty of it) will be of Great use to promote the *Reformation* now on Foot; for *we are led by Examples, more than Precepts*. . . .

As a result we get an amazingly full gallery of portraits of the time, too full indeed for inclusion in the space of one book; so that at one point Dunton resorts to names of a 'Hundred Persons, &c,' to most of which no more than an adjective is attached: 'Slovenly *Wire*—Tetchy *W—ms*—Smiling *Feltham*'; and so on, the ladies getting rather more generous shrift:

[1] John Dunton, 1659–1733, was educated at Dungrove, near Chesham; and by his father, Rector of Aston Clinton, Bucks.

'Divine *Astell*—Refin'd Lady *Masham*—That Angel in Flesh and Blood Madam *Gwillim*'; while in another place Elizabeth Singer, whom he dubbed 'the Pindaric lady' gets excited adulation. His longer portraits, however, are valuable, especially that of Defoe, with whom he more than once collaborated, and who wrote for him the panegyric on Samuel Annesley, and the Pindaric Ode on the Athenian Society when its works were gathered in book form. We hear of Settle, Gildon, and Ned Ward; of Tonson, Lintott, the unfortunate Tutchin (who was later beaten to death), Ridpath, Lesley, Abel Boyer, and others; he also, in the 'Idea of a New Life' section, ventures upon sketches of the great—Godolphin, Harley, Gilbert Burnet— who thus appear to us as seen by the ordinary man in the street. His manner is buoyant enough, somewhere between the Nashe- Dekker exuberance of Tom Brown and Ned Ward, and the more controlled vivacity of Defoe. Take, as an average sample, the character of:

> Robert Carr—A small *Poetical Insect*, Like Bays in everything but writing well—An odd Mixture of Lead and Mercury—As heavy and dull as an old Usurer, and yet as unfixt and Magoty as Parson Grubb—still changeing, displeased, unquiet, uneasy, a Perfect Contradiction to himself, and all the World: He writ *an Antidote against Lust*: and has nothing but his CHASTITY to recommend him.

He can be more scurrilous and Billingsgate; one unfortunate is a murderer of paper, who makes Helicon a puddle, not a spring. But he can more temperately hammer Lesley, whom he disliked, at the same time giving him his due; be judiciously praising of Defoe, and very warm towards Tutchin, Ridpath, and Boyer. He draws a well-modelled picture of Buckley, the printer, striking out a good aphorism by the way: 'Sam Buckley, by a liberal education, has been softened to civility; for that rugged honesty some men profess is an indigested chaos, but it wants form and matter. . . .'

His account of his own life is interesting enough in its feveredly insistent way: fact is interspersed with introspective and religious comment as we follow him leaving his parsonage home, being apprenticed to a bookseller, setting up on his own, launching the *Athenian Gazette*, which became the *Athenian Mercury*, one of the contributors to which, he notes, was 'Mr Swift, a Country Gentleman'. Involved in his life was Samuel

Wesley, who since Dutton also married one of the daughters of the noted Samuel Annesley, became his brother-in-law; not always in perfect accord with him, Dutton came to have some scorn for the 'conforming Dissenter'. This was mainly, it would seem, on account of the financial disasters in which the hopeful publisher became swamped, after a sortie to Boston, Massachusetts, and a visit to Ireland, on which he wrote a book, which not only describes his 'scuffle' in Dublin, but makes a fairly interesting travelogue. A curious figure emerges, very much self-justifying while searching out his errors, loudly protesting against the infamy of others, touchingly vaunting his conjugal affections (he married twice). Harried as he is, he is in some sort triumphant in himself, a manic-depressive type who became more and more obscure in the journalistic field, till in the end he had to beg for a royal pension. His book may not be literature, but it is near enough to earn a place as one of its wilder freaks.

If *An Account of the Conduct of the Dowager Duchess of Marlborough From her First coming to Court to the Year 1710* (1742), huddled up at odd times, and finally put together with the help of Nathaniel Hooke, is of some interest to historians, to the student of character it is sheer delight. Her Grace's style is racy, impelled by an ardent need for self-justification, and not without art; while her irony, if not very profound, is amusingly brisk, when, as a staunch, even a fanatical Whig, she is full of scorn for the clumsy Tory trick of rallying votes or keeping places by the cry 'The Church in Danger'. Such a taste as 'The last great wound given to the Church this year was by the Queen's taking the Privy Seal from the Duke of Buckingham' will serve: obvious, but in its setting very pretty. The holding power of the book, however, and it still holds, resides in the fascinating story of the passionate friendship (the word is the Queen's) between Lady Churchill, as she was when the story opens, and 'her poor, unfortunate, faithful Morley', as Queen Anne styled herself. There are some astonishing letters, and a few markedly dramatic scenes as the Duchess strove to maintain her position against Lady Masham, who by her monstrous scheming, as it appeared to the Duchess, succeeded not only in displacing her benefactress, but also, through her backstair intrigues with Harley, in undermining the Duke, shattering the Whigs, and bringing the country, as old age saw it, to ruin.

To read this document is to see the politics of the time through the distorting glasses of the emotions, generous as well as bitter, of a powerful if not very sensitive personality, the whole policy of England seeming to hinge upon the acerbities of court ladies, and the private ambitions of treacherous noblemen. The odd thing is that one world does indeed appear to reflect the other. However, this account of affairs, and of her impeccable behaviour, did not go unchallenged; there were many retorts, notably one by James Ralph (Pope's victim), in the anonymously published *The Other Side of the Question* (1742), the defence being taken up in the same year by no less a person than Henry Fielding in *A Full Vindication of the Dowager Duchess of Marlborough*.

A charming glimpse of Lady Churchill, when she was at the height of her friendship with the Princess Anne, is to be caught from another source, namely *An Apology for the Life of Mr Colley Cibber* (1740). The hopeful young son of the sculptor found himself in the service of the Earl of Devonshire at the time of the Revolution, when forces from Chatsworth were occupying Nottingham, whither the Princess and her companion, aided by the Bishop of London, had fled from the capital. Cibber, who waited at table, was dazzled by 'so clear an emanation of beauty, such a commanding grace of aspect', to such an extent that he retained the impression throughout his life. His autobiography is still engagingly readable, as the almost garrulous chatter of a clever and confessedly vain man, so vain in fact as to believe, to our benefit, that his virtues so far outweigh his faults that he can afford to tell the world about the latter. Yet he is modest enough to be quite clear on his place as a writer, and can jest at himself: his manner is absolutely right. As a professional author, naturally he knew something about writing; and his style, the good vernacular of the intelligent man of the world, deserves to be ranked, in this one manner, with that of Defoe, though with Defoe you are always aware that he is being a little too voluble on purpose. Cibber rattles along, telling the story of his stage triumphs or failures, and the whole history of the theatres in his day, on which, though his facts are not invariably quite consistent with truth, he must always remain a primary authority. Besides that, he is the first critic of the art of acting that we possess, and from him we can almost reconstruct the way the great actors presented their parts. Betterton's manner, for example, is convincingly described, the modulations of his voice, his restraint, his tact, so that we can appreciate that 'he never thought any kind of [applause] equal to an attentive Silence; that there were many ways of deceiving an Audience into a loud one; but to keep them husht and quiet, was an Applause which only Truth and Merit could arrive at'. His description of Mrs. Montfort as Melantha is a little classic of its kind:

... The first ridiculous Airs that break upon her are upon a Gallant, never seen before, who delivers her a Letter from her Father, recommending him to her good Graces as an honourable Lover. Here now, one would think she might naturally shew a little of the sexe's decent Reserve, tho' never so slightly cover'd! No, sir; not a Tittle of it; Modesty is the Virtue of a poor-soul'd Country Gentlewoman; she is too much a Court Lady, to be under so vulgar a Confusion; she reads the Letter, therefore, with a careless, dropping Lip, and an erected Brow, humming it hastily over, as if she were impatient to outgo her Father's Commands, by making a complete Conquest of him at once; and that the Letter might not embarrass her Attack, crack! she crumbles it at once into her Palm, and pours upon him her whole Artillery of Airs, Eyes and Notion; down goes her dainty, diving Body to the Ground, as if she were sinking under the conscious Load of her own Attractions. ...

Where he is exceedingly interesting, and could even now be valuable, is in his discussion of the proper use of voice and gesture.

The book as a whole is bursting with life, not deeply apprehended to be sure, but greatly enjoyed, and we follow as zestfully as we do in a novel of the narrative kind, the bothers over, say, getting Wilks to behave properly in collaboration with Doggett; we almost share the amusement of Cibber's vinous conversations with the foolish Colonel Brett (once one of Addison's favourites) as we do his sense of the difficulties with chamberlains as well as audiences. We get the sense of a thoroughly competent man of the theatre, with ability in handling his colleagues, and not too fussy about himself. Cibber is always gay and astute, really devoted to his profession; and since, without being foppish, he likes himself so well, it betokens a curmudgeonly attitude not to like him too.

On an altogether different level as regards sheer quality of writing are the *Memoirs of the Reign of King George II* (modestly prefixed by the words 'Some Materials Towards') of John, Lord

Hervey.[1] The work is a masterpiece in its kind, worthy to rank with Saint-Simon's. Pretending to be careless how he wrote, he had a clear sense of the position a writer of memoirs should occupy with respect to history; he would, he said, avoid 'the disagreeable egotisms with which almost all memoir writers so tiresomely abound', and would not arrogate to himself an effect on events that he did not have, leaving 'that useless imaginary glory' to 'those ecclesiastical heroes of their own romances, Retz and Burnet'. His manner, though largely discursive, is pulled together by summings up in epigrammatic and often antithetical form; for example: 'For so great was the difference between the King's command of his temper and the Queen's, that, whereas he would often kick whilst he obliged, she would stroke while she hated.' Or, of Lord Strafford: 'In short, there was nothing so low as his dialect except his understanding, nor anything so tiresome as his public harangues except his private conversations.' He might occasionally spit himself abroad in spite or venom, but there is no florid impotence in, for instance, the way he spoke about Bolingbroke, in a passage firmly constructed upon rhetorical lines, with a swinging change of movement, a play of vowel-sound, an antithetical succinctness where he needs it, and a final phrase that reveal a prosewriter of a very high order. He could, moreover, give any devil his due; as in the praise he gave to Bolingbroke's style quoted in a previous chapter.

The *Memoirs* cover the life of the Court, and its connexions with politics, from the accession of George II in 1727 till the death of Queen Caroline ten years later, with a tantalizing gap of two years, during which, it would seem, Hervey over-vividly and too blatantly described his quarrel with Frederick, Prince of Wales, whom he ever after abhorred with a confessedly vindictive desire for revenge. He and the royal pair so fanned each other's flames of hatred and contempt for the heir to the throne, that for most readers too much space would be taken up over this family quarrel—for this rift, though politically noisy was of not more than surface importance—were it not so dramatically presented. Hervey puts you 'there', in the middle of the scene,

[1] John, Baron Hervey of Ickworth, 1696–1743, was educated at Westminster and Clare Hall, Cambridge. He was elected M.P. in 1725, and in 1730 became Vice-Chamberlain to George II and Privy Councillor. In 1733 he was called to the House of Lords by writ, and was Lord Privy Seal until Walpole's fall in 1742.

so felicitously that a novelist tackling the theme would find most of the work of actualization done for him. For instance, when in the autumn of 1724, the Princess, after a visit to England, where she wished to stay, had to return to Holland for her lying-in, the following scene is given us, prefaced by the statement that the Queen was really ill, though nobody would credit her:

. . . Lord Hervey found her and the Princess Caroline together, drinking chocolate, drowned in tears, and choked with sighs. Whilst they were endeavouring to divert their attention by beginning a conversation with Lord Hervey on indifferent subjects, the gallery door opened, upon which the Queen said, 'Is the King here already?' and, Lord Hervey telling her it was the Prince, the Queen, not mistress of herself, and detesting the exchange of the son for the daughter, burst out anew into tears, and cried out, 'Oh! my God, this is too much.' However, she was soon relieved from this irksome company by the arrival of the King, who, finding this unusual and disagreeable guest in the gallery, broke up the breakfast, and took the Queen out to walk. Whenever the Prince was in a room with the King, it put one in mind of stories one has heard of ghosts that appear to part of the company and are invisible to the rest; and in this manner, wherever the Prince stood, though the King passed him ever so often or ever so near, it always seemed as if the King thought the place the Prince filled a void space.

The description at the end of the *Memoirs* of the last days of Queen Caroline, whom he admired and loved, is by its Stendhalian realism immensely moving, the King's very brutality being an index of his devotion, of how greatly he felt his consort to be his other, and certainly his better self; but this is a classic passage, and need not be insisted upon.

Hervey serves us up the Court dish sauced with the astringent detachment of disinterested cynicism, interspersed with some passages of warm humanitarian feeling, as when he discusses the trivial personal causes of devastatingly cruel wars. He can be generous to those whom he likes, yet he is never carried away in either direction. Much as he admired Walpole as a sane and commanding statesman, he could deplore his coarseness and his want of feeling as a person. If he loved and respected the Queen, he was aware of her failings. His keen eye let little slip by him. To the student of politics, not of the period alone, he is invaluable; he sees the little wheels which actuate the great chains of events; and if to the reader uninterested historically the long accounts of what happened over the Excise Bill, the Porteous riots, or especially the question of the allowance the Prince of Wales ought to have, may very well become tedious; if the King's (and his own) speeches are apt to pall, these can easily be skipped, though to the loss of a few brilliant *aperçus*. But a man to whom the King, the Queen, Walpole, and others poured themselves out cannot but have immensely revealing things to say; and as he comments, we become impressed by the solidity of Hervey's own character. When at the ear of Eve, the familiar toad inculcated nothing but the soundest common sense; thus to pass a few evenings with the *Memoirs*, and to read the entertaining little play Hervey wrote on the receipt of the information of his own death, is to live temporarily in the atmosphere at once of an extraordinary domestic life on the stage of international politics.

Whether or not Lady Mary Wortley Montagu's[1] death-bed remark, 'It's been very interesting; yes, it's all been very interesting' is apocryphal, it marks a distinction between this very vital person and her friend Hervey. Both of them 'intellectuals' as we would now say, she brought a zest to her consideration of life which had very little of the malicious in it. In spite of her native common sense, there is a touching vulnerability to be responded to in her early letters, especially those to Wortley just before their clandestine marriage, moving love-letters from a woman who thinks. The other early letters one reads rather for what they tell us about herself than for the light on the times (superior gossip) shed by her later correspondence; even, more than occasionally, for the very conscious forming of herself as a letter-writer as part of her self-education, and, as another side-light, her letter to Burnet enclosing her translation of the *Enchiridion* of Epictetus, done from a Latin version.

The publication in 1763 of the *Letters during Mr Wortley's Embassy to Constantinople*, from August 1716 to October 1718, is attended with some mystery, there being within a few weeks of each other two editions, followed by an additional volume in 1767. The differences are not enormous; what seems fairly certain is that these letters, originally personal, were looked

[1] Lady Mary Wortley Montagu, *née* Pierrepont, 1689–1762, was admirably educated at home. She married Edward Wortley Montagu in 1712, and went with him to Constantinople when he was appointed ambassador to the Porte. She lived most of her life abroad from 1739 to 1761.

over, and to some extent edited, by Lady Mary herself, so that the collection is to be regarded as a travel book rather than untramelled correspondence, though the style is easy enough. The letters are full of interest, even now; for Lady Mary took the trouble to learn Turkish, and penetrated deeply enough into the feminine side of Turkish life to give an intimate and convincing record. She always writes entertainingly, even wittily, not keeping herself out of the picture, but never obtruding into it, as she describes places, people, conversations, and customs. She is alert with curiosity about things ancient as well as contemporary, thus her descriptions are full of variety, colour, and movement, relieved by unprejudiced comment and lay philosophizing, the manner differing, as is proper, according to her correspondent, whether her sister, Pope, the Abbé Conti, or Lady Rich. There is, as well, one letter which ranks as a landmark in European medicine, that written to Miss Sarah Chiswell from Adrianople on 1 April 1718.

A propos of distempers, I am going to tell you a thing, that will make you wish yourself here. The *small-pox*, so fatal, and so general amongst us, is here entirely harmless by the invention of *engrafting*, which is the term they give it. [There follows a description of their method of inoculation]. Every year thousands undergo this operation: and the French Ambassador says pleasantly, that they take the small-pox here by way of diversion, as they take the waters in other countries. There is no example of anyone that has died in it, and you may believe I am well satisfied of the safety of this experiment, since I intend to try it on my dear little son. I am patriot enough to take pains to bring this useful invention into fashion in England; and I should not fail to write to some of our Doctors very particularly about it, if I knew any one of them that I thought had virtue enough to destroy such a considerable branch of their revenue for the good of mankind. But that distemper is too beneficial to them, not to expose to all their resentment the hardy wight that should undertake to put an end to it. Perhaps, if I live to return, I may, however, have courage to war with them. Upon this occasion admire the heroism in the heart of Your friend, &c.

Some of her later letters describe the battles she waged against medical and popular prejudice to get accepted this branch of preventive medicine. It may give rise to some ironic comment in the reader when we learn from a letter some ten years later that Miss Chiswell was herself 'carried off by the small-pox'.

The bulk of her letters until she went to live abroad in 1738 are addressed to her sister, Lady Mar, who joined her husband at Paris in his exile. They retail chiefly the scandal of the day, the petty surface of things, but with a vivacity which seems to increase as Lady Mary tries to induce some degree of cheerfulness into the sister whose melancholia was gradually deepening into the madness which eventually made her incapable. The literary historian may derive some amusement from such passages as

... the most considerable incident that has happened a good while, was the ardent affection that Mrs Hervey and her dear spouse took to me. They visited me twice or thrice a day, and were perpetually cooing in my room. I was complaisant a great while; but (as you know) my talent has never lain much that way, I grew at last so weary of those birds of paradise, I fled to Twicknam ... (July 1721).

He will think that it had been better for Lady Mary's peace of mind if she had always felt thus towards Lord Hervey, and avoided the fatal collaboration in the verses on Pope which goaded the poet to fury. Or it is interesting, in view of Scriblerian history, to read of *Gulliver's Travels*:

... Here is a book come out, that all our people of taste run mad about: 'tis no less than the united work of a dignified clergyman, an eminent physician, and the first poet of the age; and very wonderful it is, God knows!—great eloquence they have employed to prove themselves beasts, and shew such a veneration for horses, that, since the Essex Quaker, nobody has appeared so passionately devoted to that species ... (Nov. 1726).

We get a different interest from the same letter which begins:

I am very sorry, dear sister, for your ill health, but hope it is so entirely past, that you have by this time forgot it ... I leave the great world to girls that know no better, and do not think one bit the worse of myself for having out-lived a certain giddiness, which is sometimes excusable but never pleasing. Depend upon it, 'tis only the spleen that gives you those ideas; you may have many delightful days to come, and there is nothing more silly than to be too wise to be happy:

> If to be sad is to be wise,
> I do most heartily despise
> Whatever Socrates has said,
> Or Tully writ, or Montaigne read.

So much for philosophy.

The last letter, written, apparently, before Lady Mar finally succumbed to her mental disorder, one feels to be an almost desperate attempt to bring a smile to her sister's face by a grotesque description of personalities at the coronation of George II. Her letters are always animated, gay, like talk but '*better than talk*, easy, fluent, neither slipshod nor stilted' as Saintsbury phrased it, as one might expect from a woman who could write verse that, to quote the same appreciative authority, 'flashes with the very best paste in Dodsley'.

Of the Court journals of the time, those of Hervey are, of course, the glorious Lucullan feast; but as hors-d'œuvres, not without a touch of spice, *The Diary of Mary, Countess Cowper* offers an appetizer to the gourmet in these matters. This is more especially true, perhaps, of the second part, covering only three or four months in 1720, dealing almost entirely with the royal family quarrel (for which she blames Walpole and Townshend) which was to act as a pattern throughout the century. Lady Cowper, as Lady of the Bedchamber to the Princess of Wales, is naturally on the side of her mistress, though the King had shown her many kindnesses. To the ordinary reader, the earlier part, from October 1714 to October 1716, will be the more attractive, inducting him into the comings and goings of Court life mingled with home anxieties; he will get a sense of the pressure of personalities on the life of affairs, of the mingling of affection with formality, of politeness with irritation. Lady Cowper's own charming personality comes out incidentally, that of a humane, unambitious woman, caring greatly for her husband, the Lord Chancellor, solicitous for her children, infuriated by the intolerable Mademoiselle Schutz (probably sister or daughter of the punning Schutz of Pope's Court Ballad), who pestered her with her attentions, and insisted on borrowing her jewels for Court functions on the plea that Lady Cowper looked best 'unadorned'. She gives a compact picture of her daily life, and the life of the Court. Take, for example, the entry under 11 February 1716:

My poor *Spencer* [her son] pretty well, for which I heartily thank *God*. This Morning, before I went out, I bought a Parcel of small Rubies and Emeralds of *Mizan*. Two letters from Mademoiselle *Schutz*. 'Tis very troublesome to be writing thus at every turn. I wish she had as much Occupation as I have. I dined at Mrs *Clayton's* with Lord and Lady *Halifax*. . . . Great Complaints of the Preamble to the Land Tax Bill cooked up by Mr *Lechmere* and Lord *Coningsby* . . . my Lord Halifax said, if it was passed . . . it will be a Reproach upon the Parliament never to be blotted out. My Lady *Dorchester's* Wit makes amends for her Ugliness. She has always more to say for herself than Anybody. Sir *Isaac Newton* and Dr *Clarke* came this Afternoon, to explain Sir *Isaac's* System of Philosophy to the *Princess.* I would not stay to hear them, having left my Lord not well.

We get also a view of general life, the amusements, the theatre, footpads, ombre, the trial and execution of those who suffered for participation in the '15, of the Whig internecine squabbles, and so on. There is little literary value in this agreeable enough document, tinged with humour, as when she comments laconically about excusing herself from recommending Mrs. Howard to be a Woman of the Bedchamber; 'I would not have undertaken that Affair for all the World.'

The correspondence of Mrs. Howard herself, namely the *Letters of the Countess of Suffolk and the Hon. George Berkeley, 1712–1767*, does not tell us very much: apart from some letters of Lord Peterborough—in general a trifle silly—and some from her second husband, George Berkeley, most of the letters are to be found in other collections, those of Pope, Swift, Chesterfield, and so on. Gay is there too; and, not in the centre of the literary world, the Herveys gossiping, Miss Vane telling a thumping lie about herself, all of minor interest even to addicts of social studies. Another collection, not without some literary interest, but chiefly of use to the parliamentary historian are the *Egmont Diaries*, the papers of John Perceval, 1st Viscount Perceval, and 1st Earl of Egmont, running from 8 January 1730 to 30 August 1747. As a friend of Bishop Berkeley's he notes under 22 February 1732:

I heard the mortifying news . . . that Dean Berkley [*sic*] has missed the Deanery of Down, by a villainous letter wrote from the Primate of Ireland that the Dean is a madman and disaffected to the Government. Thus the worthiest, the learnedest, the wisest and most virtuous divine of the three kingdoms is by an unparalleled wickedness made to give way to Dean Daniel, one of the meanest in every respect.

Competently written as these papers are, it is doubtful if the literary student will find his reward in looking through the two heavy tomes of the report of the Historical Manuscripts Commission. Nor will he be luckier in perusing *The Private Diary of Lord Chancellor Cowper, 1705–1714*, though it will give him less labour.

Its interest for the general reader lies in the one or two personal touches: 'I search'd my heart, and found no Pride or Self Conceit in it', and other expressions of humility; and it contains the all too often quoted—seeing its one-sidedness—description of Harley, making him out a monster of dissimulation and cunning, with a propensity 'to love Tricks even where not necessary, but from an inward satisfaction he took in applauding his own Cunning. If any Man was born under a Necessity of being a Knave, it was he'. This of the friend of 'The Doctor and Dean, Pope, Parnell and Gay'! Nevertheless, the *Diary* is grist to the historian's mill, as are equally valuable to him the diaries and papers of, for example, Narcissus Luttrell and Lord Marchmont, and of others whose business was government or whose delight was mingling in 'the public'.

A minor work about an amiable but historically shadowy figure is *The Life and Posthumous Works of Arthur Maynwaring Esq.*, written by his friend John Oldmixon, and published in 1715. Anyone concerned with the Marlboroughs or Godolphin will have met his name, but he was more than a mere politician, and was much the friend of poets, besides being *au dernier bien* with Mrs. Oldfield, for whom he would write prologues and epilogues. Like many others he took his early verses to Walsh for correction, was included by Tonson among his translators of Horace, and aspired to an ode or two. According to Oldmixon, 'he was generally allowed to be the best Critick of our time'; but his main literary activity, apart from political tracts, was the concoction of passable satirical trifles, some of which his biographer records, in especial a line which struck him, and which may well stick in the present-day reader's mind as applicable to one or more of his acquaintance: 'His Face a Map of Jolly Ignorance.' The narrative is lively, Whiggish, and entertainingly acrid about the supposed authors of the *Examiner*, Charles Davenant's treatise on trade, and other Tory productions. Something of the intimate life of a second-grade public figure comes through the story, presented in unpretentious but dignified prose, the whole of a tactful brevity which causes the account to end before one is tired of it. Maynwaring himself had undoubted skill in writing, as may be seen from his reply to Swift's proposal to Harley for an academy, *The British Academy* (1712), which companioned Oldmixon's, but is less political. He is not to be neglected by anyone studious of the tracts of those times, or enlivened by hearing the party outcries during the troubled reign of Queen Anne; but he gains movement when his biographer paraphrases him, as, say, over the Sacheverel affair:

... Are we all to be frightened out of our Wits by such a *Scare-Crow* as *Sacheverel*? And must the Laws, the Government, and the Queen give way to this trifling *Incendiary* and his Mob? Tho' they caress him to Day, they will hang him to Morrow: True, this Whiffling *Incendiary* has not yet been *Dewitted* by his own Mob; but then it has been more his good Luck than his Cunning. ...

Perhaps the best thing to be said in his praise is that Steele dedicated to him the first volume of the *Tatler*.

In *The Letters of Sir Thomas Burnet to George Duckett (1712–19)*, we can enjoy the company of a light-weight very young man skirmishing in politics and letters on the Whig side, so intimate with his correspondent that anything can be said.[1] If Maynwaring is historically shadowy, one might say that Burnet was historically noisy for a brief while, but his political pamphlets are of no importance, while as a literary figure he exists only as a member of the Little Senate at Button's eager to yap at the heels of Pope. His letters are gay and lively, as he himself, leading a roistering life, evidently was; he could write a letter of running commentary in rhymed octosyllabic couplets, or anapaestic hendecasyllables; he talks of the works he is writing with Duckett—a good, solid country squire—including the unprovoked *Homerides*, or about his *Grumblers*. He writes good colloquial English, and we can feel the interest of the gossip of the day, from the Hamilton–Mohun duel to the changes in the ministry, the more deeply felt personal note coming in as he records the death of his father whose *History* he was later to edit. He enjoyed being involved in the life of the day, being suspected of being a Mohock, and entering the literary scene.

Addison is so outwardly fond of me, that you would be amazed at it, and we often drink together; the last time we met, I was never in a better cue and we did not part till after four in the morning;

and he could smile when he saw 'Addison caressing Pope, whom at the same Time he hates worse than Beelzebub'. When Garth invited him to dine with Pope he found the latter 'an ill-natured little false Dog, but he does not want a great deal of very

[1] Thomas Burnet, 1694–1753, was educated at Merton College, Oxford (for eight months at the age of 11), Leyden, and the Middle Temple. He became a judge of the Court of Common Pleas.

diverting Satyrical Wit'. He enjoyed being amusing, on Hoadly's side, about the Bangorian controversy. His letters throw a flickering light on the literary scene, but his letters fade in interest after his appointment as Consul at Lisbon. He could no longer plot politics with his friend, nor write to him, 'Prithee send me up some Pamphlet of yours to revise, for I am idle and want something to criticize upon.'

Very different is the scale of existence we are invited to share in the *Reliquiae Hearnianae* of that honourable Jacobite scholar Thomas Hearne,[1] whose whole life was spent at Oxford in the antiquarian researches of which he gives us a glimpse while recording the public gossip of the day. If Hervey hated the patriot 'boys' because he was a good Walpuddlian Whig, Hearne despised both parties equally, regarding the Revolution as 'wicked'. He is not to be relied on as an authority in matters of his time; his contradictory statements as to Pope's parents, for instance, invite little credence for his statement that Parnell died of too great addiction to mild ale. As a diarist he is interesting partly as a recorder of university politics, but chiefly as the painter of his own character. The present-day reader will run over his pages detachedly, growing to like the man, but not feeling involved in his prejudices. He is the stock figure of Tory 'reactionary' feelings, attractive in himself as an ardent campanologist, and a real devotee of archaeology: by his own wish his tomb bears the inscription, 'He studied and preserved antiquities.' As recorder of day-to-day popular, prejudiced Oxford opinion, he often provides amusing comment on the events and life of the time (1705–35), and though not embittered, as he might well have been, he is acerb enough. There is no literary value in his jottings, and he would not have pretended that there was, but, recluse as he might be, there is enough pulse of life in him to help us reconstruct the ethos of his day and place, and of what it might have been like to live in his England.

Oct 3 (1733) I hear of iron bedsteads in London. Dr Massey told me of them on Sat. Sept. 29, 1733. He said they were used on account of the buggs, which have, since the great fire, been very troublesome in London.

---

[1] Thomas Hearne, 1678–1735, educated at St. Edmund Hall, Oxford, became second Keeper of the Bodleian Library in 1712, of which post he was deprived in 1716 as a non-juror. He refused subsequent invitation to offices on political grounds.

We may take for what it is worth his note on 24 July 1719 that '. . . my lord Bullingbrooke is a great villain, and that king James turned him out of his court for being a spy. . .', for there speaks the disappointed Jacobite, who kept King James III's birthday as a holiday, and who despised 'Vanbrugg' if only because he was the architect of Blenheim, and who preferred to speak of King George I as the Duke of Brunswick. He is always interesting to anyone who likes gossip of any time and clime about the details of college life and of various notabilities, of say the Lady Lichfield who used, at the request of his Majesty, Charles II, to scratch the King's head while he slept in the elbow chair. It is refreshing, too, to hear speak the true scholar who despises frippery, while not fearing the charge of pedantry. When some hopeful scholar comes to discuss another edition of Theophrastus, Hearne, having helped in that of Needham, comments: 'Dutchmen are for multiplying editions to no purpose, with burthens of notes to perplex and amuse the reader.' His comment on Burnet is as entertaining as Hervey's:

Mar. 19 (1733–34) Learning is sunk so very low, that I am most certainly inform'd, that nothing is now hardly read but Burnett's romance or libel, call'd by him *The History of his Own Times.* 'Tis read by men, women, and children. Indeed it is the common table-book for ladies as well as gentlemen, especially such as are friends to the revolution scheme.

Completely opposite to Hearne, gregarious, avid of worldly activity, Aaron Hill in his letters keeps us always in the centre of the literary scene. If taking himself rather too seriously must have made him, as has been said, 'a bit of a bore', his very pretentiousness as a man of letters made him acutely to the point. His exchanges with Pope give a glimpse—delighting to those who may harbour a touch of malice in their natures—of the relations of two men who while effusive to each other attacked one another 'sneakingly', to use their own expression, in their publications. The editor of *The Plain Dealer* did not mince matters with Pope Alexander, especially in those letters concerning the initials A. H. in *The Dunciad.* To Pope's genteel equivocation he returned a sturdy reply:

Your Enemies have often told me [he wrote on 28 January 1731], that your *Spleen* was, at least, as distinguishable as your Genius . . . I will, therefore, suppose you to have been *peevish*, or in *Pain*, while you were writing me this Letter.

They came to uneasy terms, both of them adulatory, yet on guard: and we find Hill writing to Pope on 17 June 1738: 'I am charm'd, while I hear you disclaim that Propensity to *Pique* and *Contempt*, which, to speak with the Soul of a Friend, seems, to me, the only *Spot* on your Character.' His letters are unusually varied: largely literary, they also concern coffee, sugar, the tax on Madeira, and other matters of interest to an enthusiastic projector; the Bermudas alternate with Drury Lane. A correspondent of actors, such as Booth and Wilks, he is always good about the theatre, having much to say, for example, about stage delivery, and the difference between the 'weighty' and the 'pathetic'. Writing to Mallet, in all good-fellowship dispraising his *Euridice*—yet composing an epilogue for it—he says of its performance:

To speak, frankly, my sentiments on the matter, you had full justice done you by none of the players, except the two, who acted the parts of *Leonidas* and *Polydor*:—*They* were touch'd, and touch'd their *hearers*; for they spoke feelingly, that is, *naturally*, and without that *stage vice*, their eternal affection of forced tone, with which they cover and efface the passions, they are endeavouring to heighten.

His correspondence with Thomson, whom he takes to task very sensibly for the proliferation of capitals and italics in his poems, is thought-provoking. He writes, frankly, his sentiments to anybody, to Lord Oxford, to Peterborough refusing a post, to Sewell criticizing a poem of his. But he can be urbane, as when he writes to Lady Walpole about rock-gardens, discreet when he writes to Voltaire about *Zaïre*. Afraid of no man, he dares write to Walpole himself: 'Another road to popularity, tho' of less immediate *use*, because it regards the *esteem* of the World, when you will be out of reach of its *malice*, is, the encouragement of able *writers*.' He can, however, be generous, going into raptures over Richardson; his comments are always interesting, and he acts as a link with such figures of the next phase as Chesterfield, Garrick, and Samuel Johnson.

Escaping from the acerbities of scholarship, the glamour of the boards, or the hothouse of the Court, it is refreshing to enter the world of everyday middle-class life as seen and experienced for some eighteen months by an extremely competent young man who was some day to become Chief Justice, and fail to enjoy a peerage only because he died of an apoplexy on the very

night that the King signed his patent. Dudley Ryder,[1] like
Defoe the son of a dissenting draper, but like Pope, grandson of
a parson evicted in 1662, might be described as a thoroughly
normal person, serious but not too serious, moral but not fault-
less or priggish, very 'central' one would say, in the ideas of his
day; a considerable reader who loved discussion, and with a
zest for life, an interest in people, and a sense of responsibility
which are both admirable and attractive. There exists his *Diary*,
written with that frankness to which the discretion of shorthand
was congenial, from 6 June 1715 to 7 December 1716, of which
the interesting part has been given us by his editor; and it is
doubtful if any document could more easily convey the sense
of general life at the time, and the impact of thought on the
intelligent common reader. How he found the *Tatler* a guide to
self-education as a social being has already been noted; we find
him reading and absorbing Berkeley's *Principles*, to the destruction of his faith in the existence of Locke's abstract ideas; he
relishes *A Tale of a Tub*, being 'mightily pleased with the wit
and extravagant humour of it but it is too apt to give one a mean
and ridiculous idea of religion', as it well might to a young man
who would differ from his father on the question of Calvinistic
election. Horace he reads, and learns by heart; he is impressed
by Molière, and enjoys reading Rowe as much as he does seeing a Cibber comedy. Above all he dotes on Boileau's satire on
women, hoping therefrom to find some sort of guard against his
susceptible nature, for try as he will he cannot, in the society of
the women who most attract him, display that gaiety in conversation which alone seems to win their hearts. He is perhaps too
eager to form himself as a social creature, attending dancing
classes so assiduously—whenever he finds the ladies agreeable
enough—learning to talk, behave, discuss, and take remedies
against the badness of his breath. However, his practising of the
viola to accompany his rendering of Italian songs, and his playing of the flute with others, seem to have been indulged in for
sheer pleasure.

Both spartan and pleasure loving, we follow him studying
the law—pleased with the progress of his own analytical powers,
darning his socks and breeches, meeting his club when they

[1] Dudley Ryder, 1691–1756, was educated at the Dissenting Academy, Hackney,
Edinburgh University, and Leyden. He became Solicitor-General 1733, Attorney-
General 1737, and Chief Justice in the King's Bench in 1754.

have discussions, beginning as 'set', but digressing to matters naturally agitating the healthy young man, concerned about his brother and enjoying the dinners offered by relations. And in telling us about himself, Ryder gives us a brilliant picture of ordinary London life at the time, and of how a young man, a normal member of the dissenter trading class looked upon affairs, and was so violent a Whig that to talk to a Jacobite made him tremble with rage. We hear of the rebellion of '15, are taken to the trial and execution of the Lords convicted of treason; we visit the new man-of-war, the *Royal George*, when about to be completed. We know what he thought about all sorts of matters, about the wicked Tories, the virtues of the cold plunge, about Bath and Beau Gnash (as he prefers to spell it), about music and plays, love and marriage, style in preaching sermons and saying prayers—very young we feel, even naïf, and wonderfully the pattern, if not of everyman, of a great many. The diverting picture of his family that he gives is worth a dozen period novels, depicting the rash but affectionate father, the rather peevish mother who managed her house so badly, Brothers Richard and William—the latter woefully extravagant—Aunt Billio and her family, and a dozen others. In writing his diary, in a prose which is almost that of today, to make him know himself better, Ryder allows us at this remove to know him very well, and to like our acquaintance prodigiously.

To be put beside Ryder, but more widely entertaining because less concerned with himself, is John Byrom,[1] a man of enormous energy, ceaselessly inquiring into religious questions, and of a literary talent such as almost to bring him under the head of a writer. His ballad, 'My time O ye muses', has already been referred to, but though he was included by Chalmers in his collection, was edited by Nichols in 1814 and by A. W. Ward in three volumes between 1894 and 1912, little of his verse remains for general reading except for those included in the *Oxford Book of Eighteenth Century Verse*. His most famous poem is 'Christians Awake!', based on St. Bernard, which he wrote as a present for his daughter; but most people know his jape on Handel and Bononcini, where Tweedledum and Tweedledee

---

[1] John Byrom, 1692–1763, was educated at Chester, at the Merchant Taylors School, and at Trinity College, Cambridge, of which he became a Fellow. In 1716 he went to Montpellier to study medicine, but subsequently made his living by teaching shorthand.

first make their appearance, and the clever jingle about the Pretender, which Byrom, more than a little a Jacobite, produced when asked to toast the King. Except for two essays on dreams, extremely advanced for their time, which he contributed to the *Spectator*, the public knew nothing of the type of mind he represented until the publication of his journals and letters by the Cheetham Society in 1854-7. He reveals, perhaps more fully than anybody, the strong thread of religious feeling, as often as not unorthodox—his own predilection was for the mystics —which ran through the early eighteenth century. In fact his strongest private interest, apart from his deep family affection, was religious thought, which he never lost an opportunity of discussing whether in convivial coffee-house conversation, or in prolonged discussion with William Law in the grounds of the Gibbon home at Lime Grove. Wherever he went—and he travelled a good deal to diffuse his system of shorthand, the 'tychygraphy' of which he became Grand Master—he never lost an opportunity of engaging divines in talk, and we find him discoursing with the Wesleys, with Samuel Clark, and even with Joseph Butler, whom he met at his pupil's, the Duke of Queensberry, in company with David Hartley, though there he talked 'with too much impetuosity'.

What some would today call Byrom's 'contacts' were surprisingly various, from his noble pupils, such as the Duke of Devonshire or Lord Stanhope, and others ('Memorandum: the first money I received for teaching—three guineas of Lord Lonsdale'), bishops such as Hoadly, or Warburton, who wrote to Hurd that he was 'certainly a man of genius, plunged deep into the rankest fanaticism. . . . He is very libellous upon me; but I forgive him heartily, for he is not malevolent, but mad.' He frequented scientists, such as Desaguliers, was friends with Dr. Cheyne, went to boxing matches, and witnessed the great fencing contest between Figg and Sutton, on which he wrote his well-known verses; had many good dinners, which he describes with ill-concealed gusto, and occasionally set his six foot four of vigorous manhood to good physical tasks such as digging potatoes. Since he went about a good deal in pursuit of his profession we have many letters to his wife, usually beginning 'My dearest love; how do you do?', as also some to his children. But during his stays at his home in Manchester he took a full part in local politics, such as vigorously opposing the Manchester

Workhouse Bill as Whig chicanery, as well as serving the cause of literature, and, with that strong group of Jacobite Mancunians, had to tread warily during the '45. There is something of a mystery about his relations, if any, with the Pretender; certainly as a non-juror, unable to take Holy Orders, he had to relinquish his Fellowship at Trinity (he was always a stout supporter of Bentley), and went to Montpellier to study medicine for a year. But he relinquished both politics and medicine for more philosophic interests. A typical entry in his Journal, which like his letters is written in simple unaffected English, runs:

> Tuesday 4th (March 1729). . . . We went to the Bull Inn, Putney, and sent to Mr Law that we should wait on him in the afternoon, it was then near two o'clock; while we were eating mutton chop Mr Law came to us, and we went with him to Mr Gibbon's, where we walked into the gardens and upstairs into some rooms, the library, and then we sat in a parlour below with Mr Law and young G., who left us after a while over a bottle of French wine. We talked about F. Malebranche much . . .

and then about *The Serious Call*, Byrom in due course reading Law his poem 'The Pond', a paraphrase of a passage in Law's already famous book. Byrom is something of a man of great talent *manqué*, at once a perfectly normal man and the typical English eccentric, pretending to vegetarianism, given to dietary experiments. One of the most entertaining episodes in his career was when this contemner of the theatre wrote a prologue to a play, to wit, the *Hurlothrumbo, or the Super-natural*. Not only was this a squib on an activity to which he was antipathetic, but it was also by his fellow Mancunian Samuel Johnson ('the other'), whose success among the great he followed with high glee. Byrom and Ryder are equally likeable; but the latter, if more solid, would not have been half such good fun to meet, nor have been so intellectually stimulating.

To anyone interested in the social background of the countryside at this period, *The Purefoy Letters, 1735–1753*, offer an immensely varied field. Though Henry Purefoy, who wrote the bulk of the letters, was a man of some reading, the correspondence has only small literary value. The matters dealt with are the daily doings of a country family in the western home counties, the getting of food and wine, the cutting of hedges and trees, communal grazing, purlieu hunting, furniture, the grinding of razors, the inexcusable behaviour of the hunting parson

—as little typical of his age as Parson Adams—the shocking villainy of a cousin, theatre-going, and so on. Imagination aiding, they present a vivid picture of life as it was peacefully and unpolitically lived outside London; the relation of the classes, of town and country; and the everyday doings of ordinary well-do-to people. And there is a certain flavour about these letters almost wholly absent from *Blundell's Diary and Letter Book, 1702–1728*. There we have the skimpiest details of a visit to London, where a cloak was bought at eighteen shillings a yard, seeing *The Merchant of Venice* eliciting less comment: little more than the itinerary is given of a tour in Belgium. The record comes a little more alive when we read of how 'I sowed in the First Bed in the Nursery in the Visto Wood Alder Berrys, in the Second Bed I sowed Black Cherrys which had been steeped in Brandy . . .', and of the planting of flowers, or the trimming of Apricock Trees. Or of how they had 'two Fidlers at night and dansed Country Dances in the Halle'. We are given one curious glimpse of summary discipline: 'Seaven Boyes of this Towne were beaten at my Lodg Gate with stirrup Lethers, som by their Fathers, som by their Masters and others, for stealing Apples and other peevish Tricks.' In those days there were no magistrates' courts for juvenile delinquents.

Of altogether different scope, emanating as they do from persons moving in the larger world, are *The Verney Letters of the 18th Century* (1696–1799). Although such as fall within our period have little intellectual range, being concerned largely with horse-racing and such activities, they contain such lively exchanges of information, such naïf revelations of character, as to have an almost novelistic value. Take, for example, Lord Fermanagh, writing to Ralph Verney on 20 March 1707:

Deare Ralph,—I got on Tewesday night home, tho' hindered some time by the fall of my Trunck from behind. J. Scott and Perry alighting to help him, let his horse goe, soe that we were an hour in the darke in North Marston field before we could goe on, and then Scott was forst to carry the Trunck before him, which made us goe very softly to prevent other accidents. Since my return I have been very ill. . . . The Caves were here when I came but went away the next morning to dinner at Lady Cave's and so home to Stanford. Sir Tho. rec'd a letter that his gardener coming over the Bridge fell into the River and was Drown'd, being in Drincke, and that two of his horses have had Chances, I think one of 'Em was a Coalt for the Coach, the other a Mare, I bidd him fifteen pounds for his horse, he stood for sixteen, I told him no more would I give soe he said he would send him. He was in the coach with the Children when I bade him the money so that I did but just see the horse under the Postilion. My service to the young Lady and her sister. . . .

Thackeray would have rejoiced enormously in these letters had they been available when he was collecting material for *The Virginians*, and would have revelled in John Verney writing to his father from Tunbridge Wells on 31 September 1736, so vividly that we almost expect to meet young Warrington round the next corner.

2. TOURS AND TRAVELS

If Tours are not strictly speaking diaries or journals, they can plausibly be included among such, since they are for the most part clearly enough derived from jottings taken down from day to day. Certainly Celia Fiennes[1] when she wrote her accounts for her 'near relations' must have had recourse to notes, and she can open this section, for though most of her *Journeys* took place in the seventeenth century, 'The Great Journey' in 1698, her 'London and Later Journeys' are dated 1701–3. Her alert and curious mind and eye missed very little of the outward show of life; she ranges from palaces to gardens, from prisons to housewifery and clothes. Though she speaks too like a book on the constitution of the government of London, her account of 'the Lord Major's' show is as lively and specific as is that of a royal funeral:

Then after the service of burial which is done with solemn and mournful musick and singing, the sound of a drum unbraced, the breakeing of all the white staves of those that were the officers of the Queen, and flinging in the keys of the rest of the officers devoted by that badge into the tomb. . . .

or of a coronation. She visits the Tower, and notes:

Here is noe wracks or tortures nor noe slaves made, only such as are banish'd, sometymes its into our forreign plantations there to worke; we have also prisons for debtors, and some of which are privilidge places. . .

[1] Celia Fiennes (1662–1741) was the daughter of Nathaniel Fiennes, second son of William, 8th Baron and 1st Viscount Saye and Sele. As a nonconformist, she had access to societies other than the aristocratic.

She is determined to be informative, in an easy, homely way, free of any trace of assertive didacticism; and no doubt when describing members of Parliament she is voicing a certain unease which must have been widespread as membership of the House began to become a profession. Things are in a pretty way, since now by 'bribeing, by debauching by drinke and giving them money. . . would-be parliament men spend prodigious summs of money to be chosen'. But she wastes little time on moralizings or reflections, her delight being in how people lived, and she gives some attractive descriptions of houses in the country, their interior arrangements, their decorations, touching upon them as perhaps only a woman could. She is no less illuminating about gardens, such as Mr. Root's house and garden at Epsom, or Sir Thomas Cooke's, or about the grounds of the parson at Banstead, who 'is old now and doates', but who 'diverted himself in his garden' to very odd effect. Always it is how people live that interests her:

Bedford town is an old building its wash'd by the river Ouse . . . its stored with very good fish, and those which have gardens on its brinke keepes a sort of trunck or what they call them (its a receptacle of wood of a pretty size full of holes to let the water in and out) here they keep fish they catch as pike tench etc:, so they have it readye for their use. . . ;

but if it is the ordinary way of living that interests her most, she is not negligent in describing Hampton Court and Windsor.

Of quite different sensibility is a very minor author, mentioned earlier, whose writings are not unamusing, but which belong rather to the social historian than the taster of literature, John Macky, a secret service agent, who was unfortunate enough— according to his not quite orthodox version—to discover and give away the secret of Prior's visit to France when the Treaty of Utrecht was brewing. His *A Journey through England in Familiar Letters from a Gentleman Here to His Friend Abroad* (1714) in some ways complements Defoe's *Tour*, since he gives good racy description of outward manners. Pretending to be a foreigner, he dedicates his work to the English 'Nobility and Gentry', asking why they should so eagerly devour accounts of foreign countries, and ignore their own, to which he ascribes all the political and domestic glories—freedom of opinion, gentleness of manners, especially to foreigners, and so on—except that of neatness in beheading people. Though he gives adequate accounts of the institutions of the country he is supposedly visiting, such as the hospitals, Bedlam, Bridewell, Gresham College, the Royal Society, and describing also the clubs, such as the 'Kitt-Catt' and 'October', it is in the livelier details that he is most interesting, describing them in good current colloquial English. On the clubs themselves he throws a little light, telling us that 'the most diverting, or amusing of all, is the *Mug-House Club* in *Long Acre*', evidently the forerunner of the Victorian singing club such as that to which Colonel Newcome innocently took Clive, where every man had his own mug, where songs were sung and healths drunk, so that 'there is no room for *Politicks*, or any Thing that can slow Conversation'. He has no great opinion of the life led at the fashionable resorts:

The Manner of living at *Tunbridge* is very Diverting for one Week; but as there is no other Variety but in new Faces, it soon proves Tiresome to a Stranger. . . .

There is as little Ceremony here, as is at *Montpelier*; You engage with the Ladies at Play without any Introduction, only they do not admit of Visits at their Lodgings; but every Gentleman is equally received by the Fair Sex upon the Walks.

This Indistinction is attended with one Inconvenience, That Sharpers, whose Trade is to go Genteel, and with a fine Address, mix themselves in all the Diversions here; and with their false Dice very often send People from the Wells sooner than they would otherwise go.

So he jogs along, happily and informatively enough. In the second volume he dilates largely upon the Peak, copiously quoting from Cotton's verses. There he is pleasantly descriptive, but he clearly does not know the far districts so well as the home counties; and when, in the third volume, he describes Scotland, you feel he is the mere traveller, though he can be interesting, as about 'the Marshallian Academy' at Aberdeen. His other travel book, *A Journey through the Austrian Netherlands* (1725), is no more than characterless guide-book stuff.

The show-piece of this kind is, of course, Defoe's *A Tour thro' the Whole Island of Great Britain*, issued in parts (1724, 1725, and 1727), solid, varied, detailed, written as a guide-book, yet giving an illuminating personally observed account of the social and industrial life of the country at that time, the background landscape being well presented pictorially. He slips so easily from one subject to another, describing, say, a great house such as

Canons or Wilton; duck-decoying, the clothing-trade, horse-racing, Beverley Minster; a snow-thunderstorm on the Pennines, occult occurrences, local customs or antiquities, that the reader is never bored. Though perhaps primarily valuable to the social historian, it is still a book to be read almost as one reads a story, apart from its being diversified with anecdote. Defoe is always serious, whether discoursing upon population, or a kind of guillotine at Halifax (which surely was efficient enough to have satisfied even John Macky), port facilities, the beauty of horses—where he grows ecstatic—and institutions; but he is never ponderous, and his prose travels along at its firm, brisk walking-pace, which, if it hardly varies in tone, always seems appropriate. He is not the pontificating showman so much as the conversationalist: 'When I was at . . .' is a common opening. Too much stress has been laid on his main interest being trade, as though in his early journeyings as a merchant, or his later travellings as intelligence agent for Harley and Godolphin, he thought of nothing else, and therefore could talk well on no other subject. True, his guide-book had to be diversely attractive, and no doubt he mugged up his Camden and his Dugdale, referring to them both, quoting especially the latter's *Monasticon*, but he himself certainly possessed a nourished historic sense. Nor is he devoid of interest in the goings-on of nature; he discusses, for example, the migration of swallows, being here ahead of his time, for even so late as Cowper it was thought that swallows during the winter lay embedded in 'torpid state' in the mud of river banks. He can be almost rapturous about scenery.

Nevertheless it is certainly the goings-on of men, how things are done, that stir him most, especially, this must be admitted, where trade is concerned. His brilliant description of the cloth-market on the Brigg-shot (Briggate) at Leeds is a classic passage, which must have been well known to Dyer when he wrote:

> Lo, in throngs,
> For ev'ry realm, the careful factor meet,
> Whisp'ring each other. In long ranks the bales,
> Like war's bright files, beyond the sight extend.
> Straight, ere the sounding bell the signal strikes,
> Which ends the hour of traffick, they conclude
> The speedy compact; and well-pleased, transfer,
> With mutual benefit, superior wealth
> To many a kingdom's rent, or tyrant's hoard.

Defoe is less sententious:

At seven a Clock in the Morning . . . the Market Bell rings; it would surprize a Stranger to see in how few Minutes, without hurry or noise, and not the least disorder, the whole Market is fill'd; all the Boards upon the Tressels are covered with Cloth, close to one another as the Pieces can lie long ways by one another, and behind every Piece of Cloth, the Clothier standing to sell it.

This indeed is not so difficult, when we consider that the whole Quantity is brought into the Market as soon as one Piece, because the Clothiers stand ready in the Inns and Shops just behind, and that there is a Clothier to every Piece, they have no more to do, but like a Regiment drawn up in line, every one takes up his Piece, and has about five Steps to march to lay it upon the first Row of Boards, and perhaps ten to the second Row; so that upon the Market Bell ringing, in half a quarter of an hour the whole Market is fill'd, the Rows of Boards cover'd, and the Clothiers stand ready.

Then he takes us on to watch the merchants and buyers walking up and down matching colours, some with foreign orders in their hands; and how, 'when they see any Cloths to their Colours, or that suit their occasions, they reach over to the Clothier and whisper. . . .' In about half an hour all is over; the bell rings again, and everything is cleared off; deals may be completed in the inns, the gratifying result being that 'the Clothiers are constantly supplied with Money, their Workmen are duly paid, and a prodigious Sum circulates thro' the County every Week'.

But Defoe is just as alert to see how ducks are decoyed, though here we feel that he is a trifle gullible about the birds that fly to foreign parts to inveigle victims to visit them; yet when we come to the actual process of luring the duck into the nets he is amazingly actual. As he is when he tells us how dexterous the northern grooms and breeders are in looking after horses: 'Those Fellows take such indefatigable Pains with them, that they bring them out like Pictures of Horses, not a Hair amiss in them; they lye constantly in their Stables with them, and feed them by Weight and Measure.' He has a word also about the oak Charles II hid in after the Battle of Worcester, how it is surrounded by a palisadoe, since visitors used to carry away pieces of it, 'so that the Tree was litterally in Danger not to dye of Age, but to be pull'd Limb from Limb'. He can discuss the strange fires that occur in Merionethshire in years of the total eclipse of the sun as happily as the navigability of rivers. Ever and again, as might be expected, the middle-class moralist peeps out. After telling us of the great concourse of nobility and gentry at Newmarket races, he goes on:

. . . But they were all so intent, so eager, so busy upon the sharping Part of the Sport, their Wagers and Bets, that to me they seem'd just as so many Horse-coursers in *Smithfield*, descending (the greatest of them) from their high Dignity and Quality, so picking one another's Pockets, and Biting one another as much as possible, and that with such eagerness, as that it might be said they acted without respect to Faith, Honour, or good Manners.

Nor is the Dissenter entirely absent. After telling how an Archbishop of York renounced all superiority and honours to live a recluse at Beverley, he comments: 'This Story will prompt you to enquire how long ago 'twas, for you know as well as I, and will naturally observe, that very few such Bishops are to be found now; it was indeed a long time ago. . .', and with some relish he informs the reader that the good man died A.D. 721, leaving the reader to tot up the sum of years to 1726.

It may be that today the book is indispensable to the economic historian alone; yet even if it is not to be read through, it can be generously dipped into for its sense of abundant life. It was certainly much used as a guide-book during the century, an eighth edition appearing in 1778; but each successive issue was 'overlaid with insertions', to use the phrase of its editor of 1927, Mr. G. D. H. Cole. Even now the Scottish portion (the second half of the third volume) remains unedited, which though comparatively skimpy, less lively, less intimate, is never dull. There is about it, indeed, a little of the foreign tourist observing, perhaps criticizing, as when he deplores the lack of enclosures, leading to the impoverishment of the soil. Yet in the main he is friendly, he praises: the man who helped to forge the Union is not going to antagonize an important limb of Great Britain.

A very lively minnow among the more serious sprats is the extremely entertaining little work known for short as *Hogarth's Peregrination*, but which is entituled 'An Account of what seemed most remarkable in the Five Days Peregrination of the Five following Persons, Viz. Messieurs Tothall, Scott, Hogarth,

Thornhill and Forrest. Begun on Saturday, May 27th, and finished on the 31st of the same Month'. It bears the motto inscribed on the porch of Dulwich College, *Abi tu et fac similiter*, and the reader wishes that he could, so gay is the tale of what Thackeray called 'a party of tradesmen engaged in high jinks'. The frontispiece portrays the headless figure of Mr. Somebody, the tail-piece giving us Mr. Nobody, all head. The latest editor (1952), Mr. Charles Mitchell, interprets the former as the medieval hero-scapegoat, the latter as 'a sectarian and a villain', more especially the antiquary and seller of bric-à-brac who injures the living artist. Nichols calls the book 'a burlesque on the then mode of travel writing', but the title-page carries the words 'the whole being intended as a burlesque on historical writers, recording a series of insignificant events intirely uninteresting to the reader'. The journal, meant only for private handing round, was not published until 1782, the antiquary William Gostling having in the meantime paralleled it with a version in muscular Hudibrastic verse. The elected scribe, Ebenezer Forrest, a lawyer who had perpetrated a ballad-opera, writes with a natural flowing gaiety, his script being illustrated by Hogarth and the painter James Scott; John Tothall, who dealt in haberdashery, rum, and brandy, was appointed treasurer and caterer during the trip—the whole cost six guineas—while John Thornhill, also a painter, son of the great Sir James, with whose daughter Jane, Hogarth had eloped a few years earlier, acted as cartographer. The party set off on the river singing 'Why should we quarrel for riches', and gambolled through Rochester, Chatham, Gravesend, Sheerness, Queenborough and the Isle of Sheppey, eating well, drinking better, indulging in the most schoolboyish of pranks: 'Hogarth and Scott stopped and played at hop-scotch in the colonnade under the Town-hall'; they all had 'a battle-royal with sticks, pebbles and hog's dung', or enjoyed a water contest. Among high fooleries they bathed, made sketches of antiquities, slept how and where they might, often very uncomfortably; we read on one occasion of 'our lips, eyes and hands, being tormented and swelled by the biting of gnats'; we are given a drawing of them being shaved while they breakfast, and can find them discoursing with a party of sailors who had been left in the lurch by their midshipman. The whole brief thing, alive with young life, makes the most refreshing reading since it does not matter a pin to anybody.

Travels follow naturally after tours, and indeed after memoirs, since they are often recorded as journals, as was Woodes Rogers's *A Cruising Voyage Round the World*, his account, kept from 1 August 1708 until 14 October 1711, being published in the next year. It is memorable, notoriously, as containing the story of the rescue of Alexander Selkirk, a passage, from which Defoe got a great deal, too often quoted to need repetition here; but it is otherwise noteworthy. Written in 'the Language of the Sea, which is more genuine and natural for a Mariner' than 'the Stile and Method which is us'd by Authors that write ashore', it tells the adventure of a privateering expedition which had as its main object the capture of Spanish treasure, thus aiding the national effort in the War of Spanish Succession. It is not so much the descriptions—the usual curious mixture of observation and hearsay that we get, though less attractively, in Dampier a little earlier and Anson or Cook a little later—not even the stirring accounts of naval engagements and land raids that make the chief impression, but the artless revelation of human relationships. There were two ships in the expedition, the other commanded by Stephen Courtney; but Rogers, in the *Duke*, had with him no less a person than William Dampier himself, who shipped as pilot in the South Seas, and, as second captain, Thomas Dover (of Dover's Powder fame). The last later made other voyages, and was to publish in 1731 *The Ancient Physician's Legacy to his Country*, which, though containing a little adventure, is concerned with urging the use of mercury as a universal specific; he was not unamusingly answered in 1733 by Daniel Turner in *The Ancient Physician's Legacy Impartially Survey'd*. That in the future; at this time he was a tiresome colleague given to outbursts of rage, who, though totally incompetent, insisted on commanding the Manilla prize captured during the cruise. Luckily the whole expedition was governed by a Council, which, though Dover acted as titular President, was clearly dominated by Rogers, who put two other officers on board, and these actually commanded the ship, allowing Dover merely nominal supremacy. The cruise was, it goes without saying, a commercial adventure rather than a patriotic foray, for crew as much as for employers and officers, and the whole story gives an odd insight

---

[1] Woodes Rogers, d. 1732, commanded two Bristol privateersmen, and engaged in various naval exploits and forays. In 1728 he was appointed Captain-General and Governor-in-Chief of the Bahamas.

into how such a voluntary organization was made to work. Rogers had virtually the authority of a naval officer, being commissioned by Prince George of Denmark: he could have men flogged for theft, or put in irons for dereliction of duty. There were mutinies, even a fourth mate being guilty of insubordination; but usually, after a short time in irons, the men asked pardon, promised amendment, and all went on as before.

These affairs were rather like family tiffs, so that sometimes 'healing arguments' were enough to make all 'easy and quiet'. Agreements were entered into as to the shares of plunder, and one very enlightening one 'to prevent Gaming':

> We the Ship's Company belonging to the Ship *Duke* now in the *South Seas*, being Adventurers so far to improve our Fortunes in a private Man of War . . . and considering the apparent Hazard of our Lives in these remote Parts; do mutually agree to prevent the growing Evil now arising amongst us, occasion'd by frequent Gaming, Wagering, and abetting at others Gaming, so that some by chance might thus too slightly get Possession of what his Fellow-Adventurers have dangerously and painfully earn'd. To prevent this intolerable Abuse, we shall forbear and utterly detest all Practises of this kind for the future during the whole Voyage, till our safe Arrival in *Great Britain*, where good Laws of this kind take place. . . .

All the officers and men in each ship signed this document.

What we get, in short, interwoven with the ordinary travellers' reports of strange countries, old and new, of their inhabitants and their history, very vividly related, is a fascinating account of how such a community lived—the ardours and endurances, the fighting on land as well as at sea, the difficulties of victualling, or repairing ships, and so on, the whole being infused with a great sense of vigour, of courage, of a certain brutality tempered by kindness and fellow-feeling, recorded in language that is picturesque almost by its very matter-of-factness, simple and direct without being bare. There is about the book a sense of adventure, which Rogers himself does not seem to have felt; and we shall be tempted to skip only the technical navigational details, so little do any of the others come amiss. The account was popular in its own day, three editions being called for in fourteen years, and is superior to *A Voyage to the South Seas and Round the World* (also 1712) by Captain Edward Cooke, who served on this expedition as second captain on Courtney's ship, the *Dutchess*.

However brief, an account of travels in this period should include the name of William Dampier. Most of his work was published in the previous century, and he belongs to the previous volume; but his last work, *A Voyage to New Holland*, appeared in two parts in 1703 and 1709. Nor should mention be omitted of that scoundrelly privateer George Shelvocke, who issued his *Voyage Round the World* in 1726, a work which, if lacking in literary merit, at least, with its account of the shot albatross, gave Coleridge the basis for his 'Ancient Mariner'.

3. HISTORIANS AND ANTIQUARIES

It is natural that after upheavals such as the Civil War and crises such as the Revolution, men should wish to see where they stand, and that 'the wisdom of looking backwards', to adopt the title of one of White Kennett's books, should be manifest. Nor is it surprising that much of the work should have been undertaken by shining lights of the Church, the existence of which had been perilously at stake, outstanding names in learning being those of William Wake, Archbishop of Canterbury; Edmund Gibson, Bishop of London; White Kennett, Bishop of Peterborough; and Laurence Echard, Archdeacon of Stow. A number of these were scholars rather than historians; and, as might be expected given their vocation, their work was concerned largely with the relation of Church and State, the independence of Convocation, the status of Dissenters, and like matters; some labours were more general, such as Rymer's *Foedera* (1704), while an enormous amount of knowledge was harvested by the Saxonists, such as William and Elizabeth Elstob, and Humphrey Wanley, Lord Oxford's librarian. It may indeed be claimed that the years 1660–1730 constitute the grand age of scholarly and antiquarian research, as has been so admirably exhibited by Professor David Douglas in his *English Scholars*; and how fully the importance of the movement in learning begun by Camden, and continued by Dugdale and Henry Wharton, was recognized in our period is attested by the foundation in 1724 of the Regius Professorships of History at Oxford and Cambridge.

The work of the scholars cannot be discussed here, since only an expert in that field could do so without impertinence; moreover, it was conned by specialists alone, or by those—often 'occasional writers'—who were engaged in producing (which is our concern) histories to be read by the general public. The point to be made, however, is that, thanks to the example of the scholars, from now on popular history was squarely, if not always fairly, based upon documents, presumed to be written with a sense of responsibility, and presented as an attempt to arrive at the truth. But to what end? The incitement to much of the historical study was the delight of gathering fuel for factional wrangling, an imputation neither the republican Oldmixon nor the Jacobite John Banks could avoid, though Abel Boyer declared that he was never a party man. The party lines, however, are harmless enough, if only because they are clear. The occasional writers tend to be Whiggish, in varying degrees; the Churchmen, while clinging to tradition to an extent that might be called Tory, are nevertheless at one with the Whigs so far as the reign of James II is concerned, and together they are content with the Act of Settlement. Yet however much a writer might be prejudiced in his view of history (and what man that is a man can avoid interpreting the past according to his temperament and desires?), he had to make his case. Oldmixon speaks of 'The Obligation that modern Historians lie under to date all their Events'—which might be thought elementary; Strype[1] declares his *Annals of the Reformation in England* (1709; pub. 1708) to be 'Compiled faithfully out of Papers of State, Authentick Records, Publick Registers, Private Letters, and other Original Manuscripts'. Thus though much of the history written was pleading for Whig or Tory conclusions, as was inevitable given the tensions of those days, it could not afford to look too much like special pleading.

For the modern reader, indeed, who prefers his history predigested, there may seem to be a good deal too much buttressing with documents, as when Lediard[2] in his *Naval History of England* (1735) devotes several pages to details of the various quadrons engaged on both sides in a battle, grimly arranged in

[1] John Strype, 1643–1737, went from St. Paul's to Jesus College, Cambridge; but disliking the 'superstitious' religion practised there, transferred to St. Catherine's Hall. He was for a short time curate at Theydon Bois, but soon became minister of Leyton, also in Essex, and finally sinecure Rector of West Tarring, Sussex.

[2] Thomas Lediard, 1685–1743, completed his private education by serving on the staff of the Duke of Marlborough in Flanders. He was later attached to the embassy at Hamburg, and was said to have been Professor of Modern Languages in Lower Germany.

tabular form under the headings, 'Burden Tuns', 'Guns', 'Numbers of Mariners', 'of Soldiers'. In his Preface he states:

I have taken all possible Care to be exact in my Chronology, and, to that End, have reduced this Work in a great measure into Annals, and kept up a regular *Historical* and *Chronological* Connection, by an Abridgment of the most remarkable Occurrences, not only of every Reign, but of every Year.

This was to take things too far, for the result is totally sapless; he provides, rather than a history, the materials for such, his footnotes alone adding a little colour or warmth to a narrative unillumined by the faintest ray of imagination. But though the problem of dovetailing documents into a narrative giving the pulse of life was seldom resolved, even the bleakest histories serve to a greater or less extent as sources for present-day historians of the period, for the strong impulse in most of the writers was to bring their histories, not only within living memory, but up to the very year of writing. This is not so true of the ecclesiastical writers, such as Jeremy Collier with his *The Ecclesiastical History of Great Britain* (1708), of which the second part appeared in 1714, as did the third part of Burnet's *History of the Reformation*; or Daniel Neal,[1] whose *History of the Puritans* (1732) dealt with the subject from 1517 to 1584, the fourth and last volume (1738) ending with 1689. Strype's *Reformation* covers only 'the First Twelve Years of Queen Elizabeth's Happy Reign'. White Kennett, who compiled the third volume of *The Complete History of England* (1706), the 'only attempt', according to A. W. Ward, who strangely neglected Echard, 'to present a collective view of the national history' down to the earlier part of the eighteenth century, extended the story to include the reign of William and Mary. As early as 1702, Abel Boyer had produced his *History of William III*, which he continued in 1722 with his *History of Queen Anne*; in 1737 Lediard brought up to date Tindal's translation of Rapin de Thoyras's *Histoire D'Angleterre* by adding accounts of the reigns of Queen Mary and Queen Anne, while Oldmixon, in the second, 1735 volume of his *History of England*, came frankly into the contemporary scene, only in his last, 1739 volume, going back to the Tudors. Nor were there lacking writers about special occurrences of the time; one has to remember only

---

[1] Daniel Neal, 1678–1743, was educated at the Merchant Taylors School, and at the Universities of Utrecht and Leyden. He became minister of two Independent congregations in London.

Defoe's *History of the Union of Great Britain* (1709), and Swift's masterly *The History of the Last Four Years of the Queen*, which though not published till long after his death, was written in the relevant decade, and still, thanks to its inside information, has enormous value as a source book. In a somewhat different category is Boyer's *Political State of Great Britain*, which ran as a serial from 1711 to 1729, and is no more than a weekly register, a bagful of information dealing with anything from the pay of the forces, debates in Parliament, the Bangorian controversy, brandy for sailors, or statements such as that the petitions of the 'Tanners, Leather Dressers, Cutters of Leather in the Counties of *Devon, Cornwall, Pembroke, Brecon, Salop, Berks* &c, were presented to the Commons and read, complaining of the great Exportation of Oaken Bark into *Ireland* (where no Duty is paid to his Majesty for Leather)'. Much of his actual history writing is after that manner, something in the way of chronicles, just as Lediard's *Life of Marlborough* (1736) reads like a series of official dispatches.

The curious will note that it is the writers who have some special interest, as had Lediard, who are the dullest historians. Strype, whose mind was stirred only by ecclesiastical matters and in writing the lives of Archbishops down to Whitgift, and whose main object was to justify an Erastian church, is what Bagehot would have described as 'a very learned and illegible author'. Cramming his work with documents (which makes it still valuable), his attempts to give life are laboured and dismal; he seems to have thought that enumerating those who attended some function, and briefly describing their costume, would give a sense of actual being. White Kennett,[1] again, is imaginatively caught up in history (and then with no strong feeling for the past), mainly as it is ecclesiastical, politically so, it might be said; it is easy to understand Oldmixon's tart comment: 'Having no Conception that Convocation History is what Bishop *Kennett* entitles it, *The History of Religion*, I enter very little into it.' This is not to deny that their writings have a certain importance; they contributed liveliness to the controversies of the day; but though contemporaries might have to read them, to do so is a task no

---

[1] White Kennett, 1660–1728, had his elementary schooling at Elham and at Wye, proceeded to Westminster, and thence to St. Edmund Hall, Oxford. Ordained, he became curate at Bicester, and in 1691 was made Vice-Principal of St. Edmund Hall. He occupied various lecturing posts—and various livings. He became in succession Prebend in the church of Salisbury, Archdeacon of Huntingdon, Dean, and finally Bishop of Peterborough. He was one of the original members of the S.P.G.

general reader of today need burden himself with. In truth, the historians that we at this date find readable are those who had interests outside some particular investigation, and indeed other literary interests; for after all, though 'history' may resolve itself into a comparison of documents, the writing of history is an art. On this assumption Abel Boyer should have been among the readable historians, a position it would be difficult to claim for him; but if he fails in this respect, he did, in his Preface to *A History of Queen Anne*, contrive an attractive essay on the problems involved.

His own writing lacks vividness, perhaps because he took too much to heart Saint-Evremond's dictum 'That he who sets about to write the History of *England* must write the History of Parliaments'; but he is shrewdly to the point when he gleans from Raleigh that the historian must follow truth neither too near nor too far, and from Grotius 'That it is a hard Matter to write History; because if the Author be an Eye-witness, he is apt to be drawn to a Party; if not, he cannot attain a true knowledge of Affairs'. He must know, in short, how things are done in the world, and an object lesson is happily provided for us by Strype. In his *Annals of the Reformation* he describes how Cecil came to be chosen Speaker, against which some irate reader of the British Museum copy scrawled on 7 February 1708-9; 'Idle, impertinent, and impossible—only depends upon the poor man's mistaken [notion?] of wht he does not understand.' Certainly the better authors were alive to the problem of 'The Way to write History'; they had read their Lucian (Echard had even translated him), and though they did not always take heed of his precepts, some, while clearly distinguishing between poetry and history, tried to introduce the proper modicum of the former. This came out as well as anywhere in the nice concern exhibited in the place the 'character'—perhaps a relic of character-writing, the glory of seventeenth-century history— should occupy in virtuously documentary records. Possibly Clarendon, with his beautifully sinuous drawings, had stimulated the taste; but Oldmixon inveighed against the 'Affectation of continually drawing Characters'; he had no exaggerated love of psychological scalpels, and remarks witheringly when speaking of Echard:

The Character he gives of Mr *Ireton*, Lord Deputy of *Ireland*, is so monstrous, that it murders Truth and Credibility, that Part of it which he borrows from the Lord *Clarendon*, supposes his Lordship to have been in the *Inwards* of him, and to have dissected his Mind more than ever a Surgeon did a Carcass.

For his own part he preferred something more external, contenting himself, for example, when describing Walpole, with his friend Maynwaring's brief phrase: 'the best Master of Figures of any Man in his Time'. There was evidently some literary discussion about this side of historical writing, to judge from Matthew Green's Epigram comparing Laurence Echard's well-nourished, part Clarendonian figures with the somewhat arid factual portraits presented by Gilbert Burnet:

> Gil's history appears to me
> Political anatomy,
> A case of skeletons well done,
> And malefactors every one.
> His sharp and strong incision pen
> Historically cuts up men,
> And does with lucid skill impart
> Their inward ails of head and heart.
> Laurence proceeds another way,
> And well-dress'd figures does display:
> His characters are all in flesh,
> Their hands are fair, their faces fresh;
> And from his sweetning art derive
> A better scent than when alive;
> He wax-work made to please the sons,
> Whose fathers were Gil's skeletons.

This is an assessment of generosity rather than accurate analysis; for Burnet does not much probe to the inward ails, while Echard went too deep to please Oldmixon; but at any rate it bears witness to the considerable artistry of a good deal of the character-drawing of the time.

At all events the most enticing works at the present day, and indeed for the general reader at that time, are those which brought the story at least to within living memory, giving a sense of life to the whole narrative, of which, though the beginning and the middle might be interesting enough, the end was enthralling, stimulating to the prejudices. No doubt the taste for this was engendered by the publication of Clarendon's *History of the Rebellion and the Civil Wars* offered to an eagerly expectant world in 1704, stimulated again in 1723 by *Bishop Burnet's History of His Own Time*, and by histories subsequent to these, many of which, especially those by Oldmixon, are designed as refutations or supports of one or the other. Those two works, however, are largely Memoirs, and, written as they were, in the previous century—even, largely, Burnet's—belong for discussion to the volume preceding this one. The age, utilitarian though it might be in its outlook, actual in its imagination, while demanding documented facts, was not at all averse from a spice of gossip, was by no means tired of pageantry, and could appreciate the excitement of a crowded canvas. The writers who best provided this pabulum are Echard[1] and Oldmixon; they alone enter the realms of literature, and may be read as such; for though many others ordered their material as well as did these, only these two endue their work with enough vital imagination to enable the reader to participate in the action and experience some tremor of the emotions. The voluminous earlier products of Echard's vast energies need not be dwelt upon here, his ever more space-embracing geographical compendiums, his histories, mercifully shrinking in scale, of the early Church and the Roman Empire, popular as they were. He enters our present framework with his *History of England*, the most sought-after work in that field until superseded by Tindal's translation of Rapin in 1723–31. Yet the reader of today may well hesitate before venturing upon the three massive folio volumes of more than 900 pages each, the first of which was published in 1707. It is doubtful if any will wade through the first great tome which covers the years from the Roman conquest to the end of the reign of James I; but still of interest is the second, issued in 1718, which carries the story to the Restoration, and which must have found many readers, though not so many perhaps as the third, of the same year, which brings us to the establishment of William and Mary. Those would still touch the passions, fuel partisan feeling, in a way that the first volume, agreeable to dip into though it still is, would probably not. The history, apart from its possible value as a source, is in itself good reading—if the exercise is not too prolonged—and an indication of the feeling of the time, especially of its political emotions.

It might be said that the style is Clarendonian; but at any rate it is buoyant as well as dignified, mingling documentary

---

[1] Laurence Echard, 1670?–1730, was admitted a Sizar of Christ's College, Cambridge, in 1687. He was ordained, held the livings of Welkin and Elkington in Lincolnshire, and in 1712 became Archdeacon of Stow.

matter with current tales, such as Captain Lindsay's of the appearance of Satan to Cromwell on the eve of the battle of Worcester. It is diversified, moreover, with some oral tradition adding liveliness to sterner historical matter, of which one instance must suffice. He is talking of the Popish Plot.

The King, whose Inclinations were more to Popery than any other Religion, had almost from the Beginning look'd upon the Plot-Discoverers as little better than Impostors; but soon after the Beginning of this Session of Parliament, he was more fully confirm'd in it by an Accident and Passage not hitherto publish'd; but was related by the King Himself to a Person of full Credit, who communicated it to the Author of this History. The Substance of the Story was, That as soon as *Oates* was by the Parliament esteem'd the prime Discoverer of this Plot, his Reputation in the Height, and all Persons inflam'd with the Horror of it, about Twenty eminent rich Citizens, entire believers of the whole, met at a great Supper in the City, to which they invited Dr *Tongue*, Mr *Oates*, and another noted Divine, who had been often favour'd with the King's private Conversation. These three were handsomely entertain'd, and particularly caress'd by the rest of the Company; but their highest and distinguishing Compliments were paid to Mr *Oates*, and with such a seeming Derogation to the Honour of Dr *Tongue*, who valu'd himself and his Abilities as much as any Man, that there arose a verbal Quarrel between these two Confederates; which came to that Height, that the Doctor plainly told *Oates*, *That he knew nothing of the Plot, but what he had learnt from Him*. These dangerous Words disturb'd and confounded the whole Company; and had such an Effect upon one of them, who was thought to be a Spy, that the very next Morning he went to the King, and told him the whole Passage and Transaction. Upon which, his Majesty immediately sent for the foremention'd Divine, in whom he had a good confidence, and opening the Matter to him, he let him know *That he expected to hear the Particulars from Him*. But he made some Excuses, and particularly alledg'd the *Badness of his Memory*; at which the King said in a Passion, *If you are good for any Thing, it is for your Memory*; and then let him know, *That he had heard sufficient of the Matter already, but expected it all from Him*. But he still pretended not to remember it, or else gave so imperfect an Account of it, that the King incens'd, at last spoke to this effect to him: *I find there is like to be a great deal of Bloodshed about this Plot: and the Times are so troublesome and dangerous to me, that I durst not venture to pardon any that is condemn'd: Therefore their Blood be upon your Head, and not upon Mine! And I desire to see you no more*. And so he finally dismiss'd him his Presence. But to return to the Parliament.

And he returns to good solid ground, stepping over it on the whole rapidly. His narrative style is by no means despicable, if he is sometimes, as above, a little uncertain with his relative pronouns. Though a trifle long-winded, he can add plenty of colour by his use of words, and movement by his sense of phrase. Sometimes he strikes a lively note, as when, speaking of the Royalists' state of mind after Naseby, he says: 'From this great period, the King's whole Party began to fall into Convulsive Fits. . . .' There is no pomposity about him, and he can impart the temper of the nation at any time so as to carry conviction. He makes it plain that while being a good Tory he is also a good Churchman, though he feels that James II might have been more tenderly treated.

This comes out again in his *History of the Revolution and the Establishment in the Year 1688*, which appeared in 1725. There is some repetition of the third volume of his larger work, but it is not, he says, 'a repeated Old Story', being garnished with 'new and material Passages'. Moreover, it is 'attempted in such a lively and easy Manner as may be most acceptable to the Taste of the Generality of Readers'. There is, as before, considerable documentation, besides descriptions of the general feeling of the time, often neatly put, as, when discussing the birth of a royal son in 1688, he remarks: 'no Papist cou'd declare his Joy for a Prince of *Wales*, but a *Protestant* was ready to retort upon him, *The Bishops are in the Tower*.' Echard had a considerable sense of drama.

Enjoyable as Echard may have been to many of his contemporaries, he was a source of constant irritation to Oldmixon, who, according to Pope (goaded by Oldmixon's participation in *Court Poems*), was 'all his life a virulent Party-writer for hire'; yet it was only in his second phase as an author that he produced his politico-historical works, some of which are still of interest. None but the very curious will look up his earlier work as a poetaster, or as a minor dramatist, supported though this was by Purcell, Dennis, and Farquhar, but his part in *The Muses Mercury, or the Monthly Miscellany* (Jan. 1707 to Jan. 1708) should be noted. He enters our field with his main journalistic venture, *The Medley*, which was founded with Maynwaring's support in October 1710 to counteract the *Examiner*, and in which Oldmixon answered *The Conduct of the Allies*. He abominated the Harley ministry, so much so that even in his *Reflections on Dr Swift's Letter to Harley* (1712) he bases his objections to an

Academy purely on the grounds that anything suggested by a Tory must be fundamentally sinister. His first historical work, however, *The British Empire in America* (1708), is tolerably calm, and was found useful enough in its day to be frequently reprinted until 1741, though it is little more than a bundling together of the accounts of other writers, such as Archdale, Boone, and Defoe, supplemented by untrustworthy evidence from settlers in America, and is neither authentic nor entertaining to read.

But his next venture, *A Critical History of England*, 'Ecclesiastical and Civil, wherein the Errors of the Monkish Writers and Others before the Reformation are Expos'd and Corrected, As are also the Deficiency and Partiality of Later Historians', is enriched by splenetic outbursts against his *bêtes noires*, Clarendon and Echard, against anyone, indeed, who did not read history, especially recent history, through the most strongly Whig-tinted spectacles. Even the rambling (his own word for it) Essay on Criticism prefixed to the third (1728) edition is distorted by anti-Tory spleen, for though in some respects balanced enough, erring sometimes on the side of generosity with a Drydenic magnanimity, he never for a moment lets Echard off, and is flagrantly unfair. When after declaring that the unfortunate archdeacon's expressions need not be taken 'upon his bare Word for Wit' he illustrates his contention with 'the New Noddle Army', he neglects to point out that the jape was not of Echard's coining; he had merely reported that such was the Royalists' nickname for the New Model. Sometimes he waxes furious, sometimes assumes virtuous indignation. For instance, to pick up his defence of Ireton referred to earlier, he is prepared to accept all the good that Clarendon and Echard say about him, but cannot suffer it when the latter suggests that there was a good deal of blood shed during the Lord Deputy's rule. Ireton in Ireland 'did the Business there extremely well, and disciplin'd the *Irish* Rebels better than any Commander in chief had done before him in that Kingdom. This our Historian calls *Sanguinary* proceedings. . . .' Such outbursts read oddly in a work of literary criticism.

His well-documented, well-ordered *The History of England during the Reigns of the Royal House of Stuart* (1730), uniformly directed against the 'Stuartine' monarchs, and 'corrective' of horrid Tory errors and misrepresentations, is a readable work of which the sub-acid flavour may be enjoyed at the present day. His apparently business-like prose enhances the point of the dry comment. Take him, for example, describing the occasion when Charles II's letters to Monk and to Parliament were read in the House. According to Clarendon, 'so universal a Joy was never seen within those Walls'; as Oldmixon sees it, the letters 'were both read in the House with as much Joy as People, who did not very well know why they were so joyful, cou'd express'. It is entertaining, too, to compare his view of the Restoration with the magnificent panegyric, almost a paean, Echard deploys at the beginning of his second volume, describing in abundant and in its way admirable prose, the rejoicings at the turn events had taken. Here is Oldmixon's account of the result as exhibited in the reign of Charles II:

> This Reign is full of Creations, Honours, Pomps and Ceremonies, and we are to live in it like Men who feed upon Sauces. Purveyors, Cooks and Heralds are the Men of Business, unless what was carry'd on by Lord *Lauderdale* and the Ladies.

He can be beautifully contemptuous, but sometimes lands himself in difficulties, as when he tries at one and the same time to diminish Oates and maintain the reality of the Popish Plot. 'I knew *Oates* [he writes], he was dull enough, no more capable of forming the *Plot*, even as *Echard* has copied it [he can never keep his hands off Echard], than of writing *Paradise Lost*.' But, a good deal later:

> *Oates* was a passionate, rash, half-witted Fellow, and his want of Judgment might run him a little too far into Particulars: But that there was a treasonable Plot in general, &c., that the Persons he accus'd were particularly engag'd in it, there is no Room to question. . . .

But however chagrined Oldmixon may have felt at finding himself in the same voting lobby with Echard over James II, in certain passages, as when treating of the Seven Bishops, or the Earl of Lichfield's regiment, his account is similar, even for some lines together word for word the same. His second volume (1735) brings us almost to the year of publication, and written in the same ultra-Whig spirit, which derogates from its value as a source; it becomes a little wearisome. Yet he can sometimes be slashing and shrewd. When writing of the publications in 1727 he remarks:

> The most notorious of these *scandalous* Papers, was the *Weekly Libel*, call'd *The Craftsman*, publish'd by an expell'd Member of the

University of *Oxford*, every *Saturday*, full of Sophistry, Falshood, Malice, and Scandal, against the best Friends of the Government.
... These Libellers pretended to be the only *Patriots* in the Kingdom, tho' the Chief of them was one of those that had been a Fugitive abroad, under an Attainder of High Treason, several Years. ...

Oldmixon does not add much to literature (though he tells us incidentally a good deal about Defoe), but his is respectable historical writing, allowing for his somewhat fantastic partisanship; his 'revelation', for instance, of how Clarendon's *History* had been 'edited' in the Tory interest turned out to be, if not altogether without justification, something of a squib. No doubt he lacked detachment; but then a completely detached historian, besides being dull, is an inhuman monstrosity under whose pen truth is drained of its life-blood. His *Memoirs of the Press*, published posthumously in 1742, is the disappointing work of a disappointed man. Opening with a fulsome dedication to the Duchess of Marlborough (though, to be sure, dedications are an art form, not witnesses to truth), praising especially her *Conduct* which she by no means wholly wrote, it is largely an *apologia*, that of an Old Whig who finds himself spurned by the New; and even there the mangled wraiths of Clarendon and Echard haunt his pages. Whether he wrote the *Life* of Admiral Blake is doubtful, though he was brought up with his brother, and the work is impregnated with the ideas that Cromwell's great sea-captain may be supposed to have handed on to his ward.

There is little else in this active enough period of historical writing to attract the student of literature. Daniel Neal's *History of New England* (1720) was popular in America, and may amuse the curious; Warburton's *The Alliance between Church and State* (1736), which endeared the future Bishop to the Court, will no doubt remain, with the rest of his works, 'more known than read', as Jonathan Edwards put it; while students of historical controversy may be edified by the comments of Zachary Grey, the editor of *Hudibras*. So far as the general history of England goes, Tindal continued Rapin in a narrative free of party bias, and this was taken over by Smollett. Bolingbroke has already been referred to; his work is political rather than historical, as is that of Fletcher of Saltoun, who deserves recognition if only for saving the phrase, 'if a man were permitted to make all the ballads, he need not care who should make the laws of a nation'.

PART THREE

1720-1740

INTRODUCTION

THE general mental background of the second part of our period has already been touched on under philosophy; it needs perhaps only to be added that the interest in science, and the Newtonian conception of the universe, from having been matter for publicists had by this time become part of the normal world-picture, as will become clear enough—some may think almost too clear—in treating of the poets. The aspect which needs further brief comment is the general social background which most of the literature of the next twenty years will reflect.

There is no longer the sense of crisis so marked during the last phase of Queen Anne's reign, which though it continued a few years after the accession of the House of Hanover had virtually died out by 1720. Feelings which earlier were explosive enough to have produced a civil war were now replaced by such as ran only so high as to give a lively pulse to party wranglings. The country felt itself settling down into a state of stability, the great new commercial class no longer evincing an eagerness to become civilized, but rather, quietly insisting that it was so. Pride in the achievements of England as a civilized society was one of the stimuli by which men lived. The painters were turning their attention to civic glories. If Alexander van Galen's graceful picture of Queen Anne returning from the opening of her first Parliament in 1702 may have been inspired by a sense of pageantry, P. Tilleman's View from Richmond Hill (c. 1720), W. Grimbaldson's Panorama of London from Islington (c. 1730), and the view painted by Anthony Highmore (to whom Isaac Hawkins Browne addressed his poem on 'Design in Beauty') of the Canal in St. James's Park (c. 1740), reveal a satisfaction at the large graciousness that civilized society had brought into being.

Moreover the religious excitement had abated. Not only had the more vociferous heretics ceased to outrage the orthodox, hardly anyone caring to profess open infidelity, but the various Churches, save only the Catholic, were confidently settling down in their realms, and guardedly staking out further claims. If the lion did not lie down with the lamb, at least he did not try to devour it. A sense of humanitarianism was generally spreading; and though it would not be true to say that there was much awareness of the problem the Victorians were so acutely conscious of as that of 'the condition of the people', such a measure as the Gin Act of 1736, and the early movements towards prison reform, indicated by the Fleet Prison Committee of 1729, and the Charitable Corporation of 1730, bear witness to the extension of the social sense beyond an immediate clique or confraternity, as do to a large extent the paintings of Hogarth.

The aristocratic oligarchy was securely settled, and for more than a century England was to be ruled by a small number of families, the Russells, the Stanhopes, the Pelhams, the Pitts— all interconnected, their ranks being reinforced by the rising middle class, replacing some of the older stock, the City broker Dunton, for example, acquiring the Villiers property of Helmsley in Yorkshire. It was this aristocracy which built throughout the century the great country houses, beginning with Vanbrugh's Castle Howard, such houses as Stowe, Hagley, Badminton, Wentworth Woodhouse, Holkham, Lydiard Tregoz, and Harewood, together with numberless smaller gems. With these went the landscape gardens, the parks, the hills, the lakes, all contrived to make the houses like jewels in a setting, a vogue fostered by the poets from Pope to Shenstone. Here perhaps, and in the town houses which corresponded with them, was deliberately brought into existence the refined and cultured society, intensely conscious of personal relationships and of civilized values, a society very much aware of its distinction from the mass, which was still dangerously savage, as the eighteenth-century predilection for tumult shows well enough. The mobs rioted over the Gin Act, over Papal Nuncios, over Wilkes, over Lord George Gordon, over prices at Drury Lane; any excuse would seem to serve to relieve the monotony and the misery of the lives disrupted by the gathering speed of the industrial revolution. The happy few cultivated the arts partly as a barrier, though they were more than willing to help society as a whole to achieve a humane level, and were not unmindful of their responsibilities to either land or people. There were the beginnings of cultured drawing-rooms, though these did not attain prominence until the days of Elizabeth Montagu and the blue-stockings generally; Swift complained that there was no conversation to be had in London, and Chesterfield kept longing eyes fixed firmly on France. Still, this society was happy, confident, and thriving; it was in the saddle, and it was free.

It is, then, all the more surprising to find the extravagant eulogies of liberty and the agonized outcries against corruption cropping up with seeming irrelevance in the most innocent-looking play or poem, as though under the sense of stability and even self-gratulation, all was not complacency. It would seem that we tend to under-estimate the sense the early years of the century had of liberty as a precious possession lately threatened; the word at that time was not always a mere counter, but expressed how close the age felt itself to be to its tyrannic past, to the bitter struggle not yet quite determined. Nor is it easy for us to understand how poignantly some might feel the threat to liberty in the later days of Walpole's rule. To us this last phase seems absurdly exaggerated; we smile at the sharpness of eternal vigilance. Yet making all allowances, the supposition is inescapable that it was largely a matter of party cries: 'Liberty in danger' replaced the old alarm of 'The Church in danger'. What, after all, were the threats to liberty in the thirties? Certainly, as we have seen, the theatre was gagged, especially perhaps after the new Licensing Bill of 1737, which again reduced the theatres to two, chiefly for the benefit of the actors. But there was nothing to stop anyone printing the play. Chesterfield's famous speech against the Act has, admittedly, a certain validity as a warning, but it is doubtful if he would have uttered it had he not been in opposition. Much may be said about the theme of corruption, a party cry met with *apropos de bottes* in any writer attached to the malcontent Whigs. As a matter of sober fact the administration was no more corrupt than in previous epochs, indeed rather less so, if only because so much more was open to inspection than there

had been before the Cabinet system began to evolve under
George I. There was, nobody will deny, a good deal of patronage,
jobbery, even bribery; yet under the blessed William III at
least once

> . . . beneath the Patriot's cloak
> From the crack'd bag the dropping Guinea spoke,

as the nobleman in question was making his exit by the back
stairs. Corruption again, we suspect, was a party cry. And we
do not notice that party bribery was notably lessened, nor
freedom perceptibly enlarged, when the Patriots ultimately
got into power.

It is an unconscious tribute to the poets of the period, satirical
or not, that the view of a debased eighteenth century so long
held the field. The fact is that most of the poets were in one way
or another attached to the opposition, consisting mainly of
people whom Walpole found it disturbing, irritating, or useless
to employ. Calling themselves 'the Patriots' (since, as we know,
it is always the opposition that is patriotic, whereas those in
power invariably rule in the interests of party or from personal
motives), they were the oligarchy whom Walpole kept out of
the jobs they felt they would run so much better than he with
his Newcastles and Harringtons. Cultured people, some of
them poets or men of letters, and largely interrelated, many
of them possessed inspiringly lovely country places, and they
liked to 'caress' poets. A proportion of them were animated by
the Roman, Ciceronian virtues, especially Chesterfield, whom
Thomson, along with a number of other patriots, justly but a
little irrelevantly praised in the final 'Winter'. Walpole saw
through what was in many of them a pose, inherited from the
Commonwealth and Restoration periods, and still lingering in
the sub-heroic plays of our period: 'Well,' he would ask a
political aspirant, 'are you to be an old Roman? a patriot?' He
knew better than any of them at that date, that a man rules
not as he would but as he must. No doubt he exaggerated
when he said of 'the Boys', as he preferred to call the Patriots,
'All those men have their price'; still, it was an understandable
retort to make upon a group of men who were in season and
out accusing him and his administration first of corruption,
then of tyranny; and a few did indeed fall to the lure of office,
notably Pulteney and Carteret. There was some justice in

Fielding's definition of the patriot (in *Covent Garden Journal* No. 4) as a candidate for a place at Court. At all events many writers fell victims to the suasions of this clique, adorned by the brilliant Bolingbroke. No one would wish to maintain that the cultured aristocrats engaged the poets for propaganda purposes —we are not now in Queen Anne's reign—but the effect was as though they had; for the panegyrics on freedom, the tirades against corruption, occupy a good deal of space in the verse of the period. Again and again we meet laments for the decay of British virtue, morals, integrity, and valour, as at the beginning of Thomson's *Britannia*, where we find the goddess 'revolving sad' the 'faded fame' of her 'degenerate sons'. How far the poets vivified into a glorious principle matters of mere grumbling it is hard to say; but here is Arbuthnot, a steady, sensible man, writing to Swift on 13 January 1732:

I wish you had been here, though I think you are in a better country. I fancy to myself that you have some virtue and honour left, some small regard for religion. Perhaps Christianity may last with you some twenty or thirty years longer. You have no companies or stock-jobbing, are yet free of excises; you are not insulted in your poverty, and told with a sneer that you are a rich and thriving nation. Every man that takes neither place nor pension is not deemed with you a rogue, and an enemy to his country.

If he was comparing the thirties with the blamelessness of the days of their first acquaintance, he seems to have forgotten his friend's *Prospect for the Advancement of Religion*, or Shaftesbury's inveighing against corruption. His were the girdings of an old man no longer in tune with his age, comparable with the old Duchess of Marlborough's persistent panic that 'a sponge' was to be passed over the National Debt. Some really patriotic opposition to Walpole indeed there was, from those who wished the country to show a stouter face to the world, as did Pitt, a frequent visitor at Stowe; it did not occur to him that Walpole's pacifism might be as patriotic as his own belligerent policy.

Whatever Arbuthnot may have thought, the nation as a whole certainly regarded itself as rich and thriving; few Englishmen at the time felt that they were 'degenerate sons'. They were up and doing, adventuring in strange lands over perilous seas; English sailors were the best and most valorous in the world, aiding the traders to make England fabulously wealthy, and carrying peace and civilization over the whole, surely not ungrateful, globe. There was no shame in the fact that the basis of it all was wool. Did not the Chancellor, after all, sit upon the Woolsack as an emblem of England's greatness? Tracts and pamphlets on wool were continually written and devoured, and in 1757 Dyer was to sing the full glory of the wool trade in *The Fleece*. Towns were springing up and being enormously enlarged, all of which contributed to the sense of greatness and stability of the new middle classes, whose less material problems were soon to find their expression in the novel. It is not a somnolent, degenerate, or corrupt England which is the background of the literature of the third and fourth decades of the century, but an England conscious of its greatness, of its abounding energy, and actively aware of its mission.

XI

DEFOE, 1715–1731

I. THE 'MISCELLANEOUS WRITER'

THE work that Defoe considered his most important contribution to society is so stupendous in bulk that here it must be skimmed over rapidly, especially as posterity has relegated it to second place. In the last fifteen years of his life he was, as always, indefatigably busy, immersed in affairs, writing away furiously in his home at Stoke Newington, becoming progressively more prolix, since he was paid by the sheet, and his necessities decreased no more than his wide-embracing interests. Seeing that he was the most active journalist of his time, it is as well before entering upon a brief description of his labours to take some note of the whirl of ephemeral production of which he himself was often the instigator.

In the earlier part of our period, the Steele–Addison and Defoe papers, together with the *Examiner*, rise above the multitude of *Observators*, *Rehearsals*, *Grumblers* referred to in a previous section. The last journal became entirely political in 1715, at about which date appeared also such papers as the various short-lived 'Shifts', beginning in 1716 with *Robin's Last Shift or Weekly Remarks*; and finally, in 1717, *The Shift Shifted*, which Defoe stigmatized as 'a scandalous paper', and undertook *Mercurius Politicus* to oppose. That year too appeared *The Scourge*, which professed to be 'Designed as a Modest [in the British Museum copy the adjective is corrected by some peevish owner to 'Modish'] Vindication of the Church of England'. These papers varied in content and purpose; Boyer's monthly the *Political State of Great Britain*, which ran from 1711 until 1729, was factional; the *Visiter*, first on Tuesdays, then on Fridays as well, appeared between 18 June 1723 and 3 January 1724, and though moralistic and social rather than literary, exhibited many verses and poemicules; the *Tea-Table*, which lasted for nineteen numbers from 21 February was, as already seen, devoted to the raising of taste. Best of all, perhaps, was the *Plain Dealer*—23 March 1724 to 7 May 1725—which made great play of being democratic, that is, scornful of the pretensions of the nobility. Conducted in turns by Aaron Hill and William Bond, who, according to Savage, were 'the two contending powers of light and darkness' since Hill was so much better than Bond, bringing it indeed almost up to *Spectator* standard, it maintained a good philosophic-literary level. Dennis and Savage both contributed, it was here (as noted earlier) that Mallet's 'William and Margaret' first appeared, and there is some lively criticism. In due course there appeared the literary miscellany the *Gentleman's Magazine* (1731), and the *World* (1753), the Pope-inspired *Grub Street Journal* (1730-7); Bolingbroke's political the *Craftsmen* (1726). This is to give only a dim notion of the proliferation of newspapers and other journals, for which compendious bibliographies must be consulted.

This bewildering number of London sheets, daily, twice, and thrice weekly, weekly, monthly, paralleled by those in the country, serves to manifest the contentions of the early Hanoverian years, in which Defoe became entangled. He wrote actively until 1726, then, apparently, remained silent in this field, except when, in 1728, he wrote the first number of the *Universal Spectator* launched by his son-in-law, Henry Baker. It is impossible to determine exactly how far Defoe was involved in the publications with which his name is connected, to what extent even he may have owned them. Here need be mentioned, besides the *Flying Post and Medley* with which he followed up *Mercator* after Harley's defeat, only *Mercurius Politicus*, Applebee's *Original Weekly Journal* (1720-6), and Dyer's, afterwards Dormer's, *News Letter*, a hand-copied journal, the country squires' favourite pabulum. But it was outside these that his real work was done, and his energies had characteristic outlet, Defoe balancing himself on a razor-edge where a slip might mean disaster. It was as though he relished danger. He had for many years, during and just after the Harley régime, played an extremely tricky political game, narrowly escaping prison more than once, especially over the ironic Hanoverian tracts of 1713 and 1715. In 1717 he was again nearly trapped in his own meshes through his connexion with Nathaniel Mist's the *Weekly Journal; or Saturday's Post* (known as *Mist's Journal*, till being interdicted it changed its name to *Fog's*), where he acted as a new kind of secret service agent. Moderate Whig though he was, he joined the staff of *Mist's*, whose correspondents were, according to Defoe, 'Papists, Jacobites, and enraged High Tories', which stoutly, even, in the government's view, dangerously maintained the Tory, not to say Jacobite, standpoint. His function was to tone it down. 'This remarkable masquerade among the Tories of the Whig wolf in sheep's clothing', as Professor James Sutherland calls it, was not without its dangers, and there were some critical moments.

It can be argued that in all these political manœuvres Defoe proved himself a liar and a cheat, an impudent forger, scandalously caring for nothing but his own advantage. You cannot continually bow down in the house of Rimmon without becoming suspect. Yet two facts emerge: first, his constant loyalty to Harley, in whose interest, immediately before his impeachment, he published *Minutes of the Negotiations of Mons. Mesnager,* which, if genuine, cleared the minister of the imputation of double-dealing over the Treaty of Utrecht; secondly his by now thoroughly pragmatic attitude towards government. If his puritan conscience seems sometimes to have been stilled, if his actions entailed continuous deceit, he could always plead that it was he alone who was imperilled, and that he had in mind always and everywhere (or very nearly so; one must allow for the vacillations of human nature) moderation, together with the peace and prosperity of his country.

These writings illuminate the tenor of nearly all his writings. It is not only that they give significance to the main characters of his fiction, playing as they do lone hands, but that the life of invariable compromise tallies so well with the general moral atmosphere of the novels, in which moral rigour has so often to bend itself so as to comply with circumstance. Throughout, the ideal has to contend with the practical, with what is possible in life as it is lived out; and if at the end of his tales the ideal is accorded a somewhat perfunctory victory, that was in accord with life in society as Defoe had found it to be. The sense of this suffuses his literary output during the last fifteen years of his life, which was astonishingly multifarious, especially during the miraculous five or six years from 1719 to 1724, during which appeared the works he is chiefly known by today, interspersed with others. Works on travel, on rogues, on morals, on trade, on the occult, on servants, on marriage; memoirs of wars, of the plague; history and biography, he poured all out copiously, ceaselessly, at varying, but often at great length, driven not only by his daemon, but by the need to make money. Possible it may be to order them into categories, and here it will be convenient to do so to some extent; yet one set flows into the other, and during the great lustre the elements became fused together in some of his writings in such a way as to raise them to works of art.

It would not be unfair to say that Defoe's two driving interests were trade and morals, in that order if you like; but then he was interested in the moral value of trade, and, if you care to put it that way, the trade, or at least the practical, value of morals. But threading through these considerations, there is nearly always in Defoe a streak of the occult, this being one of the reasons why it is unfruitful to range his work in compartments. And over and above all these things is Defoe's intense fascination with how life is lived, with how people behave, how they make do. When, owing to what conditions it would be hopeless to guess (perhaps even financial pressure), his imagination, the practical imagination of the period, makes him one with the actuality of character in a given situation, then he achieves art. And here it is in some degree the puritan condemnation of art, as feigning, that is to say lying, that gives him his superb objectivity. Even when he is inventing, if he could be said ever to invent unless invention is an extreme instance of living-into, he is careful to assert veracity, to profess sometimes that uncertainty that gives the effect of verisimilitude. Something of this has already been touched upon in an earlier chapter, when discussing *Mrs. Veal* and *The Storm*; a last example may be taken from the *History and Reality of Apparitions* (1722). He is talking about an apparition who appeared for a certain purpose, but on one occasion

it discours'd of other Matters also; as of the *Dutch* War, and the bloody Engagement at Sea: I do not remember exactly, whether it said a bloody Engagement had been, or would be; but I think it was an Engagement that had lately been.

This work will not find many readers, nor will *The Political History of the Devil* (1726), though written with much lively humanity, nor again *A System of Magick: or, A History of the Black Art* (1727). Perhaps the brief biography of Dickory Cronke, *The Dumb Philosopher; or Great Britain's Wonder* (1719), the man who was born dumb, reflected deeply, and for a brief while before his death was granted the faculty of speech, may attract a few; but most will be repelled by the lengthy, heavily languaged *History of the Life and Adventures of Mr Duncan Campbell* (1720), the deaf-mute endowed with second sight, a work in which Defoe was helped by William Bond and perhaps Eliza Haywood. The books in the first group dealing purely with the occult may seem to us more than a little childish; yet Defoe is not infinitely gullible: he is aware of hysteria and self-delusion. Sporadically beguiled by the meaning of dreams, the effect of conscience, and so on, he is alert to the value of what we have come to call intuition. In the last two, the practical side of his nature comes out, as in the teaching of letters to Cronke and to Campbell, and it is relevant to note that his son-in-law, Henry Baker, for some time successfully directed a school for the education of deaf-mutes.

All through his work he insists that 'the ways of Providence are sovereign and superior'; this comes out again and again in all that he writes. He is given, too, to rubbing in the idea that to sin in imagination is as corrupt as to sin in actuality, and is prone to quoting or implying that 'Whoso looketh after a woman and lusteth after her, committeth adultery in his heart', dwelling upon it at the risk of wearying the reader. Moll Flanders, for instance, confesses:

. . . I never was in Bed with my Husband, but I wish'd myself in the Arms of his Brother; . . . In short, I committed Adultery and Incest with him every Day in my Desires, which without doubt, was as effectually Criminal in the Nature of the Guilt, as if I had actually done it.

His main notions continually crop up, indeed he is tiresomely repetitive, and anyone who has read one of his works will as likely as not experience a sense of familiarity when reading another. One instance, somewhat ludicrous, is that in two such differing works as *A General History of Discoveries and Improvements in Useful Arts* (four monthly numbers, from October 1726 to January 1727) and *A History of the Devil*, he traces the legend of Faustus to his having been a commercial traveller for Gutenberg in Paris, where the accuracy of the reproductions so astonished the booksellers that they attributed it to magic.

If these works offer a clue to the basis of what we may call his creative writings, it is his moralistic works which merge most readily into the novels, beginning with *The Family Instructor* (1715 and 1718) and ending with *The Complete English Gentleman*, of which only the first page was printed at the end of his life, publication being delayed until 1890. Some of these should at least be glanced at for a full understanding of what lies behind the novels; they link up extraordinarily, the same themes recurring again and again. Thus *The Family Instructor*, dealing in part with the relation of children to parents, is related to *The Protestant Monastery* (1727), in which Defoe, urged perhaps by his quarrel with his son, bitterly inveighs against the way children treat their aged progenitors. In the same way, *Conjugal Lewdness; or Matrimonial Whoredom* (1727) dovetails in with the earlier works, *Religious Courtship* (1722), *The Great Law of Subordination Consider'd* (1724), and *Everybody's Business, is No-Body's Business* (1725), all of them dealing wholly or in some part with the 'Universal Degeneracy' of servants, Defoe everywhere insisting, nevertheless, upon their proper treatment.

Since these moralizings serve as background to the novels, some will repay glancing at here. The theme of *Religious Courtship*, written mainly in dialogue form, since 'Historical Dialogues, it must be confess'd, have a very taking Elegancy in them', declares itself in the sub-title: 'on the Necessity of Marrying Religious Husbands and Wives only | As Also | Of Husbands and Wives being of the same Opinions in Religion with one another'. One of the most supposedly heartrending of the little dramas the dialogues develop into is that of the woman who found that she had married a Papist. An appendix divagates upon 'the Necessity of taking none but Religious Servants, and a Proposal for the better managing of Servants'. *Conjugal Lewdness*, which Defoe claimed to have had by him for thirty years—if so, he had early begun to gratify his taste for quoting Jeremy Taylor—if fiercely puritanical, shuddering at nakedness as the utmost horror of immodesty, is a thoroughly common-sense book. It argues that marriage should take place between persons in similar circumstances, and of congruous interests, though not for mere worldly advantage; affection, likeness of temper must be the basis of marriage, otherwise coming together is blatant concupiscence: any notion of birth control is utterly abhorrent to Defoe. Though he writes chiefly in his running, colloquial manner, he sometimes mounts into the dissenting pulpit:

Household Strife is a terrestrial Hell, at least 'tis an Emblem of real Hell; 'tis a Life of Torment, and without Redemption. Matrimony is an irreversible Decree; 'tis a Grave from whence there is no return; nothing but the King of Terrors can open the Jayl; and 'tis then but an even lay between the Man and his Wife, who goes out first; and if when the Jaylor comes, the Devil comes with him, 'tis but one to one who he calls for, nay, if they have lived the Life I speak of, as is very probable, they may even do what they never did, that is to say, agree for a Moment, and go together.

Brief, and not always very brief, sermons on choosing a partner from time to time crop up in the novels, more than once from the mouth of Moll Flanders, and once at least from that of Roxana in her fervent warning against marrying any kind of fool, 'whether a mad Fool, or a sober Fool, a wise Fool, or a silly Fool, take anything but a Fool; *nay*, be anything, be even an Old Maid, the Worst of Nature's Curses, rather than take up with a Fool'. In the same way the matter of conjugal felicity intrudes sporadically, not in the novels alone; but in the latter, since happiness calls for little comment, and leads to no dramatic action, the periods of calm and peace are rapidly passed over. It is more developed in *The Complete English Tradesman*, written in the form of 'Familiar Letters'. Concerned though it is with the business man, from his beginnings as an apprentice to his becoming 'a general in trade', in the first volume there is a long dialogue between a married couple to propagate the idea that if only husbands will tell their wives *in time* of their business troubles, sensible helpmeets will retrench their expenses, and perhaps save the situation. Later there is a warning to up-and-coming tradesmen not to burden themselves too soon with wife and family. Yet preach the ideal as he may in these moralistic conduct-books, Defoe, in common with other Dissenters, knew that you must not expect too much of fallen man. You might indicate the highest, but common sense informed you that men in general would pursue the lower, though they might be raised from the lowest.

Defoe's trade pamphlets are innumerable—literally so, since new ones are continually being brought to light; few besides economic historians will wish to read them now; enough to say here that they are always imaginative and forward-looking. But it is as well to note how many of his other works, especially the voyages, are covert advertisements for trade, for the

development of British commerce, backed by no small degree
of fervent patriotism. Yet he is careful to proclaim in his *General
History of* . . . *Useful Arts*, a kind of popular encyclopedia which
might be called a history of commerce, that from the earliest
times, trade 'knows no Parties, no Politic, no Religious Interests'; it exists, in fact, for the good of mankind, a theme not
unsung by poetasters. His *Plan of the English Commerce* (1728)
contains a panegyric upon English products and the English
workman; but, on the other hand, *Augusta Triumphans, Or, The
Way to make London the Most Flourishing City in the World* (1728)
and *The Complete English Gentleman* are moral, and especially
educational tractates, in the last of which he gives voice to the
Dissenters' hostility to the old classical education: 'the knowledge of things, not words, make a schollar'.

The themes outlined above occur again and again in the
novels, but not more pervasively than do the adventure books
which form the basis of three of his works of fiction. A vast
amount of 'research' was harvested in these, yet *Memoirs of a
Cavalier* (1720) and *Captain Carleton* (1728), now accepted as
his, are both very readable, much as the war memoirs of this
century may be in two hundred years' time. More important
are the popular voyage books, such as *The King of the Pirates.
Being an Account of the Famous Enterprises of Captain Avery, the
Mock King of Madagascar* (1720), and *The History of the Pirates*
(1724), almost certainly of his minting, though stated to be
by 'Captain Charles Johnson', which includes accounts of the
two women pirates, Mary Read and Anne Bonny. But foremost among such works, imaginary, though strictly based on
fact, is *A New Voyage round the World* (1724), full of incidents we
have met with in the novels written earlier. Containing some
inspired guess-work, Defoe, for example, discovering that sea
lay between Australia and Tasmania some decades before the
Bass Straits were mapped, it is, in effect, propaganda for setting
up trading stations, not to say founding colonies, in South
America, a matter Defoe had had much to heart from the days
of William III, and had pleaded for in his *Review*. Again and
again, in reading *Robinson Crusoe*, *Captain Singleton*, and *Colonel
Jacque* we come upon passages parallel with some to be found
in these books: the last, indeed, may in some sort be said to be a
brief compendium of the moralistic, trade, and travel-adventure
books. In these he can sometimes be a little perfunctory; but he

is never boring where his view of how life should be lived is involved; and this is what gives animation to his moralistic works.

Superbly lively among these is *The Family Instructor*, a conduct-book so much sought after in its day as to run into ten editions in some five years. It should certainly not be ignored by anyone interested in Defoe's development as a writer of fiction, owing its vogue, one might think, to its being in a sense the first of his novelistic writings, excepting possibly *Mrs. Veal*. Both volumes, of 1715 and 1718, are composed of dialogues, the first series being devoted to the family, the duties of parents, the care of apprentices and servants, and the disposing of children in marriage. Read as a whole the work may be found more than a little tedious, tending too much here and there to the horridly sentimental-pietistic; the 'little chee-ild' is as overdone as he is in Victorian melodrama. Nevertheless, there are some happy passages of life as it runs. In the fourth dialogue, for instance, we read of the girl of about eighteen who has 'ruffled' her mother and been duly admonished. The young woman complains to her brother, who, to ease the tension, suggests, '*Come Let's read a Book then*: Have you never a Play here? Come, I'll read a Play to you.' The girl goes to her closet to find that her mother has swept away all the books she 'had any Pleasure in', the collection of plays, 'all the *French* novels, all the modern Poets, *Boileau*, *Dacier* and a great many more', leaving for perusal only a Bible, a Prayer Book, *The Practice of Piety*, and *The Whole Duty of Man*. The family disturbance makes up a few pages of comedy in the happiest stage tradition.

The second book is an altogether different matter. The first part, 'Relating to Family Breaches, and their obstructing Religious Duties', consists of three dialogues, with narrative portions here and there, the whole amounting to a wavering tale; the second part is devoted to 'the great Mistake of mixing the Passions in the Managing and Correcting of Children', and here the third dialogue is a characteristic Defoe novel *in petto*. A wife has deserted her home and taken up with a wicked female friend. In due course the husband arrives with a constable to arrest the friend and expostulate with his wife. The opening scene is dramatically enough told, for Defoe was already creeping towards a method of creating tension. As the story goes on we learn that the wife 'playing with the edg'd Tools of her own

Passions', thought of going home to burn down the house with her husband in it:

> . . . But she had not Courage for that. *No*, said she to herself . . . No, *Poison him*; I won't do that, I may burn the Children too.
>
> The dreadful Word . . . was for some Days working up to a height, the Words follow'd her like a Voice, *Poison him, poison him.*

At first the suggestion appalled her, but soon 'she took up the horrid Resolution to POISON *her Husband'*. Little by little she arranged it all, admirably, one may say; but the night before her plan was to take effect she dreamt that she had done away with her husband and her two children:

> When on a suddain, she thought she saw a black Cloud, and heard a Voice as loud as Thunder out of it, which said, *That wicked Woman, his Wife, has Poison'd him and her own Children*, let her be taken and let her be burn'd.

As an appropriate result, repentance followed, and the family was blessedly reunited.

Again, if you will, not 'grace abounding', but melodrama, and at the most mediocre 'Murder in the Red Barn', 'Sweeney Tod' level, but it would seem to be crucial in the development of Defoe, a born novelist, for whom the form was not ready. Dialogue he had already resorted to in the *Review*; narrative he had employed in *Mrs. Veal*; here, for the first time, he combined them effectively. More important still, the story embodies themes that seem to have haunted him; the temptation to murder, that we find in *Moll Flanders* and *The Fortunate Mistress* (Roxana); the 'voices' that we come across in the first and in the third, possibly autobiographical, part of *Robinson Crusoe*; and so on. We meet repentance, following upon fear of the retribution that evil actions incur, such as is depicted almost everywhere, though here it is not comfortably palliated by the comforts with which a life of successful crime is concluded.

The foregoing considerations are necessary to an understanding of what Defoe imagined he was doing when he wrote his masterpieces, and set the English novel on its long and glorious course. He himself seems to have felt no difference in kind between what we have come to regard as his fiction and his more patently moralistic work. How far he may have believed that his novels were a form of conduct-book only a very bold man would hazard: the Preface to *Moll Flanders* reads suspiciously like a delicious piece of irony, notably where, speaking of his story, he says, slyly one must feel, that 'an author must be hard put to it to wrap it up so clean as not to give room, *especially for vicious readers* [the italics not his], to turn it to his disadvantage'. And again, when he points the moral, it may be thought that he is saying to himself; 'It's time I put on my Chapel voice for a sentence or two.' As early as the first *Family Instructor* he sees fit to make excuses: and similarly in *The New Family Instructor* of 1727, after he had made his contribution to imaginative literature, an argument between brother and sister revolves round the proposition that 'when the Moral of the Tale is duly annex'd, and the End directed right', fictitious stories may be of value, since theirs is 'the most pungent way of writing or speaking'—provided, it goes without saying, that 'The Fable is always made for the Moral, not the Moral for the Fable', as he announced in the Preface to *Moll Flanders*.

'The most pungent way.' Defoe had learnt a good deal about pungency: he had during his career resorted to a variety of methods; and, always adapting his style to his matter and his audience, was never slave to his habitual manner. It is one of our hereditary errors to refer to 'the plain style of Bunyan or Defoe', as though they, to begin with, were not fields apart; or to the 'simple' style of Defoe (though Aitken saw that it was only 'apparently simple'), as if he had chanced upon some happy means of communication, and never bothered his head about how he wrote. True, just as in the *Essay upon Projects*, his earliest prose piece, he had pronounced that he cared little to dress up a story with 'the exactness of style', so in one of his latest books, *The Compleat English Tradesman*, he tells his readers:

If any man was to ask me, which would be supposed to be a perfect stile, or language, I would answer, that in which a man speaking to five hundred people, of all common or various capacities, [idiots or lunaticks excepted,] should be understood by them all [in the same manner with one another, and] in the same sense which the speaker intended to be understood [, this would certainly be a most perfect stile].

That, however, it should be noticed, comes under the heading 'Of the Trading Stile'; it is not a general precept. For Defoe was not afraid of 'style'. But his conception of style does not seem to have included brevity; he was flowing, repetitive, at

times even slipshod. That there was an art to blot never
entered his feverishly energetic mind, and the editors of the
fourth (1738) edition of this work shrewdly commented:

> ... One thing we take the liberty to observe of his Writings, that,
> generally speaking they are too verbose and circumlocutory; inso-
> much that it has been well observed of them, That to have a com-
> plete work come out of his hands, it was necessary to give him so
> much *per* sheet to write it in his own way; and half as much after-
> wards to lop off its excrescences, or abstract it. . . ;

they themselves judiciously pruning away the phrases indicated by hooks in the extract quoted above.

Defoe, in short, was astonishingly varied. Keeping in mind
the overall tone of *Robinson Crusoe*, the work on which, apparently, the usual confident generalizations about his prose
are based, we may enjoy the impact of a markedly different
attack in, say, the opening passages of *Reasons against the Accession of the House of Hanover*:

> ... Why, hark ye, you Folk that call yourselves Rational, and talk of
> having Souls, is this a Token of your having such things about you,
> or of thinking Rationally; if you have, pray what is it likely will
> become of you all? Why, the Strife is gotten into your Kitchens, your
> Parlours, your Shops, your Counting-houses, nay, into your very
> Beds. You Gentlefolks, if you please to listen to your Cook-maids
> and Footmen in your Kitchens, you shall hear them scolding, and
> swearing, and scratching, and fighting, among themselves; and when
> you think the Noise is about the Beef and the Pudding, the Dish
> water, or the Kitchen-stuff, alas, you are mistaken, the Feud is about
> the more mighty Affairs of the Government, and who is for the
> Protestant Succession, and who for the Pretender.

What he could do by way of more dignified utterance can be
seen in some of his letters, as in one to Stanhope (8 March
1710) about Sacheverell:

> Nothing, Sir, has witheld me from blackening and exposing this
> insolent priest but a nicety of honour, that I thought it dishonourable
> to strike him when he was down, or to fall on when he had other
> enemies to engage.

The man who writes like that is thinking of what he is doing;
he has a sense of the sound of words, and a *cursus*-like effect.
When he is really writing for himself, as in *The Serious Reflections*

. . . *of Robinson Crusoe*, a writer strikingly different from the commonly expected Defoe emerges:

> What are the Sorrows of other Men to us? And what their Joy? Something we may be touch'd indeed with, by the Power of Sympathy, and a secret Turn of the Affections; but all the solid Reflection is directed to our selves. Our Meditations are all Solitude in Perfection; our Passions are all exercised in Retirement; we love, we hate, we covet, we enjoy, all in Privacy and Solitude: All that we communicate of those Things to any other, is but for their Assistance in the Pursuit of our Desires; the End is at Home; the Enjoyment, the Contemplation, is all Solitude and Retirement; 'tis for our selves we enjoy, and for our selves we suffer.

The building up of the sentences, the antithetical clauses followed by a run of verbs giving a variation in pace, the deepening of the tone, all denote, if not the conscious stylist, at least someone who was not unaware of how he was writing.

Indeed throughout this more meditative work he writes in the cultivated tone of the *Tatler–Spectator*, though he never attains the innate ease of those journals, even in the more relaxed passage about conversation; it would seem that he had it in him only to argue, not to converse. Yet in the final part, *A Vision of the Angelic World*, when detached from the enthralling urgencies of everyday life, he can vie with Addison's *Spectator* 565:

> When my Fancy had mounted me thus beyond the Vestiges of the Earth, and leaving the Atmosphere behind me, I had set my firm Foot upon the Verge of Infinite, when I drew no Breath, but subsisted upon pure Æther, it is not possible to express fully the Vision of the Place; first you are to conceive of Sight as unconfin'd, and you see here at least the whole solar System at one View. Nor is your Sight bounded by the narrow Circumference of one Sun, and its Attendants of Planets, whose Orbits are so appropriated to its proper System, but above and beyond, and on every side you see innumerable Suns, and attending on them, Planets, Satellites, and inferior Lights proper to their respective Systems, and all these moving in their subordinate Circumstances, without the least Confusion, with glorious Light, and Splendour inconceivable.

The reader might think that he is listening to Philonous adjuring Hylas to contemplate the heavens with all their glittering furniture, but that it lacks the grace of movement, the surprising word that alerts us in Berkeley, who, moreover, would never have committed the unlucky 'Satellites, and inferior Lights'.

But such sonority was foreign to Defoe's usual purpose; normally he varies his tone with his audience, as well as with the *persona* he is assuming, saddler, pirate, or garrulous old reprobate. His central style, perhaps, is that of his moralistic works. It is, one might say, a classless way of writing, not of the boudoir, as Addison's is, nor even of the coffee-house, as Swift's aimed at being: when he is not being autobiographical, he tends to the tub-oratorical. But at all events he renounces any appeal to the snobbery of learning, and rarely wishes to titillate the ear of the refined, or truckle to genteel forms. His is an honest-to-God, Dissenter's, market-place utterance. Yet there again a doubt intrudes. Are his occult writings possibly more faithful to the actual Defoe? Take, for instance, a passage from *Duncan Campbell*:

If one that has Speculated deep into abstruse matters, and made it his Study, not only to know, how to assign natural Reasons for some strange new Acts, that looked like Miracles by being peculiar to the individual Genius of some particular admired Man, but carrying his Enquiry to a much greater height had speculated likewise, what might possibly be achieved by human Genius in the full Perfection of Nature, and had laid it down as a *Thesis* by strong Arguments, that such Things might be compassed by a human Genius (if in its true degree of Perfection) as are the hourly Operations of the Person's Life I am writing, he would have been counted a wild, Romantick Enthusiast, instead of a Natural Philosopher.

William Bond, or Elizabeth Haywood? Surely not; the absence of periods alone makes it indubitably Defoe's. For one of his stigmata, or at least noticeable idiosyncrasies, is a certain breathlessness; others are the 'no, not' emphasis, and the catching up of an uncontrollable sentence with an 'I say', and a general characteristic density. But a plain, straight-forward, Anglo-Saxon vernacular? He is 'simple' only when speaking through the mouths of simple people, as admittedly he usually does.

2. DEFOE AND THE NOVEL

Defoe was solidly right in making the young man in *The Second Family Instructor* warn his sister 'against approving such Fables and Romances as are actually the Product of the present Age, having no such moral or justifiable End attending them' as was indicated in some of the earlier 'Fables, feigned Histories, invented Tales and even such as we call Romances'; for then there was no *Arcadia* or even *Incognita* to allure the reader to morality, the age having to boast only such scandalous *romans à clef* as Mrs. Manley's[1] *The History of Queen Zarah and the Zarazians* (1705) directed against the Marlborough faction, or her more notorious *The New Atalantis* (1709), into which the former work was absorbed, and for which she and the printers were arrested for libels on the Whigs. Assume a moral pose she did, as well as inveigh against the 'vice' of reading romances; but the attraction she held out to readers was the amusement of scandal about great figures spiced with the pleasures of pornography. This poor successor of Mrs. Behn, in her last book, *The Power of Love* (1720), did little more than retell stories from Bandello, via Painter's *Palace of Pleasure.* Except as an example of contemporary gossip her fiction may well remain unread, as may that of her successor, Mrs. Haywood,[2] at any rate in such works as *Love in Excess* (1719-20) and *Lasselia* (1723), somewhat unoriginal novels of female passion and misfortune; but again her *romans à clef, Memoirs of a Certain Island Adjacent to the Kingdom of Utopia* (1725-6) and *The Secret History of the Present Intrigues of the Court of Caramania* (1727), have a certain historical interest. Both authoresses have the liveliness of the skilled journalist, and a paucity of constructional ability disappointing in playwrights as they both were. Mrs. Haywood, however, following the lead of Mrs. Hearne, made tentative efforts at epistolary fiction; and her later works, written after she had studied Defoe and Richardson, namely *Betty Thoughtless* (1751) and *Jemmy and Jenny Jessamy* (1753), may, with a certain optimism, be said to look forward to *Evelina*, though there is no proof that Fanny Burney had read them. They are worth consideration, and will be touched upon in the next volume. Both these writers figure to some extent in literary history; Mrs. Manley from her connexion with Swift; while Mrs. Haywood, whom Swift called 'a stupid, scribbling, infamous woman', though she deserves only the second epithet, may be the Sappho in Steele's *Tatler* 23, as she certainly is the prize offered the manly contestants in Book II of *The Dunciad*, her reward for having fleered at Martha Blount in *Memoirs of a Certain Island*. Both, largely influenced by French fiction, fundamentally merely worked out variants of the Portuguese

---

[1] Mrs. Mary de la Rivière Manley, 1663–1724, wrote many *Examiners*, and two tragedies.
[2] Mrs. Elizabeth Haywood, 1690?–1756, wrote *The Female Spectator*, 1744–6.

Nun range of emotions, without achieving any individualiza-
tion, or attempting even Mrs. Behn's timid realism.

If their works, and those of some half-dozen other women
novelists, such as Mrs. Aubin, may be considered the 'romances'
of the period, the picaresque strain is represented by the many
rogue-histories, chiefly of notorious criminals, a highly popular
form of literature to which Defoe himself contributed accounts
of Jack Sheppard (1724) and Jonathan Wild (1725). These go
back to Nashe's *The Unfortunate Traveller* and the cony-catching
pamphlets, the form degenerating throughout the seventeenth
century with tales of vagabonds, highwaymen, and cheats of
both sexes, the type being Head's *The English Rogue* (Merriton
Latroon, 1665), which was developed in a series by Kirkman,
whose *The Unlucky Citizen* . . . (1673) was a supposed autobiography, all these works being reprinted in our period, the
English Rogue tradition persisting until its *Jeremy Sharp* avatar
in 1776. These, together with chap-books and broadsheets
luridly presenting accounts of executed criminals, had a tremendous vogue in Defoe's day, for the same perennial reasons
that cause delight to the devourers of certain Sunday papers in
our own era. But the nearest approach to Defoe's kind of realism
is to be found in Deloney's *Jack of Newbury*, and other tales.

Kirkman also contributed to the flow of imaginary voyages,
partly by way of parody, bringing out in 1673 *The Floating
Island*, to be followed the next year by *The Western Wonder*.
These were as much read as the actual voyages of Wafer,
Dampier, Woodes Rogers and others, if not more, the eagerness
with which all these were seized upon being a sign of the
vigorous and expansive temper of the age. Thus in choosing his
forms to write in, Defoe was catering for, one might even say
pandering to, 'the class that read *Mist's Journal*', as Professor
Sutherland says; 'the small shopkeepers and artisans, the
publicans, the footmen and servant wenches, the soldiers and
sailors, those who could read but had neither the time nor the
inclination to read very much', except, one would add, what
was easy to read and seemed to be about themselves, or events
they might be caught up in.

And always and everywhere, relying as he did on a public
that was largely dissenting, and by tradition, if nothing more,
puritanical, he was at great pains to assert the actuality of
what he wrote; he was, he would claim, simply reporting fact,

otherwise his stories would remain widely unread, and therefore little sold. And in a sense he did deal with fact, palpably so in his plague works, his military memoirs, and his voyage novels —the tabulation of his sources is enough to prove that; even his female rogue novels, for which the sources have not been much traced, were probably spun out of stories which he obtained, as did Moll Flanders, from 'long conversation with crime and with criminals ... while ... a prisoner in Newgate'. The occult episodes themselves, as when the Devil incites Moll to theft, and she says that ''twas like a voice spoke to me over my shoulder, "Take the bundle; be quick; do it this moment"'', or when her Lancashire husband heard her voice calling to him when he was twelve miles away, were for Defoe possible, not to say frequent, and therefore real occurrences, such as the one he had 'recorded' in *The Family Instructor*. He himself had heard voices, supposing 'A Vision of the Angelic World' to be in part autobiographical. There we learn that in 1715, when he was threatened with disaster on account of his libel against the Earl of Anglesey, and was in hiding, a voice imperatively told him day after day 'Write to the Judge'. It would seem that his constructive imagination was so burning that it fused fiction and fact together; one might suppose that he came to the state of not knowing what was fact, what fiction. If he always seems at pains to impress the reader that what he is telling is true, that may well be. because, to his mind, he had invented nothing; intensely interested in everything that happened, he was anxious only that the reader should share the interest. Defoe, then, we may say, dealt entirely with fact.

That all the same we relish his books may appear to some as a national limitation. In the first of his *Nuits d'Octobre*, Gérard de Nerval remarks:

> Qu'ils sont heureux, les Anglais, de pouvoir écrire et lire des chapitres d'observation dénués de tout alliage d'invention romanesque! ... L'intelligence réaliste de nos voisins se contente du vrai absolu.

But to attain the degree of *intelligence réaliste* that Defoe did is no mean achievement; it argues an intensity of what might be called realizing imagination that is very rare indeed, that one might risk even calling unique. With him, it would seem, the primary imagination, 'the living power and prime agent of all human perception' (to use Coleridge's phrase), from which we create objects out of our sense-impressions, was so acute in him as to make the observation itself a 'romantic' invention. Usually without imagery, though he can use imagery when he likes, he invests the simplest thing with a reality which gives it a significant dimension. Virginia Woolf put the point admirably in her discussion of *Robinson Crusoe*:

... Defoe, by re-iterating that nothing but a plain earthenware pot stands in the foreground, persuades us to see remote islands and the solitude of the human soul. By believing fixedly in the solidity of the pot and its earthiness, he has subdued every element to his design; he has roped the whole universe into harmony.

This is one of the characteristics that makes his 'great' works something essentially different from the tales of travel and roguery that poured out so profusely from others besides himself during the period. What matters to us, then, is not that Defoe dealt entirely with fact, but what he did with fact.

Perhaps, however, his seminal innovation was taking for his main characters quite ordinary persons, so that we can say, 'There, but for the grace of God, go I.' Similar claims have been made for previous works, such as Kirkman's *The Counterfeit Lady*, based on the life of Mary Carleton; but she is really no more than the vehicle which carries the tale of the old picaresque novel, though Kirkman's intention was serious. None of Defoe's people, naturally, has the faintest link with the idealized hero or heroine of the romance, but none of them is wholly amoral or irresponsible. The most virtuous of them would seem to be 'poor, wild, wicked Robinson Crusoe', as he is termed in Part III, but even the worst of them have generous impulses and feelings of compassion. And their brilliant actuality is achieved—and this we may think is where Defoe most indubitably reveals his genius—because he identified himself with his chief characters as had never before been done in fiction, to such a degree as almost to offset the great defect of the autobiographical method, the impossibility of seeing people, or of interpreting events, from the outside. Defoe can convince us because, even more certainly than Flaubert could say, *Madame Bovary, c'est moi*, he could have said, 'I am Moll Flanders.'

He did indeed say that he was Robinson Crusoe, in the Preface to *The Serious Reflections*, though the conjecture that he was taking up an attitude to defend his veracity against the shrewd doubts Gildon expressed in his *The Strange and Surprising Adventures of Daniel Defoe* is not unplausible. That his life 'chimes part for part and step for step with the inimitable life of Robinson Crusoe' is to carry allegorical correspondence too far; but there is this in common between the two—they both lived in isolation, as did so many other of Defoe's creations, a point which need not further be insisted upon. Thus having himself been so often thrown on his own resources enabled him to enter into the being of lonely, unsupported persons, so that he could envisage their actions in the smallest detail. 'He understands plain practical people', as Professor McKillop says, 'and is endowed with remarkable insight into primitive minds—the child, the savage, the poor and ignorant servant'. He seems to have said to himself, 'Now, this being the situation, what exactly should I do?' So when Moll Flanders robs the child in Bartholomew Close we are told what streets she went through as she slipped off; in the same way, when young Colonel Jacque picks a pocket, we know by what twisted route he made his getaway, scouring 'down Bartholomew Lane, so into Tokenhouse Yard, into the alleys which pass through from thence to London Wall, so through Moorgate, and sat down on the grass in the second of the quarters of Moorfields'. To produce a sense of verisimilitude? Not a bit of it. Because it was true.

And so the characters emerge. Just as all the time Defoe seems to be saying to himself, 'What happened? What did they do? How did they manage?', so he seems to wonder, 'What was it like to be that person? What sort of thoughts would occur to him or her?' In a sense complying with the condition that justifies the autobiographical method, he becomes that person, his or her mind open to all the little breezes of impulse, the contradictions, the vagaries of temper that make up the bundle that we call the personality. It is this that makes them so enchanting; they surprise—but then you feel that the stroke is absolutely right. Take, for example, the famous moment when Crusoe discovers the hoard of coin on the wreck:

I smil'd to my self at the Sight of this Money, O Drug! Said I aloud, what art thou good for, Thou art not worth to me, no, not the taking off of the ground, one of those Knives is worth all this Heap, I have no Manner of use for thee, e'en remain where thou art, and go to the Bottom as a Creature whose Life is not worth saving. However, upon Second Thoughts, I took it away, and wrapping all this in a Piece of Canvas, I began to think of making another Raft. . . .

The implications, especially through the lack of emphasis which Coleridge so much admired, are tremendous; the 'second thoughts' suggest the whole of the structure of the society Crusoe had been formed by. They are, by their very vagueness, just what a man so circumstanced would 'think'. Such vagueness indeed is part of the delineation of character; it gives just that little extra touch which again makes the person like one of ourselves, as when he makes Roxana say:

The Horse-Guards, or what they call them there, the *Gensd'arms*, had upon some Occasion, been either upon Duty, or been Review'd, or something (I did not understand that Part) was the Matter, that occasion'd their being there, I know not what; . . .

giving all that air of casualness about indifferent things which is common to most of us; the indifference also being that of the feminine mind relating matters which are the province of men, and that she is not expected to understand. That kind of verisimilitude which makes the reader willingly suspend his disbelief was something entirely new in perspective.

In reading through Defoe's 'fiction' it becomes clear that his main personages are built upon one model; they are outside the general structure of society; they are none of them fools; and beyond that they share a characteristic which seems to be peculiar to Defoe's idea of life. It was manifest to him that there is in man an intractable impulse, an irresistible itch to go on that no preaching can tame, a tireless daemon driving him to hazards and disaster. Defoe seems to be in some doubt whether this is a virtue or a moral defect, though, to be sure, his characters assign their misfortunes to it. So Crusoe: 'But that I was born to be my own Destroyer, cou'd no more resist the Offer than I could restrain my own rambling Designs'; and though early in his tale he informs us that it was his ill fate that pushed him on with an obstinacy that nothing could resist, in Part II he admits his own responsibility, with '. . . I who had no more Business to go to the *East Indies* than a Man at full Liberty, and having committed no Crime, has to go to the Turnkey at *Newgate*, and desire him to lock him up among the Prisoners there and starve him'. Moll Flanders more than once confesses that she might have 'left off' her evil ways, but 'cou'd not forbear going abroad again' to steal. If Roxana was not under quite the same compulsion, Jacque, more sober than most, when he in turn felt that 'Now was my time to have sat still', was goaded from within to a further trading venture that cost him a long period in exile. What then is it that rescues these people from the utmost consequences of their surrender to impulse? Not their mother-wit, but Providence, again and again given credit as prime agent of salvation. So well is this exhibited, it could be said of all the novels that, in common with *Robinson Crusoe*—as accounted for in Part III—they were in essence meant 'to convince us of the great Superintendency of Divine Providence in the minutest Affairs of this World'. How far Defoe felt that ill-controlled impulse was his own destructive principle it is impossible to say. There is much in his life to support the suggestion. That his sense of Providence derived from his schooling under Morton seems likely; at all events the combination constitutes his overriding vision of the human condition, a vision which gives his work an altogether deeper scope than any previous realistic fiction.

All his tales are 'success stories', though in a limited field; his heroes and heroines all make good, indeed reach affluence, in the end, after tottering at the edge of the abyss, the exception being Roxana, whose career he never finished, perhaps feeling it impossible to extricate her with any sense of justice. They might even be called stories of successful crime, and so at least the tale of 'blessed Mary Flanders' was considered to be by Borrow's old apple-woman on London Bridge. But the success is obtained at the price of a reformed life, accompanied by repentance, this last being the feature that places these works in the category of conduct-books. It is easy enough to be cynical about this; there is, so to speak, no sense in not repenting if you can still cling to your none-too-well-gotten gains. Singleton, it is true, to some extent expiated his crimes by endowing a poor woman, his friend William's admirable sister; Moll and Jacque sit back comfortably enough to consider their sins. But then, as Defoe saw it, it is not innate wickedness but sheer necessity that drives people to malefaction. 'Would you not rob, would you not become a whore if you were starving?' he seems all the time to be asking. Jacque's pedagogue in the Plantations has always in his mind '*Solomon* or *Agar's* Prayer, "Give me not

Poverty, lest I steal".' You can repent only if you have the leisure—'Here, I say, I had leisure to repent', Jacque tells us more than once—and the security, to contemplate God. Moreover, Defoe is always careful to distinguish between real repentance and mere fear of your sins finding you out, or even panic at the idea of divine retribution, the first being attained only after the preliminary stages of fear of various kinds. The passages in which Roxana is in agony about her sins are the tensest part of *The Fortunate Mistress*; she could not enjoy her fortune; there was a dart stuck into her liver, there was a secret hell within; when it thundered she expected the next flash would penetrate her vitals, and so on; she began to look back on her former life 'with that Horror, and that Detestation, which is the certain Companion, if not the Fore-runner of Repentance'. So also with Captain Singleton when he begins to think about his past:

My Soul was all Amazement and Surprize; I thought my self just sinking into Eternity, owing to the divine Justice of my Punishment, but not at all feeling any of the moving, softening Tokens of a sincere penitent, afflicted at the Punishment, but not at the Crime, alarmed at the Vengeance, but not terrify'd at the Guilt, having the same Gust to the Crime, tho' terrify'd to the last Degree at the Thought of the Punishment, which I concluded I was just now going to receive.

Those then are the props supporting the philosophic structure of the novels, which vary enormously one from the other in emphasis.

The great masterpieces are *Robinson Crusoe* and *Moll Flanders*, with close behind them *Captain Singleton*. Both *The Fortunate Mistress* and *Colonel Jacque* have their moments of creative depth, but they are not so consistent within themselves, while *A Journal of the Plague Year* fits into a different category, that rather of the military memoirs than of imaginative fiction. It is the first two that are of importance in the history of the development of the novel, not so much in that they directly influenced the works of Richardson and Fielding, as that they helped to create an atmosphere in which these were possible. One reason among others would seem to be that he managed, by suggestion rather than by direct statement, to endue those works with some philosophic significance, or at least induce in the reader an imaginative state where philosophic contemplation is possible. Recourse may again be had to Virginia Woolf. The idea of a desert island, she says, leads you to expect romantic scenery, the sun rising and setting, man brooding in solitude upon man. She goes on:

We read; and we are rudely contradicted on every page. There are no sunsets and no sunrises; there is no solitude and no soul. There is, on the contrary, staring us full in the face, nothing but a large earthenware pot. . . . And is there any reason, we ask as we shut the book, why the perspective that a plain earthenware pot exacts, should not satisfy us as completely, once we grasp it, as man himself, in all his sublimity standing against a background of broken mountains and tumbling oceans with stars flaming in the sky?

Whether or not you grasp the perspective depends upon from where you look at the pot; for us, still hankering after the heady stimulus the Romantics provide, it is not easy to reach the right place.

On the face of it, *The Life and Strange Surprizing Adventures of Robinson Crusoe, of York, Mariner,* is a popular voyage-adventure tale, at once so eagerly devoured that after publication in book form it ran as a serial from October 1719 to October 1720 in the *Original London Post, or Heathcote's Intelligence* (Nos. 125–289). Though its immediate origin was the account of the discovery of Selkirk in Woodes Rogers's voyage, followed up by Steele in No. 26 of the *Englishman,* the frillings, in innumerable detail, were derived not only from an enormous quantity of travel-books, but also from such other mines as one of the several translations from the Arabic of the Life of Hai Ebn Yokdan, a castaway from youth. To cover the ground here would take inordinate space, and the reader must be referred to such scholars of sources as Professors A. W. Secord, J. R. Moore, and E. A. Baker. It was, then, edited reportage of strange and surprising adventures such as the child in man is always enticed with, made edifying for the pious-minded sections of the public by interspersed moralizings.

Borrow was largely justified in saying of *Robinson Crusoe* that it is

a book which has exerted over the minds of Englishmen an influence certainly greater than any other of modern times, which has been in most people's hands, and with the contents of which even those who cannot read are to a certain extent acquainted.

It has become so much part of European literature that it is

accepted as a myth. But of what? Too much has been made of
it as a myth embodying the ideals of the successful bourgeois, the
materialistic puritanical business man, in this way even becoming, if only by implication, a criticism of the emerging
capitalist-credit society, to adopt the all too familiar jargon of
our day. It is, in truth, the myth of Man surviving in an indifferent universe, or of man struggling against circumstance,
pitting himself alone against odds, even if, as with Crusoe,
they were considerably softened. It is the eternal book for
children and adolescents, and for the child that persists in the
grown man. Yet it is as a memory rather than a present thing;
for ask most men or women whether they have read the book
since their childhood—then no doubt in a juvenile version—and
they will probably answer, No. Some will add that they believe
it to be made tedious by moralistic passages.

But though it is the fascinating book of our childhood, it
may also fascinate us in our maturity, if read attentively, so as
not to miss the little suggestions, leading to broad implications,
that Defoe continually offers. Only so can we savour the seemingly artless irony which he infuses into his story, with a sly-
ness, we may think, designed to cheat the eye of the puritanical
inquisitor. Defoe must always be read attentively if the whole
harvest of his peculiar mind is to be reaped. Here, ostensibly,
we have the daily doings and thoughts of a respectable, God-
fearing business man, earning prosperity by virtue of his industry and his observance of the Sabbath. Ordinary enough, no
doubt; the prototype of such books as the now unread *Self-
Help* of Samuel Smiles; but how deftly the major, unacknow-
ledged preoccupation is suggested, as when, not to multiply
examples, Crusoe happens upon the money in the wreck. One
of the constant pleasures in reading Defoe is to catch the irony
(whether intentional or not) so easily missed, or a criticism
almost Swiftian in its devastating completeness, both so carelessly hidden away, it would seem, that did such things not
occur so often they might be thought accidental. There are
dozens of instances; as where Crusoe prays for the first time,
and at once gets drunk on rum-impregnated tobacco; or
where, finding himself able to strut about under an umbrella,
he thanks Providence for its goodness.

Yet—and yet! After all, those are hazards, and we have no
right to accuse Defoe of lacking a sense of humane humour.

Crusoe is blamed for being materialistic; who, we may ask, would not be in those circumstances? For the part of the book that is still vibrantly alive is that where Crusoe is the castaway; the trading aspect we ignore. It is sometimes suggested that the moralistic reflections that punctuate the matter-of-factness merely confirm a meaningless puritan habit. Apart from that being nonsense, without the religious aspect the novel would lack scale, and Crusoe would be two-dimensional. It may be that the book remains, as remain it does, because all the time we are saying to ourselves—as Defoe did to himself: 'What would I do if . . . ? How does one make this thing?' or even 'What mistakes might I make?' as when Crusoe builds his canoe, and then finds he has made it so far from the sea that he is unable to launch it. It is all extremely vivid, actual. For the first time in a book of this sort the writer was not only telling about the adventure, as happening to himself or to somebody else, but seeming to write as he was experiencing the events, and so making the reader experience them too. But without the anxieties, the fears, the religious anguish, and the passionate prayers accompanying the physical activities, the story would be, literally, spiritless.

To ask how *Robinson Crusoe* can be a novel, such as we understand by the word, is to raise an awkward question, if, as will perhaps be granted, the novel is the literary form in which society views itself, of which the material is man living in society, the drama being brought about by the struggle of the individual impelled by desires and ideals against other people and, perhaps in turn, their ideals. Out of this struggle of man to fit himself into society, some philosophy, some vision of human kind has to emerge. But here we have the story of a man abstracted from society, a tale of solitude, of absolute solitude, not of being an 'outsider' within society as with Defoe's other eponymous heroes. How then is it a novel at all? The answer may possibly be found in Rousseau, the first to see in it a philosophic as opposed to an adventure story; it was the only book, we may remember, that Émile was to be allowed to read. He admits that to dwell alone on a desert island is not the state of social man, nor is it likely, he adds disarmingly, to be Émile's lot:

mais c'est sur ce même état qu'il doit apprécier tous les autres. Le plus sur moyen de s'élever au-dessus les préjugés, et d'ordonner ses

jugements sur les vrais rapports des choses, est de se mettre à la place
d'un homme isolé, et de juger tout comme cet homme en doit juger
lui même, eu égard à sa propre utilité.

And there is no doubt that the interest wanes after the rescue
of Robinson Crusoe; the latter portion of Part I and the whole
of Part II, *The Farther Adventures of Robinson Crusoe*, fall into the
adventure story category. That all this is brilliantly done in its
kind is undeniable; it is picturesque, full of varied incident, it
throws sidelights on the knowledge and the interests—particularly the trading interests—of the time. It is, you might say,
good Defoe, the imaginative travelogue at its best, since Defoe
makes creative use of his many sources, vivifying them, sometimes imparting colour and life to a dull description by the
addition of an adjective. It is, however, no more than agreeable casual reading, since Defoe does not 'live' this Crusoe, and
indeed there would be little point in his doing so. Part III, the
Serious Reflections. . ., the *Crusoe* that nobody reads, would more
fittingly be classed with his moralistic and pseudo-philosophic
works. But here he is at his deepest, his most thoughtful, and the
volume may serve to illustrate the average meditations of the
well-educated Dissenter who is also a man of the world and
of varied personal experience. As earlier quotations will have
shown, it is written without the sense of hurry we often find in
Defoe, and is free of the breathlessness which is characteristic
of much that he wrote. After the brief attempt to maintain that
the story of Robinson Crusoe is an allegorical autobiography, the
hero is hardly remembered in the extended essays of which
the book is composed. The last part, 'A Vision of the Angelik
World', might be regarded as a profession of faith uttered by a
man who refuses to be dazzled into Deism by the scientific
discoveries of his age; conscious as he is of the glory of the
physical universe, for him the centre of creation is still the man-
inhabited world. The portion dealing with spirits is his most controlled, not to say most sceptical, statement of his beliefs in that
realm, discoursing as he does with due safeguards of the Devil,
and of the 'converse of spirits' from which come strong intima-
tions, intuitions, and warnings, as well as impulses to evil. It is
by no means in the ruck of writings of that kind, though it does
not rise very far above it, and it cannot be ignored in the totality
of Defoe's work, nor as a gloss on the novel, since it enables us a
little better to grasp the perspective of the earthenware pot.

The desert island portion of the work is undoubtedly a great, one would say, achievement, if it were certain that Defoe was conscious of what he was accomplishing; at all events it is greatly inspired. But if this is a book which lives by its reputation rather than through its continuing readers, that is not the case with his superb picaresque, rather than adventure, book, *The Fortunes and Misfortunes of the Famous Moll Flanders,* the full title—which Professor Trent found unprintable—running on, 'who was born in Newgate, and during a life of continu'd variety for three-score years, besides her childhood, was twelve years a whore, five times a wife (whereof once to her own brother), twelve years a thief, eight years a transported felon in Virginia, at last grew rich, liv'd honest, and died a penitent, written from her own memorandums'. The title, naturally, would be attractive to the all too common reader, but though it may have corrupted the morals of the young—it was conned by Hogarth's idle apprentice—it is not what we would today regard as an erotic book. As Professor McKillop remarks, Moll Flanders

is after all concerned with the social and economic conditions for sexual union. She is too business-like to be either demure or lascivious, and she is so consistently on the make that she imposes strict limits on the range of Defoe's compilation.

Though that is not quite true—no generalization about Defoe is that—it is true enough to clear the book from the stigma of its title.

Here we have the unvarnished (auto-)biography of a person anyone might meet in the street. Moll Flanders is a creature entirely realized; and not only is this wicked, jolly, imperfectly repentant old woman completely alive, she is, we feel, essentially good, or at least kindly, with real qualms at some of her actions. Though to a certain degree impelled to her misdemeanours by the pressures of society around her, it is a mistake to regard her as merely a victim of these, though it may be going too far to agree with Professor Legouis that she was at heart a whore; if not lascivious, she feels no distressed reluctance. She excuses herself too easily, as when she gives her reasons for making herself out to be 'a fortune' so as to get a well-to-do husband:

This Knowledge I soon learnt by Experience (*viz*) that the State of things was altered, as to Matrimony . . . that Marriages were the Consequence of politick Schemes for forming Interests, and carr[y]-ing on Business, and that LOVE had no Share, or but very little in the Matter.

The disquisition—one of Defoe's pronouncements on marriage —proceeds for some time, followed by some very good advice on why and how women should maintain their dignity, dictated to Moll by Defoe, the advocate of women's rights. She moralizes from time to time, of course, but in the main she carries on the tale in what we are persuaded was her own language, though Defoe admits that he, to use our term, bowdlerized it.

Thus we follow her happily through her matrimonial or unsanctified adventures, her innocently contracted incestuous union, her career as pickpocket and thief, her transportation and return; ill luck, till near the very end, seems always to dog her steps. But then she is urged by the fatal, uncontrolled impulse we have already noted, which runs counter to the Christian virtue of prudence. Her enjoyment of success, her odd sense of glory, her ineffectual fits of remorse, her shrewd comment, her immense talent for lying offset by her rare genius for telling the truth (in these last she is like Defoe himself), what we might call her veracious unveracity, endear the sinful old creature to us, though we may not like the young woman so much. And in all this Defoe's personal experience, his journalistic flair, his imaginative capacity for piercing beneath the skin of other people, combine to make the writing creative. He knew all about Moll Flanders and her kind. Had he not lived five months in Newgate? Had he not himself experienced the pangs of the jail-bird, and been able to study the inmost nature of these derelicts, and ever since been close up against the rapscallion elements of the population?

He makes this scandalous criminal so entrancing largely because he endows her with supreme honesty *for the moment*. She lied in life, but she never lies to herself, nor to us. Take the scene where all her maternal instincts swell up in a passionate lament of thwarted motherhood, when she sees her own and her brother's son after a lapse of many years, but is not permitted to disclose herself.

It was a wretched thing for a Mother thus to see her own Son, a handsome comely young Gentleman in flourishing Circumstances,

and durst not make herself known to him; and durst not take any
notice of him; let any Mother of Children that reads this, consider
it, and but think with what anguish of Mind I restrain'd myself;
what yearnings of Soul I had in me to embrace him, and weep over
him; and how I thought all my Entrails turn'd within me, that my
very Bowels mov'd, and I knew not what to do; as I now know not
how to express those Agonies . . . I made as if I lay down to rest
me, . . . and lying on my Face wept, and kiss'd the Ground he had
set his Foot on.

She hadn't given this son a thought for over twenty years, had
abandoned, we forget as we read how many other children to
be left more or less as waifs and strays; yet we know that at this
meeting she felt as she says; there is no make-believe—though
whether she would have felt differently had he not been handsome, comely, and in flourishing circumstances is another
matter. At all events her instinct rises above experience, cancels
experience. What she tells us she felt at any given instant we
know she did feel; what she says of herself is true *for the moment*.
In fact Defoe's great feat in this work is the unconscious self-
revelation of his heroine. At the end, for example, when she is
parting from that son to whom she had in due course explained
their relationship, and presents him with a gold watch:

I told him, I had nothing of any value to bestow but that, and I
desir'd he would now and then kiss it for my sake; *I did not indeed tell
him* that I had stole it from a Gentlewomans side, at a Meeting-
House in *London*, that's by the way.

Half the character is compressed into that last careless phrase;
the acceptance of things as they are, putting the best face on
them, making do. Defoe, of course, leaves you to make the
comment for yourself; though he does peach on her about the
conclusion. Moll's last sentence informs us that she and her
husband resolve to spend the remainder of their years in sincere penitence for the wicked lives they had lived; but to get
Defoe's comment we have to go back to the end of his Preface:
'. . . she liv'd it seems, to be very old; but was not so extraordinary a Penitent, as she was at first; it seems only that indeed
she always spoke with abhorence of her former Life, and of
every Part of it.' It could hardly be more subtly done; but the
reader has to be alert. How much conscious irony there is in the
book it is impossible to say; we can feel it so long as we keep
outside Moll herself. Dr. Ian Watt perhaps sums it up when he

remarks: '*Moll Flanders* is undoubtedly an ironic object; but it is not a work of irony.'

No doubt Defoe, with one part of his mind, designed Moll Flanders for a warning, and regarded the book as a blow struck in the battle for the reformation of manners. The moral that he had in view at the beginning may have been that which he emphasizes in *Colonel Jacque*, an admonition to society to look after the upbringing of the young, especially those born in unlucky circumstances: Moll was born in Newgate, Jacque was a cast-off bastard. Singleton also was a waif. But whatever the case may have been, as he worked, scribbling away at unbelievable speed and, warmed by the rapidity of the motion, fusing himself with the character, something other than the moralist took charge—the creative faculty; some glow other than that of moral virtue suffused him, that of the artist rejoicing in his work. Be that as it may, *Moll Flanders*, besides being a book of inexhaustible delight, is one of first-rate importance. For there is nothing extravagant in the claim, if not pressed too far, that it marks the birth of the modern novel, if, as suggested, the peculiar mark of the novel as an art form distinct from other literary forms is that it shows the interplay of the individual and society. Previously the picaresque novel had born little relation to *common* experience, not much more, to say truth, than the romance, which had been deliberately not of the commonplace world. But here is the story of an ordinary person in the workaday world. Kirkman, it is true, had taken Mary Carleton for his *Counterfeit Lady*; but even if Defoe had based Moll Flanders on Laetitia Atkins, as we are told, the difference is great: both women were outstanding figures in their own scandalous sphere; Defoe, by sympathizing with his heroine, understanding her in a way Kirkman never approaches, keeps her on the ordinary level, gives her 'reality'.

Not of the same coherent quality, nor quite of the same kind, is *The Fortunate Mistress*. . . . *Being the Person known as The Lady Roxana*. This is not to say that it fails to be readable, even now, or that it is not dotted with good things, with delicious *aperçus*, with picturesque—and once at least with distasteful—detail, with strokes of character-drawing, and, it goes without saying, pithy and not so pithy moralizings. It is different, not only that here Defoe moves in unfamiliar higher spheres, but because it has about it a slight flavour of the erotic, and also of real tenderness. It is more complex, because besides the main figure of Roxana we have the confidante, Amy, who plays no mean part, and the more subtle Quakeress. Roxana does not simply struggle for survival, for ample security, as Crusoe and Moll Flanders do; she is not so much the victim of the itch to go on as the person with worldly ambition. It was Defoe's last attempt at novelistic fiction, and had he been able to carry it through, it might have constituted another forward step in the art; but he abandoned it, feeling perhaps that he was faced with a technical problem, as well as a moral one, that he could not solve, or had not the leisure to attempt.

Moreover, the Quakeress is not an 'ordinary' person, of the everyday kind. Defoe seems to have been fascinated by Quakers, possibly from a certain ambiguity he found in their attitude; he may have pondered the Quaker nature in that very complex figure, William Penn—Quaker, courtier, pioneer, and colonizer —who had earlier tried to save him from the pillory, and had only recently died. Such a character is lightly touched upon in *Moll Flanders*, but it is in *The Life, Adventures, and Piracies of the Famous Captain Singleton* that we get the most convincing as well as the most attractive portrait. Such a character was not altogether new in the popular literature of the period; there is even one in the memoirs of Captain Avery. But Singleton's friend, adviser, and in the end moral saviour, William Walters, is so delightful in himself, so vivid, that he lives on a different plane of actuality from the others. The book, however, is remarkable because, partly with William's help, it is the first adventure novel as opposed to the adventure story. True, it is an 'imaginary voyage', though drawn from many sources including *Captain Avery*, doing no more than giving depth, colour, detail to travellers' tales, as when he recounts the attack of the wild beasts in central Africa, describing how '. . . there was a Noise and Yelling, and Howling, and all sort of such Wilderness Musick on every Side of us, as if all the Beasts of the Desart were assembled to devour us'. Colour and incident abound, besides the Crusoe-like detail of doings, which alone make the book extremely interesting, so much being based on fact. There are, for example, the discovery of the Englishman, stark naked, who had been for some years living among the savages; the rescue of the Dutchman from the Malabars, a variant of the story of Captain Robert Knox and his son; such things happily diversify the accounts of the piracies. But all the while, giving the book its unity, there is William, pious, prudent, refusing actually to fight, but giving advice as a first-rate staff officer; worldly-wise, yet somehow retaining his Quaker integrity. Though he never takes up arms, he evidently feels no little zest in the piratical business, and has no notion of physical fear. He is, moreover, a man of action, and deals in no weak manner with Singleton when the latter suffers a nervous breakdown near the end of the book. With him Defoe, though not completely successful creatively, is a good psychologist, and the reader can wholly believe in him. Yet he will not 'feel' him as he does Moll Flanders; he is known, however piercingly, only from outside, not from within.

Still less will the reader share the being of the eponymous hero of *The History and Remarkable Life of the Truly Honourable Colonel Jacque, Commonly Call'd Col. Jack*, who aspired to die a general (in which ambition he was balked), although he had begun life as a pickpocket, without a thought that such a habit had anything wrong in it; it was merely one of the ways in which a man made his living. The first part is admirable as a thoroughly live account of *choses vues* at the pulsating heart of a certain level of London existence, of the boys especially who slept in the warm ashes of the glass factories, a reminiscence this, surely, of the time when Defoe was their inspector under William III. As a memorable passage the one may be cited in which a constable and his watch are seeking out a malefactor, who, they have been told, was to be found among the beggar-boys under the nealing arches in the glass-house.

The alarm being given, we were awaken'd in the Dead of Night with *Come out here*, ye Crew of young Devils, come out and show yourselves; so we were all produc'd, some came out rubbing their Eyes, and scratching their Heads, and others were dragg'd out; and I think there was about Seventeen of us in all, but *Wry-neck*, as they call'd him, was not among them.

The book, certainly, carries forward the narrative by means of conversation more than any other of Defoe's novels; the psychology of the boy is solidly enough built up to have elicited praise from Charles Lamb; but as we follow the growth in him of the idea of wrongdoing, he may seem a little too innately good. The part where he goes to the wars is Captain Carleton over again; the sea adventures Captain Avery once more, and the interest flags, though here and there the scenes come to life. The *Memoirs of a Cavalier* and *The Military Memoirs of Captain Carleton* will not be discussed here, since readable though they are, they made only a negligible contribution to the development of the novel. They do, however, make some advance in narrative method, to which a high tribute was paid by Sir Winston Churchill when he stated of his history of the First World War, that 'it strives to follow throughout the method and balance of Defoe's *Memoirs of a Cavalier* . . . history strung upon a fairly strong thread of personal reminiscence'. The same general description might be given of *A Journal of the Plague Year*, which might, if such grouping were convenient, be bundled together with the other memoirs, but that it stands in a class apart, and is to be ranked as a masterpiece on the level of the two great novels. And here again because Defoe, not so much from knowledge in the strict sense of the term as from childhood memories of the atmosphere of those terrible days ('I very particularly remember the last visitation of this kind which afflicted this nation in 1665'), could *be* the narrator of the *Journal* in a way that he could not live himself into the Cavalier or Carleton, or, for the matter of that, Singleton, or the mature Jacque; moreover, he could visualize London in all minute, trivial detail, as he could not the Pacific or Mexico. Yet what must have been the preliminary *Due Preparations for the Plague*, though printed later, is not at all the same thing. The process would seem to have been as follows: alarmed, as people were, at the outbreak of the plague in Marseilles in 1721, he wrote, as did others, seasonable warnings coupled with instructions. As the journalistic—and moral—pamphlet grew, in the form of a brother and sister dialogue, and he came to describe certain events, actual or fictitious, of the great plague, he warmed to the work of re-creation; as you read, you feel it becoming ever more a personal experience. Such immersion in the subject, it may safely be guessed, fired his actualizing imagination. What must it have been like to live then? How did people behave; what did they do? He would be some man at that time, and tell the story. So, living into the *persona* of the saddler, he produced his third work of genius, consulting as many documents as he could lay hands on—Bills of Mortality, religious exhortations, possibly private family diaries (his uncle Henry Foe had been a saddler)

—using them with such faithful skill that his account was taken as a genuine record, so well did it tally with ascertainable fact. The great Dr. Mead for some years quoted it as an authority.

At times it is humdrum, at others moving, terrifying, pitiful; it never flags, and can on occasion be starkly dramatic:

> The Watchman had knock'd at the Door, it seems, when he heard that Noise and Crying, as above, and no body answered, a great while: but at last one look'd out and said with an angry quick Tone, and yet a Kind of Crying Voice, or a Voice of one that was crying, 'What d'ye want, that ye make such a knocking?' He answer'd, 'I am the Watchman! How do you do? What is the Matter?' The Person answered, 'What is that to you? Stop the Dead-Cart.' This, it seems, was about one a-Clock; soon after, *as the Fellow said*, he stopped the Dead-Cart, and then knock'd again, but no Body answer'd: He continued knocking, and the Bellman cal'd out several Times, 'Bring out your Dead'; but no Body answered, till the Man that drove the Cart being call'd to other Houses, would stay no longer, and drove away.

There is, besides the inescapable moralizing, a deal of practical advice, or implication, together with some criticism of the policy of shutting up houses. There would not seem to be much need of his tricks—if they were tricks—for assuring the reader of the truth of his statements; but even here, 'in telling some of the more startling of the anecdotes', Aitken pointed out, 'the saddler is careful to say that as regards these matters he is relating what he heard, not what he himself saw, and here and there he hints that he himself feels doubtful whether the incident really occurred'. It is all done with consummate art, till we feel the horror of the whole thing, the delirium, the violence—as when a family blows up the watchman so as to escape from their house; we hear of people being buried alive, of the mockers in taverns, of the religious folk who dared assemble in churches in spite of the risk of crowds. It is in no way subtle, as some of the other works often are. It has no need to be: the starkness is enough.

However seminal these works of Defoe may be granted to be, they are, obviously, only embryonic as 'novels' properly speaking; they lack form. Apart from the rough moral scaffolding, they have hardly any structure: they just start, and go on to the end. Not that there is altogether a want of connexion between events and their consequences; Moll Flanders's marriage with her half-brother is made possible by their mother's life in Newgate; and again, the 'Lancashire husband' to whom she is briefly wedded reappears to tie up the whole story. Moreover, as Dr. Ian Watt remarks:

Although the events described are actually recounted decades after they happened to Crusoe, Moll Flanders, and Roxana, they are set upon a general autobiographical time scale which is presented in some detail. The main events are so narrated as to give the impression of their occurring in the historic present, and the details of these events are depicted through a closer or more discriminated time-dimension than had previously been embodied in narrative.

And Dr. Watt also points out that he is at some pains to particularize place. But there is no structure in the sense of change of speed, no tension, no preparation for a scene followed by that scene; no climax, and therefore no emotional node. Whereas in most novels expectation is aroused as to what will happen as the result of this or that action or decision, with Defoe that particular excitement is wanting, except possibly with Roxana; there the reader does indeed find himself eager to know whether she will be caught by the daughter who pursues her Erinnically in her later years. Again, beyond the common cupidities, remorse, and religious fears, Defoe is not interested in feelings; he hardly glances at the saving impulses of the heart, the affections, or what we have come to call 'the personal relation'; yet here too there are slight indications—in Roxana with her prince, in Moll Flanders's affection for her 'Lancashire husband', in Jacque's taking back of his first wife. His passionate curiosity was directed upon what people did, with all the minute details of how they did it, and to what extent they succeeded; in this the spring of his creative faculty was not unlike Balzac's. And if he was often forgetful, contradictory, careless about leaving loose ends hanging in the air, the pressure is such that in rapid reading these things are no more noticed than, apparently, Defoe noticed them in his hurried writing.

It is, however, untrue to say, as is often said, that he showed no capacity to paint the social scene, or that his novels are devoid of conversation. They abound, indeed, with the latter. The social scene, to be sure, is rather crudely portrayed; Defoe was no frequenter of drawing-rooms, nor was he a Jane Austen;

but by no means lacking in accomplishment is the scene where
the family in which Moll Flanders is a servant are, at table,
discussing her illness, and whether it was love-sickness. A few
interchanges in the middle of the conversation must serve as
illustration.

'I would she was in Love with me', says Robin; 'I'd quickly put
her out of her Pain.'

'What d'ye mean by that Son', says the old Lady, 'How can you
talk so?'

'Why madam', says Robin again, very honestly, 'Do you think I'd
let the poor Girl Die for Love, and of one that is near at hand to be
had too.'

'Fye Brother', says the second Sister, 'how can you talk so? would
you take a Creature that has not a Groat in the World?'

'Prethee Child', says Robin, 'Beauties a Portion, and good-
Humour with it, is a double Portion; I wish thou hadst half her
Stock of both for thy Portion': So there was her Mouth stopp'd.

'I find', says the eldest Sister, 'if *Betty* is not in Love, my Brother is;
I wonder he has not broke his Mind to *Betty*, I warrant she won't say
NO.'

The whole two or three pages gives no dull sense of family
discussion, while in it there appears the first hint of Moll's
character, when she as narrator (at that time she was Betty),
interjects 'So there was her mouth stopp'd.

Defoe's was only a first step in the art, even though the decisive one. As Mrs. Jack remarks with some justice:

Because he has a place in histories of literature which would give
no place to Warwick Deeping, his seriousness has often been mistaken for the seriousness of art. In fact he was one of the first writers to
take upon themselves the task of reinforcing prejudice and prudence
while at the same time offering escape from the burden of reality.
To pass off fiction as fact is not the same thing as to pursue imaginative truth.

Which brings us up sharp against the fact that, however much
the creative genius breaks through, Defoe's fictional works are
the outcrop of his puritan conduct-books. In some ways the
most commonplace, in others the most extravagantly odd figure
among English writers, he was, as Professor Trent put it, 'a
Proteus both in literature and affairs, who when he is viewed
in the totality of his powers and performances, seems to be an
almost titanic genius'. In respect of fiction, he carried the

narrative method to a point it has never surpassed, established the realistic novel, and gave a pointer to the psychological brand. 'He is', Virginia Woolf said, 'of the school of Crabbe and Gissing, and not merely a fellow-pupil in the same place of learning, but its founder and master.' No doubt he would have wished to be remembered as a political thinker, an economist, an inspirer of colonial expansion, and above all, as a moralist; we, however, salute him as an artist.

XII

SWIFT, 1715–1745

I. THE IRISH PATRIOT

SWIFT's world crumbled around him in 1714, and he had retreated to Ireland from Letcombe, a man defeated and dismayed, but two great supports remained; his religion—one may say boldly his religion, not his churchmanship—and his deep affection for Esther Johnson. After a period of profound depression, a real disease of the spirit exhibited in such poems as 'In Sickness', he threw off, with amazing resilience, his feeling of being sent to 'die like a poisoned rat in a hole', and recovered his status with himself as a human being, that is as 'a smart Dean', a friend, a civilized companion in a draggled society. But it was some years before he regained the surplus energy necessary for creative work, for something more urgent, of more universal scope, than the justifications of the fallen ministry with which, in his 'few hours of health and leisure', he had tried to plug the gap in time. He then entered upon a period of literary activity of enormous importance, of an inner quality different from any he had before shown himself capable of; and between the years 1720 and 1729 comes to be revealed, not so much the man of many interests and a brilliant skill in controversial prose and intellectual satire, as the artist whose cause is finally one with that of humanity.

It is a humanizing experience to watch his gradual revival and reintegration. In October 1718 Arbuthnot wrote to him: 'In your last [letter] I think, you desired me to let you alone to enjoy your own spleen', the reference being to some three years back. But now he is making a circle of new friends in Ireland, beginning to correspond more freely with his old ones in England, and playing with poetry, which at first is sardonic and unsanctified. And, although beginning unpromisingly, it is in this decade that we see Swift at his greatest, not as a writer alone, though it is the period of the Drapier, of *Gulliver*, of *A Modest Proposal*, together with much lively verse, but also as a great public figure, a companion who will bring gaiety into any gathering, a whole-hearted friend to his old cronies in

England, whom he at last feels able to visit, and a touchingly devoted lover.

Perhaps it was through the contests within his Chapter that Swift came to feel that he must once more bestir himself in public affairs—'I will own they raise my Passions whenever they come in my way' he confessed to Ford at the end of 1719; and in 1720 he broke his six years' silence, and his vow of 'never medling with Irish Politicks'—so to Ford in 1714—with his warmly indignant *Proposal for the Universal Use of Irish Manufacture*. In this he took up so caustically as to cause legal reactions, the theme he was never altogether to drop, of the injustice done to Ireland by England; nor did he ignore the callous connivance of a good many of the Irish themselves, whose snobbery forbade them to use home-woven cloths. Not that the theme was new to him; it appears in his early letters, it is not wholly absent from his political writings in the reign of Queen Anne. In 1707 he had written *The Story of the Injured Lady*, a prose fable on this very point, which was not, however, published till just after his death, and there is a bitter paragraph in the *Matter concerning the Sacramental Test*. At this time also he began once more to attack his old enemy the moneyed interest, which he 'ever abominated', and by means of squibs now unreadable, and hardly to be understood except by the expert, was instrumental in defeating the proposal to inaugurate a bank in Dublin.

But of most purely literary interest at this period are the two papers to young people (we may have, a little regretfully, to abandon as wholly his a third, the *Advice to a Young Poet*). Both are full of that common sense which to the sentimental may seem harsh, but to the sensitive are delicate because they do not shirk facts, and are addressed to equals; though admonitory, they do not patronize. The *Letter to a Young Gentleman lately entered into Holy Orders* (1721) has the added interest of being Swift's most important pronouncement on style, to be read together with his *Tatler* 230, his *Proposal for Correcting, Improving, and Ascertaining the English Tongue* (1712), and, in a sense, *Polite Conversation* (1738) with its Introduction. For though all the time we feel his solicitude for the young man—it reads as though addressed to an individual and not to an abstraction— the pleasure for us lies in its critical validity. But it is sometimes forgotten that Swift was suggesting rules for a spoken composition, rules which do not necessarily apply to works meant chiefly to be read. He is not pretending to cover style as a whole: 'Proper words in proper Places, makes the true Definition of a Stile.' Yes; 'But', he continues, 'this would require too ample a Disquisition to be now dwelt on.' Proper for what? is the question he does not tackle. He deals only with what is needed for, or spoils, a good effective sermon. Too much stress has been placed on the famous phrase, 'In short, that Simplicity without which no human Performance can arrive to any great Perfection. . .', and too little on his strictures upon 'a flat kind of Phraseology', and 'the Frequency of flat unnecessary Epithets', for baldness is not at all what he was recommending. The *Letter* is interesting from other points of view: Swift's attitude at this stage to religion, which will be discussed with his sermons, and his sense of what was pedantic. Averse as he was from mental gymnastics, with a hatred of false learning and affectation, it is noteworthy that he wishes the young man could have stayed ten years longer at the university so as to acquire further learning, and that he remarks, 'The fear of being thought Pedants hath been of pernicious Consequence to young Divines'. The whole essay is common sense raised to the degree of clarifying wisdom.

And so is the *Letter to a Young Lady on her Marriage* (1723); but here it is tenderness and solicitude for happiness that is the efficient cause of the essay, written in beautifully modulated phrases. It is, as Mr. Herbert Davis says, 'a very charming letter welcoming to the Deanery circle a very young lady, whose parents and husband were alike Swift's particular friends', to wit the Stauntons and John Rochfort of that Gaulston where he passed so many happy days, and of which he wrote such laughing verses. The common sense here is that which sees that a woman must be a companion to her husband, must read, think, be gracious, have a sense of what is fitting. 'The grand Affair of your Life', he tells her, 'will be to gain and preserve the Friendship and Esteem of your Husband . . . but neither Good-nature, nor Virtue, will suffer him to esteem you against his Judgment. . .', and so on. It shows a great respect, not for the generality of her sex, for which he confesses he has little, but for the individual woman. There is just a touch of avuncular playfulness in the authority he assumes, which could excuse what might seem impertinence but actually is a beautiful honesty and a winnowing of experience.

But these domestic interludes, we might call them, in his writing were calm backwaters in his main literary activities of these years, the *Travels*, and the great political battle which brought out all his powers, and which perhaps nourished the *Travels*. To these we shall return, taking now, as the grand example of the struggle of the next few years, the famous writings which smashed the attempt to introduce Wood's halfpence into Ireland.

As a preliminary it is helpful to look at the *Letter to Mr. Pope* dated 10 January 1721, a letter which never reached the poet, and seems to have been meant as a public declaration. It is of first importance as an *apologia*, but is of most interest here as a statement of some of Swift's political principles; his dislike of the party system, his hatred of 'that scheme of politicks, (now about thirty years old) in setting up a monied Interest in opposition to the landed'; his fear of any attack upon freedom, and his respect for law except when it becomes tyrannical. What most aroused his ire was the monstrous tyranny which England at that time exerted over Ireland, by which, as he had said in the pamphlet referred to earlier, using the spider image as he had in *The Battle of the Books*, 'the greatest Part of our *Bowels and Vitals* is extracted, without allowing us the Liberty of *spinning* and *weaving* them'. The occasions of Wood's halfpence fuelled him doubly, for the scheme was not only, as he thought, clearly in the moneyed interest, but was a direct violation of the fundamental liberties of the Irish in that the whole transaction had been launched without the least reference to the inhabitants themselves.

In July 1722, on the assumption that there was a shortage of small coin in Ireland, the English Government granted a mine-owning iron-merchant, William Wood, the right to coin the exaggerated amount of over £100,000 worth of copper. The Irish commissioners of Revenue objected to the patent (suspected moreover to be of benefit to the King's mistress); Parliament, after a gap of eight years, reassembled, and on 28 September 1723 both Houses addressed the King in protest. In December the King promised an inquiry, which opened in London early in April 1724. But by then, in March, there had appeared in Dublin 'A Letter to the *Shop-keepers, Tradesmen, Farmers*, and *Common-People* of IRELAND, Concerning the Brass Half-Pence Coined by Mr. Woods . . . Very Proper to be kept in every FAMILY', by M. B. Drapier (who before very long was universally known to be Swift), which fanned the flame of excitement, and either inaugurated or made effective the boycott of the new coins. In many ways it reads like an amusing squib, for Swift a little gave rein to his two favourite amusements of pushing things to an absurd logical extreme, and of doing sums. Having calculated the actual (not nominal) value of the coins as he makes it out to be; having taken for granted what we know as Gresham's Law that bad money drives out good, by 'exuberant logic' Mr. Quintana calls it, he comes to delightfully fantastic conclusions:

> They say Squire Connolly has *Sixteen Thousand Pounds a Year*; now if he send for his *Rent* to Town, *as it is likely he does*, he must have *Two Hundred and Fifty Horses* to bring up his *Half Year's Rent*, and two or three great *Cellars* in his House for Stowage.

Any lady going out to shop must be 'followed by a Car loaded with Mr. Wood's Money'; a banker will need twelve hundred horses to carry the cash he needs in his bank. The main argument, however, is deadly serious, and goes to show, with solid support from authority, that this money cannot legally be forced on anybody, copper not being a royally sponsored specie; and that if the Irish take it they will be utterly undone. This is rousing enough as far as it goes, but Swift has another shot in his locker—contempt for Wood, appeal to pride, which he stirs up by expressing indignation that Wood's interests should be allowed to count against those of a kingdom. And throughout *The Drapier Letters*, Swift, usually so sparing of adjectives, reiterates them, with all the more force because of their rarity, whenever he mentions Wood. The phrases act as a little goad applied every now and then, lest the stupid cattle he is driving should grow weary by the way. The supreme example of the use of invective of this kind, a beautiful model of how the thing should be done, appears in the second letter, 'To Mr. Harding, the printer':

> First, Observe this little impudent *Hard-Ware-Man* turning into ridicule *the Direful apprehensions of a whole Kingdom*, priding himself as the Cause of them, and daring to prescribe what no King of *England* ever attempted, how far a whole Nation shall be obliged to take his Brass Coin. And he had Reason to insult; for sure there was never an Example in History, of a great Kingdom kept in Awe for above a

Year, in daily Dread of utter Destruction; not by a powerful Invader at the Head of Twenty thousand Men; not by a Plague or a
Famine; not by a tyrannical Prince (for we never had one more
Gracious) or a corrupt Administration; but by one single, diminutive,
insignificant Mechanick.

Having by this superbly rhythmed and pointed paragraph got
such a notion firmly into the heads, or rather hearts, bile, and
liver (or wherever indignation may lie) of his readers, he feels
that in future an occasional reminder will do. In the fourth
letter, where the whole matter is more urgently treated, 'one
obscure Ironmonger' is judged to be enough.

The skill, one may say the final mastery (even with *The
Conduct of the Allies* in mind), can be tasted only by considering
the *Letters* in relation to the movement of events, and taking
them as a whole. We note the change of tone according as the
draper is addressing the shopkeepers, the printer Harding, the
gentry and nobility, for instance the variation in the third
letter, where the debate may be thought to rise above both the
sphere and the capacity to understand of the average tradesman. The *persona* has to be maintained, and he accounts for
his own knowledge as a mere shopkeeper by explaining how he
has obtained the information and the argument from people
whose business it is to know about that sort of thing. But here
the appeal is not to the pocket, but altogether to pride, not to
finance, but to the sense of freedom. If in the progress of the
letter reason and justice are called upon in the calmest of
tones, not far from the beginning is the sort of thunder that
Swift alone of his contemporaries knew how to generate:

Were not the people of *Ireland* born as *free* as those of *England?*
How have they forfeited their Freedom? Is not their *Parliament* as
fair a *Representative* of the *People,* as that of *England?* And hath not
their Privy Council as great, or a greater Share in the Administration of publick Affairs? Are they not subjects of the same King?
Does not the same *Sun* shine over them? And have they not the same
God for their Protector? Am I a *Free-man* in *England,* and do I become
a *Slave* in six Hours by crossing the Channel?

In considering the battle, note must be taken also of his verses—
most of them abominable doggerel—and his private labours, as
for instance his letter to his old acquaintance Lord Carteret,
who was about to occupy the post of Lord Lieutenant, and

whom he warned as to the strength of feeling in the country. Then on the day Carteret landed—26 October—there was published the greatest of all the letters, the one, not to a section, but 'To the Whole People of Ireland'.

Certainly if Carteret needed to be told of the state of feeling, this magnificent polemic so perfectly adjusted in movement would have told him. Professedly a spur to the people to keep up their spirits, it reiterates the political arguments, removes fears as to flouting the royal prerogative, rouses once more the libertarian emotions in treating again of 'dependence', now and again throws little spirts of scorn at the 'obscure iron-monger', and answers the English pamphlets in defence of Wood. Swift is at the top of his form, because he feels that the battle is going well, so that after some strenuous argument he can afford to give a loose to his sense of the ludicrous. Referring to the report that Walpole had been heard to say that he would make the Irish swallow Wood's copper as fire-balls, he takes it all literally, indulges in a trifle of arithmetic, and with delicious solemnity comes to the conclusion that 'considering the *Squeamishness* of some Stomachs, and the *Peevishness* of *Young* Children', fifty thousand operators will be needed, so that 'under Correction of better Judgments, I think the Trouble and Charge of such an Experiment, would exceed the Profit'. He ends up with a sardonic if unjustified allusion to the greatness and integrity of Walpole.

Carteret, unable to ignore the pamphlet, issued edicts for the arrest of the author, with a reward of £300 for information laid against him. The secret was an open one, but officially in-violable, men, women, and children getting by rote the verse from *The Book of Samuel*:

And the people said unto Saul, Shall Jonathan die, who hath wrought this great salvation in Israel? God forbid: as the Lord liveth, there shall not one hair of his head fall to the ground, for he hath wrought with God this day. So the people rescued Jonathan, that he died not.

But they could not prevent the printer from being indicted; whereupon Swift wrote his unequivocal *Seasonable Advice to the Grand-Jury*, who, thus encouraged, refused to commit. The Chief Justice, Whitshed, thereupon (21 November) dissolved the Grand Jury; but Swift countered this move by swiftly

of the very
they were
me effort,
nfute the
nplies. It
injured,
The last-

ple. The
Families
ss upon
ir Feet,
em . . .

ch he

one
ture.
zzle
the
d a
ge-
old
ds.
in
he
a
d

bate in the House of Commons in
hief Justice to dissolve Grand Juries
ry to the law; and the new jury,
y feeling, instead of finding a Bill
denounced Wood's halfpence. Whit-
e Swift the opportunity of addressing a
own ultra-Whig, Lord Molesworth, in
ort for his anti-coinage pamphlets on the
This is quieter, since the situation is less
as effective, being at once a dignified
osition, and a keeping intact of the battle-
ndeed, been another letter, to the Chan-
ton, in which, avowing his authorship, he
fence against the charges of preaching sedi-
arently advised to withdraw this, which he
r paper, a more general attack upon those who
esses of Ireland, in the form of an address to
Parliament; for before this could be published,
ugust 1725, the official news came from England
d been caused to surrender his grant. The victory

to what extent Swift had been instrumental in
about can never be assessed. It is certain that he
ble helpers, as it is clear that the populace gave him
nce, so that for the rest of his life he was the people's
. his personal triumph—for such to a large extent it
ve to his more considered work a resilience it might
e have lacked. It probably affected the final revision of
s *Travels* which he carried out in 1725, and gave a
r sureness to his other political pamphlets, the *Maxims
lled [checked by what happens] in Ireland* (1724?), *The Present
rable State of Ireland*, if it be his, (late 1726?), and *A Short
v of the State of Ireland* (1728).

t is sometimes said that when Swift fought for the Irish he
as thinking only of the English in Ireland, their rights as
nglishmen, their prosperity; and that he cared nothing for the
wild Popish inhabitants'. If this seems to be so, it is only
because the ruling section alone could put up any kind of
political fight. That he felt for the miseries of the Irish wretches
is shown again and again, and it is no argument to say that in
a sermon or two he told the poor that they were themselves

responsible for their miseries. Even supposing some
poorest came to hear him—and most would not sinc
Catholics—how else could he induce them to make s
retain some self-respect? These pamphlets alone c
view, for his protest was far deeper than the view i
was the cry of a man injured because humanity is
outraged because the spirit in man is being denied.
named pamphlet is heavy with unhappiness at seeing

... The miserable Dress, and Dyet, and Dwelling of the Pec
general Desolation in most Parts of the Kingdom. .. The
of Farmers who pay great Rents, living in Filth and Nastin
Butter-milk and Potatoes, without a Shoe or Stocking to the
or a House so convenient as an *English* Hog-sty to receive th

and he cannot, he confesses, continue the irony with wh
set out to write the paper.

But to think of Swift merely as a political writer, o
always pondering human wrongs, is to nurture a false pio
The old Swift has largely returned, the Swift who could d
with his charm and gaiety, be interested in his garden,
Naboth's Vineyard, which cost him so much money to bui
wall around. His letters of the time are full of vigour and la
ness of vision, whether to Pope and Bolingbroke and other
Scriblerians, such as Gay and Arbuthnot, or to his Irish frien
There was life in the Deanery, verbal games with Delany
Dublin, fun at Quilca and Loughgall with the Sheridans and t
Copes, and a couple or so of other houses and families. To get
complete view of Swift the letters of those days must be read; an
the charming, tender, and deeply felt birthday poems to Stella

At this time he made his last two journeys to England, ir
1726 and 1728, to see his friends in the first instance, and then
to plot the clandestine publication of *Gulliver's Travels* and to
edit his *Miscellanies* with Pope; and also, perhaps, to make one
last bid for employment in England. But at any rate, especially
when at Twickenham with Pope, he could forget the politician
(in spite of an interview with Walpole to try to make him
realize the miseries which English injustice was causing in
Ireland) and be the man of letters, the philosopher, the
historian. It was maybe the last gleam of happiness in his
life, but both visits were marred not only by Stella's illness,
but also by his own. He suffered more and more from

giddiness and deafness, and was finding himself to be no fit companion. There is hardly anything more moving in the history of literature than the farewell letters exchanged between himself and Pope, both imbued with so gallant an acceptance of the pessimistic view of life, so deeply affectionate, yet restrained, respectful of personality. The final submission to exile does something to explain the colour of Swift's latest writings.

But before turning to those, it is worth while to look at his sermons, since most of those we possess were probably written during the decade we are considering, and those we know to have been composed sooner offer no variants in outlook or belief. Some are occasional, as is the one *On Doing Good*, preached in connexion with Wood's project, or the one on the miseries of the Irish people. They are simple, well-ordered, the reverse of flashy, even oddly defensive of religion, which he seems to guard from attack even from himself. We do not therefore find much doctrine in the sermons, which follow rather the precept he laid down for the Young Clergyman: 'As I take it, the two principal Branches of Preaching, are first to tell the People what is their Duty, and then to convince them that it is so.' There is to be no curious searching into the mind of God. His attitude towards the mysteries is plain enough in the most interesting of his sermons, the one on the Trinity. There, if anywhere, and in his 'Thoughts on Religion', his anti-intellectualism is apparent, that is, his objection to the reason's having pretensions in spheres where it cannot operate, thus making religion 'a fantastick and unintelligible thing'. 'It would be as well', he states, 'if People would not lay so much Weight on their own Reason in Matters of Religion, as to think every thing impossible and absurd which they cannot conceive.' Swift as the spokesman of his time is eager to define the limits of reason. And again, as a child of his age, he accepts revelation by the analogy which Butler was by no means the first to invent, but was to express the most completely. Half-way through the sermon *On the Trinity* we read 'How little do those who quarrel with mysteries, know of the commonest Actions of Nature?', and towards the end:

God commandeth us, by our Dependence upon his Truth and his holy Word, to believe a Fact that we do not understand. And, this is not more than what we do every Day in the Works of Nature, upon the Credit of Men of Learning.

It is the doctrine of implicit belief, without which, in the daily life of nature, we could not live. It is also the argument from scepticism, and it helps to humiliate man. 'It is an old and true Distinction', Swift says, 'that things may be above our Reason without being contrary to it.' How wholly Swift believed we cannot say; we know only that if he had doubts he felt it his duty to conceal them—since after all the doubts were only intellectual, and what was the intellect? But the feeling behind the prayers for Stella argues a sentiment that is stronger than hope, whatever the wording: 'And if thou wilt soon take her to thyself, turn our Thoughts rather upon that Felicity, which we hope she shall enjoy, than upon that unspeakable Loss we shall endure.' There was to be no selfish self-pity: this is dissolved by faith.

And it was Esther Johnson's death in 1728 that occasioned his most moving piece of intimate prose, known as the 'Character of Stella'. But even now, with increasing illness, giddiness, and deafness his old stoicism came to reassert itself; he could still, a little later, impart his old courageous gaiety, the *vive la bagatelle* spirit. It was only courage, and perhaps a more settled religious faith than he is usually allowed, which enabled him to hide, and perhaps temporarily overcome, the almost unbearable despair which breaks out sometimes in his letters, the deep rage he occasionally unleashes in his political work (which went on almost to the end), and the scabrous verses in which he seems to take revenge upon himself for being that animal called man. And once again, at least, the rage gave rise to a masterpiece, the splendidly macabre *A Modest Proposal for preventing the Children of Poor People from being a Burthen to their Parents, or the Country, and for making them Beneficial to the Publick.*

The title is almost exactly that of many pamphlets of the time, which put forth the economic doctrines against which the whole tract is a vehement outburst. That Swift's mind had been exercised by these matters is clear from his various other projects, and the numbers of the *Intelligencer* that he wrote together with Sheridan, especially No. 17, which refers to Fynes Moryson's account of Tyrone's rebellion, during which cannibalism actually took place. In this outraged protest, written when he was 62, Swift displays all his command of an irony so smooth and bland as to make the twist of the knife almost a caress. It surpasses *An Argument against the Abolishing of Christianity* because the impelling emotion is a *saeva indignatio* he felt at seeing the wretchedness of the people of Ireland, the sordor of their dwellings, the forced animality of their lives, which had already taught him how to describe Yahoos, or the beggars in Brobdingnag. Animality; that is the clue to the peculiar form which the beast myth—always so readily at hand in Swift's armoury of symbols—took on this occasion. The humans are never called beasts or allegorized; it is merely that one term used about them is a farmyard term: 'It is true that a Child, *just dropt from its Dam* [the italics are Swift's], may be supported by her Milk, for a Solar year, with little other Nourishment'; the note is struck fairly early. But there is no clanging of it, and such an animal term is hardly used again, since we soon have enough to show us how detachedly benevolent the argument is going to be; and now it is surely the most natural thing in the world to say: 'I am assured by our Merchants, that a Boy or Girl, before twelve Years old, is no saleable Commodity . . .', and so on. It is all very forthright and no nonsense; the writer, so one would say at first, is evidently a dull rogue with his arithmetical computations; so the reader is laid open to the full horror of:

I shall now therefore humbly propose my own Thoughts, which I hope will not be liable to the least Objection.

I have been assured by a very knowing *American* of my acquaintance in *London*, that a young healthy Child well nursed, is, at a Year old, a most delicious, nourishing, and wholesome Food, whether *Stewed, Roasted, Baked,* or *Boiled,* and I make no doubt that it will equally serve in a *Fricasie* or *Ragoust.*

And so the whole scheme of selling children as butchers' meat is developed, with immense plausibility, variants of it refuted as not really serving the purpose, or being open to some objection. Occasionally the lash sweeps across someone's shoulders so that one can be sure the attack is directed: 'I grant this food will be somewhat dear, and therefore very *proper for landlords,* who, as they have already devoured most of the Parents, seem to have the best Title to the Children'; but at once we return to a detached 'Infants Flesh will be in Season throughout the Year. . .' and are brought back to an abominable iciness of stockyard calculations. Only once is the character of the cool economist, the well-wishing projector, broken through. After referring to a Formosan girl of fifteen, who was eaten having been condemned as a traitor, he goes on:

Neither indeed can I deny, that if the same Use were made of several plump young Girls in this Town, who without one single Groat to their Fortunes, cannot stir Abroad without a Chair, and appear at the *Play-house*, and *Assemblies* in foreign Fineries, which they never will Pay for; the Kingdom would not be the worse.

But he passes swiftly on to how relieved he is not to have to think about the aged, diseased or maimed, 'because it is very well known that they are every Day *dying*, and *rotting*, by *Cold*, and *Famine*, and *Filth*, and *Vermin*, as fast as can be reasonably expected'.

The paper is the most savage and despairing of all his attacks on the treatment of Ireland by the English, as comes out most strongly when he answers the probable objection that his scheme would lessen the population. That, from the point of view of the orthodox economist or mercantilist of the day, would have been the most damning criticism. At least from the time of Charles II it had been accepted that people were the riches of the nation; and Swift was prepared to accept that doctrine for any country but the one he lived in; he had begun to call in doubt its applicability to that unhappy nation in his *Maxims Controlled in Ireland*. For, the argument implies, England's treatment of a kingdom which, to Swift's fury, it insisted on regarding as dependent, had been so to transform it that the usual laws of nature and of nations did not apply. Such a criticism of his modest proposal would have been valid in any other country, but as Swift says at the head of a mostly italicized passage, where he abandons all the other schemes he had put forward: 'I desire the Reader will observe, that I calculate my Remedy *for this one individual kingdom of* IRELAND, *and for no other that ever was, is, or I think, can ever be upon Earth.*' The indictment is scathing, more so than in any of his many other pamphlets. No doubt Swift the artist obtained a deep satisfaction from the resolution of its problems, the very perfection of the way his mind worked on it must have given relief from the agony of his contemplation. He is indulging his favourite tactic of pushing a proposition to an absurdly logical conclusion, he is giving pleasure to his mind in the arithmetical computations he always took so much delight in, but at the same time nothing can conceal the bitterness in his heart, which comes out finally in the sad despairing cadences of the last paragraph.

For us today it is perhaps difficult to assess this piece. The initial horror has little more than the gruesomeness of an ogreish tale, and our sentiment must be one of pleasure, such as we may perhaps get from an Italian Renaissance picture of the Massacre of the Innocents. How can one not relish the beautiful conduct of the whole complex operation? or fail to respond to the perfection of 'After all, I am not so violently bent upon my own Opinion, as to reject any Offer, proposed by wise Men, which shall be found equally innocent, cheap, easy and effectual. . .', with its gliding transition to a statement of the miseries of existence? Yet all the time we cannot but be conscious that it is a great statement, an assertion even, if you will, of Christian principles against the economic theories of the day. It is the cry of protest of a suffering spirit, for whom there is no private release; yet it expresses not merely frustration and rage, but a deep despair. There is not the faintest perfume of hope in the document; nothing will happen; no one will stir a finger, but there is no acceptance in it, neither Stoic nor Christian. It is the control, the courageous will disciplining and shaping the justifiably bitter emotions, that makes of it a consummate, a great, almost a noble work of art.

2. GULLIVER'S TRAVELS

Gulliver's Travels began light-heartedly, in the Scriblerian days of 1713–14, as an attack upon pedantry, including the scientific brand, and in the form of voyages. Swift carried away the idea and a few written portions to dwell for some time in the profound gloom of his mind during his first exiled years at the Deanery; but when his powers once more stirred, the idea of *Gulliver* began to move. Though he did not bring the finished work over to England until 1726, we know from his letters to Ford that he was at work on it early in 1721; that it was written, patched, laboured at, and revised through the time that he was waging the battle of Wood's halfpence, and going through the emotional crises of Vanessa's death and his deepest feelings for Stella. Thus Swift was leading his fullest life, in the enjoyment of his richest imagination, and at the height of his intellectual powers, when he wrote the book which he could declare with the irony of complete detachment would 'very much mend the world'.

Apparently a good deal of the first voyage and parts of the third had been sketched out in 1714, but it had all to be revised, brought up to date, fitted in with the form and temper of the reconceived work. The early parts had been filled out by an enormous amount of reading, the most important sources being Lucian, especially the *True History* and d'Ablancourt's additions, Rabelais, Cyrano de Bergerac's *Comic History of the Moon* and of the *Sun*, with hints from innumerable other sources, classical and modern. In nearly all his borrowings Swift altered not only the scope but the bearing of the original passages, making them subserve his own humorous or satirical purpose; but as it took later shape, into all this was embroidered a vast amount of current political allusion and satire, and again a steady, even a rigorous reading, of the *Transactions of the Royal Society*. However, to concern ourselves here with sources would be to take us too far out of our way; nor are we concerned with the immediate political allusions which no doubt tickled the contemporary reader, nor the satire on the science of the time; our quest is Swift's general attitude towards politics, science, and man; and to see how far his vehicle makes his ideas valid for us now. We need, however, to know that we cannot fully appreciate either the immense virtuosity of the work, or its satire, or its real fun, unless we take the trouble to be a little acquainted with its raw materials.

Gulliver's Travels, then, is the most mature, the most pondered, of all Swift's works, and the most complex; for though it has in many ways a deceptive air of simplicity, as compared, say, with the more fuliginous *Tale of a Tub*, in the later book was packed a lifetime of experience to add to the brilliant bookishness of the earlier. For if in either case the injunction given to the reader is: 'Look! whatever you may think, this is what things are really like', in the earlier book it amounts to no more than a sturdy and rather hubristic 'Clear your minds of cant', in the later it is, rather, a stoical 'clear your hearts of hope and your spirits of pride'. And what makes it a healthy book, a challenge to react rightly, is not only its detachment (a detachment of release, not of indifference), not only its magnificent control in view of 'the *accepted* hells beneath', to use the phrase Saintsbury borrowed from Whitman to illustrate Swift's greatness, but its emotional complexity. So much of Swift is here; not Gulliver alone, but Dean, Drapier, Bickerstaff, by turns choosing Cervantes' serious air, or shaking with Rabelaisian laughter; the rounded man is before you, in movement, varying in mood and in response, with all the surprises of a living human being, with the gaiety and the tragedy of a great one.

For *Gulliver* is, in a sense, a tragic work, as near a tragic work as the age ever got, in that it is the picture of man's collapse before his corrupt nature, and of his defiance in face of the collapse. It is the tragedy of unreason, but the tragic is frustrated by the satire. For if in a sense the pessimism of the book is that Christian pessimism which sees man as a fallen creature, Swift shows him as irredeemably fallen; he is to be bereft of all pride, so that even Stoicism is denied him—at least in the Yahoos, if not in Gulliver himself, who is no Yahoo. For if Swift would seem to argue that reason is the one saving virtue, he also shows that this human quality is not to be found in man —and that is the tragedy. Swift was a real rationalist, believing in reason (within its proper sphere), and he was infuriated to find the irrational, not only in the hearts of men, but at the heart of things. It is true that he turned this accusation upon his friends. '. . . I do not hate mankind' he wrote to Pope on 26 November 1725, 'it is *vous autres* who hate them, because you would have them reasonable animals, and are angry for being disappointed'; but the counter-accusation does not carry conviction. Sometimes he seems almost to rage in horror and impotence; but then, with superb control, he pulls himself up, saved by that form of self-criticism we know as humour. Take, for example, the scene, impregnated with all the loathing of the human body which he felt to a pathological degree, where the female Yahoo embraces Gulliver; the appalled hero comforts himself a little with the thought that 'her countenance did not make an Appearance altogether so hideous as the rest of her kind'.

Complex as the book is, stuffed with personal, political, and philosophic criticisms and dicta, crammed with personal and literary allusions, the story is unified, as it is made vital, by the tremendous urgency of the desire to humble human pride. The whole work converges with a devastating precision to the two final paragraphs:

My reconcilement to the *Yahoo*-kind in general might not be so difficult, if they would be content with those Vices and Follies only which Nature hath entitled them to. . . . But, when I behold a Lump of Deformity, and Diseases both in Body and Mind, smitten with *Pride*, it immediately breaks all the Measures of my Patience; neither shall I be ever able to comprehend how such an Animal and such a Vice could tally together. . . .
. . . therefore I here intreat those who have any Tincture of this absurd Vice, that they will not presume to appear in my Sight.

There is no mistaking the point of this scathing sermon on humility. To reduce human pride had, of course, always been one of the clearest objectives of the Scriblerians; but the *Travels* are aimed, with deadly singleness of purpose, at divesting man of the least shred of excuse for being proud of any of his moral or intellectual achievements, or of his physical graces.

The world, in the shape of some of its most liberal writers, has now for a long time professed itself shocked at the degrading picture of human nature presented in the last Book; Swift's contemporaries, in the main, seem to have sustained the blow more easily though there were some who, like Orrery, thought he had carried things too far; there was nothing new to them in the idea of the belittlement of man; his moral wretchedness had been preached for centuries, his insignificance proved by the new cosmography. Readers were accustomed to hearing man compared to his disadvantage with the beasts, perhaps in Montaigne's *Apology* for Raimond Sebond, Boileau's eighth *Satire*, certainly in *Tatler* 108 and *Spectator* 209. Moreover the last Book, which follows naturally on the second (the third may be regarded as an illustrative interpolation) does no more than repeat what had already been stated in two forms by the events at Lilliput and the conversations at Brobdingnag. What may shock some is the violence of the last Book, not so much in Swift's statement as in the spectacle of his despair. But is not this to be a little blind as to what Swift was after here? For stripping the last part of all its trappings, what he is doing is to show us how dreadful man would be if he let go of all reason, and what even beasts could be if they were given reason. He is not saying that man is a Yahoo. Here is man without mind, he is saying: better an animal with it; yet he is, of course, at the same time at his old amusing game of taking a proposition and pushing it to its absurdly logical conclusion. The work exists on different levels, the reasonableness of it is shot with moods, and we have all the time to be aware that Swift is a great artist constructing his object with the ruthless logic of the creator, whose supreme value is the value of his artistic intuition at the moment, his exploration to the uttermost of the suggestion made him by the imagination.

Given a knowledge of Swift's literary and scientific sources, of the political allegory, and so on, what strikes us as we read is the amazing consistency of the art, and the intensity of the imaginative flame which welds all the diverse elements into a unity. It is the kind of actualizing imagination of which Defoe also was a vehicle. Up to a point, the method of both is the same—an attention to detail about details which no one would question, so as to act as support for things beyond knowing. But the comparison must not be stretched too far. For however deeply Defoe may look into Moll Flanders or Robinson Crusoe, however much he may be looking into himself as he looks into them, he is doing so with a normal eye. To achieve naturalistic verisimilitude as he does is indeed a brilliant act of creative imagination; but to look at yourself with an abnormal eye, with, in Coleridge's phrase, 'an intense half self-deceived humourism', through telescope or microscope or distorting spyglass as Swift did when he looked at Lilliputians, Brobdingnagians, and Yahoos, and then to achieve verisimilitude is imagination of a different order, a formative rather than an interpretive one.

It was brilliant of Swift to do so many things at the same time as he did in each portion of the book, but perhaps the brilliance is so dazzling as to defeat its own end. The proof of this may well be that though the book was written to vex the world and not to divert it, divert it it did. But then Swift as he wrote was himself diverted, certainly in the first three books. This is clear enough from Gulliver's prefatory letter to Captain Sympson, and Swift's lack of protest at Pope's Gulliverian verses. Whatever his literary sources may have been for the Lilliputians, he had always been delighted in the tiny, as we know from his poems on Vanbrugh's house, and the little house at Castlenock; and had always loved travel literature. His real formative source then was his own immense amusement; and if he borrowed some details, say from Philostratus's account of the capture of the sleeping Hercules by the pygmies, from Ctesias, from Sir John Mandeville, and from a dozen other fancied or reputedly authentic tales, the constructive consistency was his, the keeping of everything to exact scale—one inch to a foot— so that even the number of coverlets which go to make up one for Gulliver is perfectly computed to allow for the ends being turned in when they are sewn together. Once more he found fun in doing absurd sums. His task in the earlier chapters was fairly easy to be sure, for thus far he was intent only to make the most of a good story in adorning it with all the details, to ram home with Swiftian thoroughness the idea of relativity which he had himself nourished, and which he found developed to some degree in Rabelais and Cyrano de Bergerac. (He did not really need Berkeley's *New Theory of Vision* here.) This much he had probably attempted in the early draft, but his difficulties began when he wished to introduce political allegory into the story; yet the skill with which the dovetailing is performed, so that England is seen in little, with Gulliver as a gigantic St. John, and the rest, so blindfolds the reader that he is not aware of what is happening to him. Nevertheless the entanglements begin, and the allegory—which mercifully never reads like deliberate allegory—becomes dual, and then ever more complicated. It may be possible that we are inclined to read too much into the *Travels*. Gulliver's method of putting out the fire in the palace is adapted from Rabelais, and would be just the sort of thing to amuse Swift; it may well be doubted whether it was meant to stand for the *Tale of a Tub*, which the Queen never forgave and so denied him preferment. At all events the Voyage to Lilliput had necessarily to be in the first place entertaining, since if it were dull nobody would read the rest; moreover it is only part of the argument from relativity which it needed the next book to complete.

But Chapter VI is, confessedly, a little awkward; a new element is introduced. So far Swift has been reworking the old pure Scriblerus fun, giving rein to the little residue of the child-like which always remained with him, being good-temperedly and quite detachedly political, representing the Lilliputians and therefore the English as silly little insignificant creatures with here and there some rather nasty traits in them—in fact not too brutally castigating pride; but here he suddenly brings in a new version of the Utopian travel-book, and discovers in the Lilliputians admirable qualities absent from the English, in, for instance, their treatment of children, which consists of an odd mixture of rational common sense and a Swiftian mistrust amounting to dislike of human sentiments. Swift, artist that he was, noticed the discrepancy; but the philosopher overcame the artist, and he retained the chapter with the lame excuse that these moral splendours existed only in the memory of the Lilliputians, who had since a couple of generations undergone the usual corruption of mankind—another commonplace of the imaginary voyage. The chapter by itself is fascinating because it is leavened with humour, the delightful light humour which seems to have characterized Swift's converse with his friends:

... their Manner of Writing is very peculiar; being neither from the Left to the Right, like the *Europeans*; nor from the Right to the Left, like the *Arabians*; nor from up to down, like the *Chinese*; nor from down to up, like the *Cascagians*; but aslant from one Corner of the Paper to the other, like the Ladies in *England*;

so the more profoundly moral, and ideally quite sound precepts, seem fun rather than satire, and the chapter is excellently rounded off with the solemn asseverations regarding the honour of a Lilliputian lady who, Gulliver swears, never visited him alone. The shift back in his mind as he writes his *Travels* and calls all his Lilliputian servants to bear witness to this is a superb *tour de force*; we relish the brilliant inconsistency, and on the whole conclude the first Book with a delighted sense of satisfied fantasy. By itself it has no great weight, but it is essential to the force of the next.

The second travel is beautifully consistent; nothing ruffles us as we read; it is perfectly conceived and rounded, and there is no sense of invention being strained to bring out a point; the sources are all completely digested, and there is no feeling of patchwork, no uneasy sense of palimpsest. The form and the idiom are perfectly adapted to what Swift had to say, which was something far more profoundly felt and realized than anything he wished to convey in the first travel. He is now ready to handle, not the surface of society merely, but its foundations in the human make-up. 'Lilliput', really, is all fun; what do Walpole and politicians generally really matter? (The Drapier had not come into play when this was written.) 'Brobdingnag', though fun is not absent, swells to being a sustained attack upon human behaviour and motives; yet the two Books are linked

together, since unless you knew what a Lilliputian looked like
to a human, you would not know what it felt like to be a human
among the Brobdingnagians; nor, unless you had seen what a
repugnant mass of flesh a giant seemed to a human, would you
realize how gross a human would appear to a pygmy. And
perhaps the most remarkable part of the sheer technique of the
second travel is the way the transitions are carried out, from
the adventure story, where humanity is implicitly criticized, to
criticizing humanity in the giants, and from that point to the
giants themselves criticizing humanity, the medium of trans-
ference being a mixture of the burlesque and the horrifying, the
cynical and the affectionate. There is no overstatement, for
even the most devastating attacks are performed with that
bland suavity we associate with Swift's irony; yet here the
mode is not that of irony.

If style is the manipulation of the reader's mind—or subduing
it—then the style of this Book is perfect, since all the while we
are at Swift's mercy, his plaything, from the opening Scriblerian
making fun of sailors' jargon in the almost word for word
account of the storm from Sturmy's *Mariner's Magazine* (1679),
to Gulliver's final difficulties with scale when he gets back to
England. By always keeping the fantasy intact, backed by
verisimilitude; by humanizing the giants as far as he wants to—
they have all the amiable thoughtlessness of the average un-
intellectual man who happens to be happily placed—he can
make us accept anything from them; by continually keeping
our visual sense in play he maintains our alertness. He appeals
to us on several levels in each of the realms of humour, disgust,
thought, or revulsion; but sometimes it is the child in us he
speaks to, sometimes the disillusioned adult—and never for a
moment does he seem to be preaching to us.

Apart from occasional side-issues, sufficiently scourging of
man, Swift is talking about three main things, all of them
central to his attitude to life: man's pretensions with regard to
his mind, man's pleasure in his own body, and the monstrous
behaviour of man in society; all themes, we see, are an attack
upon human pride.

It has been argued that when in Chapter VII Swift decries
the learning of the Brobdingnagians, he is adopting the usual
classical and imaginary travellers' assumption that giants are
often ogreish though possibly good-natured (as both Gran-

gousier and the King of Brobdingnag were), but certainly rather stupid. He does indeed say:

> The Learning of this People is very defective; consisting only in Morality, History, Poetry and Mathematicks; wherein they must be allowed to excel. But, the last of these is wholly applied to what may be useful in Life; to the Improvement of Agriculture and all mechanical Arts; so that among us it would be little esteemed. And as to Ideas, Entities, Abstractions and Transcendentals, I could never drive the least Conception into their Heads;

but the paragraph is merely a plain statement of his constant anti-intellectualism; here again, the giants are superior to ourselves. One has only to notice the placing of the paragraph—after the King's horror at the description of gunpowder, and his inability to understand the science of politics. As for Man's pride and delight in the human form divine, this was as incomprehensible to Swift as, authorities tell us, was any mystic sense or experience. It may have been partly due to the relics of medieval theology in Swift as well as a personal revulsion, but it enabled him to lash man's pride. The third tail to the lash is perhaps the most famous, when the King remarks after Gulliver's panegyric upon his country that

> . . . I cannot but conclude the Bulk of your Natives, to be the most pernicious Race of little odious Vermin that Nature ever suffered to crawl upon the Surface of the Earth.

It is this judgement that, apart from the descriptions of the Yahoos, has most infuriated Swift's detractors, the Macaulays and the Thackerays, and has brought down upon him the charge of loathsome and unforgivable cynicism and misanthropy.

It was not this statement of Swift's that most pained those very few of his contemporaries who did not wholly applaud the *Travels*; the outcry on this point arose in the period of Victorian optimism, when progress, it seemed (to all but the most distinguished Victorians), was proceeding so rapidly that Utopia was only just round the corner. Nobody today, with the events of the years 1910–60 in mind, would seriously dispute Swift's view. And, after all, the notorious expression of the royal mind does not necessarily involve misanthropy, or even a non-Christian feeling; it is, on the contrary, Christian, since the whole basis of Christianity is that man is a wretched and fallen being, and that love alone is the instrument of grace.

I have ever hated all Nations, professions, and Communityes [Swift wrote to Pope on September 29th, 1725, just after the final revision of the *Travels*], and all my love is towards individuals: for instance, I hate the tribe of Lawyers, but I love Councellor such a one, and judge such a one: for so with physicians—I will not Speak of my own Trade—Soldiers, English, Scotch, French, and the rest. But principally I hate and detest that animal called man, although I heartily love John, Peter, Thomas and so forth. . . . I have got Materials Toward a Treatis proving the falsity of that Definition *animal rationale*; and to show it should be only *rationis capax*. Upon this great foundation of misanthropy, though not [in] Timon's manner, the whole building of my Travells is erected. . . .

Here Swift is true to form; but his misanthropy is not expressed in Timon's manner,

> As my Method of Reforming
> Is by Laughing, not by Storming.

Yet it must be seen that Swift's misanthropy is a tragic one; man could be governed by reason; man ought to be governed by reason; it is the nations, professions, and communities, representing something lower than himself, which ruin him— and that is one of the underlying themes of all tragedy—something fine being spattered by something less fine; the individual being destroyed by the thing which enables him to live. *Le cœur a des raisons que la raison* thinks it best to ignore—and it was the logic of the emotions that took Swift in the writing of the *Travels* from Brobdingnag to Houyhnhnmland. The mind's logic would next have dealt with man's intellectual pride—and Swift returned to write Book III and fit it into its proper mental place; but the creative warmth engendered in writing of the giants drove him from the comparative detachment of that episode to the deeper phase of the Yahoos. That was the emotional movement; but it behoves us to look at the object with which Swift presented us, for that is the way he wanted to manipulate our minds, so it is to Laputa that we must go next. This voyage has never been popular, even Arbuthnot was disappointed in it; it seems at first sight too much of a rag-bag of all the left-overs in Swift's satirical armoury; both the scientific references and the political ones are at once too contemporary and too recondite. To the student of Swift it is fascinating, especially since it has been discovered how closely Swift had followed the *Transactions of the Royal*

Society, how he had fused the immediately political with the rest, and had spoofed the more solemn asseverations of idealists. The Book has classical, literary, scientific, political, and philosophic sources, all welded together in this amazing fantasia; it is a nightmare which the dreamer does not feel to be such. We are wrong to require more unity than a nightmare possesses; we should be thankful that it is so miraculously gay.

Swift's main purpose in this book, apart from his political strokes which refer more especially to England's treatment of Ireland, was to take to a ridiculous logical conclusion the suggestions made by the scientists. It is great fun and is often very funny; how far there is real prevision in it may be matter for doubt. It is true that the Laputans discovered the satellites of Mars more than a century and a half before the scientists of Europe did; but it is also true that a great many things that Swift mocked at as chimerical have come to pass—we do, for example, extract sunshine from cucumbers, though we put it into globules and call it Vitamin C. We make fruits ripen at all seasons of the year. Much of the joke, alas, depends upon our knowing the references; though some are fairly obvious to anybody of average reading. For instance Sprat, in his *History of the Royal Society*, had enunciated his famous dictum that the ideal of prose was to deliver 'so many "Things", almost in an equal number of "Words"'; at the Academy of Projectors this becomes the sages with the 'Scheme for entirely abolishing all Words whatsoever' by carrying round sackfuls of objects. In the same way, all but one or two of his fooleries of this kind are drawn direct from the *Transactions*, though it makes for clarity to note that Swift divided his projectors into the mechanical and the political. But since his political observations do not differ from those in the other books, although they have their particular comic angle and the deadly serious reference to England's treatment of Ireland, what emerges in this book and nowhere else in the *Travels* is his attitude towards science, and, of course, to the old despised pedantries.

It is the ghost of Aristotle in Glubbdubdrib who states the argument against science:

He said, that new Systems of Nature were but new Fashions, which would vary in every Age; and even those who pretended to demonstrate them from Mathematical Principles, would flourish but a short Period of Time, and be out of Vogue when that was determined.

That, in a sense, is true, as we now realize; but it is also irrelevant. What matters is that man at any given time should have a conception of the universe—of, if you like, the way God's mind works in so far as any particular thing is concerned—on a level with his physical experience. Swift, as far as we know, did not despise science; what he objected to was the self-glorification of the petty virtuoso dissecting flies, and the absurd pretensions of the second-rate scientist to 'explain' the inexplicable. In the ridicule he cast upon the whole Academy, and on the Laputan philosophers, he was proclaiming that none of these things really matter; what does matter is man's realization of his duty to man. The fool in any sphere is meat for the satirist; but Swift, while including the petty strutter, was aiming at something far more fundamental. He was really asking the question, 'What is the proper object of man's most strenuous intellectual attention?'; and since this is a question that should be asked all the time, there is still a freshness about this part of the *Travels* in spite of the very specific references for almost every absurdity with which he amused the readers of his own day.

The third Book may not in itself be very coherent, but it is a necessary gap in the emotional sequence, for in it Swift can use a certain relieving lightness he could not for a moment risk in the last. The satire is sometimes good-humoured chaff, as when he speaks of the 'very common Infirmity of human Nature, inclining us to be more curious and conceited in Matters where we have least Concern, and for which we are least adapted either by Study or Nature', a theme taken up more fiercely in 'The Beast's Confession' (1732). This Book is necessary again for another reason, namely that our sense of actuality has to be shifted. The first two Books, fantastic as they are, strain our belief beyond the probable, no doubt, but not beyond the possible; there are, after all, pygmies, and there are, or at least have been, giants. In Book IV (already written) we are going to be presented with something it will be very difficult for us to accept; but compared with Book III, the Houyhnhnms and Yahoos are easy to swallow; in Book III Swift might have said as frankly as Lucian did, 'I humbly solicit my readers' incredulity'; and if we can allow our fancy to be held captive in any of those islands even for a minute, we shall be susceptible of being trapped into feeling a sense of reality about the following and most serious part of the whole work.

And there is one further point where the Voyage to Laputa is essential—in the description of the Struldbrugs. Whether their source be classical—especially through the Tithonus myth—or the then recent account of the tribe in 'Casmere' that lives to an advanced and horrible, desireless old age does not matter. The description, and the whole episode, is, of course, valuable in itself; our dreams of a wise old age are illusory, and Swift brings out every atom of the eternal human comedy. But there is more purpose in it than that; for the statement in this part is, 'You want desperately to live', and in the next part we hear the inexorable voice asking, 'Very well then; under what conditions will you accept life?'

It is the most profound question possible, and it is a little difficult to see why the last voyage has produced such hysterical, frenzied outbursts even from men who have claimed to interpret Swift; much of what it has to say is implicit in his other writings, some of it even directly stated, especially in his letters. It might be regarded as a gloss on the Stoic dilemma, which Swift may have pondered on in St. Augustine's *De peccato originale*:

For although man, set up in a place of honour, and not understanding, is likened to the beasts, and becomes like unto them; yet he is not so like as to be a beast. For he is likened unto them by a fault or defect, not by his nature; not a fault or defect in the beast, but in his nature. For man is so much more excellent than the beast, that what is fault or defect in man is nature in the beast: but not for that is the nature of man become that of the beast.

Thus one cannot but feel that what the men of the nineteenth century revolted against was not the moral degradation of the Yahoos—after all, the King of Brobdingnag had left man without a particle of virtue—but the physical filth; it was in their animal vanity that they were hurt, as people still are. It is perhaps healthy, biologically right, to feel in this way about the whole treatment of man and the use here made of the beast myth. Had the Victorians been more familiar with possible sources their revolt might not have been so violent; Cyrano de Bergerac and the relevant passages of Plutarch were perhaps not read much in those days, and Rabelais was out of fashion. But quite apart from that, however animally healthy the revulsion may be, it is imaginatively stupid, for the vision of man here is not merely a scabrous, defiling vision, but, in a queer distorted way, a tragic one. Swift is not rejoicing in the Yahoos; he is horrified to think that, but for reason, there is man, and how slender a guard is reason. And the tragedy lies in the abuse of reason. Gulliver's master in Houyhnhnmland after hearing about the English had remarked that:

> he looked upon us as a sort of Animals to whose Share, by what Accident he could not conjecture, some small Pittance of *Reason* had fallen, whereof we made no other Use than by its Assistance to aggravate our *natural* Corruptions, and to acquire new ones which Nature had not given us.

How closely connected this may be with what he saw of the poor wretches into which the Irish peasantry had been deformed it is hard to say; the *Modest Proposal* may give us pause.

It is, however, not altogether easy to see what Swift was doing in this last voyage, since he was, after all, doing so many things—apart from superbly carrying on the narrative. He is, basically, making use of one of the recognized methods of disputation, presenting the extreme logical end of a case, while quite aware that this is not the whole case, and that there is another point of view that might be maintained. And it is the extreme logical end, not as with More's *Utopia*, of which R. W. Chambers said the inhabitants represented man with reason, certainly, but without revelation; for the Houyhnhnms never having fallen could not need revelation. Since they had no passions they had no sin, nor sense of sin. But the logical argument is not coldly carried out, it is variously warmed with Swift's anger, frozen with all the frigidity of his horror, or again lightened with his gayest humour as in the derogatory remarks that Gulliver's 'master' makes about the absurdity of the human body, or when Gulliver takes his leave; or maybe shot with his bitterest irony, an irony which yet jerks you into laughter:

> And, to set forth the Valour of my own dear Countrymen, I assured him, that I had seen them blow up a Hundred Enemies at once in a Siege, and as many in a Ship; and beheld the dead Bodies drop down in Pieces from the Clouds, to the great Diversion of all the Spectators.

It is, perhaps, passages of that sort that give the clue; for here Swift is pushing further his criticism of man than he has in the other Books. Whereas earlier he had condemned standing armies, here all war is condemned. And just as in earlier Books the distortions of law had been scourged, here the very existence of such an institution is regarded as a symptom of social disease, after the manner of the most innocent anarchist. This book, possibly, is more pessimistic even than the others: Gulliver himself is affected, for whereas in the first books he loudly maintains man's superiority, here he is miserably on the defensive, and soon completely surrenders. Yet though Swift is, if you like, enraged at man for being what he is, he is in the main so calm, so aloof even, in spite of the spurts of anger, that the appeal is throughout to reason: the thoroughly sympathetic Don Pedro at the end is proof enough of that.

But if it is a plea for man to use his reason, he is not really arguing that man could be, or even should be, without the element of irrationality which makes him able to recognize the divine. For though it might be pleasanter to dwell among his horses than among his anthropoid apes (he is careful to make the distinction between civilized man and the Yahoos), to be a Houyhnhnm might be a good deal duller than to be a Yahoo. Here again he is only driving further home the point he began to make in gentler form in the first voyage, and has been deepening all through, just as he hammers home still more powerfully his criticisms of current economics (still very largely our own), the moneyed interest, the treatment of Ireland by England, attacking not only social but also moral values in a way that may at first arouse laughter, but afterwards induces thought. Think, for example, of the implications of lumping together such activities as he does in the following passage; he is not just laying wildly about him; he is thinking very precisely, directing his blows with an assured aim:

. . . in order to feed the Luxury and Intemperance of the Males, and the Vanity of the Females, we sent away the greatest Part of our necessary Things to other Countries, from whence in return we brought the Materials of Disease, Folly, and Vice, to spend among ourselves. Hence it follows of Necessity, that vast Numbers of our People are compelled to seek their Livelihood by Begging, Robbing, Stealing, Cheating, Pimping, Forswearing, Flattering, Suborning, Forging, Gaming, Lying, Fawning, Hectoring, Voting, Scribling, Stargazing, Poysoning, Whoring, Canting, Libelling, Freethinking, and the like Occupations. . . .

Everything Swift hated is there.

What eventually counts is not so much the intellectual statement of a work of this sort as the total mood imposed on the reader, and in this extremely complex work the response is as various as the matter. *Gulliver's Travels* is a terrible book, perhaps a ruthless book, but it is not a horrible one. It is true that it does not flatter man; it is not optimistic; it contains no Christian comfort, and it leaves us conscious of having 'too much weakness for the Stoic's pride'; but it is, in essence, a challenge. It is not a gloomy, or despairing, or blasphemous book, and it teaches at least that half of Stoicism which tells us that

. . . unless he can,
Above himself erect himself, how poor a thing is man.

It is not a reviling of man's indignity, but a passionate plea for the dignity of man, in spite of his loathsome body, his absurd mind, his ridiculous political pretensions, his arrogant ignorance. The only hope of salvation, Swift tells us, is to rid ourselves of our cruel illusions, to be aware of, and to accept the hells beneath, so that we may not subside into them. If it is first and foremost and most profoundly a moral challenge, as all tragedy is, it is also an intellectual one; and it remains a warning against the pretentiousness of our claim to have arrived much nearer to the ultimate mystery of creation, or even the organizing of mankind. As to politics, who dare today contradict Swift's assertions? The only way to do so is to become more like Swift, and face the fact that civilization is a precarious frontier state—there is where the challenge of his political scourgings lies; the only part which is at all unhealthy is the attempt, assuming it was made, to bring man to be disgustful of his own body, an attempt which will fail till the race is ready to die out. One might say with Pascal, 'Il est dangereux de trop faire voir à l'homme combien il est égal aux bêtes, sans lui montrer sa grandeur'; but to be horrified by the book, to rave in revulsion, is to confess that one cannot rise to the challenge of the masterpiece bequeathed us by a terrifyingly clearsighted genius.

3. THE FINAL PHASE. POETRY

It was on 11 August 1729 that Swift, 'more moved than perhaps becomes a clergyman, and a piece of a philosopher', wrote to Pope of the miseries of Ireland, his intense realization of which at that time forced from him *A Modest Proposal*. It was to be his last great prose work. He had confessed to Pope more than a year earlier (1 June 1728) that, as far as he was a patriot, '. . . what I do is owing to perfect rage and resentment, and the mortifying sight of slavery, folly, and baseness about me, among which I am forced to live'; and as his energies died out, his 'itch of meddling with the public', so he informed Bolingbroke (5 April 1729), was subdued by his worsening attacks of deafness and giddiness; and as the last hope of ever getting transferred to England flickered out, his efforts, though they were not altogether to cease for some ten years, grew ever more spasmodic. If in his outward existence he was still the man with whom the word 'mirth' was so often bracketed, the death of Esther Johnson had struck a shattering blow at the whole structure of his life. He might go bravely on with his friends, but nobody who has read the letters which he wrote when in 1727 he thought Mrs. Johnson might die, nobody who has read what he put down on the night of her funeral, who has pondered the 'Prayers for Stella' or her 'Character', can doubt how deeply he was affected. The steady energy, the direction, the purposefulness went out of him, as though life had lost much of its meaning. His general state of being he expressed clearly to Bolingbroke—to whom he seems to have been most self-revelatory—in his letter of 21 March 1730:

. . . I find myself disposed every year, or rather every month, to be more angry and revengeful; and my rage is so ignoble, that it descends even to resent the folly and baseness of the enslaved people among whom I live. . . . When I was of your age I often thought of death, but now, after a dozen years more, it is never out of my mind, and terrifies me less. I conclude that Providence has ordered our fears to decrease with our spirits; and yet I love *la bagatelle* better than ever, for, finding it troublesome to read at night, and the company here growing tasteless, I am always writing bad prose, or worse verses, either of rage or raillery, whereof some few escape to give offence, or mirth, and the rest are burnt.

And near the end of the letter there occurs the phrase already quoted: 'die here in a rage, like a poisoned rat in a hole.'

One has, then, a sense of instability; the tremendous complex machine is running down; parts are getting out of gear. At moments there is a marvellous mature balance; a geniality such as we get in the humorous '*Libel on* D—— D——' of 1730, and this is the period of his most superb verse; but the balance is precarious. There is the yearning for, the passionate belief in, friendship, but none of the tenderness which informs the Stella birthday poems. If there is splendid poise in the 'Verses on the Death of Dr. Swift', Tighe and Allen rouse him to vituperation, a mood which rises to its height in 'The Legion Club'; and every now and again there is an outbreak of the scatology which for us disfigures a proportion of what Swift wrote. It would seem to be a symptom of rage against the very conditions of animal existence more than an intellectual striking at romance (or sentimentality), more than a medieval impulse to see the body as a mass of corruption. It would seem to be a physical revulsion. Swift could never become reconciled to human effluvia, to the notion that man is an organism that has to be voided. It is not merely that he uses this fact as an instrument for humbling man's pride; he takes rough pleasure in forcing his readers to accept it; he rubs their nose in the filth as one may do with a puppy when training it. Or perhaps by deliberately facing the fact, he is absorbing some shock which has made his aversion to the physical almost if not quite pathological. In *Human Ordure, Botanically Considered*—if it is his, and a good case can be made out for its being so—he is trying to humorize it, as he is in *An Examination of Abuses* . . . (1732) where the scatological element is incongruously brought in, and, to us, brutally developed; and again so unexpectedly in what should have been, and still largely is, one of the most graceful of the poems from Market Hill, 'A Panegyrick on the Dean'. The scatological had been an element in Swift's work ever since 'The Problem' of 1699, but it is marked just at this period, not, as Delany suggested, as a result of Pope's influence (the latter's scatology is far more controlled and directed— and directed from, not towards himself), but, one may think, as an outcome of Esther Johnson's death. The decay, the collapse of the body, how appalling! his own vertigo, how humiliating! how nauseating the whole business of physical being! Yet if this is the human body, the condition of existence, very well then, he will accept it (it is one of the hells beneath), he will face it, defeat it by outfacing it. What is abnormal about this attitude is not its rarity, but its intensity; the intensity itself is the abnormality, as it is in much that Swift wrote. He, above all people, must see the object as it really is.

The subject can be dropped in discussing Swift's contribution to literature (though not if discussing Swift himself); but there is just one comment to be made with respect to one of the malodorous poems of the period—'A Beautiful Young Nymph going to Bed'. It is besides an expression of contempt for the body, a scourging of sham and pretence; but beyond that, such a poem is in a tradition, almost, one might say, a 'kind'. Swift was not the only person at this time to write that sort of poem: we get it in Prior, Parnell, and others. In England it possibly derives first from Otter's description of his wife in *Epicœne*, then, with more disgust, from Killigrew's Lady Love-All in *The Parson's Wedding* (*c.* 1653):

> I peep'd once to see what she did before she went to bed: and by this light, her maids were dissecting her: and when they had done, they brought some of her to bed, and the rest they either pinn'd or hung up, and so she lay dismember'd till Morning: in which time her Chamber was strew'd all over like an Anatomy school. (IV. i.)

Like a good deal of the verse and prose printed during this period, it is what we might term schoolboy rather than anything else. The age, of course, was less squeamish than ours— it had to be or die of aromatic pain, not of a rose; and it may be as well to remember that Lady Acheson was expected to be amused at the scatological portions of the Market Hill poem referred to. Having said that, we can return to a consideration of Swift's more central contributions to literature.

The main driving motives of his life still continued to operate: his hatred of injustice and oppression, and his contempt for cant and humbug. A 'born idealist' as Whibley called him, and one who refused to veil what he did not like, or pretend that it did not exist, the man of action in him used all his powers for betterment by storming as well as by laughing, and as often as not by plain common-sense statement. It was these motives, combined with the love of his friends, that enabled him to go on so bravely after 1728; the *Intelligencers* which he shared with Sheridan, helped him at the first; but there were no great popular issues, or shall we say no proper foci of attack to crystallize his rage into masterpieces. The state of Ireland he did indeed continue to write about, but compared with *A Modest Proposal* his later prose writings seem tame, as do his attacks —speaking again of prose only—directed against those who wished to tamper with tithes, or abolish the Test. The pamphlets are still beautifully clear; occasionally the old humour— light or sardonic—breaks out; but though it would not be quite fair to say that they are long-winded, one can at least say that they lack brevity, though conciseness still governs the phrase. And at the end a note of futility, of disillusion creeps in. In the final paragraph of what would appear to be his last tract, *A Proposal for giving Badges to the Beggars in all the Parishes of Dublin* of 1737, one is aware of a tired old man voicing his fatigue:

. . . as I am a Desponder in my Nature, and have tolerably well discovered the Disposition of our People, who never will move a Step toward easing themselves from any one single Grievance; it will be thought, that I have already said too much, and to little or no Purpose, which has often been the Fate, or fortune of the Writer.

It is as though the virulent verses of 'The Legion Club' of the year before had exhausted the last spark of characteristic energy.

There are, however, two prose pieces which still survive as fairly common literary reading, the *Polite Conversation* (1738) and *Directions to Servants* (1745), two old projects which Swift was already refurbishing in 1731. The first was finished in 1737, the second was never completed, though there is enough of it as it stands to make the point. As a humorous satire on the abundance of flavourless banalities of which much 'polite' talk is even today composed, *A Complete Collection of Genteel and Ingenious Conversation . . .* to give a part of its true title, is amusingly readable, though we may think that it is here and there a little heavy, and that it goes on too long. If in Swift's earlier and best work the artist took charge and shaped perfectly the tool which was to perform certain functions, it would seem that here the artist has misjudged the importance of the function, and has made too weighty a tool; the craftsman we feel, is obtaining delight from the actual process of forging the weapon, defeating melancholy with *la bagatelle*, and a little losing sight of its final shape and purpose. The Introduction is superb, and still valuable (it is, we may note, by Simon Wagstaff): one 'scene' would have been illustration enough of the general fatuity of ordinary talk. It does for conversation what the *Tritical Essay* did for composition, but does it too much. Similarly with the *Directions to Servants*, though here the attack is even more obvious, if perhaps more amusing, since the idea of writing from a vicious servant's point of view is carried out with a plausibility which almost amounts to the bland irony of some of the earlier great pieces. Each idea was worth a squib; but in each one feels the effect of misdirected mastery. Here and there the old inimitable trenchancy, the suavity in uttering the ridiculous, brings the special alertness which Swift alone can arouse, with passages of happy badinage (one thinks of the last few paragraphs of the Introduction); but though these pieces may serve a little to round off the figure of Swift, they do not add to his stature. Nor for that matter does the more slashing *Serious and Useful Scheme to make a Hospital for Incurables* (1733), amusing and terrifying enough as some of it variously is, for it is too sweeping in aim, too disrupted, too diffuse.

The fact would seem to be that at this period of Swift's life, a period of moods and instability, the medium of prose could not carry what he wanted to say; and it is remarkable that it was at this time, especially in about 1731, that he attained his finest, his most loaded achievements in verse. But once he had flung off the Pindaric, high-falutin style, verse was for him as natural a medium of expression as prose, and in some spheres far more effective for emotional release. Though he may not have added anything of the utmost importance to our poetic canon, much of what he did is individual, unmatched, while a little of it has something of that kind of value we should feel the poorer for being without. And whether or not you admit him to the higher ranks of the minor poets, you must concede that he was at least a masterly versifier, and a brilliant rhymster whose supremacy in that field is threatened only by Byron, who, whenever he felt his own springs running dry, would come to the bubbling wells of felicitous syllable-juggling provided by Swift. Anybody who takes an innocent delight in what pranks words can be made to play can enjoy Swift's verses for that not disgraceful reason alone. Swift would seem at times to have used verse because, besides finding himself able to say 'something in verse as true as prose', it happened that even in his hands

> Truth shines the brighter clad in Verse,

provided, of course, that the verse was compact enough, without padding, or meretricious 'imaginative' effects.

His *Tatler* verses, the 'City Shower' and 'Description of a Morning', were emancipatory, defiantly anti-poetic, the latter poem, for example, describing nothing that the common run of poets would seize on. With them he parts company from his second phase, the Addisonian 'Baucis' or the Prioresque 'Biddy Floyd'. The political squibs of the immediately succeeding period were to give him practice and all the freedom he needed, and it is in these till almost the end, together with his flippant bantering verses to Sheridan, Delany, and others, that he achieves some of his most surprising and entertaining prosodic effects. The range of his metre is astonishing. Nearly all the verse that can be classed as poetry is in the favourite metre of the time, the loose octosyllable; but there is hardly any form, apart from blank verse, that he did not try. Moreover all his verse, or poetry, has the same qualities of controlled metre, of vigour, of concentration. Whether you take the 'Excellent New Ballad. . .' style, or the common metre of

> *Pope* has the Talent well to speak
> But not to reach the ear;
> His loudest Voice is low and weak,
> The *Dean* too deaf to hear

or the rollicking, ingeniously rhymed 'An Answer to the Bally-spellin Ballad' of Sheridan, or the anapaestic hendecasyllable of 'Advice to a Parson':

> Wou'd you rise in the *Church*, be *Stupid* and *Dull*,
> Be empty of *Learning*, of *Insolence* full. . .

still better used, perhaps, in *The Grand Question Debated*; the lively trochaic measure of *Helter-Skelter*:

> Now the active young Attornies
> Briskly travel on their Journies,
> Looking big as any Gyants,
> On the Horses of their Clients. . .

in the triplet or in the use of a refrain, you always feel the discipline of the craftsman. So with his more serious poems, you are confident that he has chosen the metre which best suits himself in relation to the subject.

It is convenient for purposes of discussion to divide Swift's later poetry into groups. The bulk of his verse, the most important group, is what might be called genial satire; this leads to the next largest group, sterner satire which can often be classed as bitter; smaller groups are the vituperative and the scatological; but a group larger than either of the last two, almost equal to the second, might be classed as tender, or at least deeply affectionate. There are, moreover, the political poems, street cries, riddles, and so on, which will interest the student of Swift rather than the amateur of literature. The very complexity of this sketchy classification may serve to illustrate how readily Swift relied on verse to release his exuberance or relieve his oppression.

The boundaries of the groups, naturally, cannot be rigidly defined; a given poem, particularly in the last period, may slide from one group into another. Yet the framework will serve, more especially as the genial satire contains all but a minimal amount of his autobiographical verses. These may be said to begin with the first imitation of Horace (I. vii), *Quinque dies*, of 1713, where he complains to Harley that becoming a Dean has put him woefully out of pocket, and to end with the masterly *Verses on the Death of Dr. Swift* written in 1731. They all have something of the Horatian detachment combined with a Prioresque ability to look at himself as others might see him, broken across by streaks of self-defence which are not untinged by the application to his own person of a little of that almost caressing irony which had become at his most commanding moments almost second nature to apply. It may well be argued that it is in these verses that he wrote his best poetry, for our pleasure in them, the delight they impart, is due as much to his control of the medium in perfectly responding to the subject-matter, as in the matter itself. A work such as the *Verses on the Death of Dr. Swift* has to be read complete to appreciate the changes of tempo, the pressure which forces the phrasing into a lilt which if not exactly singing is a kind of delighted crooning. In the result, what is achieved is a poem of forgiveness, of wisdom, of an acceptance that is seldom found in poetry which is ostensibly satire—certainly not in Pope in whom indignation is never quite submerged, or quite lost sight of even in the great aura of friendship. You do not get it in Swift's other work, in, say, his reproofs to Delany, or in the 'Epistle upon an Epistle'. But this first group insensibly merges into the purer satire on the one hand, that of the rod-wielder, and on the other into the tender.

Remarkable also about Swift's satire is the range of emotion which impels it, from the sheer hatred of his early 'Salamander' verses or his very late 'The Legion Club', expressing itself in scarcely controlled vituperation, or the almost cynical gloom of 'The Day of Judgment', to the light-hearted half-affectionate contempt of literary forms, as in his Market Hill 'Pastoral Dialogue' or the 'Love Song in the Modern Taste'. But it will probably be agreed that his most holding work is that in which the moods vary, as they nearly always do in that great group he wrote after 1729, from which date he seems to have found verse a more flexible medium than prose, one in which emotion did not always have to appear so consistently to be reason, and the personal could so easily be turned into the channel of the political. We could take as examples the poem to Gay or the 'Epistle to a Lady'; or again where the literary turns into the political, as in the great 'On Poetry: a Rapsody'. But what makes the verse of this period unlike anything else in our literature is the way that in a very short space Swift can bind together a medley of emotions and make a unified thing of the poem. Take the 'Epistle', which mixes a little satire on women with some passages of self-mockery and some of political gibing: it is welded into a unity by a sense of the wholeness of being of the writer who cannot even for the moment be only satirist and not a complete human being; it is humane because it really is a personal letter, and not a public utterance as, say, Pope's *Epistle to Arbuthnot*, which too expresses wholeness, but aims consciously at expressing it. The latter is an apologia, which Swift's, even half-mockingly, is not. Take again the 'Rapsody' where sardonic advice to a poet becomes a swingeing attack upon Walpole together with mockery of the king which approaches in quality Pope's passage on George II in the *Epistle to Augustus*, though the texture is very different. Swift's passage is blunter, less wide in its references: it really is the poetry of statement (or misstatement), whereas Pope's only makes believe to be so, being actually the poetry of implication. Indeed the virtue of Swift's poems resides largely in their directness; and certainly where politics were concerned he would have to be direct, for at this stage the flow of poetic creation seems to have swept him on willy-nilly into politics. There was no need for either the rather affectionately humorous 'Epistle to a Lady' or the humorous satire and criticism of the rhapsody 'On Poetry' to have gone on to politics at all, and in fact in its first form the 'Epistle' did not contain the political passages. But now Swift could not help dwelling on the subject. Yet even here, where he seems to have been helplessly in the grip of his by now almost ruling passion, he is in control, and can interrupt the poem to let the addressee, Lady Acheson, break in with:

> Deuce is in you, Mr. Dean;
> What can all this Passion mean?
> Mention Courts, you'll ne'er be quiet;
> On Corruptions running Riot.

So, even when giving rein to the somewhat too innocent anarchism he voiced in the last Book of *Gulliver's Travels*, he is detached, and self-observant.

Where he is not detached, but giving his fury full rein, is in his last and most terrible poem, 'The Legion Club'. It is hardly satire, it is sheer invective, couched in language of extraordinary vigour; it is an outburst of rage the nearest approach to which in English verse is in some of the vituperative verses of Skelton, or of the ageing Landor. The bitter intensity of the emotion gives the lines a human quality; and, after all, the emotion was an indignation which any Churchman might well think righteous, seeing that what Swift is enraged at is a further whittling away of the tithes of his poorer brethren. Here he completely abandoned his conviction—at least as expressed in the 'Epistle of a Lady'—that he encountered Vice with Mirth:

> Keeper, show me where to fix
> On the Puppy pair of *Dicks*;
> By their lanthorn jaws and Leathern,
> You might swear they both are Brethren:
> *Dick Fitz-Baker, Dick* the Player,
> Old Acquaintance, are you there?
> Dear Companions hug and kiss,
> Toast *old Glorious* in your Piss.
> Tye them Keeper in a Tether,
> Let them stare and stink together;
> Both are apt to be unruly,

> Lash them daily, lash them duly,
> Though 'tis hopeless to reclaim them,
> Scorpion Rods perhaps may tame them.

Whether a reader finds those verses enjoyable or not will depend upon his temper at the time of reading; but to deny force to the poem, and the very few similar ones or small portions of others, a force that prose could not have, is to be insensitive to the power of verse. For the whole conduct of the piece is admirable, with its startling horrific vision in the earlier part of

> *Poverty*, and *Grief* and *Care*,
> Causeless *Joy*, and true *Despair*;
> *Discord* periwigg'd with Snakes

through the monstrous Hogarthian presentation of the Irish House of Commons, to the contemptuous deliberately low-toned conclusion. There may be 'demoniacal inspiration' about it, as Jeffrey suggested; but if so, it was Swift's own perfectly disciplined daemon that not only inspired it, but also directed it with beautiful precision.

And if more complex, 'On Poetry' is just as precise, although its virtue lies in generalization. Here Swift is making, not a limited attack, but a general statement about poetasters and patrons in any age; he weaves into it much that will be found in other poems, 'The Beast's Confession' for instance, and, of course, in the 'Directions for a Birthday Song', in the poem to Gay, and the 'Libel' on Dr. Delany; indeed there are not really very many themes in Swift's poetry, though there are many variations on them. Nor is this poem unrelated to both Pope's *Essay on Criticism* and *The Dunciad*—the relationship with the latter being best illustrated by one of the most famous passages in the Swift canon:

> . . . search among the rhiming Race,
> The brave are worried by the Base.
> If on *Parnassus'* Top you sit,
> You rarely bite, are always bit:
> Each Poet of inferior Size
> On you shall rail and criticize;
> And strive to tear you Limb from Limb.
> While others do as much for him.
>
> The Vermin only teaze and pinch
> Their Foes superior by an Inch.
> So, Nat'ralists observe, a Flea

Hath smaller Fleas that on him prey,
And these have smaller Fleas to bite 'em,
And so proceed *ad infinitum*. . . .

Swift might be trusted to make an 'unpoetic' use of the microscope, and he uses it, not as the master of disgust, as he so often
is, but, almost equally with Pope, a master of contempt, and
more cool than Pope usually allows himself to be.

The comparison with Pope, however, is more interesting in
the field of the Horatian satire or epistle, though comparison
in any detail would demand too much space here: it must be
enough to say that in his apologia, *Verses on the Death of Dr.
Swift*, Swift apparently uses a calm, detached irony against
himself, whereas Pope in the *Prologue to the Satires* lashes his
enemies. Swift gives us no Sporus or Atticus, but with what
might be called a sympathetic, indeed a soothing irony, the
portrait of every man and every woman:

> My female Friends, whose tender Hearts
> Have better learn'd to act their Parts,
> Receive the News in *doleful Dumps*,
> 'The Dean is dead, (*and what is Trumps?*)
> 'Then Lord have Mercy on his Soul.
> '(Ladies I'll venture for the *Vole*.)
> 'Six Deans they say must bear the Pall.
> '(I wish I know what *King* to call.)
> 'Madam, your Husband will attend
> 'The Funeral of so good a Friend.
> 'No Madam, 'tis a shocking Sight,
> 'And he's engag'd To-morrow Night!
> 'My Lady *Club* wou'd take it ill,
> 'If he shou'd fail at her *Quadrill*.
> 'He lov'd the Dean. (*I lead a Heart.*)
> 'But dearest Friends, they say, must part.
> 'His Time was come, he ran his Race;
> 'We hope he's in a better Place.

His satire is all the more searching because he himself seems so
little scathed. Pope, in the *Prologue*, is never so uninvolved; we
feel he protests too much. But then Swift had worked tremendously at this poem, for the very purpose we might think, of
gaining this distance. He told Gay on 1 December, 1731:

I have been several months writing near five hundred lines on a
pleasant subject, only to tell what my friends and enemies will say

on me after I am dead. I shall finish it soon, for I add two lines every week, and blot out four and alter eight. I have brought in you and my other friends, as well as enemies and detractors.

But he had made other attempts at an apologia: the dialogue 'alluding to' Horace Satire II. i:

> Since there are persons who complain
> There's too much satire in my vein. . .

(comparison with Pope's 'Epistle to Mr. Fortescue' is profitable); the 'very scrub' libel against himself known as 'A Panegyric on the Reverend D—n S—t' (we might perhaps add the Market Hill 'Panegyric on the Dean') and 'The Life and Character of Dean Swift', which leads off with the same reference to La Rochefoucauld, is dedicated to Pope, and was used by Pope and King when they produced the London copy of the 'Verses'. The whole conduct of the poem makes it an enchanting master-piece; the movement, the changes of tempo, the differences in depth, are handled so that the reader is beautifully led from one phase to another, and the conclusion—even with the sharp drop in tone of the last two lines which is usual with Swift— leaves him in no doubt as to the meaning or temper of the communication.

As individual, and as unlike anything else in our language as the 'Verses' are the 'tender' poems, beginning, we may think, with *Cadenus and Vanessa*, and going on to the last of the Stella poems: though we need not stop short there, since a good deal of the same element enters into many of the Market Hill group where Sir Arthur and Lady Acheson, especially the latter, are concerned. It is in these poems that Swift made certain areas of receptivity more sensitive. *Cadenus and Vanessa* needs too detailed an examination to be treated in brief; moreover Swift, we feel, is here and there too much on the defensive; but where the Stella poems are concerned no reservations need intrude. They are beautifully frank statements of a lovely and difficult relationship, deeply and sincerely felt: they push Stoic accep-tance almost to the height of romance. The birthday poems, 'Stella at Wood-Park', 'A Receipt to Restore Stella's Youth', are love-poetry of a deep order. The last one for 13 March 1727, composed of 'tender and beautiful lines' to borrow a phrase from Sir Harold Williams, written when Stella was sure soon to

die, is profoundly moving, if only for the way it faces the fact of
death. There is room to quote the last paragraph:

> O then, whatever Heav'n intends,
> Take Pity on your pitying Friends;
> Nor let your Ills affect your Mind,
> To fancy they can be unkind.
> Me, surely me, you ought to spare,
> Who gladly would your Suff'rings share;
> Or give my Scrap of Life to you,
> And think it far beneath your Due;
> You, to whose care so oft I owe,
> That I'm alive to tell you so.

It is perhaps a tribute to the poem to notice that, isolated in this
way, the paragraph loses half its force: as with all good poetry
the effect is cumulative.

But if these poems are without quite their like in our literature,
they are not too distantly related to Ben Jonson's work. The
virtues in either case are much the same: colloquial speech, and
rather heavily stressed colloquial rhythms, not counterpointing
the prosodic stress as with Donne, but, except for some adept
fingering here and there, fitting in with it. Swift seldom approaches the lyrical, though in his later work there is at intervals a lilt which is almost singing, and which is carefully braked
after a few lines, lest something in the verse should belie the
truth of the prose. Skilful as he is in metre, however, where
Swift falls short is in the appeal to the eye; he hardly offers the
reader any visual imagery, none of the metaphorical imagery
which gives poetry its wings, again perhaps deliberately. What
he offers—except in such a furious outburst in 'The Legion
Club'—is a succession of facts, and ideas, or of emotions he
makes no attempt to impart. The reader is sometimes uncomfortably conscious that Swift is all the while over-aware of what
he is doing. He falls short again in the quality of his music—
here too perhaps deliberately, for in 'A Love-Song in the
Modern Taste' he is as mellifluous as anyone could wish. You
are never to be enchanted as you are with Pope; you are never
at any time to be carried away (except once or twice with rage);
but you are to be presented as clearly, as brutally, or as
delicately as the case may require with the actuality. Brutal
Swift could be, but his brutality has been exaggerated; delicate
he could be; the humanity of his feeling cannot be exaggerated.

The man who broke off a letter when he heard of Prior's death, who would not open the one which brought him the news of Gay's because he had a premonition, is a man whose affection was as rare as his genius was great, and it is manifest in his verse as it is in his letters.

Swift's last years, until he fell into darkness and complete silence some two years before his death, were increasingly ridden by his dread, not of death, but of the vertigo which made it impossible for him to direct his own affairs after 1740. Yet to the end of his responsible days he was himself, the self that had emerged in the last decade of the previous century, the man who had determined that some day he would make vice and folly bleed; the self that had developed in the first decade of the new century, the man of reason, knowing the limits of reason, suspicious of 'systems', and believing politically that power resided in the people as a whole; the self who had fought so valiantly in the twenties, hotly indignant at the miseries forced upon the people of Ireland; and always the man to whom friendship meant more than any other good in the world, the man who cannot be known except through a familiarity with his correspondence, as close as with his work. Stoic and Roman Republican, perhaps, rather than a Christian Englishman (though that he also was), he is, in many ways, the completest man the century produced, a man whose stern morals did not prevent his abundant charity, whose deep pessimism seemed only to give body to his irresistible gaiety. He towers head and shoulders above all his contemporaries both as a writer and as a man; his amazing energy continues to impart itself to any reader who admires him enough to criticize him, and is humble enough to do him homage; he is a man for the unsentimental to love, as he was loved by Pope and Prior, Gay and Bolingbroke, by Arbuthnot and by Stella. And his writings retain their disturbing impact on the imagination.

XIII

POETRY, 1720–1740

I. THOMSON

IT was during the twenties that the poetry of our period took definite shape, the expression of men living in the time that they did. It is to be valued as existing in its own right, not merely as faintly heralding the romantic movement. We might hazard a general description by saying that the poetry from about 1720—it had its forerunners, of course—was chiefly of the compendious kind—contemplative, philosophic, variously didactic, and intrepidly descriptive. In replacing the epic, it took all knowledge for its province and attempted a synthesis, so that we have presented to us what seems an inordinate number of poems about creation or the cosmos, sometimes in blank verse, but also in couplets and even in quatrains. These poems were necessarily objective, even when divagating on the human mind; never, we might think, was a period of poetry so little egocentric. It follows that, ignoring the individual soul it could not use emotion as its material; so it does not much move the post-romantic mind. In so far as it allowed itself to be emotive, the emotions it worked upon were such as might be derived from seeing the glory of the Divinity impelling the universe, or, to use the title of Ray's book, from grasping 'the wisdom of God manifested in the works of the creation'.

The poetry of the first two decades had to some extent been a fading echo of seventeenth-century thought and feeling, and had been largely occasional. That generation, working within an old sensibility, had passed; Prior, Parnell, Congreve, Lady Winchilsea had died; or they had faded from the poetic scene as did Tickell and Ambrose Philips; and though Gay went on writing, one feels that his *Fables* could have been written under Queen Anne as readily as under Queen Caroline. Pope, by far the most highly geared of his contemporaries, alone moved on. The change was gradual, though we now see it to have been radical. It is not only, as Mr. T. S. Eliot has said, that poetry ceased to be courtly, and came to seem as though it were all written by country parsons (as a good deal of it was), but that the poets with whom we now have to do were men daring to desert the individual in a narrow society as their usual subject, and follow Newton into strange seas of thought, or to venture into landscape painting. They were, in fact, consciously or not, reacting against Hobbes's dictum, hitherto complied with, that 'the subject of a poem is the manners of men, not natural causes'. We see them rapt with the mystery of colour and light as revealed to them in the *Opticks*, delighted with what geographers or botanists had to tell them, carried away by the excitement of mercantile expansion, loud in praise of liberty, moved by a sense of patriotism, and boldly declaring for domesticity. Naturally much of what they had to say had already been adumbrated by their forebears; but being less curious about the soul they gained a firmer grip of external nature, and a much firmer technique—surer though more crude —based on a freer mastery of Milton, and less funk of Spenser.

To the non-co-operative reader much of this poetry is dull, except for selected passages; he will skip with Thomson, yawn over Dyer apart from *Grongar Hill*, and—here quite rightly —touch Young's nocturnal vapourings very gingerly. Being largely didactic it can add little to the sensibility of the man of today, since, except with a major poet such as Pope, what is taught is always transient. We know about the rainbow and the comet, the springs and micro-organisms, and know it differently. The patriotism is often oddly stressed, too much inspired by faction; and the theme of commerce no longer warms our poetic fires. Nor does this poetry seek to reconcile opposites; the imagination, filled by what the mind discerned, is contemplative rather than creative; the symbols of the emotions are the things which themselves caused the emotions. 'There is a poetry', Goethe remarked, 'without figures of speech, which is a single figure of speech', and it is to this category that much of the poetry of this time belongs. Thus figurative imagery is largely out of place, and this poetry too lacks metaphysical tension. It reasons certainly, but the reason is treated, in Montesquieu's phrase, as 'le plus noble, le plus parfait, le plus exquis de nos sens'. Thus, for anyone prepared to take the trouble to apply the form of criticism that Mr. R. P. Blackmur has dubbed 'elucidation of scripture', it can give lively pleasure and acquire positive value; while to those who are delighted and enriched, or even entertained by understanding how a generation felt, and strove to express itself, the period can teach much, if only moderation, tolerance, and, yes, humility before so real an achievement.

Moreover there is here the interest of watching the new sensibility trying to find the medium in which to express itself. The Pindaric would not do—it was too clumsy; the eclogue, besides being of the wrong scale, had been laughed out of court, and so on; there seemed nothing for it but experiments with Milton, and bashful attempts to see if something could not be got out of that quaint old poet Spenser; as Thomson remarked prefacing *The Castle of Indolence*, 'the obsolete words, and simplicity of diction in some of the lines, which borders on the ludicrous, were necessary to make the imitation more perfect'. It was, of course, some time before imitation became unconscious, and thus modified become a valid instrument in the living tradition, which along that line of development had its end with Wordsworth. Yet it must be recognized that in accepting the older dictions as valid, the poets of the century may have denied themselves the full expression of what they had to say. Neither Spenserian nor Miltonic verse would seem the best expression for the complex of emotions, domestic, humanitarian, or contemplatively religious by which the century lived. It was an age of consolidation, using the terms of an age of exploration or of struggle. Abandoning the older tradition of which Pope was the last exponent, with its logico-dialectical inner structure, with its fierce, dramatic colloquialism, in attempting to universalize, the poets tended to stifle the more disturbing emotions of the domestic scene, which remain to be best expressed in such aberrant appearances as—after our period—Mrs. Greville's delicate 'Prayer for Indifference'. In substituting an externally organized style for one intellectually built up from within, they sacrificed the sense of tension. But if their poetry is low-toned, it repays attentive listening; it is not to be read in the same way as that of the preceding century; its wheels, to adopt Coleridge's phrase regarding the poetry of Donne and Dryden, do not grow hot with the rapidity of their motion. The sympathetic reader, however, will supply the warmth.

Dyer[1] may serve as a vantage point from which to attack the vast array of poems; he is an interesting 'case', for though to

---

[1] John Dyer, 1699–1757, was educated at Westminster, and though designed for the law, abandoned its study for art. He later travelled in Italy, and in 1741 took Orders, and became Vicar of Catthorpe in Leicestershire.

begin with he corresponded technically to his contemporaries
(he later fell well behind), he was not trying to say what,
for example, Thomson or Savage or Glover were anxious to
declare, though in some ways they come nearest him. His
interest for us at this point lies in his technical innovation, and
his example as a landscape poet. Finding that the Pindaric form
would not convey what he wished of his painter's sensations
when climbing Grongar Hill, he broke back to Miltonics of the
Allegro sort, beautifully varying his cadences, and achieved
a happy, successful poem of just the right verse density for
what he felt. It is illuminating to read the three available versions, beginning with the Pindaric which appeared in Savage's
Miscellany in 1726, going on to the tetrameter version which,
though written later, had been printed by Warner in 1725.
This, though it may be treated as an unpolished (and carelessly
printed) copy of the poem familiar today, Lewis having included it in his *Miscellany* of 1726, has some interesting variants.
We can see what is happening. Dyer is ridding himself of stale
forms, hereditary diction, and, what is more, inflated abstractions, all of which muffled his direct contact with what he
wanted to enjoy, and thus prevented him from singing about it.
A few lines from each form will illustrate the process; first the
Pindaric:

I

Fancy! Nymph, that loves to lye
On the lonely Eminence;
Darting Notice thro' the Eye,
Forming Thought, and feasting Sense:
Thou! that must lend Imagination Wings,
And stamp Distinction, on all worldly Things!
Come, and with thy various Hues,
Paint and adorn thy Sister Muse.
Now, while the Sun's hot Coursers, bounding high;
Shake lustre on the Earth, and burn, along the Sky.

II

More than Olympus animates my Lays,
Aid me, o'er labour'd, in its wide surveys;
And crown its Summit with immortal praise:
Thou, aweful Grongar! in whose mossy cells
Sweetly-musing Quiet dwells . . .

which is making distinctly heavy weather of it; you hardly feel
he is enjoying himself, as he so clearly is in the final version:

> *Silent Nymph*, with curious Eye!
> Who, the purple Ev'ning, lye
> On the Mountain's lonely Van,
> Beyond the Noise of busy Man,
> Painting fair the form of Things,
> While the yellow Linnet sings;
> Or the tuneful Nightingale
> Charms the Forest with her Tale;
> Come with all thy various Hues,
> Come and aid thy Sister Muse;
> Now while *Phoebus* riding high
> Gives lustre to the Land and Sky!
> *Grongar Hill* invites my Song,
> Draw the Landskip bright and strong;
> *Grongar*, in whose Mossie cells
> Sweetly-musing Quiet dwells . . .

the abstractions, it is true, have not quite gone, but they are
homely and understandable, and are not compelled to carry
ponderous philosophic conceptions: the hackneyed catchwords,
as Saintsbury suggested, are *un*hackneyed into propriety and
personality. If the main originality of the poem lies in its approach, the charm of the final version is the unifying swing of
the whole, the pace getting faster, the excitement increasing, as
Dyer walks higher and higher to get an ever more extended
view. Something had been done in this poem to free country
poetry, and it was done by the sheer exuberance of the metre
married to the novelty of the vision.

We shall revert to Dyer later in another connexion, noting
here what is most significant for us at the moment about the
passage quoted, namely the appeal from the muse of poetry to
her sister muse of painting to come and help her. The country
poem is ceasing to be a Georgic, or a 'place', or 'estate' poem,
or merely décor—and becoming a picture, a subject in its own
right: the writers are going to try to convert to poetry

> Whate'er *Lorrain* light-touch'd with softening hue,
> Or savage *Rosa* dash'd, or learned *Poussin* drew,

and luckily at that very moment they discovered for their
palettes the whole spectrum which Newton had revealed to

them in his *Opticks*. As Professor Marjorie Nicolson has brilliantly shown, from about 1725 the *Opticks* and its implications became almost a major theme in poetry for some decades, or, as the first excitement lapsed, a structural-decorative part of much minor philosophical poetry. In the earlier years of the century the country had been taken for granted; it was part of everybody's life, the poets had no separate consciousness of it; thus most of the rural poetry written was rustically didactic. Now, however, that the landscape painters had drawn attention to a possible new visual treatment, and the scientists had added an inner vision of how nature worked in such a way as to produce a renascence of wonder, the poets felt that they had something exciting here to work with. The difficulty was to find an adequate vehicle in which to express this. In going back to Milton rather than attempting to continue the Pindaric tradition (the heroic couplet, one may remark parenthetically, had before the turn of the century ceased to exercise whatever 'tyranny' it may ever have been able to impose), their instinct was right—or so we say, judging after the event. But what they did not all notice, or forgot, was that to employ the whole battery of the Miltonic poetic implies that you have something as important to say as Milton had, and as strong a poetic pressure moving you. Some tried to supply a deficiency of ideas by using elevated language, the result often being to produce that sort of stupor to which the term 'academic' best applies, a devastating effect of the platitudinous. Here, for instance, is Thomson, no mere poetaster, telling us that it is nice to sit down in the shade on a hot summer's day:

> Welcome, ye Shades! ye bowery Thickets, hail!
> Ye lofty Pines! ye venerable Oaks!
> Ye Ashes wild, resounding o'er the Steep!
> Delicious is your Shelter to the Soul,
> As to the hunted Hart the sallying Spring,
> Or Stream full-flowing, that his swelling Sides
> Laves, as he floats along the herbag'd Brink.
> Cool, thro' the Nerves, your pleasing Comfort glides;
> The Heart beats glad; the fresh-expanded Eye
> And Ear resume their watch; the Sinews knit;
> And Life shoots swift thro' all the lighten'd Limbs.

A dire result, we may think, of trying to adapt a form evolved for the conveying of an old ethos to fit a new sensibility.

A heavy price has to be paid by the generation that sets itself
to undergo a necessary discipline. Here and there certainly,
the innovating generation reaps the benefit as when Thomson
is setting the scene for his tumultuous birds:

> Or, where the NORTHERN ocean, in vast whirls
> Boils round the naked, melancholy isles
> Of farthest THULE, and th' ATLANTIC surge
> Pours in among the stormy HEBRIDES.

The metric—together with the borrowing from *Lycidas*—we
feel is justified. Thomson, moreover, had learnt to vary and
develop the metres, as we can see in continuing the passage:

> Who can recount what transmigrations there
> Are annual made? what nations come and go?
> And how the living clouds on clouds arise?
> Infinite wings! till all the plume-dark air,
> And white resounding shore are one wild cry.

That superb iamb-spondee conclusion is certainly not Miltonic.
Sometimes, in *The Seasons*, there is a complete break away from
the master into a colloquialism which shows, at least momentarily, an unshackled freedom within the form.

In the main, however, the Miltonics of this time—oddly
enough after the freedom attained earlier by John Philips—
produce a dulling effect upon the mind; it is—tell it not in
Gath—with some relief that we turn even to such obvious
satiric material as Young's *Universal Passion* to enjoy the sureness and conciseness of the couplet, which did at least bound
and circumscribe the often too conscientious fancy. We might
say they were too involved (just as Keats was to be) when they
went to Milton, though they could be 'artful' enough, detached enough, when playing with Spenser as Thomson did in
The Castle of Indolence, and Shenstone in *The Schoolmistress*. They
were, moreover, too plainly imitative, and laboured too much
under the yoke of the 'sublime'—this last may account partly
for the turgidity of the first quotation from Thomson—to do
more than here and there reveal the authentic poet. Dyer is a
case in point. Though *The Ruins of Rome* and *The Fleece* belong
to the next phase, it is interesting to note that instead of adapting Miltonic verse to what he had to say, he more and more
crushed his material under the weight of an inappropriate form,
though indeed *Paradise Regain'd* does not serve the former poem

badly. But it is no use to treat traffic on the high seas, as Dyer does in *The Fleece*, as sonorously as if it were the trafficking of the Archangels in the Miltonic cosmos. The passages of musical and imposing proper names fail to produce the sense of sublimity, and the line

> Woods, tow'rs, vales, caves, dells, cliffs, and torrent floods,

evokes, not the picture of the shepherd climbing Bredon after a kidling, but, with a smile, Satan skirting

> Rocks, caves, lakes, fens, bogs, dens, and shades of death,

while the stress on an important word beginning a line often becomes a reiterated thump. This is not to decry *The Fleece* as a whole; it is, in its way, an admirable construct, eruptive of poetry, sometimes in flashes attaining real vividness; it has here been unfairly treated to illustrate the kind of bondage from which Thomson at his best broke free.

For it is James Thomson who, Pope apart, is the outstanding poet of this phase; and since he transcends it less than Pope does, being more innocent, he is in some ways more representative. He belongs more surely to the eighteenth century, not only in its thraldom to Newtonian physics (seeking comfort in Derham and like thinkers with him), but also in its sentimentality: his Shaftesburian optimism does not feel the restraints that Pope imposed upon his own variant. Beginning with perfectly happy natural reactions to the enchanting countryside of Teviotdale in which he was brought up, he never had to struggle for his philosophy, any more than he had to probe deep for his symbolic subject-matter, as his 'Juvenilia' make plain. That is where his weakness lies. There is no battling for his intellectual or moral position, and even his abandonment of a career in the Church seems to have caused no alarming qualms; while the solution of the problem of evil he took happily from current Physico- and Astro-Theology. Born in 1700, third son of the manse, in 1712 he was sent to the Grammar School at Jedburgh, not far from his home at Southdean, in both places indulging in the country pursuits of a healthy boy. He also made the acquaintance of a farmer at Earlshaugh, Robert Riccaltoun, an amiable poetaster (he later took orders) who wrote a poem 'A Winter's Day', which 'first put the design' of his own *Winter* into Thomson's head, and though it has not been identified for certain, is probably that published in Savage's 1726 *Miscellany*. In 1715 he entered Edinburgh University, his home being in that town after the loss of his father who died in the process of exorcising a ghost. At the age of twenty he became a Divinity student, but not impressing his teachers as being a very favourable subject, at the end of February 1725, having published some poems in the Edinburgh press, he set out for London, and never saw Scotland again.

His 'Juvenilia' already exhibit the figure in his carpet, and it is interesting to have it pointed out, as it has been by Professor Herbert Drennon, that this execrably clumsy blank-verse poem, 'The Works and Wonders of Almighty Power', is almost a transcript of a passage in Shaftesbury's *Moralists*, while 'Upon Happiness' derives from John Norris of Bemerton. Very much a harbinger too is a poem in quite neat couplets comparatively free of 'poetic diction', 'Of a Country Life', published in the *Edinburgh Miscellany* in 1720. This has some agreeably vivid description, born of participating enjoyment, of the sights and sounds of the countryside. In it Thomson applauds rural sports in a way he would later reject, but foreshadows what was to be his major life-work by a description of the seasons which clearly enough indicates his preferences, since he gives four lines each to Spring and Summer, two to Autumn, and no less than sixteen excitedly appreciative ones to Winter. Again, the 'Hymn on the Power of God', in common measure, though not so Deistic as the Hymn which was to conclude *The Seasons* in 1730, asks us to praise 'The God of Nature', and is an earnest of the religious colouring which was to be diffused over so much of Thomson's work.

Religious colouring rather than any deep religious sense, which it would be useless to demand from this amiable scientific-rationalist, moved to a sentimental Deism only a bigot need be annoyed by. He was all that is stated in Stanza 68 of the first Canto of *The Castle of Indolence*, engaging, easy-going, genial, soft-hearted, sensitive to the charms of nature, and interested, one might add, in any and every current philosophy without criticizing its sources or pursuing its implications. If his only completely successful works are the first *Winter*, *To the Memory of Sir Isaac Newton*, and *A Hymn on the Seasons*, there is no reason why the rest of his poetry should be put aside as flat or faded, spurious, or disgustingly didactic.

Evidently it is by that widely influential and for long immensely popular but chaotic poem *The Seasons* that Thomson must be judged. It is extremely uneven in performance because the impulse formative of the various parts springs from such different levels of awareness and response; and since it was so much a matter of patchwork and insertions no one can guess what incongruity is coming next. The purpose as it seems to have formulated itself gradually in Thomson's mind was to show the workings of Creative Nature: that, together with the framework of the progression of the year, is what holds the poem together at all, coherence being given by a certain inner rhythm of movement from, in each morsel, the material to the spiritual. To judge from the first 1726 version of *Winter*, Thomson seems to have begun as a landscape painter sensitive to light and 'feel', by the very act of creating the harmony necessary for a picture led into a sense of the Deity, a sense that all was well, which in turn drew him on to the somewhat oddly emergent and totally unconvincing solution of the problem of evil which concludes the poem. The earliest version is a charming spontaneous thing, not too long, and there is just the right modicum of 'philosophy' to give it substance. Then something disastrous happened, and the Scottish border poem became a didactic work, a kind of *Essay on Man*.

In the Preface which Thomson added to the second 1726 edition of *Winter*, after deploring the decay of poetry in his day, its triviality, he exalts nature as a great and serious subject; it contains 'all that enlarges and transports the soul'. Although this Preface is, amusingly enough, a close adaptation of Norris of Bemerton's address 'To the Reader' in his 1687 *Collection of Miscellanies*, it is the differences rather than the likenesses that are significant; for whereas Norris declares that he will raise poetry to its height by treating of 'Divine and Moral Subjects', Thomson is going to rely on 'wild romantic country' and 'the Works of Nature', though he will not reject the help of the *Georgics*. This, of course, is where the disaster which had overtaken Thomson becomes apparent. He is about to assume the mantle of the theosophic-rationalist preacher. Everything has to be 'philosophically', that is, scientifically solved. 'Frost or the moral order, it makes little difference which,' Professor Drennon remarks, 'he always feels it incumbent on him to give a rationalistic explanation.' The Preface indicates that he is to become—among other things—a lay Derham to whom many sorts of different knowledge were to be added. There was really no need for Thomson to justify himself; there was nothing startlingly new about the kind of poetry he had given the reading world, so that we can regard the Preface rather as the symptom of what had happened to him. He had become entangled with the intelligentsia, beginning with his Scotch friends Mallet (or Malloch) and Murdoch, going on to Aaron Hill, Thomas Rundle, and others, and being made at home among the rich intellectuals such as Lord Binning, whose son he tutored, and Bubb Dodington. Their subjects of conversation were the latest scientific discoveries and pseudo-scientific speculations with their bearings on the old attitudes, the most recent travels into remote regions, the latest artistic finds in Italy, in short all the things which mentally active, cultivated, civilized beings with a sense of values would naturally talk about. Unluckily Thomson was not of the calibre to order things of such diverse scope, to fuse all this material satisfactorily into a poem; and just as many poets of our own yesterday clogged themselves with Marx and depth-psychology and anthropological vistas, so Thomson became lost and embrangled in a mass of material which excited him enormously, but not all of which he could intuitively apprehend. So as his knowledge grew—led by an ever-active curiosity—he fitted in new bits, and enlarged or corrected existing pieces; and thus the poem swelled, not indeed so catastrophically as did in the next century Bailey's *Festus* or Tupper's *Proverbial Philosophy*, but enough to destroy whatever organic unity the poem might have had. Thus *The Seasons* became in the end the most extraordinary hotchpotch of direct observation and the poet's nervous response, landscape painting, with or without figures, moralizing, praises of that wedded love denied him by the obduracy of Miss Elizabeth Young, sentimental anecdote and humanitarianism, light satire, history and geography, patriotism and panegyrics on politicians, applied science, a looking back to a golden age incompatible with an almost simultaneous progressivist looking forward to a similar perfection of living ('What cannot active Government perform, New-moulding Man?'). Added to these are the latest events and discoveries, the aurora borealis of March 1716, Newton with prism and telescope, the plague at Marseilles, botanists with microscopes, prison reformers, travellers' reports, and so on.

The innumerous details are faggoted together, you might say, by an extraordinary rope of difficult concepts and conflicting assumptions twisted close, with, as a dimly pervasive thread, especially in the *Hymn*, a sentimental 'optimistic' Deism, based partly on the Stoics, partly on the latest results of natural philosophy. 'And over these complexities', Professor A. D. McKillop a little mournfully remarks, 'the poet meditates without agony or rigour, sometimes pedestrian, always conciliatory, genial and eclectic.'

Thomson, to put it plainly, was no thinker, and he tried to do far too much. There is no driving force in the poem to give it direction such as informs Pope's at least equally complex *Essay on Man*, no brilliant mind, no formative energy as we can feel there fusing the incompatible elements. Pope is all the time selecting, criticizing, arguing; his poem is, of course, from first to last a moral argument, whereas Thomson simply imparts any piece of popular philosophy he thinks picturesque. It is the very lack of limitations that limits his vision, makes it less intense; thus nobody would quote *The Seasons* to describe the human situation today as Sir Winston Churchill in 1949 was able to quote the *Essay*.

Yet the poem has some delightful passages, often extensive, either where Thomson is intensely interested, as when he tries to describe the various qualities of light—then he becomes succinct; or when he lets the man of sentiment have unabashed play—then he is likeable; or when his Deistic fervour, however 'optimistic' it may be, carries him along with notable speed and intensity. If his Miltonism may now and again be tiresome (it is absurd to argue with Dr. Johnson that there is no tang of Milton in his versification), it often has about it much of the rude sweetness of a Scottish tune. It is harder, perhaps, to get over some of his craggy latinisms and his pet words—his diffusives, effusives, amusives, and so on—or again his too frequent use of adjectives in place of adverbs; but once you get used to the idiom the variations within it become attractive and, what is more, expressive, as do departures from his sometimes monotonous prosody such as the surprising and effective

And shiver ev'ry Feather with Desire.

It becomes a positive value to go with him, to adventure with him to see how he makes his none too flexible medium begin to express the sensibility of his time, as in the domestic-love passage in 'Autumn', or when he praises the social virtues; it is a positive value because it is, when embraced in this way, an exploration of reality. There are times when, stirred by his personal discovery of natural scenery, together with other people's discoveries of how nature works, he presents us with an object nobody else offers us in that sort of way, together with an invitation to share that particular sensibility. It would be non-sensical to claim this as a great poem: it is readable *in toto* only by the curious and the scholar; nevertheless, it need not be insisted, it contains a very great deal that should delight the reasonable reader.

Nobody can fail to admire the immense industry, not only in the rearranging and the rewriting that went to this poem, but in reading. It is a work of enormous erudition, a compendium of lore and learning; the literary and philosophic sources traced by Professor McKillop represent a library, and it is just to say that Thomson's description of the subjects he would like to spend evenings discussing with his friends very fairly describes the scope of the poem. Not indeed, the original scope, but such as it appeared to Thomson to have been when he made the 1730 revision of *Winter*, where a pretty stiff conversational programme is suggested, covering metaphysics, science, ethics, history, and geography. To us, with our ideal of specialized knowledge for its own sake, it seems monstrous; but to Thomson's contemporaries our procedure, leading to an admirably segregated sterility, would, perhaps with some justice, have engendered scorn. For there was, after all, some object in all this labour:

> As thus we talk'd
> Our hearts would burn within us, would inhale
> That portion of divinity, that ray
> Of purest heaven, which lights the glorious flame
> Of patriots and of heroes. But if doom'd
> In powerless humble fortune, to repress
> These ardent risings of the kindling soul;
> Then, even superior to ambition, we
> Would learn the private virtues . . .

and if this should be thought too priggish or intense, wit, and humour, and laughter 'deep-shaking every nerve' is to act as relief.

The whole passage is calmly and happily serious. Thomson is

talking; he has forgotten Milton, since there is no need to reach
for the sublime. It is the statement of 'progressivism', evolution-
ary Deism we might call it, which we have already met at the
conclusion of the Hymn (see Chapter I). And it is time to ask
ourselves how that passage taken with the whole theme of
'fittingness' differs in essentials from:

> How exquisitely the individual Mind
> (And the progressive powers perhaps no less
> Of the whole species) to the external World
> Is fitted:—and how exquisitely, too—
> Theme this but little heard of among men—
> The external World is fitted to the Mind;
> And the creation (by no lower name
> Can it be called) which they with blended might
> Accomplish:—this is our high argument.

One would say that in *The Recluse*, at any rate, Wordsworth's
philosophy differs from Thomson's only in the sense—somewhat faint—of the creative capacity of the mind. But Wordsworth could not help feeling what he did; Thomson, had he
lived in a different age, might, we think, have felt otherwise;
but both began with much the same reaction towards nature.
Thomson, however, never gets very near to describing the
actual impact of the external things upon the nerves; the
following is possibly as close as he ever does get:

> 'Tis *Harmony*, that World-attuning Power
> By which all Beings are adjusted, each
> To all around, impelling and impell'd
> In endless Circulation, that inspires
> This universal Smile. Thus the glad Skies,
> The wide-rejoycing Earth, the Woods, the Streams
> With every *Life* they hold, down to the Flower
> That paints the lowly Vale, or Insect-Wing
> Wav'd o'er the Shepherds' Slumber, touch the Mind
> To Nature tun'd, with a light-flying Hand,
> Invisible; quick-urging, thro' the Nerves,
> The glittering Spirits, in a Flood of Day.

That passage, dropped in 1744, expresses the kind of sentiment
later generations have wished he had explored and developed;
but even had he felt impelled to do so, it is doubtful whether
the prosody into which he had built his sensations, and the

diction he had so whole-heartedly inherited, could have communicated it.

At the present day there are, it seems, two schools; those who regard Thomson primarily as a 'nature poet', and those who conceive his main interest to have been philosophical. But the argument is idle, because it is quite likely that Thomson, after the first flush of youthful reaction, found nature by herself not enough and wished to deepen his theme. The argument, moreover, is meaningless, since it was only through philosophy that nature could mean anything; nature and philosophy were the same. This was altogether in the line of thought of Ray and others, and had been long enough popularized by Steele and Addison. What the poets such as Thomson (who was one among many) were doing was to express the ethos of the time, its apprehension of the universe. So when we say that something disastrous happened to Thomson, that is only from our point of view; for him and his contemporaries the development was only right and proper. After all, the business of the poet was to instruct, and it was the new natural philosophy that his readers wished to be instructed in; thus Pemberton:

Every Gentleman, who has a moderate Degree of Literature or Politeness, may by this assistance [he is here referring to his own popularization of Newton, but the remark covers wider ground] form a comprehensive View of the stupendous Frame of Nature, and the Structure of the Universe . . . without engaging in the minute and tedious Calculations necessary to their Production;

and every polite, that is educated, gentleman would be expected to know these things, just as he was to have acquired 'a Taste of the Magnificence of a Plan of Architecture, or the elegance of a beautiful Plantation'.

Thomson, it is evident, was profoundly stirred by the revelation afforded by Newton of how Creative Divinity works. In the poem *To the Memory of Sir Isaac Newton* he asks:

> Did ever Poet image aught so fair,
> Dreaming in whispering Groves by the hoarse Brook?
> Or Prophet, to whose Rapture Heaven descends!

And it is hardly Thomson's fault that the occasion of this pæan, namely the justice and beauteousness of the refractive law, does not appeal to us in the same way as it did to him. The rainbow was lovely, as Thomson saw; but what was really marvellous was the way it happened. That was the stupendous thing. In due course people became accustomed to this, and we can understand, though we need not excuse, the exuberance at Haydon's 'immortal' dinner, when he with Keats, Lamb, and Wordsworth drank confusion to mathematics, after Keats had declared that the prism had destroyed all the poetry in the rainbow. Naturally, if Keats had had the spectrum drummed into him at school he might well write

> There was an awful rainbow once in heaven
> We know her woof and texture; she is given:
> In the dull catalogue of common things.
> Philosophy will clip an angel's wings . . .

But Thomson and his generation would simply not have understood this attitude; they might, alas! have regarded it as immature, and have said with Coleridge: 'In wonder all philosophy began; in wonder it ends; but the first wonder is the offspring of ignorance, the last is the parent of adoration.' For what was happening in the poetry of the twenties was a renascence of the second kind of wonder, that of most of the Romantics would have seemed to the earlier poets like the gaping of country bumpkins. Yet wonder was not enough. The thinking man could go beyond this to a conception of the moral governance of the universe. Happy the man who can know the causes of things—the Virgilian tag echoes through much of *The Seasons*—for then, to his contemplative mind, a great deal will be revealed. To such, endowed with an 'exalting eye',

> a fairer World
> Of which the Vulgar never had a Glimpse
> Displays its Charms; whose Minds are richly fraught
> With Philosophic Stores, superior Light.

To the philosopher, but not to the vulgar, it is evident that there is an analogy between the natural and moral world. And since to a man of Thomson's nature and real love of beauty the natural world declared benevolence as its principle, benevolence must be the ruling factor in the moral order. The essential goodness of God being granted, it followed that the happier man was, the better pleased God would be, a point of view based perhaps on what such divines as Barrow and Tillotson had said; there was at least that much orthodox support. The argument from analogy—not the same that would be developed by Butler, its opposite indeed—had been argued at least as early as Joseph Glanvill, who seems to be echoed at the end of *Winter*, where there intrudes another form of optimism, briefly stated perhaps as the belief that the justice of God corresponded with man's idea of justice. To some extent all this was derivable from Clarke's *Being and Attributes of God* (1705), for Clarke's second law of righteousness was benevolence, a benevolence manifested in the created world order. To the modern reader the argument at the end of *Winter* seems an amazing *non sequitur*, and therefore an unconvincing solution of the problem of evil. The argument, however, would seem to be mainly one for immortality; nature 'dies' in winter, but spring is not far behind; if this was not also true of man, nature would not be a reflection of the moral order. Also, since to be judged by only one life would be unjust, there must be a succession of lives (this also fits in with the rising scale of being), and it is an easy step from there to the Pythagoreanism which Thomson expressed more clearly in *Liberty* than in *The Seasons*. This faith was not uncommon in that part of the century, and was discussed by Soame Jenyns in No. CLXIII of *The World*, 12 February 1756, as though it were a commonplace.

None of this much matters to us wishing to enjoy in the poem what Thomson alone has to give, but even so very light an 'elucidation of scripture' is necessary if we are to get unobstructed the enjoyment open to us; and it would seem clear that Thomson's own original enjoyment, which helped to produce his philosophy, was enormously sharpened, made more tense and exciting, by the philosophy itself. He had achieved, if not synthesis, or a unified vision, at least a syncretism; there was no split, no dualism such as Butler was to insist upon, and he could sail happily away, feeling that anything he put into his poem was appropriate, adding more and more 'as books or conversation extended his knowledge and opened his prospects'. So the modest 405 lines of the 1726 *Winter* became 1,069 lines in 1744, and the first *Seasons* of 1730 (where *Winter* was already nearly doubled), containing 4,464 lines, expanded some eleven hundred by the final revision of 1746, which was the last that Thomson attempted.

The present-day reader probably finds most exciting not the well-known set pieces such as the snowstorm, the thunderstorm, the sandstorm, and so on, nor even the landscapes, where

Thomson sometimes fails to distinguish between description and cataloguing, nor the sentimental stories; but those occasional lines or short passages where by some kind of magic Thomson opens doors he himself does not seem to be aware of. Apparently he thinks he is describing; he is really lifting the shutter of intensely imaginative vision. The reader comes across these things with a shock of delighted surprise, as at the end of the Siberian passage in the 1730 editions of *Winter*. The passage first occurs in the second 1726 edition, where we see

> the *Bear*
> Rough *Tenant* of these Shades! shaggy with Ice
> And dangling Snow, stalks thro' the Woods, forlorn.

But in 1730, after the bear we have:

> While tempted vigorous o'er the marble waste,
> On sleds reclin'd, the furry Russian sits;
> And by his rain-deer drawn, behind him throws
> A shining kingdom in a winter's day,

a connotative glimpse which easily makes up for the bear shaggy with ice having become 'the shaggy bear with dangling ice all horrid'. But, and this is why we suspect his unawareness, in the 1744 version the bear becomes merely 'shapeless', and the furry Russian is extinguished, in the interests of 'accuracy'. Or take again the passage in *Spring* where Thomson, using Burnet's *Theory of the Earth*, gives a vision of the time when nature was deemed to have changed her course, a kind of terrene 'Fall' to correspond with the Fall of man:

> Hence in old time, they say, a deluge came;
> When the disparting orb of earth, which arch'd
> Th' imprisoned deep around, impetuous rush'd,
> With ruin inconceivable, at once
> Into the gulph, and o'er the highest hills
> Wide-dash'd the waves in undulation vast;

and so far the effect is a little laboured; but then we get a transition which brings us to a last line which is miraculous, even though it may be derived from Milton:

> Till, from the centre to the streaming clouds
> A shoreless ocean tumbled round the globe.

And here it was not science that captivated Thomson, for by then even popular opinion was beginning to reject Burnet; and, moreover, no optimist could accept him seeing that if the world had once been better than it now is, all cannot be for the best in the best of all possible worlds: Thomson himself referred to 'fabling Burnet'. What spurred him was the sudden vision, and here, perhaps, is the clearest example of Thomson exploring his imagination, and so releasing that of the reader.

Yet if we read Thomson with an eye for this sort of stimulus, we shall lose sight of the after all rather important fact that this is a poem about climate, and that what interests Thomson most about climate is light, and the effect of light, colour itself being light analysed. The obvious rotation of the seasons is of course illustrated, the flowers in woodland or garden change as do the crops; sheep need different attention; there is a time for work and a time for love, for labour and for feasting. Men endure the heat of the tropics or the rigours of Lapland, the birds migrate, avalanches wipe out brigades of unfortunate soldiers, and everything in due course lends itself to moralizing, especially when stories are told, such as the Lavinia variant of the Ruth story, or the one of the lover struck by lightning, or the pater-familias meeting his death in the snow. And if these stories all come from traceable sources, they are none the less impressive for that, and equally well illustrate the weather. But although Thomson evidently likes all this well enough, and feels it to be good material for poetry, it is only when he is describing light that we feel he could not but write poetry; he is absorbed in watching its changes, filled with delight and wonder, sensing in its behaviour some revelation of the divine, something which puts him in touch with the inapprehensible. Already in the first *Winter*, although it is full of the noise of storm and tempest where 'Huge Uproar lords it wide', we feel Thomson's almost mystic sense of light, at this season of the year more particularly of light as whiteness. Throughout the poem we feel that Thomson is moved by

> the fair power
> Of light to kindle and create the whole

and it is in his rapt attention to the changes of light and colour, far more than in the apostrophes and invocations—a little too reminiscent of Milton—that we are immediately aware of the depth of his response, a depth it cannot offend anyone to call religious.

It is revealing to look for a moment at the sort of thing Thomson was doing in some of his revisions. To begin with there were enormous additions. Sometimes they were admirable, and in tone; when they stuck to the theme of the seasons, which is after all that of the poem, they were valuable contributions, as are the fishing scene, and the flower-pieces in *Winter*. Often the corrections of words or phrases are great improvements, as when in *Winter* he alters 'Is all one dazzling Waste' to 'Is one wild dazzling Waste'. But it is the larger alterations we must consider. What is happening? we ask. Abstraction, personification, metaphor, and classical reference have ousted objectivity and sensitiveness. It is all done, we imagine, in the interests of 'the sublime'. Can we blame Lyttelton, who had a finger in the later versions? Probably not; 'the age', it seems, was tending in that direction, or at least one part of it was, moving towards Gray's Odes and Burke *On the Sublime*, and more and more to that generalization which was not so much the expression of common experience, as the refusal with Imlac in *Rasselas* to number the streaks of the tulip, or with Sir Joshua Reynolds to notice 'particularities, and details of every kind'. Lyttelton, that perfect good boy of his time, was no doubt in part responsible; but his influence lay rather in the fields of religious or moral thinking, struggling as he used to do to convert Thomson to Christianity. Yet there does not seem to be much retrenchment of Deistic statement, or intrusion of a specifically Christian ethos. Lyttelton seems to have urged a higher degree of intensity, but his influence appears for the more part to have told in the direction of a prudery the mid-nineteenth century would have approved. In the closing passages of *Winter*, for example, 'Those Nights of secret Guilt' become 'Those gay-spent, festive Nights', which makes us wonder why Virtue should have been dragged in as a contrast a few lines later. Again, in *Summer*, the story of Damon, first introduced in 1730 as a healthy, happy story, is in 1744 made vulgar and even slightly salacious in the interests of 'morality'; it appears too from the manuscript corrections that Lyttelton would have expunged from *Spring* the line which states that beauty 'is when unadorn'd adorn'd the most'.

But it is not such revisions that make it difficult for us to grasp the poem as an entity; it is the extravagant amount and variety of material inserted. Thomson is a perfect jackdaw; he goes about making finds, and adding them to the treasures he hoards in his nest. He is so charmingly eager in his discoveries, from the Psalms to Maupertuis, that he has to tell us everything, and the man who tells everything becomes a bore. Thomson incurs the danger of being such, even to those naturalized in his idiom; for the organic sense is dissipated, as it is not in the *Essay on Man*. The fact is that he confused the 'kinds'; and 'the confusion of kinds', as Henry James remarked, 'is the inelegance of letters and the stultification of values'. And since the values in *The Seasons* from this very cause tend to become blurred, the bulk militates against our grasping the object whole. Try as we will the poem obstinately resolves itself into separate morsels, many of them indubitably fine, others touching; some, it would be foolish to deny, either emotionally or poetically unworthy. Here and there the work is intolerably slack; Dr. Johnson could read passages aloud omitting every other line, to the 'highest admiration' of Shiels, and G. C. Macaulay gave an example of how this might be done. Yet if it is not a poem of the first order, it is one that we would not do without; and, after all, a work which had so much effect on European poetry and which was praised by Goethe demands respect. It contains magnificences and felicities; it is above all a friendly poem, and to converse with it is not always to miss exaltation, and at least we often share the excitement of sharpened recognition. A good portion of what it has essentially to impart can be derived from the admirable poem *To the Memory of Sir Isaac Newton*, written in 1727, the year Newton died, after *Winter* had appeared and while *Summer* was being composed. We may think that scientific fact is incompletely absorbed, but a little sympathetic imagination can dissolve the particles foreign to poetry.

It succeeds then; and it is sad to note that in the same year Thomson perpetrated *Britannia*, which was not published until 1729. In our modern jargon we should call it a blatantly war-mongering poem. It cannot be denied a certain vigour; it is not the work of a hack-poet, and contains such things as

—where loud the Northern main
Howls through the fractur'd *Caledonian* isles;

but indignation aroused by Walpole's refusal to make war did not bring forth first-rate verses in any quantity. And here we come upon the most disastrous part of Thomson's social milieu, for he had become absorbed in the gifted circle which formed the opposition. Again and again we meet laments for the decay of British virtue, morals, integrity, and valour. Even the later versions of *The Seasons* are infected. The prevailing atmosphere in that coterie led Pope himself into some absurdities, and the effect on Thomson was lamentable in that it induced him to waste a great deal of time and energy on the long elaborate poem *Liberty*, published at intervals in five parts during 1735 and 1736. It has not the narrative and epic interest of *Leonidas*, yet it is a far better poem than any others on that theme. Thomson, however, tried to do far too much in it. It is really a history of civilization, which can flourish only where freedom exists, as it did with such vigour in England until Walpole's fatal accession to power. Goethe found it bad because in it Thomson had given himself over to party feeling, and it is true that the worst portions are those devoted to 'corruption'. It is a pity that the pleasurable parts, which are those where Thomson praises the countryside and looks forward to a happy, prosperous, golden-age England, should be overlaid by so much tedious historical matter—though even that becomes livelier where Britain comes into view and the poet writes good Whig history. It is not altogether just that it should be relegated to the shelf where Dr. Johnson consigned it 'to harbour spiders and to gather dust', for it repays a first careful reading so that enjoyable lines may be marked. Here again we may think Thomson erred in confusing the kinds; for it is not a travel poem as is Addison's *Letter from Italy*, nor strictly historical, nor mainly political; it fails now as it did at its birth, because it has not the force to unify and give single direction to the emotional responses it was meant to call forth.

There is no such error either in the conception or the contrivance of *The Castle of Indolence*, at any rate as far as the first canto goes. Born of a mood of idleness and friendship, cast in a form chosen because it was fun to fool about with quaint old versification and diction, it·has an ease and spontaneity, a freedom from rhetoric, in the bad sense, which makes it delightful; and delightfully easy reading, provided always that you will enter into the game. Half-hearted Spenserians may revolt at the flippancy, but true worshippers will no more mind this than the Dryden devotee objects to *The Rehearsal* or the Montague-Prior *jeu d'esprit*; the general reader may resent eftsoons, ne and moe, depainted and yblent, not to mention the occa-

sional grotesqueness of phrase, until he realizes that he is not
meant to take them seriously. And when, carried away by the
theme, Thomson forgets all the frippery of imitation, he really
exudes something of the original, a sensuous music, and a simple
directness of expression, combined with a freedom from contemporary poetic diction, which are refreshing. It is possible to
say that this is Thomson's best poem, though it is not his most
important, if best means most immediately apprehensible and
enjoyable, and one in which the kinds are not confused. Where
he does not attempt any archaisms he speaks the language of
his day, which is almost that of ours. A few of his happier
favourite expressions remain; the streams bicker, the word
serene is used as a verb, and he occasionally invents (enough has
not been made of Thomson as an inventor in this sense), or
adapts from Milton's prose as when he refers to 'the wretch who
slugs his life away'. Exquisite? No; that is too high distinction.
It is not too much to say that it provides a charming pleasaunce.

It appears to have begun as a joke among friends enjoying
laziness, Thomson himself, 'more fat than bard beseems', Quin
the actor, the amiable poetaster Patterson, Forbes, the 'joyous
youth', Murdoch, 'A little, round, fat, oily man of God',
Lyttelton (genteelly on the outskirts), and others. Most important perhaps, John Armstrong, whose unpublished poem on
winter Thomson had generously pilfered, who wrote the cave of
spleen stanzas at the end of Canto I, and had in 1744 published
his blank verse poem *On the Art of Preserving Health*. The
organized poem, however, shows no sign of scrappiness, and
soon after the enchanter Indolence begins his seductive singing
we are caught up in the atmosphere of the idle Abbaye de
Thelème. Indolence is no fool; he knows that to offer sensuous
joys is not enough for the intelligent man; some higher general
principle must be appealed to:

> What, what is Virtue but Repose of Mind?
> A pure ethereal Calm! that knows no Storm,
> Above the Reach of wild Ambition's Wind,
> Above those Passions that this World deform,
> And torture Man, a proud malignant Worm!
> But here, instead, soft Gales of Passion play,
> And gently stir the Heart, thereby to form
> A quicker Sense of Joy; as Breezes stray
> Across th' enlivened Skies, and make them still more gay.

There is movement in the canto, a little light satire (we have momentary forebodings when we read of 'the patriot's noble rage, Dashing corruption down through every worthless age', but the danger soon passes), and throughout there is a general feeling of richness, of luxury, of a *fays-ce que voudras* life in which boredom is guarded against, though not, alas, hypochondria, gout, apoplexy, and other ailments of the rich not unusual in a society in which Addison plaintively complained, 'How can a man help his being fat who eats proper to his quality?' It is a good lotus-eating world, which it is pleasant to inhabit for a time. And the moral of it?

Well, the moral is round the corner, not so much in the hidden hospital for incurables, which is obviously worth risking, but in the second canto, where the Knight of Arts and Industry, somewhat oddly begotten by savagery on poverty, breaks up the sham paradise. It is often complained that Thomson spoilt the poem by forcing the moral forward in this way; but Thomson is not being puritanically moral. Canto II is not so much a set of moralizing stanzas as a poem on industry and commerce, one of the very many of that age; it was a theme Thomson could believe in. Poems of that family will be touched upon later; what is worth noticing here is a new note, a different pace, of which one would not have thought Thomson capable; the verse has forgotten sublimity but has a vigour and an ease, almost one would say a lordly Byronic assumption of careless power, not it is true sustained, but never far away. The third stanza, for example:

> I care not, Fortune, what you me deny:
> You cannot rob me of free Nature's Grace;
> You cannot shut the Windows of the Sky,
> Through which *Aurora* shows her brightening Face:
> You cannot bar my constant Feet to trace
> The Woods and Lawns, by living Stream, at Eve.
> Let health my nerves and finer Fibres brace,
> And I their toys to the *great children* leave:
> Of Fancy, Reason, Virtue, nought can me bereave.

But alas, only some four months after the poem was published, in May 1748, Thomson died, an event celebrated in Collins's famous tribute. Yet *The Castle of Indolence* happily rounds off a varied enough body of poetry—the plays have been treated in the section on drama—which any writer not of first rank might look upon with satisfaction. His smaller poems and occasional

verses call for no especial comment; they are neat, they breathe
a delicacy of feeling rather than any passion of love or fervour of
friendship. It is worth noting that Thomson was adept enough
in the quatrain or rhymed stanza, but his couplets, as instanced
say by his humorous lines on Murdoch, 'the incomparable
soporific doctor' (who seems to have been able to stand any
amount of chaff), lack variety of movement or attack. Some of
his shorter pieces should be better known, but it is unlikely that
Thomson will ever again be a popular poet, though he will
always be read by a circle considerably larger than that of
student or historian.

2. SCIENTIFIC VERSE

Thomson is central to the large group of poets, poetasters, and
mere versifiers spurred on by the discoveries of Newton and the
system of Locke to write poems about the cosmos. Never was there
such a spate of philosophic verse as burdened the bookstalls
from, say, the appearance of John Reynolds's[1] *Death's Vision*
in 1709 till after the middle of the century. They were not, of
course, the first cosmic poems; after all, leaving *Paradise Lost*
aside, there was the Du Bartas–Sylvester *Divine Weeks and
Works*, to which Henry More's *Song of the Soul* might be added;
but the new writers went back to Lucretius (the translation by
Creech was much reprinted) rather than any Christian cosmogony, and if few of them were poets, they represent the
effort the age made to accept the current concepts of the universe
and of man. Add here and there a little descriptive nature
poetry, and what they said might as well have been uttered in
prose. But in reading them the sense all the time comes through
that these men were profoundly excited, and that if Newton
voyaged in perilous seas of thought alone he towed behind
his noble vessel an inordinate number of skiffs, the Derhams of
verse. Not that all of them by any means shared Derham's
orthodoxy in matters of faith; if few were so openly deistic as
Thomson, many of them exhibiting the oddest mixture of new
science and old theology, all were to some extent dazzled by
the immensity of the universe, its beautiful fitness, and the

[1] John Reynolds, 1667–1727, went up to Pembroke College, Oxford, from the
Free School at Stourbridge. He took no degree, but was ordained, being temporarily a trinitarian. He soon reverted to dissent, and became pastor in various
places.

neatness of the way it worked physically and morally. In a sense all these poems are hymns of praise to God, or whatever name they liked to call him, the First Cause, the Creative Principle or anything else. With few is it a question of mere description, the business was to teach. What else was poetry for? many of them would seem to ask. The author of a moralistic poem *An Essay on Human Life* (2nd edition 1736) wrote in his Preface:

> Of all Kinds of Poetry the *Didascalic* is the most valuable . . . the descriptive Kind is like a fine Landskip, where you meet with two or three principal Figures; the rest is all Rocks, Rivulets, hanging Woods and verdant Lawns, amusing to the Eye, shewing the Taste of the Painter, but carrying little Instruction along with it . . .

a sentiment shared by Pope and Thomson. Reynolds, indeed, frankly confessed: 'I could never allow myself to study the laws of Poetry, or the accuracies of a poem.' In view of such a situation it is interesting to inquire for whom these poems were written, and why these works were composed in verse rather than in prose. It did not matter to him, since his work was popular enough. It was reprinted in 1716 and again in 1719, was expanded for a further edition in 1725, now entitled *A View of Death*, and reissued later. Intermediately there had been some dozen or so cosmic poems, culminating in *The Seasons*, and, if you like, *The Essay on Man*, though Pope obviously lays stress on man and his position in the universe rather than on the universe itself. They are, it may be suggested, the popular expression of the Enlightenment, the ideas of physical science and psychology being made available to the ordinary polite reader of whom there was an ever-growing number; they are a symptom of the coalescence of the reading publics referred to in the first chapter. And just as, according to the parson-poet Diaper, moral reflections were more readily transmitted in verse than in prose, so were the ideas set out in scientific treatises which the common man would find deterrent reading; these poems were more attractive, and less labour, than the *Principia*, the *Opticks*, which at any rate remained in Latin for some years, and the *Essay on Human Understanding*. By the time of Newton's death in 1727 it became almost obligatory to mention Newton in a poem, on whatever subject, so much so that Somerville[1]

---

[1] William Somerville, 1675–1742, was educated at Winchester and New College, Oxford, of which he was elected Fellow. He was for some time a student at the Middle Temple, but lived a country and sporting life enriched by literary interests.

rounded off with some lines upon him even that agreeable hunting poem *The Chase*. Indeed a poem on Newton seemed to the young poets the first step up Parnassus, as it was with Glover,[1] on which theme his 'advent'rous muse with trembling pinions soared'. A few of the lines of that too lengthy and too classically ornamented poem (written in his sixteenth year) are worth quoting to illustrate the whole phase:

> Newton, who first th' Almighty's works display'd,
> And smooth'd that mirror, in whose polish'd face
> The great Creator now conspicuous shines;
> Who open'd nature's adamantine gates,
> And to our minds her secret powers expos'd;
> Newton demands the Muse; his sacred hand
> Shall guide her infant steps; his sacred hand
> Shall raise her to the Heliconian height,
> Where, on its lofty top enthron'd, her head
> Shall mingle with the stars.

Thus though these poems were basically scientific popularizations, they appealed to the imagination rather than to the reason—so far at least they deserve the name of poetry— Reynolds's work, on which some of the succeeding poems were modelled, being in the form of voyages of the soul through infinite space, journeys so exciting as to make an early demise subject for joy rather than lamentation. 'Learn'd death', Reynolds apostrophizes:

> Learn'd death! that in one hour informs me more
> Than all the academic aids could do,

exalting him, he proceeds, to being 'a more than Newton in abstruse philosophy'. What the various aspects of this abstruse philosophy were need not be followed here; each would seem to demand a special study, such as Professor Marjorie Nicolson has provided in her brilliant and entertaining *Newton Demands the Muse* which is concerned mainly with the poets' reaction to the theories of light. This, even more than the infinitude of space, was the subject-matter of the poets, this and the prism, since after all it involved colour, to which the poets of that day were peculiarly sensitive, their alertness having been aroused

[1] Richard Glover, 1712–1785, was schooled at Cheam in Surrey, and entered the business of his father, a Hamburg merchant in London. He made his living in business, and in 1761 entered the House of Commons as Member for Weymouth.

by the attention paid to landscape painting. Thomson again is
the most exciting exemplar, ending his admirable and moving
poem on Newton by the exclamation

How just, how beauteous, the refractive law!

which for us has a deflationary effect (perhaps because our own
imaginations are dulled), as has also Blackmore's immortal
couplet

Let curious Minds, who would the Air inspect
On its Elastic Energy reflect,

but in neither case is it fair to judge the poem by such lapses.
For Blackmore's *The Creation*, which he published in 1712, and
which was to vie for popularity with Derham's *Astro-Theology*
and *Physico-Theology* (though the sales of these latter may
possibly be due to their use as textbooks), is more than versified
science. Whether its being the best of Blackmore's poems is due
to his having abandoned his normal haughty indifference to
criticism and submitted it to the revision of a club of wits, or to
his having been more deeply gripped by his subject than in his
interminable epics, no one can say; but the fact remains that it is
well constructed, well argued, and though prolix and repetitive,
not unreadable; once it is plunged into, it is difficult to put
down if only in hopes of finding passages which to us seem
funny. It is no mere acceptance of Newton and Locke. In his
anxiety to get his knife into poor unoffending Lucretius, in fear
lest an atomized universe should lead to the sty of Epicurus, he
throws doubts upon Newton's atomic-corpuscular theory, and
is sharp in detecting how it tells against the theory of light as
tentatively put forward in the *Opticks*. Like Reynolds, who remarks that no fixed system could account for the Deluge, he
is anti-mechanistic, though in his argument for a Creator he
insists upon the beautiful fitness of things, sometimes to a comic
extent, as when in Book I he gives a picture of what the world
would be like if the mysterious 'magnetic force' (Gravity) were
either greater or less than it actually is. 'All men, like statues,
on the earth would stand', or, conversely, mountains, whirled
from the globe, would scatter through the sky. In Book II he
very sensibly observes that the mere invention of new names
cannot oust God. Speaking of the heavenly bodies, he argues:

If some, you say, prest with a pondrous load,
Of Gravity, move slower in their Road,

> Because, with Weight encumber'd and opprest,
> These sluggish Orbs th' Attractive Sun resist;
> Till you can Weight and Gravity explain,
> Those Words are insignificant and vain.

This is scarcely poetry; but in Book IV his passage on the minuteness of atoms stirs the imagination. Examples of the thrill this downward extension of the chain of being caused in the contemporary mind we have already noticed, and it continued to the end of our period. At the end of the twenties Henry Baker[1]—Defoe's son-in-law—that strange F.R.S., who translated Molière with James Miller (still current in 'Everyman's Library') and compiled in English a considerable anthology of classical authors, pointed out in his *The Universe*, that 'Were millions [of microscopic creatures] joyn'd, one Sand would over-top them all', and goes on

> They too are pain'd with Love;—address the Fair,
> And with their Rivals wage destructive war.

So Henry Brooke[2] writes on the theme already familiar through Diaper

> Of azure *Tribes* that in the Damson bloom,
> And paint the Regions of the rip'ning Plum.

Again, Moses Browne, whose other later poems consist mainly of poorish, mildly satirical light verse, in his *Essay on the Universe* (1735) is staggered by the minuteness of microbes:

> In one small humid Drop the curious Eye (c)
> Can millions of their little Forms descry.

the footnote (c) explaining that:

With the Microscope Dr. *Hook* discovered no less than 8,280,000 Animalculae in one single Drop of Water, and he suspects Millions of Millions might be contained in it.

---

[1] Henry Baker, 1698–1744, was apprenticed as a bookseller, but made his fortune by teaching the deaf and dumb. As a naturalist, an authority on microscopy, he became F.R.S. in 1740, and in the same year a Fellow of the Society of Antiquaries. He was one of the founders of the Society of Arts in 1754, but posterity's chief debt to him is as the introducer of rhubarb into England.

[2] Henry Brooke, c. 1703–83, was possibly tutored by Sheridan (Swift's friend), but entered Trinity College, Dublin, as a pupil in Dr. Jones's school. He became a student at the Temple, spent some time in England, but in 1740 returned to Dublin, where he became barrack-master in about 1745. He pressed for the relaxation of the penal laws against Roman Catholics in Ireland.

But in the main it was the magnificence of the heavens which moved the scientists and the minor poets to their best efforts; they were stirred by its size, its order, its perfect fitness. Here again Moses Browne may serve as the first illustration, as his dull couplets move to a slightly more spirited measure:

> Convenient Form, that round his *central Sun*
> The circling Planet might his period run;
> That purging *Tides* might unresisted flow,
> And seasons change, (a) and genial Breezes blow;

(a) Those things are demonstrably impossible were the Earth *plane, angular*, or any way contrary to the present figure. [Ray's *Wisdom of God.*]

Reynolds asked his readers to wonder at the heavenly bodies and note

> How they are chain'd in this *elliptic* Race,
> Nor gallop out into the Fields of Neighb'ring Space.

Blackmore, naturally, has some lines on the subject: speaking of 'the Orbs sublime in Æther born' he evoked a more vivid vision of the universe:

> None by Collision from their Course are driv'n,
> No Shocks, no Conflicts, break the Peace of Heaven;
> No shatter'd Globes, no glowing Fragments fall,
> No Worlds o'erturned, crush this terrestrial Ball;
> In beauteous Order all the Orbs advance,
> And in their mazy complicated Dance,
> Not in one part of all the Pathless Sky,
> Did ever any halt, or step awry.

But it is David Mallet[1] who provides the most evocative passage.

That so mediocre, one cannot say downright bad, a poet should so bravely have sustained two cantos of a cosmic poem reveals how deeply the Newtonian cosmogony stirred the average intelligent man of those days; and Mallet was in-

---

[1] David Mallet, originally Malloch, *c.* 1705-65, educated in the parish school, Crieff, spent much of his life as tutor to young aristocrats, and was such when he entered the University of Edinburgh, which he left without taking a degree. In 1742 he was made secretary to Frederick, Prince of Wales, a post he did not hold for long. In 1763 he became Inspector of Exchequer Book in the outports of London, a comfortable sinecure.

telligent, as is evidenced by his Preface to an edition of Bacon, and his being chosen by Bolingbroke to handle his *Works*. Mallet's poem, *The Excursion* (1728), was to be comprehensive enough. Written after the manner of Reynolds as a voyage, the first canto treated of this terrene globe, the second was concerned with the solar system, and—*excusez du peu*—of the fixed stars. 'Sublimity', Thomson wrote to him (2 August 1726), 'must be the characteristic of your piece', and, so to speak, handed over to him an earthquake and a volcano, together with a famine, though this last gift was not taken up. Mallet, however, was first in the field with a thunderstorm, even more deadly than Thomson's, since it could count two victims, besides striking terror into the hearts of the guilty. Mallet belabours his unfortunately overladen Pegasus, but, at any rate in the first canto, cannot get the poor beast to rise into the air. The descriptions of the arctic regions and the deserts of Tartary, and some southern European country, 'say Italy', fail to move the reader, as do the dutiful detailings of nature at morning, evening, noon, and night, though it is interesting to note how he tries to make use of colour to add liveliness to his flocculent landscape. In the whole canto there are only two lines that stir, when the earthquake is impending, and

> a sighing cold
> Winters the shadow'd air;

the rest being rhetoric in the bad sense of the word. The problem of evil he refuses to face; all that Reason can do in the face of the promiscuous horror of a city engulfed is with due praise to acknowledge the Almighty, and adore 'His will, unerring, wisest, justest, best'. The romantic trappings will be commented on later; all that need be further noted with respect to Canto I are certain pilferings from Pope's *Essay on Criticism* in an amusingly unexpected context.

The second canto can, however, be taken a little more seriously; not that it is always much better as poetry, but here at least Mallet knew what he wanted to say, and now and again achieved poetry in a sub-Miltonic manner strongly influenced by Thomson, as might be expected, since he was in close contact with him while the first draft of *The Seasons* was being written. The lines on 'the blue profundity of heaven' constitute his peak:

Unfathomable, endless of extent!
Where unknown *suns* to unknown *systems* rise,
Whose numbers who shall tell? Stupendous host!
In flaming millions thro the vacant hung,
Sun beyond sun, and world to world unseen,
Measureless distance, unconceiv'd by thought!
Awful their order; each the central fire
Of his surrounding stars, whose whirling speed,
Solemn and silent, thro the pathless void,
Nor change, nor error knows.

You feel he is moved by a tremendous vision, more intense than
that of Blackmore, and not unlike that of Shelley (the most
scientific of the Romantics) in *Queen Mab*, when 'the Daemon
and the Spirit Approached the overhanging battlement'. It will
be noted that all these passages are plain statement, the thing
was the symbol; you never get the particularized image as you
do, say, with Rossetti's glimpse of the world spinning 'like a
fretful midge'; there is a sense of grandeur, but not of terror as
you get in Tennyson's Lucretian vision of

> the flaring atom-streams
> Ruining along the illimitable inane;

and though Mallet notes the silence of the astral dance, there is
no hint that he is terrified by it. He feels what Addison might
have called 'a secret pleasure and complacency' at the spectacle;
yet he is warmed as in the lines to Newton; there is a sense of
glory, as in the apostrophe to the sun, much improved upon,
however, when rewritten in 1747 as Aurelius's prayer to the
Creator of light in *Amyntor and Theodora* (II. 100 seq.). The
inset on the train of beings, as he phrases it, reveals how he too,
in common with his age, had one foot in the medieval world
while the other is in that of Newton.

It would be tedious to run through many of these cosmic
poems, though a few may be noted. There was John Hughes's
The Ecstacy, in couplets, posthumously published in 1720;
Hinchcliffe's *The Seasons* (1718); Aaron Hill's pindaric *Creation*
(1720), and although this is largely a paraphrase of *Genesis*
and preaches humility, it has traces of Newton, for whom he
later wrote an epitaph. This was followed in 1725 by Bezaleel
Morrice's quatrains *An Essay on the Universe*, for him a development, since in his poem 'On Human Condition', published in

Miscellanies and Amusements in Prose and Verse (1712), he had
written:

> If study be thy Care and Conduct such,
> As not to think too little or too much;
> Try well the Knowledge of thy self to find,
> And seek the useful Knowledge of thy Kind . . .

the proper study of mankind obviously being man. Richard
Collins's *Nature Displayed* was again in couplets, but by 1728,
when Mallet and Thomson had set the pace, Samuel Edwards
produced his essay on *The Copernican System*. 'As to the Style of
this Poem,' he prefaces his work, an intolerable muddle of
Newtonianism and the classics in which he insists on the pre-
saging value of the stars, 'I wish it were an Imitation of the
Sacred MILTON, whose every Work is Praise.' For sheer bad
poetry, the most entertaining example is the work of J. T.
Desaguliers, F.R.S., *The Newtonian System of the World, the best
Model for Government. An Allegorical Poem.* It was no doubt well
liked, since the system fitted in very well with the governmental
idea of the country oligarchy. After discussing various systems,
including that of Pythagoras—

> The Musick of the Spheres did represent
> That ancient Harmony of Government —

he turns to Newton, with the invocation:

> But now my cautious Muse, consider well,
> How nice it is to draw the Parallel

(though the 'nicety' of the parallel may not seem to need much
caution) and he includes lines on the fitness of things, how right
it is that we should have only five senses, since our state could
not bear more, and passing through meteorology and astronomy,
rejoices that the pull of gravity should be such as to produce an
acceleration of thirty-two feet per second per second. It is not
surprising that in the next decade the poets should begin to
turn away from sheer unadulterated science, and begin to
query once more the limits of reason, as did Walter Harte[1] in his
Essay on Reason (1735): Paradise, no doubt, was a place 'Where

---

[1] Walter Harte, 1709–74, proceeded from the Grammar School at Marlborough
to St. Mary Hall, Oxford, of which he became Vice-Principal in 1740. He was for
some time Vicar of Gosfield in Essex, travelled abroad as tutor to Philip Stanhope,
Chesterfield's son, and in 1756 was made Canon of Windsor.

Truth was almost felt as well as seen', but on this sublunary globe care had to be used:

> Reason, like Virtue, in a Medium lies;
> A hairs-breadth more might make us *mad* not *wise*,
> Out-know ev'n Knowledge, and out-polish Art,
> Till *Newton* drops down giddy—a *Descartes*!

Poor Descartes; he got short shrift from most of the scientific poets of the age. Moses Browne had a slap at him in one of his footnotes, and Collins, in his *Nature Display'd* (1727), a medico-psychological treatise, in which, incidentally he tackles the difficult theme of laughter, revolts against Descartes's mechanical theory of the mind:

> The Frenchman has, with Def'rence to his Merit,
> Raised in his Scull, a Work-house for a Spirit.

Yet these cosmic or otherwise scientific works were not all, or altogether, mere dull popularization of Newton and Locke. Not only were the writers authors of other works more sensuously motivated, they sometimes included descriptive lines amid their sterner stuff, or definitely abjured the more pleasant objects of contemplation. Moses Browne opens his cosmic poem by warning the reader:

> No more a *Fisher*, by the Reedy Streams
> [A reference to his *Piscatory Eclogues*]
> To easy Notes I chaunt the Rural Themes,
> These pleas'd me once, when, artless in the Shade,
> I Nature, first, in Simplest Charms survey'd.
> To gaze o'er all her Prospects now I soar;
> The Streams, and Shades, confine my Haunts no more;

though he sometimes lapsed. He also adds, as many did, a *benedicite*, which virtually is what Samuel Boyse,[1] who helped in 1741 to modernize the *Canterbury Tales*, almost altogether confines himself to in *Deity: a Poem* (1739), which can yet, however, be ranked as a cosmic poem. Unfortunately his prayer, 'O grant me Wisdom—and I ask no more!' was not altogether answered. The poet who most nearly made a real poem out of science was, however, Henry Brooke who followed up his

---

[1] Samuel Boyse, 1708–49, received his schooling at a private establishment in Dublin, and proceeded to Glasgow University. He took no degree, entered no profession, and, bungling all his opportunities, died in poverty.

Design and Beauty: an Epistle of 1734, with his *Universal Beauty*, published in six parts from 1734 to 1736. The first Book, a scientifico-philosophical Deistic-moralistic eulogy on the perfection of design in the universe—the fittingness of everything— ends with a poetical rhapsody, but it is not until Book II that the poem gathers way, and becomes pleasant reading, if only because Brooke could manage the couplet with some skill, and a certain variety of movement, not to be illustrated by a snippet.

The phase continued well beyond our period, but in a failing degree. It did, however, though probably only to a small extent, nourish the idea of the sublimity of mountain scenery. The notion should be dispelled that all men and women of the early eighteenth century regarded anything more than a gentle hill as a 'horrid Alp', a sense perhaps encouraged by Burnet's *Theory of the Earth* (it is only in the Latin title that the word 'sacred' appears), which showed that mountains were a mistake, the result of a natural Fall paralleling that of man. It is only fair, however, to note that Burnet admitted that these 'majestic ruins' cast the mind 'into a pleasing kind of stupor and admiration', just as Sprat in his *Cowley* (1668) had derived pleasure from the sight of 'a precipice or a rising wave'. So also Dennis in 1688 had regarded the Alps with 'delightful horrour and terrible joy'. By no means all, then, shared the dislike of wildness; they rejoiced in mountains, and not for Defoe's reason that they formed useful trade boundaries. John Philips in *Cider* ventured to suggest:

> Nor are the Hills unamiable, whose Tops
> To Heav'n aspire, affording Prospect sweet,
> To Human Ken,

while Blackmore is far bolder:

> The Mountains more sublime in *Ether* rise,
> Transfix the Clouds, and tow'r amidst the Skies;
> The snowy Fleeces, which their Heads involve,
> Still stay in part, and still in part dissolve.
> Torrents and loud impetuous Cataracts
> Thro' Roads abrupt, and rude unfashion'd Tracts
> Roll down the lofty Mountain's channell'd Sides,
> And unto the Vale convey their foaming Tides.

Similarly, Berkeley's Philonous asked Hylas:

At the Prospect of the wide and deep Ocean, or some huge

Mountain whose Top is lost in the Sky, or of an old gloomy Forrest, are not our Minds filled with a pleasing Horror? Even in Rocks and Deserts, is there not an agreeable Wildness?

How far the common reader shared this taste may be checked by keeping in mind the phrase Aaron Hill (probably) used in *The Plain Dealer*: 'That Blood-curdling, chilling Influence of Nature, working on our Passions (which Criticks call the *Sublime*).' The majority, it would seem, preferred with Thomson

> softly swelling Hills
> On which the Power of Cultivation lies;

yet if Mallet agreed with him, he got some satisfaction also out of the Caucasus

> Pale glitt'ring with eternal Snows to Heav'n,

just as Moses Browne got a thrill from the 'shudd'ring Horror' that precipices and torrents frowned on his aching sight. Yet that the sublimity of mountain scenery impressed the average polite reader can be gathered strikingly enough from the most unexpected person in that world, the very urban Horace Walpole, who, writing to West in September 1739, breaks out about 'Precipices, mountains, torrents, wolves, rumblings, Salvator Rosa . . . here we are, the lonely lords of glorious desolate prospects . . .'; and two days later, forgetting the 'picturesque':

But the road, West, the road! Winding round a prodigious mountain, and surrounded with others, all shagged with hanging woods, obscured with pines, or lost in clouds! Below, a torrent breaking through cliffs, and tumbling through fragments of rocks! Sheets of cascades forcing their silver speed down channelled precipices, and hasting into the roughened river at the bottom.

That is real; a direct and honest reaction.

Indeed it may be said that, in a sense, the cosmic poem took the place of the epic, supplying the sense of sublimity that the age demanded, free, moreover, from the heroic atmosphere against which the age reacted so strongly, accepting it only in its mock or burlesque forms. Yet the epic was not entirely absent. In addition to Blackmore, who overlapped into the eighteenth century with his heavily soporific tales of Renaissance or medieval grandeur, his *Eliza* of 1705 in ten Books, and

his *Alfred* of 1723 in twelve, which gained little if any contemporary applause, we have the incomplete *Davideis* (1712) by
Milton's delightful Quaker friend, Thomas Ellwood, which,
dreary as it seems to us, was often reprinted, though John
Bulkeley's *The Last Day* (1720), in twelve Books of Miltonic
blanks, suffered much the same fate as Blackmore's lucubrations. Mallet's *Amyntor and Theodora*—already mentioned
—has, with its sub-title, *The Hermit*, no heroic ring, while the
sentimentality with which the separated lovers are wafted
together is likely to remind the post-Shandean reader of
'Amandus he, Amanda she; he East, she West. . .'. It is now
'lost in forgetfulness' as it was already in Dr. Johnson's day,
although, as he added, it is clothed in 'copiousness and elegance
of language', both the copiousness and the elegance being
Thomsonian. It has its verbal felicities, its occasional happy
freedom with words, and though his descriptions are somewhat
overwrought in the interests of sublimity, his account of the
shipwreck is vivid enough, the best perhaps before Falconer.
Dr. Johnson might have found it agreeable—'But it is in blank
verse'; and indeed, when Mallet's exercises in octosyllables are
read, it is permissible to echo Aaron Hill's somewhat splenetic
remark on receiving the latest recension of *The Seasons*: 'The
more I read these eruptions in blank verse, the more beautifully
necessary I perceive the yoke of rhyming.' Glover's *Leonidas*
(1737) is far more readable, and today unduly despised, for it
is at least a sustained effort in Miltonics, lacking neither vigour
nor imagery. It does, perhaps, read a little too much like a
translation of some Homer–Virgil, but the rhetoric is not
unpalatable, though an enemy might call it woolly fustian, and
the reader may come to feel himself too much in the presence of
a Muse alert to pounce on any opportunity offered to embark on
an extended simile. Both poems can mildly entertain the reader
of today, once he will accept the idiom, but they will not
awaken him to any fresh awareness either of the human dilemma
or of the time in which they were written. They are, rather,
curious extravagations; and it is not difficult to understand
how, when the superb old Duchess of Marlborough commissioned Mallet and Glover to write the Life of her hero the Duke,
she should have made it a condition that not a line of it should
be in verse.

3. VARIOUS TRENDS

Allied with these works, for the delectation of the more thoughtful, may be numbered the contemplative poems best exemplified, perhaps, by Savage's[1] *The Wanderer* (1729), a long, rambling, derivative 'eruption' as Hill might have said, in which the yoke of the couplet had little restraining influence. It is true that his statement 'O'er ample Nature I extend my Views' is hardly borne out by what follows, though to be sure he visits various climes from the arctic to the torrid zones. The appeal is rather to the 'creative skill' of Contemplation (the adjective is interesting) when confronted by human life. The moral, which emerges faintly, is stated in the couplet:

> Justly to know thy self peruse Mankind!
> To know thy God, paint Nature on thy Mind!

Mankind is to some extent perused, and nature painted in sometimes attractive lines. The poem, however, tends to resolve itself into phrases which were commonplace even in Savage's day, though now and again he uses or invents a rare word, as in the line about the stars which as they

> Cross *Ether* swift elance the vivid Fires!

or when he describes how

> . . . berries blacken on the virid Thorn.

It cannot be said that he keeps the mind or the eye alert, but it may be argued that he keeps them occupied. His description of the comet nicely balances visual effect with contemplation, and his passage on the spectrum is a happy attempt to popularize science. Sometimes he slightly surprises:

> The interval 'twixt Night and Morn is nigh,
> Winter more nitrous chills the shadow'd Sky:
> Springs with soft Heats no more give Borders green,
> Nor smoking breathe along the whiten'd Scene;
> While steamy Currents sweet in Prospect charm
> Like Veins blue-winding on a Fair-one's Arm,

while his answer to the supposed question, 'Can a mother's

---

[1] Richard Savage, d. 1743, unsuccessfully claimed to be the illegitimate son of the fourth Earl Rivers and Lady Macclesfield. After he had written *The Bastard*, in 1728, Lord Tyrconnel gave him a pension by way of hush-money. He was also pensioned by Queen Caroline, and styled himself 'volunteer laureate'.

tender care, Cease towards the child she bare', is a vigorously
and bitterly phrased 'Yes' of some lines, if unwanted bastards
are in question, ever a sore point with Savage.

But if this heap of shining materials thrown together by
accident, to use Dr. Johnson's phrase—Saintsbury analysing
the material as tinsel—can only occasionally cause a vibration
of any kind in the reader of today, it is not difficult to see why it
appealed to Savage's contemporaries. It contained, even though
'thrown together', so many of the elements they either were
accustomed to, or hankered after. Apart from lines in praise
of his contemporaries, and astonishingly adoring ones to 'fair
Wortley', there was the obvious scientific interest, the nature
descriptions, which had by then become almost accustomed
fare, together with the usual attempt to solve the problem of
evil by making it the generator of good; but beyond that they
found the romantic or pseudo-romantic elements they were
acquiring a taste for. In this very social age, the idea of the
hermit, the central figure of the poem, was evidently attractive
to the imagination; his acquaintance had been made through
Parnell, Mallet was to use this convenient person in his
Amyntor and Theodora, and he was to reappear in *Rasselas*. With
Savage he is useful as a guide and narrator, but also as a highly
romantic figure, the young man aged by sorrow in love, stricken
by the death of his Olympia, abandoning a patrimony, dwelling
in a cave adorned with all the luxuries of symbolic art, and
finally transformed into some sort of an angel, a variation of
Parnell's story. There was plenty of matter there for the yearnings of domestic sentimentality. And beyond that the poem has
a further interest as showing, together with Mallet's *Excursion*
of the same date, the growing liking for what may be called
romantic trappings. Dyer had perhaps begun their popularization two or three years earlier—that it had never been entirely
absent since Milton is evidenced by some passages in *Eloisa
to Abelard*—and they continued popular till they found their
culmination in Collins's *Ode to Evening* and Gray's *Elegy* on the
one hand, and in the Gothic novel on the other. The trappings
here referred to are ruins (ivied or not), with the lurking creatures
and ominous fowl which were considered their appropriate
accompaniment, such things being happily congruous with the
'graveyard' trend, again begun by Parnell, followed up successfully by Blair, again culminating with Gray.

We may begin with Dyer (though indeed Garth's 'Claremont' has its bat, and its beetle-infested ivied ruin), indulging in a fairly long quotation so as to recover the flavour of verse that can give delight. He has brought us to the ruined tower on Grongar Hill, 'Whose ragged Walls the Ivy creeps':

> 'Tis now the Raven's bleak Abode;
> 'Tis now th'Appartment of the Toad;
> And there the Fox securely feeds;
> And there the pois'nous Adder breeds,
> Conceal'd in Ruins, Moss and Weeds:
> While, ever and anon, there falls,
> Huge heaps of hoary moulder'd Walls.

A moral naturally there must be (of all kinds of poetry the didascalic is the most valuable), but Dyer carries it off with a poetic swing, a lilt that is almost a song, which necessarily makes the attempts of his successors seem more than a little leaden:

> Yet Time has seen, that lifts the low,
> And level lays the lofty Brow,
> Has seen this broken Pile compleat,
> Big with the Vanity of State;
> But transient is the Smile of Fate!
> A little Rule, a little Sway,
> A Sun-beam in a Winter's Day
> Is all the Proud and Mighty have,
> Between the Cradle and the Grave.

Mallet, as might be expected, is more wordy; he has no specific ruin, but a place 'where Ruin dreary dwells', where the ivy twines on walls, and the column is grey with moss:

> All is dread silence here, and undisturb'd,
> Save what the wind sighs, and the wailing owl
> Screams solitary to the mournful moon.

From Savage we get the same picture:

> The roof is now the Daw's, or Raven's Haunt,
> And loathsome Toads in the dark Entrance pant,
> Or Snakes that lurk to snap the heedless fly,
> And fated Bird, that oft' comes flutt'ring by.

The scene was being set for the mid-century.

So it was, also, by such works as *Cato Major*, by Samuel
Catherall (1725), a poem in four Books 'Upon the model of
Tully's Essay of Old Age'. This amiable Fellow of Oriel and
Prebend of Worcester, dissatisfied with Denham's version, tried
his own hand at an 'imitation', notable not only because it appeared timely, but because it is written in surprisingly fresh,
effectively colloquial, flexible blank verse. On the other hand,
nothing could be more prosaic and prosy than William Melmoth's not even amusingly bad *Of Active and Retired Life* (1735),
which nevertheless Dodsley thought worth while to reprint in
his 1748 Miscellany. It is studded with such copy-book maxims as:

> Grave precepts fleeting notions may impart,
> But bright examples best instruct the heart,

inducing the reader readily to believe that

> Yet of the various tasks mankind employ,
> 'Tis sure the hardest, leisure to enjoy.

Such works perhaps led up to the most portentously heavy of all
the contemplative poems of the time, Young's *Night Thoughts*
(1742-6), which though by date of publication belonging to the
next period, in ethos hovers—if so weighty an object can be
said to hover—between the two. Expressed in rambling, formless, indisciplined blank verse, it is an ironic illustration of his
later dictum in *Conjectures on Original Composition* (1759), that
blank verse is 'verse unfallen, uncurst; verse reclaimed, re-
inthroned in the true language of the gods.' It is not a philosophic work, but one in which thought is gently soothed down
into musing, though now and again the old epigrammatist of *The
Universal Passion* peeps out. Nothing could be a greater contrast
than the happy moralizing which Matthew Green[1] uttered so
gaily in *The Spleen* (1737), a heartening release from the didactic
poems 'which so fearfully overcast or overbilge the poetry of the
time'. It was, perhaps, a little out of date when it appeared,
since it belongs to the family of Pomfret's *The Choice*, and the
whole 'retirement' group of the first years of the century; but
it is so fresh and lively in its flexibility, in its light-hearted
octosyllabics, that anyone may enjoy it with ease. The poem,
of course, aims at a far shallower level of apprehension than

---

[1] Matthew Green, 1696-1737, came of a dissenting family, and held a place in
the Customs House.

Young's, but on that level—that of the contented Stoic, 'Never becalm'd, nor over-blown'—it achieves complete success. Green never falters, never dwells too long on one subject, indulges in a little genial satire, occasionally uses the entertaining word or expression, for example, 'tarantulated by a tune', and tinkles as merrily in the close as he did in the beginning. The poem is as typical of the century in one aspect as Young's is in another. Green expresses a consciously felt stability, free of any doubts to cause him uneasiness; Young is harried all the time by something resembling an inner conflict, a sense of frustration not to be altogether ascribed to his failure to achieve a bishopric. If Young solitary writes by night in the rectory of Welwyn, by the dim beams, as legend has it, of a candle stuck in a skull, Green scribbles away in full sunshine at a table set in his garden,

> Nor wanting the dispersive bowl
> Of cloudy weather in the soul

nor the friend to share it with him. He did not experience Melmoth's difficulty in enjoying leisure.

If the philosophico-contemplative poems, the rare epics, and more still the spate of poems about the universe were the stock reading of the more thoughtful, sublimity and the cosmos did not provide so popular a theme as patriotism. It crops up in the most unexpected places, sometimes in a ludicrous way. Isaac Watts might well excuse his beginning his version of Psalm lxvii with

> Shine, mighty God! on Britain shine

by appealing to current theories of translation; but that Solomon, in Prior's poem of that name, should have a vision of Britannia, and that Laelius should prophesy over the corpse of Thomson's Sophonisba that in farthest Britain patriots would arise—an unlikely thought to occur to a man some two hundred years before Christ—is symptomatic of either deep feeling or profound irritation.

As George Eliot remarked, 'one is afraid to think of all that the genus "patriot" embraces', but it is necessary here to distinguish what is merely adventitious, such as the eygre of patriotic poems which swept up Fleet Street to submerge the bookstalls when Marlborough triumphed over the national foes, or even when the Union with Scotland took place, or when feelings against Spain raised the temperature of those born with tumultuary blood. The feelings we are concerned with were less ephemeral, based on instincts rather less primitive, though at that time as deeply felt, namely the passion for liberty, and the vistas of glory of all kinds opened up by commerce. The former has already been commented upon, and here, as illustration, we may note that Cooke, in prefacing his edition of Glover's *Leonidas*, tells us that its brief success 'has been imputed not solely to its intrinsic merits, but in part to a zeal, or, as some persons term it, a rage for liberty, which at that time prevailed in England'; and since Leonidas laid him down

in honourable rest
To seal his country's liberty by death,

Lyttelton was led to declare in *Common Sense* No. 10, that 'Never yet was an epic poem wrote with so noble and so useful a design'. Commerce appears a less likely theme, but poems on the subject gave vent to the pulsating energy of an age of mercantile expansion, with everywhere a bursting sense of something doing, of being alive in a terrifically exciting world of practical affairs. These differing emotions were to some extent welded together by the patriotism which Renan defines as the sense of a people having accomplished great things together, and intent on doing more. This was an emotion pointed by the growth of the historical sense, more immediate no doubt as to the past century, but spreading further back through the writings of serious historians such as Echard, antiquaries such as Wanley, and even linguists such as Elizabeth Elstob, who in her Preface to *The Rudiments of Grammar for the English-Saxon Tongue* (1715) evinced the justness and propriety of Anglo-Saxon as proof of the good sense of the early nation. All the long nature poems, *Windsor Forest, Cider, Dryades*, and Thomson's *Summer*, somewhere catalogue various national heroes in a sketchy 'retrospect of ages past', the heroes being mainly associated with liberty as a peculiarly British product. This patriotic poetry cannot all be dismissed as mere 'Whig panegyric'; the themes are too constant and too various, and are as fervently carolled by the most arrant Tories as by the most aggressive or aggrieved Whigs; Dodsley's first *Miscellany* is more than half occupied by verses on this theme.

There was nothing jingoistic or restricted in the praises of patriotism, except in the hymns to victory already noted.

Britain was celebrated by the poets for nobler reasons, as a place where civil strife was at an end, and where refugees could harbour. Thus, to reduce examples, Fenton in his irregular Pindaric Ode in glorification of Marlborough (1707), a poem somewhat oddly entitled *Ode to the Sun*, cried out:

> Iö, Britannia, fix'd on foreign wars,
> Guiltless of civil rage extend thy name . . .

and Croxall in *The Vision*, speaking of St. Paul's:

> From foreign Climes see injur'd People come,
> Invoking Aid beneath its ample Dome;
> And hospitably form a safe Retreat
> From the fierce Flames of persecuting Heat,

while Thomson in *Liberty* enlarged the humane conception to the gay Colonies,

> the calm retreat
> Of undeserv'd distress, the better home
> Of those whom bigots chase from foreign lands.

But behind all these feelings there lay a more fundamental instinct, the passionate love of what freedom will permit a man to enjoy, namely the countryside itself, in all its strange loveliness and all its familiarity. The sentiment is pervasive, appearing strongly in Philips's *Cider*, in Thomson's *Summer*, and in his *Liberty*, through descriptions expressing love of the countryside because it is above all the English scene.

Yet stronger than all these themes, at least more specifically expressed, is the glorying in England on account of her commerce. It begins, as far as we are concerned in this volume, in 1700, with, as we might expect, wool, in Prior's *Carmen Seculare*:

> Through various Climes, and to each distant Pole
> In happy Tides, let active Commerce rowl:
> Let BRITAIN's Ships export an Annual Fleece,
> Richer than ARGOS brought to Ancient GREECE;
> Returning loaden with the shining Stores,
> Which lye profuse on either INDIA's Shores.

It was to reach its climax as a poetic theme in Dyer's *The Fleece* (1757), in many ways the greatest patriotic poem in the language, bursting with the energy which characterized the country at that time, when 'the redd'ning fields, of busy Manchester', Sheffield, and Birmingham rose and enlarged their suburbs—an event which today is not universally applauded. Indeed in our own period there were warning voices, and Aaron Hill, writing to Thomson on 17 February 1735, bade him: 'Think seriously . . . and try, if in all your intimate acquaintance with past ages, you can find a people long, at once retaining *public virtue* and *extended commerce*.'

Public virtue; the poets were not altogether unmindful of that; public works were frequently extolled in verse, Savage going so far as to write a poem upon the subject. And as to the danger that Hill had suggested, was not commerce the great peace-bringer? Was it not the business of a great commercial country 'to fold the world with harmony', as Dyer was to put it? Commerce alone, especially if directed by Britain, would ensure universal peace; the theme sings out already at the end of *Annus Mirabilis*, it inspires the conclusion of *Windsor Forest*, it is on this point that even so short a poem as 'Rule Britannia', which Thomson wrote for *Alfred* in 1740, had its climax. Fenton, once more, in his *Verses to the Queen on her Birthday*, tells his monarch that she longs 'to give the lab'ring world repose', so that

> Commerce beneath the southern stars shall thrive,
> Intestine feuds expire, and arts revive . . .

thus voicing the further theme of commerce as the mother of the Muses, which others developed; while another body of poets, after the manner of Thorowgood in *The London Merchant*, sang not only of its benefit to the arts, but also of its parentage of society. Thus Young, who had voiced more general patriotism in *The Instalment* (1726), gave utterance to the further sentiment in *Imperium Pelagi* (1729, pub. 1730), a naval poem, which he suppressed in his collected works:

> COMMERCE gives *Arts*, as well as *Gain*;
> By Commerce wafted o'er the main,
> They barbarous Climes enlighten as they run;
> Arts the rich Traffick of the Soul!
> May travel thus from Pole to Pole,
> And gild the World, with Learning's brighter Sun.

And Glover, in *London: or, The Progress of Commerce* (1739):

> Thou gracious Commerce, from his cheerless caves
> In horrid rocks and solitary woods,
> The helpless wanderer, man, forlorn and wild,
> Did'st charm to sweet society . . .

Who can say that they were wrong? The question is, did the excitement caused by such realizations produce enough tension to give birth to poetry?

Those, then, were the themes peculiar to the time; in no other age of our history could such themes have been the mainstay of the vast body of verse. The direct versification of science went out, perhaps, with Darwin's *Botanic Garden* at the end of the century, barely revived by Sarah Hoare's *Poems of Conchology and Botany* (1831); poets, those at any rate since Tennyson, integrate it more with their general consciousness, as does, for instance, Mr. Auden at the present day. Patriotism no longer calls upon commerce: it has taken different forms, in the present century preferring rather to warn responsibly, as did Kipling in 'Recessional', following a tradition which dates at least from Cowper, or indeed Sylvester. Yet these themes, which seemed so vastly important at the time, were, after all, but adventitious, and the more usual streams of poetry ran on, a little placidly, perhaps, more it would seem as undercurrents. Pope and Thomson apart, there was no one yet of any stature wholly given to letters, and, unless we include Johnson, whose *London* appeared in 1738, no hint of lesser, but indubitably good poets such as usually throng the lower slopes of Parnassus. It seems curiously like a period of slack tide. That there were plenty of surface ripples is abundantly plain from the number of miscellanies that appeared, notably *The Vocal Miscellany* (1734) and *The Choice* (1737), nearly all of them containing items constructed with vivacity and skill (many of them figure in our own anthologies), but as a rule with no great sense of conviction. It was as though men inclined to literature no longer felt the writing of poems to be a natural activity, and had not yet come to the notion of writing poetry (the distinction is Professor Sutherland's); or, to put it another way, the conception of 'kinds' was dying out as the neo-classical ideal dwindled away in the new attitude towards poetry engendered by Locke's 'sensationalism'. The kinds, indeed, continued to be recognized, and even practised, but (apart of course from Pope) in enervated form. Take, for example, the mock-heroic as put out by Anthony Whistler in his *The Shuttlecock* (1736), clearly the work of a man who had read *The Rape of the Lock*, and used something of its diction in competent couplets; it is a confused story of Cupid robbed of his arrows, and is devoid of any hint of epic structure. Or again there appeared sporadically variations of the *Ars Poetica* applied to other activities, after the manner of William King's *The Art of Cookery*; such, for instance, were Bramston's[1] *The Art of Politicks* (1729) and Soame Jenyns's[2] *The Art of Dancing* (also 1729). The first is evidently the work of a man of lively intelligence, ready to use verse to supply comment on what at the moment interested the average reader. His *Man of Taste* (1733), good light verse addressed to Pope, is persiflage on current ideas rather than satire, which he reserves for the obvious moral butts. The title itself indicates the way minds were moving, thus giving the poem a certain reflected interest for us. His Horatian piece is better managed. In spite of his digressions—where, for instance, the subject of diction lures him gaily out of his prescribed path—he pursues his subject with admirable rapidity:

> Whoe'er you are that have a Seat secure,
> Duly return'd, and from *Petition* sure,
> Stick to your Friends in whatsoe'er you say;
> With strong aversion shun the Middle way:
> The Middle way the best we sometimes call,
> But 'tis in Politicks no way at all.

He is often more pithily epigrammatic than when advising his reader to toe the party line. Jenyns's exhibits that mixture of the 'kinds' that Dr. Johnson was to declare inevitable. It is partly mock-heroic, adorned with Proposition and Invocation, but slips into being a hand-book of drawing-room dancing and a guide-book to folk-dancing, though within that framework it must have amused the contemporary reader with its somewhat obvious parodies—if that was the intention—of the *Essay on Criticism* in such morsels as:

> True dancing, like true Wit, is best exprest
> By Nature, only to Advantage drest;

or:

> The *Dance* and *Musick* must so nicely meet
> Each note must seem an Echo to your Feet.

It is today negligible, except in so far as it is indicative of what

---

[1] James Bramston, 1694?–1744, was educated at Westminster and Christ Church, Oxford. He became Rector of Lurgashall, Sussex, and later of Hartley, Kent.

[2] Soame Jenyns, 1704–87, sojourned at St. John's College, Cambridge, but took no degree. He represented Cambridgeshire in Parliament from 1742 to 1754, and Dunwich from 1760 to 1780. He was made a Commissioner of Trade.

was happening; and it may be thought just as well that the young frequenter of ball-rooms should have lapsed into the prosy moralist of his later years. Among other declining kinds the Pindaric had fallen into the doldrums of Cibber's Birthday Odes, from which Collins and Gray were to revive it by blowing the winds of new aesthetic doctrine and wilder material. The epistle had ceased to have any flavour of its own, though the title was common enough; it became merely any poem named for an individual, rather than a confidential missive which could have been addressed to one person alone, as was, say, Congreve's to Lord Cobham. The word was used as Green used it at the head of *The Spleen*, as Young did for his muffled invective against writers, which he dedicated to Pope.

And here the mention of Young is a reminder that, alas! no history of the literature of this period can omit a separate treatment of his verse, though his most considerable contribution to letters, not forgetting even *Night Thoughts*, consists in his prose *Conjectures on Original Composition* (1759). His verse, it can be said, never falls below a certain level, and here and there for a line or two suggests vivacity; nor are his themes trivial, being such as 'The Last Day', and 'The Force of Religion; or Vanquish'd Love' (1714); but in spite of the versified praise of the first by Thomas Warton the elder, written when at Oxford, and the dramatic subject of the second, namely the story of Lady Jane Grey, the total effect is soporific. Had Young possessed, if only in a small degree, the art to blot, the effect might have been vivid; but descents into bathos such as

> Deep was her anguish, but she bore it well,

together with passages of commonplace thought and threadbare imagery, smother what was personal to Young himself. Landor was not accurate when he described Young as 'the dreariest droll of puffy short-breathed writers', since it was precisely that he could endlessly maintain his exhalations that make the reading of him wearisome. Yet agreement is readily forthcoming when Landor writes:

> *'A Paraphrase on Job'* we see
> By Young: it loads the shelf:
> He who can read one half must be
> Patient as Job himself.

For it is more than a paraphrase. 'I have omitted, added, and transposed', Young informs his readers: 'The *mountain*, the *comet*, and the *sun*, and other parts are entirely added: those upon the *peacock*, the *lion*, etc. are much enlarged.' They are. Yet in all these works there is just a hint which makes the reader hope for something better, and go on. But though it may be felt that there are the makings of a poet in what Young exhibits, his failure to be precise enough muffles the merit.

Yet, after all, as Spence remarked in the first historical sketch of English poetry ever written (in about 1733): 'Young est plus heureux dans ses Satires, que dans ses autres écrits.' If his satire 'Concerning the Authors of the Age' is far too generalized to be effective, and the condemnation too sweeping, in *The Love of Fame, or the Universal Passion* (1725) he is more particular, aiming, if not at portraits, at least at 'characters'. To ignore the work would be to flout the opinion of Dr. Johnson and of Saintsbury, both of whom took pleasure in the epigrammatic quality which imparts to it the pepper which a marked deficiency of salt would seem to demand. Even so, it must be read in short snatches if it is to be enjoyed; otherwise, like the rest of Young's verse, it invites slumber. There is no movement, no change of pace, no alteration in tension; and the reason would seem to be that Young had no real sense of the evils he set himself up to attack. He erected Aunt Sallies which he had no difficulty in knocking down, old relics of innumerable fairs. There is nothing fresh or freshly conceived about them, and the immediate popularity of the work may well be ascribed to the fact that its readers were able to welcome old friends in it. Its continuing reputation can be due only to the epigrams, such as

> LUCIA thinks happiness consists in state;
> She weds an *ideot*, but she eats in *plate*,

which so far is well enough; the heavily italicized passage which follows adds nothing:

> The goods of fortune, which her soul possess,
> Are but the *ground* of *unmade* happiness;
> The rude *material: wisdom* adds to *this*,
> *Wisdom*, the sole *artificer* of bliss.

The reading public, apparently, was taken in by this sapless drooling; those who appointed to bishoprics were not.

For the lighter-minded reader of the day, who liked good literature but avoided either portentousness or too athletic a following of ideas, a little relief may have been gained by parody, such as was offered by Isaac Hawkins Browne[1] in his *A Pipe of Tobacco* (1735). If Cibber was his easiest game, his most readable verses are those in the manner of Thomson and of Young, though it is the parody of Pope that is quoted in *Mansfield Park*. From Thomson's *Liberty* he was able to take, or almost take, whole lines; but as parody his Young is his best. Confining himself to *The Love of Fame* he made play with the whole idea of the poem, as well as successfully imitating the 'characters'. His collection adds one to the number of verses mocking Ambrose Philips's Namby-pamby pieces (of which Carey's is the most triumphant), though this item was 'sent to him by an ingenious friend'. Parody, however, somewhat oddly it would seem in so socially alert an age which might be thought propitious to this mild form of criticism, never developed to any great extent; it was overborne, supposedly by the more terrific onslaughts of satire, or absorbed in the greater scope of the mock-heroic.

Social awareness did, however, set its stamp upon one form, namely the lyric, especially the love-lyric, the kind in which you might least expect to find it. If in the earlier part of the century the song had lost its poise, it found it again in a manner which makes it the most distinctive, and possibly the most permanent contribution made by the age, permanent if only because the theme is so, since however much the social pressure of his circumstances may cause man to alter his expression, it does not alter his nature. The love theme also was now treated in such a way as to mark it of its time, imbued with a strong sense of the social, even of the domestic; it was thus no joyous or argumentative utterance defiant of any would-be listener, no general declaration to the world. It no longer had the Cavalier or Restoration attack of Suckling, of Rochester, or of Dryden, which had persisted as late as Congreve's 'False though she be to me and love', a poem which itself, however, softens to social acceptance with the conclusion:

> For though the present I regret,
> I'm grateful for the past.

---

[1] Isaac Hawkins Browne, 1705-60, was educated first at Lichfield, then at Westminster, from which he went to Trinity College, Cambridge. He studied law at Lincoln's Inn, but never practised. In 1744 he was elected M.P. for Wenlock. He was a F.R.S.

There is no poem written in England with the lovely freshness of Allan Ramsay's[1] 'My Peggy is a young thing' that, with other songs only slightly less victorious, animates the pastoral play of *The Gentle Shepherd*, which though written in 1725 remained virtually unacted until 1747, for reasons obvious to any stage producer. Even Carey's[2] justly popular 'Sally in our Alley' lacks, with its rather too conscious plebeianism, the real sense of pent-up emotion seeking release, more nearly approached in *The Beggar's Opera*.

Henry Carey is worth a paragraph. He was merciless with Philips's

> Namby-Pamby's little rhimes,
> Little jingles, little chimes,

and indeed the 'Naughty-Paughty, Jack-a-Dandy' poem is extremely funny. This amiable musician has great merits as a light, fluent, and easy writer in a number of metres, which make up in vigour and what one can rightly call 'jolliness' for their small interest in prosodic virtuosity. Most of his poems are meant to be sung, and as songs they have as much point, meaning, or originality as the average of the period, which do not bear comparison with the poems of the song-writers of a hundred years earlier, Campion, Dowland, and a dozen others. For him, as he said in the Preface to the 1729 edition of *Poems on Several Occasions*, poetry was an amusement, not a profession, and his work has the charm that belongs to that of the gifted amateur, without pretensions, ignoring models, unhampered by classical predilections which his shoulders are not broad enough to carry. Thus he is always readable, except in his attempts at the heroic couplet, where, save in his prologues and epilogues to plays which serve their purpose happily enough, he tried to clamber a little higher up Parnassus than he was fitted to do. His satire is mild and agreeably obvious; there is humour but no bite in his *fabliaux*; where he really did break new ground was in the modern ballad, or the ballad song. If he owed a good deal to

---

[1] Allan Ramsay, 1686-1758, began his career as an Edinburgh wig-maker, but in about 1717, after being a leading member of a Jacobite club, transferred his energies to bookselling. He ceased to write in about 1730, and in 1755 retired from business.

[2] Henry Carey, c. 1687-1743, was possibly the son of Henry Savile. He received his education, including the rudiments of music, at his mother's school in Yorkshire; after learning from various teachers, he made his living by teaching music in boarding-schools.

Gay, certainly Goldsmith and Cowper came to owe much to him, so he is in the line of succession, and can still give pleasure. But his chief form of expression was music; only in the pieces on the daughter who died is there any depth of feeling, though almost everywhere there is a lightness of touch which indicates sensitiveness. There is a naturalness and humanity in him which can be counted upon to give refreshment.

The song, however, found its compensations, a new balance determined by the assumed presence of intimate listeners, and by the consciousness of many of the writers that they stood for a high level of social behaviour, of delicacy, of refinement in social relations, as dwellers in a world contrasting sharply with the crude, even savage, world of the great mass of the people. In an age which had achieved stability, and valued it, passion however deeply felt must be read between the lines. As Hawkins Browne declared in his poem 'On Design and Beauty',

> True elegance appears with mild restraint,
> Decent, discreet, and proper, yet not quaint.

And since the poems of this somewhat intemperate man were composed of commonplaces, his voice may be taken as typical. All this is, if you like, poetry of the drawing-room, in which woman must be wooed by graceful concessions rather than by a triumphant masculinity. Thus it is not surprising that it should often have been written by aristocrats, by amateurs who are more than competent, by Peterborough in his delightful 'I said to my heart between sleeping and waking', an early example, as is Walsh's 'Of all the Torments, all the Cares'; by Chesterfield in 'Mistaken fair, lay *Sherlock* by', and in the lines to 'the beautiful Molly Lepel' (Lady Hervey) he wrote with that eminent diplomat Charles Hanbury Williams; by Lyttelton in 'When Delia on the plain appears'. Its subtlest expression is to be found in Pope's epistle to Martha Blount.

But domesticity easily creeps in to the realm of delicacy, a sense which, as in other spheres, was almost to make a little kind of its own. Carey's best verses, as noted, are those on the death of his daughter. Yet it is where domesticity crept in rather than was stated that it is most effective, as in Ambrose Philips's poems to the Pulteney children. Domesticity permeates rather than is expressed in Broome's 'Queen of fragrance, lovely rose'. Within its framework the poem is carried out with a beautiful delicacy;

read as verse meant to be feelingly spoken, it reveals happy prosodic subtleties; written ostensibly on the 'Gather ye rosebuds' theme, in sentiment it is nearer 'My noble, lovely little Peggy', though Broome had not Prior's sense of knowing exactly where he stood in relation either to the subject of the poem or to the reader. It might be said that for its theme it is too personal, whereas Herrick's exhortation is public; and though that of Catullus' *Vivamus mea Lesbia* is perhaps personal enough, it is hardly private. But if in Broome there is only a slight flavour of sentimentality, the sentiment comes out clearly in Samuel Wesley's domestic and private version of the theme, 'To a Young Lady on her Birthday, being the First of April'. Published in Lewis's Miscellany of 1730, it was written at about the time Wesley's brothers John and Charles were enjoying their romantic flirtation with the Granville sisters. Two lines and a stanza will serve to give the atmosphere of a poem which can be called, if nothing else, lightly and delightfully tender:

> . . . Forget not Earnest in your Play
> For Youth is but an *April* Day.

> When Piety and Fortune move
> Your Heart to try the Bands of Love,
> As far as Duty gives You Pow'r,
> Guiltless enjoy the present Hour:
> 'Gather your Rose-buds while You may,'
> For Love is but an *April* Day.

But in the main even that amount of singing note is rare in the lyric of the time. Anyone looking through the Contents of the works by, say, Fenton, Broome, Mallet, Hammond, Christopher Pitt, and the unlucky Stephen Duck (of whose poems it is not quite fair to say with Saintsbury that they were dead before their author died, since 'The Thresher's Labour' is realistic and lively) will meet Odes, Epistles (so-called), Paraphrases, Imitations, and Translations galore, with a few satires, epitaphs, and complimentary addresses, but scarcely a lyric, or song.

Such was the poetry which serves as background to the outstanding figure of Pope. Though the lesser poets may still provide pleasure, and add to the sense of life, of none of them can it be said, as it has been of Pope, that those who read him at all read him over and over. To him we can now return.

XIV

POPE, 1725–1744

WITH Shakespeare off his hands in March 1725, with three volumes of the *Odyssey* published in April, and the other two nearing completion for their appearance in the next June, Pope began to turn his feverishly active mind to consider what he should do next. Writing to Swift on 14 September he suggests vaguely that two or three of the friends of former days might divert themselves, and the world too if it pleased, by 'at the worst laughing at others innocently and unhurtfully'. He declared he would make no further travels abroad: 'I mean no more translations, but something domestic, fit for my own country, and for my own time.' He evidently had something Scriblerian in view, and a month later (15 Oct.) refers to 'one of my satires', in which he had tried to 'correct the taste of the town in wit and criticism'. In the next year, with Swift visiting him at Twickenham to arrange for the garnering of the *Miscellanies*, and an urgency given to the need for correcting the taste of the Town in criticism by the appearance in March of Theobald's *Shakespeare Restored*, direction and sharpness might well have been given to Pope's search for a subject. Talking over the state of the world with Swift—and now and again with Bolingbroke—talking over also the state of 'wit' with Arbuthnot and Gay, the subject-matter of the new poem would become defined.

With Pope, however, the crying problem would be what form the material was to take to make it most expressive. He was evidently becoming aware that his talent lay in satire. It is arguable that great satire needs two conditions, deep irritation within the satirist, and an object of large enough scope to give the satire a certain degree of universality. If Pope was going to correct the taste of the Town in criticism, the irritation was abundantly provided, partly by the ceaseless flow of vituperation to which he was subject, nearly all unjustified, and partly by the very much justified, moderate, and thus more galling strictures provided by Theobald. The universality was another matter—for the world of letters is not the whole world. The claim can be made that it represents the whole world, since it is its voice, and this is the tacit ground upon which Pope worked. He is often blamed for devoting so much attention to the dunces; but that is to ignore both the ethos of the time and Pope's real anxiety to maintain the standards of literature. To him as to Swift, it appeared that the world of wit, that is, of imaginative writing, was in decline. There was no poet of anything like the stature of Milton or Dryden; descriptive nature poetry, now enormously popular, would for them lack the necessary philosophic lacing, while the philosophic poetry, of which there was no famine, did not rise to a level that either would consider tolerable. Criticism which had certainly not yet 'smoothed its brow' had descended to verbal minutiae, and science to apparently meaningless minute particulars; the drama was in visible decline. Their view, of course, was partial, as is that of any literary clique which accomplishes anything; and, as Dr. Johnson put it:

In the letters of both Swift and Pope there appears such narrowness of mind, as makes them insensible to any excellence that has not some affinity with their own, and confines their esteem and approbation to so small a number, that whoever should form an opinion of the age from their representation, would suppose them to have lived amidst ignorance and barbarity, unable to find among their contemporaries either virtue or intelligence, and persecuted by those that could not understand them.

That is exaggeration; but universal tolerance is not a prerequisite for a great work of art. How far Pope believed that such a poem would sweep away the dross of literature it is impossible to guess; but that the attempt was approved by his friends there is no doubt: they perhaps looked upon it as the final grand assault made by the Scriblerians on the fortress of distorted and misapplied learning. Some may at this date regret that he should have wasted, as they think, so much of his genius on an attempt that was clearly doomed to failure, since you cannot cure mankind of being itself. Yet, at least, the work can be regarded as the one in which he first found his most satisfying field of action.

But what of the form? However skilfully strung together, odd paragraphs, such as the lines on Addison possibly written in 1716 and piratically published from 1722, a few lines on Ambrose Philips, 'backs of letters, filled with hints, and interlined',

as Swift put it, would not make a poem. It was certainly a happy
idea of Pope's to pretend, as explained with elaborate solemnity
by Martinus Scriblerus in a Preface, that he felt it 'in some sort
his duty' to complete his translation of Homer by 'imitating' the
lost *Margites*, and inspirited by 'the jocose Dean', Pope would
be able to amuse himself enormously, in a way that would also
'dissuade the dull and punish the malicious, the *only way that
was left*'. But if he was already beginning to think of satire in
terms of the 'sacred weapon', his method would not here admit
of the searing controlled vituperation he was already mastering:
genial mockery would be far more appropriate. In spite of the
vivid rage aroused in him by the intemperate onslaughts made
upon him, Pope was always in control; and even if the demands
of his art had not counted with him far more than the exigencies
of his bile, he would know that it was no way to get rid of these
insects to exalt them to the stature of figures deserving of his
heaviest artillery. They must be overwhelmed with ridicule. And
certainly, although in our mealy-mouthed age we may regard
the attack as savage, compared with the brutal way his enemies
treated him the retort strikes us as almost mild. He wanted
to destroy Theobald's credit since he could not confute his
criticism; but the most he did was to make him, with his other
enemies, look ridiculous: none of them did he accuse of base
crimes. A tincture of malice here and there informs the picture,
but it is all dissolved in laughter, of a sort more easily yielded
to in 1728 than now. There is enormous fun in *The Dunciad*;
and if it is only by means of close study of the notes that we
can always escape boredom as we read it through, that is the
fate of most work of which the material is mainly an attack
upon persons.

But though, generally speaking, the mock-epic would seem
to be a convenient 'kind', even if not acquainted with the foreign
models the reading public would be familiar with *The Dispensary* and naturally with *Mac Flecknoe*, where dullness had been
duly scarified in fragmentary mock-epic style. Pope would feel
on safe traditional ground, and be sure that a great part of his
readers would be aware of the echoes of Homer and Virgil,
and of the brilliant way in which passages had been dovetailed
in, as they would seize upon the adapted ('parodied' is not
quite the right word) lines from Denham, Milton, Waller,
Dryden, Cowley, Garth, and even himself. It was especially, as

Mr. Aubrey Williams has shown, his adaptation of passages from Dryden's *Aeneid* that enabled him to use the action, the transferring of sovereignty from the City (Troynovant) to Westminster—'The Smithfield Muses to the Ear of Kings'—as Aeneas had from Troy to Latium. On us, with a different set of literary references, a large proportion of the joke must be lost, unless we study the notes; and then we gain delight. It is not a poetic delight in the full sense of the term, but it is an aesthetic delight in the sense that any game beautifully played conveys that quality. And Pope continually merges his satiric purpose in the deeper impulse to produce a good poem.

His problem as an artist was how to make unpromising material into poetry. In *The Rape of the Lock* his purpose—never mind Caryll's—had primarily been to produce something charming; whereas here the beauty, if beauty there should be, would be either incidental or in the structure: the stuff itself was not 'poetic'. Yet, Pope might have asked himself, what is 'poetic stuff'?, and he would, we think, have welcomed Flaubert's saying:

Donc cherchons à voir les choses comme elles sont, et ne voulons pas avoir plus d'esprit que le bon Dieu. Autrefois on croyait que la canne à sucre seule donnait le sucre, on en tire à peu près de tout maintenant; et il en est de même de la poésie; extrayons-la de n'importe quoi, car elle gît en tout et partout. Pas un atome de matière qui ne contienne la poésie, et habituons-nous à considérer le monde comme une œuvre d'art, dont il faut reproduire les procédés dans nos œuvres.

For the mockery of the epic form was even less to the purpose here than in the earlier piece; the problem now was to create poetry out of the follies of people whom Pope thought to be lesser grubs—in short, to provide the preservative amber.

Again and again, even in the first two books where this element is least noticeable, we come across a line, a couplet, or even more, which apart from the meaning sings out from its context; and these passages increase in number till we feel in Book III that Pope has forgotten his individual victims, forgotten almost Dulness herself, except as an instrument for his art; so eagerly does he contemplate the feathers, he forgets to kill the bird. What dwells in our memory from the first Book is the passage describing confusion, where the visual image is as of some curious confection under a glass dome, and the auditory image is extraordinarily evocative:

> Here gay Description Ægypt glads with showers;
> Or gives to Zembla fruits, to Barca flowers;
> Glitt'ring with ice here hoary hills are seen,
> There painted vallies of eternal green,
> On cold December fragrant chaplets blow,
> And heavy harvests nod beneath the snow.

We remember in the second book

> As when a dab-chick waddles thro' the copse,
> On feet and wings, and flies, and wades, and hops,

and perhaps there pause to consider the layers of consciousness to which the couplet can simultaneously appeal. For here, still, Pope was in that respect a Metaphysical. The first obvious appeal is that of Lintot looking ridiculous as he flounders along in the race, for this is part of the Games in the Epic. Or, with some readers the first appeal may be to the beautifully observed nature inset; then again it has reference to the verses in *Paradise Lost* where Satan skirts the nether regions, so once more referring the poem to the epic, but through another channel. This gives some idea of the immense complexity of the work, the extraordinary artistry that went to its making. There is, for instance, the turgid speech by which, as Professor Wilson Knight has pointed out, he on occasion deliberately slows down the pace and thickens the texture and atmosphere of the poem. And all the while we are amusedly conscious of the blows dealt the victims, never the impersonal *coup de grâce* that Dryden knew how to dispatch his with, for in these earlier Books at least we feel that his victims are always nagging a little at Pope's elbow.

It is not until Book III, where Pope, rising more and more above the individuals who compose his picture, perhaps getting a little wearied of the ridicule, launches out into generalizations, that we really hear the singing note, become sensible of incantation. The splendid, sombre passage summing up the downfall of learning on the collapse of the Roman Empire does not stand out glaringly, as an isolated gem: it is led up to, and seems to arise naturally from the texture of the poem; but for the reader the satiric intent is likely to get lost. He is enthralled by the vision:

> How little, mark! that portion of the ball,
> Where, faint at best, the beams of Science fall.

> Soon as they dawn, from Hyperborean skies,
> Embody'd dark, what clouds of Vandals rise!
> Lo where Mœotis sleeps, and hardly flows
> The freezing Tanais thro' a waste of Snows,
> The North by myriads pours her mighty sons,
> Great nurse of Goths, of Alans, and of Huns...

and even when Pope returns to the matter in hand, and the Goddess of Dulness once more takes possession of England, the magical words evoke a lovely image which itself cuts across the whole ethos of the book:

> This fav'rite Isle, long sever'd from her reign,
> Dove-like, she gathers to her wings again;

and perhaps the weakness of the poem lies precisely in the fact that no coherent emotional unity is built up in the reader. It may, on the other hand, be argued that Pope is deliberately leading us from the petty squabbles and dirty intrigues of Grub Street, with its foul dung- and mud-impregnated atmosphere all too palpably put before us in Book II—a book which extravagantly stinks—to major themes, a vision, even, of the human condition, shot with irony and pity, leading us finally to the dread warning uttered at the end of Book III. These passages are great poetry, and however dazzling the skill in interweaving the more trivial elements, prevent the poem having any real unity of atmosphere. For though you may fairly easily yoke incongruous images violently together and achieve an emotional whole, it is far harder to take the further step and fuse incongruous emotions into a stable attitude.

As Professor Tillotson has admirably put it, *The Rape of the Lock* is 'an exquisitely diminished shadow cast by an entire epic poem', whereas *The Dunciad* is 'the ludicrous, grotesque, life-size shadow cast by a piece of an epic poem'. Thus the poem does not exist alone. It was probably never intended to, in spite of the edition Pope so astutely had pirated, which, lacking the notes, even Swift found largely incomprehensible. But then this 'spurious' edition was merely a part of the tremendous preparation for the poem, following the appearance of *Peri Bathous; or the Art of Sinking in Poetry*, an essay by Martinus Scriblerus which appeared in the 'Last' *Miscellany* of 1728, and served, as Professor Sutherland has suggested, as a kind of ground-bait to provoke fools to further folly and to catch more

gudgeon; then there were the carefully fostered rumours that
Pope was going to produce a work on 'The Progress of Dulness'.
So this edition, followed by others in Dublin which filled in
some of the blanks somewhat haphazardly, gave Pope an
excuse for publishing an 'authorized' edition—containing the
friendly dedication to Swift (the first great burlesque note-
writer, in *A Tale of a Tub*)—which was 'attended with *Proeme,
Prolegomena, Testimonia Scriptorum, Index Authorum* and *Notes
Variorum*'. In fact, the poem itself is only a portion of the sport;
the burlesque apparatus, with its notes by Scriblerus-Theobald-
Bentley, is itself an important part, not only of the satire, but
also of the self-justification. It may even be said that if the poem
itself is a good-humoured thing, its sting resides in the enormous
tail of comment. It must have been of this rather than of the
verse that Cibber was thinking when he wrote in his *Letter from
Mr. Cibber to Mr. Pope* of 1742:

> You seem in your *Dunciad*, to have been angry at the rain for
> wetting you, why then would you go into it? You could not but
> know that an Author, when he publishes a Work, exposes himself
> to all weathers;

sound common sense, appropriate even today (though it took
no account of the purely personal attacks on Pope); for it is in
the apparatus that the more deadly blows are given, and in
which Pope reveals his wounds. And the more we soak ourselves
in the poem, the more extraordinary the object appears. Supported by the massive notes (here others may have helped), in
which the personages assume a baffling character, part-real,
part-ghostly, imparting another, deeper dimension, the whole,
in fact made more weighty by a superstructure which might be
regarded as a heavy donnish joke, the poem, itself written for
so many different levels of response, seems sometimes to cry
out emotionally. It is the most fluid of literary contrivances,
susceptible of being ceaselessly tampered with and added to.
Indeed Pope did tinker at it for some twelve or more years, till
he absorbed the *New Dunciad* into the body of the work in 1743.
But since Book IV, the most important part of the epic, belongs
to Pope's final phase, it will be more suitably discussed at the
end of our consideration of his work, which it does in a sense
conclude.

After the first *Dunciad* in 1728, and up to and including

the *New*, Pope's poetical work, except for odds and ends, is homogeneous. It is all one 'moralized' song. In the main this work is sustained on two structural props, one that of direct moralizing as in the *Essay on Man* together with the *Moral Essays*; the other the satirical *Epistles* together with the *Satires*; the frontiers are hazy if only because satire is, at any rate in part, moralizing. And here really is his great contribution to the corpus of English poetry: it is what is distinctively Pope. We should miss a great deal of pleasure, something rare, should *The Rape of the Lock* and *Eloisa to Abelard* be swept out of existence; but were we to lose the work of the last decade or so of Pope's work, we should miss all that is valuable as his distinctive poetic criticism of life: and the final mastery in certain directions.

Once *The Dunciad* was, for the moment at least, over, Pope asked himself to what he was to turn his hand. The discipline, the deepening apprehension of values, perhaps even the fatigue of translating Homer and editing Shakespeare, would obviously make it difficult to take up where he had left off in 1717. Pope, over forty years old, forced by his physique to think rather than be, compelled by political circumstances to philosophize rather than to act, would, we suppose, turn naturally to moralizing, to doing something that would be 'of use'. After all, he had passed the formative years of his adolescence in the great utilitarian decade 1705-14; he had early revealed himself a moralist. Moreover *The Dunciad*, in which he backed up his passionate taste with moral rationalizing, may have shown him where, for the next ten years, perhaps, his genius might be fruitful. And for a year or so we see him clarifying in his letters the state of mind he was to indulge in writing the first of his 'Moral Essays', which we know as the fourth, the *Epistle to Lord Burlington*, published in December 1731.

Thus he writes to Caryll in December 1730:

As to your question, if I am writing, I really very rarely dip my pen. The vanity is over: and unless I could hope to do it with some good end, or to a better pitch than I've hitherto done, I would never return to the lists. But the truth is, it is now in my hopes (God knows whether it may ever prove in my power) to contribute to some honest and moral purposes in writing on human life and manners, not exclusive of religious regards, and I have many fragments which I am beginning to put together . . .

and satire, he comes more and more to insist, perhaps with

Young's satires to encourage the thought, is the only way in which any good can be done in a corrupt age. No doubt the letter quoted above is a fair enough statement of what he was feeling; and to moralize his song he would have to 'stoop to truth', pounce on actual living as all men realized it; Belindas and Eloisas would no longer serve his turn. But Pope's moralizings are, of course, Pope's; they are not, like Dryden's, the result of a search after a solution of personal dilemmas; they are the moralizings of a man who wants to be a moralist, not necessarily a meaner ambition, but springing from a different impulse. We never get the sense of a personal struggle, never a hint, say, of confession, such as we get near the beginning of *The Hind and the Panther*. There is, instead, the self-justification of a man who acted (in the main) according to principles which he never doubted. They were, after all, the principles everybody agreed to; they represented the *communis sensus* of generations brought up on the dual systems of Christian belief and Roman virtue. It is not therefore to be expected that the poems should give us any fresh contribution to the problems of ethics, or unexpected revelation as to the workings of the hearts of men.

But why should we look for these? The age had solved the ethical problems; the Enlightenment—at least as far as Pope absorbed it—was taken for granted. If Shaftesbury's 'optimism' is tempered, Butler's 'pessimism' had not yet—at least till 1736—made itself 'popularly' accepted, and then it was too late to affect Pope, who at any rate had heard it all before from Swift. What Pope was doing, as always, was to sum up the findings of the educated world, illustrate them brilliantly with examples and object lessons, and by the very virtue of his verse give the reader's contemplation of the human scene a higher tension or a certain valuable detachment—the comic detachment if you like, appreciated by men who would know that comedy also sometimes thunders.

Yet it is not to be wondered at that Pope himself did not achieve this detachment, or that he used his personal enemies for illustration of vices. He was almost forced to do the latter, because if he did not he was charged either with ingratitude, as when the Duke of Chandos was (wrongly) recognized in Timon, or of making unprovoked attacks, which, so long ago, Dennis had accused him of doing. He was in the same sort of dilemma between using the living and the dead: was it worse to attack

Addison, who had been dead some time, and so would not feel the smart (though, of course, *de mortuis nil nisi bonum*), or the active Lord Hervey, who would probably writhe, and might be materially injured? The dilemma is admirably put in the first of the Horace 'Imitations', the 'Epistle to Fortescue', and crops up amusingly here and there right through to the second part of the Epilogue. In any event, 'characters', even satirical characters, cannot be born out of the blue; if they are, a Theophrastian chill descends upon them, and they die. A poet must take his material from life, not from literary models; thus Pope did, as Dryden had done before him, and as Swift had said that you must. Yet so far as he could he generalized, or exaggerated beyond the proportions of verisimilitude; sometimes he combined two persons in one character, as with Atossa. He distorted for the sake of art. If the original gave him all he wanted, was in itself rich enough for the poetic purpose, the portrait, as with the Atticus–Addison one, was lifelike and perfect; with the Sporus–Hervey one it was kept in proportion but raised to a higher power.

It is clear that, rather fitfully, Pope conceived all the work of this period, not as bits which might be patched into a whole, but as a grandiose structure of which the *Essay on Man* was the first book, the four Moral Essays that we have being fragments of the third and fourth Epistles of the second book, or, if we accept Warburton's division as explained in his 1751 Preface, of a fourth book which was to deal with 'private ethics or practical morality'. Certainly in 1734 Pope saw the *Essay on Man* as the First Book (in four parts) of the *Ethic Epistles*, as explained in a scheme prefixed, according to Spence, to 'about a dozen' copies; the second, which would also deal with the limitations of man's reason, would contain some of the Moral Essays, some matter which Pope never dealt with, and some which was caught up into the *New Dunciad*. The scheme had not varied very much when Pope wrote to Swift about it on 25 March 1736. Thus it is of some interest, because it is a help in critical appreciation, to follow the bibliography and see in exactly what order the various works appeared. What is especially to be noted is that just before the first Epistle of *An Essay on Man* crept fearfully and anonymously into the world, Pope had hurriedly and happily scribbled off, and with trumpeting published, the first Imitation of Horace, and that similar

Imitations seem to have broken through his plan, so congenial did this sort of work become. Finally, in March 1742 Pope gathered up into the *New Dunciad* whatever he could salve from the grand scheme.

No one can be blamed for considering that here and there the *Moral Essays* glow less brightly, as they are certainly and confessedly the most laboured of all Pope's writings. They are lit up by passages of vivid satire, of delightful humour, or sheer sensuous beauty; to a reader intimate with Pope the positive intuitions can be construed into them. But in the main we read them for their 'prose' meaning; and, again in the main, they live in the memory for the brilliant 'character' passages, instinct with poetry—Timon, Villiers, Wharton, Atossa, Chloe. In these epistles Pope seems really to have been working with the motive of constructing (horrid prospect!) one of the works of the great *summa* of which the *Essay on Man* was the first; that is to say, the impulse was too consciously intellectual, they are too determinedly corrective, Nor are the morals more than obvious. 'Whatever service Pope may have meditated to the philosophy of morals', De Quincey remarked, 'he has certainly performed none.' There is, to be sure, nothing very original about the thought in any of the *Ethic Epistles*, but there is no reason why there should be. It is not the business of a poet to be a good philosopher, but to be a good poet, that is, to give whatever philosophy he may intuitively accept the intensity of poetic apprehension. What Pope was actually doing, and it was not necessarily an ignoble sport, was to make the pretentious rich uncomfortable, the sexually erring ridiculous, against the accepted moral background. In so far as his standards were aesthetic standards he is justified, and the much-howled-at description of Timon's villa was disliked—especially when the Epistle was called 'On Taste'—precisely because always 'a hundred smart in Timon and in Balaam'. Thus when the essay became the second one on 'The Use of Riches', its point was largely blunted. What we are concerned with, however, is how far these things are poetry for us here and now (given we have a little understanding of and feeling for the period in which they are written), that is, how far they can delight, and give us a more vivid apprehension of the quality of living.

For there is always the question of how far directly didactic poetry can be poetry at all; for if poetry teaches, it does so, as

De Quincey stated in arguing the matter out over Pope himself, indirectly, lurkingly, 'only as nature teaches, as forests teach, as the sea teaches, as infancy teaches, viz., by deep impulse, by hieroglyphic suggestion'. It is not for the poet to 'address the *insulated* understanding'. The artistic problem (and this with Pope was mercifully always the final and the fundamental problem, whatever his protestations) was how to integrate the illustrations of the moral with its abstract exposition; how to fuse the quivering modes of his sensibility, sometimes his personal resentment, with the cooler atmosphere of acceptance of an obvious ethical system; or sometimes more flatteringly, with an appeal to the alert intellect. Pope accomplished the fusion in two ways: either by a careful leading up to the brilliant passage—usually one of the rises, and often containing the lilt—with or without an easing away after it was over; or by suffusing the whole with humour, as, for example, in the Sir Balaam or the Halifax–Bubb passages. The methods, naturally, might be combined, and often were. If the abstract matter could legitimately give occasion for warmth, so much the better.

It is, then, by the portraits and the self-revelation that the poems of this period live—the Ethic Epistles and the Imitations of Horace—not by their philosophy. But the *Essay on Man*, which may be considered central to this whole group of poems—for they all revolve round it whether or not we take Warburton's 1751 Preface literally—contains no portrait, and is alive; at all events, it is still read with pleasure. 'I am just now writing, or rather planning a book,' Pope wrote to Swift in June 1730, 'to make mankind look upon this life with comfort and pleasure, and put morality in a good humour.' Taken immediately after *The Dunciad*, it seems in a sense to be a counterbalancing answer to it. And since the morality of all the other poems depends upon the philosophy expounded in this one, it may, though not the first to be published, be considered before the others.

In embarking upon the *Essay on Man*, Pope was not only completing the pattern of the Augustan poet, of which the exemplar had been Dryden, whose *Religio Laici* and *Hind and Panther* might be said to constitute a philosophic apologia, but he was also challenging Milton, or perhaps complementing his work, though it is not easy to guess what implication may lurk in *vindicating* rather than *justifying* the ways of God to man. At all events, since the Fall was declaredly outside his field, as also was the Revelation, Pope, in this new explanation of the reason for the Deity's treatment of man, would be able to jettison all the scholastic lumber which (in his view) had clogged Milton, and sail away freely on the full breeze of the Enlightenment. Whatever may be thought of the philosophic validity of the poem, it certainly was a remarkable achievement, for it was a brilliant compression of the 'polite' philosophy of the day as sketched earlier in this volume. We need no longer accept the 'silly idea', as John Laird called it, that Pope 'simply put into tuneful rhyme material in prose which Bolingbroke supplied for the purpose', though it certainly contains the sort of thing you would expect men such as Pope and Bolingbroke to talk about when they met. Bolingbroke we know had been immersed in philosophy ever since he had quitted the Pretender, and reported to Swift in 1730 that he was 'deep in metaphysics' with Pope. To us (but we must bear in mind the assumptions of those days) the work seems self-contradictory, and indeed Pope himself stated in his Introduction the difficulty of 'steering between the extremes of doctrines seemingly opposite'.

The plain common sense of it is that both the poet and the 'master of the poet and the song' derived their ideas from the same sources, the general ethos being the Deistic view as expressed variously by thinkers from Herbert of Cherbury, strongly tinctured by Shaftesburian optimism and the philosophy of 'plastic nature'; both perhaps had recently read King's *De Origine Mali* to which fresh attention had been drawn by Law's translation, and Cudworth's *Eternal and Immutable Morality*, not published till 1731. Though Bolingbroke kept records of many of their conversations, and set out his own views on paper, Pope by no means always adhered to them; indeed many of the ideas he now put into verse occur in his correspondence with Caryll from 1713, and some of them, as already noted, may be met as early as in the *Essay on Criticism*. Pope told Spence that he submitted the 'plan' to his 'guide, philosopher, and friend'; and the latter no doubt contributed suggestions as to the ordonnance of the poem. It is doubtful if Pope realized how unorthodox were many of the doctrines he derived from reading and conversation; and though his friend warned him 'you will know how to screen yourself . . . against any direct charge of heterodoxy', Bolingbroke stated later that the poet 'understood nothing of his own principles nor saw to what they naturally tended'. Certainly Pope was surprised and hurt when Crousaz and others attacked him for Spinozism and other unforgivable heresies, and was much relieved when Warburton snatched his opinions back for some sort of orthodoxy. Bolingbroke, the retired statesman, may have contributed something in the political part of the disquisition, as when in the poem we get an echo of the passage in *Of the State of the Nation* which runs:

> There is a political as well as a natural self-love; and the former ought to be, to every member of a commonwealth, the same determining principle of action, where public interest is concerned, that the latter will be to him most certainly wherever his private interest is concerned.

'Self-love and social are the same' (the poem is threaded with Stoicism in spite of Pope's denials), but it is likely that this sort of thing was much discussed among the haycocks at Dawley or in the grotto at Twickenham, as it is made much of in Butler's sermons.

In the main Pope gives a vision of the clockwork universe implied, if not exactly stated, by Locke; but throughout he balances the mechanistic sense with one of organic creation, constantly reminding us of it as he does in:

> Whate'er of life, all-quick'ning æther keeps,
> Or breathes thro' air, or shoots beneath the deeps,
> Or pours profuse on earth; one nature feeds
> The vital flame, and swells the genial seeds.

It contains all sorts of other ingredients, such as the problem of evil, the limits of man's reason and the strength of the subconscious, the great Chain of Being, the pleasing picture of man learning from the animals what to do with his faculties— from Montaigne this, apparently, as was the 'pampered goose'. It is a learned poem, though constructed out of a learning of little use to us today as either philosophy or religion. Pope, in trying to formulate the traditional background philosophy of his time, possibly chained himself too narrowly. But there is in the *Essay*, as Professor Wilson Knight properly insists, a communication which transcends all the intellectual presentations, which still speaks to us as human beings, and which can only be called poetry. It glows with something of the wonder which characterized the poets of the third and fourth decades of the century whenever they approached a contemplation of how nature worked; and for Pope Nature was God, or at least, as Addison phrased it in his most enduring verses, all things in Nature 'Their great Original proclaim'. The poem is not all at the same level; it is not always the exciting response to a vision of the universe; sometimes it does no more than state in couplets almost too pithily compressed a notion that has been arrived at with intellectual effort; there is, in short, what Professor Renwick has called 'uneven transformation'. Yet, as so much in Pope, it is in many ways deceptively simple in appearance. The superb passage at the beginning of the second Epistle with its description of man, ending

> Sole judge of Truth, in endless Error hurl'd,
> The glory, jest, and riddle of the world!

has undeniable poetic dynamic, though derived, it may be, from Basil Kennet's translation of Pascal: 'A profess'd Judge of all Things, yet a feeble Worm of the Earth, the great Depository and Guardian of Truth, and yet a meer Huddle of Uncertainty: the Glory and the Scandal of the Universe.' Even so, when looked into closely, especially with reference to the satirically ironic passage which follows, it reveals more than a little 'metaphysical' complexity.

It is surprising that the poem can attain such tension, given the deliberately unpompous style and diction, the easy only slightly formalized colloquialism and the touches of humour of the familiar epistle—Pope's form of the 'unpolished rugged verse' Dryden chose for his ratiocinative pieces. The *Essay* makes its way forward by means of a logical, argumentative structure, and so the progress the reader makes through it is an intellectual rather than an imaginative one. It is true that the repetitions and echoes in the last four lines of the poem are possibly little emotional hammer-taps rather than mental conclusions; but imaginative movement is abundantly there, in the warmth or tempo of the various parts, not to be guessed from the argument prefixed to each. Many of the sections, as Professor R. K. Root has shown, are of sonnet, or nearly sonnet size, with an intense and exquisite effect. Pope's feeling-thought normally resolved itself into paragraphs of about this length—he constructed in this way rather than in couplets—and such weakness as he shows lies not in the weaving together of the couplets, but in the

joining together of the paragraphs. The opening of each Epistle
is a brisk challenge (that of the third Epistle the least so), at a
high level of poetic evocation; passages of ratiocination ensue,
gradually rising, or suddenly plunging into the most emotional
part of the chapter, occurring usually towards the end, which
drops down to a level of calm, rich contemplation, all intellectual passion spent. The Epistles, in fact, follow the usual pattern
of Pope's work, with its rise or rises, and its lilts. The tone varies
a little. The first may be judged the most perfect. The attack, the
invocation to St. John, swings us straight into the subject with
a grand inviting gesture; Sections I and II are spirited rhetorical
argument, and it is not till Section III that the poetic imagination is called upon, but then how grandly:

> Oh blindness to the future! kindly giv'n,
> That each may fill the circle mark'd by Heav'n;
> Who sees with equal eye, as God of all,
> A hero perish, or a sparrow fall,
> Atoms or systems into ruin hurl'd
> And now a bubble burst, and now a world,

the transition to the next passage being beautifully made.

There are undeniably lovely things, some famous couplets,
and the touching 'poor Indian' passage; but the rise begins
in Section VIII with 'Vast chain of being!...' to reach its
climax in IX when we meet the impact of 'All are but parts
of one stupendous whole', the lilt occurring in this part with
another reminder of organic creativeness:

> Warms in the sun, refreshes in the breeze,
> Glows in the stars, and blossoms in the trees;
> Lives thro' all life, extends thro' all extent;
> Spreads undivided, operates unspent!

The withdrawal to calmness comes in Section X, which concludes so ringingly with:

> And, spite of Pride, in erring Reason's spite,
> One truth is clear, 'Whatever IS, is RIGHT.'

the placing of the Panglossian statement giving it an undoubted
if brittle glory. The second Book begins with one of the loveliest,
most nostalgic paragraphs, one of the most packed and evocative; yet the last four lines of the Epistle leave us with a sense
not so much of quiet as of deflation, so harshly has the moral

tag been dragged in. The third, the least impressive of all, is mainly contemplative, and the rise is comparatively weak. The tone of the fourth is imparted largely by muted rhetoric, while most of its notable passages are satirical.

Structure alone, however, cannot give validity to a poem, as distinct from a philosophic discourse; validity it achieves by the texture all through, the sensuous appeal, and the imaginative evocation. These are seldom absent for long in the *Essay*, though sometimes the claims of 'perspicuity'—to use his own excuse— bring us to passages which are laboured and are now dead, as the conclusion of Epistle II, though even out of that there suddenly springs

> In Folly's cup, still laughs the bubble, Joy.

Moreover, in this work as everywhere else in Pope, we are constantly reminded of older poets, more particularly Dryden; passages in Epistle II, for example, are full of reminiscences of *Aureng-Zebe* or of Dryden's 'Lucretius on the Fear of Death'. Pope always knew how to enrich his appeal by quotations he could suppose his reader to be aware of, so providing overtones; but the *Essay on Man* largely makes its effect, apart from the wider movement, by the continual stimuli to the nerves and the senses, by the wider generalizations which are uttered with that amazing compression of which Pope was the master, a compression which imparts so much vividness that many of his couplets, or single lines, have passed into the language through the stage of being popular quotations. Such things as these are so well known that we forget where they come from:

> Hope springs eternal in the human breast:
> Man never Is, but always To be blest—   (I. 95)

a thought which he might have culled from Pascal's 'Le présent n'est jamais notre but. Le passé et le présent sont nos moyens; le seul avenir est notre objet. Ainsi nous ne vivons jamais: mais nous espérons de vivre.' Or the often but usually irrelevantly quoted:

> Die of a rose in aromatic pain?   (I. 200)

Or the lovely little nature inset, recently popularized:

> The spider's touch, how exquisitely fine!
> Feels at each thread, and lives along the line.   (I. 217)

The attention may rise, perhaps, at such clinching lines as

> Or, meteor-like, flame lawless thro' the void   (II. 65)

and

> With all the rash dexterity of Wit;   (II. 84)

or become delightedly alert at the still fresh satire of:

> . . . the Politic and Wise:
> All sly slow things, with circumspective eyes.   (IV. 225)

It is by such things, constantly occurring, that the poem is step by step carried along, even where the broader sweeps flag.

It is not easy to assess what the poem means to us now, since the philosophico-scientific premisses no longer hold, while some even strike us as absurd. But even though De Quincey called this a *hortus siccus* of pet notions, that does not matter so long as the notions produce poetry. And in more than one respect it is at all times to the point, in for instance the call to intellectual humility, and where the pretensions of science to explain the universe are roughly handled. It is, after all, a vision of humanity, of man's place in nature, though optimistic and lacking in the sense of tragedy, as it is (of careful set purpose) in the Christian ethos. But if it presents a rationalistic view of the universe, it is full of wonderment and delight, and that excitement of apprehending a whole with that part of man's nature we have no choice but to call poetic. There was, we know, little philosophic consistency about Pope; philosophic 'systems' at any rate are repugnant to the chameleon poet, and it is not to be held against him that he was eclectic, for he confessed in his Imitation of Horace Epistle I. i, addressed to Bolingbroke:

> But ask not to what Doctors I apply?
> Sworn to no Master, of no Sect am I:
> As drives the storm, at any door I knock;
> And house with Montagne now, or now with Lock.

And though, no doubt, philosophically this is an unforgivable sin, in the last analysis it is Pope's own emotion in face of the problem of existence that is moving, that gives the work its imaginative quality. It is not Pope the thinker we respond to, but Pope the ordinary puzzled human being whom we meet, like, and unavoidably echo.

At least he invites to introspection: the final 'Know Thyself', more pessimistically felt perhaps than the Gnostics intended, is always good advice. It is at the smallest a protection against complacency; and here Pope is interesting enough, his feeling-thought complex being by no means so simple or so superficial as is normally (far too carelessly) maintained. For wherever Pope succeeds in teaching it is by purely poetic means, by sharpening our apprehension, as in such a line as 'By turns we catch the vital breath, and die' (such lines must of course be read in their context); or by a change of movement which imparts a dramatic quality to the whole sense of the thing. This is perhaps most easily illustrated when at the end of the poem he breaks from a set of strictly antithetical couplets into the magnificently swinging measure of the generous peroration addressed to Bolingbroke, within which again the movement is brilliantly varied. These things bring into the intellectual argument a warmth which gives the reader an impulse vigorous enough to carry the mood with him, after, a few lines later, he has come upon the end of the poem.

It is this warmth which gives the *Essay* its positive quality, by which it enlarges and enriches our experience. Moreover it is important because it is central to all the rest of the Great Moral Poem, so to name almost the whole of the corpus of work produced from the 'Epistle to Burlington' onwards. In it are to be found the premises used as parts of the structural fabric of the various poems: the place of self-love, the ruling passion, the social impulses, the part played by corrective reason, and so on, figure largely throughout the remainder of the canon.

Take, for example, what is now the first *Moral Essay*, 'Of the Knowledge and Characters of Men', which more than the other Epistles resembles the greater *Essay*. It is not very profound or illuminating; and poetically the most sustained passage, the character of Wharton, is too reminiscent of its brilliant forebear, the character of Zimri, much to move astonishment. It is interesting that, in describing man as an unstable bundle of emotions and principle, it should postulate the subconscious:

> As the last image of that troubled heap,
> When Sense subsides, and Fancy sports in sleep,
> (Tho' past the recollection of the thought)
> Becomes the stuff of which our dream is wrought:
> Something as dim to our internal view,
> Is thus, perhaps, the cause of most we do.

It would, however, be tedious to follow these Epistles in detail seriatim. The next, on the Character of Women, is, in the main, cheap: we read it now for Atossa. The third, to Bathurst, which incidentally gives us a friendly little dramatic view of that genial, not very intellectual nobleman, we read for the characters, for Cotta, and especially for the inaccurate but magnificent picture of the end of Villiers (Zimri on his death-bed). We avoid if we can, well-placed though it is, the character of John Kyrle, unless we maliciously delight in the bathos of:

> Who taught that heav'n-directed spire to rise?
> 'The Man of Ross', each lisping babe replies,

avoiding, too, the rather absurd, semi-Mandevillian economics. There is, of course, the fun of people being condemned out of their own mouths: 'Bond damns the Poor', and

> The grave Sir Gilbert holds it for a rule,
> That 'every man in want is knave or fool';

the phrases being historically attested. There are numerous witty and pungent strokes; but the incessant girding at the obvious abuse of riches, in spite of the pieces of rapid narrative, makes it for some a trifle tedious in comparison with the 'Imitations', though many will always enjoy the fable of Sir Balaam, no better and no worse than the usual fable of the day, with at least the happy

> 'Live like yourself,' was soon my Lady's word;
> And lo! two puddings smoak'd upon the board.

But on the whole it is overburdened: it 'abounds in moral example, for which reason it must be obnoxious in this age. God send it does any good', so Pope wrote to Caryll (Jan. 1732-3) and his fears may well apply now. The last, in time the first, is in some ways the most interesting since it is partly an essay on taste in landscape gardening (he referred to it as 'the gardening poem') which beautifully sets out the current ideas of the time, and indeed explains a good deal of what Pope himself was trying to do, on a tiny scale, at Twickenham. And suddenly, near the end, after some more Mandevillian economics, we are for a moment back again in the romantic mood of *Eloisa*, the *eheu fugaces* mood of the *Rape*, together with the theme of creative plenitude:

> Another age shall see the golden Ear
> Imbrown the Slope, and nod on the Parterre,
> Deep Harvests bury all his pride has plann'd,
> And laughing Ceres re-assume the land,

making a beautiful transition to the utilitarian-patriotic ending, reminiscent, perhaps on purpose, of the conclusion of *Windsor Forest*, which connotes a feeling that was in Pope deep and constant. But disillusion had clouded the earlier vision; the rapacious money-grabbers, the vulgar *nouveaux riches*, had given birth to the feelings that provoked the bitter mockery of the last two Epistles.

The four Epistles exhibit, naturally, all the technical skill which Pope had by this time acquired; we can take pleasure in the pyrotechnics, and be willing to pay for them by the discomfort here and there caused by too great compression, a tightened 'correctness' leading often to an ambiguity which is far from correct. But the delight we may get from them is not a poetic delight in the full sense. Pope, we feel, was uncomfortable in this sort of pulpit, and when we come upon the graceful ease, outvying Swift's, with which the first Imitation of Horace sails away, we know that here Pope has found his real medium, his most personal utterance, and we are by no means surprised to find him writing to Caryll that 'it was a slight thing, the work of two days, [a harmless inaccuracy, as we now know] whereas that to Lord Bathurst was the work of two years by intervals'. It is not astonishing that it met with 'such a flood of favour, that [his] ears need[ed] no more flattery for a twelve month' because here he was free of fetters, talking as he wished to talk, and singing when it came upon him to sing.

We must, however, distinguish between the groups of these Imitations. Putting aside the two lyrics from the Odes—only one of which, *Inter missa Venus diu* is complete, a nostalgic confession, the emotions beautifully imparted, and a graceful tribute to the future Lord Mansfield—there are those which are personal defences of his position, and those which are generally speaking moral-satirical. It might be possible to split them up into the political and the neutral, but it turns out that towards the end the political ones tend also to be the personal. It is not that we need take Pope's politics very seriously. As a Catholic he would be likely to support the Tory side, or failing them, the Whigs who were not, or had ceased to be, of the faction that

triumphed at the death of Queen Anne. Many of these happened
to be his personal friends, such as Burlington and Cobham,
whose taste in architecture and gardening he admired. There
were Chesterfield and Pulteney, and the various groups Walpole could do without; while at the centre of them—from time
to time—there stood Pope's close and almost idolized friend
Bolingbroke. It is not easy to say how far Pope was really taken
in by the political propaganda of this clique, which, as always,
was partly the victim of its own propaganda; but the attitude he
was enabled to adopt of being the flail of the corrupt, the reverence with which he declared he regarded the sacred weapon
of satire, the excuse it all gave him of writing in the form and
manner best suited to his genius, fell in very well with his
temper at that time. The complex of emotions engendered by
his love for his friends, his vision of the political situation, his
sense of growing corruption and the decline of his age (however
little it may have been justified) created a tension of feeling
which in its turn produced the pressure without which there
can be no good or effective poetry.

But to be at its most effective, the poet must feel above his
material; what usually relieves the dullness of mere moralizing
is the poet's delight in his craft. Pope, when in good spirits, may
remind us of Marvell's soul gliding into the boughs of the fruit
trees:

> There like a bird it sits and sings,
> There whets, and combs its silver wings;
> And, till prepar'd for longer flight,
> Waves in its plumes the various Light.

Certainly in his first Imitation he is all iridescence; preparing
for the longer flights of the *Essay on Man*, and, perhaps, the
Epistle to Augustus; we feel he is in holiday mood, not at all that
of the Moral Essays he has just published, or of the first part of
the great *Essay* which is about to appear. He is so gay, so
genial, that one feels here, what one very rarely feels with Pope,
the *careless* ease of the giant: how natural to be what he is!

> Fools rush into my head, and so I write;

or

> Who-e'er offends, at some unlucky Time
> Slides into Verse, and hitches in a Rhyme.

He is happy, he is bland, he is ironical; he is enjoying his attacks

with impish glee, though for the most part his satire is mellower
than usual; he scribbles off his now charming self-justifications
with his tongue at least half in his cheek. And after all, it was
part of the 'rhetoric' of satire for the author to make himself
out to be the Stoical *vir bonus*: Pope could assume the *persona*
when he wished. There is a hint of the country retreat motif,
more than a hint of the theme that to enjoy the society of one's
friends is the highest good, and the whole is so musically woven
together, seems to spring so much from one impulse that we have
no sense at all of translation, as in the others we sometimes do.

The really triumphant Imitations are those which have no
direct basis in Horace (except for an occasional passage),
namely the masterly *Epistle to Dr. Arbuthnot*, and the two dialogues which form the *Epilogue to the Satires*. The *Prologue* is,
more than any other single piece, the poem which establishes
Pope as having added something essential, something rarely
individual, to the canon of English poetry. The beautiful
colloquialism which never degenerates from poetry, never becomes chat; the internal movement, the management of the
'rises' and the placing of the 'lilts'; the brilliant fusion of castiga-
tion and song, the modulation of the imagery which ensures that
for each kind of passage the communication shall be of the
right vividness, make of this particular poem a lasting object
of delight. Besides, it is really not only Pope's most telling
Dunciad, except that Dunces were not his mark, it is also his
most profound moral essay. For all the time, what he is doing
from within the warm fortress of a long and respected friendship
is to attack the negative and sterile, the things which detract
from life. Some of the emotions no doubt arose in the first
instance from personal resentment, as did the Atticus passage;
but this, deadly true so far as it goes, now concerned a man
fifteen years dead; and, moreover, Pope knew that it was only
part of the picture, witness his reference in the *Epistle to Augustus*,
and his poem at the head of Tickell's edition of the latter's
hero; what Pope was aiming at now was the generalized picture
of negative 'virtue'. Pope gave every credit to the man of letters,
deploring that the same man should have so distasteful (to put
it mildly) a character. He had been disillusioned, wounded.
Sporus had his origin in the hideous hatred Pope felt for Lord
Hervey, but the object of attack is futile sterility; and so on.
Thanks largely to its autobiographical snatches, it gives us the

complete picture of a man, the man of battle, the positive man, in whom, however, the passages of Horatian 'retirement' are at this stage perfectly genuine.

If we turn to it directly after reading *Sober Advice from Horace*, which immediately preceded it, we are struck by the difference in tone. Though the Horatian 'sermon'—this from Horace I. ii. —is intended to be colloquial, the liberating ease of the *Epistle to Dr. Arbuthnot* places the latter on an altogether different level. To speak in the way Pope does here is almost to sing. Or at least to walk in this way is all the while to be on the verge of dancing. It is perhaps this which makes the changes of movement so easily accomplished, for basically some of the transitions are as abrupt as is common with Horace. One of the startlingly interesting things technically about this poem is that when thought about visually—as remembered poems do present themselves in the memory—it is extraordinarily three-dimensional. Pope himself and his interlocutor—whether or not we regard the piece as a duologue—weave a kind of variegated background, composed in depth, against which the main figures, Atticus, Sporus, and Bufo, stand out starkly, and lesser figures, Dennis, Gildon, and so on, occupy intermediate positions. The verse in the great portraits, though as beautifully modulated as in the friendly or affectionate passages—look at the miraculous changes of stress and tempo in the Sporus portrait, the almost fiendish skill of the vowel values—rings out more as a public utterance than the more intimate communication. The opening lines are, in a sense, ordinary prose speech, but so pointed, so economical, so sure in movement that they are self-elected into poetry. It is necessary to make once more this point, which might have been thought at this date to need no comment, since critics who ought to know better still refer to 'the monotonous litany of the rhymed couplet'. Think only of

> Pretty! in Amber to observe the forms
> Of hairs, or straws, or dirt, or grubs, or worms;
> The things, we know, are neither rich nor rare,
> But wonder how the Devil they got there?

Monotonous? A litany? You may say, if you will, that this is to hum delightedly rather than to sing: but then:

> Peace to all such! but were there One whose fires
> True Genius kindles, and fair Fame inspires,
> Blest with each Talent . . .

and so on in ringing tones which are too well known to need
repetition, though further acquaintance with the passage reveals,
as always with Pope, further delights of reference—as, for example, the brilliant adaptation of Phineas Fletcher's personification of Envy:

> When needs he must, yet faintly then, he praises
> Somewhat the deed, but more the means he raises,
> So maketh what he makes, and praising most dispraises.

Yet what is perhaps most remarkable in the Epistle is the variety
of tone introduced into this single piece, the irritation of the
beginning, Pope's tribute and gratitude to Arbuthnot, his
homage to his father, his deep affection for his mother, as well
as the good-humoured brief contempt for the lesser figures, and
the molten lead for his enemies. The self-justification following
straight upon the Sporus lines—an awkward transition there—
is likely to make the reader a little uneasy, and perhaps Pope
himself felt a little uneasy here. Certainly he was later to play
this particular tune with far more confidence and brio in the
Epilogue, developing the vein of humour directed against
himself already hinted at in his first Imitation.

After the *Epistle to Dr. Arbuthnot* all Pope's work, except for
the *New Dunciad*, was Horatian (it seems likely that Moral
Essay II 'On the Character of Women' was ready before he
hurriedly completed his poem to his friend, lest the latter's
death should prevent the tribute); and in it, though literary
criticism occasionally occurs, notably in the *Epistle to Augustus*,
the personal apologia and political themes grow in importance,
together with the town-country opposition to which Professor
Butt has drawn attention, and for the sake of which he originally
chose for 'versifying', in 1713, Donne's second satire. Rehand-
ling this for his *Collected Works* in 1735 enabled him to suggest the
general spread of corruption from town to country, while his
earlier versification of Donne's Fourth Satire in 1733 had
enabled him merely to state his dislike for the Court party, to
which his friends did not at the moment happen to belong.
Every poet is entitled to his own politics; but it is only fair to
point out that posterity has too easily accepted brilliant satire
as truth *au pied de la lettre*; and though we kindle to Pope for the
warm support he gave his friends, it cannot be said that these
were immaculate. Pope's work has all the exaggeration of the

satirist, as well as the violent partisanship of the man who does not really know what the fuss is all about; it did not altogether do to carry *l'esprit simpliste* into the complex politics of the formative struggles of English cabinet government. But it is this very innocence which gives these satires their pure quality, and makes it easy for us to take in our stride such obvious nonsense as 'That not to be corrupted is the shame'; it is the innocence of fact, combined with the fine eagerness of intention, that raises what might be vituperation into the region of poetry.

The most daring political satire occurs in the *Epistle to Augustus*; but to make play with mock praise is an irony too easy to be very enduring, and to anyone with knowledge of the reality a great deal too callow. Pope was welcome to the satisfaction of angering Walpole by his couplet on Swift, but we may well doubt if the First Minister was really deeply galled by a reference to an event of a decade earlier. The political part is certainly readable, chiefly as extremely skilful, and thus very enjoyable, light verse; but it must be confessed that the snorted revulsion against flattery and flatterers which brings the piece to a conclusion *con brio* may raise a smile that Pope never intended. Yet let us beware, for by now Pope was in a strong enough position to allow a little self-critical humour to intrude; and at all events, the tempo and the tone are just what is needed to round off the direct hitting. Yet whatever may be said about the political satire, the interest of the piece is almost entirely in the addition the literary passages make to the *Essay on Criticism*, passages from which it is still almost impossible not to borrow quotations when discussing the writers of the earlier age; an interest too will always remain in such a transcription from Horace—far closer to translation than Rochester's well-known 'Allusion to Horace'—for those who care to read it side by side with the original (as Pope meant us to), and enjoy Pope's skill, nearly always vivifying, in adapting what Horace wrote to suit the different time and clime. This is true for all the Imitations, though the *Nil admirari* rendering most readers will find disappointing, while the *Hoc erat in votis* satire is probably mainly Swift's; and in the *Quinque dies* 'Imitated in the manner of Dr. Swift', we feel that Pope is trying to dance in slippers which do not fit him.

In the Imitation of Epistle I. i, however, addressed to Bolingbroke, we feel that Pope has once more found his measure;

he seems again to give freely of himself in talking of himself. The country-Court opposition is happily dealt with, and if the moral is a little obvious, as the satire also is in part, the latter is given pungency by such couplets as:

> While with the silent growth of ten per Cent,
> In Dirt and darkness hundreds stink content.

But it is not until we come to *One Thousand Seven Hundred and Thirty Eight. A Dialogue Something like Horace* of May 1738, to be followed by Dialogue II in July, the two together being known as the Epilogue to the Satires, that we again find Pope at his very best, in the fascinating complexity of his fullest freedom. They are largely politico-moral poems, overstressing to our minds the theme of corruption; but here, again, what matters is not how far Pope may have been right or wrong, but the strength of feeling behind the statement. What matters is not the verdict of history (which may itself be distorted), but rather:

> *Vice* is undone, if she forgets her Birth,
> And stoops from Angels to the Dregs of Earth:
> But 'tis the *Fall* degrades her to a Whore;
> Let *Greatness* own her, and she's mean no more:
> Her Birth, her Beauty, Crowds and Courts confess,
> Chaste Matrons praise her, and grave Bishops bless:
> In golden Chains the willing World she draws,
> And hers the Gospel is, and hers the Laws:
> Mounts the Tribunal, lifts her scarlet head,
> And sees pale Virtue carted in her stead!

Pope has been described as the master of rage, with Dryden and Swift as masters respectively of contempt and disgust; but here he rivals his seniors, though his voice is not so much that of the recording spirit or of the judge as of the prophet crying *Ichabod*. It comes, moreover, as a climax to the previous passages of argument in defence of satire, somewhat arid and formal as compared either with his first apologia in the 'Epistle to Fortescue', or with the splendid defiant singing which was to come in the second part of the Epilogue.

As a swan song (as this last may in some sort be considered, since *The Dunciad* was already largely sung, bellowed, or screeched) it is superb. It is a *defensio* rather than an *apologia*; and never was defence more aggressive, never did indignation,

laced with a plentiful brew of self-justification, make more
ringing verses. It would be misleading, however, to describe it
merely in terms of those two impulses, since so much flows
from them—clear thinking about the issues, admiration of his
Patriot friends, and homage to them, the whole bound together,
not so much by indignation, as by humour, both in the swing of
the admirably colloquial verses, the *va et vient* of the conversation,
and the detachment with which Pope views himself until he
makes his final arrogantly humble declaration. The number of
levels on which the poem moves, not quite simultaneously—
though that kind of depth is not lacking—requires of the reader
either an astonishing agility, or better, a complete surrender to
the rapid movement. It may even be said that nearly all the
mature Pope, the Pope who had ceased to wander in the maze
of delighted fancy, may be found from the stomach-turning
simile of the hogs of Westphaly (not originally Pope's) to the
'tinsel insects' passage. We may take it up from the slightly
pompous statement

> Ask you what Provocation I have had?
> The strong Antipathy of Good to Bad,

when Pope, applying a little saving humour to himself, makes
the Friend say:

> *Fr.* You're strangely proud.

Then the cymbal clashes:

> *P.*   So proud, I am no Slave:
> So impudent, I own myself no Knave:
> So odd, my Country's Ruin makes me grave.
> Yes, I am proud; I must be proud to see
> Men not afraid of God, afraid of me:
> Safe from the Bar, the Pulpit, and the Throne,
> Yet touch'd and sham'd by *Ridicule* alone.
> O sacred Weapon! left for Truth's defence,
> Sole Dread of Folly, Vice and Insolence!
> To all but Heav'n-directed hands deny'd,
> The Muse may give thee, but the Gods must guide.
> Rev'rent I touch thee! but with honest zeal;
> To rowze the Watchmen of the Publick Weal,
> To Virtue's Work provoke the tardy Hall,
> And goad the Prelate slumb'ring in his Stall.

Then the indifference of supreme contempt gives him lyrical
impetus:
> Ye tinsel Insects! whom a Court maintains,
> That counts your Beauties only by your Stains,
> Spin all your Cobwebs o'er the Eye of Day!
> The Muse's wing shall brush you all away;

the last springing line proclaiming the primacy of poetry in
intuition and in power, before he drops back into the vein of
Horatian 'sermonizing'. The poem with its skill, its sinewy verve,
its shapeliness, was a fine full close to the last of the Imitations
which, if Warburton's remark to Charles Yorke really represented Pope's feelings, Pope was getting tired of, as indeed the
final couplet and his own note would seem to testify.

Whether or no Pope intended 'more Essays on Man', it
would seem that towards 1740 he began to think it was time to
bring his work to a close, rather than complete his blank verse
epic *Brutus*. He was becoming, indeed had become, spiritually,
if not socially, isolated. If he still had such friends as Bethel,
Allen, and Martha Blount, if he still had the aristocratic world
to move in, all his old literary friends were either dead, or dead
to him, with Swift failing in Ireland, and Bolingbroke hardly
ever at home. Remained only the gentle appreciative Spence,
who from 1740 gave way more and more to the heavy-minded
Warburton, 'the most impudent man alive' according to
Bolingbroke. Perhaps, however, we owe it to Warburton's
bustle that Pope produced his last two works, the first of which
was *The Memoirs of Martinus Scriblerus*, which he issued in 1741.
However much of this may originally have been written by
Arbuthnot, with passages by Gay and hints from Swift, it was
all wholly revised and rewritten by Pope. Engendered in the
old Scriblerian days of Queen Anne, it was in many ways out
of date before it appeared; but it has enough of the universal in it
to make it readable even now, for anybody interested either in
Pope or in the history of ideas. The 'tale' itself is entertaining
enough; the absurdities of pedantry are amusingly fooled, and
the story of 'the double marriage' (to one of Siamese twins) gives
opportunity for a deal of parody of solemn nonsense, legal as
well as scholastic. If it is readable now mainly by the student
alone, it is nevertheless an important document as being the
arch between *Gulliver's Travels* and the *Dunciad*.

Perhaps even *The New Dunciad; as found in 1741*, the other of

Pope's last two works. Realizing that now he would not have the time, nor perhaps the constant inspiration, to complete his great system of didactic poetry, in this poem he blended a good deal of what he had intended to say in the form of moral essays, with what remained over for him to do in the way of satire. The result was this *New Dunciad*, different not only in scope and target from the old, but also in tone. Yet it is evident that from its first conception he meant it to form an organic part of the old poem, with which it was incorporated in 1743 as Book IV; it continues on from the old Book III, and the famous conclusion is transferred from that book to the end of the combined version. He was not, however, at liberty to tamper with the old until the expiration of the fourteen-year contract under which Lawton Gilliver had taken over the copyright from the three peers to whom Pope had originally protectively assigned it. In the meantime he reworked the original poem, here and there making improvements, but with the main intention of substituting Cibber for Theobald as King of the Dunces. The usurpation was on the whole smoothly accomplished, and the tone of light banter, of almost genial good-humour—except in the notes—was maintained.

But the *New Dunciad*, or Book IV, is another thing. The tone is altogether more urgent, more serious; the scope is far wider, and personalities as such almost entirely disappear. Pope deals either with the whole nation, or with groups; and if here and there individuals are singled out, such as Bentley or the young Duke of Kingston, it is as representatives of their class, of pedants in the one case (a brief sketch of what was to have been one of the stanchions of this modern *summa*), in the other of young nobles debauched by the Grand Tour. The poem is immensely rich, enormously varied; it is like a great organ fugue concluding the oratorio, in which all the resources of the diapason are brought into play. Pope sings more continuously, and more consistently appeals to the poetic imagination, than he does in the other three books. The movement is swifter, and even more superbly controlled than in the other parts, so although it is possibly wittier and even more genially humorous, it is both profounder and more far-reaching in its effect. Pope is writing in all deep seriousness, criticizing as profoundly as he can the society which he, a little too gullibly no doubt, sees through the eyes of the Patriots. Satire has at last become the sacred weapon. In short, to use De Quincey's dichotomy with regard to this, which he considered the greatest of Pope's works, it more wholly belongs to the literature of power than the rest of the philosophical or moral poems; it has less to do with the literature of knowledge. It is, indeed, hardly didactic at all, unless any expression of a sense of values is to be classed as didacticism. We feel that the attacks are at least emotionally justified, and moreover, *mutatis mutandis*, applicable today, so broad have the implications become. Besides, the emotions are coherent, and, however unlike in origin, fused together in one complete effect.

If the *Essay on Man* is taken to be Pope's general survey of existence, the *Prologue* and the *Epilogues* his lasting self-justification, the *New Dunciad* might be regarded as his final statement with respect to the relation between the *Essay* and everything satirical that he wrote; for here he most clearly expresses his philosophy of wholeness, and his sense of the creative principle. When after the celebrated passage of the botanists and the entomologist, done with a delicious lightness that takes us back to *The Rape of the Lock*, the goddess perorates,

> O! would the Sons of Men once think their Eyes
> And Reason giv'n them but to study *Flies*!
> See Nature in some partial narrow shape,
> And let the Author of the Whole escape,

she is really stating the core of the intuitive argument. The charge against the educationists is the same:

> Plac'd at the door of Learning, youth to guide,
> We never suffer it to stand too wide . . .
> We ply the Memory, we load the brain,
> Bind rebel Wit, and double chain on chain,
> Confine the thought, to exercise the breath;
> And keep them in the pale of Words till death;

but the whole of the long passage, which replaced what should have been one of the Ethic Epistles, is a brilliant attack on pedantry at any time, and in some respects is as relevant today as when it was written. And when we look at the magnificently sombre conclusion, too familiar to need quotation, it is brought home to us that the main charge against all that he had been arraigning is that it is sterile,

> Light dies before thy uncreating word

the word uncreating being the key which reveals the meaning of the whole chaotic scene.

This is perhaps the most weightily serious, the most genuinely and deeply felt of all the poems of his maturity; and it is amazing how the yeast of wit and of humour leavens the whole poem to make it light, and how the delicacy of poetic fingering renders each part enchanting to the speech. To appreciate it to the full you must read it aloud. Admittedly just here and there we meet with, not *longueurs* but slight *lourdeurs*, particularly when, perhaps under pressure from Warburton, Pope seems anxious to re-establish his orthodoxy, notably in the passage about the 'gloomy clerk'. There is actually little likeness to a mock epic in this portion; but there is an inner unity, a progression from one class of dunce to another, each constituting a criticism of society rather than of persons. All the while, of course, there are the deliciously witty references, as when Dulness remarks:

> —'Thus revive the Wits!
> But murder first, and mince them all to bits;
> As erst Medea (cruel, so to save!)
> A new Edition of old Æson gave,
> Let standard-Authors, thus, like trophies born,
> Appear more glorious as more hack'd and torn,
> And you, my Critics! in the chequer'd shade,
> Admire new light thro' holes yourselves have made.'

The double allusion in the last couplet to Milton and Waller would immediately appeal to readers to whom both poems concerned were familiar, and who would appreciate the gibe at critics. Or again there is the famous pun, when Pope, after referring to Cambridge colleges, remarks:

> Where Bentley late tempestuous wont to sport
> In troubled waters, but now sleeps in Port.

Or again there is the sensuous passage, beginning with the most damning of all couplets about the rakish young nobleman on the grand tour:

> Intrepid then, o'er seas and lands he flew:
> Europe he saw, and Europe saw him too.

Then follows, unexpectedly, in a 'rise' accompanied by a 'lilt':

> There all thy gifts and graces we display,
> Thou, only thou, directing all our way!

> To where the Seine, obsequious as she runs,
> Pours at great Bourbon's feet her silken sons;
> Or Tyber, now no longer Roman, rolls,
> Vain of Italian Arts, Italian Souls;
> To happy Convents, bosom'd deep in vines,
> Where slumber Abbots, purple as their wines:
> To Isles of fragrance, lily-silver'd vales,
> Diffusing languour in the panting gales:
> To lands of singing, or of dancing slaves,
> Love-whisp'ring woods, and lute-resounding waves . . .

and again we experience the amazing effect, not of heterogeneous ideas yoked violently together, but heterogeneous emotions submitting to the same process, and pulling together. Pope, we realize, has succeeded in creating a comic poem without ever writing what we would call comic verse, or even burlesque. The assumptions, the reversals of values, are so complete that the verse itself can afford to have its proper value as verse. See, for example, the passage (ll. 549-62), breathtaking in its blasphemy, where money values take the place of religious ones; and when the goddess makes her crucial utterance:

> 'Go Children of my care!
> To Practice now from Theory repair.
> All my commands are easy, short, and full:
> My Sons! be proud, be selfish, and be dull.'

No extraneous verbal trickery ruffles the surface; however comic or burlesque the matter, the verse retains the evocative power of poetry, at the end, of course, of great poetry. The emotional colour of the lines

> As one by one, at dread Medea's strain,
> The sick'ning stars fade off th' ethereal plain

gives a grand intensity as well as a sense of space to the whole intellectual picture which seems almost to assume palpable reality. To Pope, who saw the whole scale of European values tottering, the confusion of realms which since Bacon had been carefully and progressively divided, seemed disastrous. It struck him with horror, as it struck Swift with disgust, that mystery should fly to mathematics, physic of metaphysic beg defence, or that philosophy, which used to lean on Heaven, should shrink to her second cause. We today are familiar with the state of affairs, but it does not follow that it is a healthy one. As at the end of *The Rape of the Lock* all satirical intention seems to have been fused into a deeper, far more commonly felt sense, which is here a sense of cosmic dread, of some inevitable catastrophe of impending ghoul-ridden death.

It may usually be only a momentary glimpse of some kind or another that Pope gives us from the time he ceased to wander in fancy's maze, but we fail to respond properly if we do not treat, first each poem, then the entire canon, as a whole. We have to obey his constant objurgation not to see a thing in parts:

> 'Tis not a lip or eye we beauty call,
> But the joint force and full result of all,

as he insisted in the *Essay on Criticism*. Up to *Eloisa to Abelard* we can claim for him what Mr. Wilson Knight has called a 'coherent romanticism', the poems are one; but from *The Dunciad* onward there is not at first reading 'the balance or reconciliation of discordant qualities' which for most of us constitutes poetry, for these remain unfused. As often as not it is the very discordance of the lovely and the sordid, of the positive and the sterile, which produces 'the sense of novelty and freshness'. And though there may be generated in us a state of 'more than usual order', the possession by 'a more than usual state of emotion' is problematical, if by emotion, is meant unrelated excitement. For with Pope we do not as a rule touch the fringes of what seems to ordinary mortals to be the inapprehensible; nor in his expression of factual truth—the truth of experience—does he give the illusion of opening the door on another, a more comprehensive reality. Here he seems to fall short of the greatest popular poets, or rather, he belongs to a different family. If he rarely carries the reader to the heights of ecstasy, and seldom touches the deeps of mysticism, if he is not, in short, a poet of illumination—a pale-eyed prophet dreaming —in his own field he provides an intensity of awareness of a kind no other poet offers. This may be because, though speaking with the voice of his age, he is still writing in the tradition of 'wit'. At all events we get (to return to Coleridge) 'judgment ever awake and steady self-possession' to a degree it would be difficult to match, the exquisite accuracy, of touch, of fitting the word to the emotion, and the emotion to the object, causing in us that detachment from immediacy which it is one of the characteristics of great poetry to give. It is, perhaps, only in snatches that we can at first wholly rejoice in the later poetry, namely that for which he is most to be valued; but that amount of joy at least is a permanent possession, and of no mean value, for it steadily sings the theme of wholeness and the creative principle.

Pope was, we may think, the last of our poets to belong to the old European Renaissance tradition, with its belief that Nature was perfect and that Reason might be supreme; the tradition of 'optimism' derived from Plato, and familiar in Pope's day through Leibnitz and Shaftesbury is one which lacks the sense of original sin, and holds that morality may be based on 'common' sense. Pope perhaps was himself not quite fully European, though his affinities are with Boileau as well as with Dryden, who was magnificently so; but after him, beginning even with Dyer and Thomson, we enter the Anglo-Provincial tradition, only now, possibly, becoming reintegrated with the thought and literature of Europe, though this may be a false dawn as it was with Byron and again with Matthew Arnold.

CONCLUSION

NEVERTHELESS, much of the verse of the age, though negligible if judged *sub specie aeternitatis*, is animated by a gaiety which is sometimes infectious. It was written by men with alert and amused minds, and healthily active senses, who made the mental and social life of their time spin along more briskly, and still provide a slight stirring for ours. Concurrently, however, there lies before us a placid ocean of dullness. It would be tedious to mention the dozens of poetasters of either sex, who, like draggled bees too tired to forage among the flowers, buzzed about the honey-pot of poetry to ooze out in turn an insipid gummy liquid. Their works are remarkably alike, and the names on the title-pages might be exchanged without harm being done to any memory. In each volume there are probably a wilting pindaric, a social love-song, a toothless satire, exercises in blanks, in quatrains and in couplets. There is no need to mock at this work; its counterpart adorns the journals of today; it is possibly an essential marsh to nourish the stream, and may be taken for granted.

Yet there were signs of something stirring; the lesser poets, as Professor Renwick has remarked, 'touch most things that make up what Wordsworth and Coleridge would call "the goings-on of life"'. The rural theme was turning from the Georgic to the hunting poem, such as Somerville's *The Chase* (1735), a lively exercise in Thomsonian Miltonics, full enough of observation and lasting vigour to keep it popular until well into the nineteenth century, Mr. Jorrocks culling from it his favourite quotation on hunting as 'the sport of kings, The image of war', the sagacious City merchant adding, 'and with only twenty-five per cent. of its danger'. Fielding, who contributed to this theme his still sung 'The dusky night rides down the sky', also, with Richard Leveridge, explored the poetic possibilities of the roast beef of old England, a curious variety of the patriotic theme. These latter things are of little importance, for though they still appear in anthologies, they led to no development.

But there were variations of more importance, since they opened new routes. For together with the threads of fairly clearly defined subject-matter implying fairly definable sentiments, such as have been noted, there were also threads composed of less neatly docketed feelings, bordering on sentimentality, as we might think. The age is seeking expression for a sensibility well understood in the moral ambit of the newly dominant middle class—puritanism and sugar, perhaps—and finding it either in artless ditties about domestic happiness, or in poems (or passages in poems), about the lower classes. In the latter there is often, as Professor James Sutherland shows, a certain amount of amused patronage; but that was not the only element. And patronage, so long as it is amused, carries with it that touch of self-critical irony which admits that there is another way of looking at these people; it assumes a sort of equality. From the formal point of view it would seem as though the pastoral having died, at least in its eclogue form, something had to be devised to take its place in so far as 'simpleness' went. What was invented was the ballad, the ballad-song, or the pastoral ballad, which was a taking over by 'literature' of the popular or street-song of the broadside and ballad variety. Though not so complex as the pastoral—there is no question here of courtiers pretending to be peasants—it was nevertheless tremendously sophisticated. The old ballad was already a matter for connoisseurs, for collectors such as the Pepys's, the Dorsets, and the Harleys of this world, though Addison's patronage of 'Chevy Chase' in *Spectators* 70 and 74, as though he would wheedle folk into liking it through comparisons with Virgil, may have brought it into more general favour. Prior's alarming elaboration of 'The Nut-Brown Maid' must have had the opposite effect, however, and we may wonder how far Addison's plea for the 'despicable simplicity' of the verse of 'The Babes in the Wood' (*Spectator* 85) attracted the reader. At all events it was the ballad-song rather than the ballad that became popular in the first instance, with such things as John Byrom's 'pastoral' 'My time, O ye Muses, was happily spent', praised by Addison in the *Spectator*, where it appeared (No. 603, 6 October 1714), as 'so original' that he did not much doubt that it would divert his readers. The originality may have lain in the fact that the Phoebe of the poem was Bentley's daughter, for it cannot have been in the anapaestic metre which is after all that of Dryden's 'The Lady's Song'; for us at least its artificiality is still that of the eclogue. Soon, however, we get Rowe's 'Colin's Complaint', published as a broadside in about 1715, and, in pleasant enough octosyllabic anapaests, introduces the death-from-a-broken-heart theme which was largely characteristic of this development; and if Gay parodied the nascent form in the delicious ' 'Twas when the Seas were roaring' of *The What D' Ye Call It* (1715), his own 'Sweet William's Farewell to Black-Eyed Susan' of 1720 bears just that relation to the new ballad-song which his *Shepherd's Week* did to the eclogue, that is, gave it a reality which pierced through the spoof. In the *Musical Miscellany* of 1729, we get both Tickell's 'Colin and Lucy' (once more forsaken love and the grave, published earlier) and Carey's 'Sally', this time, domestic happiness. These are in iambics, but Shenstone, whose 'pastoral Ballad' was written in 1743, by bringing un-disguisedly back into this form the convention of the eclogue, ruined the idea, just as by over-jigging it he ruined the anapaests Byrom had quite tactfully and charmingly used. The form died out, or, rather, became the drawing-room ballad familiar to the Victorians at home and concert hall. It did, however, in its day produce what Lord Mahon referred to as 'the noblest song perhaps ever called forth by any British victory, except Mr. Campbell's "Battle of the Baltic" ', to wit Glover's 'Hosier's Ghost', which long proved popular, though the anti-Walpole propaganda motive of the ballad must soon have grown stale. Its verse seems to try to catch the *naïveté* of a broadside ballad written to the address of 'our gallant tars'. Published in 1740, this by no means inept sample may close our concern with the form.

Less competent than the above—most of them are to be found in current anthologies—but ultimately of more importance, is the ballad written in the old manner of narrative quatrains, since the revival of the form has endured. In 1723 Ambrose Philips published a collection of ballads, and it may have been these which spurred Mallet to his still well-known 'William and Margaret', for it was written in that year, issued as an anony-mous black-letter broadside, appearing eventually in Hill's *Plain Dealer* of July 1724. To us it may seem just an exercise in the sham ballad, falsely simple and simply sentimental, neat enough to induce Percy to include it in his *Reliques*. If, as Saintsbury suggested, it was a good shoehorn to draw on the romantic movement, it reflects no credit on the movement. Still more repellent is his 'Edwin and Emma', which is, however, a rather touching story as told in a letter from 'a curate at Bowes' printed with the ballad in Mallet's *Works*. A poem of real merit, however, is William Hamilton of Bangour's 'The Braes of Yarrow', avowedly 'in imitation of the ancient Scottish manner'. Published in Allan Ramsay's *The Tea-Table Miscellany* of 1724, it has an authentic ring of melancholy and terror, getting its effect from the rhythm and the vowel sounds, and the use of words to mean what they do mean without any affectation of 'simplicity' or any attempt to heighten the tragedy by wormy graves, so that the spectre comes as the proper emanation of the girl's agonized sorrow. It is a heart-rending lament:

> Long maun she weep, long maun she, maun she weep,
> Long maun she weep with dule and sorrow,
> And long maun I nae mair weil be seen
> Puing the birks on the Braes of Yarrow.

It reads as though it came from a still living, not a revived, tradition. Indeed the whole of that Miscellany is flavoured with both the sense of tradition, kept active perhaps by Ramsay's *The Ever-Green* collection of 1724, and of live poetic quality, largely absent from minor English work; the Scottish Muse could still sing, and provide encouragement for Fergusson and for Burns.

Much of the English ballad stuff seems to us monstrous and absurd. If in 1724 Mallet's spectre can tell the faithless lover of the deserted maid

> The hungry *worm* my *sister* is;
> The *winding-sheet* I wear:
> And cold and weary lasts our *night*,
> Till that *last morn* appear . . .

it was, we feel, only to be expected that some day someone would sing:

> The worms they crept in, and the worms they crept out,
> And sported his eyes and his temples about,

as 'Monk' Lewis did in 1795, thus exploding the convention as 'poetry'; in fact much of this balladry, especially with Mallet who was addicted that way, smells of the graveyard poetry which had its own contribution to make. Here, evidently, was a clumsy attempt to express some kind of sensibility not otherwise catered for. The ballad proper itself never quite died out;

we have it with us today, though it is a conscious 'literary' form, and as sophisticated as it was in the early eighteenth century, if more vigorous. What, it would appear, this sentimental ballad was trying to express found its vehicle in *Clarissa* on the one hand, and on the other in the Gothic horror novel, as also in Strawberry Hill, a hankering (at first shy and to be treated as a joke) after the medieval period, the taste for which the Enlightenment had failed to eradicate, a hankering which was to bear full fruit in the next phase, with Gray, Percy, and 'Ossian' Macpherson.

Those were 'movements' within the period; but the age had exhausted its characteristic means of expression. It had not been inventive in poetic form, except for the ballad-opera, but it had reinvigorated some of the old forms by both pungency and ease of expression. Its achievement was to have absorbed, and put within common reach, the revolution in thought that had begun in the seventeenth century. It had expressed an attitude of man to his surroundings very different from that of the earlier age. Not only had it grappled successfully with the moral problems engendered by the new scientific outlook, it had begun to express a different personal sensibility. A new sense of the functions of poetry was heralded by Johnson's *London* (1738), the first of the flood of contemplative poems which was to make its way from Young's *Night Thoughts* (1742–5), through Dyer's *Ruins of Rome* (1740) and *The Fleece* (1757), Akenside's *Pleasures of the Imagination* (1744 and 1757), Gray's *Elegy* (1751), Cowper's *The Task* (1785), and achieve its culmination in Wordsworth's two long poems. The century passed from considering the cosmos, the universality of things, to discursions upon society—Crabbe is the final exponent in this field; and, further narrowing its ostensible subject-matter but not its scope, to the egocentric poetry of the Romantics. At the same time its fading sense of being was revivified from Collins through Smart to Keats.

It was in prose that it had been most inventive of form; it created the journalistic essay, the leading article, the cultured magazine, and, above all, the novel as a serious form of reading. Its admirable prose, at once colloquial and figurative, direct, yet securely built on rhetorical lines, was soon to give way to the more grandiose voices of Johnson, Gibbon, and Burke. In three important fields it had given birth to writers whose thought is still our own; in poetry to Pope, in prose to Swift, in philosophy to Berkeley. If it produced no major figure in criticism, the critics of the time, Shaftesbury and Dennis especially, opened doors through which later critics unceremoniously passed. Only in the drama was it sterile, in this realm doing nothing to express the thought of the age, and imperfectly absorbing its sentiment. It can, however, be said that the age gave being to certain enduring attitudes of mankind; and if later generations were to give utterance to others, no less eternal, these are not necessarily more important.

CHRONOLOGICAL TABLE
1700–1740

Date	Public Events	Literary History	Verse
1700	Last Statute against Papists. Attacks on Somers and Burnet. Irish Forfeitures Dispute. Act of Resumption. Death of Duke of Gloucester. Partition Treaty. Death of King of Spain. Bombardment of Copenhagen.	Dryden d. James Thomson b. Dyer b. ? Fénelon *Dialogue des Morts*.	Dryden, *Fables*. *Secular Masque*. Blackmore, *Satire against Wit*. Pomfret, *The Choice*. *Reason*. Prior, *Carmen Seculare*. Tate, *Panacea: a Poem on Tea*.
1701	General Election — Tory Triumph. Somers impeached. Kentish petition. Society for the Propagation of the Gospel. French invade Low Countries. James II d. Pretender recognized by Louis XIV. Act of Settlement. Bounties first given on raw material from Colonies. General Election — Whig Recovery. Truck Act.	Sedley d.	Dryden, *Collected Poems*. Addison, *Letter to Halifax* (written). Defoe, *True-born Englishman*. Gildon, *New Miscellany of Poems* (mainly by poets of the previous age, but including Lady Winchilsea's *The Spleen*). John Philips, *The Splendid Shilling*.
1702	William III d. Anne accedes. Tory government and House of Commons. Godolphin–Marlborough influence. Harley Speaker. War declared on France—Grand Alliance. War of Spanish Succession. Provisional Union of E. India Companies (confirmed 1708). Union with Scotland set in train.	John Pomfret d. Philip Doddridge b.	Pomfret, *Collected Poems*. *Poems on Affairs of State* (1702-1707) [one of the principal editions].
1703	First Occasional Conformity Bill defeated in Lords. Savoy joins the Allies. Campaign in Flanders. General Election in Scotland. Great Storm (Nov. 27th).	Pepys d. St. Evremond d. Henry Brooke b. (?) Robert Dodsley b. John Wesley b. Gilbert West b. Defoe imprisoned, pilloried and released.	Addison, *Letter to Halifax* (printed). Defoe, *Hymn to the Pillory*.
1704	Q. Anne's Bounty. Nottingham faction resigns. Harley Sec. of State. St. John Sec. at War. Battle of Blenheim. Capture of Gibraltar. Scottish Act of Security. Press Gang authorized by Statute.	Thomas Brown d. Roger L'Estrange d. Locke d.	Defoe, *Hymn to Victory*. Wycherley, *Miscellany Poems*. *Poetical Miscellanies* v (Dryden's, publ. Tonson).

Prose

Halifax (Marquess of, d. 1695), *Works.*
Harrington (d. 1677), *Collected Works.* Life
by Toland. Temple (d. 1699), *Letters,* ed.
Swift, vols. i, ii. Defoe, *Enquiry into Occasional
Conformity.* Motteux, trs. *Don Quixote,* vol. i.
Ned Ward, *London Spy* (12 parts).

Drama (date of acting)

Burnaby, *Reform'd Wife.* Centlivre, *Perjur'd
Husband.* Cibber, *Richard III. Love Makes a
Man.* Congreve, *Way of the World.* Dennis,
Iphigenia. Farquhar, *Inconstant Couple.* C. John-
son, *The Gentleman-Cully.* Rowe, *Ambitious
Stepmother.* Southerne, *Fate of Capua.* Van-
brugh, *Pilgrim.*

Temple, *Miscellanea,* iii, ed. Swift (i in 1680,
ii in 1692). Whichcote (d. 1683), *Several Discourses.* C. Davenant, *Essay on the Balance
of Power.* Defoe, *Original Power. Legion's
Memorial. Kentish Petition.* Dennis, *Advancement of Modern Poetry.* Gildon, *Examen Miscel-
laneum.* Norris, *Ideal and Intelligible World,* i
(part ii, 1704). Steele, *Christian Hero.* Swift,
Contests in Athens and Rome.

Dryden, *Collected Plays.* Burnaby, *Ladies'
Visiting Day.* Congreve, *Judgment of Paris.*
D'Urfey, *The Bath.* Farquhar, *Sir Harry Wild-
air.* Gildon, *Love's Victim.* Granville, Lord
Lansdowne, *Jew of Venice.* Motteux, *Acis and
Galatea.* Rowe, *Tamerlane.* Steele, *Funeral.*
Settle, *Virgin Prophetess.*

Clarendon (d. 1674), *History of Great Rebellion*
(concl. 1704). Bysshe, *Art of English Poetry.*
T. Brown, *Letters from the Dead.* Defoe,
Shortest Way with Dissenters. Dennis, *Large
Account of the Taste in Poetry.* Echard, *General
Ecclesiastical History.* Gildon, *Comparison be-
tween the Two Stages.* King, *De Origine Mali.*
Mather, Cotton, *Magnalia Christi Americana.*
Penn, *Primitive Christianity Revived.* Shaftes-
bury, *Paradoxes of State. Daily Courant* begins
(to 1735). *Observator* begins (to 1712).

Burnaby, *Modish Husband.* Centlivre, *Stolen
Heiress.* Cibber, *She Wou'd and She Wou'd Not.
Schoolboy.* Farquhar, *Inconstant. Twin Rivals.*
Vanbrugh, *False Friend.*

Temple, *Letters,* iii, ed. Swift. Hearne, *Re-
liquiæ Bodleianæ.* Boyer, *History of the Reign of
Queen Anne* (concl. 1720). Defoe, *Peace without Union.* Hickes, *Thesaurus.* Whichcote (d.
1683), *Moral and Religious Aphorisms.* White
Kennett, *Complete History of England.* Ned
Ward, *London Spy* (Collected: 18 monthly
parts, from Nov. 1698).

Burnaby, *Love Betrayed.* Centlivre, *Love's Contrivance.* Gildon, *The Patriot.* Rowe, *Fair Penitent.* Steele, *Lying Lover.* Vanbrugh, *Country
House.*

T. Brown, *Dialogues.* Burnet, *Tracts and Dis-
courses.* Dennis, *Grounds of Criticism in Poetry.*
Fletcher, *Right Regulation of Governments.*
Newton, *Optics* (1st Engl. trs.). Psalmanazar,
Description of Formosa. Rymer and Sander-
son, *Foedera* (concl. 1735). Swift, *Tale of a
Tub. Battle of the Books.* Defoe's *Review* begins
(to 1712).

Cibber, *Careless Husband.* Congreve, Van-
brugh, and Walsh, *Squire Trelooby.* Dennis,
Liberty Asserted. Farquhar, *Stage Coach.* Rowe,
The Biter. Trapp, *Abra-Mule.*

Date	Public Events	Literary History	Verse
1705	Whig Success in Elections. 'Whig Junto.' Marlborough pierces lines of Brabant. Scottish Act for a Treaty with England. 'The Church in Danger.'	Stephen Duck b. David Hartley b. David Mallet b. (?) Abraham Tucker b. Vanbrugh opens Haymarket Opera House. Addison made Commissioner of Appeals.	Addison, *Campaign*. Blackmore, *Eliza*. Coppinger, *Session of the Poets*. Mandeville, *The Grumbling Hive*. John Philips, *Blenheim* and corrected *Splendid Shilling*. Ward, *Hudibras Redivivus*.
1706	Union with Scotland—terms defined. (Act of Succession.) Battle of Ramillies. Sunderland Sec. of State.	Evelyn d. Benjamin Franklin b. Steele made Gazetteer.	John Philips, *Cerealia*. Watts, *Horæ Lyricæ*. Watson, *Choice Collection of Scottish Poems*.
1707	Union with Scotland ratified. Attack on Toulon. Failure in Spain. 1st Union Parliament meets — Whig domination. Walpole on Admiralty Board.	Farquhar d. Fielding b. Charles Wesley b. Buffon, b. Lesage, *Diable Boiteux*.	Sedley, *Poetical Works and Speeches*. John Philips, *Ode to Bolingbroke*. Prior, *Poems on Several Occasions* (pirated). Tickell, *Oxford*. Watts, *Hymns*.
1708	Battle of Oudenarde. Harley and St. John resign. Campaign in Catalonia. Somers returns to office. Naturalization Act. Addison Keeper of Records, Dublin.		Wm. King, *Art o, ‿ okery*. John Philips, *Cyder*. Swift, *Elegy upon Partridge*.
1709	Peace Negotiations. Battle of Malplaquet. Charles XII defeated at Pultawa. Sacheverell Sermon.	John Philips d. John Armstrong b. Samuel Johnson b. George Lyttelton b. First Copyright Act, with penalties for infringement (14 years, renewable for another 14 if author is alive). Steele dismissed *Gazette*. Lesage, *Turcaret*.	King, *Art of Love*. Prior, *Poems on Several Occasions*. Swift, *Baucis and Philemon*. *Poetical Miscellanies*, vi (Dryden's, ed. Tonson. Contains the *Pastorals* of Pope and A. Philips.)

Prose

Addison, *Remarks on Italy*. Clarke, *Being and Attributes of God*. Dunton, *Life and Errors*. Toland, *Socinianism Truly Stated*. Defoe, *Consolidator*.

Drama (*date of acting*)

Centlivre, *The Gamester. Love at a Venture. The Bassett Table*. Clayton, *Arsinoë*. H. Norris, *Royal Merchant*. Rowe, *Ulysses*. Steele, *Tender Husband*. Vanbrugh, *Confederacy*.

Locke, *Conduct of Understanding. Miracles. Fourth Letter on Toleration*. Defoe, *Apparition of Mrs Veal*. Dennis, *Operas after the Italian Manner*. Hughes, *History of England*. Kennett, *Complete History of England* (completed 1719).

Addison, *Rosamond*. Centlivre, *Platonick Lady*. D'Urfey, *Wonders in the Sun*. Farquhar, *Recruiting Officer*. Granville, *The British Enchanters*. Manley, *Almyna*.

T. Brown, *Works* (complete ed. 1760). Defoe, *Modest Vindication of the Present Ministry*. Echard, *History of England*, i. Newton, *Arithmetica Universalis. The Muses' Mercury* (1707–8).

Cibber, *Comical Lovers. Double Gallant. Lady's Last Stake*. Dennis, *Orpheus and Eurydice*. Farquhar, *Beaux' Stratagem*. Granville, *Jew of Venice*. Rowe, *Royal Convert*. Settle, *Siege of Troy*.

Locke, *Letters*. Bingham, *Origines Ecclesiasticæ*. Collier, *Ecclesiastical History of Great Britain*, (ii, 1714). Downes, *Roscius Anglicanus*. Urquhart and Motteux, *Rabelais* (trs.). Hughes, *Fontenelle's Dialogues of the Dead* (trs.). Oldmixon, *British Empire in America*. Shaftesbury, *Letter Concerning Enthusiasm*. Swift, *Predictions or 1708. Account of Partridge's Death. Sentiments of a Church of England Man. Argument against Abolishing Christianity*.

Theobald, *Persian Princess*.

Temple, *Memoirs*, iii (ed. Swift). Whitelocke (d. 1675), *Memorials of English Affairs*. Berkeley, *New Theory of Vision*. Defoe, *History of the Union of Great Britain*. Mrs. Manley, *The New Atalantis*, i, ii. Strype, *Annals of the Reformation* (concl. 1731). Shaftesbury, *Moralists*. Swift, *Project for Advancement of Religion*. Steele, *Tatler* begins 12 April.

Rowe's 'Shakespeare' (concl. 1710). Centlivre, *Busybody*. Dennis, *Appius and Virginia*.

Date	Public Events	Literary History	Verse
1710	Trial of Sacheverell. Peace Conference at Gertruydenberg. Fall of the Whigs. Triumph of Harley and St. John. Tory Commons. Stanhope defeated at Brihuega.	Thomas Reid b. First edition of Bayle's *Dictionary* in English.	Congreve, *Collected Works.* Swift, *City Shower.*
1711	Death of the Emperor. Expedition against Quebec. Whig coalition with Nottingham under Nottingham. Occasional Conformity Act. Dismissal of D. of Marlborough. Creation of 12 Peers.	Bp. Ken d. John Norris d. David Hume b. Prior sent to France. Boileau d. King made Gazeteer.	Waller (d. 1687), *Collected Works* (also 1729). Blackmore, *Nature of Man.* Pope, *Essay on Criticism.* Swift, *Miscellanies in Prose and Verse.*
1712	Barrier Treaty. Negotiations at Utrecht.	Edward Moore b. Richard Glover b. Stamp Act: Papers. Rousseau b. Fénelon, *Existence de Dieu.* Fontenelle, *Eloge des Académiciens.*	Granville, *Poems upon Several Occasions.* Blackmore, *Creation.* Diaper, *Nereides.* Pope, *Rape of the Lock. To a Young Lady. Messiah.* Tickell, *To the Lord Privy Seal.*
1713	Treaty of Utrecht.	Thomas Rymer d. Bishop Sprat d. 3rd Earl of Shaftesbury d. Sterne b. Scriblerus Club formed. Swift Dean of St. Patrick's. Hamilton, *Mémoires de Grammont.*	Carey, *Poems on Severa Occasions.* Diaper, *Dryades.* Gay, *Rural Sports.* Parnell, *Essay on Different Styles of Poetry.* Pope, *Windsor Forest. Ode for Music.* Lady Winchilsea, *Miscellany Poems.*
1714	Schism Act. Death of Queen Anne. Accession of George I. The Whigs in office.	Shenstone b. Whitefield b. James Hervey b. Leibnitz, *Monadologie.*	Gay, *Shepherd's Week. The Fan.* Pope, *Wife of Bath. Rape of the Lock* (final form). Young, *Force of Religion.*

Prose	*Drama (date of acting)*
Hearne's edition of Leland's *Itinerary* (concl. 1712). Stillingfleet, *Works* (ed. Bentley). Berkeley, *Principles of Human Knowledge*. Burnet, *Exposition of Church Catechism*. Gildon, *Life of Betterton. Remarks on Shakespeare*. Mrs. Manley, *Memoirs of Europe* (later iii and iv of *New Atalantis*). King, *Historical Account of Heathen Gods and Heroes*. Swift, *Meditations upon a Broomstick*. Strype, *Life of Grindall*. Addison, *Whig Examiner*, Sept., Oct. *The Examiner* (Swift, St. John, Prior, &c.).	Congreve, *Collected Works*. Centlivre, *The Man's Bewitched*. Hill, *Elfrid* (see also 1732, *Elfrid* rewritten as *Athelwold*). *Walking Statue*. Shadwell, *Fair Quaker of Deal*.
Drummond of Hawthornden (d. 1649), *Collected Works*. William Alexander (d. 1640), *Anacrisis*. Atterbury, *Representation of the State of Religion*. Dennis, *On the Genius and Writings of Shakespeare. Essay upon Public Spirit*. Shaftesbury, *Characteristics*. Swift, *Conduct of the Allies*. Strype, *Life of Parker*. Whiston, *Primitive Christianity Revived* (concl. 1712). Boyer, *Political State of Great Britain* (concl. 1729). Steele, *Tatler* ends January. Addison, *Spectator* (1 March to 6 December 1712).	Centlivre, *Marplot*. Cibber, *Hob; or, the Country Wake*.
Browne (d. 1682), *Posthumous Works*. Arbuthnot, *Art of Political Lying. History of John Bull*. Motteux, *Don Quixote* (tr.). Swift, *Advice to Members of October Club. Barrier Treaty. Proposal for Correcting the English Tongue*.	Gay, *Mohocks*. Hughes, *Calypso and Telemachus*. C. Johnson, *Wife's Relief*. A. Philips, *Distressed Mother*.
Bentley, *Remarks upon a Discourse of Freethinking*. Collins, *Discourse of Free-thinking*. Dennis, *Remarks upon Cato*. Berkeley, *Three Dialogues of Hylas and Philonous*. Collins, *Discourse*. Defoe, *Reasons against Accession of House of Hanover. What if the Pretender should come?* Swift, *Importance of the Guardian considered*. Steele, *Guardian* (begins 12 March).	Addison, *Cato*. Cibber, *Ximena*. Gay, *Wife of Bath*. Shadwell, *Humours of the Army*.
Ellwood (d. 1713), *History of his own Life*. Locke (d. 1704), *Works*. Steele, *The Ladies' Library. The Crisis*. Mandeville, *Fable of the Bees. Guardian* ends (February). *The Englishman*. Swift, *Public Spirit of the Whigs*.	Centlivre, *The Wonder! A Woman keeps a Secret*. Rowe, *Jane Shore*. Theobald, *Electra*.

Date	Public Events	Literary History	Verse
1715	Jacobite rebellion. Louis XIV d.	Gilbert Burnet d. Prior sent to the Tower. Rowe poet laureate. Lesage, *Gil Blas* (concl. 1735).	Cotton (d. 1687), *Collected Works*. Garth, *Claremont*. Pope, *Temple of Fame*. *Homer's Iliad I*. Tickell, *Homer's Iliad I*. Watts, *Divine Songs for Children*.
1716	Treaty with Denmark against Sweden. Townshend loses seals. Rise of Prince of Wales' Party. Septennial Act.	South d. Wycherley d. Thomas Gray b. Leibnitz d.	Lady M. W. Montagu, *Town Eclogues*. Blackmore, *Poems on Various Subjects*. Gay, *Trivia*. Pope, *Epistle to Jervas* (in ed. of Du Fresnoy's *Art of Painting*). Hill, Gideon. Pope, Gay, &c., *Court Poems*.
1717	Triple Alliance between England, France, and Holland. Townshend dismissed. Walpole resigns. Impeachment of Oxford stopped. Alberoni in Spain. Convocation ceased till 1850.	David Garrick b. Horace Walpole b. Addison becomes Secretary of State. Prior released. The Bangorian Controversy 1717–20.	Congreve's ed. of *Dryden's Works*. Fenton, *Poems on Several Occasions*. Garth ed. *Ovid's Metamorphoses* (by Dryden, &c.). Parnell, *Homer's Battle of Frogs and Mice*. Pope, *Collected Works* (incl. *Unfortunate Lady* and *Eloisa to Abelard*). Purney, *Pastorals*. Roscommon, *Poetical Works*. Tickell, *Epistle from a Lady in England*.
1718	Quadruple Alliance (England, France, Holland, the Emperor). Byng defeats Spanish fleet at Cape Passaro. Death of Charles XII. France and England declare war on Spain.	Parnell d. Cumberland d. Penn d. Rowe d. Motteux d. Addison resigns. Eusden poet laureate. Society of Antiquaries refounded. Voltaire, *Œdipe*.	Prior, *Poems* (incl. *Alma* and *Solomon*). Ramsay, *Christ's Kirk on the Green*. Rowe, *Lucan* (tr.).
1719	Repeal of Schism Act. Hispano-Jacobite landing in Scotland. Defeat of Spain. Peace concluded. Alberoni banished. Stanhope at head of Foreign Affairs. Peerage Bill.	Addison d. Garth d. La Motte, *Fables*.	Ramsay, *Scots' Songs*. Tickell, *Elegy on Addison*. Young, *Letter to Tickell* (on Addison's death).

Prose	*Drama (date of acting)*
Defoe, *Appeal to Honour and Justice. Family Instructor,* i. Derham, *Astro-Theology.* Addison, *Freeholder* begins (December).	Bullock, *Woman's Revenge.* Carey, *Contrivances.* Cibber, *Venus and Adonis.* Gay, *The What d'ye call It.* Rowe, *Lady Jane Grey.* C. Johnson, *Country Lasses.*
Browne (d. 1682), *Christian Morals* (ed. Jeffrey). Blackmore, *Essays.* Pope, *Harsh and Barbarous Revenge . . . on Curll.* Oldmixon, *Critical History of England.* Shaftesbury, *Letters to a Student at the University.* Addison, *Freeholder* ends (June).	Addison, *The Drummer.* Hill, *Fatal Vision.*
Dennis, *Remarks upon Pope's Homer.* Hoadly, *Nature of Christ's Kingdom.* Ashmole, *Memoirs.* Law, *Letters* (i, ii) *to Bishop of Bangor* (Hoadly).	Cibber, *Non-Juror.* Gay, Pope, &c., *Three Hours after Marriage.* Manley, *Lucius.*
Defoe, *Family Instructor,* ii. Gildon, *Complete Art of Poetry.*	Centlivre, *Bold Stroke for a Wife.* Theobald, *Pan and Syrinx.*
Defoe, *Robinson Crusoe. Further Adventures.* Law, *Letter III to Bishop of Bangor.* D'Urfey, *Wit and Mirth or Pills to Purge Melancholy.* Jacob, *Poetical Register,* i. Addison, *Old Whig.* Steele, *Plebeian.*	Young, *Busiris.* Southerne, *Spartan Dame.*

Date	Public Events	Literary History	Verse
1720	Walpole Paymaster. Townshend Lord President. South Sea Bubble and Bill. War with Spain (to 1729).	John Hughes d. Lady Winchilsea d. Samuel Foote b. Richard Hurd b. Charlotte Lennox b. Mrs. Elizabeth Montagu b. Gilbert White b. Marivaux, *Arlequin*.	Gay, *Collected Poems*. Hill, *The Creation*. Pope, *Iliad*, vol. 6 (the last). With others *Hammond's Miscellany* (incl. Pope on *Lady M. W. Montagu*). Ramsay, *Poems*.
1721	Sunderland resigns. Walpole Lord Treasurer. Death of Stanhope. Proceedings against South Sea suspects.	Prior d. John Sheffield, Duke of Buckingham d. William Collins b. Akenside b. William Robertson b. Smollett b. Montesquieu, *Lettres Persanes*.	Pope, *To Mr. Addison* (in *Collected Works* of Addison). *To Robert, Earl of Oxford*.
1722	Sunderland d. Marlborough d. Walpole's reign begins. Young Pretender b. Atterbury Plot. Taxes on Roman Catholics. Compulsory oath of allegiance.	Toland d. Christopher Smart b. Joseph Warton b.	Parnell, *Poems*, ed. Pope. Diaper and Jones, *Halieuticks* of Oppian. Tickell, *To Sir Godfrey Kneller*. *Kensington Gardens*.
1723	Exile of Atterbury. Return of Bolingbroke.	Centlivre d. D'Urfey d. Blackstone b. Joshua Reynolds b. Adam Smith b. Voltaire, *Henriade*.	Mallet, *William and Margaret*. Prior, *Down Hall*.
1724	Carteret dismissed. Wood's Halfpence: Ireland. Malt Tax Disturbances in Scotland.	Elkanah Settle d. Charles Gildon d. Frances Brooke b. William Mason b.	Ramsay, *Ever Green. Tea Table Miscellany*, i (ii 1726, iii 1727).
1725	Death of Peter the Great. Treaty of Vienna (Empire and Spain). Treaty of Hanover (England, France, Prussia). Walpole and Townshend rivals. Jacobite intrigues in France.	William Kenrick b. (?).	T. Cooke, *Battle of the Poets*. Pope, *Odyssey*, i–iii (completed 1726) with Broome and Fenton. Somerville, *The Two Springs*. Young, *Universal Passion*, Parts i to iv (collected as *Love of Fame* 1728).

Prose

Drama (date of acting)

Defoe, *Duncan Campbell. Captain Singleton.* Jacob, *Poetical Register*, ii. Mandeville, *Free Thoughts on Religion.* Swift, *Proposal for the Universal Use of Irish Manufactures.* Strype's edition of Stow's *Survey.*

Hughes, *Siege of Damascus.*

Addison, *Collected Works*, ed. Tickell (incl. *Dialogue on Ancient Medals* and *Evidences of the Christian Religion*). Dennis, *Original Letters.* Gildon, *Laws of Poetry.* Swift, *Letter to a Young Gentleman lately entered into Holy Orders. Letter of Advice to a Young Poet.* Bailey's *Universal Etymological English Dictionary.*

Haywood, *Fair Captive.* Young, *Revenge.*

Works of Buckingham (d. 1721), ed. Pope. Croxall, *Fables of Æsop and others.* Defoe, *Plague Year. History of Peter the Great. Colonel Jack. Moll Flanders.*

A. Philips, *The Briton.* Steele, *Conscious Lovers.*

Burnet, *History of My Own Time*, i (completed 1735). Mandeville, *Fable of the Bees*, 2nd edit. (with *Essay on Charity* and *Search into Nature of Society*). Law, *Remarks on the Fable of the Bees.*

Centlivre, *The Artifice.* Fenton, *Mariamne.* Haywood, *A Wife to be Let.* A. Philips, *Humphrey, Duke of Gloucester.* Savage, *Sir Thomas Overbury.*

Boyle, *State Letters.* Anthony Collins, *Grounds of the Christian Religion.* Defoe, *Roxana. Tour through Great Britain*, i (concl. 1726). Eliza Haywood, *Memoirs of a Certain Island.* Charles Johnson, *General History of . . . the Pirates.* Oldmixon, *Critical History of England.* Swift, *Drapier Letters.*

Gay, *Captives.*

Mandeville, Sir John, *Travels* (first English version). Berkeley, *Proposal for Converting the Savage Americans.* Defoe, *New Voyage Round the World. Complete English Tradesman* (concl. 1727). *Jonathan Wild.* Echard, *History of the Revolution.* Hutcheson, *Original of our Ideas of Beauty and Virtue.* Tindal, trs. of Rapin, *History of England* (begun). Watts, *Logic.*

Pope, *Shakespeare* (2nd ed. 1728). Ramsay, *Gentle Shepherd.*

Date	Public Events	Literary History	Verse
1726	Fleury becomes French premier. Ripperda (Spain) dismissed.	Jeremy Collier d. Sir J. Vanbrugh d. W. Wotton d. Charles Burney b. Maurice Morgann b. Voltaire in England.	Dyer, *Grongar Hill* (as Ode in Miscellaneous Poems. Revised in Lewis's). Thomson, *Winter*. Swift, *Cadenus, and Vanessa*.
1727	Siege of Gibraltar. Preliminaries of peace with the Emperor signed at Paris. George I dies. George II accedes.	Isaac Newton d. Arthur Murphy b. John Wilkes b.	Dyer, *Grongar Hill* (final). Gay, *Fables*, i (ii 1738, complete 1750). Harte, *Poems on Several Occasions*. Pope, Swift, Arbuthnot, &c., *Miscellanies*, i and ii (iii 1728, contains *Bathos*; iv 1732, v 1735, Motte's Misc.). Somerville, *Poems, Translations and Tales*. Thomson, *Summer*.
1728	Preliminaries signed with Spain. Congress of Soissons.	T. Warton, Jr. b. Robert Bage b.	Blair, *Poem to Wm. Law*. Pope, *Dunciad* (i–iii). Ramsay, *Poems*. Savage, *Nature in Perfection. The Bastard*. Thomson, *Spring*. Young, *Ocean*.
1729	Treaty of Seville.	Steele d. Congreve d. Blackmore d. Clarke d. Burke b. Percy b. Clara Reeve b. Trans. of Perrault's *Contes*. Lessing b.	Waller, *Collected Works*, ed. Fenton. Carey, *Poems on Several Occasions* (3rd ed. enlarged. *Namby-Pamby* and *Sally in our Alley*). Pope, *Dunciad* (rev. ed. Book IV 1742, Final 1743). Savage, *Wanderer*. Thomson, *Britannia*.
1730	Townshend resigns. 'Methodist Society', Oxford.	Echard d. Eusden d. Cibber poet laureate. Goldsmith b. Voltaire, *Brutus* and Preface. Marivaux, *Le Jeu de l'Amour et du Hasard*.	Ramsay, *Fables*. Thomson, *The Seasons* (with *Autumn*).

Prose	*Drama (date of acting)*
Penn, *Works* (ed. Besse). Atterbury, *Sermons.* Butler, *Fifteen Sermons.* Bentley, *On Latin Metres.* Defoe, *History of the Devil.* Law, *Treatise upon Christian Perfection. Unlawfulness of Stage Entertainments* answered by Dennis, *The Stage Defended.* Swift, *Gulliver's Travels.* Theobald, *Shakespeare Restored. Craftsman* begins (Bolingbroke, Chesterfield, Pulteney, &c.).	Hill, *Fatal Extravagance.* Welsted, *Dissembled Wanton.*
Newton, *Principia* (1st English trs.). Defoe, *History and Reality of Apparitions.* Dorrington, *The Hermit, or the History and Adventures of Philip Quarll.* Lardner, *Credibility of the Gospel History* (last vol. 1757). Spence, *Essay on Pope's Odyssey.* Warburton, *Inquiry into Prodigies.* . . .	Theobald, *Double Falsehood.*
Defoe, *Captain Carleton.* Hutcheson, *Nature and Conduct of the Passions and Affections.* Law, *Serious Call.* Mrs. Rowe, *Friendship in Death.* Swift, *Short View of the State of Ireland.* Young, *Vindication of Providence.* Ephraim Chambers, *Cyclopædia. Intelligencer* (1728–9).	Cibber's *Provok'd Husband,* completion of Vanbrugh's *Journey to London.* Fielding, *Love in Several Masques.* Gay, *Beggar's Opera.*
Mandeville, *Fable of the Bees,* ii. Oldmixon, *History of England* (concl. 1739). Swift, *Modest Proposal.*	Cibber, *Damon and Phillida.* Coffey, *Beggar's Wedding* (Dublin). Hippisley, *Flora.* C. Johnson, *Village Opera.* S. Johnson, *Hurlothrumbo.*
Bacon, *Works* (1st Collected ed. Blackbourne). Bolingbroke, *Remarks upon History* (in *Craftsman*). Tindal, *Christianity as Old as the Creation.* Watts, *Catechisms. Grub-Street Journal* (1730–7).	Fielding, *Temple Beau. Author's Farce. Pleasures of the Town. Rape upon Rape. Coffee House Politician. Tom Thumb.* Thomson, *Sophonisba.*

Date	Public Events	Literary History	Verse
1731	Walpole supreme. English substituted for Latin in legal proceedings. Inquiry into prisons.	Defoe d. Cowper b. Erasmus Darwin b. C. Churchill b. Marivaux, *Marianne*.	Pope, *Epistle on Taste* (later *False Taste*. Moral Essay iv).
1732	'The Patriots' as opposition.	Gay d. Atterbury d. G. Colman, Sr. b. Falconer b. R. Cumberland b. B. Franklin, *Poor Richard's Almanac* (to 1757). Voltaire, *Zaïre*. Destouches, *Glorieux*.	Bentley's ed. of *Paradise Lost*. Dodsley, *Muse in Livery*. W. King, *The Toast*. Lyttelton, *Progress of Love*. Pope, *Use of Riches* (Moral Essay iii).
1733	Walpole's Excise Scheme. War for the Crown of Poland.	Mandeville d. Tindal d. Joseph Priestley b.	Pope, *Essay on Man. Epistle on the Characters of Men*, (Moral Essay i). *First Satire of 2nd Book Horace imitated. The Impertinent*. Swift, *On Poetry; a rapsody*.
1734	Motion for repeal of Septennial Act.	Roger North d. Dennis d. Voltaire, *Lettres Anglaises*. Montesquieu, *Grandeur et Décadence des Romains*.	Pope, *Second Satire of 2nd Book Horace*.
1735	Peace preliminaries. Polish war concluded.	Arbuthnot d. J. Beattie b. Prévost, *Manon Lescaut*. Marivaux, *Paysan Parvenu*	H. Brooke, *Universal Beauty*. Dodsley, *Beauty or the Art of Charming*. Pope, *Characters of Women* (Moral Essay ii). *Ep. to Arbuthnot. Satires of Donne. Collected Works*, ii. *Miscellanies*, v (see 1727). Savage, *Progress of a Divine*. Somerville, *The Chace*. Thomson, *Liberty*, i, ii, and iii.
1736	Dissenters attempt to repeal Test Act. Bill for relief of Quakers. Mortmain Act. Gin Act. Porteous Riots.	Budgell d. James Macpherson b. George Steevens b. Voltaire, *Enfant Prodigue*.	Armstrong, *Œconomy of Love I*. Browne, *A Pipe of Tobacco*. Duck, *Poems on Several Occasions*. Pope, *Bounce to Fop*. Thomson, *Liberty* (iv and v and complete). Swift, *Legion Club*.

Prose	*Drama (date of acting)*
Cudworth, (d. 1688), *Eternal and Immutable Morality.* Law, *The Case of Reason. Gentleman's Magazine* (to 1907). *Daily Advertiser.*	Fielding, *Tom Thumb* (enlarged 'Tragedy of Tragedies'). *The Letter Writers.* Lillo, *George Barnwell.* Mallett, *Eurydice.*
Berkeley, *Alciphron.* Mandeville, *Origin of Honour. Letter to Dion.* Neal, *History of the Puritans,* i and ii (iii and iv 1738). Watts, *Scripture History. London Magazine* (to 1785).	Fielding, *Covent Garden Tragedy. Modern Husband. Mock Doctor.* Hill, *Athelwold* ('Elfrid' 1710 rewritten).
Bolingbroke, *Dissertation upon Parties (Craftsman).* Swift, *Life and Genuine Character of Dr. Swift. The Bee* (Feb. 1733–June 1735).	Fielding, *Miser.* Gay, *Achilles.* C. Johnson, *Caelia.* Havard, *Scanderbeg.*
Atterbury, *Sermons.* Bacon, *Letters and Remains,* ed. Stephens. Reresby, *Memoirs.* C. Johnson, *Famous Highwaymen.* Sale's trs. of *The Koran. General Advertiser.*	Theobald's ed. of *Shakespeare.* Carey, *Chrononhotonthologos.* Fielding, *Don Quixote in England. Intriguing Chambermaid.* Miller, *Mother-in-Law.*
Berkeley, *Querist,* i (ii 1736, iii 1737). Johnson, *Voyage to Abyssinia* (trs. from Jerome Lobo). Lyttelton, *Letters from a Persian in England.* Pope, *Letters* (unacknowledged, ed. Curll). Swift, *Collected Works* (Faulkner 4 vols., 1738 6 vols., 1746 8vols). Wesley, *Journal* begins (to 1790). *Daily Gazetteer* (to 1748).	Carey, *Honest Yorkshire-man.* Dodsley, *Toy Shop.* Fielding, *An Old Man Taught Wisdom.* Lillo, *Christian Hero.* Miller, *Man of Taste.*
Newton, *Method of Fluxions.* Butler, *Analogy of Religion.* Carte, *Life of D. of Ormond.* Oldys, *Life of Raleigh.* Warburton, *Alliance between Church and State.*	Fielding, *Pasquin.* Hill, *Zara. Alzira* (both from Voltaire). Lillo, *Fatal Curiosity.*

Date	Public Events	Literary History	Verse
1737	Frederick Prince of Wales, heads opposition. Death of Queen Caroline.	Strype d. Green d. Gibbon b. Playhouse Act.	Glover, *Leonidas*. Green, *Spleen*. Hill, *Tears of the Muses*. Pope, Ep.VI, Book I. Ep. I of Book I. Eps. I and II of Book II imit. *Horace. Ode to Venus*. Shenstone, *Poems on Various Occasions*. Thomson, *Mem. of Lord Talbot*. J. and S. Wesley, *Psalms and Hymns*.
1738	Treaty of Vienna (Polish Succession). England isolated.	J. Wolcot (Peter Pindar) b. Voltaire, *Discours sur l'homme*. Piron, *Métromanie*.	Gay, *Fables*. Akenside, *A British Philippic*. Johnson, *London*. Pope, *Universal Prayer*. Seventeen thirty eight (*Epilogue to Satires*).
1739	War with Spain. Capture of Porto Bello.	Lillo d. Hugh Kelly b.	Boyse, *The Deity*. Glover, *London, or the Progress of Commerce*. Swift, *Verses on the Death of Dr. Swift*.
1740	Frederick II starts War of Pragmatic Sanction. France joins. England helps Maria Theresa.	Tickell d. Boswell b. Saint-Simon, *Mémoires*.	Prior, *Miscellaneous Works*, Dyer, *Ruins of Rome*. C. Pitt. *Æneid* (trs.). Somerville, *Hobbinol*.

Prose

Cruden, *Biblical Concordance*. Edwards, *Surprising Work of God*. Oldys, *British Librarian* (originally in parts January to June). Pope, *Letters* (authenticated). Warburton, *Divine Legation of Moses* (concl. 1741).

Drama (date of acting)

Carey, *Dragon of Wantley*. Dodsley, *King and Miller of Mansfield*. Fielding, *Historical Register 1736*. Havard, *King Charles I*.

Edwards, *Discourses*. Swift, *Genteel Conversation*. Watts, *World to Come*. Whitefield begins *Journals* (concl. 1741).

Carey, *Margery (The Dragoness)*. Thomson, *Agamemnon*.

Hume, *Treatise of Human Nature* (concl. 1740). Johnson, *Marmor Norfolciense*. *Compleat Vindication of Licensers of the Stage*. W. Smith, trs. of *Longinus on the Sublime*. Warburton, *Commentary on Pope's Essay on Man* (revised 1741). *Scots Magazine* started.

Brooke, *Gustavus Vasa ('prohibited)*. Carey, *Nancy*. Mallet, *Mustapha*. Thomson, *Edward and Leonora*.

Bacon *Works*, ed. Mallet. R. North, *Examen*. Cibber, *Apology*. Richardson, *Pamela*. Stukeley, *Stonehenge*. Whitefield, *Short Account, etc.* *Christian History*.

Garrick, *Lethe*. Lillo, *Elmerick*. Thomson and Mallett, *Alfred* (contains *Rule, Britannia*).

BIBLIOGRAPHY

THIS bibliography is selective, and makes no pretence to completeness. Its object is to enable a reader interested in any particular author to see, generally, the scope of that author's work; and to name the chief authorities and comments of interest.

CONTENTS:

ABBREVIATIONS:

Ang	*Anglia*
CBEL	*Cambridge Bibliography of English Literature*
CHEL	*Cambridge History of English Literature*
DNB	*Dictionary of National Biography*
E & S	*Essays and Studies by Members of the English Association*
EHR	*English Historical Review*
E in C	*Essays in Criticism*
EL	*Everyman's Library*
ELH	*English Literary History*
HLQ	*Huntington Library Quarterly*
JEGP	*Journal of English and Germanic Philology*
JHI	*Journal of the History of Ideas*
JMH	*Journal of Modern History*
MHRA	*Modern Humanities Research Association* (Annual Bibliography of English Language and Literature)

MLN	Modern Language Notes
MP	Modern Philology
MLQ	Modern Language Quarterly
MLR	Modern Language Review
N & Q	Notes and Queries
PBSA	Papers of the Bibliographical Society of America
PMLA	Publications of the Modern Language Association of America
PQ	Philological Quarterly
Quart. Rev.	Quarterly Review
RES	Review of English Studies
SP	Studies in Philology
WC	World's Classics

Other abbreviations used are:

Cibber	Theophilus Cibber and Robert Shiels: *The Lives of the Poets*
Jacob	Giles Jacob: *Poetical Register*
Kippis	Andrew Kippis: *Biographica Britannica*
Nichols	John Nichols: *Literary Anecdotes of the Eighteenth Century*

I. GENERAL BIBLIOGRAPHIES AND WORKS OF REFERENCE

Two works of the first importance are: *DNB*; and *CBEL* ed. F. W. Bateson, 4 vols., 1940: *Supplement* ed. G. Watson, 1957. Vol. iii of *The Term Catalogues, 1668–1709*, ed. E. Arber, 1906, contains relevant material: as does *A Transcript of the Registers of the Stationers, 1640–1708*, ed. G. E. B. Eyre, 3 vols., 1913–14. The two most useful catalogues of printed texts are the *General Catalogue of Printed Books* published by the British Museum, 1931 ff. (a new edition is in hand); and *A Catalog of Books represented by Library of Congress Printed Cards*, 167 vols., Ann Arbor, 1942–6; *Supplement*, 42 vols., 1948 (still in progress). *The Rothschild Library. A Catalogue of the Collection of Eighteenth-Century Printed Books and Manuscripts formed by Lord Rothschild*, 2 vols., 1954, is a valuable record of a private collection. *The Britwell Handlist*, 2 vols., 1933, should also be consulted. Other similar works include: R. Bowes, *A Catalogue of Books printed at or relating to the University, Town and County of Cambridge*, 2 parts, 1894; C. E. Sayle, *A Catalogue of the Bradshaw Collection of Irish Books*, 3 vols., 1916; and for political and social writing, *The Kress Library of Business and Economics Catalogue*, 2 vols., Boston, 1940–56. The catalogues of the Ashley, Hoe, and Wrenn Libraries are also of some use. R. Watt's *Bibliotheca Britannica*, 4 vols., 1824, is valuable for its subject index.

Bibliographical help may be obtained from the following: W. T. Lowndes, *The Bibliographer's Manual of English Literature*, rev. ed. H. G. Bohn, 6 vols., 1869; C. S. Northup, *A Register of Bibliographies of the English Language and Literature*, New Haven, 1925; J. W. Spargo, *A Bibliographical Manual*, 2nd ed., Chicago, 1941; and T. P. Cross, *Bibliographical Guide to English Studies*, 10th ed., Chicago, 1951. Three books in this category dealing more specifically with our period are: J. E. Tobin, *Eighteenth Century Literature and its Cultural Background*, N.Y., 1939; F. Cordasco, *A Register of 18th Century Bibliographies and References*, Chicago, 1950; and H. V. D. Dyson and J. E. Butt, *Augustans and Romantics*, 2nd ed., 1950.

Indispensable annual bibliographies are: the current bibliography 'English Literature, 1660–1800', published annually in *PQ* since 1926, which covers articles as well as books; *The Year's Work in English Studies*, published by the English Association to cover the years 1919–20 and onwards; the *Bibliography of English Language and Literature*, published by the Modern Humanities Research Association for the period beginning 1920; and the bibliography included in *PMLA* since 1922.

Some miscellaneous works of reference are: Halkett and Laing, *Dictionary of Anonymous and Pseudonymous English Literature*, rev. ed., 1926 ff.; P. Harvey, *The Oxford Companion to English Literature*, 3rd ed., 1946, and the abridgement, *The Concise Oxford Dictionary of English Literature*, 1939; and J. C. Ghosh and E. G. Withycombe, *Annals of English Literature, 1475–1925*, 1935.

In addition to *DNB*, the following are useful sources of biographical detail: Giles Jacob, *The Poetical Register*, 2 vols., 1719, 1720; Andrew Kippis, *Biographia Britannica*, 6 vols. (in 7 parts), 1747–66, and 6 vols., corrected and enlarged, 1778–93. T. Cibber and R. Shiels, *The Lives of the Poets of Great Britain and Ireland, to the Time of Dean Swift*, 5 vols., 1753; J. Nichols, *Literary Anecdotes of the Eighteenth Century*, 9 vols., 1812–15, and

Illustrations of the Literary History of the Eighteenth Century, 8 vols., 1817–58; and Spence's *Anecdotes*, &c., edited in 1820 by both E. Malone and C. Singer. More recent works are: J. Foster, *Alumni Oxonienses . . . 1500–1714*, 4 vols., 1891–2, together with the continuation, *Alumni Oxonienses . . . 1715–1886*, 4 vols., 1887–8; J. Venn and A. J. Venn, *Alumni Cantabrigienses . . . to 1751*, 4 vols., 1922–7; and S. J. Kunitz and H. Haycraft, *British Authors before 1800*, N.Y., 1952.

II. GENERAL COLLECTIONS AND ANTHOLOGIES

The collections of English verse began with *The British Poets*, 44 vols., Edinburgh, 1773–6. Also issued in Edinburgh was J. Bell's *The Poets of Great Britain complete from Chaucer to Churchill*, with biographical and critical prefaces, 109 vols., 1777–83. S. Johnson's *The Works of the English Poets. With Prefaces, biographical and critical*, amounted to 68 vols. in the 1779–81 edition, and to 75 vols. in 1790. R. Anderson's *The Works of the British Poets*, also with prefaces, was issued in 13 vols. in Edinburgh from 1792 to 1795. A. Chalmers's edition, from Chaucer to Cowper, with Johnson's prefaces, and some new ones by himself, appeared in 1810. *The British Poets*, 100 vols., 1822, contains 'lives', as does R. Bell's *The Annotated Edition of the English Poets*, 29 vols., 1854–7. *The Aldine Edition of the British Poets* was issued in 41 vols., 1891–7. *Minor Poets of the Eighteenth Century*, ed. H. I'A. Faussett, *EL* 1930, contains the poems of Lady Winchilsea, Parnell, Dyer, and Green.

For contemporary anthologies see A. E. Case, *English Poetical Miscellanies*, 1935, and the various editions of R. Dodsley's *A Collection of Poems*, from 1748 to 1770, which are elucidated by *Dodsley's Collection of Poetry. Its contents and contributors*, ed. W. P. Courtney, 1910. Material will be found in *The Oxford Book of Eighteenth Century Verse*, ed. D. Nichol Smith, 1926. *Before the Romantics*, ed. G. Grigson, 1946, gives a useful selection.

Ballads of the period will be found in the various collections, such as F. J. Child, *English and Scottish Popular Ballads*, 5 vols., Boston and N.Y., 1882–98; *English and Scottish Popular Ballads . . . from the collection of Francis James Child*, ed. H. C. Sargent and G. L. Kittredge, Boston and N.Y., 1904. A more restricted collection is that by W. W. Wilkins's, *Political Ballads of the Seventeenth and Eighteenth Centuries*, 2 vols., 1860.

Collections of essays begin with [James] Harrison's *British Classics*, 8 vols., 1796–7; followed by N. Drake's *Essays . . . Illustrative of the Tatler, Spectator and Guardian* 3 vols., 1805; and *The Gleaner*, 4 vols., 1811, of which vol. i is relevant here; more compendious collections under the title of *British Essayists* appeared later, the first being that edited by A. Chalmers, 45 vols., 1817, and 38 vols., 1823. Intermediately there had appeared that by J. Ferguson, 40 vols., 1819. These were followed by the collection edited by R. Lynam, 30 vols., 1827. The Pelican *Eighteenth Century Prose, 1700–1780*, ed. D. W. Jefferson, 1956, gives suitable extracts from prose of various kinds. For other collections see under special headings, criticism, travel, art, &c.

III. GENERAL LITERARY HISTORY AND CRITICISM

This section consists of three divisions: 1. Common; 2. History and Criticism of Prose; 3. History and Criticism of Verse; 4. History and Criticism of Drama; 5. History and Criticism of Fiction.

1. COMMON

CHEL ix, 1912, and x, 1913, provide the fullest history. Other good accounts of literary development are: E. Legouis and L. Cazamian, *Histoire de la littérature anglaise*, Paris, 1924; trans. revised ed., 1957; W. F. Schirmer, *Geschichte der englischen Literatur*, Halle, 1937; and the compact if somewhat dated *Concise Cambridge History of English Literature*, by G. Sampson, 1941. *A Literary History of England*, ed. A. C. Baugh, N.Y., 1948, contains an excellent section by G. Sherburn, 'The Restoration and Eighteenth Century'.

Among works confining themselves more narrowly to the eighteenth century, four older books deserve mention: E. Gosse, *A History of Eighteenth Century Literature*, 1889; J. Dennis, *The Age of Pope*, 1894; O. Elton, *The Augustan Age*, 1899; and G. Saintsbury, *The Peace of the Augustans*, 1916; *WC* 1946. Two recent perceptive handbooks are: J. E. Butt, *The Augustan Age*,

1950; and *From Dryden to Johnson*, ed. B. Ford, Pelican, 1957, which includes a useful short bibliography.

Social and intellectual factors are given more prominence in A. Beljame, *Le Public et les hommes de lettres en Angleterre au dix-huitième siècle*, Paris, 1881, 2nd ed. 1897; English trans. by E. O. Lorimer, 1948. W. P. Ker has a brief but valuable sketch entitled 'The Eighteenth Century' in vol. i of his *Collected Essays*, 1925; W. Ebisch and L. L. Schücking have compiled a useful 'Bibliographie zur Geschichte des literarischen Geschmacks in England' in *Ang.* lxiii, 1939.

Among books offering relevant material, the more prominent are: A. Dobson, *Eighteenth Century Vignettes*, 3 vols., 1892–6; H. G. de Maar, *A History of Modern English Romanticism*, 1924, a substantial, although unfinished discussion; S. Vines, *The Course of English Classicism*, 1930; and F. Gallaway, *Reason, Rule, and Revolt in English Classicism*, N.Y., 1940, a good general account of the subject. Studies effectively comparing French and English literary ideas are: F. C. Green, *Minuet*, 1935; and K. E. Wheatley, *Racine and English Classicism*, Univ. of Texas Press, 1956. W. Empson's three books, *Seven Types of Ambiguity*, rev. ed., 1947; *Some Versions of Pastoral*, 1935; and *The Structure of Complex Words*, 1951, also handle Augustan concepts, but with a markedly different technique. J. E. Mason's study of courtesy literature, *Gentlefolk in the Making*, Philadelphia, 1935, and C. A. Moore, *Backgrounds of English Literature, 1700–60*, Minneapolis, 1953, help to fill out the picture.

Collections of essays containing further criticism include: B. Dobrée, *Variety of Ways*, 1932; *Essays on the Eighteenth Century presented to David Nichol Smith*, ed. J. Sutherland and F. P. Wilson, 1945; and *Pope and his Contemporaries, Essays presented to George Sherburn*, ed. J. L. Clifford and L. A. Landa, 1949. M. H. Nicolson has written two first-rate books dealing with cross-currents from the world of science (see under v. 4), while K. Maclean has commented upon another important literary trend in *John Locke and English Literature of the Eighteenth Century*, New Haven, 1936. Shorter studies in periodicals abound, but the following deserve special attention, and cover a large part of the field: R. D. Havens, 'Romantic Aspects of the Age of Pope', *PMLA* xxvii, 1912; O. Elton, 'Reason and Enthusiasm in the Eighteenth Century', *E & S* x, 1924; P. S. Wood, 'Native Elements in English Neo-Classicism', *MP* xxiv, 1926;

R. S. Crane, 'Suggestions towards a Genealogy of the "Man of Feeling"', *ELH* i, 1934; L. Babb, 'The Cave of Spleen', *RES* xii, 1936; and two contributions by J. W. Draper, 'The Rise of English Neo-Classicism', *Revue anglo-américaine* x, 1933, and 'The Theory of the Comic in Eighteenth-Century England', *JEGP* xxxvii, 1938. For Scottish literature see: H. Walker, *Three Centuries of Scottish Literature*, 2 vols., 1893; T. F. Henderson, *Scottish Vernacular Literature*, 3rd ed., 1910; J. H. Millar, *A Literary History of Scotland*, 1903; G. G. Smith, *Scottish Literature*, 1919; and *Scottish Poetry*, ed. J. Kinsley, 1955. For Wales may be consulted: W. J. Hughes, *Wales and the Welsh in English Literature from Shakespeare to Scott*, 1924; J. S. Lewis, *A School of Welsh Augustans*, 1924; and T. Parry, *A History of Welsh Literature*, trans. H. I. Bell, 1955.

2. History and Criticism of Prose

General studies of prose include: P. Fijn van Draat, *Rhythm in English Prose*, Heidelberg, 1910, supplemented by the same author's article in *Ang.* xxxvi, 1912; G. Saintsbury, *A History of English Prose Rhythm*, 1912; A. C. Clark, *Prose Rhythm in English*, 1913; W. M. Patterson, *The Rhythm of Prose*, 2nd ed., N.Y., 1917; O. Elton, 'English Prose Numbers' in his *Sheaf of Papers*, 1922; N. R. Tempest, *The Rhythm of English Prose*, 1930; J. R. Sutherland, *On English Prose*, 1957, and his 'Some Aspects of Eighteenth-Century Prose' in *Essays . . . presented to David Nichol Smith*, 1945; and H. Read, *English Prose Style*, rev. ed., 1952. The rhetorical tradition is surveyed in M. W. Croll's 'The Cadence of English Oratorical Prose', *SP* xvi, 1919, and in W. P. Sandford's *English Theories of Public Address*, Columbus, 1931. R. P. Bond considers work in progress in 'Eighteenth Century Correspondence', *SP* xxxiii, 1936; J. A. K. Thomson, *Classical Influences on English Prose*, 1956, gives a concise account of a large topic, as does H. Fisch in 'The Puritans and the Reform of Prose Style', *ELH* xix, 1952. D. W. Jefferson has a useful introductory essay in *Eighteenth-Century Prose* (see p. 590). The achievement North of the border is considered in J. H. Millar's *Scottish Prose of the Seventeenth and Eighteenth Centuries*, 1912.

Essays are included in the collections cited in II above. R. Withington's *Essays and Characters: Montaigne to Goldsmith,*

N.Y., 1933, may be usefully added. For studies of individual essayists see under author-bibliographies. Hazlitt's critique, 'On the Periodical Essayists' in *Lectures on the English Comic Writers*, 1819, *EL*, 1910, still provides a convenient introduction. H. Walker in *The English Essay and Essayists*, 1915, has a wide, discursive approach; G. S. Marr's *The Periodical Essayists of the Eighteenth Century*, 1923, surveys a more limited field.

3. HISTORY AND CRITICISM OF VERSE

W. J. Courthope, *A History of English Poetry*, 6 vols., 1895–1910, although lacking in incisiveness, still provides a useful starting-point. Two other general histories, more compact in presentation, are: O. Elton, *The English Muse*, 1933, and H. Grierson and J. C. Smith, *A Critical Study of English Poetry*, 1944. F. R. Leavis, *Revaluation*, 1936, has stimulating chapters on 'Pope' and on 'The Augustan Tradition'; while among books devoted more narrowly to our period the following are especially good: D. Nichol Smith, *Some Observations on Eighteenth Century Poetry*, 1937; J. R. Sutherland, *A Preface to Eighteenth Century Poetry*, 1948; I. Jack, *Augustan Satire*, 1952; W. L. Renwick, 'Notes on Some Lesser Poets of the Eighteenth Century' in *Essays . . . presented to D. Nichol Smith*, 1945.

Metrics are dealt with in G. Saintsbury's *History of English Prosody*, 3 vols., 1906–10; and in T. S. Omond's *A Study of Metre*, 1907. The poetic handling of language, and kindred subjects, are variously treated by: H. C. Wyld, *Studies in English Rhymes from Surrey to Pope*, 1923; T. Quayle, *Poetic Diction*, 1924; Owen Barfield, *Poetic Diction*, 1928; F. W. Bateson, *English Poetry and the English Language*, 1934, a brisk but not negligible book; C. Brooks and R. P. Warren, *Understanding Poetry*, N.Y., 1938, an anthology with some revealing passages of critical analysis; G. Tillotson, 'Eighteenth-Century Poetic Diction' in his *Essays in Criticism and Research*, 1942; E. M. W. Tillyard, *Poetry Direct and Oblique*, rev. ed., 1945; G. Tillotson's Warton Lecture, *The Manner of Proceeding in Certain Eighteenth- and Early Nineteenth-Century Poems*, 1950; and B. Groom, *The Diction of Poetry from Spenser to Bridges*, Toronto, 1955.

The elusive topic of 'nature' in Augustan poetry has received a wealth of treatment. Some of the most important discussions are: M. Reynolds, *The Treatment of Nature in English Poetry between Pope and Wordsworth*, 2nd ed., Chicago, 1909, a book still not out-dated; G. G. Williams, 'The Beginnings of Nature Poetry in the Eighteenth Century', *SP* xxvii, 1930; C. V. Deane, *Aspects of Eighteenth Century Nature Poetry*, 1935, a well-balanced essay on the subject; and J. Arthos, *The Language of Natural Description in Eighteenth-Century Poetry*, Ann Arbor, 1949, a large part of which is devoted to the listing of significant usages.

Consideration of the techniques and implications of various poetic genres is important for this period; a number of books and articles offer guidance, including: C. W. Previté-Orton, *Political Satire in English Poetry*, 1910; R. H. Griffith, 'Progress Pieces of the 18th Century', *Texas Rev.* v, 1919–20; M. K. Bragg, *The Formal Eclogue in Eighteenth-Century England*, Orono, 1926; J. W. Draper, *The Funeral Elegy and the Rise of English Romanticism*, N.Y., 1929; R. P. Bond, *English Burlesque Poetry, 1700–1750*, Cambridge, Mass., 1932; R. A. Aubin, *Topographical Poetry in XVIII-Century England*, N.Y., 1936, a book which in common with the preceding has useful bibliographical material; G. N. Shuster, *The English Ode from Milton to Keats*, N.Y., 1940; H. T. Swedenberg, *The Theory of the Epic in England, 1650–1800*, Berkeley and Los Angeles, 1944; and J. E. Congleton, *Theories of Pastoral Poetry in England, 1684–1798*, Gainesville, 1952. The lyric has also been surveyed, notably in O. Doughty, *English Lyric in the Age of Reason*, 1922; V. Lange, *Die Lyrik und ihr Publikum im England des 18. Jahrhunderts*, Weimar, 1935; and C. W. Peltz, 'The Neo-Classic Lyric, 1660–1725', *ELH* xi, 1944.

Among works dealing mainly with problems of literary background rather than of poetic convention are: H. A. Beers, *A History of English Romanticism in the Eighteenth Century*, 1899, a book in some ways outmoded but not wholly superseded; R. D. Havens, *The Influence of Milton on English Poetry*, Cambridge, Mass., 1922, a comprehensive study of the subject; A. L. Reed, *The Background of Gray's Elegy*, N.Y., 1924, which discusses poetic melancholy in the first half of the century; I. A. Williams, 'Some Poetical Miscellanies of the Early Eighteenth Century', *Library*, 4th series, x, 1930, which is mainly bibliographical in emphasis; C. Davies, 'Ut Pictura Poesis', *MLR* xx, 1935; M. K. Whelan, *Enthusiasm in English Poetry of the Eighteenth Century*, Washington, 1935; A. R. Humphreys, 'A Classical Education and Eighteenth-Century Poetry',

Scrutiny viii, 1939; H. N. Fairchild, *Religious Trends in English Poetry*, vol. i, N.Y., 1939; M. M. Fitzgerald, *First Follow Nature. Primitivism in English Poetry, 1725–1750*, N.Y., 1947. C. F. Chapin's *Personification in Eighteenth-Century English Poetry*, N.Y., 1955, treats of a debatable feature of this poetry; while M. H. Nicolson, in her valuable *Newton Demands the Muse*, Princeton, 1946, reveals the relationship between science and the poetic imagination, with particular reference to the impact of Newton's *Opticks* upon the poets of the eighteenth century. This approach is developed in J. Butt's 'Science and Man in Eighteenth-Century Poetry', *Durham Univ. Journ.* xxxix, 1947, and D. Bush's *Science and English Poetry*, N.Y., 1950.

D. F. Foxon has in hand a much-needed *Check List of English Poetical Pieces, 1701–1750*.

4. History and Criticism of Drama

After *Jacob*, the first attempt at dramatic history was that made by John Mottley, 'A List of all the Dramatic Authors . . . and of all the Dramatic Pieces . . . to the Year 1747', added to the edition of T. Whincop's *Scanderbeg*, 1747; followed in 1759 by Thomas Wilkes, *A General View of the Stage*. Standard reference books are: D. E. Baker, *A Companion to the Playhouse . . . down to 1764*, 2 vols., 1764, edited as *Biographia Dramatica* by S. Jones, *et al.*, 3 vols. in 4, 1812–13; and J. Genest, *Some Account of the English Stage from 1660–1830*, 10 vols., 1832. The best modern reference book is Allardyce Nicoll, *A History of Early Eighteenth Century Drama, 1700–1750*, 1925, rev. ed. 1952, to which may be added his *British Drama*, 1925. Vol. iii of A. W. Ward's *A History of English Dramatic Literature*, 3 vols., 1899, is, however, still useful.

Books dealing with Restoration drama usually include the drama up to 1720: J. Palmer, *The Comedy of Manners*, 1913; B. Dobrée, *Restoration Comedy*, 1924, and *Restoration Tragedy*, 1929. Devoted wholly to the eighteenth century are: F. W. Bateson, *English Comic Drama, 1700–1750*, 1929, and F. S. Boas, *An Introduction to Eighteenth Century Drama, 1700–1780*, 1953. More specialized studies are: E. Bernbaum, *The Drama of Sensibility*, Boston, Mass., 1915; C. C. Green, *The Neo-Classic Theory of Tragedy in England during the Eighteenth Century*, Cambridge, Mass.,

1934; S. Rosenfeld, *Strolling Players and Drama in the Provinces, 1660–1765*, 1939; and W. S. Clark, *The Early Irish Stage: the Beginnings to 1720*, 1955. Articles include: O. Waterhouse, 'The Development of English Sentimental Comedy in the Eighteenth Century', *Ang.* xxx, 1907, and J. R. Sutherland, 'Shakespeare's Imitators in the Eighteenth Century', *MLR* xxviii, 1933.

5. HISTORY AND CRITICISM OF FICTION

The standard bibliography of primary material is A. Esdaile's *List of English Tales and Prose Romances printed before 1740*, 1912. A useful list of secondary works is F. Cordasco's *The 18th Century Novel*, Brooklyn, 1950; a similar though brief survey is E. Bernbaum's 'Recent Works on Prose Fiction before 1800', *MLN* li, lii, 1936, 1937. General histories include: J. C. Dunlop, *History of Prose Fiction*, 3 vols., Edinburgh, 1814, rev. ed., Bohn, 2 vols., 1888; E. A. Baker, *The History of the English Novel*, vol. iii, 1929, a comprehensive, factual account; J. R. Foster, *History of the Pre-Romantic Novel in England*, N.Y., 1949; A. C. Kettle, *An Introduction to the English Novel*, vol. i, 1951, Marxist in outlook, but containing some useful criticism. Two thoughtful critical studies are: A. D. McKillop, *The Early Masters of English Fiction*, Univ. of Kansas Press, 1956; and I. Watt, *The Rise of the Novel*, 1957.

The feminine contribution to English fiction of this period is considered by J. M. Horner in *The English Women Novelists and their Connection with the Feminist Movement, 1688–1797*, Northampton, Mass., 1930; and by B. G. MacCarthy in vol. i of *The Female Pen*, 2 vols. Cork, 1944. Five books which isolate different strains in the novel are: M. P. Conant, *The Oriental Tale in England in the Eighteenth-Century*, N.Y., 1908; C. E. Morgan, *The Rise of the Novel of Manners*, N.Y., 1911; U. Habel, *Die Nachwirkung des picaresken Romans in England*, Breslau and Oppeln, 1930; T. P. Haviland, *The Roman de Longue Haleine on English Soil*, Philadelphia, 1931; and G. F. Singer, *The Epistolary Novel*, Philadelphia, 1933. A. J. Tieje comments on an important aspect in *The Theory of Characterization in Prose Fiction prior to 1740*, Minneapolis, 1916; and P. B. Gove discusses a recurrent theme in *The Imaginary Voyage in Prose Fiction*, N.Y., 1941, which includes a useful check-list of eighteenth-century examples. See also, E. Pons, *Le Voyage, genre littéraire au XVIIIe siècle*, Strasbourg, 1926.

IV. SPECIAL STUDIES

This section contains: Language; Popular Literature; Journalism; History and Biography; Translations; Contemporary Criticism; Printing and Publishing.

1. LANGUAGE

The standard bibliography is A. G. Kennedy's *A Bibliography of Writings on the English Language*, Cambridge, Mass., and New Haven, 1927. *A New English Dictionary*, ed. J. A. H. Murray *et al.*, 1884–1933; corrected reissue, 13 vols., 1933, abridged as *The Shorter Oxford English Dictionary*, 3rd ed., 1955, is esssential. There are general histories by G. H. McKnight, *Modern English in the Making*, N.Y., 1928; O. Jespersen, *Growth and Structure of the English Language*, 9th ed., 1948; S. Potter, *Our Language*, Pelican, 1950; A. C. Baugh, *A History of the English Language*, 1951; and H. C. Wyld, *A History of Modern Colloquial English*, 3rd ed., 1953. L. P. Smith's *Words and Idioms*, 4th ed., 1933, is slighter in scope. A. S. Collins's 'Language 1660–1784' in *From Dryden to Johnson*, Pelican, 1957, is a masterly piece of compression.

Dictionaries form the subject of the following: J. A. H. Murray, *The Evolution of English Lexicography*, 1900; M. Segar, 'Dictionary Making in the Early Eighteenth Century', *RES* vii, 1931; M. M. Mathews, *A Survey of English Dictionaries*, 1933; and D. T. Starnes and G. E. Noyes, *The English Dictionary from Cawdrey to Johnson*, Chapel Hill, 1946. Two contemporary works, both of which ran through many editions, may be instanced here for the influence they exerted throughout the period: T. Dyche, *A Guide to the English Tongue*, 2nd ed., 1710; and N. Bailey, *An Universal Etymological English Dictionary*, 1721.

Writings on other relevant topics include: E. N. Adams, *Old English Scholarship in England*, New Haven, 1917; S. A. Leonard, *The Doctrine of Correctness in English Usage, 1700–1800*, Madison, 1929; H. Kökeritz, 'English Pronunciation as described in Shorthand Systems of the 17th and 18th Centuries', *Studia Neophilologica* vii, 1935; and W. Matthews, 'Some Eighteenth-Century Phonetic Spellings', *RES* xii, 1936. An interesting contemporary item is the rhyming dictionary of E. Bysshe included in his *The Art of Poetry*, 1702.

2. POPULAR LITERATURE

A number of catalogues provide help, notably: J. O. Halliwell [-Phillipps], *Catalogue of Chap-books, Garlands, and Popular Histories*, 1849; R. Lemon, *Catalogue of a Collection of Printed Broadsides in the Possession of the Society of Antiquaries of London*, 1866; *Bibliotheca Lindesiana. Catalogue of English Broadsides*, 1898; and the *Catalogue of English and American Chap-Books and Broadside Ballads in Harvard College Library*, Cambridge, Mass., 1905. *The Common Muse*, by V. de S. Pinto and A. E. Rodway, 1957, provides some interesting examples. Other relevant works of reference include: G. L. Apperson, *English Proverbs and Proverbial Phrases*, 1929; W. Bonser, *Proverb Literature*, 1930; W. G. Smith, *The Oxford Dictionary of English Proverbs*, 2nd ed. rev. P. Harvey, 1948; and I. and P. Opie, *The Oxford Dictionary of Nursery Rhymes*, rev. ed. 1952.

Further information on chap-books and related subjects is to be found in J. Ashton's *Chap-Books of the Eighteenth Century*, 1882; and F. W. Chandler's *The Literature of Roguery*, 2 vols., Boston, 1907. For Scotland there is J. Fraser, *The Humorous Chapbooks of Scotland*, 2 parts, N.Y., 1873; and W. Harvey, *Scottish Chapbook Literature*, 1903. Although the great efflorescence of children's books belongs to a later age, F. V. Barry's *A Century of Children's Books*, 1922, is focused on the eighteenth century, and the following touch in varying degrees upon our period: G. Andrede, *The Dawn of Juvenile Literature in England*, Amsterdam, 1925; F. J. H. Darton, *Children's Books in England*, 1932, the best general account; and P. H. Muir's lavishly illustrated, *English Children's Books*, 1954.

R. Nevill surveys another kind of popular literature in *Old English Sporting Books*, 1924; while the broadest sense of the term provides the subject of L. Whitney's *Primitivism and the Idea of Progress in English Popular Literature of the Eighteenth Century*, Baltimore, 1934. A. D. McKillop in 'English Circulating Libraries, 1725–50', *Library*, 4th series, xiv, 1934, offers a link with the study of fiction. For still readable contemporary popular literature see under Edward Ward.

3. JOURNALISM

The most comprehensive list for this period is *A Census of British Newspapers and Periodicals*, by R. S. Crane and F. B. Kaye, Chapel Hill, 1927; this is supported by *Studies of British Newspapers and Periodicals from the Beginning to 1800*, by K. K. Weed, R. P. Bond, and M. E. Prior, Chapel Hill, 1946. Of considerable value is *The Times* [J. G. Muddiman] *Tercentenary Handlist of English and Welsh Newspapers, Magazines and Reviews*, 1920. Section I: London and Suburban. Section II: Provincial. For these latter see also G. A. Cranfield, *A Handlist of English Provincial Newspapers and Periodicals, 1700–1760*, Cambridge Bibliographical Society, 1952.

The earliest useful work on this subject is H. Andrews's *The History of British Journalism from the Foundation of the Newspaper Press in England to the Repeal of the Stamp Act in 1855*, 2 vols., 1859. Recent works include: J. R. Sutherland, 'The Circulation of Newspapers and Literary Periodicals, 1700–1730' *The Library*, 4th series, xv, 1934; W. B. Ewald, Jr., *The Newsmen of Queen Anne*, 1956; and R. P. Bond *et al.*, *Studies in Early English Periodicals*, Chapel Hill, 1957. These may be supplemented by W. Graham's *The Beginnings of English Literary Periodicals, 1665–1715*, 1926. An important issue is covered by L. Hanson's *Government and the Press, 1695–1763*, 1931; and F. S. Siebert's *Freedom of the Press in England, 1476–1776*, Urbana, 1952.

4. HISTORY AND BIOGRAPHY

This sub-section comprises historical writing, biography, autobiography, diaries, and letters.

For the study of historiography, J. W. Thompson's *History of Historical Writing*, 2 vols., N.Y., 1942, is invaluable. The bibliographies cited in Section V. i include historical writing of the period; the bibliographies of individual historians in Section VI should also be consulted. Two rich sources for the study of antiquarianism and allied topics are T. Hearne's writings (see under Hearne); and *Remarks and Collections of Thomas Hearne*, ed. C. E. Doble *et al.*, Oxford Historical Society, 11 vols., 1885–1921. Commentaries on this subject are to be found in: H. B. Walters, *The English Antiquaries of the Sixteenth, Seventeenth and Eighteenth Centuries*, 1934; and D. C. Douglas, *English Scholars, 1660–1730*, 2nd ed., 1951.

On biography a sketch is provided by H. Nicolson's *The Development of English Biography*, 1927; the subject is more fully documented in M. Longaker's *English Biography in the Eighteenth Century*, Philadelphia, 1931; but most important of all is D. A. Stauffer's *Art of Biography in Eighteenth Century England*, 2 vols., Princeton, 1941, which includes a bibliographical supplement. J. Birnbaum's *Die 'Memoirs' um 1700*, Halle, 1934; and J. C. Major's *The Role of Personal Memoirs in English Biography and Novel*, Philadelphia, 1935, provide introductions to such weightier works as: W. Shumaker, *English Autobiography*, Berkeley and Los Angeles, 1954; and the annotated bibliography by W. Matthews, *British Autobiographies*, Berkeley and Los Angeles, 1955.

W. Matthews also compiled a comprehensive bibliography of *British Diaries*, Berkeley and Los Angeles, 1950; and Lord Ponsonby gives a series of extracts in *English Diaries*, 1923, *More English Diaries*, 1927, and *Scottish and Irish Diaries*, 1927. Two important collections of letters are: H. Ellis, *Original Letters of Eminent Literary Men of the Sixteenth, Seventeenth, and Eighteenth Centuries*, Camden Society, 1843; and J. Aitken, *English Letters of the XVIII Century*, Pelican, 1946. For commentary there is K. G. Hornbeak's *Complete Letter-Writer in English, 1568–1800*, Northampton, Mass., 1934, of which S. Richardson's *Letters written to and for Particular Friends*, 1741, ed. B. W. Downs, 1928, may serve as an example.

5. TRANSLATIONS

This sub-section also covers classical and foreign relations.

Two critical studies are: F. R. Amos, *Early Theories of Translation*, N.Y., 1920; and J. W. Draper, 'The Theory of Translation in the Eighteenth Century', *Neophilologus*, vi, 1921.

Bibliographical information on translations of the ancient classics is to be found in: F. M. K. Foster, *English Translations from the Greek*, N.Y., 1918; F. S. Smith, *The Classics in Translation*, 1930, which offers a selective listing; and the valuable work by H. Brown, 'The Classical Tradition in English Literature', *Harvard Studies and Notes in Philology and Literature* xviii, 1935. General surveys are: the collection of essays ed. G. S. Gordon, *English Literature and the Classics*, 1912; J. E. Sandys, *A History of Classical Scholarship*, ii, 1908; and J. A. K. Thomson, *Classical Influences in English Prose*, 1956.

The influence of individual Greek and Roman authors is treated of in: R. T. Kerlin, *Theocritus in English Literature*, Lynchburg, 1910; C. Goad, *Horace in the English Literature of the Eighteenth Century*, New Haven, 1918; E. Nitchie, *Vergil and the English Poets*, N.Y., 1919; E. S. Duckett, *Catullus in English Poetry*, Northampton, Mass., 1925; and D. L. Durling, *Georgic Tradition in English Poetry*, N.Y., 1935. One aspect of neo-Latin writing is discussed in L. Bradner, *Musae Anglicanae: A History of Anglo-Latin Poetry, 1500–1925*, N.Y., 1940.

Two general accounts of European influences may be named: T. G. Tucker, *The Foreign Debt of English Literature*, 1907; and L. Magnus, *English Literature in its Foreign Relations*, 1927. For France there are: A. F. B. Clark, *Boileau and the French Classical Critics in England*, Paris, 1925; and U. T. Holmes, *The French Novel in English Translation*, Chapel Hill, 1930, which gives bibliographical help. A comprehensive record of the counter-movement is C. A. Rochedieu's *Bibliography of French Translations of English Works, 1700–1800*, Chicago, 1948; for Germany there is B. Q. Morgan, *A Critical Bibliography of German Literature in English Translation, 1481–1927*, 2nd ed., Stanford, 1938; for Spain, R. U. Pane's bibliography, *English Translations from the Spanish, 1484–1943*, New Brunswick, 1944. Two other books may be mentioned here: T. de Vries, *Holland's Influence on English Language and Literature*, Chicago, 1916; and E. J. Simmons, *English Literature and Culture in Russia (1553–1840)*, Cambridge, Mass., 1935.

6. CONTEMPORARY CRITICISM

The standard collection of texts is *Critical Essays of the Eighteenth Century, 1700–1725*, ed. W. H. Durham, New Haven, 1915. Other collections illustrating this period in varying degrees are: G. Saintsbury, *Loci Critici*, 1903; R. P. Cowl, *The Theory of Poetry in England*, 1914; D. Nichol Smith, *Eighteenth Century Essays on Shakespeare*, 1903, and *Shakespeare Criticism*, 1916, *WC*; and E. D. Jones, *English Critical Essays (Sixteenth, Seventeenth, and Eighteenth Centuries)*, 1922, *WC*. H. A. Needham's *Taste and Criticism in the Eighteenth Century*, 1952, contains some useful extracts.

G. Saintsbury's *History of Criticism and Literary Taste in Europe*, 3 vols., 1900–4, and *History of English Criticism*, rev. ed.,

1949, give a general impressionistic account; a more sober presentation is offered by J. W. H. Atkins's *English Literary Criticism: 17th and 18th Centuries*, 1951. There is also useful material in the incisive account by W. K. Wimsatt, Jnr., and C. Brooks, *Literary Criticism. A Short History*, N.Y., 1957. To these should be added R. S. Crane's 'English Neoclassical Criticism' in *Critics and Criticism, Ancient and Modern*, ed. R. S. Crane, Chicago, 1952. Other works of a fairly general character are: T. S. Omond, *English Metrists*, 1921; and the two thoughtful discussions by R. Wellek, *The Rise of English Literary History*, Chapel Hill, 1941, and, by R. Wellek and A. Warren, *Theory of Literature*, 1949.

Shakespearian criticism is considered in D. Nichol Smith's *Shakespeare in the Eighteenth Century*, 1928; and in H. S. Robinson's *English Shakesperian Criticism in the Eighteenth Century*, N.Y., 1932. Classical influences are studied in: A. Rosenberg, *Longinus in England bis zum Ende des 18. Jahrhunderts*, Berlin, 1917; T. R. Henn, *Longinus and English Criticism*, 1934; J. W. Draper, 'Aristotelian "Mimesis" in Eighteenth Century England', *PMLA* xxxvi, 1921; M. T. Herrick, *The Poetics of Aristotle in England*, New Haven, 1930.

Useful in defining general characteristics of eighteenth-century criticism may be noted: P. Hamelius, *Die Kritik in der englischen Literatur des 17. und 18. Jahrhunderts*, Leipzig, 1897; J. G. Robertson, *Studies in the Genesis of Romantic Theory in the Eighteenth Century*, 1923, which has the advantage of not confining itself to English developments; W. Folkierski, *Entre le classicisme et le romantisme*, Paris, 1925; and W. J. Bate, *From Classic to Romantic*, Cambridge, Mass., 1946, a rewarding study of critical premises. Other important subjects of a more circumscribed kind are handled in the following: G. M. Miller, *The Historical Point of View in English Literary Criticism from 1570–1770*, Heidelberg, 1913; R. H. Wollstein, *English Opinions of French Poetry, 1660–1750*, N.Y., 1923; O. Seeger, *Die Auseinandersetzung zwischen Antike und Moderne in England*, Leipzig, 1927; J. B. Heidler, *The History, from 1700 to 1800, of English Criticism of Prose Fiction*, Urbana, 1928; R. D. Havens, 'Changing Taste in the Eighteenth Century', *PMLA* xliv, 1929; R. W. Babcock, 'The Idea of Taste in the Eighteenth Century', *PMLA* l, 1935; S. H. Monk, *The Sublime. A Study of Critical Theories in XVIII-Century England*, N.Y., 1935, a particularly useful summary of a central theme; and E. R. Wasserman, *Elizabethan Poetry in the Eighteenth Century*, Urbana, 1947, which includes useful material on the critical attitude of the period.

7. PRINTING AND PUBLISHING

Bibliographical technique may be studied in: R. B. Mc-Kerrow, *An Introduction to Bibliography*, 1927; 1948; F. T. Bowers, *Principles of Bibliographical Description*, Princeton, 1949, an advanced work on the subject; and A. Esdaile, *A Student's Manual of Bibliography*, 3rd ed., 1954. Assistance is also to be found in *Transactions of the Bibliographical Society*, 1893 ff., incorporating from 1920 *The Library*, 4th and 5th series; and the publications of the Bibliographical Societies of America, Cambridge, Edinburgh, Oxford, and Virginia. Relevant works of reference include: C. H. Timperley, *A Dictionary of Printers and Printing*, 1839; E. C. Bigmore and C. W. H. Wyman, *A Bibliography of Printing*, 3 vols., 1880–6; A. Growoll and W. Eames, *Three Centuries of English Booktrade Bibliography*, N.Y., 1903; and the two compilations by H. R. Plomer *et al.*, *A Dictionary of . . . Printers and Booksellers . . . 1668 to 1725*, 1922, and its continuation covering from 1726 to 1775, 1932.

Of books and articles on printing the following are especially worth attention: F. A. Pottle, 'Printers' Copy in the Eighteenth Century', *Papers of the Bibliographical Society of America* xxvii, 1933; P. Simpson, *Proof-reading in the Sixteenth, Seventeenth, and Eighteenth Centuries*, 1935; W. T. Berry and A. F. Johnson, *Catalogue of Specimens of Printing Types*, 1935; *A History of the Printed Book*, ed. L. C. Wroth, Dolphin No. 3., N.Y., 1938; S. Morison, *Four Centuries of Fine Printing*, 2nd ed., 1949; P. Gaskell, 'Printing the Classics in the Eighteenth Century', *Book Collector* i, 1952; S. H. Steinberg, *Five Hundred Years of Printing*, Pelican, 1955.

Publishing and bookselling are treated in: W. Roberts, *The Earlier History of English Bookselling*, 1889; C. Knight, *Shadows of the Old Booksellers*, 1927; R. W. Chapman, 'Eighteenth-Century Booksellers', *Book-Collector's Quarterly* ix, 1933, containing supplementary notes to Plomer; M. Plant, *The English Book Trade*, 1939, an excellent all-round account; and F. A. Mumby, *Publishing and Bookselling*, rev. ed., 1954.

For an account of publishing outside London, there is S. C.

Roberts's *A History of the Cambridge University Press, 1521–1921*, 1921. I. A. Williams has written a good account of 'English Book-Illustration, 1700–1775', *Library*, 4th series, xvii, 1937; C. Atto has thrown light on an interesting publishing venture in 'The Society for the Encouragement of Learning', *Library*, 4th series, xix, 1939; and W. B. Todd has contributed a good commentary on 'Bibliography and the Editorial Problem in the Eighteenth Century', *Studies in Bibliography* iv, 1951–2. An intricate and important phase of publishing history is well analysed by P. M. Wiles, in *Serial Publication in England before 1750*, 1957.

V. THE BACKGROUND OF LITERATURE

This section comprises: History and Political Thought; Philosophy and Religion; Science; Travel; Social Life; Education; The Arts.

1. HISTORY AND POLITICAL THOUGHT

Writings for the period are covered by: *A Bibliography of British History, 1700–1715*, 5 vols., by W. T. Morgan, Bloomington, Indiana, 1934–42; *A Select Bibliography of British History, 1660–1670*, by C. L. Grose, Chicago, 1939, and the same author's 'Studies of 1931–40 on British History, 1660–1760', *JMH* xii, 1940; and by *Bibliography of British History, The Eighteenth Century, 1714–1789*, by S. Pargellis and D. J. Medley, 1951. For an excellent general history see W. Michael, *Englische Geschichte im Achtzehnten Jahrhundert*, 5 vols., 1896–1955, the first two volumes of which have been translated as *The Beginnings of the Hanoverian Dynasty*, 1936, and *The Quadruple Alliance*, 1939, both under the editorship of L. Namier.

Although Macaulay's *History of England*, vol. v, 1861, stops short with William III, it provides an admirable background for what was to follow. A standard work is G. M. Trevelyan's *England under Queen Anne*, 3 vols., 1930–4, and W. E. H. Lecky's *A History of England in the Eighteenth Century*, rev. ed., 7 vols., 1892, carries the story further. A good general popular history is still *The History of England from the Peace of Utrecht to the Peace of Aix-la-Chapelle*, by Lord Mahon (P. H. Stanhope, later Earl Stanhope), 7 vols., 1836–54. Recent authoritative histories covering two periods are G. N. Clark's *The Later Stuarts, 1660–1714*, 2nd ed. 1955; and B. Williams's *The Whig Supremacy, 1714–1760*, 1939. The period is possibly best understood by studies of various statesmen, of which a few may be noted: F. S. Oliver, *The Endless Adventure*, 3 vols., 1930, 1931, 1935, which studies Walpole's problems; T. Lever, *Sidney Godolphin*, 1952; B. Williams, *Stanhope*, 1932; and J. H. Plumb, *Sir Robert Walpole*, vol. i, 1956. An interesting contemporary item is *The Matrial Atchievements of the Scots Nation*, by P. Abercromby, 2 vols., Edinburgh, 1721.

H. J. Laski's compact *Political Thought in England from Locke to Bentham*, 1920, should be complemented with R. Walcott's *English Politics in the Early Eighteenth Century*, 1956. Other works to be consulted include: F. J. C. Hearnshaw (ed.), *The Social and Political Ideas of some English Thinkers of the Augustan Age, 1650–1750*, 1928; J. B. Bury, *The Idea of Progress*, 1920; G. H. Sabine, *A History of Political Theory*, 3rd ed., 1928, which though it jumps from Locke to Hume provides a useful general framework; R. H. Tawney, *Religion and the Rise of Capitalism*, 1926; K. G. Feiling, *A History of the Tory Party, 1640–1714*, 1924, followed by his *The Second Tory Party, 1714–1832*, 1938; C. B. Realey, *Early Opposition to Sir Robert Walpole*, Kansas, 1931; and W. T. Laprade, *Public Opinion and Politics in Eighteenth-Century England*, N.Y., 1936.

Economics is too specialized a study to be covered here, but two examples may be given: T. S. Ashton, *An Economic History of England. The Eighteenth Century*, 1955; and, as showing the early development of engineering, and the use of coke, A. Raiswick, *Dynasty of Ironfounders*, 1953. The excellent brief bibliography compiled by C. J. Horne for the Pelican *From Dryden to Johnson*, 1957, may be consulted.

2. PHILOSOPHY

Two works are of primary importance under this head: L. Stephen, *History of English Thought in the Eighteenth Century*, 2 vols., 1876–80, which is still valid; and B. Willey, *The Eighteenth Century Background*, 1940. Especially useful for continental links is Paul Hazard, *La Crise de la conscience européenne, 1680–1715*, Paris, 1935, trans. 1953, and *La pensée européenne au XVIIIᵉ siècle, de Montesquieu à Lessing*, Paris, 1947, with which may be read C. L. Becker, *The Heavenly City of the Eighteenth Century Philosophers*, New Haven, 1932; and E. Cassirer, *The Philosophy of the Enlightenment*, Princeton, 1951. For general current ideas should be read A. O. Lovejoy's two works, *The Great Chain of Being*, Cambridge, Mass., 1936, and *Essays in the History of Ideas*, Baltimore, 1948. C. Sherrington's *Man on his Nature*, 1940, contains much that is of interest in this period; more definitely focused is D. G. James's *The Life of Reason*, 1949, which includes Bolingbroke. A useful collection of essays from writers chiefly of the eighteenth century is L. S. Bigge's *British Moralists*, 2 vols., 1897. A. R. Humphreys's ' "The Eternal Fitness of Things". An Aspect of Eighteenth-Century Thought', *MLR* xii, 1947, treats of an important item. See also under Berkeley, Hutcheson, Mandeville, Shaftesbury, *et al*.

There is a considerable literature discussing religious thought at this period, of which the following may be noted: J. M. Creed and J. S. Boys Smith, eds., *Religious Thought in the Eighteenth Century*, 1934; W. K. L. Clarke, *Eighteenth Century Piety*, 1944; J. Hunt, *Religious Thought in England*, ii–iii, 1871–3. Opposite religious views are recorded on the one hand by W. H. Hutton, *The English Church, 1625–1714*, 1903, with J. W. Legg, *English Church Life from the Restoration to the Tractarian Movement*, 1914, and J. H. Overton, *Life in the English Church 1660–1714*, 1885; and on the other by H. W. Clark, *History of English Nonconformity*, 1911, and J. H. Overton, *The Nonjurors, Their Lives, Principles and Writings*, 1902. Shorter essays include M. Pattison, 'Tendencies of Religious Thought in England, 1688–1750', a chapter in *Essays and Reviews*, 1860; and R. S. Crane, 'Anglican Apologists and the Idea of Progress', *MP* xxxi, 1934. The political aspect is represented by N. Sykes, *Church and State in England in the XVIIIth Century*, 1934. Valuable biographies by the same author are: *Edmund Gibson, Bishop of London*, 1926; and *William Wake, Archbishop of Canterbury*, 1957. See also under Butler, Law, *et al*.

3. SCIENCE AND SCIENTIFIC THOUGHT

The actual science of the period can best be studied in the *Transactions of the Royal Society* of the relevant years. A useful general history is H. Lyons's *The Royal Society, 1660–1940*, 1944. A gloss on the whole is provided by A. N. Whitehead's

Science and the Modern World, 1926, though the chapter on the eighteenth century is devoted mainly to the later French scientists and to Berkeley. Useful are *A History of Science, Technology and Philosophy in the Eighteenth Century*, by A. Wolf, rev. D. McKie, 1952; and *The Origins of Modern Science*, by H. Butterfield, 1949, to which may be added W. C. Dampier's *A Shorter History of Science*, 1944. The effect of science on thought and literature has been much studied in recent years, as in: W. C. Dampier, *A History of Science and its Relations with Philosophy and Religion,* 3rd ed., 1952; two books by M. H. Nicolson, *The Microscope and English Imagination*, Northampton, Mass., 1935, and *A World in the Moon. A Study of Changing Attitudes towards the Moon*, Northampton, Mass., 1936. Its relation to poetry are treated of by D. Bush, *Science and English Poetry*, N.Y., 1950; by J. Butt, 'Science and Man in Eighteenth Century Poetry', *Durham Univ. Journal* xxxix, 1947; and by B. Dobrée in *The Broken Cistern*, 1954. Three interesting articles by R. F. Jones may be noted: 'Science and English Prose Style', *PMLA* xlv, 1930; 'Science and Criticism in the Neo-Classical Age of English Literature', *JHI* i, 1940; and 'The Background of the Attack on Science in the Age of Pope' in *Pope and his Contemporaries* (p. 591). Since the ideas of science take a generation or two to percolate, two studies of late seventeenth-century scientists throw an interesting light on our period: C. E. Raven, *John Ray, Naturalist*, 1942; and M. 'Espinasse, *Robert Hooke*, 1956. See also under Derham.

4. TRAVEL

The standard bibliography for travel books is E. G. Cox's *A Reference Guide to the Literature of Travel*, Seattle; Vol. I. The Old World, 1935; Vol. II. The New World, 1938; Vol. III. Great Britain, 1949.

Individual works not mentioned in the text include: Martin, *A Description of the Western Islands of Scotland*, 1703, and *A Late Voyage to St. Kilda*, 1718, both ed. D. J. Macleod, 1935; W. Betagh, *Voyage Round the World, Being an Account of a remarkable Enterprize begun in 1719*, &c. 1728, refuting as 'spurious' much of what Shelvocke had written; J. Monck, *An Account of a Most Dangerous Voyage*, &c., 1732, dealing with the North-West Passage; J. Atkins, *A Voyage to Guinea, Brasil, and the West Indies*, &c., 1735.

Collections produced during this period, or including works written during the period, are of considerable value: A. and J. Churchill, *A Collection of Voyages and Travels, some now first printed from Original Manuscripts, others translated out of Foreign Languages*, &c., 4 vols., 1704; 6 vols., 1732 and 1744–6; 8 vols., 1745 and 1752. The Preface is probably by John Locke. This was followed in rivalry by J. Harris's *Navigantium atque Itinerantium Bibliotheca. A Compleat Collection of Voyages and Travels, consisting of above 400 of the most authentick Writers*, 2 vols., 1705, and of above 600 authors in 2 vols., 1764, noteworthy for their maps. From 1709 there was issued monthly *A New Collection of Voyages and Travels*, collected in 2 vols., 1710.

In 1715 J. Campbell published in 2 vols. an enlarged edition of Harris's book; and in 1744–8 he issued a collection, *Voyages and Travels*, &c., 2 vols., bringing the account down to Anson. In 1729 W. Dampier published *A Collection of Voyages and Travels*, which included some of his own. In 1745 T. Osborne issued *A Collection of Voyages and Travels*, 2 vols. The largest collection was that edited by T. Green, but produced under the name of the publisher, T. Astley, *A New General Collection of Voyages and Travels*, 4 vols., 1745–7, a work of which the Abbé Prevost's *Histoire Générale des Voyages*, 18 vols., 1746–8, is chiefly composed. For our purpose here the list may conclude with T. Smollett's *A Compendium of Authentic and Entertaining Voyages*, 7 vols., 1756. The specialist should consult the publications of the Hakluyt Society, particularly *Richard Hakluyt and his Successors*, Series II, No. xciii, 1946, containing a bibliography of the Society's publications.

5. SOCIAL LIFE

What London was like in this period we have at first hand from Gay's *Trivia*, *1716*, and from *London in 1731*, by 'Don Manoel Gonzales', first printed in the *Harleian Miscellany*, 1744–6, often reprinted, last in Cassell's National Library, 1888. A wider picture is obtainable from W. Besant's *London in the Eighteenth Century*, 1903, a more architectural view being given by J. Summerson in *Georgian London*, 1946.

Standard works on social life comprise: J. Ashton, *Social Life in the Reign of Queen Anne*, 2 vols., 1882; *Social England*, ed. H. D. Traill and J. S. Mann, 1893–7, iv, 1663–1714; v, 1714–1815;

G. M. Trevelyan, *Illustrated English Social History*, iii, The Eighteenth Century, 1951. Useful works to be added are: M. D. George, *English Social Life in the Eighteenth Century*, 1923; and *London Life in the XVIIIth Century*, 1925; A. S. Turberville, *English Men and Manners in the 18th Century*, 1926; D. Marshall, *English People in the Eighteenth Century*, 1956. As regards writers the classic study is Leslie Stephen's *English Literature and Society in the Eighteenth Century*, 1904, with which may be consulted A. R. Humphreys's *The Augustan World: Life and Letters in 18th Century England*, 1954. J. R. Sutherland studies a few representative figures in *Background for Queen Anne*, 1939. An admirable contemporary document for London is *The Diary of Dudley Ryder, 1715–1716*, ed. W. Matthews, 1939; the country may be looked at in G. E. Fussell, *Village Life in the Eighteenth Century*, 1947. Good pictures of the later part of our period are given by: H. B. Wheatley, *Hogarth's London*, 1909; and P. Quennell, *Hogarth's Progress*, 1955. An important aspect is treated by: J. R. Allen, *The Clubs of Augustan London*, Cambridge, Mass., 1933; and A. Ellis, *The Penny Universities. A history of the coffee-houses*, 1956. Another aspect is pursued by G. N. Clark, *Science and Social Welfare in the Age of Newton*, 1937.

6. EDUCATION

The influence of Locke upon educational thought in this period is of major importance. There is a convenient edition of both *Some Thoughts Concerning Education*, 1693, and *Of the Conduct of the Understanding*, 1706, in *The Educational Writings of John Locke*, ed. J. W. Adamson, 1912, 2nd ed. 1922. Other contemporary works of interest are: F. Brokesby, *Of Education*, 1701; L. Maidwell, *An Essay upon the Necessity and Excellency of Education*, 1705, reprinted in 1955 by the Augustan Reprint Society, Los Angeles, which makes special reference to mathematics; J. Talbott, *The Christian School-Master*, 1707, dealing particularly with charity-schools; J. Essex, *The Young Ladies Conduct*, 1722; I. Watts, *The Improvement of the Mind*, 1741; and G. Turnbull, *Observations upon Liberal Education*, 1742.

Histories of the subject include: S. S. Laurie, *Studies in the History of Educational Opinion from the Renaissance*, 1903; J. W. Adamson, *A Short History of Education*, 1919; A. E. Dobbs,

Education and Social Movements, 1700–1850, 1919; N. Hans, *New Trends in Education in the Eighteenth Century*, 1951; and S. J. Curtis, *History of Education in Great Britain*, 3rd ed., 1953. University education is dealt with in: A. D. Godley, *Oxford in the Eighteenth Century*, 1908; C. Mallet, *A History of the University of Oxford*, 3 vols., 1924–7; and D. A. Winstanley, *Unreformed Cambridge*, 1935. C. Wordsworth described conditions at both universities in his two books, *Social Life at the English Universities in the Eighteenth Century*, 1874, and *Scholae Academicae*, 1877. Histories of individual colleges are also rich in information. The Nonconformist tradition has been studied by: I. Parker, *Dissenting Academies in England*, 1914; H. McLachlan, *English Education under the Test Acts*, 1931; and J. W. A. Smith, *The Birth of Modern Education*, 1954. A thorough account of *The Charity School Movement* was made by M. G. Jones, 1938; female education is given prominence in M. Reynolds's *The Learned Lady in England, 1650–1760*, Boston and N.Y., 1920; M. Phillips and W. S. Tomkinson, 'Women's Education in the Eighteenth Century' in their *English Women in Life and Letters*, 1926; and D. Gardiner, *English Girlhood at School*, 1929, a thorough survey. Relevant to many aspects of school life are the numerous histories of famous and less well-known schools: R. Bayne-Powell provides a general framework in *The English Child in the Eighteenth Century*, 1939. Other works probably most usefully included here are: A. Heal, *The English Writing-Masters and their Copy-Books, 1570–1800*, 1931, containing a wealth of biographical and bibliographical detail; and M. L. Clarke, *Greek Studies in England 1700–1830*, 1945.

7. THE ARTS

Of overall importance is J. W. Draper's *Eighteenth Century English Aesthetics. A Bibliography*, Heidelberg, 1951, usefully supplemented by W. D. Templeman's 'Contributions to the Bibliography of Eighteenth Century Aesthetics', *MP* xxx, 1933. For general framework see B. Bosanquet, *A History of Aesthetic*, 1892; B. S. Allen, *Tides in English Taste, 1619–1800*, 2 vols., Cambridge, Mass., 1937; with which may be consulted, *The Artist; a Collection of Essays on Painting, Poetry, Sculpture, Architecture and the Drama*, ed. Prince Hoare, 1810; A. Cunningham, *The Lives of the Most Eminent British Painters, Sculptors and*

Architects, 6 vols., 1829–33; rev. ed. 3 vols., 1879–80; and *A Calendar of English Taste*, ed. E. F. Carritt, 1949. (The Picturesque, which developed later, is omitted here.)

In architecture, the grand production of the period was the superbly illustrated *Vitruvius Britannicus; or, the British Architect*, 3 vols., 1717–25. Architectural change in general is covered by: R. Blomfield, *A History of Renaissance Architecture in England, 1500–1800*, 2 vols., 1897; J. N. Summerson, *Architecture in Britain, 1530–1830*, Pelican, 1953; G. Scott, *The Architecture of Humanism*, 1914; and A. E. Richardson, *An Introduction to Georgian Architecture*, 1949. More concentrated studies are: B. Little, *The Building of Bath*, 1947; J. N. Summerson, *Sir Christopher Wren*, 1953; M. Jourdain, *The Work of William Kent*, 1948; and C. Barman, *Sir John Vanbrugh*, 1924. The private house is treated of by J. A. Gotch, *The English Home from Charles I to George IV*, 1918; and H. A. Tipping, *English Homes*, Periods IV–V, 1921–6. Its appurtenances are considered in M. Jourdain, *English Interior Decoration, 1500–1830*, 1950; and F. Lenygon in *Decoration in England, 1640–1760*, rev. ed., 1927, and *Furniture in England, 1660–1760*, 1920. Church architecture may be studied in M. Whiffen, *Stuart and Georgian Churches*, 1948, and one aspect of sculpture in K. A. Esdaile's two books, *English Monumental Sculpture*, 1927, and *English Church Monuments*, 1946.

An interesting contemporary item in music is R. North's *The Musicall Grammarian*, ed. H. Andrews, 1925. General histories include: E. W. Hadow, *The Oxford History of Music*, 6 vols., 1901–5, iii and iv; and E. Walker, *A History of Music in England*, 1907. G. Grove's *Dictionary of Music and Musicians*, 5th ed. by E. Blom, 1954, gives details of individual musicians. Relevant articles are: S. A. E. Betz, 'The Operatic Criticism of the "Tatler" and "Spectator"', *Musical Quart.* xxxi, 1945; and H. M. Schueller, 'Literature and Music as Sister Arts: an Aspect of Aesthetic Theory in Eighteenth-Century Britain', *PQ* xxvi, 1947; and 'The Use and Decorum of Music as Described in British Literature, 1700–1800', *JHI* xiii, 1952.

The most interesting work by a practising painter before W. Hogarth's *Analysis of Beauty*, 1753, is J. Richardson's *Essays on the Theory of Painting*, 1715. *The Vertue Notebooks* of G. Vertue, ed. K. A. Esdaile, 1930–57, were largely made use of by Horace Walpole in his famous *Anecdotes of Painting in England*, 4 vols., 1762–80; reprinted 5 vols., 1888. A work to the purpose here is C. R. Grundy's *English Art in the Eighteenth Century*, 1928, to which the relevant part of E. K. Waterhouse's *Painting in Britain, 1530–1790*, Pelican, 1953, may be added. More special studies are: E. W. Manwaring, *Italian Landscape in Eighteenth-century England*, N.Y., 1925; and B. Taylor's *Animal Painting in England*, Pelican, 1955. *The Rule of Taste from George I to George IV*, by J. Steegman, 1936, may be supplemented by C. B. Tinker's *Painter and Poet: Studies in the Literary Relations of English Painting*, Cambridge, Mass., 1938.

VI. INDIVIDUAL AUTHORS

ADDISON, JOSEPH, 1672–1719

The 1689 collection, *Vota Oxoniensia Pro Guilhelmo Rege*, contained Addison's first poem, 'Inauguratio Regis'. His first English poem, 'To Mr Dryden', appeared in Dryden's third Miscellany, *Examen Poeticum*, 1693. The next year's *Annual Miscellany* contained his translation of the fourth *Georgic*, 'A Song for St. Cecilia's Day', and other items. 'A Poem to his Majesty, presented to the Lord Keeper' was separately printed in 1695. *Poetical Miscellanies: The Fifth Part*, of 1704 presented 'A Letter from Italy to Lord Hallifax' (separately printed without authority in 1709); and *The Campaign* appeared in 1705. His other verses occur either as prologues or epilogues, or in his periodicals.

The Poetical Works of the Right Hon. Joseph Addison, Esq., Glasgow, 1750, heralded three further Glasgow editions, in 1751, 1760, and 1770. In 1773 Addison's verse was printed in vol. xxiii of *The British Poets* (Edinburgh). See also *Johnson* xxiii; *Anderson* vii; and *Chalmers* ix.

Rosamond. An Opera appeared on the stage and in print in 1707, as did *Cato. A Tragedy* in 1713. *The Drummer, or, the Haunted House*, anonymously produced in 1716, was printed that year with a brief Preface by Steele. The 1722 edition contained Steele's full Preface.

The Dramatic Works were published at Glasgow in 1750.

Addison contributed 46 numbers to the *Tatler. By Isaac Bickerstaff Esq.*, from 12 Apr. 1709 to 2 Jan. 1711. He wrote the 5 numbers of the *Whig Examiner*, 14 Sept.–12 Oct. 1710; 274 numbers, over the initial C. L. I. or O. of the *Spec-*

tator, which ran from 1 Mar. 1711 to 6 Dec. 1712; and 24 numbers of vol. viii, which ran from 18 June to 29 Sept. 1714. He also contributed 51 numbers to the *Guardian*, 12 Mar.–1 Oct. 1713; numbers 10 and 39 to the *Lover. By Marmaduke Myrtle, Gent.*; numbers 3 and 4 to the *Reader* (for these see under Steele). He entirely wrote the *Free-Holder, or Political Essays*, 55 numbers from 23 Dec. 1715 to 29 June 1716; and the 2 numbers of the *Old Whig*, 1719. This last was reprinted by Nichols in *The Lover and Reader*, 1789. For this, and first collected editions, see under Steele.

Addison's other main works consist of: *Nova Philosophia Veteri Præferenda*, 1693; 'An Essay on Virgil's Georgics' in Dryden's translation *The Works of Virgil*, 1697; *Remarks on Several Parts of Italy*, &c., 1705 (revised 1718); political pamphlets, *The Present State of the War*, &c., 1708; and *The Late Tryal and Conviction of Count Tariff*, 1713. There appeared posthumously in Tickell's edition (see below), *Dialogues upon the Usefulness of Ancient Medals*, and *The Evidences of the Christian Religion*, which latter was republished with considerable additions in 1730. *A Discourse on Ancient and Modern Learning*, 'prepared and corrected by himself', was published at Glasgow, 1739.

Addison's letters began to appear in the 1735 edition of Pope's letters; the next addition of any bulk was *The Correspondence of John Hughes and Mr. Addison*, 1773. They were not all collected until 1941 when W. Graham produced the definitive *The Letters of Joseph Addison*, which contains more than three and a half times the number printed by Bohn in vols. v and vi of *British Classics*.

The Works of the Right Honourable Joseph Addison, Esq., edited by T. Tickell, appeared in 4 vols. in 1721. *The Miscellaneous Works in Verse and Prose*, &c., was published in 3 vols. in 1726, often reprinted. The 2-vol. edition by A. C. Guthkelch, 1914, adds some Poems and Poemata, and Latin prose works, not included by Tickell, adds the plays, but excludes the periodical essays.

A bibliography of Addison's works by C. N. Greenhough may be found in *Selections from the Writings of Joseph Addison*, edited by B. Wendell and C. N. Greenhough, Boston, 1905, pp. xlvii–lxi.

Memoirs of the Life of the Rt. Hon. J. Addison, with an Account of

his Writings, 1719, a Grub Street affair, preceded the authoritative Preface that Tickell wrote for his 1721 edition of the *Works*.
He is treated of by Steele in *Jacob*, 1724; in *Cibber*, vol.
iii, 1753; in *Kippis*, i; and in *Johnson*. Full scale biographies are:
Nathaniel Ogle, *The Life of Addison*, 1826; Lucy Aikin, *The
Life of Joseph Addison*, 2 vols., 1843; W. J. Courthope, *Addison*,
1884 (English Men of Letters), and finally *The Life of Joseph
Addison* by P. Smithers, 1954, the most scholarly and thorough
of all as regards biography. Long essays, to a greater or lesser
degree biographical, are to be found in Macaulay's *Essays*,
1843, 'The Life and Writings of Addison' being prompted by
Lucy Aikin's *Life*; in A. Beljame (p. 591), 1948; in *Essays in
Biography, 1680–1726*, by B. Dobrée, 1925; and in J. R. Sutherland's *Background for Queen Anne*, 1939, 'The Last Years of
Addison'.

Criticism, laudatory and adverse, began early, with on the
one hand Gay's *The Present State of Wit*, and on the other
Dennis's *Essays upon Shakespear: with some Letters to the Spectator*,
1712, and *Remarks upon Cato, a Tragedy*, 1713. After Johnson's,
the first detailed criticism was that of T. Tyers in *An Historical
Essay upon Mr Addison*, 1783. He is treated of in Hazlitt's
Lectures on the English Comic Writers, 1819; and in Thackeray's
The English Humourists of the Eighteenth Century, 1853.

More specialized studies are: H. Blair, *Lectures on Rhetoric and
Belles Lettres*, 2 vols., 1783; C. de W. Thorpe, 'Addison and
Hutcheson on the Imagination', *ELH* ii, 1935; C. S. Lewis,
'Addison' in *Essays on the Eighteenth Century presented to David
Nichol Smith*, 1945; J. Lannering, *Studies in the Prose Style of
Addison*, Upsala, 1951; and C. D. Thorpe, 'Addison's Contri-
bution to Criticism' in *The Seventeenth Century: Studies by R. F.
Jones and Others in his Honor*, Palo Alto, 1951.

ARBUTHNOT, JOHN, 1667–1735

Arbuthnot's scientific and medical works need not be noted
here. He comes into purview in 1712, with various works all
published in that year anon. at Edinburgh. The abbrevi-
ated titles are: *Law is a Bottomless Pit; John Bull in his Senses;
John Bull still in his Senses; An Appendix to John Bull still
in his Senses*; and *Lewis Baboon turned Honest, and John Bull
Politician*, which were gathered together under the title of
The History of John Bull, and followed by *Proposals for Printing a*

very curious Discourse in Two Volumes in Quarto, entitled ΨΕΥ-
ΔΟΛΟΓΊΑ ΠΟΛΙΤΙΚΗ'; *or A Treatise of the Art of Political
Lying.* In 1722 he published *Annus Mirabilis; or the Wonderful
Effects of the Approaching Conjunction of the Planets Jupiter, Mars,
and Saturn. By Abraham Gunter, Philomath.* He wrote at least the
earlier parts of *It Cannot Rain but it Pours; Or, London strow'd
with Rarities*, &c., 1726, still anonymously.

He probably contributed to the *Craftsman* in 1726–7, and
certainly to the notes in *The Dunciad Variorum* of 1729. To
vol. iii of the Pope–Swift *Miscellanies* he contributed *An Essay
of the Learned Martinus Scriblerus concerning the Origin of Sciences* in
1732, and probably wrote a good deal of Pope's volume, 1741
(see under Pope).

His only poem of note is ΓΝΩΘΙ ΣΕ'ΑΥΤΟΝ. *Know Yourself.
A Poem*, published anonymously in 1734. A great number of
works is attributed to him (see *CBEL* ii. 579 seq.).

His *Miscellanies in Prose and Verse* appeared in 4 vols., 1727–
32, with a Preface by Swift and Pope. *A Supplement to Dr. Swift's
and Mr. Pope's Works, Now first Collected into one Volume*, Dublin,
1739, contains many pieces by Arbuthnot. *The Miscellaneous
Works of the late Dr. Arbuthnot*, 2 vols., Glasgow, 1751, was followed by a corrected *Miscellanies in Prose and Verse, by Dr.
Arbuthnot*, Glasgow, 1766. G. A. Aitken's *Life and Works*, 1892,
contains the chief satirical pieces, and an excellent bibliography.

His letters remain uncollected, but appear in many places
(see *CBEL* ii. 580).

Early criticism of Arbuthnot is of the contemporary sportive
kind. The first serious study occurs in *Kippis*, i, 1778. The best
and still definitive large work is Aitken (*supra*). H. Teerink
investigates the composition, publication, and authorship of the
'John Bull' writings in *The History of John Bull, for the First
Time faithfully re-issued from the Original Pamphlets, 1712*, Amsterdam, 1925. The latest full work is L. M. Beattie's *John Arbuthnot,
Mathematician and Satirist*, Cambridge, Mass., 1935.

BAKER, HENRY, 1698–1774

His scientific works will not be included here. His poetical
works begin with *An Invocation to Health. A Poem*, 1723. This he
followed with *Original Poems: serious and humorous* in 1725, to
which he added *Second Part of Original Poems* in 1726. *The*

Universe. A Poem intended to restrain the Pride of Man, appeared *c.* 1734.

He also wrote *The Universal Spectator. By Henry Stonecastle*, which, originally issued periodically from 12 Oct. 1728 to 22 Feb. 1746 (907 numbers), was collected in 4 vols., 1747. With James Miller he translated *The Works of Molière*, 8 vols., 1739, now available in *EL*; and he edited *Medulla Poetarum Romanorum: or the most beautiful and instructive Passages of the Roman-Poets with translations in English Verse*, 2 vols., 1737.

BANKS, or BANCKS, JOHN, 1709–51

The second volume of his *Miscellaneous Works*, 2 vols., 1738, has as Preface 'A Discourse Concerning Language, Especially the English'. A writer of histories, his *Short Critical Review of Oliver Cromwell*, 1739, was the most often reprinted. He edited the works of Prior, q.v.

BERKELEY, GEORGE, 1685–1753.

Berkeley's early mathematical works, in Latin, were published in Dublin in 1707. His most important work in this field, *De Motu: sive de Motus principio et Natura, et de Causa communicationis Motuum*, appeared in 1721; *The Analyst; or a Discourse addressed to an Infidel Mathematician* in 1734; and *A Defence of Free-Thinking in Mathematics* in 1735.

His first philosophical work, *An Essay Towards a New Theory of Vision*, was published in Dublin in 1709; and in 1710, also in Dublin, *A Treatise Concerning the Principles of Human Knowledge*, followed by *Three Dialogues between Hylas and Philonous*, 1713. *Alciphron: or, The Minute Philosopher. In Seven Dialogues*, 2 vols., appeared in 1732, and in the next year *The Theory of Vision, or Visual Language, shewing the Immediate Presence and Providence of a Deity, Vindicated and Explained*. His first tar-water essay, *A Chain of Philosophical Reflexions and Inquiries Concerning the Uses of Tar-Water*, 1744, was renamed as *Siris: A Chain, &c.*, and printed in Dublin in the same year. His last was *Farther Thoughts on Tar-Water*, published in the *Miscellany* of 1752.

His socio-political works begin with *Passive Obedience, or, the Christian Doctrine Of Not Resisting the Supreme Power, Proved and Vindicated upon the Principles of the Law of Nature*, 1712. *An Essay Towards Preventing the Ruin of Great Britain* was published in 1721; and in 1725 *A Proposal for the better Supplying of Churches in our Foreign Plantations, and for Converting the Savage Americans to Christianity. By a College to be erected in the Summer Islands, otherwise called the Isles of Bermudas,* followed up in 1732 with *A Sermon Preached before the Incorporated Society for the Propagation of the Gospel in Foreign Parts.* His more directly political and economic publications began with *A Discourse addressed to Magistrates and Men in Authority,* Dublin, 1732, followed by *The Querist, containing Several Queries, Proposed to the Consideration of the Public,* which appeared in Dublin in 3 parts, 1735–7. He pleaded with the Roman Catholic clergy in two essays: *A Letter to the Roman Catholics of the Diocese of Cloyne,* published in 1745 in connexion with the rebellion; and *A Word to the Wise: or, An Exhortation to the Roman Catholic Clergy of Ireland* in 1749. *Maxims Concerning Patriotism. By a Lady,* Dublin, 1750, differs slightly from the text Berkeley published in *A Miscellany,* Dublin, 1752. The *Commonplace Book,* which was first printed in Fraser's edition (see below), was first published separately, ed. G. A. Johnston, 1930, as *Berkeley's Commonplace Book,* and again, ed. A. A. Luce, 1944, as *Philosophical Commentaries, Generally called 'the Commonplace Book'.*

The first collected edition, *The Works. To which is added a Life and several letters to T. Prior, Dean Gervais, and Mr Pope,* was published, probably by Joseph Stock, 2 vols., Dublin, 1784, and 3 vols., 1820, Stock having previously in 1776 published a memoir, which was reprinted in *Kippis,* ii, 1780. *The Works* were ed. G. N. Wright, 2 vols., 1843; but the standard edition for a long time was *The Works of George Berkeley, formerly Bishop of Cloyne, Including Many of his Writings hitherto unpublished. With Prefaces, Annotations, His Life and Letters, and an Account of his Philosophy* by A. C. Fraser, 4 vols., 1871, revised 1901. George Sampson published *The Works,* 3 vols., 1897–8; but all these have been superseded by the edition by A. A. Luce and T. E. Jessop, Edinburgh, 9 vols., 1948–57.

Useful introductions are: *Selections from Berkeley,* ed. A. C. Fraser, 1874 (often reprinted); and *Berkeley: Philosophical Writings,* selected T. E. Jessop, 1952.

The only separate collection of letters is by Benjamin Rand, *Berkeley and Percival. The Correspondence of George Berkeley afterwards Bishop of Cloyne and Sir John Percival afterwards Earl of Egmont,* 1914, a main biographical source.

Mind xli, 1932, contains a catalogue of his library by R. I. Aaron.

See also *A Bibliography of George Berkeley* by H. R. Mead, Berkeley, 1910; and T. E. Jessop, *A Bibliography of George Berkeley. With an Inventory of Berkeley's Manuscript Remains* by A. A. Luce, 1934, which is supplemented by J. Lameere *et al.* in *Revue internationale de philosophie* vii, 1953. An interesting item is the *Catalogue of Manuscript Books and Berkeleiana* printed for Trinity College, Dublin, 1953.

The first Life after Stocks's memoir (see above) was J. N. Norton's *Life of Bishop Berkeley*, 1861; this was followed by A. C. Fraser's *Berkeley* in 1881. There have been others, but the standard one is that by A. A. Luce, *The Life of Berkeley*, Edinburgh, 1949.

Special studies, of which there are many, begin with A. Joussain, *Critique de la Philosophie de Berkeley*, Paris, 1920; A. Levi, *La Filosofia di Giorgio Berkeley*, Turin, 1922; A. J. Balfour's *Essays and Addresses*, 1893, in 1894 he was treated of by T. H. Huxley in *Hume, with Aids to the Study of Berkeley*. Other works are: R. Metz, *George Berkeley, Leben und Lehre*, Stuttgart, 1925; J. M. Hone and M. M. Rossi, *Bishop Berkeley, his Life, Writings and Philosophy*, 1931; M. M. Rossi, *Saggio sul rimorso*, Turin, 1933; C. D. Broad, *Berkeley's Argument about Material Substance*, 1942; N. Baladi, *La Pensée religieuse de Berkeley et l'unité de sa philosophie*, Cairo, 1945; G. J. Warnock, *Berkeley*, 1953, Pelican. A. A. Luce has further contributed *Berkeley and Malebranche*, 1934, and *Berkeley's Immaterialism: a Commentary on his 'A Treatise'*, &c., Edinburgh, 1945, besides a number of essays in *Hermathena* and *Mind*. Other essays include: T. E. Jessop, 'Berkeley', *Philosophy* xii, 1937; and *'L'esse est percipi de Berkeley'*, *Revue philosophique* cxliii, 1953; E. D. Leyburn, 'The Querist', *Proc. Royal Irish Acad.* xliv, 1937, announcing a forgotten pamphlet; J. Johnston, 'A Synopsis of Berkeley's Monetary Philosophy', *Hermathena* lv, 1940; C. Lehec, 'Trente années d'études Berkeleyennes', *Revue philosophique* cxliii, 1953. The whole number of *Hermathena* lxxxii, 1953, is devoted to addresses on Berkeley delivered at the bicentenary celebrations at Dublin in that year.

BLACKMORE, SIR RICHARD, *c.* 1650–1729

Blackmore's literary works, so to exclude his medical and political writings, opened with *Prince Arthur: An Heroic Poem*, 1695, with a Preface reprinted in vol. iii of J. E. Spingarn's

Critical Essays of the Seventeenth Century, 1909. His second epic, *King Arthur: An Heroick Poem*, followed in 1697. Early in 1700 he published *A Satyr against Wit*, which was taken up in March of that year by a number of writers in *Commendatory Verses, on the Author of the Two Arthurs, and the Satyr against Wit*, which was retorted to a month later by Blackmore in *Discommendatory Verses, on Those Which are Truly Commendatory, on the Author of the Two Arthurs, and the Satyr against Wit*. (For the last two see *Sir Richard Blackmore and the Wits*, by R. C. Boys, University of Michigan Press, being Number 13 of *Contributions in Modern Philology*, June 1949: this reprints, with critical apparatus, the verses of the attackers and Blackmore's retorts.) *A Paraphrase on the Book of Job*, &c., appeared in the same year. *A Hymn to the Light of the World, with a short description of the Cartoons of Raphael Urbin, in the Gallery at Hampton Court* appeared in 1703. His next heroic poem, *Eliza: an Epick Poem*, was published in 1705. *Advice to the Poets. A Poem. Occasioned by the Wonderful Success of her Majesty's Arms in Flanders*, 1706, was immediately followed by another edition 'corrected'. Two lighter pieces then appeared: *The Kit-Cats. A Poem*, 1708, and *Instructions to Vander Bank. A Sequel to the Advice to the Poets*, 1709. After these, two more portentous works appeared: *The Nature of Man: A Poem, in Three Books*, 1711, and *Creation: A Philosophical Poem, in Seven Books*, 1712. (The last may be found in *Johnson* xxiv, *Anderson* vi, and *Chalmers* x.) He published further: *A Collection of Poems on Various Subjects*, 1718; *A New Version of the Psalms of David*, 1721; *Redemption. A Divine Poem, in Six Books. To which is added a Hymn to Christ the Redeemer*, 1722; and *Alfred. An Epick Poem*, 1723.

The Lay Monastery, 1714, contains his essays in the tri-weekly periodical, the *Lay Monk*, which he issued with John Hughes from 16 Nov. 1713, to 15 Feb. 1714. He also published *Essays upon Several Subjects*, 1716, including 'An Essay upon Epic Poetry'. *The Accomplished Preacher; or an Essay on Divine Eloquence*, was edited by J. White, and published in 1731. His *Essay on Wit*, 1716, was edited by R. C. Boys, Ann Arbor, 1946, Augustan Reprint Society.

For contemporary comment see *Jacob*. A Life is to be found in *Johnson*, and in A. Rosenberg, *Sir Richard Blackmore*, Lincoln, Nebraska, 1953. He is treated of at some length in Scott's *Dryden*.

Other studies include: O. Liss, *Die Arthurepen des Sir Richard Blackmore*, Strasburg, 1911; B. Boyce, '"The Dispensary", Blackmore and the Captain of the Wits', *RES* xiv, 1938; L. Douglas, 'A Severe Animadversion on Bossu', *PMLA* lxii, 1947 (Blackmore as the butt of Pope's 'Receipt to Make an Epic Poem'); J. R. Moore, 'Gay's Burlesque of Blackmore's Poetry', *JEGP* l, 1951.

BOLINGBROKE, HENRY ST. JOHN, VISCOUNT, 1678–1751

Much of Bolingbroke's writing is political journalism, beginning in 1710 with *A Letter to the Examiner* (anon.), continuing from 1726 onwards in the *Craftsman*, under the pseudonym of Caleb D'Anvers. His most important contributions were gathered in the volumes *A Dissertation upon Parties*, 1735 (anon.), and *Remarks on the History of England. From the Minutes of Humphrey Oldcastle*, 1743. Anonymous also was *Letters on the Spirit of Patriotism: On the Idea of a Patriot King: and On the State of Parties*, 1749. This was followed in 1752 by *Letters on the Study and Use of History*, which also contained the letters headed 'A Sketch of the History and State of Europe' and 'Of the True Use of Retirement and Study', and the 'Reflections upon Exile'. In the same year there appeared in Edinburgh *Letters on the Study and Use of History. To which are added Two other Letters*, namely the material noted above, in 2 vols. *Reflections concerning Innate Moral Principles. Written in French* was also published in 1752, in both French and English; and in 1753 there appeared *A Letter to Sir William Windham. II. Some Reflections on the Present State of the Nation. III. A Letter to Mr. Pope*.

Letters and Correspondence, public and private, during the time he was Secretary of State to Queen Anne, were edited by G. Parke in 1798, 2 vols. 4to and 4 vols. 8vo. In 1817 R. Warner printed *Original Letters from Bolingbroke*. P. Baratier edited *Lettres inédites de Bolingbroke à Lord Stair, 1716–1720*, Trévoux, 1939.

David Mallet edited *Works*, 5 vols., 1754, often reprinted with various additions until it appeared in 11 vols., 1786.

Early criticism is that of W. Warburton in *A Letter to the Editor of the Letters on the Spirit of Patriotism*, 1749, anon. as were other contemporary writings: *An Examination of Lord Bolingbroke's Letters on History*, 2nd ed., 1753; *Some Remarks on the Famous Letter to Sir William Windham*, 1753 (by Philalethes); *Critical Remarks upon Letters on the Study and Use of History*, 1754;

and *The Freethinker's Criteria Exemplified*, &c., 1755 (by Philologus Cantabrigiensis).

The first full-length study was made by G. W. Cooke, *Memoirs of Lord Bolingbroke*, 2 vols., 1835. Subsequent ones include those by: R. Harrop, 1884; A. Hassall, 1889; W. Sichel, 1901, followed up with *A Sequel*, 1902, which contains a bibliography; C. Petrie, 1937. Other studies in book form have been critical rather than biographical: P. Baratier, *Bolingbroke; ses écrits politiques*, Paris, 1939; W. M. Merrill, *From Statesman to Philosopher: a Study in Bolingbroke's Deism*, New York, 1949; and D. G. James, *The Life of Reason: Hobbes, Locke, Bolingbroke*, 1949.

Shorter studies are: W. Bagehot, 1863, in *Biographical Studies*, ed. R. B. Hutton, 1880; C. Whibley in *The Criterion*, i, nos. 3 and 4, April and July 1923; articles by H. N. Fieldhouse in *EHR* lii, 1937; and in *History* xxiii, 1938; C. Petrie, 'Bolingbroke and his Influence on English Politics', *Quart. Rev.* cclxxxix, 1951.

BOYER, ABEL, 1667–1729

Boyer wrote a number of educational works, some on the learning of French, to which he added a French-English Dictionary, some on manners, and a number of translations, largely educational. His most important work lies in his historical books, beginning with *The History of King William III*, 3 vols., 1702–3. His *The History of the Reign of Queen Anne, Digested into Annals*, was published from 1703 to 1713, making 11 vols. He published *The History of the Life and Reign of Queen Anne* in 1722. From 1705 to 1709 Boyer edited *The Post Boy* and from 1711 to 1729 was responsible for *The Political State of Great Britain*, which had achieved 60 vols. when it was discontinued in 1740. In 1714 he issued *Memoirs of the Life and Negotiations of Sir W. Temple*. A second edition of *A Compleat and Impartial History of the Impeachments of the Last Ministry* appeared in 1716, followed in 1717 by *An Impartial History of the Occasional Conformity and Schism Bills*. Various other political tracts came from his pen.

BOYSE, SAMUEL, 1708–49

Both *Translations and Poems Written on Several Subjects*, 1731, and *Verses occasioned by seeing the Palace and Park of Dalkeith*, 1732, were published in Edinburgh. Other poems of interest are: *The Olive: an Ode Occasion'd by the auspicious Success of His Majesty's Counsels, in the Stanza of Spenser*, 1737; *Deity*, 1739; and *Albion's Triumph*, 1743. See *Anderson* x; and *Chalmers* xiv.

His prose works comprise: *An Historical Review of the Transactions of Europe* . . . *1739* . . . *1745*, 2 vols., 1747; *Impartial History of the late Rebellion in 1745 from Authentic Memoirs*, &c., 1748; and *A New Pantheon, or Fabulous History of the Heathen Gods*, 1753.

He is treated in *Cibber*, v, 1753, and *Kippis*, ii, 1780. 'Boyse's Albion's Triumph' is discussed by R. H. Griffith in *Texas University Studies* xiii, 1933.

BRAMSTON, JAMES, *c.* 1694–1744

Bramston's two earliest works were first published anonymously: *The Art of Politicks, in Imitation of Horace's Art of Poetry* in 1729; and *The Man of Taste. Occasion'd by an Epistle of Mr Pope's On that Subject* in 1733. *The Crooked Sixpence* appeared in 1743.

BROOKE, HENRY, *c.* 1703–83

His works to be noted for this period are: *Universal Beauty. A Poem* (6 pts.), 1735; his translation *Tasso's Jerusalem, an Epic Poem*, 1738 [Books I and II only]; and his version of 'The Man of Lawe's Tale' in Ogle's *The Canterbury Tales of Chaucer, Modernis'd by several hands*, 1741.

The Poetical Works of Henry Brooke Esq., Revised and corrected, with his life by Charlotte Brooke, was published in Dublin, 4 vols., 1792.

His plays consist of *Gustavus Vasa, The Deliverer of His Country, As it was to have been Acted at the Theatre-Royal in Drury Lane*, 1739, acted as *The Patriot* at Smock Alley in Dublin in 1744; and *The Earl of Essex*, acted in Dublin in 1750, published in London and Dublin, 1761. *A Collection of Plays and Poems* appeared in 4 vols., 1778.

He published a considerable number of other works, largely dealing with Dublin; see the Bibliography of the next volume.

In 1804 C. H. Wilson published *Brookiana. Anecdotes of Henry Brooke*, 2 vols.; and in 1816 Isaac D'Olier produced at Dublin *Memoirs of the Life of the Late Excellent and Pious Mr Henry Brooke*. The latest biography is that by H. M. Scurr, *Henry Brooke*, Minneapolis, 1927.

Special studies include: R. S. Brooke, 'Henry Brooke',

Dublin University Magazine, Feb. 1852; H. Wright, 'Henry Brooke's Gustavus Vasa', *MLR* xiv, 1919; H. M. Stevenson, 'Brooke's Universal Beauty and Modern Thought', *PMLA* xliii, 1928; and E. Gillett, 'The Fool of Quality' [1764–70], *London Mercury* xxx, 1934.

BROOME, WILLIAM, 1689–1745

Broome published occasionally in Miscellanies from 1714; his *Poems on Several Occasions,* with a critical preface of his own, were collected in 1727, an enlarged edition following in 1739. He collaborated with Oldisworth and Ozell in a prose translation from the French of the *Iliad,* 5 vols., 1712; and one in blank verse from the Greek in 1714. He contributed eight Books to Pope's *Odyssey,* viz. ii, vi, viii, xi, xii, xvi, xviii, xxiii. See *Johnson* xliii (with Life); *Anderson* viii; *Chalmers* xii. See *Memoirs of Broome with a selection from his Works,* by T. W. Barlow, 1885.

BROWNE, ISAAC HAWKINS, 1705–60

His first work, *The Fire-Side: a Pastoral Soliloquy,* probably 1735, was followed by *Of Smoking. Four Poems in Praise of Tobacco* in 1736, a pirated part-version of *A Pipe of Tobacco* published in the same year. This was edited by H. F. B. Brett-Smith in 1923. *De Animi Immortalitate. Poema,* 1754, was translated in the same year by William Hay, and by Richard Grey; and in 1765 by J. Cranwell.

Poems upon Various Subjects, Latin and English, which includes the above, was published by his son in 1768.

BROWNE, MOSES, 1704–87

He began in 1721 with *The Throne of Justice, a Pindaric Ode,* and in 1722 he published *The Richmond Beauties,* which contains three other poems, two of them by Browne. *Piscatory Eclogues,* 1729, was renamed *Angling Sports* in the third edition of 1773. *Poems on Various Subjects Many never printed before* appeared in 1739; and *Percy-Lodge, a descriptive poem* in 1755.

In 1723 he published *Polidus or Distress'd Love, A Tragedy. With a Farce call'd All Bedevil'd or the House in a Hurry;* and in 1750 he edited *The Compleat Angler* by Cotton and Walton.

He also produced two religious works, the more important of which is *The Universe,* &c., 1752; and some sermons.

See further: E. R. Wasserman: 'Browne, and the 1783 Edition of Giles and Phineas Fletcher', *MLN* lvi, 1941.

BROWNE, PETER, *c.* 1665–1735

His writings consist of: *Letter in answer to a Book entitled Christianity not Mysterious*, 1699; *Procedure, Extent and Limits of the Human Understanding*, 1728; and *Things Divine and Supernatural conceived by Analogy with Things Natural and Human*, 1733.

BURNABY, WILLIAM, *c.* 1672–1706

Burnaby, whose plays were unsuccessful, was responsible for: *The Reform'd Wife*, 1700; *The Ladies Visiting Day*, 1701; *The Modish Husband*, 1702; and *Love Betray'd: or, The Agreeable Disappointment*, 1703, all printed in the year of their performance, and all anon., causing his work to be ascribed to his brother Charles. They are collected in *The Dramatic Works*, ed. F. E. Budd, 1931, with a biographical, bibliographical, and critical Introduction.

In 1694 he and 'another Hand' produced a translation of the *Satyricon* of Petronius. See *Jacob, Genest, Whincop*, and *Nicoll*.

BUTLER, JOSEPH, 1692–1752

Fifteen Sermons preached at the Chapel of the Rolls Court, 1726, was augmented in the 1749 edition by six sermons preached on public occasions. These were published 1765 in 2 vols. corrected, 1769, &c., and were ed. W. R. Matthews in 1914. *The Analogy of Religion, Natural and Revealed, to the Constitution and Course of Nature*, was published in 1736, and 'corrected' in the same year. It was ed. H. Morley in 1884, and by R. Bayne *EL* 1906, *WC* 1907. *Some Remains (hitherto unpublished) of Bishop Butler* were gathered by E. Steere in 1853.

The *Works* were ed. S. Halifax, 2 vols., Edinburgh, 1804; by W. E. Gladstone, 2 vols., in 1896, added to by *Studies Subsidiary* in 1897; and by J. H. Bernard, 2 vols., in 1900.

Butler appears in *Kippis*, 1753, but there is no adequate Life, the only approach being that by Thomas Bartlett, 1839. Some added information is given in *Stanhope Memorials of Bishop Butler*, by W. M. Egglestone, 1878.

Discussion of his philosophy may be found in Sir J. Mackintosh's *On the Progress of Ethical Philosophy during the XVIIth and XVIIIth Centuries*, 1830 (revised 1872); Sir J. Napier's *Lectures on Butler's Analogy*, 1864; W. Bagehot's 'Bishop Butler' (reviewing Steere) in *The Prospective Review*, Oct. 1854, reprinted in *Literary Studies*, iii, 1895; J. F. D. Maurice, *The Conscience*, 1872; Leslie Stephen, *English Thought in the Eighteenth Century*, 1876; J. R. J. Eaton, *Bishop Butler and his Critics*, 1878. Matthew Arnold's 'Bishop Butler and the Zeitgeist' appeared in *Last Essays on Church and Religion*, 1877.

See C. D. Broad, *Five Types of Ethical Theory*, 1930; E. C. Mossner, *Bishop Butler and the Age of Reason*, 1936; and A. Duncan-Jones, *Butler's Moral Philosophy*, 1952, Pelican. Of interest is A. E. Taylor's 'Some Features of Butler's Ethics', *Mind* xxxv, 1926.

BYROM, JOHN, 1692–1763

A Pastoral appeared in the *Spectator* of 6 Oct. 1714. Among separate publications were *An Epistle to a gentleman of the Temple*, 1749; and *Enthusiasm; a Poetical Essay*, 1751: but the bulk of his work appeared in *Miscellaneous Poems*, 2 vols., 1773, and again, edited by J. Nichols, in 1814. In 1774 Francis Okely collected his *Seasonable, Alarming, and Humiliating Truths*, versifications of passages from William Law.

The Poems of John Byrom were edited by A. W. Ward, 2 vols., Chetham Society, 1894–5. A third volume was added in 1912. See also *Chalmers* xv.

The Private Journals and Literary Remains of John Byrom were edited by R. Parkinson, 4 vols., Chetham Society, 1854–7. *John Byrom*, a selection from his journals and papers, by Henri Talon, 1950, contains a memoir and a brief bibliography.

Lives are given by Chalmers and Nichols. He is treated of in *Byrom and the Wesleys* by the Rev. Dr. Hoole, 1864; in Leslie Stephen's *Studies of a Biographer*, vol. i, 1898; and by S. Hobhouse in *William Law and Eighteenth Century Quakerism*, 1927, which contains some fragments and letters. A catalogue of his library was published in 1848.

CAREY, HENRY, c. 1687–1743

In 1710 Carey published anon. 12 numbers of the *Records of Love, Or, Weekly Amusements for the Fair Sex*, in prose. His

Poems on Several Occasions, first printed in 1713, were enlarged for another edition in 1720, and again enlarged in 1729. *Namby-Pamby A Panegyrick on the New Versification to A[mbrose] P[hilips] Esq.* appeared anonymously in 1725; and in 1735, *Of Stage Tyrants: An Epistle*, to Chesterfield, on the rejection of *The Honest Yorkshire-man.* In 1737 there appeared the first issue of *The Musical Century, in one hundred English ballads*, with Carey's own settings. *An Ode to Mankind, Address'd to the Prince of Wales*, 1741, was the last publication during his life. In 1748 was published *Cupid and Hymen. A Voyage to the Isles of Love and Matrimony . . . In Prose and Verse . . . by the Facetious Harry Carey, and other Persons of Wit and Humour*, &c., with appendixes probably all by Carey.

In 1924 M. Gibbings edited a selection of *Songs and Poems by Henry Carey*: a full edition, produced by F. T. Wood in 1930, *The Poems of Henry Carey*, includes a biographical Introduction.

His first play, *The Contrivances; or, More Ways than One*, was acted and printed anonymously in 1715. Recast as a ballad opera, it appeared in 1729. *Hanging and Marriage; or, the Dead-Man's Wedding*, acted in 1722, became the ballad opera *Betty, or the Country Bumpkin* in 1732, the songs being printed in 1739. *Amelia. A New English Opera* was acted and printed anonymously in 1732. *The Tragedy of Chrononhotonthologos* appeared on the stage and in print in 1734; *The Honest Yorkshire-Man*, acted 1735, was printed 1736, and *The Dragon of Wantley* was acted and published 1737. His last play was *Nancy; or The Parting Lovers*, 1739. *The Dramatick Works of Henry Carey* appeared in 1743.

In 1726 he published *A Learned Dissertation on Dumpling*, &c. In 1902 W. H. Cummings treated of Carey in *God Save the King*; W. H. Hudson discussed him in *A Quiet Corner in a Library*, 1915; and his dramatic work is covered in F. W. Bateson's *English Comic Drama, 1700–1750*, 1929.

He is also to be found in musical treatises and dictionaries.

CENTLIVRE, or CARROLL, SUSANNA, *c.* 1670–1723

Of Mrs. Centlivre's nineteen plays, beginning with *The Perjur'd Husband: or, The Adventures of Venice*, 1700, the following popular ones may be picked out: *The Gamester*, 1705; *The Busie-Body*, 1709, ed. by J. Byrd, Los Angeles, 1949 (Augustan Reprint Society); *The Wonder: A Woman Keeps a Secret,*

1714; and *A Bold Stroke for a Wife*, 1718. Her last play was *The Artifice*, 1722, printed 1723. *The Gotham Election*, 1715 was unacted, and appeared as *The Humours of Elections* when reprinted in 1737.

Her four poems, written between 1713 and 1720, were included in *The Works of the celebrated Mrs Centlivre, With a New Account of her Life*, 3 vols., 1761–2, reprinted 1872 as *The Dramatic Works*.

Jacob treats of her, and she is discussed by Hazlitt in *A View of the English Stage*, 1818; and *Lectures on the English Comic Writers*, 1819; by F. Hohrmann in 'Das Verhältnis Susanne Centlivres zu Molière und Regnard' in *Zeitschrift für vergleichende Litteratur-Geschichte* xiv, 1900; and by F. W. Bateson in *English Comic Drama, 1700–1750*, 1929. Journals also contain: P. B. Anderson, 'Mrs. Centlivre and the Female Tatler', *PQ* xvi, 1937; J. R. Sutherland, 'The Progress of Error: Mrs Centlivre and the Biographers', *RES* xviii, 1942.

For bibliography see J. E. Norton, 'Some Uncollected Authors, Susanna Centlivre', in *The Book Collector*, Summer 1957, and Autumn 1957.

CHEYNE, GEORGE, 1671–1743

His *Philosophical Principles of Natural Religion*, 1705, was enlarged for the edition of 1715. *Dr. Cheyne's own Account of Himself and his Writings* appeared in 1743.

The Letters of Dr. George Cheyne to [Samuel] Richardson (1733–43) were ed. C. F. Mullett, Columbia, Missouri, 1943.

CIBBER, COLLEY, 1671–1757

Cibber wrote in all some twenty-four stage pieces, of which only the more successful will be noted here. His first play, *Love's Last Shift; or, The Fool in Fashion*, appeared in 1696, followed in the same year by *Woman's Wit: or, The Lady in Fashion*, printed 1697. His other comedies include: *Love Makes a Man; or, The Fop's Fortune*, acted 1700, published 1701; *She Wou'd and She Wou'd Not*, 1702, printed 1703; *The Careless Husband*, 1704, printed 1705; *The Double Gallant: or, The Sick Lady's Cure*, 1707; *The Non-Juror*, 1717, printed 1718; and the play concluded from Vanbrugh's manuscript, *The Provok'd Husband; or, A Journey to London*, 1728.

The Tragical History of King Richard III, acted and published

1700, was his only successful play in that form. *Ximena; or, The Heroick Daughter*, acted several times in 1712, was not published until 1719. His last theatrical piece was *Papal Tyranny in the Reign of King John*, 1745.

He also wrote masques, a popular farce, *The School-Boy: or, The Comical Rivals*, 1702, though not published until 1707, and two ballad-operas, the successful one being *Damon and Phillida*, 1729.

Plays, 10 plays, appeared in 2 vols., 1721. *The Dramatic Works*, 4 vols., 1760, contains an anonymous Life; and the ed. 5 vols., 1777, is headed with a Life by D. E. Baker.

His first published work, however, was *A Poem on the Death of Our Late Sovereign Queen Mary*, 1695. In 1731, as Poet Laureate, he produced *An Ode to His Majesty for the New Year*, and *An Ode for His Majesty's Birthday 1731*. A broadside, *The Blind Boy*, was printed *c.* 1735. *A Rhapsody upon the Marvellous: Arising from the First Odes of Horace and Pindar*, 1751, was followed by his last poem, *Verses to the Memory of Mr. Pelham*, 1754.

He published his now most famous work, *An Apology for the Life of Mr. Colley Cibber, Comedian*, first in 1740; again in 2 vols., 1750 (with Account of the English Stage and a Dialogue on Old Plays), and finally in 2 vols., 1756, with a List of Dramatic Authors. It was edited by E. Bellchambers in 1822, and by R. W. Lowe, 2 vols., 1889. It is included in *EL*. In 1742 there appeared *A Letter from Mr. Cibber to Mr. Pope. Inquiring into the Motives that might induce him in his Satyrical Works to be so frequently fond of Mr. Cibber's Name*. In 1743 there followed *A Second Letter from Mr. Cibber to Mr. Pope*, rounded off in 1744 by *Another Occasional Letter From Mr. Cibber to Mr. Pope*. Intermediately, in 1743, he had written *The Egotist: or, Colley upon Cibber*. In 1747 he published *The Character and Conduct of Cicero Considered from the History of his Life, by Dr Middleton*; and finally, in 1748, *The Lady's Lecture. A Theatrical Dialogue between Sir Charles Easy and his Marriageable Daughter*.

Jacob writes on him, but the first complete biography is that of F. D. Senior, *The Life and Times of Colley Cibber*, 1928, soon followed by R. H. Barker's *Mr Cibber of Drury Lane*, New York, 1939. He is treated of in: Thomas Davies, *Dramatic Miscellanies*, 3 vols., 1783–4; I. D' Israeli, *Quarrels of Authors*, 3 vols., 1814; Hazlitt (p. 614); E. Bernbaum, *The Drama of Sensibility*, Boston, 1915; and F. W. Bateson, *English Comic Drama, 1700–1750*, 1929.

Articles include: D. H. Miles, 'The Original of the Non-Juror', *PMLA* xxix, 1914; C. W. Nichols, 'Fielding and the Cibbers', *PQ* i, 1922; De W. C. Croissant, 'A Note on The Egotist, or Colley upon Cibber', *PQ* iii, 1924; A. C. Sprague, 'A New Scene in Colley Cibber's *Richard III*', *MLN* xlii, 1927.

CLARKE, SAMUEL, 1675-1729

His great work is composed of two courses of Boyle Lectures given in 1704–5, *A Discourse Concerning the Being and Attributes of God*, &c., published in 1705–6. *Scripture Doctrine of the Trinity* appeared in 1712, and *Seventeen Sermons* in 1724. Philosophical Transactions, No. 401, 1728, contains *A Letter to Benjamin Hoadly, F.R.S., occasioned by the controversy relating to the proportion of Velocity and Force in Bodies in Motion*.

Works, 4 vols., 1738, is prefaced with a Life by Hoadly.

He is considered by: J. E. Le Rossignol in *Ethical Philosophy of S. Clarke*, Leipzig, 1892; by G. von Leroy in *Die philosophischen Probleme in dem Briefwechsel zwischen Leibniz und Clarke*, Giessen, 1893; and by E. Albee in 'Clarke's Ethical Philosophy', *Philosophical Rev.* xxxvii, 1928.

COLLIER, JEREMY, 1650-1726

Collier's *Miscellanies*, in 2 parts, were published in 1694–5, and these were followed by *Essays upon several Moral Subjects*, in 3 parts, 1698–1705. His famous *A Short View of the Immorality and Profaneness of the English Stage: Together with the Sense of Antiquity upon this Argument* appeared in 1698, backed up in the next year by his answer to the replies of Congreve and Vanbrugh, *A Defence of the Short View*, &c., followed in 1701 by *A Second Defence*. In 1701 he published *The Great Historical, Geographical, Genealogical and Poetical Dictionary. Collected from Historians, especially L. Morery*, 2 vols., and *The Emperor Marcus Antoninus his Conversation with Himself*, a translation of the *Meditations*, praised by Matthew Arnold, together with a Life of Marcus Aurelius. In 1708 he returned to the charge against the theatre with *A Farther Vindication of the Short View*; and from 1708 to 1714 produced in 2 vols. *The Ecclesiastical History of Great Britain, chiefly of England. With a Brief Account of the Affairs of Religion in Ireland*.

For the 'Collier Controversy' see J. W. Krutch, *Comedy and Conscience after the Restoration*, New York, 1924.

COLLINS, ANTHONY, 1676–1729

His philosophic writings consist of: *Essay Concerning the use of Reason in propositions the evidence whereof depends on Human Testimony*, 1707; *Priestcraft in Perfection*, 1709; *A Discourse of Freethinking occasioned by the Rise and Growth of a Sect called Freethinkers*, 1713; *Inquiry Concerning Human Liberty and Necessity*, 1715, a theme taken up again in *Liberty and Necessity*, 1729; and *A Discourse of the Grounds and Reasons of the Christian Religion*, 1724. His contribution to literary theory is *A Discourse concerning Ridicule and Irony in Writing*, 1729.

CONGREVE, WILLIAM, 1670–1729

Except for a masque, *The Judgement of Paris*, 1701, and the opera *Semele* which was printed with his *Works* in 1710, Congreve wrote nothing for the theatre after *The Way of the World* in 1700. His writings after that date are confined to: *A Hymn to Harmony*, 1703; *The Tears of Amaryllis for Amyntas. A Pastoral*, 1703; and *A Pindarique Ode on the Victorious Progress of Her Majesties Arms*, 1706, which included his useful 'prefatory Discourse of the Pindarique Ode'. His *Works* of 1710 contains many poems on several occasions. *An Impossible Thing, A Tale*, was published in 1720; and *A Letter from Mr Congreve to the Viscount Cobham* in 1729.

A handy complete edition is that in 2 vols., WC 1925 and 1928, ed. B. Dobrée. For a full bibliography see the previous volume

CROXALL, SAMUEL, d. 1752

An Original Canto of Spencer Design'd as Part of his Fairy Queen but never printed. Now made Publick. By Nestor Ironside, 1714, was followed by *Another Original Canto of Spencer* in 1714. His best poem, *The Vision*, 1715, and *The Fair Circassian. A Dramatic Performance done from the Original by a Gentleman Commoner of Oxford*, a warm version of the Song of Solomon which appeared in 1720, together with the 'Several Occasional Poems' added in the edition of 1721 constitute his poetic contribution apart from his translations of the 6th, and parts of the 8th, 10th, 11th, and 13th books of *Ovid's Metamorphoses* in Garth's edition, 1717, &c. His chief prose works are *The Fables of Aesop and others Newly done into English with an Application to each fable*, 1722, and

Scripture Politics, 1735. He also published a number of sermons. He appears in *Jacob*, in *Kippis*, iv, 1780, and in H. de Maar's *A History of Modern English Romanticism*, 1924, vol. i. 6.

DEFOE, DANIEL, *c.* 1660–1731

Defoe's first work, in verse, *The Meditations of Daniel Defoe*, written in 1681, was first printed in 1946, ed. G. H. Healey. Other early publications were also in verse, *A New Discovery of an Old Intreague*, 1691, and *The Character of Dr Samuel Annesley* 1697. His first book was *An Essay upon Projects*, 1697, followed by the pamphlets *An Enquiry into the Occasional Conformity of Dissenters in Cases of Preferment*, 1698, *The Poor Man's Plea*, 1698, *An Argument Shewing that a Standing Army, with Consent of Parliament, is not Inconsistent with a Free Government*, 1698, and *The Two Great Questions Consider'd. I. What the French King will do, with Respect to the Spanish Monarchy. II. What Measures the English ought to Take*, 1700. *The Pacificator. A Poem*, 1700. In 1701 he published the pamphlets: *The Six Distinguishing Characters of a Parliament-Man*; *The Free-Holders Plea against Stock-Jobbing Elections of Parliament Men*; *The Villainy of Stock-Jobbers Detected*; the broadsheet *Legion's Memorial to the House of Commons*, followed by the relevant pamphlet *The History of the Kentish Petition*, having intermediately produced the verse *The True-Born Englishman. A Satyr*. In 1702 there were two verse productions: *The Mock-Mourners. A Satyr. By Way of Elegy on King William*, and *Reformation of Manners. A Satyr*; more important, *The Shortest Way with the Dissenters: Or Proposals for the Establishment of the Church*, and *A New Test of the Church of England's Loyalty*. In 1703 he brought out more verse: *Ode to the Athenian Society: More Reformation. A Satyr upon Himself. By the Author of The True-Born Englishman*, and *A Hymn to the Pillory*; and the pamphlet *The Shortest Way to Peace and Union*. Two more pamphlets distinguish the year 1704: *More Short Ways With The Dissenters*, and *Giving Alms no Charity, And Employing the Poor a Grievance to the Nation*, to which year belongs the book *The Storm: Or, A Collection of the Most Remarkable Casualties and Disasters which Happen'd in the Late Dreadful Tempest, Both by Sea and Land*. In this year also was launched *A Review of the Affairs of France: And of All Europe, as Influenced by that Nation*, which began on 19 Feb. 1704, and ran under its shortened titles until 11 June 1713. The satirical work, *The Consolidator: Or Memoirs of Sundry Transac-*

tions from the World in the Moon also appeared in 1705. Followed in 1705 the pamphlet *The Experiment: Or the Shortest Way with the Dissenters Exemplified*, and the verse *The Dyet of Poland. A Satyr.* Two books of verse appeared in the next year: *Jure Divino: A Satyr. In Twelve Books*, and *Caledonia. A Poem in Honour of Scotland, and the Scots Nation*, Edinburgh and London 1707, the notable work, however, being *A True Relation of the Apparition of One Mrs. Veal, the Next Day after Her Death, to One Mrs. Bargrave at Canterbury, the 8th of September, 1705*. The next few years are sparse: *The History of the Union of Great Britain*, Edinburgh, 1709. *The Present State of the Parties in Great Britain: Particularly an Enquiry into the State of Dissenters in England*, 1712, and *An Essay on the South-Sea Trade*, 1712. *A General History of Trade* 1713, and in that year the three ironical pamphlets: *An Answer to a Question that No Body Thinks of, viz., What if the Queen should Die?*; *Reasons Against the Succession of the House of Hanover*; and *What if the Pretender Should Come? Or some Considerations of the Advantages and Real Consequences of the Pretender's Possessing the Crown of Great Britain*. Defoe's personal political writings may be said to end with *The Secret History of the White Staff, being an Account of Affairs Under the Conduct of Some Late Ministers*, 1714; *An Appeal to Honour and Justice, Tho' it be of his Worst Enemies. By Daniel Defoe. Being a True Account of his Conduct in Publick Affairs*, 1715, and *Minutes of the Negotiations of Monsr. Mesnager, at the Court of England*, 1717.

His moralistic conduct-books can be said to begin with *The Family Instructor*, 1715; vol. ii, 1718; but for the moment there followed a spate of historical and biographical works: *The History of the Wars of His Present Majesty Charles XII King of Sweden*, 1715; *Memoirs of the Church of Scotland*, 1717; *Life and Death of Count Paktul*, 1717; *Memoirs of the Duke of Shrewsbury* 1718, and *Memoirs of Daniel Williams*, 1718. In the next year his great phase begins. *The Life and Strange Surprizing Adventures of Robinson Crusoe, of York, Mariner*, 1719 and within a few weeks, *The Farther Adventures of Robinson Crusoe*. Also in 1719, *The Anatomy of Exchange-Alley: Or a System of Stock-Jobbing*; *The Life of Baron de Goertz*; *The Dumb Philosopher; Or, Great Britain's Wonder* (Dickory Cronke); *The King of Pirates: Being an Account of the Famous Captain Avery, The Mock King of Madagascar*. In 1720 come *A Translation of Du Fresnoy's Art of Painting*, in verse, doubtfully his; *The Supernatural Philosopher; Or the Mysteries of Magick; The History of the Life and Adventures of Mr Duncan Campbell; Memoirs of a Cavalier: Or a Military Journal of the Wars in Germany, and the Wars in England; The Life, Adventures, and Pyracies of the Famous Captain Singleton;* and finally *Serious Reflections During the Life and Surprising Adventures of Robinson Crusoe: With his Visions of the Angelick World. Written by Himself.* The next year is void of anything important, but in 1722 there appeared *The Fortunes and Misfortunes of the Famous Moll Flanders; Due Preparations for the Plague;* and *A Journal of the Plague Year,* between the two last being sandwiched *Religious Courtship: Being Historical Discourses, On the Necessity of Marrying Religious Husbands and Wives only,* and finally *The History and Remarkable Life of the Truly Honourable Colonel Jacque, Commonly Call'd Col. Jack.* Followed *The History of Peter the Great,* 1723; *The Fortunate Mistress: Or a History of the Life and Vast Variety of Fortunes of Mademoiselle de Beleau, Afterwards Call'd the Countess of Wintselsheim, in Germany. Being the Person Known by the Name of the Lady Roxana, in the Time of King Charles II,* 1724; *The Great Law of Subordination Consider'd, Or the Insolence and Unsufferable Behaviour of Servants in England Duly Enquir'd into,* 1724; *A Tour Thro' the Whole Island of Great Britain. Divided into Circuits or Journies,* 1724; vol. ii, 1725; vol. iii, 1727; *A New Voyage Round the World, By a Course Never Sailed Before,* 1724; and *A Narrative of All the Robberies, Escapes, Etc., of John Sheppard,* 1724.

Defoe did not return to novel writing. In 1725 there appeared *Every-Body's Business, is No-Body's Business; Or, Private Abuses, Publick Grievances: Exemplified in the Pride, Insolence and Exorbitant Wages of Our Women-Servants, Footmen Etc.* In the next there appeared *The Complete English Tradesman* (vol. ii, 1727); otherwise 1726 produced moral or occult works: *Mere Nature Delineated* (Peter, the Wild Boy); *The Political History of the Devil, As Well Ancient as Modern;* and the first three of the four numbers of *A General History of the Principal Discoveries and Improvements.* This phase continued through 1727, with *The Protestant Monastery, Or a Complaint against the Brutality of the Present Age: A New Family Instructor; A History of Magick: Or a History of the Black Art; Conjugal Lewdness, Or, Matrimonial Whoredom;* and *An Essay on the History and Reality of Apparitions.* In 1728 there appeared *An Account of Jonathan Wild; Augusta Triumphans, Or, The Way to Make London the Most Flourishing City in the*

Universe, followed by *A Plan of the English Commerce.* This year also contained two works on thieving, *Street Robberies Consider'd,* and *Second Thoughts are Best.* In 1729 he reverted to an earlier kind with *The Military Memoirs of Captain George Carleton,* and, almost certainly his, *Madagascar: Or, Robert Drury's Journal,* and showed his lasting interest in commerce with *A Humble Proposal to the People of England for Increase of Trade.* The manuscript of· *The Compleat English Gentleman* was edited by K. D. Bülbring in 1895, and *The Letters of Daniel Defoe* by G. H. Healey in 1955.

Professor J. R. Moore, who ascribes *Madagascar* to Defoe, contrary to the opinion of A. W. Secord, makes out a good case also for including in the canon, *A General History of the Robberies and Murders of the Most Notorious Pirates* by 'Captain Charles Johnson', 1724 which was doubled in size by the time of the fourth edition in 1726, and portions of *The Voyage of Don Manoel Gonzales,* issued from the Harleian Collection in 1745.

The above list contains only a proportion of the writings of Defoe, which amount to above 400. There is little doubt about any of them, though there is about many not mentioned here.

Defoe's *Works* first appeared in 1703 as *A Collection of the Writings of the Author of the True-Born Englishman,* to be followed a few weeks later by *A True Collection . . . ,* the second omitting two tracts, and adding eleven. Later collections have varied in their arrangement, but not greatly in what they have included. They are: *The Novels of Daniel Defoe,* ed. Sir Walter Scott, 12 vols., Edinburgh, 1810. *Novels and Miscellaneous Works* appeared in 20 vols., 1840–1, the last volume being a Life by G. Chalmers; and in Bohn's British Classics in 7 vols., from 1854 to 1867. *The Earlier Life and the Chief Earlier Works,* ed. H. Morley, 1889. *Selections from Defoe's Minor Novels,* ed. G. Saintsbury, Edinburgh, 1892. *Romances and Narratives,* ed. G. A. Aitken, 16 vols., 1895. *Works,* ed. G. H. Maynadier, 16 vols., New York, 1903–4. *Novels and Selected Writings,* 14 vols., Oxford, 1927–8. A complete facsimile of the *Review* in 22 vols., ed. A. W. Secord, was printed for the Facsimile Text Society, Columbia University Press, 1938. The same Press published *An Index to Defoe's Review,* ed. W. L. Payne, 1948.

A certain amount of contemporary information about Defoe

can be gleaned from Dunton's *Life and Errors*. The first *Life* is that by G. Chalmers, 1785, published separately with the author's name in 1790. Other *Lives* are those by W. Wilson, *Memoirs of the Life and Times of Daniel Defoe*, 3 vols., 1830. W. Lee, *Daniel Defoe: His Life and Recently Discovered Writings*, 3 vols., 1869, which contains selections from periodicals. W. Minto, *Daniel Defoe*, English Men of Letters series, 1879. Paul Dottin, *Daniel Defoe et ses romans*, 3 vols., Paris, 1924, vol. i of which was translated by L. Ragan, 1928. J. Sutherland, *Defoe*, 1937, 2nd ed. 1950; and J. R. Moore, 1958.

The first important critical study is W. P. Trent, *Daniel Defoe: How to Know Him*, Indianapolis, 1916. Close criticism and source-hunting was begun by A. W. Secord in *Studies in the Narrative Method of Defoe*, Illinois University, 1924, though *Historical Sources of the Journal of the Plague Year*, by Watson Nicholson, Boston, 1919, is useful in that field, as is G. Roorda, *Realism in Defoe's Narratives of Adventure*, Wageningen, 1930. An important contribution is J. R. Moore, *Defoe in the Pillory, and Other Studies*, Indiana, 1939. See also W. L. Payne, *Mr. Review*, N.Y., 1947, and C. Sen, *Daniel Defoe: His Mind and Art*, Calcutta, 1948.

Comments on sources will be found in most editions in recent times, beginning with G. A. Aitken's edition noted above, and his Introductions to separate editions, such as *A Journal of the Plague Year* (*EL*) and *Captain Singleton* (Aldine ed.). Vol. iii of Ernest A. Baker's *History of the English Novel*, 1929, contains much information, while chapter i of A. D. McKillop's *The Early Masters of English Fiction*, University of Kansas, 1956, is illuminating, as is Ian Watt's *The Rise of the Novel*, 1957. Other studies are: R. G. Stamm, *Der aufgeklärte Puritanismus Daniel Defoes*, Zürich and Leipzig, 1936; E. A. Baker, 'Defoe as a Sociological Novelist', *Academy*, 86. v. 1906. Virginia Woolf, 'Defoe', in *The Common Reader*, i, 1925, and 'Robinson Crusoe' in *The Common Reader*, ii, 1932. P. Dottin, 'Daniel Defoe, Mystificateur', *Revue Germanique*, July 1923. Pierre Legouis, 'Marion Flanders, est-elle une Victime de la Société?', *Revue de l'Enseignement des Langues Vivantes*, July 1931. Articles by J. R. Moore include, 'Defoe and the Eighteenth Century Pamphlets on London', *PQ*, Jan. 1941; 'Defoe and the South Sea Company', *Boston Public Library Quarterly*, Oct. 1953; 'Daniel Defoe: Star Reporter', ibid., Oct. 1954.

DENNIS, JOHN, 1657–1734

Dennis's most important work is in criticism. His *Preface to the Passion of Byblis*, 1692, and the Introduction to *Miscellanies in Verse and Prose*, 1693, brief enough, were followed in 1693 by the dialogue *The Impartial Critick* of the same year. A selection only of subsequent works can be given, the most important being: *Remarks on a Book Entituled, Prince Arthur*, 1696; *The Usefulness of the Stage*, 1698, these, after some lesser work, being succeeded by his most important original contributions: *The Advancement and Reformation of Modern Poetry*, 1701; *A Large Account of the Taste in Poetry*, 1702, and *The Grounds of Criticism in Poetry*, 1704. Thereafter the criticism tends to become more specific, and he published *Reflections Critical and Satyrical, upon a Late Rhapsody, Call'd, An Essay upon Criticism*, 1711, the first of his attacks on Pope; *An Essay on the Genius and Writings of Shakespear*, 1712, and his attack on Addison in *Remarks upon Cato, a Tragedy*, 1713. Pope received further attention in *A True Character of Mr Pope and his Writings*, 1716; *Remarks upon Mr Pope's Translation of Homer*, 1717, and *Remarks on Mr. Pope's Rape of the Lock*, 1728. Intermediately Steele had come up for comment in *The Characters and Conduct of Sir John Edgar*, in two parts, both 1720, and *Remarks on a Play, Call'd, The Conscious Lovers, a Comedy*, 1723, which together with his *Letters on Milton and Wycherley*, 1722 (?), and his *Defence of Sir Fopling Flutter*, 1722, make up his contribution to the idea of comedy, prefaced as they are by his *To Henry Cromwell, Esq: On the Vis Comica*, 1721. Good comments are to be found in his *Original Letters, Familiar, Moral, and Critical*, gathered together in 1721.

His poems are largely patriotic, beginning with *Upon our Victory at Sea*, 1692, continuing with *The Nuptials of Britain's Genius and Fame*, 1697; *Britannia Triumphans*, 1704; and *The Battle of Ramillia*, 1706; apart from *Poems in Burlesque*, 1692, and *Miscellanies*, 1693, his poems are mainly commemorative of sovereigns: *The Court of Death*, 1695, being Pindarics on the death of Queen Mary; *The Monument*, 1702, lamenting William III, and finally *Poem upon the Death of . . . Queen Anne*, 1714. He probably had a hand in the *Commendatory Verses*, 1700, attacking Blackmore.

A Plot and No Plot, 1697, was Dennis's first play, followed in 1698 and 1699 by the tragedies *Rinaldo and Armida* and

Iphigenia. He 'improved' Shakespeare in *The Comical Gallant: or, The Amours of Sir John Falstaffe,* 1702, and *The Invader of his Country,* 1705, a rehash of *Coriolanus,* which though not printed until 1720 had occasioned the *Essay . . . Shakespeare.* A further comedy was *Gibraltar: Or, The Spanish Adventure,* 1705, his other tragedies being *Liberty Asserted,* 1704, his most popular play, acted several times, and *Appius and Virginia,* 1709. A contribution to musical drama, astonishing, given his views on opera, was his *Orpheus and Eurydice,* 1707.

Tracts, political and other, appear with the titles: *The Danger of Priestcraft to Religion and Government,* 1702, at the beginning of the Sacheverell controversy; *An Essay on the Navy,* 1702, with which may be linked *A Proposal for Putting a Speedy End to the War,* 1703. The political troubles of 1711 are reflected in *An Essay upon Publick Spirit* of that year; while in 1715 he returned to his first subject in *Priestcraft Distinguish'd from Christianity.* He replied to Mandeville in *Vice and Luxury Public Mischiefs,* 1724.

Dennis's *Select Works* appeared in two volumes in 1718–19, but since then there has been no collection except for E. N. Hooker's magisterial *Critical Works of John Dennis,* Baltimore (Johns Hopkins), 2 vols., 1939, 1943, containing all Dennis's critical writings, with, in ii, a masterly introduction, and Explanatory Notes.

The first Life, apart from *Jacob,* and 'not by Curll', appeared in 1734; there is something about him in the biographical material added to Whincop's *Scanderbeg,* 1747; he is treated of in *Cibber,* in *Genest* (p. 595) and in *Kippis,* 1793. D' Israeli treats of him in both *Calamities of Authors* and *Quarrels of Authors.* No further Life appeared until a thoughtful one was produced by H. G. Paul, *John Dennis, His Life and Criticism,* Columbia University Press, 1911, which has a bibliography, and the study by Hermann Lenz, *John Dennis. Sein Leben und seine Werke,* Halle, 1913.

A few articles have appeared recently. 'Notes on the Life of Dennis', by Fred Tupper, *ELH* v, 1938; E. N. Hooker, 'Pope and Dennis', *ELH* vii, 1940; 'The Jonsonian Tradition in the Comedies of John Dennis', by C. B. Graham, *MLN* lvi, 1941, followed by an article by L. N. Bredvold, *MLN* lix.

DERHAM, WILLIAM, 1657–1738

Derham followed up his Boyle Lectures, *Physico-Theology,* 1713, with *Astro-Theology: or, a Demonstration of the Being and*

Attributes of God, from a Survey of the Heavens, 1715, rounding off the series with *Christo-Theology* in 1730.

DIAPER, WILLIAM, 1685–1717

Diaper's longest original works, *Nereides: or Sea-Eclogues*, and *Dryades: or, The Nymphs Prophecy. A Poem*, were both published in 1712, the latter dated 1713. In the same year he collaborated with Rowe, Sewell, and Cobb in translating *Callipædia*, of which he did most of Book IV. *An Imitation of the Seventeenth Epistle of the First Book of Horace* (addressed to Swift) appeared in 1714, while his translation of Part I, in two Books, of *Oppian's Halieuticks*, the remainder being by John Jones, appeared in 1722. His earliest poem, *Brent*, was not published until 1727, in a pirated incorrect version, by Curll in his *Miscellanea*, i. A corrected version appeared in Samuel Bowden's *Poems on Various Subjects*, 1754. A complete edition, with an excellent biographical and critical Introduction, and scholarly apparatus, by Dorothy Broughton, 1951, is the only collected edition. He appears in the *Journal to Stella*, in *Jacob*, and *Nichols*.

DUCK, STEPHEN, 1705–56

There were seven editions of Duck's *Poems on Several Subjects* in 1730, the sixth and later editions having a Life. In the same year Duck produced *Royal Benevolence, a Poem, To which is annexed a Poem on Providence*. Further poems are included in *Poems on Several Occasions*, 1736, which contains Spence's Life (see below). *The Vision, a poem on the death of her most gracious Majesty Queen Caroline* appeared in 1737. His last works were, *An Ode on the Battle of Dettingen*, 1743; and *Caesar's Camp: or, St George's Hill*, 1755. *The Beautiful Works of Stephen Duck* appeared in 1753.

In 1731 J. Spence printed *A Full and Authentick Account of Stephen Duck*; and in 1927 R. M. Davies published *Stephen Duck, the Thresher Poet* at Orono, Maine. He is discussed by R. Southey in *Lives of Uneducated Poets*, 1836, ed. J. S. Childers, 1925; and by E. Blunden in *Nature in Literature*, 1929.

DUKE, RICHARD, 1658–1711

Duke commenced poet with *An Epithalamium upon the Marriage of Captain William Bedloe*, published anon. in 1679, which was followed in the next year by *Funeral Tears upon the*

Death of Captain William Bedloe, also anon. The satirical *A Panegyrick upon Oates*, 1680, is doubtfully his. He contributed to Dryden's translations of Juvenal and Plutarch, and to the 1683 version of Ovid's *Heroides*. His *Poems on Several Occasions* were appended to *Poems by the Earl of Roscommon*, 1717. See *Jacob*; *Johnson* xi; *Anderson* vi; and *Chalmers* ix. He also published several sermons.

DUNTON, JOHN, 1659–1733

Dunton is chiefly known by his *Athenian Gazette or Casuistical Mercury*, Mar. 1690, Feb. 1696.

In addition to his editing of journals, such as *The Athenian Oracle*, i and ii of which appeared in 1703, iii in 1704, and i to iv, 3rd edn., in 1728, Dunton produced in 1699 *The Dublin Scuffle*, ed. J. Nichols, 1818, and *An Account of Ireland*. His most interesting work, *The Life and Errors of John Dunton*, appeared in 1705, and was ed. J. Nichols, 1818, with a Memoir. Vol. i of *Dunton's Whipping-Post, or a Satire upon Every body* was printed in 1706. A second volume does not seem to have been achieved. In 1710 he published *Athenianism. Or, The New Projects of Mr John Dunton. . . . Being Six Hundred distinct Treatises (in Prose and Verse)*.

DYER, JOHN, c. 1700–58

There are three versions of *Grongar Hill*. The first, in 174 lines of octosyllabics, appeared in 1726 in T. Warner's *A New Miscellany, Being a Collection of Pieces of Poetry from Bath, Tunbridge, Oxford, Epsom and other places in 1725*; the pindaric version, with other shorter poems of Dyer, was printed in R. Savage's *Miscellaneous Poems and Translations*, 1726; the final version in 157 octosyllabic lines occurs in D. Lewis's *Miscellaneous Poems by Several Hands*, also 1726. It was separately edited by R. C. Boys, Baltimore, 1941. *The Ruins of Rome, a Poem*, was printed 1740; and *The Fleece: a Poem, in four books* 1757.

Poems, 1761, contains the three long poems, which reappeared in 1765 as *The Poetical Works*. In 1855 R. A. Wilmot edited *The Poetical Works of Mark Akenside and John Dyer*. Dyer's *Poems* were again edited by E. Thomas in 1903; the *Minor Poets of the Eighteenth Century*, EL, 1930, ed. H. I'A. Faussett, includes all Dyer's poems. See also *Johnson* liii; *Anderson* ix; and *Chalmers* xiii.

There are some letters from Dyer in vol. iii of *Letters to Several*

Eminent Persons, including the Correspondence of John Hughes, ed. W. Duncombe, 3 vols.; 2nd ed., 1771.

Apart from Johnson's, there is no account of Dyer. He is treated of in: John Scott of Amwell's, *Critical Essays on some of the Poems of several English Poets*, 1785; G. Greever, 'The Two Versions of Grongar Hill', *JEGP* xiv, 1917; R. M. Williams, 'Thomson and Dyer: Poet and Painter' in *The Age of Johnson: Essays presented to C. B. Tinker*, New Haven, 1949.

ECHARD (or EACHARD), LAURENCE, *c.* 1670–1730

Echard's work before 1700—geography and translations from the classics—will not be noted here, with the exception of *The Roman History, from the Building of the City, to the Perfect Settlement of the Empire by Augustus*, 1695; vol. ii, *From Augustus to Constantine*, 1698, produced in 2 vols., 1699 (4th ed.). In 1702 he published his first historical study, *A General Ecclesiastical History, from the Nativity of our Blessed Saviour to the First Establishment of Christianity by Humane Laws under the Emperour Constantine the Great*, which was followed in 1707 by the first two vols. of *The History of England*. The title of the first vol. continues: *from the First Entrance of Julius Caesar and the Romans, To the End of the Reign of King James the First, Containing the Space of 1678 Years*. The second vol. runs *From the Beginning of the Reign of King Charles the First to the Restoration of King Charles II, Containing the Space of above 35 Years*, and appeared in 1718 with the third vol. *From the Restoration of King Charles the Second, To the Conclusion of the Reign of King James the Second, and Establishment of King William and Queen Mary, Containing the Space of near 29 Years*. In 1725 he brought his series to an end with *History of the Revolution and the Establishment of England in the Year 1688*.

See *Jacob* i for his translations from Terence and Plautus.

FARQUHAR, GEORGE, 1678–1707

Both *Love and a Bottle* and *The Constant Couple; or a Trip to the Jubilee* were acted and published in 1699. *Sir Harry Wildair: Being the Sequel of the Trip to the Jubilee* was acted and printed in 1701; and *The Inconstant: or the Way to Win Him* in 1702. *The Twin Rivals* was acted in 1702, published in 1703; *The Stage Coach*, acted in 1704, was printed in Dublin in the same year, and in London in 1705. *The Recruiting Officer* was acted and published in 1706, and *The Beaux' Stratagem* in 1707.

It is impossible to divide the rest of his work neatly. Some of his letters appeared in Abel Boyer's *Letters of Wit, Politicks and Morality*, 1701, and in *Familiar and Courtly Letters*. The most important of his other productions is *Love and Business in a Collection of Occasionary Verse and Epistolary Prose. A Discourse likewise upon Comedy in Reference to the English Stage. In a Familiar Letter*, 1702 (d. 1701). His widow published his *Barcellona. A Poem. Or The Spanish Expedition* in 1710.

The Works of the late Ingenious Mr George Farquhar: Containing all his Poems, Letters, Essays and Comedies appeared in 2 vols., 1711. This was reprinted at various times until the Dublin edition of 1775, with a Life by T. Wilkes. *The Dramatic Works of George Farquhar*, ed. E. C. Ewald, 2 vols., appeared in 1892, and the complete *Works* were ed. C. Stonehill, 2 vols., 1930, which includes Wilkes's memoir.

The first book devoted to him is *George Farquhar*, by D. Schmid, Vienna, 1904, the most recent being *Young George Farquhar* by W. Connely, 1949. Criticism may be found in Hazlitt (p. 614), 1819; John Palmer, *The Comedy of Manners*, 1913, and in William Archer's Introduction to the Mermaid edition, 1906, which contains four plays; in Allardyce Nicoll's *Restoration Drama*, 1923, and *A History of Early Eighteenth Century Drama*, 1925; B. Dobrée in *Restoration Comedy*, 1924, and in H. T. E. Perry, *The Comic Spirit in Restoration Drama*, New Haven, 1925.

FELTON, HENRY, 1679–1740

Apart from religious works, of which the most important is *The Christian Faith asserted against Deists, Arians, and Socinians*, &c., 1732, with a large 'Preface concerning the Light and Law of Nature, and the Expediency and Necessity of Revelation', Felton's only publications are: *A Dissertation on Reading the Classics, and forming a Just Style*, 1713; and 'Of Genius' in *Occasional Papers*, iii, no. 10.

A sketch of his Life was written by his son, William Felton, in 1748. See also R. S. Crane: 'Imitations of Spenser and Milton in the Early Eighteenth Century', *Stud. Phil.* xv, 1918.

FENTON, ELIJAH, 1683–1730

Fenton's poetic output was small, consisting mainly of contributions to Miscellanies. Separately published among others were: *An Ode to the Sun, for the New Year*, 1707; *To the Queen*,

On Her Majesty's Birthday, 1710?; *An Epistle to Mr Southerne*, &c., 1717. He translated Books I, IV, XIX, and XXII of Pope's *Odyssey*, 1725–6. See *Jacob* i; *Johnson* xxix; *Anderson* vii; and *Chalmers* x.

His one play is *Mariamne. A Tragedy*, 1723.

He wrote the *Life of John Milton* prefixed to a 1725 edition of *Paradise Lost*; and *Observations on the Life of Edmund Waller*, 1729, which also prefaced his edition of Waller in that year.

Lives, besides Johnson's, are: W. W. Lloyd, *Elijah Fenton. His Poetry and Friends*, ed. G. L. Fenton, with Life by R. Fenton, 1894; and E. Harlan, *Elijah Fenton*, Philadelphia, 1937.

GARTH, SAMUEL, 1661–1719

Garth published his most famous poem, *The Dispensary*, in 1699, added to in editions up to 1714. He wrote some complimentary verses, but his only other interesting works are 'Claremont', 1715, and in the same year, *Ovid's Metamorphoses*, which he edited, and partly translated. See *Johnson* xx, *Anderson* vii, and *Chalmers* ix: also *Cibber*.

The only critical work solely devoted to him is *Sir Samuel Garth und seine Stellung zum komischen Epos*, by T. Schenk, Heidelberg, 1900.

GAY, JOHN, 1685–1732

Gay preluded his major occasional poetry with *Wine* (anon.), 1708. *Rural Sports* appeared in 1713, and *The Fan*, followed by *The Shepherd's Week. In Six Pastorals*, in 1714. *Trivia: or the Art of Walking the Streets of London* came out in 1716. His last noteworthy occasional piece, *To a Lady on her Passion for Old China*, was published in 1725, but this kind of verse was succeeded by *Fables*, 1727, and *Fables. Volume the Second* in 1738. The volumes were issued together in 1750.

The first collected edition was his own *Poems on Several Occasions*, 2 vols., 1720, a revised text being issued in 1731. *Poems and Fables*, 2 vols., Aberdeen, 1772, stimulated a rival ed. 2 vols., Edinburgh, 1773, to be followed by *The Poetical Works*, 3 vols., 1777. In the nineteenth century, *The Poetical Works*, 2 vols., Boston, 1854, was followed by *The Poetical Works*, ed. John Underhill, 2 vols., 1893. *Poems by John Gay*, ed. Francis Bickley, appeared in 1923, and *Selected Poems*, ed. A. Ross, in 1950. See *Johnson* xxxix, xl; *Anderson* viii; *Chalmers* x.

Of his plays were published: *The Mohocks. A Tragi-Comical Farce* (unacted), 1712; *The Wife of Bath. A Comedy*, 1713; and *The What d'ye call it: A Tragi-Comi-Pastoral Farce* in 1715. His collaboration with Pope and Arbuthnot, *Three Hours After Marriage*, acted 1717, was published that year. *The Captives* appeared in 1724, *The Beggar's Opera* in 1728, and *Polly. An Opera* (unacted) in 1729. *Acis and Galatea: An English Pastoral Opera*, acted in 1731, was published in the next year; and *Achilles: An Opera* in 1733. *The Distress'd Wife*, acted in 1734, was not printed until 1743; the unacted *The Rehearsal at Goatham* in 1754.

The Present State of Wit, in a Letter to a Friend in the Country appeared anon. in 1711, and may be found ed. Churton Collins, in *An English Garner*, 1903, and ed. D. F. Bond, Ann Arbor, 1947, among the publications of the Augustan Reprint Society.

The Works of Mr John Gay, 4 vols., with Life, appeared in Dublin, 1770: *The Poetical, Dramatic, and Miscellaneous Works of John Gay*, which includes Johnson's Introduction, appeared in 6 vols., 1795. *The Poetical Works of John Gay, Including 'Polly', 'The Beggar's Opera', and Selections from the other Dramatic Work*, 1926, was ed. G. C. Faber, who in the same year published *The Poetical Works of John Gay* with a full bibliography (pp. xxxv–xlvii).

The Life of Mr John Gay, 1733, was a Curll production, the first serious attempt being Johnson's in 1781. Other Lives are: L. Melville, *Life and Letters of John Gay*, 1921, and Phoebe Fenwick Gaye, *John Gay*, 1938.

Criticism opens with Hazlitt's *Lectures on the English Poets*, 1818, an example followed by Thackeray in *English Humourists of the Eighteenth Century*, 1853, and by Austin Dobson in *A Paladin of Philanthropy and Other Papers*, 1899. There are many specialist studies, among which may be noted: F. Kidson, *The Beggar's Opera: Its Predecessors and Successors*, 1922; F. W. Bateson in *English Comic Drama, 1700–1750*, 1929; W. Empson in *Some Versions of Pastoral*, 1936; A. V. Berger, 'The Beggar's Opera, the Burlesque, and Italian Opera', *Music and Letters* xvii, 1936; J. R. Sutherland 'John Gay' in *Pope and his Contemporaries*, ed. J. L. Clifford and L. A. Landa, 1949; R. C. Boys, *Sir Richard Blackmore and the Wits*, Univ. of Michigan Press, 1949; J. R. Moore, 'Gay's Burlesque of Sir Richard Blackmore's Poetry', *JEGP* l, 1951; and F. S. Boas in *Introduction to Eighteenth Century Drama*, 1953.

GILDON, CHARLES, 1665–1724

Of poems Gildon published *Threnodia Virginea* . . . *1708,* printed in that year; *Libertas Triumphans,* 1708; and *Canons: or, The Vision. Address'd to the Right Honourable James Earl of Caenarvan,* 1717. His plays, all acted and published anon., consist of *The Roman Bride's Revenge. A Tragedy,* 1697; *Phaeton: Or, The Fatal Divorce,* 1698; *Measure for Measure, or Beauty the Best Advocate. A Comedy,* acted 1699, printed 1700; *Love's Victim: Or, The Queen of Wales. A Tragedy,* 1701; and (an adaptation of Lee's *Lucius Jumius Brutus*) *The Patriot, or the Italian Conspiracy. A Tragedy,* 1703.

His most important work is his criticism, which began in 1692 with *A Letter to Mr D'Urfey, occasion'd by his Play Called the Marriage-Hater Match'd,* which was prefixed to the edition of D'Urfey's play. He edited and partly wrote *Miscellaneous Letters and Essays on Several Subjects, Philosophical, Moral, Historical, Critical, Amorous etc., in Prose and Verse,* 1694 (see Durham (p. 602) and J. E. Spingarn's *Critical Essays of the Seventeenth Century,* iii, 1909). Almost certainly his is *A Comparison Between the Two Stages,* 1702, though this is contested by S. B. Wells in 'An Eighteenth Century Attribution', *JEGP* xxxviii, 1939. In 1710 Curll added to Rowe's edition of Shakespeare Gildon's *An Essay on the Art, Rise and Progress of the Stage in Greece, Rome and England. Remarks on the Plays of Shakespear. Remarks on the Poems of Shakespear.* In 1714 Gildon anonymously attacked Pope and Rowe in *A New Rehearsal, or Bays the Younger.* His big work was *The Complete Art of Poetry,* 2 vols., 1718, which he followed with *The Laws of Poetry, As laid down by the Duke of Buckinghamshire, the Earl of Roscommon, And by the Lord Landsdowne,* 1721. In criticism may be included *A Grammar of the English Tongue,* 1711, published anon., as was *The Life and Strange Surprizing Adventures of Mr D[aniel] De F[oe],* 1719 (reprinted by P. Dottin, 1923, with an essay on Gildon's life).

His Deistic and anti-Deistic works comprise: *Nuncius Infernalis: or, A New Account from Below,* 1692; *The Oracles of Reason,* with Charles Blount and others, 1693; and *The Deist's Manual,* 1705.

As a biographer, he anonymously continued Langbaine's *The Lives and Characters of the English Dramatick Poets,* 1699; *The Life of Thomas Betterton,* 1710, by G. C.; and, anon., *Memoirs of the Life of William Wycherley Esq.*, 1718, a Curll production bound up with Lansdowne's 'Character of his Writings'.

His translations comprise *The New Metamorphosis: or, The Pleasant Transformation: Being the Golden Ass of Apuleius of Medaura. Alter'd and Improv'd to the Modern Times and Manners*, anon. 2 vols., 2nd ed. 1709; and two sections in ii of *The Works of Lucian*, 4 vols., 1711.

He published several collections of letters under the titles of: *The Post-boy rob'd of His Mail: or, The Pacquet Broke-Open*, 1692, with a second volume in 1693; both were reissued in 1 vol. in 1706, with additions and subtractions; and *The Post-Man Robb'd of his Mail: Or, The Packet broke open*, anon. 1719.

His editorial work was considerable. Apart from producing various miscellanies, he put to the press *The Histories and Novels of the late Ingenious Mrs Behn*, 1696, besides her play *The Younger Brother*, which he re-handled in 1696; and the letters of Rochester, 2 vols., 1697.

Besides P. Dottin's Essay (see above), the following special studies may be noted: F. E. Litz, 'The Sources of Gildon's "Complete Art of Poetry"', *ELH* ix, 1942; and B. Boyce, 'Pope, Gildon and Salamanders', *N & Q*, 8 Jan. 1949 (on Gildon's *Post-boy Rob'd of His Mail* as a source for *The Rape of the Lock*).

GLOVER, RICHARD, 1712–85

Glover, whose 'A Poem on Newton' appeared in Henry Pemberton's *A View of Sir Isaac Newton's Philosophy*, 1728, became famous through his *Leonidas, A Poem*, 1737, the nine books of which he expanded to twelve in his edition of 1770. *London: or, the Progress of Commerce*, appeared in 1739, his ballad *Admiral Hosier's Ghost* in 1740. In 1787 he published *The Athenaid, a poem*. His *Poetical Works* were ed. T. Park, 2 vols. 1805. See *Anderson* xi and *Chalmers* xvii.

He also wrote several plays.

The Athenaid was reviewed by W. Cowper in *The Analytical Review*, Feb. 1789, and discussed in *The Retrospective Review* ii, 1820. The only full work on him is that of J. G. Schaaf, *Richard Glover. Leben und Werke*, Leipzig, 1900.

GRANVILLE, GEORGE, BARON LANSDOWNE, 1667–1735

Granville produced a comedy, *The She-Gallants*, 1695, printed 1696; a tragedy, *Heroick Love*, 1697, printed 1698; a tragi-comedy *The Jew of Venice*, acted and printed 1707; and an opera, *The British Enchanters; or, No Magick like Love*, produced anonymously in 1706, and printed in the same year. *Three Plays* were collected in 1713, and *Four Plays* in 1732, and his *Poems on Several Occasions* was published in 1712. See *Johnson* iii.

His political writings include *A Letter from a Nobleman Abroad to his Friend in England*, 1722; and *A Letter to the Author of Reflexions Historical and Political*, 1732.

Biography, apart from Johnson, consists of E. Handasyde, *Granville the Polite*, 1933. His tragi-comedy is discussed by J. A. Wilson, 'Granville's "Stock-Jobbing Jew"', *PQ* xiii, 1934.

GREEN, MATTHEW, 1696–1737

Green made his first poetical venture in 1733 with the privately printed *The Grotto, A Poem. Written by Peter Drake, Fisherman of Brentford*. His famous poem, *The Spleen. An Epistle Inscrib'd to his particular Friend Mr. C. J.*, appeared posthumously, edited by Glover, in 1737. An edition in the next year added 'Some other pieces by the same hand'. See *Anderson* x and *Chalmers* xv.

The Spleen, and Other Poems, with a Prefatory Essay by J. Aikin ('twaddle without facts') was published in 1796, and ed. R. K. Wood, 1925. His work is represented in *The Poems of Gray, Parnell, Collins, Green and Warton*, edited by R. A. Willmott, 1853; and the *Minor Poets of the Eighteenth Century*, *EL*, edited by H.I'A. Faussett contains all his poems.

He is briefly discussed by N. Callan in the chapter 'Augustan Reflective Poetry', vol. iv of 'The Pelican Guide to English Literature', *From Dryden to Johnson*, ed. B. Ford, 1957.

HARTE, WALTER, 1709–74

Harte ventured his *Poems on Several Occasions* as early as 1727. His *An Essay on Satire. Particularly on the Dunciad*, 1730, was followed by *An Epistle to Mr Pope on Reading his Iliad*, 1731. He also published *An Essay on Reason*, 1735; and *The Amaranth; or Religious Poems*, 1767.

His prose works consist of *History of the Life of Gustavus Adolphus, sirnamed the Great*, 2 vols., 1759, generally despised, but said to read well in German; and his agreeable *Essays on Husbandry*, 1764.

HAYWOOD, ELIZA, *c.* 1693–1756

Mrs. Haywood's first publication was *Love in Excess; or The Fatal Enquiry. A Novel*, 1719. Her other works include *Idalia: or The Unfortunate Mistress*, 1723; and in the same year, *Lasselia; or, the Self-Abandoned. A Novel*; *A Spy upon the Conjurer: or, A Collection of Surprising Stories*, &c., 1724, which contains matter on Duncan Campbell; *Memoirs of a Certain Island Adjacent to the Kingdom of Utopia*, 2 vols., 1725; *The Mercenary Lover; or, The Unfortunate Heiresses*, 1726; *The Fruitless Enquiry*, &c. (stories), 1727; *The History of Miss Betty Thoughtless*, 1751; *The History of Jemmy and Jenny Jessamy*, 1753.

Her plays consist of: *The Fair Captive*, acted and printed 1721; *A Wife to be Lett*, 1723, printed 1724; and *Frederick, Duke of Brunswick-Lunenburgh*, acted and printed, 1729.

Her verse is represented by *Poems on Several Occasions*, 1724.

Her periodical publications are the *Tea Table*, 35 numbers from 21 Feb. to 22 June 1724; the *Parrot*, 4 numbers, 25 Sept.–16 Oct. 1728, with a second series of 9 numbers, 2 Aug.–4 Oct. 1746. The *Female Spectator* ran for 24 numbers, from Apr. 1744 to Mar. 1746, printed Dublin, 4 vols., 1747.

For biography and criticism see G. F. Whicher, *The Life and Romances of Mrs Eliza Haywood*, New York, 1915; and *The Female Spectator*, a selection, with a critical introduction by J. B. Priestley, 1929.

HEARNE, THOMAS, 1678–1735

A great deal of his work was written in Latin; only the English works will be mentioned here. These begin with *Reliquiae Bodleianae: or some Genuine Remains of Sir Thomas Bodley*, 1703. *A Letter, containing an Account of some Antiques between Windsor and Oxford* was printed in the *Monthly Miscellany* of Dec. 1708 and Jan. 1709. *The Life of Aelfred the Great, By Sir John Spelman: with considerable additions*, appeared in 1709. *The Itinerary of Sir John Leland, the Antiquary* was published in 9 vols., 1710–12. *A Collection of Curious Discourses, Written by Eminent Antiquaries*, 1720, was enlarged to 2 vols. in the edition of 1771. *The History of the Antiquities of Glastonbury* appeared in 1722; *Robert of Gloucester's Chronicle*, 2 parts, in 1724; *Peter Langtoft's Chronicle*, 2 vols., in 1725. In 1731 he published *A Vindication of those who take the Oath of Allegiance, To His Present Majestie.*

His autobiography appears in *The Lives of John Leland, Thomas Hearne, and Anthony à Wood*, 2 vols., 1772. Two extracts from Diaries appear in *Letters Written by Eminent Persons*, vol. ii, 1813. *Reliquiae Hernianae: The Remains of Thomas Hearne* was ed. P. Bliss, 2 vols., 1857, 3 vols., 1869. *Remarks and Collections of Thomas Hearne*, ed. C. E. Doble, D. W. Rannie and others, was printed in 11 vols. by the Oxford Historical Society, 1885–1921.

There is a good 'Portrait of Hearne' by D. C. Douglas in his *English Scholars*, 1939.

HERVEY, JOHN LORD HERVEY OF ICKWORTH, 1696–1743

Harvey wrote a considerable number of ephemeral political pamphlets, of which *Ancient and Modern Liberty Stated and Compared*, 1734, may serve as an example. Probably his most important contribution was *Observations on the Writings of the Craftsman*, published anonymously in 1730. He also wrote a quantity of verse, his most notorious piece, concocted perhaps with Lady Mary Wortley Montagu, being *Verses Addressed to the Imitator of Horace*, 1733. His verses appear in the Dodsley of 1782, iii, iv, and v, and were collected with those of Hammond in 1808.

His most important works were *Some Remarks on the Minute Philosopher*, 1732; *Letters between Lord Hervey and Dr Middleton concerning the Roman Senate*, ed. T. Knowles, 1778; and his great work *Memoirs of the Reign of George II*, ed. J. W. Croker, 2 vols., 1848, 3 vols., 1884, the standard edition of which is that edited with a memoir by R. Sedgwick, 3 vols., 1931, revised 1952.

Hervey and his Friends, 1726–38: Based on Letters from Holland House, Melbury and Ickworth, was ed. the Earl of Ilchester, 1950.

Studies comprise: R. Shafter, 'Hervey's Memoirs', *American Review* ii, 1933; and in G. P. Gooch, *Courts and Cabinets*, 1944.

HILL, AARON, 1685–1750

Hill published his feeble *Full Account of the Ottoman Empire* in 1709, and in the same year *Camillus*, complimentary verses to Peterborough. His major poetic works consist of his cosmic piece, *The Creation*, 1720 (with a Preface, edited 1949 by G. Pahl: Augustan Reprint Society, Los Angeles), *The Tears of the Muses*, 1737, and two books of an epic, *Gideon the Patriot*, 1741. His lighter verse includes *Advice to Poets*, 1731, and *The Fanciad*, 1743.

The *Plain Dealer*, the periodical that he produced with William Bond from 23 Mar. 1724 to 7 May 1725 (117 numbers), was collected in 2 vols., 1730. He was responsible for the *Prompter*, which ran from 12 Nov. 1734 to 2 July 1736 (173 numbers). His pamphlets setting forth his projects are of no literary interest.

His first stage piece, *Elfrid: or The Fair Inconstant*, was staged and published in 1710, having attached to it a farce, *The Walking Statue; or, The Devil in the Wine Cellar.* In that year he also wrote the libretto of Handel's *Rinaldo.* These were followed by: *The Fatal Vision; or, The Fall of Siam*, 1716; *The Fatal Extravagance*, printed 1720, acted 1721; and *King Henry the Fifth: or, The Conquest of France, By the English*, 1723. In 1731 he rehashed his first play as *Athelwold*, which was printed in 1732. He then turned to free translations, almost adaptations, of Voltaire's dramas, producing *The Tragedy of Zara*, 1736; *Alzira*, 1736; and *Merope*, 1749. His *Dramatic Works* were collected in 2 vols., 1760.

A Collection of Letters between Mr Aaron Hill, Pope and Others appeared in 1751, and his *Works* in 4 vols., 1753.

He is treated of in *Cibber* v, 1753, and a Life by J. K. was prefixed to his *Dramatic Works*; *Genest* may also be consulted. Recent full studies are: H. Ludwig, *The Life and Works of Aaron Hill*, 1911; D. Brewster, *Aaron Hill, Poet, Dramatist, Projector*, N.Y., 1913. Austin Dobson discussed him in *Rosalba's Journal and other Papers*, 1915.

HUGHES, JOHN, 1677–1720

Hughes began his poetical career in 1698 with *The Triumph of Peace*, followed in the next year by *The Court of Neptune*. He then turned to odes, pindaric and otherwise, variously addressed: to *The House of Nassau*, 1702; in *Praise of Music*, 1703; to the *Creator of the World* (anon.), 1713; to the *Princess of Wales*, 1716; and *The Ecstacy*, 1720. They may be found in *Johnson* xxii; *Anderson* vii; and *Chalmers* x. See also *Jacob*.

Poems on Several Occasions, with some select Essays in Prose, 2 vols., was ed. W. Duncombe in 1735. See Bell, *The Poets of Great Britain*, 1782, vols. 71 and 72.

As regards the theatre, his *Calypso and Telemachus. An Opera*, was acted and printed in 1712; and *Apollo and Daphne. A Masque set to Musick*, in 1716. His *Orestes* was unacted, but printed in 1717; *The Siege of Damascus. A Tragedy*, was acted and published in 1720. In history he collected the material for White Kennett's *Complete History* (see under White Kennett), and in 1716 compiled *The Complicated Guilt of the late Rebellion*, but this was not published until 1745. In journalism he was partly responsible for *The Lay Monastery*, 1714 (see under Blackmore). His most notable works are his renderings from the French: Fontenelle's *Dialogues of the Dead, Translated from the French. And Two Original Dialogues*, 1708; and *The Letters of Abelard and Heloise. Extracted chiefly from Monsieur Bayle. Translated from the French*, 1722. His most praiseworthy labour is *The Works of Mr Edmund Spenser. With a glossary explaining the old and obscure words*, 6 vols., 1715. 'Remarks . . .' are reprinted in Durham (p. 602).

Letters by Several Eminent Persons Deceased, edited by John Duncombe in 1772, contains Hughes's correspondence.

A. D. McKillop discusses 'Some Newtonian Verses in "Poor Richard"', in the *New England Quarterly* xxi, 1948.

HUTCHESON, FRANCIS, 1694–1747

An Inquiry into the Original of our Ideas of Beauty and Virtue, in two treatises, &c., appeared in 1725; and from 1725 to 1728 Hutcheson contributed various essays to *Hibernicus's Letters*, a Dublin periodical, such as 'Thoughts on Laughter' and 'Observations on the Fable of the Bees', which were collected and printed in 1 vol., 1735. *An Essay on the Nature and Conduct of the Passions and Affections, with Illustrations of the Moral Sense* was published in 1728, and *A System of Moral Philosophy*, 2 vols., Glasgow, in 1742. See T. E. Jessop, *A Bibliography of Hume and of Scottish Philosophy from Hutcheson to Lord Balfour*, 1938.

Books on Hutcheson include *Shaftesbury and Hutcheson*, by T. Fowler, 1882, and *Francis Hutcheson*, by W. R. Scott, 1900. See also J. Bonar, *Moral Sense*, 1930.

Special studies are those by C. de W. Thorpe, 'Addison and Hutcheson on the Imagination', *ELH* ii, 1935; A. O. Aldridge, 'A Preview of Hutcheson's Ethics', *MLN* lxi, 1946; and M. Kallich, 'The Associationist Criticism of Hutcheson and Hume', *SP* xliii, 1946.

JENYNS, SOAME, 1704–87

Jenyns began his poetical career with *The Art of Dancing. A Poem. In Three Cantos*, 1729. This was followed by *Versus inopes Rerum Nugaeque Canorae: Commonly call'd Poems on Several Occasions*, in about 1730. His last poem in this period, *An Epistle to Lord Lovelace*, 1735, heralded various other poems between 1746 and 1780. See *Anderson* xi; and *Chalmers* xvii. His prose works, largely philosophical, began to appear in 1757. *The Works* was edited with a Memoir by C. N. Cole, 1790.

KENNETT, WHITE, 1660–1728

His works are to a large extent specialized writing on Church government, or sermons, which he entered upon in 1701 with *An Occasional Letter on the Subject of English Convocations*. His historical work began with *Parochial Antiquities Attempted in the History of Ambrosden, Burcester, and Other Adjacent Parts in the Counties of Oxford and Bucks*, 1695, which was greatly enlarged by B. Bandinel in 1818, 2 vols. His major work is the third volume of *The History of England from the Commencement of the Reign of Charles I to the End of the Reign of William III*, 1706 (enlarged to include the reign of Anne in 1719). He also wrote *Memoirs of the Family of Cavendish*, 1708. His last work, *An Historical Account of the Discipline and Jurisdiction of the Church of England*, appeared posthumously in 1730.

Biographies are by W. Newton, *The Life of White Kennett. With several original letters*, 1730; and G. V. Bennett, *White Kennett, 1660–1728, Bishop of Peterborough*, 1957.

KING, WILLIAM, Student of Christ Church, Oxford, 1663–1712

For the purposes of this volume, King's first publication of interest is *Dialogues of the Dead, relating to the present controversy concerning the Letters of Phalaris*, issued anonymously in 1699 (to be found in K. N. Colville's *A Miscellany of Wits*, 1920).

His poems consist of: *The Furmetary. A Very Innocent and Harmless Poem. In Three Cantos*, 1699; *Mully of Mountown. By the Author of the Tale of a Tub*, 1704 (d. 1702); *The Fairy Feast*, 1704; *Miscellanies in Prose and Verse*, 1707; *The Art of Cookery. In Imitation of Horace's Art of Poetry*, &c., anon. 1708; and *The Art of Love. In Imitation of Ovid*, 1709. *Apple-Pye*, an imitation Georgic, was printed in *The Works of the Most Celebrated Minor Poets*, vol. iii, 1750.

The Poetical Works of Dr King. With the Life of the Author was issued in Edinburgh, 2 vols., 1781. See also *Johnson* xx; *Anderson* vi; and *Chalmers* ix.

In 1700 he produced a satire on Sir Hans Sloane, *The Transactioneer, with some of his Philosophical Fancies, in two Dialogues*. In 1709 he published anonymously *Useful Transactions in Philosophy, And other sorts of Learning*, monthly, Jan.–Sept., in three parts, 1709. His less 'scientific' works include *Some Remarks on the Tale of a Tub*, &c., 1704, which contains the complete and authorized versions of 'Mully of Mountown' and 'The Fairy Feast', here renamed 'Orpheus and Eurydice'. He contributed to the *Tatler* and the *Examiner*. In 1711 he produced *An Historical Account of the Heathen Gods and Heroes*; and in the next year *Rufinus, or an Historical Essay on the favourite Ministry under Theodosius the Great, and his son Arcadius*. His *Remains* were published in 1732, and in 1734 as *Posthumous Works*.

The Original Works, ed. J. Nichols assisted by I. Reed, with a detailed memoir, was issued 3 vols., 1776.

G. G. Williams contributed 'Dr William King, Humorist' to the *Sewanee Review* xxxv, 1927. See also C. J. Horne, 'Early Parody of Scientific Jargon: Some Notes for O.E.D.', *N & Q*, 30 Jan. 1943. See also *Jacob*.

KING, WILLIAM, Archbishop of Dublin 1650–1729

His *De Origine Mali*, Dublin and London, 1702, was translated by Edmund Law, in 1731. He also published among other works and sermons *The State of Protestants in Ireland under King James's Government*, 1691; and *A Key to Divinity, or a Philosophical Essay on Free Will*, 1715.

A Great Archbishop of Dublin, William King, D.D., by Sir C. S. King, Bt., was published in 1908.

LAW, WILLIAM, 1686–1761

His first published work was *A Sermon Preach'd at Harpingfield, On Tuesday, July 7th, 1713*. His important work begins with *The Bishop of Bangor's Late Sermon, and his letter to Dr Snape in Defence of it, Answer'd*, 1717, followed in the same year by *A Second Letter to the Bishop of Bangor*, and, in 1719, *A Reply to the Bishop of Bangor's Answer*. . . . In 1723 he wrote his *Remarks upon A Late Book, Entituled, The Fable of the Bees*; and in 1726,

The Absolute Unlawfulness of the Stage-Entertainment Fully Demonstrated. The most important of his further works are: *A Practical Treatise upon Christian Perfection*, 1726; *A Serious Call to a Devout and Holy Life*, 1728; *A Demonstration of the Gross and Fundamental Errors of a late Book called a 'Plain Account &c. of the Lord's Supper'*, 1737; *An Earnest and Serious Answer to Dr Trapp's Discourse of the Folly, Sin, and Danger, of being Righteous over-much*, 1740; *The Way to Divine Knowledge*, 1752; and *The Spirit of Love*, 2 parts, 1752–4. His last work was *An Humble, Earnest and Affectionate Address to the Clergy*, 1761.

His *Works*, 9 vols. (omitting the *Sermon*), were edited by G. B. Morgan, from 1753 to 1776, and by Brockenhurst, 1892–3. The *Serious Call* has been frequently reprinted. A good notion of Law's position can be obtained from *Selected Mystical Writings of William Law*, by S. Hobhouse, 1938.

The first biography was that by William Tighe, *A Short Account of the Life and Writings of William Law*, 1781, and he was included in *Chalmers B.D.*, vol. xx, 1815. *Notes and Materials for an adequate Biography of Law*, by Christopher Walton, appeared in 1854, to be made use of by J. H. Overton in *William Law, Non-Juror and Mystic*, 1881. S. Hobhouse, *William Law and Eighteenth Century Quakerism*, 1927, is a more specialized study. To be noted is *William Law. A Study in Literary Craftsmanship*, by H. Talon, 1953.

LEDIARD, THOMAS, 1685–1743

Lediard published *Britannia. An English Opera* in 1732, before embarking upon *The Naval History of England, In all its Branches; from the Norman Conquest 1066, to the Conclusion of 1734*, 2 vols., 1735. *The Life of John, Duke of Marlborough* appeared in 3 vols., 1736. He continued Rapin de Thoyras's *History of England* to include the reigns of William III and Mary, and of Anne, vol. iii, 1737.

LESLIE, CHARLES, 1650–1722

Until 1700, approximately, his works are theological, afterwards politico-theological, from the standpoint of an Anglican non-juring Jacobite. The earliest and most famous of these is *A Short and Easie Method with the Deists*, 1698, followed in the same year with similar advice about Jews. This was clinched by a *Vindication* of the above in 1711. In the meantime his

pamphlet, *The Good Old Cause, or Lying in Truth*, being proceeded against, led to his flight abroad. From Aug. 1704 until
Mar. 1709 he produced *The Rehearsal*—collected in 1750—in
opposition to Tutchin's *Observator* and Defoe's *Review*.
His *Theological Works* was published in 2 vols., 1721, and in
7 vols. in 1832. A Life accompanied the latter edition; and in
1885 John Leslie published his *Life and Writings*.

LILLO, GEORGE, 1693–1739

His opera *Silvia; or, The Country Burial* was acted in London,
1730, piratically and anonymously printed in Dublin in that
year, an authorized edition following in 1731. *The London
Merchant: or the History of George Barnwell* was acted and printed
in 1731; *The Christian Hero*, in 1735; *Fatal Curiosity*, acted
1736, was printed 1737; *Marina*, 1738; *Elmerick, or Justice
Triumphant*, 1740. In this year *Britannia and Batavia* was printed,
but it was not acted. John Hoadly completed his *Arden of
Feversham*, which was acted in 1759, but not published till
1762.

The Works of the late Mr. George Lillo, 1740, was edited by
T. Davies, 2 vols., 1755, 'with some Account of his Life'.

The London Merchant and *Fatal Curiosity* were edited by A. W.
Ward in 1906, and the first by B. Dobrée with an Introduction
in 1949 (d. 1948).

The completest study is by G. Lossack, *Lillo und seine Bedeu-
tung für die Geschichte des Englischen Dramas*, Göttingen, 1939.
D. B. Pallette contributed 'Notes for a Biography of Lillo' to
PQ xix, 1940. He was discussed by W. H. Hudson in *A Quiet
Corner in a Library*, 1915. Articles include: T. V. Benn, 'Notes
sur la Fortune de Lillo en France', *Revue de littérature com-
parée*, Oct. 1926; L. M. Price, 'George Barnwell on the German
Stage', *Monatshefte für deutschen Unterricht* xxxv, 1943; and
'George Barnwell abroad', *Comparative Literature* ii, 1950; G. B.
Rodman, 'Sentimentalism in "The London Merchant"', *ELH*
xii, 1945, answered by R. D. Havens, ibid.

LYTTELTON, GEORGE, BARON LYTTELTON, 1709–73

His poetry falls almost wholly within this period: *Bleinheim*,
1728; *An Epistle to Mr Pope, from a young gentleman at Rome*,
1730; *The Progress of Love, in four Eclogues*, 1732; *Advice to a
Lady*, 1733. *To the Memory of a Lady lately deceased. A Monody*

appeared in 1747. See *Johnson* lvi; *Anderson* x; and *Chalmers* xiv.

His *Letters from a Persian in England to his Friend at Ispahan* appeared in 1735; and *Observations on the Life of Cicero* in 1741. Among many subsequent prose works, his best, *Dialogues of the Dead*, was printed in 1760, and *Four New Dialogues of the Dead* in 1765. Between 1731 and 1743 he contributed to *Common Sense*.

Original Letters was ed. R. Warner, 1817; *Memoirs and Correspondence*, 2 vols., 1845, was produced by R. J. Phillimore.

The Works of George, Lord Lyttelton, now first collected together; with some other pieces never before printed, was ed. G. E. Ayscough, 1774.

Biographies consist of: S. C. Roberts, *An Eighteenth Century Gentleman*, 1930; A. V. Rao, *A Minor Augustan*, Calcutta, 1934; and R. M. Davis, *The Good Lord Lyttelton*, Bethlehem, Pa., 1939. Austin Dobson discussed 'Lyttelton as Man of Letters' in *In Old Kensington Palace and Other Papers*, 1910, as did F. P. Johnson in *PQ* vii, 1928.

MALLET, (originally MALLOCH), DAVID, *c.* 1705–65

His earlier poems consist of: *William and Margaret. An Old Ballad*, published anonymously as a broadside in about 1723; *A Poem in Imitation of Donaides*, 1725; his cosmic poem, *The Excursion. A Poem in Two Parts*, 1728; *Of Verbal Criticism: An Epistle to Mr Pope. Occasion'd by Theobald's Shakespear, and Bentley's Milton*, 1733; and, with W. Harte, *Verses Presented to the Prince of Orange. On his Visiting Oxford*, 1734. He published *Poems on Several Occasions* in 1743, and then his most popular work, *Amyntor and Theodora; or, The Hermit. A Poem. In Three Cantos*, 1747. *Edwin and Emma* appeared in 1760, and in the same year *Verses on the Death of Lady Anson*. An entirely new *Poems on Several Occasions* appeared in 1762. F. Dimsdale edited *Ballads and Songs* in 1857. See *Johnson* lviii; *Anderson* ix; and *Chalmers* xiv.

His tragedies consist of: *Eurydice*, 1731; *Mustapha*, 1739; and *Elvira*, 1763. The masque *Alfred* which he wrote with Thomson appeared in 1740; the version written entirely by himself in 1751. His other masque, *Britannia*, was printed in 1755.

He wrote *The Life of Francis Bacon*, 1740; and he edited Bolingbroke's *Letters on the Spirit of Patriotism: on the Idea of a Patriot King* in 1749, and he followed this with an edition of *The Works of Lord Bolingbroke*, 1754.

The Works of Mr Mallet, 4 parts, 1743, and 'corrected' 3 vols., in 1759.

D'Israeli discusses 'Bolingbroke and Mallet's Posthumous Quarrel with Pope' in *Quarrels of Authors*, 1814.

MANDEVILLE, BERNARD (DE), 1670–1733

Ignoring medical treatises in Latin published in the previous century in Holland, Mandeville's first production was *Some Fables after the Easie and Familiar Method of Monsieur de la Fontaine*, 1703, reissued in 1704 with additions as *Æsop Dress'd or a Collection of Fables Writ in Familiar Verse*. In 1703 there also appeared anon., but probably by Mandeville, *The Pamphleteers, a Satyr*. In 1704 he produced *Typhon: or the War between the Gods and Giants: A Burlesque Poem in Imitation of the Comical Mons. Scarron*; and in 1705 his famous *The Grumbling Hive: or, Knaves Turn'd Honest*. His last verse production was *Wishes to a Godson, with other Miscellany Poems*, 1712.

His first prose treatise was *The Virgin Unmask'd: or, Female Dialogues between an Elderly Maiden Lady, and her Niece*, &c., 1709, which in 1714 was reissued as *The Mysteries of Virginity*. He next produced *A Treatise of the Hypochondriack and Hysteric Passions, Vulgarly Call'd the Hypo in Men and Vapours in Women*, 1711, enlarged 1730 as *A Treatise of the Hypochondriack and Hysterick Diseases in Three Dialogues*. His great contentious work, *The Fable of the Bees: or, Private Vices, Publick Benefits*, appeared in 1714. This contained *The Grumbling Hive*, followed by an essay 'An Enquiry into the Origin of Moral Virtue' which prefaced the twenty Remarks explanatory of the poem. Another edition in 1723 contained the Remarks much enlarged, 'An Essay on Charity and Charity Schools' and 'A Search into the Nature of Society'. This was followed in 1728 (d. 1729) by *The Fable of the Bees. Part II. By the Author of the First*, made up of a Preface and six dialogues. From 1734 the two parts were published together. He further produced: *Free Thoughts on Religion, the Church, and National Happiness*, 1720; *A Modest Defence of Publick Stews: or, An Essay upon Whoring, as it is now Practis'd in these Kingdoms*, 1724; *An Enquiry into the Causes of the Frequent Executions at Tyburn*, 1725; *An Enquiry into the Origin of Honour, and the Usefulness of Christianity in War*, 1732; and finally *A Letter to Dion, Occasion'd by his Book Call'd Alciphron, or The Minute Philosopher*, also 1732.

For bibliography see F. B. Kaye. 'The Writings of Bernard Mandeville', *JEGP* xx, 1921; and 'The Mandeville Canon: A Supplement', *N & Q*, 3 May 1924.

F. B. Kaye's *The Fable of the Bees: or Private Vices, Publick Benefits . . . With a Commentary Critical, Historical, and Explanatory*, 2 vols., 1924, is the only modern reprint, and remains the classic study of the work. It does not, however, include *A Letter to Dion*, which was ed. B. Dobrée, 1954, and in the same year by the Augustan Reprint Society, Ann Arbor.

Early replies are noted under Dennis, Law, Hutcheson, and Watts; to these may be added Archibald Campbell's *An Enquiry into the Original of Moral Virtue*, 1733. Mandeville began to attract serious attention late in the nineteenth century, from Leslie Stephen's 'Mandeville's Fable of the Bees' in *Essays on Freethinking and Plainspeaking*, 1873, and his *History of English Thought in the Eighteenth Century*, 2 vols., 1876. J. M. Robertson discussed him in *Essays towards a Critical Method*, 1889, expanding his comment in *Pioneer Humanists*, 1907.

Books on Mandeville are: A. Morize, *L'Apologie du luxe au XVIIIᵉ siècle et Le mondain de Voltaire*, Paris, 1909; and W. Deckelmann, *Untersuchungen zur Bienenfabel Mandevilles und zu ihrer Entstehungsgeschichte im Hinblick auf die Bienenfabelthese*, Hamburg, 1933.

Articles and chapters include: W. Hasbach, 'La Rochefoucault und Mandeville', *Schmoller's Jahrbuch* xiv, 1890; N. Wilde, 'Mandeville's Place in English Thought', *Mind* vii, 1898; F. B. Kaye, 'Mandeville on the Origin of Language', *MLN* xxxix, 1924; and J. C. Maxwell, 'Ethics and Politics in Mandeville', *Philosophy* xxvi, 1951.

MANLEY, MARY DE LA RIVIÈRE, 1663–1724

Of Mrs. Manley's plays, the first two were acted and printed in 1696: *The Lost Lover; or the Jealous Husband*, a comedy; and *The Royal Mischief*, a tragedy. These were succeeded by two tragedies: *Almyna: or, The Arabian Vow*, 1706, printed 1707; and *Lucius, the First Christian King of Britain*, 1717.

Her first attempt at fiction was 'A Letter from a supposed Nun in Portugal', included in *Letters Written by Mrs Manley . . . by Colonel Pack*, 1696. Her most famous work, *The Secret History of Queen Zarah and the Zarazians; being a Looking-Glass for — in the Kingdom of Albigion. Faithfully translated*, &c., appeared in

1705 as printed in Albigion. *Secret Memoirs and Manners of Several Persons of Quality, of Both Sexes. From the New Atalantis, an Island in the Mediterranean. Written originally in Italian* in 1709. *The Adventures of Rivella; or, the History of the Author of the Atalantis*, &c., in 1714. *The Power of Love, in Seven Novels* appeared in 1720. Succeeding Swift as editor of the *Examiner* in 1711, she wrote, with help from Swift, 'A True Narrative of what passed at the Examination of Guiscard': 'A Comment on Dr Hare's Sermon'; and, unaided, 'The Duke of M—h's Vindication'. In 1713 she wrote in reply to Steele, *The Honour and Prerogative of the Queen's Majesty Vindicated and Defended against the Unexampled Insolence of the Author of the Guardian*; and, in 1714, *A Modest Enquiry into the Reasons of the Joy expressed by a certain Set of People upon the Spreading of a Report of Her Majesty's Death*.

'Mistress Delariviere Manley's Biography' was contributed by P. B. Anderson to *MP* xxxiii, 1936.

MILLER, JAMES, 1706–44

Miller published most of his verse anon., beginning with *Harlequin-Horace*, 1731, continuing with *Seasonable Reproof, A Satire*, 1735; *Of Politics: An Epistle*, 1738; and *Are These Things So?*, 1740. His only immediately acknowledged poem was *The Art of Life. In Imitation of Horace's Art of Poetry. Epistle the First*, 1739. He did not continue.

He wrote in all nine pieces for the stage, beginning with *The Humours of Oxford*, acted and printed, 1730. This also was anon., as were two other of his plays. His most successful piece was *The Man of Taste*, acted and printed 1735. In his only tragedy, *Mahomet the Impostor*, acted and printed 1744, he collaborated with John Hoadly. His last venture, a ballad-opera, *The Picture: or, The Cuckold in Conceit*, was produced and published posthumously in 1745. In conjunction with Henry Baker he produced a translation of *The Works of Molière*, 10 vols., 1739, a version still current in *EL*.

Miscellaneous Works in Verse and Prose, vol. i, including his first four plays, appeared in 1741. The collection was not continued.

MONTAGU, LADY MARY (PIERREPONT) WORTLEY, 1689–1762

Curll seized the *Town Eclogues*, published as such in 1747, and piratically produced them in 1716 as *Court Poems; By a Lady of Quality.* Her poems remained scattered till edited by I. Reed as *The Poetical Works* in 1768.

The anonymous periodical, the *Nonsense of Common Sense,* 8 nos., mainly written by Lady Mary, ran from 16 Dec. 1737 to 21 Feb. 1738. It was edited by R. Halsband in 1947 (Evanston). *Letters of Rt. Hon. Lady M—y W—y M—e written during her travels,* 3 vols., 1763, were published without authority with a preface by M[ary] A[stell]. *Letters from the Levant,* ed. J. A. St. John appeared in 1838; and *Letters from Lady Mary Wortley Montagu,* ed. R. B. Johnson, *EL,* in 1906.

Her *Works,* including her correspondence, were edited by J. Dallaway, 5 vols., 1837; the standard edition is her *Letters and Works* edited by Lord Wharncliffe, 3 vols., 1837; enlarged in 1861, when edited with new memoir by W. Moy Thomas.

C. W. Dilke included a chapter on her in *Papers of a Critic,* vol. i, 1875. Full-length biographies, with varied selections from the letters, occur frequently, now superseded by R. Halsband's *Life of Lady Mary Wortley Montagu,* 1956, which contains much new material, and gives a list of manuscript sources.

Of interest are: G. Tillotson, 'Lady Mary Wortley Montagu and Pope's "Elegy to an Unfortunate Lady"', *RES* xii, 1936; and R. Halsband, 'Pope, Lady Mary, and the Court Poems', *PMLA* lxviii, 1953.

MORRICE, BEZALEEL, *c.* 1675–1749

His first book, *The Muses' Treat,* appeared in 1702, and his *Miscellanies and Amusements in Prose and Verse* in 1712. In 1721 Morrice published *An Epistle to Mr Welsted,* on the character of his verse, and a *Satyre on the English translations of Homer.* In the same year appeared *An Essay on the Poets.* He printed *All is Fish, that comes to Net* in Dublin, 1735. *The Present Corruption of Britons,* a 'paraphrase' in verse of Pope's *One Thousand Seven Hundred and Thirty Eight* was printed in 1738.

For further details see the Biographical Appendix to vol. v of the Twickenham ed. of Pope.

NEAL, DANIEL, 1678–1743

Neal published *The History of New-England,* 2 vols., in 1720. *The History of the Puritans or Protestant Non-Conformists, from the Reformation to the Act of Toleration* appeared in 4 vols. from 1732 to 1738. A 5-vol. edition edited by J. Toulmin, 1793–7, contains a Life of Neal. Neal also published sermons.

NORTH, ROGER, 1653–1734

The only work published during his lifetime was *A Discourse of Fish and Fish-Ponds, By a Person of Honour*, 1713. His posthumously published works are: *Examen; or an Enquiry into the Veracity of a Pretended Complete History*, &c., 1740; *The Life of Francis North, Baron of Guilford*, 1742; *The Life of Sir Dudley North, and of Dr. John North*, 1744. Later publications consist of: *A Discourse on the Study of the Laws*, 1824; *Memoirs of Musick*, edited by E. F. Rimbault, 1846; *Autobiography*, edited by A. Jessopp, 1887; *The Musicall Grammarian*, edited by H. Andrews, 1925. The three Lives were published in 3 vols., 1826, and these, together with the *Autobiography*, were published in 3 vols., 1890, edited by A. Jessopp.
See R. W. Kelton-Cremer, *E & S*, 1959.

OLDMIXON, JOHN, 1673–1742

His early work is that of a poetaster and very minor playwright, opening in 1696 with *Poems on Several Occasions*, in the manner of Anacreon, continuing with two theatrical pieces, *Amyntas* in 1698, a pastoral play with a prologue by Dennis, and in 1700, *The Grove, or Love's Paradice*, with music by Purcell, and an epilogue by Farquhar. He may have written *Reflections on the Stage*, 1699. In 1712, with Maynwaring's *The British Academy*, he published *Reflections on Dr Swift's Letter to Harley*, ed. L. A. Landa, the Augustan Reprint Society, Ann Arbor, 1948. He was concerned with *The Court of Atalantis, Intermixt with Fables and Epistles in Verse and Prose, By Several Hands*, 1714, reissued as *Court Tales; or a History of the Amours of the Present Nobility. To which is added a Compleat Key*, 1717.

His historical work began with *The British Empire in America*, 1708, revised 1741; a chapter from the latter edition, 'The History of the Isle of Providence', was ed. R. Kent, 1949. His political trend became apparent in *The Medley* of 1710, other anti-Tory exercises being *A Secret History of Europe*, 1712, in two parts, a third appearing in 1713, and a fourth in 1714. In this year he produced also *Arcana Gallica; or the Secret History of France*, equally a piece of party polemics. *The Critical History of England*, 2 vols., 1724, reached a third edition in 1728, when the

Essay on Criticism was added, and again published separately in that year with its full title, *As it regards Design, Thought, and Expression, in Prose and Verse.* His major work, *The History of England during the reigns of the Royal House of Stuart. Wherein the Errors of Late Histories are Discover'd and Corrected,* issued in 1730 (d. 1729), was continued in *The History of England during the Reigns of William and Mary,* 1735, and concluded in 1739 with a volume devoted to the Tudors. *Memoirs of the Press, Historical and Political, for Thirty Years past, from 1710–1740,* was posthumously published in 1742.

He is included in *Baker* and in *Cibber*. D'Israeli discusses him in *Calamities of Authors.*

PARNELL, THOMAS, 1679–1718

Except for *An Essay on the Different Stiles of Poetry,* little of Parnell's verse was printed in his lifetime, though some was included in Steele's *Poetical Miscellanies,* 1714. *Poems on Several Occasions. Published by Mr Pope,* appeared in 1722. There have been a number of collected editions: *Works in Verse and Prose,* Glasgow, 1755; *The Posthumous Works,* Dublin, 1758; *The Poetical Works,* Glasgow, 1786. His poems were ed. J. Mitford, 1833; R. A. Wilmot, 1854; G. A. Aitken, 1894; L. Robinson, Dublin, 1927; and H. I'A. Faussett in *Minor Poets of the Eighteenth Century,* EL, 1930, who included all of them. See also *Johnson* xliv, *Anderson* vii, *Chalmers* ix.

Parnell contributed essays to the *Spectator,* nos. 460, 501, and the *Guardian,* nos. 56, 66. *An Essay on the Life, Writings, and Learning of Homer* prefaced Pope's *Iliad,* 1715; and *Homer's Battle of Frogs and Mice, with the Remarks of Zoilus, to which is prefix'd the Life of the said Zoilus,* 1717, was later added as a preface to Pope's *Iliad and Odyssey.*

Goldsmith wrote a Life (with Works) in 1770. For criticism, besides *Johnson,* see R. W. Jackson, 'Parnell, the Poet', *Dublin Mag.* xx, 1945.

PHILIPS, AMBROSE, c. 1675–1749

Philips published *Persian Tales* (for half a crown) in 1709. His *Pastorals,* which had first appeared seriatim in various Miscellanies from 1706, were issued in 1710, his 'Winter Piece', 'To the Earl of Dorset' having been printed in the *Tatler,* 5–7 May 1709. There subsequently appeared *An Epistle to the*

Right Honourable Lord Halifax, 1714, and *An Epistle to the Honourable James Craggs*, 1716. His 'namby-pamby' poems were printed, Dublin, 1725, 1726, and 1727. In 1748 he published *Pastorals, Odes and other original Poems, with translations from Pindar, Anacreon, and Sappho*. See *Johnson* xliv; *Anderson* ix; and *Chalmers* xiii.

His first play, *The Distrest Mother*, was acted and printed in 1712; *The Briton* in 1722, and *Humfrey, Duke of Gloucester* in 1723. These were collected in *Three Tragedies*, 1725.

He also edited *A Collection of Old Ballads*, 3 vols., 1723, seq., reprinted 1872. He was chief contributor to *The Grumbler*, 1715, and edited and mainly wrote *The Freethinker*, twice weekly, 24 Mar. 1718–28 July 1721.

A Variorum Text of Four Pastorals was ed. R. H. Griffiths, *Texas Univ. Studies* xii, 1932; *The Poems of Ambrose Philips*, admirably edited with Life by M. G. Segar, appeared in 1937.

Recent studies include: L. de la T. Bueno, 'The Canon of Philips: *PQ* xix, 1940; A. J. Bryan, 'Humphrey, Duke of Gloucester', in *Studies for W. A. Read*, Baton Rouge, 1940; and K. E. Wheatley, 'Andromaque as the "Distrest Mother"', *Romanic Rev.* xxxix, 1948.

PHILIPS, JOHN, 1676–1709

Philips's first poem, *The Splendid Shilling*, appeared originally in *A Collection of Poems*, an anthology issued by Daniel Brown and Benjamin Tooke, in 1701. A spurious separate edition appeared in 1705, to be followed almost immediately by a correct one. *Bleinheim* was published very early in 1705, possibly at the end of the previous year. There were three more editions in 1705, one in 1709, and one in 1713. *Cerealia* was printed once in 1706, and the *Ode to Henry St John* in 1707. *Cyder. A Poem* was published in 1708, and appeared again in the same year with a few other poems, a collection reprinted in the next year.

The Works were first collected in 1712; *Poems* in 1713, and other collocations appeared, containing different selections, that of 1714 including the *Pastorals* of Ambrose Philips. *The Whole Works* was produced by Tonson in 1720. See *Johnson* xxi; *Chalmers* viii; and *Anderson* vi.

Sewell's Life appeared with his edition in 1712, and *The Life and Character of Mr. John Philips. Written by Mr Sewell*

was issued together with *The Splendid Shilling* and *Bleinheim* by
Curll in 1715. See also *Jacob*.

The most recent edition of *The Poems of John Philips* is that
by M. G. Lloyd Thomas, 1927, containing an Introduction
covering his life and reputation among his contemporaries,
and a full bibliography up to 1720.

A separate study, *John Philips*, was made by L. A. Harrach,
Kreuznach, 1906; and 'The Life and Works of John Philips'
constitutes chapter x of H. de Maar's *A History of Modern
English Romantics*, 1924.

PITT, CHRISTOPHER, 1699–1748

Pitt published *A Poem on the death of the late Earl Stanhope* in
1721, and in 1725 *Vida's Art of Poetry, translated into English
Verse*, followed by his *Poems and Translations*, 1727. *An Essay on
Virgil's Æneid, being a translation of the First Book* appeared in
1728, and *The Æneid of Virgil, Translated*, 2 vols., 1740. *Poems
by the celebrated translator of Virgil's Æneid* was published in 1756.

See also *Johnson* xliii; *Anderson* xii, which includes *The Æneid*;
and *Chalmers* xix, which reprints the *Vida*. Life by Johnson.

POMFRET, JOHN, 1667–1702

Nearly all Pomfret's work falls within this period; earlier
there are only *An Epistle to Charles, Earl of Dorset*, 1690, and
The Sceptical Muse, 1699. *The Prospect of Death*, written in 1700,
was printed with Lady Winchilsea's *The Spleen* in 1709. *Reason*
and *The Choice or Wish* appeared in 1700, and *Two Love Poems*
in 1701. See also *Johnson* xxi; *Anderson* vi; and *Chalmers* viii.

Criticism is to be found in E. E. Kellett's *Reconsiderations*,
1928.

POPE, ALEXANDER, 1688–1744

Pope first appeared in Tonson's *Poetical Miscellanies*, part vi,
2 vols., 1709, with 'January and May', from Chaucer's 'The
Merchant's Tale', 'The Episode of Sarpedon' from the *Iliad*,
and 'Pastorals'. In 1711 he issued, anonymously in the first
instance, *An Essay on Criticism*; and in 1712 Tonson included
'Sappho to Phaon' in his 8th edition of *Ovid's Epistles*. In the
same year Lintot, in *Miscellaneous Poems and Translations. By
Several Hands*, printed among other poems by Pope, 'To a
Young Lady, with the Works of Voiture', and 'The Rape of the

Locke', the early version in two cantos. 'The Messiah' appeared in the *Spectator* of 14 May. In 1713 were printed *Windsor Forest*, the Prologue to Addison's *Cato*, and the 'Ode for Musick, on St Cecilia's Day'. The enlarged version of *The Rape of the Lock*, in five cantos, appeared in 1714, and in that year Steele's *Poetical Miscellanies* contained 'The Wife of Bath' from Chaucer, and 'The Arrival of Ulysses in Ithaca' together with 'The Gardens of Alcinous' from the 13th and 7th Books of the *Odyssey*. Books I–IV of the *Iliad* were published in 1715, Books V–VIII in 1716, Books IX–XII in 1717, Books XIII–XVI in 1718, and Books XVII–XXIV in 1720. Pope meanwhile wrote much light verse: 'A Farewell to London. In the Year 1715' (not published till 1775); 'To Mr John Moore, Author of the Celebrated Worm-Powder'; 'A Roman Catholick Version of the First Psalm', &c., 1716. 'The Court Ballad' appeared in 1717, in which year Pope issued his *Works*, which contained the final version of 'The Rape of the Lock', 'Eloisa to Abelard', 'Verses to the Memory of an Unfortunate Lady', and the 'Epistle to a Lady on her leaving the Town after the Coronation'. His 'To Mr Addison, Occasioned by his Dialogue on Medals' appeared in Tickell's edition of Addison's *Works*, 1721, and his 'Epistle to the Earl of Oxford' prefaced his edition of Parnell's *Poems*, 1722. The *Odyssey* was published in 5 vols., three in 1725, two in 1726. Vols. i and ii of the Pope–Swift *Miscellanies* appeared 1727, vol. iii, called 'the last', 1728, containing 'Sandys's Ghost', 'Macer', and 'Umbra'. Vol. iv appeared in 1732, the whole being issued in 6 vols. in 1736. 'To Quinbus Flestrin' and the other 'Gulliver' pieces were printed in *Several Copies of Verses on Occasion of Mr Gulliver's Travels*, 1727.

The Dunciad, An Heroic Poem in Three Books appeared in May 1728, in rival 'first' editions, one said to be printed at Dublin, *The Dunciad Variorum, with the Prolegomena of Scriblerus*, April 1729. The first version of 'The Dying Christian to his Soul' was printed in Lewis's 1730 *Miscellaneous Poems*, and various epigrams and inscriptions appeared in the *Grub-Street Journal* from 1730 to 1737. The Moral Essays began with *Of Taste, An Epistle to the Right Honourable the Earl of Burlington*, 1731, later named 'Of False Taste', and finally 'Of the Use of Riches', becoming the fourth Moral Essay. The second Epistle, *To Allen, Lord Bathurst*, also called 'Of the Use of Riches', afterwards the third Moral Essay, appeared Jan. 1733, in the same year as, anon. the first and separate issue of Donne's fourth Satire, *The Impertinent. Or a Visit to the Court*, the first Imitation of Horace (*Sat.* II. i) *To Mr Fortescue*, and, anon. the first three Epistles of *An Essay on Man*. The fourth Epistle appeared in the next year, as did a collected edition. In 1734 Pope also published the Epistle *To Richard Temple, Viscount Cobham*, which became Moral Essay I, 'Of the Knowledge and Characters of Men'; Horace, *Sat.* II. ii *To Mr Bethell*; and *Sober Advice from Horace, to the Young Gentlemen about Town. As deliver'd in his Second Sermon. Imitated in the Manner of Mr Pope*. In 1735 was published *An Epistle from Mr Pope to Dr Arbuthnot*, later called 'The Prologue to the Satires' and *Of the Characters of Women: An Epistle to a Lady*, afterwards the second Moral Essay; and *Works*, ii, which contained the Donne satires. The imitation of Horace's *Epistle* II. ii, as did that of Epistle II. i, commonly known as *The Epistle to Augustus*, and the *Ode to Venus* (Horace, *Odes* IV. i) came out in 1737. In the next year appeared the imitation of Horace, *Ode* I. vi, *To Mr Murray*; the version of Satire II. vi, partly done by Swift and published in the *Miscellanies* of 1727, now completed by Pope; Horace, *Epistle* I. i *To L. Bolingbroke*. In 1738 there also appeared the two parts of the *Epilogue to the Satires*, issued separately as *One Thousand Seven Hundred and Thirty Eight, Dialogue I* and *Dialogue II*. In 1742 Pope produced *The New Dunciad*, which was incorporated as Book IV of the final version of *The Dunciad*, 1743 (with Cibber as hero instead of Theobald).

There have been many collections of Pope's poems, beginning with his own *Works* of 1717 and 1735, and they appear in all the series of British Poets, see especially *Johnson* xxxii–xxxviii; *Anderson* viii; and *Chalmers* xi and xii, which includes the Homer. They were edited by A. Dyce, 3 vols., 1831, revised by G. R. Dennis, 1891; there is the Bohn edition of 1847; the Globe ed. A. W. Ward, 1869, and *The Complete Poetical Works* ed. H. W. Boynton, Boston, 1903. Not quite complete is the *EL* volume, ed. E. Rhys, 1924, revised B. Dobrée, 1956. Separate editions of *Pope's Homer* have also been printed.

The standard edition is now the scholarly Twickenham Edition, of which the General Editor is J. Butt, each volume containing Introductions and critical apparatus and notes. Vol. i has not yet appeared; it will contain *Pastoral Poetry* and *An Essay on Criticism*; vol. ii, *The Rape of the Lock and Other Poems*,

ed. G. Tillotson, 1940; vol. iii, part i, *An Essay on Man*, ed.
M. Mack, 1950; part ii, *Epistles to Several Persons* (Moral Essays),
ed. F. W. Bateson, 1951; vol. iv, *Imitations of Horace* (including
the Donne satires), ed. J. Butt, 1939; vol. v, *The Dunciad*, ed.
J. Sutherland, 1943; vol. vi, *Minor Poems*, ed. N. Ault and J. Butt,
1954. The 'Homer' is in preparation.

Pope's essays in the *Guardian*, nos. 4, 11, 40, 61, 78, 91, 92, and
173, appeared in 1713. In that year also appeared *The Narrative of Dr Robert Norris concerning the strange and deplorable Frenzy
of Mr John Denn—An Officer of the Custom House*, &c. In 1715,
besides the Preface to the translation of the *Iliad*, Pope published *A Key to the Lock. By Esdras Barnivelt.* There followed in
1716 *A Full and True Account of a Horrid and Barbarous Revenge by
Poison on the Body of Mr Edmund Curll*, and *God's Revenge against
Punning.* Apart from the Preface to his *Works* 1717, which also
contained 'A Discourse on Pastoral Poetry' no other prose
writing appeared until the Preface to his edition of Shakespeare,
1725, and the Preface to the *Miscellanies* he wrote with Swift,
1727; *Peri Bathous* was printed in the 'last' volume of the series,
1728, ed. E. L. Steeves, 1952. This first Scriblerus essay was
the forerunner of *Memoirs Of the Extraordinary Life, Works, and
Discoveries of Martinus Scriblerus* which appeared in *The Works
of Mr Alexander Pope, in Prose*, vol. ii, 1741, ed. C. Kerby-Miller,
1950. *A Letter to a Noble Lord* was first printed in Warburton's
edition (see below). The only modern collection of *Prose Works*
is that of N. Ault, i, 1936.

Pope collaborated with Gay and Arbuthnot in *Three Hours
After Marriage*, 1717. See under Gay.

His editorial work comprised: Thomas Parnell's *Poems on
Several Occasions. Published by Mr Pope*, 1722; *The Works of John
Sheffield, Earl of Mulgrave, Marquis of Normanby, and Duke of
Buckingham*, 1725; and *The Works of Shakspear Collated and Cor-
rected by the former Editions*, 1725.

Many of Pope's letters appeared during his life. Curll in his
Miscellanea, 2 vols., 1727, printed, without authorization, the
correspondence with Cromwell. Pope's edition of Wycherley
(see below), 1729, contained the Wycherley correspondence.
In 1735 there were issued various collections: *Letters of Mr
Pope, and Several Eminent Persons*; *Mr Pope's Literary Correspondence*,
3 vols. of the latter appearing in that year, a fourth in 1736, and
a fifth in 1737. In 1735 George Faulkner reprinted one of the

editions of the *Several Eminent Persons* publications, Dublin, and
*Letters from Alexander Pope, Esq: and the Right Hon. the Lord
Bolingbroke, to the Reverend Dr. Swift, D.S.P.D....*, Dublin, 1737,
stated to be reprinted from London. In 1737 Pope himself took
a hand, and apart from largely overseeing octavo editions of
The Works of Alexander Pope Esq., v and vi, was responsible for
a quarto and a folio edition. The Curll and Faulkner editions
of Swift's letters in 1741 added more. (For details see Sherburn
below, pp. xviii–xxv). The Aaron Hill correspondence appeared in *A Collection of Letters*, 1751; and the Judith Cowper
Madan correspondence in *Letters to a Lady*, 1769. The Elwin-
Courthope edition of the *Works*, 1871–89, contained many new
letters in vi to ix. But the definitive edition is the superb one
The Correspondence of Alexander Pope, edited by George Sherburn,
5 vols., 1956.

W. Warburton had been helped considerably by Pope himself in preparing his great edition of the *Works*, 9 vols., 1751,
which included some unpublished material. Other editions
followed: by Joseph Warton, 9 vols., 1797; by William Bowles,
10 vols., 1806; by William Roscoe, with a new Life, 10 vols.,
1824; and finally by W. Elwin and W. J. Courthope, 10 vols.,
1871–89.

The standard bibliography is the masterly *Alexander Pope;
a Bibliography*, by R. H. Griffith, vol. i in two parts, Austin,
Texas, 1922. *Pope and his Critics*, by W. L. Macdonald, 1951,
will be found useful. Also to be consulted are T. J. Wise's
A Catalogue of the Ashley Library, vol. iv, 1923; and *A Pope
Library. A Catalogue of Plays, Poems and Prose Writings by Alexander
Pope*, 1931.

The first Life of Pope, probably by himself, is to be found in
Jacob. Those by W. Ayre, 1745, and Owen Ruffhead, 1769, are
of little value (for these and others see Sherburn below: Introduction. Earlier Biographies). The first good Life was that in
Johnson, which, in common with the previous ones, owed a good
deal to Spence's *Anecdotes* (see under Spence), though these
were not published until 1820. The Life that Bowles prefixed to
his edition is worthless, and not much more useful is that of
R. Carruthers, 2 vols., 1853, revised 1858. C. W. Dilke's *Papers
of a Critic*, 2 vols., 1875, are of the first importance, especially as
regards the fantastic imbroglio of the letters; they should be read
together with the slightly prejudiced *Pope* by Leslie Stephen,

1880 ('English Men of Letters'), though this adds little to the Elwin–Courthope Life prefixed to their edition in 1871. The first sympathetic study was that by Edith Sitwell, *Alexander Pope*, 1930; but the classic Life up to 1728 is G. Sherburn's *The Early Career of Alexander Pope*, 1934. *New Light on Pope* by N. Ault, 1949, makes useful additions. B. Dobrée, *Alexander Pope*, 1951, is brief, embodying previous findings.

A certain amount of incidental detail is to be gleaned from *Nichols*, from the letters of Lady Mary Wortley Montagu, from Chesterfield's 'Characters'; from Cibber's *Apology*, 1470, and *A Letter From Mr. Cibber to Mr. Pope*, 1742. A good account of one side of Pope is given in I. D'Israeli's *Quarrels of Authors*, 1814. Dilke and W. J. Thoms in mid-nineteenth century sprinkled the *Athenaeum* and *N & Q* with valuable notes and commentaries.

Pope early became subject to criticism, but the only contemporary criticism of any weight is that of Dennis (see under Dennis) and Spence's appreciative *An Essay on Pope's Odyssey*, 1726–7, unless J. P. de Crousaz's *Examen de l'Essai de M. Pope sur l'Homme*, Lausanne, 1737, translated by Elizabeth Carter, 1738, be included. There is, naturally, some criticism in Warburton's edition, but the first general work of any value is Joseph Warton's *An Essay on the Writings and Genius of Mr Pope*, i, 1756; ii, 1782. Johnson's *Life* contains much interesting criticism. The counter to Warton was Percival Stockdale's *An Enquiry into the Nature and General Laws of Poetry, including a particular Defence of the Writings and Genius of Mr Pope*, 1778. Bowles's edition, 1806, called forth several replies, notably from Byron, more especially in his *Letter to John Murray, Esq. on The Rev. W. L. Bowles's Strictures on the Life and Writings of Pope*. In this connexion Bowles published *Observations, etc.* and replied to Byron specifically in *Two Letters to the Right Honourable Lord Byron etc.* Byron replied in a second letter to Murray, *Observations upon 'Observations'*, all 1821. He was treated of by Hazlitt in *Lectures on the English Poets*, 1818, and by De Quincey in his article in the *Encyclopaedia Britannica*, 1838–9, though this is largely biographical. (See De Quincey's *Works*, Edinburgh, 1863, vol. xv, and in other places, see D. Masson's edition, 1889–90, vols. iv and xi.) Leslie Stephen, in addition to his biography, discussed him in *Hours in a Library*, 1874; *History of English Thought in the Eighteenth Century*, 2 vols., 1876; and *English Literature and Society in the 18th Century*, 1904. A. Beljame (p. 591) will be found useful.

Recent major studies include: A. Warren, *Alexander Pope as a Critic and Humanist*, Princeton, 1929; G. Tillotson, *On the Poetry of Pope*, 1938, rev. ed. 1950; R. K. Root, *The Poetical Career of Pope*, Princeton, 1938; G. Tillotson, *The Moral Poetry of Pope*, 1946, and *Pope and Human Nature*, 1958. N. Ault's *New Light on Pope* is useful here also. Interesting works are *Windsor Forest, 1712, a Study of the Washington University Holograph*, by R. M. Schmitz, St. Louis, 1952, and D. M. Knight, *Pope and the Heroic Tradition: a Critical Study of his Iliad*, New Haven, 1951. Less specialized is G. W. Knight's *The Laureate of Peace*, 1954. *Pope's Dunciad*, by A. L. Williams, 1955, may be read in connexion with R. W. Rogers's *The Major Satires of Pope*, 1955.

Many important studies in chapter form are to be found in: F. R. Leavis, *Revaluations*, 1936; in *Essays on the Eighteenth Century* (p. 591), namely 'Pope at Work' by G. Sherburn, and 'The Inspiration of Pope's Poetry' by J. Butt; *Pope and His Contemporaries* (p. 591), J. Laird's *Philosophical Incursions into English Literature*, 1946; 'Essay on Man' reprinted from *RES* xx, 1944; *The Well-Wrought Urn*, by Cleanth Brooks, N.Y., 1947; W. Empson's 'Wit in the Essay on Criticism' in *The Structure of Complex Words*, 1951; I. Jack's *Augustan Satire: Intention and Idiom*, 1951; and *The Seventeenth Century: Studies in the History of English Thought and Literature from Bacon to Pope*, by R. F. Jones *et al.*, Stanford, 1951, notably E. N. Hooker's 'Pope on Wit: the Essay on Criticism'.

Essays in journals include: J. R. Sutherland, 'Wordsworth and Pope', *Proc. Brit. Acad.* xxx, 1944; V. A. Dearing, 'The First Printing of the Letters of Pope and Swift', *Library*, 4th series, xxiv, 1944; J. M. Cameron, 'Doctrinal to an Age: Notes towards a Revaluation of Pope's Essay on Man', *Dublin Review* ccxxv, 1951; and J. Butt, 'Pope's Poetical Manuscripts', *Proc. Brit. Acad.* xl, 1954.

PRIOR, MATTHEW, 1664–1721

The Hind and Panther Transvers'd to the Story of the Country Mouse and the City Mouse, written with Charles Montagu, was first published anon. in 1687. It was included in the *State Poems* of 1703, and separately published in 1709. Prior's next important contribution was *An English Ballad: in answer to Mr. Despreaux's Pindarique Ode on the Taking of Namur*, 1695, followed in 1700 by

Carmen Saeculare for the Year 1700. Other poems appeared in various miscellanies, such as 'Hans Carvel' in *A Collection of Poems*, 1702, and 'An Epistle to Fleetwood Shepherd Esq.', 1689, in the 1703–4 *Dryden Miscellany.* Separate publications included *To a Young Gentleman in Love*, 1702; *A Letter to Monsieur Boileau Despreaux; occasion'd by the Victory at Blenheim* (anon.), 1704; *An English Padlock*, 1705; and *An Ode Humbly Inscrib'd to the Queen*, 1706. *Earl Robert's Mice: A Poem in Imitation of Chaucer* was twice printed in 1712, the first copy being pirated; and in the same year was included with 'Susannah and the Two Elders' in *Two Imitations of Chaucer. The Conversation. A Tale* appeared in 1720, and *Colin's Mistake: Written in Imitation of Spenser's Style* in 1721. Posthumously there were printed in 1723 *The Turtle and the Sparrow* and *Down Hall: A Poem.* Further poems appeared in *A New Collection of Miscellaneous Poems by Mr Prior, and Others* of 1725; and in 1741 there was published *Lyric Poems: Being Twenty-four Songs (never before printed)*, now known as 'Songs Set to Music'.

Curll pirated a collected edition in 1707, which was followed by Tonson's authorized *Poems on Several Occasions* in 1709. In 1716 Roberts pirated a collection, superseded by the superb folio of 1718, which included 'Alma' and 'Solomon'.

The Poetical Works were ed. T. Evans, 2 vols., 1779, by J. Mitford, 1835, and by Gilfillan, 1858, Edinburgh. See also *Johnson* xxx, xxxi; *Anderson* vii; *Chalmers* x.

In 1740 (Dublin, 1739) J. Bancks compiled from the papers of Prior's executor, Adrian Drift, *Miscellaneous Works*, 2 vols., the second being a *History of His Own Time.* In 1905 A. R. Waller published *Poems on Several Occasions*, in 1907, *Dialogues of the Dead and Other Works.* This contains the hitherto unpublished 'Poems from the Longleat MSS.', and the two essays 'Upon Learning' and 'Upon Utopia'. This edition has full critical apparatus. *The Literary Works*, ed. H. B. Wright and M. K. Spears, 2 vols., 1959, is the fullest.

Memoirs of the Life of M. Prior, with a Copy of his Will appeared in 1722; he appears in *Jacob* and *Cibber*; but there was no Life, apart from Johnson's, until Francis Bickley produced his *Life* in 1914, which he followed up in 1921 by *Matthew Prior: a Study of his Public Career and Correspondence.* C. W. Legg's biographical study appeared 1921, and C. K. Eves's in 1939.

He is considered by: Thackeray (p. 614), J. Dennis in *Studies in English Literature*, 1876; and Austin Dobson in *Eighteenth Century Vignettes* (2nd ser.), 1894. Articles are: G. A. Aitken, *Contemporary Review*, May 1890; O. Doughty, 'The Poet of the "Familiar Style"', *ES* vii, 1925. W. P. Barrett, 'Matthew Prior's Alma', *MLR* xxvii, 1932, is complemented by 'The Meaning of Prior's "Alma"', *ELH* xiii, 1946, by M. K. Spears, whose other studies 'Prior's Attitude toward Natural Science', *PMLA* lxiii, 1948; 'Prior's Religion', *PQ* xxvii, 1948, and 'Ethical Aspects of Prior's Poetry', *SP* xlv, 1948 are equally important.

'PSALMANAZAR, GEORGE', *c.* 1679–1763

He opened his hoax with *An Historical and Geographical History of Formosa*, &c., in 1704, following this up in 1707 with *A Dialogue between a Japanese and a Formosan about some points of the religion of the time*. In 1732 he produced *A General History of Printing* (by S. Palmer), and in 1736 *An Universal History*. His later work includes *Essays, On the Reality of Miracles*, &c., 1753, and his *Memoirs*, published in 1764.

PURNEY, THOMAS, 1695–1728?

Pastorals. After the Simple Manner of Theocritus, 1717, were followed in the same year by *Pastorals: viz. The Bashful Swain: and Beauty in Simplicity*, and in 1718 by *Chevalier de St George: An Heroi-Comick Poem in six Cantos*. He contributed a critical Preface to *The Last Day. A Poem in xii Books by the late J. Bulkeley*, 1720.

The Works was published in 1933 by H. O. White, who also contributed 'Thomas Purney, a Forgotten Poet and Critic to *E & S* xv, 1929. The essay which went with the second set of pastorals, *A Full Enquiry into the True Nature of the Pastoral*, was published by the Augustan Reprint Society, Ann Arbor, 1948, ed. E. R. Wasserman.

RAMSAY, ALLAN, 1686–1758

A Poem to the Memory of the Famous Archibald Pitcairn, M.D., 1713, was followed until 1729, after which Ramsay hardly wrote at all, by a large number of poems, mainly short, often in broadside form, sometimes anonymous, such as *The Young Laird and Edinburgh Katie*, 1720. Among occasional pieces may be mentioned his printing of *Christ's Kirk on the Green*, 1718, to which he added a second canto; *Richy and Sandy. A Pastoral on the Death of Mr Joseph Addison*, 1719; and *Robert, Richy and Sandy. A Pastoral on the Death of Matthew Prior Esq.*, 1721. Especially to be noted are: *Patie and Roger: A Pastoral*, &c., 1720; and *Jenny and Meggy. A Pastoral, Being a Sequel to Patie and Roger*, 1723, as leading up to his best-known work, *The Gentle Shepherd. A Scots Pastoral Comedy*, 1725 (acted 1729). Among his more considerable poems is *The Fair Assembly*, 1723.

He also issued certain collections: *Scots Songs*, 1718, consisting of seven songs, increased to twenty-one in 1720. *Poems*, i, was issued in 1721, ii in 1728. The *Fables and Tales* of 1722, contained fifteen pieces, increased to thirty by 1730. In the meantime there had appeared *Miscellaneous Works*, Dublin, 1724. From 1724 to 1727 he issued *The Tea-Table Miscellany*, 3 vols., a fourth issued in 1740 being doubtfully his. He also, in 1724, edited *The Ever Green, Being a Collection of Scots Poems, Wrote by the Ingenious before 1600*, 2 vols. All the above, except where otherwise noted, were published in Edinburgh. *The Gentle Shepherd* with glossary and tunes was published in Glasgow, 1758.

The Poems, Glasgow, 2 vols., 1797, was the first posthumous edition, followed in 1800 by Chalmers's edn. Other edns. are: W. Tennant, 1819, and C. Mackay, 1866–8. There are selections by J. Logie Robertson, 1887, and H. H. Wood, 1940. A complete *Works* in 4 vols., ed. B. Martin and J. W. Oliver is in process of publication; i, 1951; ii, 1953.

Manuscripts are to be found in B. M. Egerton 2023; in the National Library of Scotland, at the Library of the University of Edinburgh, and at the Huntington Library, California.

'Memoirs of the Life of Allan Ramsay', by 'Philo-Scoticus', appeared in the *Scots Magazine*, Feb. 1797. Chalmers prefixed a Life to his 1800 edition. Ramsay is to be found in various biographical dictionaries or histories of Scottish literature (p. 592). Books comprise: A. Gibson, *A New Light on Allan Ramsay*, Belfast, 1927; B. Martin, *Allan Ramsay*, Cambridge, Mass., 1931.

The first noteworthy criticism appeared in the *Scots Magazine*, 'To the Memory of Allan Ramsay', Feb. 1758. Much criticism is concerned to formulate the relative merits of Ramsay and Robert Fergusson; e.g. E. Picker and A. Wilson, *The Laurel Disputed*, &c., Edinburgh, 1791; and in the same year, also Edinburgh, R. Cummings, *Essay on the Question: Whether have the exertions of Allan Ramsay or Robert Fergusson done the most honour to Scottish Poetry.* Leigh Hunt discussed him in *A Jar of Honey from Mount Hybla*, 1848, as did D. T. Holmes in *Lectures on Scottish Literature*, 1904. See also: J. Veitch, *Feeling for Nature in Scottish Poetry*, ii, 1887; J. W. Mackail, 'Allan Ramsay and the Romantic Revival', *E & S* x, 1924.

REYNOLDS, JOHN, 1667–1727

Death's Vision represented in a Philosophical Sacred Poem appeared in 1709, his *Sermons* in 1714, and a third ed. of his *A Collection of Divine Hymns and Poems upon several occasions*, 1719. He also published *An Inquiry concerning the State and Œconomy of the Angelical Worlds*, 1723. He is treated of in *Newton demands the Muse* by M. H. Nicolson, Princeton, 1946.

RICHARDSON, JONATHAN, the elder, 1665–1745

Besides producing *Essays on the Theory of Painting*, 1715, and *Two Discourses*, especially 'An essay on Criticism as it relates to painting', 1719, he combined with JONATHAN RICHARDSON, the younger (1694–1771), to issue *Explanatory Notes and Remarks on Milton's Paradise Lost*, 1734, himself contributing a Life of Milton and a discourse on the poem.

ROWE, ELIZABETH (*née* SINGER), 1674–1737

Poems on Several Occasions, by Philomela, appeared in 1696; and *The History of Joseph. A Poem. In eight books*, 1736. Verse mingles with prose in *Friendship in Death, in twenty Letters from the Dead to the Living*, 1728. Her book of prayers, *Devout Exercises of the Heart*, was revised and edited by Isaac Watts, 1737.

Miscellaneous Works appeared in 2 vols., 1739, enlarged 4 vols., 1796, with a Life by Theophilus Rowe, reprinted in *Cibber*.

The *Life*, by Thomas Jackson, may be found in x et seq. of *A Library of Christian Biography*, 1837. Apart from Johnson's scattered remarks, the only criticism would seem to be that of T. Velter in *Die göttliche Rowe*, Zürich, 1894, and of J. H. S. Hughes in *PMLA*, lix, 1944.

ROWE, NICHOLAS, 1674–1718

His first play, *The Ambitious Step-Mother*, acted in Dec. 1700, was printed early in 1701. *Tamerlane*, acted in Dec. 1701, was published 1702; and *The Fair Penitent* was acted and published in 1703. His one comedy, or farce, *The Biter*, appeared in 1704, being printed in 1705. *Ulysses*, acted in 1705, was published in 1706; *The Royal Convert* was acted in 1707, and printed in 1708; *The Tragedy of Jane Shore, Written in Imitation of Shakespear's Style* was acted and printed in 1714; and *The Tragedy of Lady Jane Gray* was acted and published in 1715. *The Tragedies* appeared in 2 vols. in 1714, and *The Dramatick Works*, 2 vols., in 1720. *Plays Written by Nicholas Rowe*, 2 vols., in 1736.

In 1709 he issued *The Works of Mr William Shakespear, Revis'd and Corrected*, 6 vols. In 1710 Gildon produced a 7th vol. with his essay and the poems—perhaps unauthorized—and this was reprinted in Rowe's 9-vol. edition, 1714.

Rowe's poetic output is not large. His first verse publication, *A Poem Upon the Late Glorious Successes of her Majesty's Arms*, appeared in 1707, his last, *Ode to the Thames for the Year 1719*, in 1719. Intermediately there had been printed *Poems on Several Occasions*. As Laureate he produced Odes for the years '16 and '17, and Odes to the King. Much of his verse output is translation. He provided 'The Golden Verses of Pythagoras' for a translation of Dacier's *Life of Pythagoras*, 1707; he helped Ozell in his translation of *Le Lutrin*, 1708, and prefixed 'some Account of Boileau's Writings'; he was one of those—Sewell, Cobb, and Diaper being the others—who translated *Callipaedia. A Poem. Written in Latin by Claudius Quillet*, 1712. After his death in 1718 appeared his *Lucan's Pharsalia. Translated into English Verse*, 2 vols. He also edited Nos. 5 and 6 of the Dryden *Poetical Miscellanies*, 1704 and 1709.

The Works, ed. Anne Deanes Devenish, 2 vols., 1747, contains the *Miscellaneous Poems*, but not *The Biter*, nor the longer translations. There was a further edition in 4 vols., 1756.

His translation of Lucan is prefaced with a Life by James Welwood, which was reprinted by Anne Devenish in her edition, and he appears in Johnson's *Lives*. The only book wholly devoted to him is that of O. Intze, *Nicholas Rowe*, Leipzig, 1910. J. R. Sutherland's edition of *Three Plays*, 1929, contains a biographical introduction and a bibliography.

Criticism occurs as early as Gildon's (?) *A Comparison Between the Two Stages*, 1702, and in his *A New Rehearsal; or, Bays the Younger*, 1714, added to in 1715. Walter Scott made 'A Comparison of *The Fair Penitent* with Massinger's *The Fatal Dowry*' in the *Observer*, Nos. 88, 89, and 90 in 1790, a matter taken up by D. B. Clark in 'An Eighteenth-Century Adaptation of Massinger' in *MLQ* xii, 1952. Of interest are: A. Jackson 'Rowe's Historical Tragedies', *Ang.* liv, 1930; G. W. Whiting 'Rowe's Debt to "Paradise Lost"', *MP* xxxii, 1935; and W. Thorpe, 'A Key to Rowe's "Tamerlane"', *JEGP* xxxix, 1940.

SAVAGE, RICHARD, *c.* 1696–1742

Savage brought out his youthful work, *The Convocation: or, a Battle of Pamphlets. A Poem*, in 1717. A gap ensued until the publication of *A Poem to the Glorious Memory of King George*, 1727. Followed in rapid succession, *Nature in Perfection; or, The Mother Unveil'd*, 1728; *The Bastard*, 1728; and *The Wanderer: a poem in five cantos*, 1729, in which Aaron Hill may have had a hand. *The Volunteer Laureat. A poem to her Majesty on her Birthday*, 1732, was the first of an annual series which continued until 1728, in which year he also wrote *A Poem Sacred to the Memory of Her Majesty*. In the meantime there appeared *The Progress of a Divine, a satire*, 1735; *Of Public Spirit in regard to Public Works*, 1737. There appeared posthumously *London and Bristol Compar'd. A Satire*, 1744. *Various Poems*, &c., appeared in 1761; *Works*, 2 vols., 1775, contained Johnson's *Life*. See *Johnson* xlv; *Anderson* viii; and *Chalmers* ix.

Savage also wrote two plays: *Love in a Veil. A Comedy*, acted 1718, printed 1719; and *The Tragedy of Sir Thomas Overbury*, 1723, published 1724.

The Life of Mr Richard Savage appeared in 1727; Johnson's famous *Account* was printed in 1744, and was reprinted with the *Lives*. Of interest is S. V. Makower's *Richard Savage: A Mystery in Biography*, 1909. A recent work is *The Artificial Bastard*, by C. Tracy, 1953.

SEWELL, GEORGE, d. 1726

Sewell began with a pro-Walpole effusion, *The Patriot*, 1712. *Poems on Several Occasions* appeared in 1719; and *A New Collection of Original Poems* in 1720, his last metrical work being *Verses to the Right Honble. the Lord Carteret*, 1721.

The Tragedy of Sir Walter Raleigh was acted and printed in 1719; but he left unfinished *The Tragedy of Richard I*, ed. and published by Gregory Sewell, 1728.

His best-known prose work is *The Life and Character of Mr John Philips*, 1712; he defended *Cato* on many occasions. He edited

Surrey's poems in 1717 and added a supplementary 7th vol. containing Shakespeare's poems to Pope's ed. 1725. *Posthumous Works* was ed. Gregory Sewell in 1728.

SHADWELL, CHARLES, d. 1720

Shadwell had a brief career as a playwright. His *The Fair Quaker of Deal, or, The Humours of the Navy*, his only success, was acted and printed in 1710; and *The Humours of the Army* in 1712. *The Hasty Wedding; or, The Intriguing Squire* was published Dublin, 1717. *Five New Plays* (which included *The Hasty Wedding*) and *The Works*, 2 vols., with a brief Life, were both printed Dublin, 1720.

SHAFTESBURY, ANTHONY ASHLEY COOPER, 3rd Earl of, 1671–1713

Shaftesbury heralded his career by writing a Preface to the *Select Sermons* of Benjamin Whichcote, 1698; and in 1699 Toland published an unauthorized version of *An Inquiry concerning Virtue*. In 1708 Shaftesbury issued his *Letter Concerning Enthusiasm*, which was followed in the next year by *Sensus Communis; an essay on the Freedom of Wit and Humour*, and *The Moralists*. In 1710 there appeared *Soliloquy, or Advice to an Author*. All these, with the exception of the Preface, were gathered together in the first, 1711, edition of *Characteristicks of Men, Manners, Opinions, Times*, 3 vols., with which was included *Miscellaneous Reflections on the preceding Treatises, and other Critical Subjects*. A second edition of *Characteristicks*, with a revised text, appeared in 1714, with the addition of *Historical Draught or Tablature of the Judgment of Hercules*, which had been published in the previous year. This had not been intended for inclusion in *Characteristicks*, nor had been *A Letter Concerning Design*, included in the edition of 1723. It was not until 1914 that B. Rand published Shaftesbury's unfinished work, now entitled *Second Characters, or the Language of Forms*.

In 1716 there was published *Several Letters, written by a Noble Lord to a Young Man at the University*, and in 1721, *Letters from the late Earl of Shaftesbury to R. Molesworth Esq.* In 1830 T. Forster issued *The Original Letters of Locke, Sidney and Shaftesbury*, the latest addition being *The Life, Unpublished Letters, and Philosophic Regimen of Anthony, Earl of Shaftesbury*, 1900. A modern edition of *Characteristicks* is that of J. M. Robertson, 1900.

Shaftesbury's views attracted attention early in the century, notably that of Robert Day; see 'Shaftesbury's Earliest Critic', by A. O. Aldridge, *MP* xliv, 1946; the first important work, however, being *Essays on the Characteristicks*, by John Brown, 1751. Later studies are: G. Spicker, *Die Philosophie des Grafen von Shaftesbury*, Freiburg, 1872; T. Fowler, *Shaftesbury*, 1881, and *Shaftesbury and Hutcheson*, 1882. Books of the present century are: *Moral Sense*, by J. Bonar, 1930; *Shaftesbury: etica e religione—la morale del sentimento*, by L. Bandini, Bari, 1930; an excellent study in eighteenth-century literary theory, *The Third Earl of Shaftesbury*, by R. L. Brett, 1951; and F. H. Heinemann's *The Philosopher of Enthusiasm, with Material Hitherto Unpublished*, *Revue internationale de philosophie*, vi, 1952.

Among interesting studies in journals may be noted: C. A. Moore, 'Shaftesbury and the Ethical Poets in England, 1700–1760', *PMLA* xxxi, 1916; and 'The Return to Nature in English Poetry', *SP* xiv, 1917; W. E. Alderman, 'Shaftesbury and the Doctrine of Moral Sense in the Eighteenth Century', *PMLA* xlvi, 1931, and 'Shaftesbury and the Doctrine of Optimism in the Eighteenth Century', *Trans. Wisconsin Acad.* xxviii, 1933; E. Casati 'Hérauts et Commentateurs de Shaftesbury en France', *Rev. de littérature comparée* xiv, 1934, and 'Un Carnet de Shaftesbury', ibid. xvi, 1936; and E. Tuveson, The Importance of Shaftesbury', *ELH* xx, 1953.

SMITH, EDMUND NEALE, 1672–1710

Adapted Racine's *Phèdre* as *Phaedra and Hippolitus*, 1707; and in 1708 (?) printed *A Poem on the Death of Mr John Philips*.

The *Works*, 1714, included a 'Character of Mr Smith by Mr Oldisworth'. See *Johnson* xxi; *Anderson* vi; and *Chalmers* ix.

SMITH, JOHN, *fl.* 1713.

Published *Poems upon Several Occasions*, 1713.

SOMERVILLE (or SOMERVILE), WILLIAM, 1675–1742

The Two Springs. A Fable, was published in 1725, and *Occasional Poems, Translations, Fables, Tales* &c., in 1727. His well-known work, *The Chace, a Poem*, was printed in 1735, and appeared in 1749 'in Heroick Verse. Written originally in blank Verse.' *Hobbinol, or the Rural Games. A Burlesque Poem, in blank Verse* was published in 1740; and *Field Sports, a Poem* in 1742. See *The Poetical Works*, 2 vols., Glasgow, 1766, and *Johnson* xlvii; *Anderson* viii; *Chalmers* xi. *A Collection of Miscellaneous Poetry*, edited by F. G. Waldron, 1809, gives the first version of *Hobbinol*, 'The Wicker Chair'. R. D. Havens discusses 'William Somervile's Earliest Poem' in *MLN* xli, 1926.

SPENCE, JOSEPH, 1699–1768

Spence first came to notice with *An Essay on Pope's Odyssey; in which some particular Beauties and Blemishes of that Work are considered*, 2 pts. 1726–7. His next publication was *A Full and authentick Account of Stephen Duck, the Wiltshire Poet*, 1731, which was reprinted with Duck's poems from 1736. Among various learned works, or contributions to such, he published *Polymetis; or an Enquiry concerning the Agreement between the Works of the Roman Poets and the Remains of the antient Artists; in ten books*, 1747; *Crito: or, a Dialogue on Beauty. By Sir Harry Beaumont* (pseud.), 1752; and *Moralities: or, Essays, Letters, Fables, and Translations; by Sir Harry Beaumont*, 1753. J. Nichols published his verse in *A Select Collection of Poems*, viii, 1782.

Works unpublished during his life are: *The Charliad*, a mock epic, printed by A. Wright in *PMLA* xlvi, 1931; and 'Quelques Remarques Hist: sur les Poëts Anglois', ed. J. M. Osborn in *Pope and his Contemporaries* (p. 591). Two editions of his indispensable *Ancedotes* appeared in 1820, the one compiled by Malone, and posthumously printed, the other by S. W. Singer, usually referred to. These editions were reviewed together by Hazlitt in the *Edinburgh Review*, May 1820; and by D'Israeli in the *Quarterly Review*, July 1820. A. Dobson discussed the 'Ancedotes' in *Eighteenth Century Vignettes*, 1st series, 1892. C. H. Beale's *Catherine Hutton and her Friends*, 1895, contains some pages on Spence and his correspondence.

Little has been written about him. He was first treated of in James Ridley's *Tales of the Genii*, 2 vols., 1764, where he figures as 'Phesoi Ecneps'. A. Wright published a *Critical Biography*, 1950, Chicago.

STEELE, SIR RICHARD, 1672–1729

Steele's first venture into literature was *The Procession. A Poem on Her Majesty's Funeral. By a Gentleman in the Army*, 1695. Except for the *Prologue to the University of Oxford*, 1706, and the *Epilogue to the Town*, 1721, all his verse appeared in his plays or periodicals, or in miscellanies, including the *Poetical Miscellanies* he himself edited in 1713 (misdated 1714). They have been collected in an admirable edition by R. Blanchard, 1952.

His first play, *The Funeral: or Grief à-la-mode* was acted 1701, published 1702; *The Lying Lover: or The Ladies' Friendship,* acted 1703, published 1704; *The Tender Husband; or The Accomplish'd Fools,* acted and published 1705; and finally *The Conscious Lovers,* acted 1722 and published 1723. Fragments were printed by J. Nichols in *Epistolary Correspondence,* 1809. The complete acted *Dramatic Works* appeared in 1734; G. A. Aitken's edition, 1894, Mermaid, includes the fragments.

His most important work, the periodical publications, opened with *The Tatler. By Isaac Bickerstaff, Esq.,* 271 nos. (188 by Steele alone), running 12 Apr. 1709–2 Jan. 1711; the *Spectator,* to which Steele contributed about 236 papers, ran 1 Mar. 1711–6 Dec. 1712; *The Guardian. By Nestor Ironside,* 175 numbers, largely by Steele, 12 Mar.–1 Oct. 1713; and *The Englishman: Being the Sequel to the Guardian,* contained 56 numbers in vol. i, which ran 6 Oct. 1713–11 Feb. 1714, No. 57 of 15 Feb. being a separate issue. Vol. ii included 38 numbers, 11 July–21 Nov. 1715. This periodical was almost wholly by Steele. *The Plebeian. By a Member of the House of Commons,* lasted only 4 nos., Mar.– Apr. 1719. His most considerable later journal, *The Theatre. By Sir John Edgar,* went to 28 nos., 2 Jan.–5 Apr. 1720. Lesser journalistic ventures include *The Lover,* 40 numbers, and *The Reader,* 9 nos., both 1714, and *Town-Talk,* 1715–16.

The *Tatler* appeared in 4 vols., 1710–11; the *Spectator,* 8 vols., 1712–15; the *Guardian,* 2 vols., 1714. These have often been edited and reprinted, a useful collection being the first 11 vols. of the *British Essayists,* ed. R. Lynam, 1827. Part I of the *Englishman* was published in volume form in 1714, Part II in 1716. They were published together in a critical edition, 1955, by R. Blanchard, who also published *The Lover, The Reader,* and *Town-Talk,* &c., 1959. *The Lover* and *The Reader* were collected together in 1715, and edited by J. Nichols in 1789, who also in the same year edited *Town-Talk* with various pamphlets, and with additions in 1790. *The Theatre* was edited by John Loftis, 1962.

Steele's political writings open in 1712 with *The Englishman's Thanks to the Duke of Marlborough.* His influential ones were: *The Importance of Dunkirk Considered,* 1713; *The Crisis. With Some Seasonable Remarks on the Danger of a Popish Successor*; and, more personal, *Mr Steele's Apology for Himself and his Writings: Occasioned by his Expulsion from the House of Commons*, 1714. Two tracts concerning the Peerage Bill were printed in 1719: *The Joint and Humble Address*, and *A Letter to the Earl of O——d*. His most important occasional piece is *The Christian Hero:* 1701. Valuable to the historian of the theatre is *The State of the Case between the Lord Chamberlain of His Majesty's Household and the Governor of the Royal Company of Comedians*, 1720. Others include projectors' pieces: *An Account of the Fish Pool*, 1718; and *A Nation a Family . . . or a Plan for the Improvement of the South Sea Proposal*, 1720. Apart from Nichols (see above), many papers remained uncollected until the publication by R. Blanchard of *Steele's Tracts and Pamphlets*, Baltimore, 1944.

J. Nichols edited *The Epistolary Correspondence*, 2 vols., 1787, republished with additional letters in 1809. The standard edition is *The Correspondence*, ed. R. Blanchard, 1941.

There is as yet no complete edition of Steele's works, though this is gradually being accomplished by R. Blanchard, whose edition of *The Christian Hero* contains a bibliography, as does Aitken's biography. *Library* x, 1929, may also be consulted.

The earliest Life of Steele was a Curll production, *Memoirs of the Life and Writings of Sir Richard Steele*, 1731. He appears in *Kippis*, vi, 1763, and in B. Victor's *Original Letters*, &c., i, 1776. J. Nichols contributed biographical and critical matter to the volumes of miscellaneous writings he edited from 1789 to 1809; but the first considerable biography was H. R. Montgomery's *Memoirs*, 2 vols., Edinburgh, 1865. Subsequent ones are: A. Dobson, 1886; the monumental *Life*, 2 vols., 1889, by G. A. Aitken; and W. Connely, 1934.

The earliest critical notice of Steele is that of Gay in *The Present State of Wit*, 1711, followed by laudatory mentions by Felton, Porter, and others (see text IV. i), and strictures by J. Dennis in *Remarks on a Play called The Conscious Lovers*, 1723. Essays may be found in N. Drake's *Essays Biographical, Critical, and Historical, Illustrative of the Tatler, Spectator and Guardian*, 3 vols., 1805; in Hazlitt (p. 614) and in Thackeray; in C. W. Dilke's *Papers of a Critic*, 2 vols., 1875; G. S. Marr, *The Periodical Essayists of the Eighteenth Century*, 1923; W. Graham, (p. 599); F. W. Bateson (p. 595); A. Nicoll (p. 595); B. Dobrée, *Variety of Ways*, 1932; and 'The Songs in Steele's Plays' by R. Blanchard in *Pope and his Contemporaries* (p. 591).

Other special studies are the volume *Steele and Drury Lane*, by J. Loftis, Berkeley, 1952; R. A. Aubin, 'Beyond Steele's Satire on Undertakers', *PMLA* lxiv, 1949; J. Loftis, 'Steele's Censorium', *HLQ* xiv, 1950; J. R. Moore, 'Defoe, Steele and the Demolition of Dunkirk', *HLQ* xiii, 1950; J. C. Stephens, 'Steele and the Bishop of St. Asaph's Preface', *PMLA* lxvii, 1952.

STRYPE, JOHN, 1643–1737

His first publication was *Memorials of Thomas Cranmer*, 1694, edited in 3 vols., 1848–54. His great work, *Annals of the Reformation and Establishment of Religion, And other Various Occurrences in the Church of England; During the First Twelve Years of Queen Elizabeth's Happy Reign*, appeared in two parts 1708–9, and in 3 vols., 1725–8, which continued the history till 1588. In 1731 *Brief Annals*, &c., continued the documentation to 1612. This became vol. iv of the third edition of *Annals*, 1735–7. Intermediately he published *Life and Acts of Matthew Parker, The First Archbishop of Canterbury in the Reign of Queen Elizabeth*, 1711, which was followed by a similar *Whitgift* in 1718. *Ecclesiastical Memorials*, &c., in the reigns of Henry VIII, Edward VI, and Queen Mary, was published in 3 vols., 1721. All his works were reprinted in 19 vols., 1812–24.

S. R. Maitland produced *Remarks on Strype's Cranmer*, i, 1848, and *Notes on Strype*, 1858. *John Strype, F.S.A.*, by A. P. Wire, 1902, includes a full bibliography.

SWIFT, JONATHAN, 1667–1745

The earliest of Swift's published writings was the 'Ode to the Athenian Society', published by Dunton in the Supplement to the *Athenian Gazette* v, 1691–2. Apart from 'A Description of the Morning' and 'A Description of a City Shower', which appeared in *Tatlers* 9 and 238, Apr. 1709 and Oct. 1710, the only authoritative publications of the poems are in *Miscellanies in Prose and Verse*, 1711, the *Miscellanies* published by Pope in 4 vols., 1727–32, and the second volume of the *Works* printed by Faulkner, Dublin, 1735. Faulkner added further items in successive editions. For details see H. Williams below, Introduction.

Here it is possible to give only a sparse selection of separate publications. *Baucis and Philemon . . . Together with Mrs Harris's Earnest Petition*, 1709; the Imitations of *Part of the Seventh Epistle of the First Book of Horace*, and *The First Ode of the Second Book of Horace* were published in 1713 and 1714 respectively. *Cadenus and Vanessa*, written in 1712 (rather than 1713), was printed Dublin, 1726. The *Journal of a Modern Lady* first appeared in Dublin in 1728. *The Life and Genuine Character of Doctor Swift* of 1731 was published in London 1733, but *Verses on the Death of Dr Swift*, also written in 1731, was delayed until 1739. *An Epistle to a Lady*, and *On Poetry: A Rapsody*, were both issued separately in 1733. 'The Legion Club' first appeared in *S——t contra omnes* in 1736.

Volumes in the various editions of his collected *Works* were devoted to his poems, but these were first separately published by Thomas Park, 4 vols., 1806–7. An excellent Pickering edition (Aldine Poets) appeared in 3 vols., 1833–4. In 1910 W. E. Browning edited *The Poems of Jonathan Swift*, 2 vols., but these have been superseded by the definitive edition by H. Williams, 3 vols., 1937, 2nd ed. 1958, containing full bibliographical details, including the whereabouts of MS. versions, together with full critical apparatus. See also *Johnson* xxxix, xl; *Anderson* ix; *Chalmers* xi; and the other big collections.

A Discourse of the Contests and Dissensions Between the Nobles and the Commons in Athens and Rome, 1701, was the first of Swift's political writings, which were to be developed some seven years later. Intermediately there appeared *A Tale of a Tub*, bound up with 'An Account of a Battel between the Ancient and Modern Books in St James's Library' and A Discourse Concerning the Mechanical Operation of the Spirit', 1704, the 'Apology' being added in the fifth edition, 1710; and the 'Partridge' papers, by 'Isaac Bickerstaff', viz. *Predictions for the Year 1708*, and *The Accomplishment of the First of Mr Bickerstaff's Predictions*, both 1708; and in 1709, *A Vindication of Isaac Bickerstaff, Esq*. During this period he wrote the politico-religious tracts, *The Sentiments of a Church-of-England Man*, and *An Argument to prove that the Abolishing of Christianity in England, may, as Things now stand, be attended with some Inconveniences, and, perhaps, not produce those many good Effects proposed thereby*, though they did not appear until the publication of his *Miscellanies* in 1711. *A Project for the Advancement of Religion, and the Reformation of Manners* was published in 1709, as was *A Letter from a Member of the House of Commons in Ireland to a Member of the House of Commons in England, Concerning the Sacramental Test*. In 1710 he contributed No. ccxxx of the

Tatler, and in the next year Nos. 5 and 20 of Harrison's continuation of that journal.

His great political phase began in 1710 with No. 13 of the *Examiner* (2 Nov.), his contributions ceasing with No. 45, 14 June 1711. In that year there followed in rapid succession: *A Short Character of His Ex[cellency] T[he] E[arl] of W[harton] L[ord] L[ieutenant] of I[reland]*; *Some Remarks upon a Pamphlet, entitl'd, A Letter to the Seven Lords of the Committee, appointed to Examine Gregg*, by 'The author of the Examiner'; *A New Journey to Paris: Together with some Secret Transactions Between the Fr—h K—g, and an Eng— Gentleman*. By the Sieur du Baudrier. Translated from the French; and *The Conduct of the Allies, and of the Late Ministry in Beginning and Carrying on the Present War*. He pursued the campaign in the next three years with *Some Remarks on the Barrier Treaty, Between Her Majesty and the States-General*, 1712; *The Importance of the Guardian Considered*, 1713, and *The Publick Spirit of the Whigs*, &c., 1714. Other works written at this time were not published till later; *Some Free Thoughts upon the Present State of Affairs* did not appear until 1741, and *The History of the Four Last Years of the Queen* was delayed until 1758, when it was printed in London and Dublin.

On his return to Ireland Swift composed his two more pondered pamphlets, *Memoirs Relating to that Change which Happened in the Queen's Ministry in 1710*, and *An Enquiry into the Behaviour of the Queen's Last Ministry*, concluded in about 1721, but not appearing until 1765 in Hawkesworth, viii, ed. Deane Swift. Then began the phase of his Irish pamphlets, *A Proposal for the Use of Irish Manufacture*, 1720, followed in 1723 by *Some Arguments against enlarging the Power of Bishops*. These heralded the *Drapier's Letters*, five of them being published from Mar. to Dec. 1724. The two remaining letters did not appear until *Works*, iv, 1735.

In 1726 Swift visited London, and on 28 Oct. of that year there appeared *Travels into several Remote Nations of the World* ... This edition by Motte was considerably tampered with, the now accepted version being that printed by Faulkner as *Works*, iii, Dublin, 1735. After his return to Ireland, Swift produced a number of papers, of which the most important (all printed in Dublin) are: *A Short View of the State of Ireland*, 1727–8; i, v, vii, ix, xix of the *Intelligencer*, 1728. There followed in the next year *A Modest Proposal For preventing the Children of Poor People From being a Burthen to their Parents, or the Country, and For making them*

Beneficial to the Publick. Though written at about this time, *Maxims Controlled in Ireland* was first printed by Deane Swift, *Works,* viii, London, 1765. *A Vindication of his Ex[cellenc]y the Lord C[arteret] from the Charge of favouring none but Toryes, High-Churchmen, and Jacobites* appeared in London, Dublin, in 1730. There were several shorter pamphlets, dealing with the Church and the condition of the Irish people, among which may be named *An Examination of Certain Abuses, Corruptions, and Enormities, in the City of Dublin,* 1732, *The Presbyterians Plea of Merit; In Order to take off the Test, Impartially Examined,* 1733, and *A Proposal for giving Badges to the Beggars . . . of Dublin,* 1737. Three of Swift's *Sermons* were published in 1744, to which a fourth was added in a 2nd ed. of the same year.

Apart from these 'involved' pieces of writing (*Gulliver's Travels* is partly so), Swift wrote several major pieces of more general applicability, namely: *A Letter to a Young Gentleman Lately enter'd into Holy Orders,* 1721; *A Letter of Advice to a Young Poet; Together with a Proposal for the Encouragement of Poetry in this Kingdom,* Dublin, 1721, though Herbert Davis doubts the authenticity of this work (see *Essays on the Eighteenth Century, presented to D. Nichol Smith,* 1945); *A Letter to a Very Young Lady on her Marriage,* printed in the Miscellanies of 1727; *A Serious and Useful Scheme, To make an Hospital for Incurables, of Universal Benefit to all His Majesty's Subjects,* 1733, in Dublin as well as London; *A Complete Collection of Genteel and Ingenious Conversation . . . In Three Dialogues. By* 'Simon Wagstaff, Esq.:' 1738; and *Directions to Servants in General; And in Particular to the Butler, Cook . . . Governess,* 1745.

Miscellanies in Prose and Verse, 1711, contains most of Swift's work up to that date, excluding the Pindarics, &c., and *A Tale of a Tub.* More of his writings appear in the *Miscellanies* compiled by Pope, Swift, and probably Arbuthnot, 3 vols., 1727, attaining 6 vols. in the edition of 1736–8, and 13 in 1753.

The Drapier's Miscellany, Dublin, 1733, contained pamphlets and verse relating to Irish affairs, but the first edition of the *Works* as a whole was published by Faulkner in Dublin in 1735, 4 vols., with Swift's approval, extended to 6 vols. in 1738. In 1746 this grew to 8 vols., in 1763 to 11, in 1769, with letters, to 20. Hawkesworth attempted to rival these editions with one in 6 vols. quarto and 12 vols. octavo in 1755, later increased to 14 vols. quarto and 25 octavo. In 1784 T. Sheridan produced an edition in 17 vols., based on Hawkesworth's text; Sheridan's edition 'corrected and revised' by John Nichols appeared in 19 vols. in 1801, all these being superseded by Sir Walter Scott's 19-vol. edition of 1814, Edinburgh, 2nd ed. 1824. From 1897 to 1908, Temple Scott issued the *Prose Works*, the twelfth and last volume being a bibliography by W. S. Jackson. The definitive edition of the prose works is that of Herbert Davis in 14 vols., 1939, in progress ('Shakespeare Head' and popular editions, identical in text), including valuable introductions, full bibliographical notes, and textual variants.

Some separate editions should be noted. There are many of *Gulliver's Travels*. The Faulkner text is now considered the 'good' one, and was first reproduced in *Gulliver's Travels and Selected Prose and Verse*, ed. John Hayward, 1934, and is the one printed in the Davis edition. In 1926 H. Williams produced an edition of the 1726 version, First Edition Club. *A Tale of a Tub* was properly edited for the first time by A. C. Guthkelch and D. Nichol Smith in 1920, revised ed. 1958. In 1935 H. Davis edited *The Drapier's Letters*.

Letters to and from Dr Swift, 1714–1728 were published in 1741, became vol. vii of Faulkner's 1746 ed. of *Works*. A collection was published in 1766 by Hawkesworth, who with Deane Swift comprised them in his edition of 1768–9. *Unpublished Letters* were ed. G. B. Hill in 1899, the great available edition being at the present date *The Correspondence*, ed. F. Elrington Ball, 6 vols., 1910–14 now being enlarged and revised by H. Williams. Ball's edition must be supplemented by *Vanessa and her Correspondence with Swift*, ed. A. M. Freeman in 1921, where the intimate letters of Swift with Esther Vanhomrigh appear for the first time, and by *Letters of Jonathan Swift to Charles Ford*, ed. D. Nichol Smith, 1935. The letters to Esther Johnson, known as *The Journal to Stella*, were first used by Hawkesworth in a 1766 edition of Swift's correspondence, and were variously treated by successive editors. Modern editions have been those by F. Ryland, 1897, G. A. Aitken, 1901, and R. K. Moorhead, 1924, the definitive edition being H. Williams's, 2 vols., 1948, with full critical apparatus.

Personal, but not very reliable, reminiscences of Swift may be found in the *Memoirs* of Laetitia Pilkington, 1748–54; more reliable are the *Remarks on the Life and Writings of Swift*, by John, Earl of Orrery (*The Orrery Papers*, 2 vols., 1903, should be read in connexion with the *Remarks*), to be checked by Patrick Delany's *Observations on Lord Orrery's Remarks*, 1754. Hawkesworth, i, 1755, was published separately in the same year, as was Deane Swift's *Essay upon the Life, Writings and Character of Dr. Jonathan Swift*. Other publications during the century, to some extent based on personal knowledge, are: W. H. Dilworth's *Life*, 1758; Johnson's in vol. iii, 1781; and that by Thomas Sheridan in 1784. *An Essay on the Earlier Part of the Life of Swift*, by J. Barrett, 1808, was balanced by Sir W. Wilde's *The Closing Years of Dean Swift's Life*, 1849. Intermediately there had appeared Scott's *Life* in the first volume of his edition, 1814, reprinted in Paris, 2 vols., 1826, as *Memoirs of Swift*. There were many Lives of Swift during the nineteenth century: *Swift: Sa Vie et ses Œuvres*, by L. Prevost-Paradol, Paris, 1856; vol. i of J. Forster's *Life*, 1875; Leslie Stephen in the English Men of Letters series, 1882; H. Craik, 1892, in 2 vols. in 1894; J. Churton Collins and G. P. Moriarty, 1893. Critical biographies written in the present century are: *Swift: Les Années de jeunesse et 'Le Conte du Tonneau'*, by E. Pons, Strasbourg, 1925; *The Skull of Swift*, by S. Leslie, 1928; *Swift*, by C. Van Doren, New York, 1930, London, 1931; *Swift: A Critical Essay*, by W. D. Taylor, 1933. These were followed by the illuminating *The Mind and Art of Jonathan Swift*, by R. Quintana, N.Y. and London, 1936, rev. ed. 1954. This contains an excellent bibliography of writings about Swift. In 1937 there appeared *Swift* by B. Newman, and in 1954 *Swift* by J. M. Murry, which is interpretive rather than critical.

There are numerous special studies in book form, among which should be noted: *A Critical Study of Gulliver's Travels*, by W. A. Eddy, Princeton and London, 1923; *Stella*, by H. Davis, N.Y. 1942, and his *The Satire of Jonathan Swift*, N.Y. 1947; *Four Essays on Gulliver's Travels*, by A. E. Case, Princeton, 1945, London, 1947; C. Looten, *La Pensée religieuse de Swift, et ses antinomies*, Lille, 1935; M. K. Starkman, *Swift's Satire on Learning in 'A Tale of a Tub'*, Princeton, 1950; Louis L. Landa, *Swift and the Church of Ireland*, 1954; W. B. Ewald, Jr., *The Masks of Jonathan Swift*; and *Satiric Allegory: Mirror of Man*, by E. D. Leyburn, Yale and London, 1956.

Separate criticism of Swift's verse is not common. In 1929 F. Elrington Ball issued *Swift's Verse, An Essay*; H. Davis on 'Swift's View of Poetry', *Studies in English*, Toronto, 1931; and

M. Johnson, *The Sin of Wit*, Syracuse, 1950, an appreciative study.

Among general essays contained in books a few are: W. M. Thackeray, (p. 614); C. W. Dilke in *Papers of a Critic*, 1875; A. Birrell in *Essays about Men, Women and Books*, 1894; P. H. Frey in *Literary Reviews and Criticisms*, N.Y. and London, 1908; C. Whibley, *Jonathan Swift*, the Leslie Stephen Lecture, 1917, reprinted in *Literary Studies*, 1919; H. Read in *The Sense of Glory*, 1929; D. Nichol Smith, *Jonathan Swift*, a lecture delivered in the University of Liverpool, 1930; John Hayward in *From Anne to Victoria*, ed. B. Dobrée, 1937; G. Orwell in *Shooting an Elephant*, 1950.

Articles and essays on various points are innumerable; only a few can be given here. In 1797 W. Godwin wrote about *Gulliver's Travels* in the *Enquirer*. In 1816 Francis Jeffrey reviewed Scott's edition in *Edinburgh Review* xxvii, which was taken up by E. Berwick in *A Defence of Jonathan Swift* in 1819. Further discussions of *Gulliver's Travels* dealing with special points are C. H. Firth's 'The Political Significance of "Gulliver's Travels"', *Proceedings of the British Academy*, 1919–20, reprinted in *Essays Historical and Literary*, 1938; articles by M. Nicolson and N. M. Mohler on the scientific background of the voyage to Laputa appeared in *Annals of Science*, vol. ii, nos. 3 and 4, July and Oct. 1937. *A Modest Proposal* was examined by L. A. Landa in *MP* Nov. 1942, and by G. Wittkowsky, 'Swift's *Modest Proposal*' in *JHI*, vol. iv, no. 1, 1943. L. A. Landa's 'Swift, the Mysteries, and Deism', appeared in *Studies in English*, Univ. of Texas, 1944. E. Pons contributed 'Swift et Pascal' to *Langues Modernes*, Mar.–Apr. 1951, and *Études Anglaises*, Nov. 1952. 'The Irony of Swift', by F. R. Leavis in *The Common Pursuit*, 1952, is an interesting study reprinted from *Scrutiny*, No. 2.

Jackson's bibliography noted above may be supplemented by *Bibliography of the Writings in Prose and Verse*, by H. Teerink, The Hague, 1937. *The Reputation of Swift, 1781–1882*, by D. M. Berwick, Philadelphia, 1941, was followed by *A List of Critical Studies* of Swift by L. A. Landa and J. E. Tobin, N.Y., 1945, a valuable guide to articles in learned journals which may be continued up to date by consulting *PQ*, 'English Literature 1660–1800'.

Many of Swift's manuscripts are in the Forster collection in the Victoria and Albert Museum, in the Rothschild collection in Cambridge, see vol. ii of *The Rothschild Library*, 2 vols., 1954, in the British Museum, and at Trinity College, Dublin. Those in American libraries are described by H. Davis in *A List of Critical Studies* (see above).

THEOBALD, LEWIS, 1688–1744

A Pindarick Ode on the Union appeared in 1707, but his poetical works are few, concluding with *The Grove, or a Collection of Original Poems*, 1721, with some translations from the Greek.

His plays include *The Faithful Bride of Granada*, anon. 1704; *The Persian Princess, or The Royal Villain*, 1708, printed 1715; and the curious *Double Falshood: or The Distrest Lovers. Written originally by Shakespeare, and now revised*, 1727, printed 1728. This was edited by Walter Graham, Cleveland, 1920. He was concerned not only with tragedy, but also with opera, such as *Orestes*, 1731, and pantomime, such as *The Rape of Proserpine*, 1727.

His prose works include: *A Complete Key to the last new Farce, The What d'ye call it. To which is prefix'd a hypercritical Preface on the Nature of Burlesque*, anon., 1715; *The Censor*, papers contributed to *Mist's Weekly Journal*, 1717; and *Memoirs of Sir Walter Raleigh*, 1719.

He published a number of translations from the Greek between 1713 and 1717, ushered in by *The Life and Character of Marcus Portius Cato collected from Plutarch, Lucan, Salust, Lucius Florus and other Authors. Designed for the readers of Cato, a Tragedy*, 1713, the 2nd ed. of the same year being enlarged. His translation of Plato's *Phaedo*, 1773, was followed by those of three plays of Sophocles and two of Aristophanes.

His lasting reputation rests upon his editorial work, heralded by *Shakespeare restored; or, a Specimen of the many Errors as well committed as unamended by Mr Pope, in his late Edition of this Poet*, 1726. His own edition, *The Works of Shakespeare, Collated with the oldest Copies and corrected. With Notes, explanatory and critical*, appeared in 7 vols., 1733, and in 10 vols., 1740. He also edited *The Posthumous Works of William Wycherley, Esq.*, &c., with a prefatory Memoir by Major Pack, 2 vols., 1728–9; and vol. i and parts of vols. ii and iii of *The Works of Beaumont and Fletcher, with Notes critical and explanatory*, 10 vols., 1750, his collaborators being Seward and Sympson.

Most of the writing on Theobald concerns his Shakespearian

scholarship, though he occurs in J. Nichols, *Literary Illus-trations*, ii, 1817. Studies begin with J. C. Collins, 'Lewis Theobald, the Porson of Shakespearean Criticism', *Quart. Rev.* clxxv, 1892, to be followed by T. R. Lounsbury, *The First Editors of Shakespeare* (to wit Pope and Theobald), 1906; R. F. Jones, *Lewis Theobald, his Contribution to English Scholarship, with some Unpublished Letters*, N.Y., 1919; in the February of which year E. H. C. Oliphant contributed 'Shakespeare, Fletcher and Theobald' to *N & Q*; W. Mertz, *Die Shakespeare Ausgabe von Theobald*, Giessen, 1925. Theobald's Preface to his edition of Shakespeare (1733) was published by the Augustan Reprint Society, Los Angeles, 1949, ed. H. G. Dick, but the Preface had previously been reprinted in *Eighteenth Century Essays on Shakespeare*, Glasgow, 1903, ed. D. Nichol Smith, who discusses Theobald in *Shakespeare in the Eighteenth Century*, 1928.

His 'Shakespeare' play was last treated of by J. Cadwalader, 'Theobald's Alleged Shakespeare Manuscript', *MLN* lv, 1940.

THOMSON, JAMES, 1700–48

The Edinburgh Miscellany of 1720 contained three poems by Thomson, notably 'Of a Country Life'.

The work known collectively as *The Seasons* appeared as follows: *Winter: A Poem* (405 lines), 1726, another ed. of the same year (463 lines) including a Preface; *Summer* (1,146 lines), 1727; *Spring* (1,082 lines), 1728; and *The Seasons*, including 'Autumn' (1,269 lines), and *A Hymn on the Seasons*, 1730, in which year there also appeared a separate ed. of *Autumn*. In the final, 1746, ed. of *The Seasons*, 'Winter' consists of 1,069 lines, 'Summer' of 1,805, 'Spring' of 1,176, and 'Autumn' of 1,373. A recent text is that ed. Otto Zippel, *The Seasons. Critical, Original and Variorum Edition*, Palaestra lxvi, Berlin, 1908.

A Poem Sacred to the Memory of Sir Isaac Newton appeared in 1727. In 1729 Thomson published *Britannia. A Poem*, and, anonymously (if it be his), *A Poem to the Memory of Mr Congreve*. In that year also the *Hymn on Solitude* appeared in Ralph's *Miscellaneous Poems by Several Hands*, together with three others. *Liberty* also appeared in several parts, to wit: *Antient and Modern Italy Compared: Being the First Part; Greece: Being the Second Part; Rome: Being the Third Part*, all 1735; *Britain: Being the Fourth Part; The Prospect: Being the Fifth Part*, in 1736. The whole was printed as *Liberty: A Poem*, in 1738. Intermediately, in 1737, Thomson published *A Poem, To the Memory of the Right Honourable The Lord Talbot, Late Chancellor of Great Britain.* Finally, *The Castle of Indolence: an Allegorical Poem. Written in Imitation of Spenser* appeared in 1748. *Poems on Several Occasions* was published in 1750.

The Poetical Works, edited by H. Nicolas, was issued 2 vols. 1830, revised P. Cunningham 1860, and by D. C. Tovey in 1897. Other eds. are: G. Gilfillan, Edinburgh, 1853, C. Cowden Clarke, 1868, W. M. Rossetti, 1873. The standard edition is that in the Oxford Poets, *The Complete Poetical Works*, ed. J. Logie Robertson, 1908, which as far as *The Seasons* is concerned is a variorum ed. the first *Winter* being added. See also *Johnson* xlviii, xlix; *Anderson* ix; and *Chalmers* xii.

Thomson's first play, *The Tragedy of Sophonisba*, was acted and printed in 1730; *Agamemnon* in 1738; *Edward and Leonora . . . As it was to have been acted at the Theatre-Royal in Covent-Garden* was published in 1739; *Tancred and Sigismunda* was acted and printed in 1745; and *Coriolanus* in 1749.

Vol. ii of *The Works of Mr Thomson*—*The Seasons* of 1730 being accounted vol. i—appeared in 1736, the whole in 2 vols., 1738; 2 vols., 1744, and 3 vols., 1749, these being largely composed of separate works bound up together. The first edition of the *Works* proper is that of Lord Lyttelton, *With his last Corrections, Additions, and Improvements*, 4 vols., 1750. Patrick Murdoch's ed., 4 vols. 1766, was prefaced by 'An Account of the Life and Writings . . . .' and Collins's *Ode on the Death of Mr Thomson.*

A Collection of Letters written to Aaron Hill Esq., 1751, contains fourteen letters from Thomson, and there are further letters from him in *The English Gentleman's Library Manual*, 1827. The latest collection is in *Unpublished Letters from Thomson to Mallett*, edited by P. Cunningham, in *Philobiblion Soc. Misc.*, vol. iv, 1854.

The first biographical memoir is that of Patrick Murdoch, noted above, separately published in 1762. After the Life in *Johnson*, 1781, there followed *Essays on the Lives and Writings of Fletcher of Saltoun and the Poet Thomson* by D. S. Erskine (Earl of Buchan), 1792. Other biographical studies include: Léon Morel, *James Thomson, sa Vie et ses Œuvres*, Paris, 1895, and G. C. Macaulay, *James Thomson* (English Men of Letters), 1908.

Critical studies begin with Jacob More's *Strictures, Critical and Sentimental, on Thomson's Seasons*, &c., 1777, to be followed by John Aikin's *Essay on the Plan and Character of Thomson's Seasons*, 1778, and, apart from Johnson, John Scott of Amwell's *Critical Essays on some of the Poems of several English Poets*, 1785. He is treated of in: J. C. Shairp, *On Poetic Interpretation of Nature*, Edinburgh, 1877; K. Gjerset, *Der Einfluss von James Thomsons Jahreszeiten auf die deutsche Literatur des achtzehnten Jahrhunderts*, Heidelberg, 1898; W. J. Courthope, *History of English Poetry*, v, 1905; A. Blau, *James Thomsons Seasons. Eine genetische Stiluntersuchung*, Berlin, 1910; J. W. Mackail, 'The Poet of the Seasons' in *Studies of English Poets*, 1926; M. M. Cameron, *L'Influence des Saisons de Thomson sur la poésie descriptive en France, 1759–1810*, Paris, 1927; and F. S. Boas, in *Introduction to Eighteenth Century Drama*, 1953.

Essays include: G. R. Potter, 'James Thomson and the Evolution of Spirits', *E. Studien* lxi, 1926; R. D. Havens, 'Primitivism and 'the Idea of Progress in Thomson', *SP* xxix, 1932; a series of valuable articles by H. Drennon in *MP* xxxii, 1934; *SP* xxxi, 1934; *PMLA* xlix, 1934; *PQ* xiv, 1935; *E. Studien* lxx, 1936; *PMLA* liii, 1938; J. E. Wells, 'Thomson's "Britannia"', *MP* xl, 1943; a number of illuminating studies by A. D. McKillop, from which may be singled out: *The Background of Thomson's Seasons*, Minneapolis, 1942; 'Ethics and Political History in Thomson's Liberty' in *Pope and his Contemporaries* (p. 591); *The Background of Thomson's Liberty*, Rice Institute Pamphlet xxxviii, Houston, Texas, 1951; and H. E. Hamilton, '"The Seasons": Shifts in the Treatment of Popular Subject Matter', *ELH* xv, 1948.

TICKELL, THOMAS, 1686–1740

His first poem, *Oxford*, was published anonymously in 1707. His next important poem, *On the Prospect of Peace*, appeared in 1712 (d. 1713), 6th ed., 1714. Intermediately some shorter pieces were published in Tonson's *Miscellany* of 1709, and Lintot's of 1712. In 1713 his essays on the pastoral appeared in the *Guardian. The First Book of Homer's Iliad* came out in 1715, two days after Pope's. *An Epistle from a Lady in England; to a Gentleman at Avignon*, 1717. The poem *To the . . . Earl of Warwick* on Addison's death, with its appendage commemorating Craggs, appeared in 1721, in his edition of Addison's *Works* as well as separately. Lewis printed 'The Horn Book' in his 1726 *Mis-*

cellany; and in 1733 appeared the last poem printed in his life-time, *On Her Majesty's Re-building the Lodgings of the Black Prince*, &c.

His poems were first collected by Cogan, 1759, in vol. ii of *The Works of the most celebrated Minor Poets*. They also appeared in Tonson's *The Works of Celebrated Authors*, 1750, in *Johnson* xxvi, *Anderson* viii, *Chalmers* xi, and in *The British Poets*, 1822. The first separate edition of his poems was a volume in Bell's *Poets of Great Britain*, 1781. Cooke edited them in 1796, and T. Park in 1807, reprd., 1808. His poems have been printed in the U.S.A. in E. Sanford's *The Works of the ` British Poets*, Philadelphia, 1819, and with Johnson's *Life*, Boston, 1854.

A complete bibliography will be found in R. E. Tickell's book listed below, and in 'Notes for a Bibliography of Thomas Tickell' by J. E. Butt in the *Bodleian Quarterly Record*, vol. v, no. 59, Dec. 1928.

A good complete Life, with new letters, and some extra poetical matter, is *Thomas Tickell and the 18th Century Poets, 1685–1740*, by R. E. Tickell, 1931.

TRAPP, JOSEPH, 1679–1747

He opened his poetical career with *Aedes Badmintonianae. A Poem*, 1701, his best-known piece being *Peace: A Poem*, 1713, his most ambitious *Thoughts upon the Four Last Things: Death; Heaven; Judgment; Hell*, issued in four parts, 1734–5. One play, *Abra-Mule; or, Love and Empire. A Tragedy*, 1704, had considerable success. He translated the *Æneis* of Virgil, 2 vols., 1718-20, and the complete works, 3 vols., 1731.

His Oxford lectures on poetry, *Praelectiones Poeticae*, 2 vols., 1711–15, were translated by W. Clarke and W. Bowyer in 1742 as *Lectures on Poetry*. An interesting point is made in V. Friemark's 'Joseph Trapp's Advanced Conception of Meta-phor', *PQ* xxix, 1950.

VANBRUGH, SIR JOHN, 1664–1726

Both *The Relapse* and the first part of *Æsop* were acted 1696, and printed 1697, as was *The Provok'd Wife*, acted 1697. *The Pilgrim*, a re-hash of Fletcher, notable for containing Dryden's 'Secular Masque', was acted 1700. *The False Friend* was acted and printed in 1702, and *The Confederacy* 1705. *The Country House*, acted 1703, was not published until 1715; *The*

Mistake, which appeared in 1705, waited for printing until 1726; and *A Journey to London*, printed in 1728, was acted in that year, as revised by Cibber, under the title of *The Provok'd Husband*. *The Plays* was published 2 vols. 1719. This edition, reprinted several times, omits *The Pilgrim*, and until 1735 did not include *The Country House*. He was ed. Leigh Hunt in *The Dramatic Works of Wycherley, Congreve, Vanbrugh, and Farquhar*, 1840. W. C. Ward again omitted *The Pilgrim* in his 2-vol. ed. of 1893. The Mermaid edition, by A. E. H. Swaen, 1896, contains the four major plays.

Vanbrugh's answer to Collier, *A Short Vindication of the Relapse and the Provok'd Wife, from Immorality and Prophaneness. By the Author*, appeared in 1698; and *Sir John Vanbrugh's Justification, Of what he depos'd in the Dutchess of Marlborough's late Tryal* in 1718.

The Complete Works, including the letters, was ed. B. Dobrée and G. Webb, 4 vols., 1927.

Biographical studies include: M. Dametz, *John Vanbrugh's Leben und Werke*, Vienna, 1898; G. H. Lovegrove, *The Life, Work, and Influence of Sir John Vanbrugh*, 1902, which is mainly architectural; B. Dobrée in *Essays in Biography*, 1925; and L. Whistler, *Sir John Vanbrugh, Architect and Dramatist*, 1938.

More wholly critical or specialized studies are to be found in Hazlitt's *A View of the English Stage*, 1818, and his *Lectures on the English Comic Writers*, 1819. Isaac D'Israeli deals with 'The Secret History of the Building of Blenheim' in the second series of *Curiosities of Literature*, 3 vols., 1825. He is discussed by John Palmer in *The Comedy of Manners*, 1913; by B. Dobrée in *Restoration Comedy*, 1924; and by Henry Ten Eyck Perry in *The Comic Spirit in Restoration Drama*, New Haven, 1925.

WARD, EDWARD, 1667–1731

He produced a large number of works, mostly anonymous, or 'By the Author of the London Spy', which was originally issued in 18 monthly parts, 1698–1700. Collections were printed in 1700, known as Parts I and II, the whole in 1703. This still readable work, more like Elizabethan than Augustan journalism, was reprinted in 1924, with an Introduction by Ralph Straus, and by A. L. Hayward, expurgated, in 1927.

Among his numerous prose works may be noted *A Trip to Jamaica*, 1698; *The Secret History of the Calves-head Club*, 1703, which reached an enlarged 7th ed. in 1709; and, as a side-light on social life, *The History of the London Clubs, or the citizen's pastime*, Part I, 1711; Part II, c. 1720. Of value is his *The Wooden World Dissected in the Character of a Ship of War*, 1707, reaching a 7th ed. 1756. It was reprinted 1807 and 1929.

Hudibras Redivivus; or, a Burlesque Poem on the Times, issued in 24 parts, 1705-7, was continued in *Vulgus Britannicus, or the British Hudibras*, in 15 cantos, 1710. He also wrote some plays, and is mentioned in *Baker*. His *Miscellaneous Writings* appeared in 6 vols., 1717-24.

The only complete study is that by H. W. Troyer, *Ned Ward of Grubstreet*, Cambridge, Mass., 1946, which contains a bibliography. Articles consist of R. Bourne, 'The Wooden World Dissected', *Pacific Hist. Rec.* xiv, 1945; and C. E. Jones, 'Short-Title Check-List of Works attributed to Ward', *N & Q* 6 Apr. 1946.

WATTS, ISAAC, 1674–1748

His earliest production was *The First Catechism* (prayers for little children), 1692. He wrote a number of religious works, among them *The Christian Doctrine of the Trinity . . . asserted and prov'd*, 1722; *Logick; or the Right use of Reason in the Enquiry after Truth*, 1725; his answer to Mandeville's complete *Fable of the Bees*, namely *An Essay towards the Encouragement of Charity Schools*, appeared in 1728; and *A Caveat against Infidelity*, 1729; his last work being *Useful and Important Questions concerning Jesus, the Son of God*, 1746. His notable secular prose work is *The Art of Reading and Writing English*, 1721.

His verse began with *Horae Lyricae. Poems chiefly of the Lyric kind*, which, first published 1706, was 'much enlarged' for the 1709 ed. *Hymns and Spiritual Songs*, 1707, appeared again 'corrected and much enlarged' in 1709. *Divine Songs Attempted in Easy Language for the Use of Children* was published 1715; and *The Psalms of David Imitated* 1719. *Sermons on Various Subjects*, 3 vols., 1721-7, contains some hymns; *Reliquiae Juveniles: Miscellaneous Thoughts in Prose and Verse*, 1734, was his last publication. See also *Johnson* xlvi; *Anderson* ix; and *Chalmers* xiii.

His *Works* were collected and edited by D. Jennings and P. Doddridge, 6 vols., 1753; *Posthumous Works* in 1773 and a further instalment in 1779. A new edition, ed. G. Burder, was produced in 1810–11, in 6 vols.; and in 9 vols., 1812–13.

Lives are those by: T. Milner, 1834; E. P. Hood, 1875; and

A. P. Davis, N.Y., 1943. He is to be found in Thomas Wright's
Lives of the British Hymn Writers, iii, 1914; and in J. Laird's *Philosophical Incursions into English Literature*, 1946.

Smaller studies include: V. de S. Pinto, 'Isaac Watts and the
Adventurous Muse', *E & S* xx, 1935; and 'Watts and Blake',
RES xx, 1944; R. Stevenson, 'Dr Watts' "Flights of Fancy"',
Harvard Theological Rev. xlii, 1949.

WELSTED, LEONARD, 1688–1747

His first appearance was in *A Poem on Apple-Pye*, 1704,
followed by *A Poem Occasioned by the Late Famous Victory of
Audenard*, 1709; *A Poem to the Memory of the Incomparable Mr
[John] Philips*, 1710, and others, the most individual being
ΟΙΚΟΓΡΑΦΙΑ, 1725, addressed to Dorset, describing the charm
of his house and the emptiness of his cellar. His most important
work after his *Longinus* of 1712 is the 'Dissertation concerning
the Perfection of the English Language and the State of
Poetry' which went with *Odes, Epistles*, &c., 1724, and may
be found in Durham (p. 601). *On False Fame, an Epistle*, ap-
peared in 1732, and his last poem, *The Summum Bonum; or
Wisest Philosophy* in 1741. His play, *The Dissembled Wanton, or
My Son get Money*, was produced in 1726.

His *Works*, with Historical Notes and Memoirs, was issued by
J. Nichols in 1787.

See 'Welsted's "Apple-Pye"', by J. C. Horne, *N & Q*, 17 Nov.
1945.

WINCHILSEA, ANNE FINCH, COUNTESS OF, 1661–1720

Her first appearance in print was in 1701, when 'The Spleen'
and three other poems were published in Gildon's *Miscellany*.
The only early collection is *Miscellany Poems, on Several Occasions*, 1713. Modern editions which reprint the *Miscellany Poems*
and poems from manuscripts have been edited by Myra Reynolds, 1903, Chicago, and H. I'A. Fausset in *Minor Poets of
the Eighteenth Century, EL*, 1930. A selection with an essay
by J. M. Murry was published in 1928. She is first mentioned
in *Cibber*, but the fullest biography is in the edition by Myra
Reynolds. There are essays by E. Gosse in *Gossip in a Library*,
1891, and by E. Dowden in *Essays, Modern and Elizabethan*, 1910.
See also R. A. Brower, 'Lady Winchelsea and the Poetic Tradition of the Seventeenth Century', *SP* xlii, 1945.

YOUNG, EDWARD, 1683–1765

Young's contributions during this period are: *An Epistle to the Right Honourable the Lord Landsdown*, 1713, and in the same year, *A Poem on the Last Day*; *The Force of Religion, or Vanquish'd Love*, 1714; *A Paraphrase on a part of the Book of Job*, 1719, and in the same year *A Letter to Mr. Tickell* on Addison's death. *The Universal Passion* appeared serially: *Satires* i, ii, iii, and iv separately in 1725, and *Satire The Last* in 1726. These were supplemented by *Satires* v and vi, both *On Women*, in 1727 and 1728, the whole being published as *Love of Fame, the Universal Passion, in seven characteristical Satires, the second edition, corrected and alter'd*, 1728. *The Instalment. To the Right Honble. Sir Robert Walpole* appeared in 1726, and *Cynthio* in 1727. The patriotic poems, *Ocean. An Ode*, and *Imperium Pelagi. A Naval Lyrick*, were printed in 1728 and 1729 respectively. *Two Epistles to Mr. Pope, concerning the Authors of the Age* appeared in 1730.

The *Poetical Works* was published in 2 vols., 1741.

Busiris, King of Egypt. A Tragedy, appeared in 1719, and *The Revenge. A Tragedy*, in 1721.

For his later works, collections, biography, criticism, &c., see the bibliography in the next volume.

INDEX

Main entries are in bold type; an asterisk indicates a biographical note. Dates are given for individuals within the period, where not otherwise stated. Modern authors have initials only. Pp. 570 et seq. are in the Chronological Tables or the Bibliographies.